Nation, Language, and the Ethics of Translation

D0143892

TRANSLATION | TRANSNATION

EDITED BY EMILY APTER

Nation, Language, and the Ethics of Translation

EDITED BY SANDRA BERMANN AND MICHAEL WOOD

PRINCETON UNIVERSITY PRESS

PRINCETON AND OXFORD

Copyright © 2005 by Princeton University Press
Published by Princeton University Press, 41 William Street, Princeton, New Jersey 08540
In the United Kingdom: Princeton University Press, 3 Market Place, Woodstock,
Oxfordshire OX20 1SY

All Rights Reserved

LIBRARY OF CONGRESS CATALOGING-IN-PUBLICATION DATA

Nation, language, and the ethics of translation / edited by Sandra Bermann and Michael Wood.
    p.   cm. — (Translation/transnation)
  Includes bibliographical references and index.
  ISBN 0-691-11608-3 (alk. paper) — ISBN 0-691-11609-1 (pbk. : alk. paper)
  1. Translating and interpreting. I. Bermann, Sandra, 1947– II. Wood, Michael,
1936– III. Series.
P306.N367 2005
418′.02—dc22   2004061697

British Library Cataloging-in-Publication Data is available

Publication of this book has been aided by the Princeton University Committee on
Research in the Humanities and Social Sciences

This book has been composed in Goudy

Printed on acid-free paper. ∞

pup.princeton.edu

Printed in the United States of America

10 9 8 7 6 5 4 3 2

ISBN13: 978-0-691-11609-9

CONTENTS

ACKNOWLEDGMENTS

We offer our warmest thanks to Emily Apter and Mary Murrell, whose firm and thoughtful support was important to us at every stage, and to Hanne Winarsky who joined the project near the end. We are also immensely grateful to Amanda Irwin Wilkins, whose practical help has been invaluable. In fall 2002, we were fortunate to have the opportunity to collaborate on this volume at the Institute for Advanced Study; we thank those who made that stay possible. We are also grateful to the two anonymous readers for Princeton University Press, who made shrewd and welcome critical suggestions, and to the University Committee on Research in the Humanities and Social Sciences for the subvention of this volume.

Individual acknowledgments accompany each essay.

Nation, Language, and the Ethics of Translation

Introduction

SANDRA BERMANN

There has probably never been a time when issues of nation, language, and translation have been more important or more troubling than they are today. In a world where individual nation-states are increasingly enmeshed in financial and information networks, where multiple linguistic and national identities can inhabit a single state's borders or exceed them in vast diasporas, where globalization has its serious—and often violent—discontents, and where terrorism and war transform distrust into destruction, language and translation play central, if often unacknowledged, roles. Though the reasons for this are undeniably complex, they are, at least in broad terms, understandable. Waves of migrating peoples have made the contemporary nation-state, and especially its urban centers, into global sites with multiplicities of languages and cultures.[1] At the same time, the international trade, finance, and information technologies that support these sites both depend upon and often seek to bypass translation for economic growth within world and regional markets.

The global reach of international law and politics only heightens the importance of language and translation. Military networks, governmental agencies, as well as international entities such as the United Nations, the United Arab Emirates, and the European Union translate for purposes of intelligence, negotiation, and the dissemination of information or propaganda, as do the growing number of nongovernmental (NGOs) agencies, be they religious or secular. Global media and information networks provide news and interviews on a minute-to-minute basis to serve multiple linguistic constituencies as well as specific cultural and political purposes.

In a world of rapidly transforming populations and technologies, where language and citizenship are caught up in tightly woven webs of economic, military, and cultural power, language and translation operate at every juncture. Indeed so central is translation's role that, as Ilan Stavans recently noted, with only a hint of hyperbole, "modernity . . . is not lived through nationality but . . . through translationality."[2]

Yet if language and translation have become increasingly important in national and international relations, and in the processes of "globalization" more

Parts of this essay were presented at the American Comparative Literature Association Convention in 2004. I am indebted to colleagues there as well as to Michael Wood and to the readers for Princeton University Press for their very helpful suggestions.

generally, their role as cultural as well as linguistic entities is only beginning to be theorized. The social sciences, that have so well described our political, economic, military, and information networks, have, for the most part, ignored these issues or considered them simply a necessary interface. This is most likely because, in their very texture, these linguistic matters belong so fully to what we traditionally think of as the humanities. Yet closely considered, language and translation in fact open up the unavoidable complexities, the historically ingrained problems and prejudices, and the intense day-to-day negotiations that occupy our interwoven global communities, setting into stark relief the difficult suturing of global networks and the over-stressed joints of the international body politic. They tend to raise questions about linguistic power and the dissemination of texts in various media; they bring to the fore issues of human rights as well as intellectual property; they also illuminate disparities among states, nations, and local traditions, and the often tragic problems of linguistic and cultural diasporas; they reveal complex multiplicities in the shadow of apparent unity.

Only a more deeply nuanced understanding of these linguistic ligatures, and a heightened awareness of their relationship to the national as well as to the "postnational," and "subnational," can begin to parse the painful dialectics of local and global, past and present, that cross the contemporary world. Pursued in greater detail, they might begin to sketch a humanistic complement to the theorization of today's economic and information complex by the social sciences and urge, in the process, a very different, more reflective, and more culturally variegated "global consciousness."

The essays in this collection afford an opportunity to rethink national, subnational, and international connections and conflicts, their histories and their futures, from the specific standpoint of language and translation. Though the essays consider a large range of texts, languages, and cultures, all circle around the same densely interwoven issues: (1) the nation, both its discursive construction and its dismantling; (2) language, as a site of power, a means of active communication, and a scene of epistemological reflection; and (3) the ethics of translation, a topic that, as each of these contributions in one way or another reveals, underlies and amplifies our understanding of both of the other, apparently broader, themes.

The Legacy of Cultural Studies and Literary Theory

Wide-ranging in subject matter and diverse in approach, these essays depend upon a recognizable legacy of thought from both cultural studies and literary theory. The work of Benedict Anderson, Timothy Brennan, Partha Chatterjee, Neil Lazarus, Bruce Robbins, Edward Said, Gayatri Chakravorty Spivak, Gauri Viswanathan, Robert J. C. Young, and others has brought to our attention the many ways in which nationhood inevitably depends upon cultural—and specifically linguistic—means for its creation, its colonial and imperialist extension, and also its dismantling.[3] Benedict Anderson's well-known description of the nation as an "imagined community," Edward Said's discussion of Orientalism, and Michel Foucault's notion of "discursive formations,"[4] have underscored the cultural—and especially linguistic—build, maintenance, and "unbundling" of national identities. Though foundational narratives might claim an originary moment and underlying unity, these more recent critical voices show that nationhood is better described as a never-ending, conflictual process driven by changing cultural practices. They reveal, moreover, that a "nation" need not be syonymous with a "state." The two are often articulated in frankly problematic ways, as any number of territorial disputes attest.

The role of language in the process of nationhood is both powerful and complex. As a means of communication that is notably tied to the *demos* (the "we-creating" sense of belonging invoked in essentialist descriptions of the nation)[5] language has always been a defining feature of national identity, even—especially—when this "nation" has become diasporic. Nor is language a neutral element. Consciously or unconsciously, it performs deft feats of appropriation and exclusion, supported by a dialectic of otherness. Creating and relying upon notions of cultural difference, groups underscore our "we," our identity and our solidarity. Through what Said has identified as Orientalism, through racism in its multiple forms, or through apparently more benign forms of ethnic, religious, or national enthusiasm, we create solidarity by excluding, marginalizing, if not vilifying and making enemies of, groups identified as other. The rhetoric of war or of propaganda provides ready examples of this strategy. Yet, as Hegel and his heirs have taught us, the "other" so firmly rejected thereby invariably inhabits any sense of self, any notion of identity. It is a strategy we live with in the public world, as in our private lives, on a daily basis.

From this awareness of language's role in the creation of identities have emerged powerful literary and cultural critiques of nationalism, colonialism, and imperialism, and an intellectual vigilance about the complex heteronomy that inheres in all of our constructed solidarities. Seeking to describe, interpret, and ultimately emancipate cultures and literatures suppressed by a legacy of more powerful groups, values, and paradigms, literary and cultural critiques have opened new paths. This has been particularly notable in studies described by the debated term "postcolonialism," a multifaceted approach seeking to understand and rectify the literary and cultural consequences of colonialism in both colonizing and colonized countries, now and in the past.[6]

As is well known, language has often been implicated in efforts to mute a past and, with it, a sense of cultural identity. In the current era, the problem of linguistic 'colonialism' continues in a specific form. Compelled by financial and literary pressure, authors seek to write in English or in one of the other major commercial languages—or else to be quickly translated. Yet despite what is known as "global English," and other locally hegemonic tongues (French, for instance, in parts of Africa and the Middle East, and Mandarin in East Asia), liberatory efforts to assert historical languages and their literary traditions nonetheless persist.

Though efforts to retrieve past languages and literatures extend to cultures and discourses of Asia, Africa, and Latin America as well as to those buried within dominant cultures in Europe and North America, they may also include gender-specific and class-specific languages and literatures that have failed to find a "home" in the Euro-American space. The importance of such archaeologies, undertaken by peoples around the globe, can hardly be overstated. Unearthing forgotten or excluded linguistic traditions, noting their inevitable interactions with other, more powerful ones, and bringing this knowledge into current discussion are surely some of the most compelling tasks faced in the history of literary studies.[7] Such critiques raise explicit, and often difficult, ethical and political questions concerning the relationship of the national to the international as well as to the subnational, the local to the global, and the esthetic to the political. More self-reflectively, they also highlight ways in which categories of critical analysis can unwittingly subsume the very historical and local particulars they mean to reveal.[8]

Though the discursive reality of nationhood and its dialectic of otherness often drives the literary or cultural critic, the very complexity of language as often makes her pause. For one, language remains radically contingent upon specific local histories and contexts. Cultural practices produce and sustain—and are in turn sustained by—the lexicon and syntax of a given language. Highly particularized cultural markers must therefore be taken into account in any linguistic interpretation—in principle, an infinite task, and a necessarily self-reflective one. Interpreters can always find yet another access to meaning, another pertinent insight, as language weaves its way through dense and rapidly changing webs of culture.

Contemporary epistemological reflections further the sense of a complex alterity at work within language. Inquiries developed throughout the twentieth century in the philosophy of language, psychoanalysis, literary theory, and especially deconstruction, underscore a shared awareness that language can never be viewed as a simple mental tool, or as a transparent medium of representation.[9] On the contrary. Conceived as a process of difference and deferral, scripted by the unconscious, by memory, and by texts and contexts immemorial, language neither mirrors a pure "truth," nor simply reflects discrete referential meanings. Language remains radically impure, haunted by endless semantic contexts and, as emphasized by Derrida and DeMan, an insuperable undecidability. Harboring its own epistemological "otherness," language imposes internal barriers to appropriative understanding as well as to transparent communication. Translation only multiplies this awareness of otherness that inhabits languages as it inhabits human society more generally.

Translation and the Ethical

Indeed, translation (commonly defined as "the rendering from one language into another")[10] illuminates both the *cultural otherness* at stake in contemporary studies of nationhood and the *epistemological otherness* at work in language itself. Engaging both with "nation" *and* with "language," with "cultural studies" *and* with "theory," as well as with more traditional literary history, with close reading and, not the least, with everyday experience in a global context, translation has itself become an important border concept in the humanities, affecting some of the most salient intellectual and ethical issues of our time. It requires attention to cultural values, to economic and political inequalities, to individual choices and, perhaps most obviously, to otherness in its linguistic and cultural forms. In the process, it foregrounds some explicitly ethical questions.

From Schleiermacher's early discussion of the role of translation in the creation of German nationhood (analyzed by Venuti)[11] to twenty-first-century "legal transplants" (discussed here by Legrand), the study of translation has raised important cultural issues of local homelands and "foreign" nations, of national or ethnic histories and global aspirations, as well as of changing power relations. Translators have long agreed that the effort to render one language system into another requires a keen awareness of broad cultural as well as specific linguistic values. It also requires existential choices that are bound to have wide-ranging repercussions for the text and its audience. How much of the "otherness" of the "foreign" should the translator highlight? How much of the foreign should he mute or erase in order to make texts easier for the "home" (target) audience to assimilate? The problems posed demand judgment calls as ethical as they are practical or cognitive.

Translation's distinctive ability to offer insight into the language process itself aligns it with ethics and the question of the foreign in a different, though not unrelated, way. As is frequently noted, translation's etymology—*trans* (across) and *latus*, the past participle of *ferre* (to carry)—suggests a transportation of meaning, a physical displacement. The German *übersetzen* implies the same.[12] Yet only if we conceive of language as a surface element, ready to collapse into meanings that could take a commanding role and, moreover, be fixed in some univocal way, could translation be a simple "carrying across" of concepts from one signifying system to another. The very impossibility of such a feat, long recognized in the history of translation studies, argues for the need to envision language in the more complicated fashion common to twentieth-century theorists. Here, each language bears its own vast and endlessly transforming intertext of socially and historically grafted meanings, along with their graphic and acoustic imagery. Though different languages clearly provide some semantic 'overlap' in their efforts to relate to the referential world, this overlap is only partial, as is attested by Benjamin's famous example of "*Brot*" versus "pain" or Saussure's equally well-known discussion of "*mouton*" versus the English "mutton" *and* "sheep."[13] If language is not a simple nomenclature for pre-established and universally recognized "meanings," as most contemporary language philosophers agree, translation can never be a complete or transparent transferal of semantic content. Yet even in its imperfect, or simply creative negotiations of difference, translation provides a necessary linguistic supplement that bridges cultural chasms and allows for intellectual passage and exchange.

Such linguistic reflections raise intriguing philosophical as well as practical questions. If, for instance, both translation and the "original" text are, in Ben-

jamin's words, "recognizable as the fragments of a greater language, just as fragments are parts of a vessel," what is the nature of this "greater language"?[14] Does
it refer to an archaic essence, or rather to a harmony, where differences and Derridean "différance," with its endless deferral of meaning and therefore of
"essence," persist?[15] Though the former describes a return to divine origins, the
latter suggests that translation participates in an ongoing creative process, in
which the outlines of a greater human language are drawn through the work of
translation itself, as each new rendering contributes to the virtually endless delineation of language and understanding. Or might Benjamin's phrase open up
an even broader concern, the greater language of human experience in which
Levinas's "face of the Other" will be found? In this case, the noncognitive horizon of otherness that human being and language present—and to which we are
ultimately responsible—stretches within and beyond each linguistic sign and
each effort at translation.[16] Regardless of one's views, the very nature of such
questions suggests that the "exorbitant" quality of language, that which remains
mysteriously "other" within it, is never more salient—or perturbing—than in
the culturally other-directed work of translation. It also suggests that the translator's task is inevitably an ethical one. In attempts to translate, we become most
aware of linguistic and cultural differences, of the historical "hauntings," and of
experiential responsibilities that make our languages what they are and that directly affect our attitudes toward the world.

Highlighting the difficult alterity within language that makes any transparent
or "literal" translation "impossible," Western contemporary theory nonetheless
makes strong claims for translation's necessity. According to Benjamin, translation is essential to the "living on" of texts.[17] Indeed, without translation, and its
close kin, interpretation, the original will die. As translation reinterprets the
original for different audiences, it provides for its continued flourishing and, in
the process, for the future of national and transnational cultures.

Indeed, translation might be effectively re-thought in historical and temporal
terms rather than only in ontological and spatial ones. Though traditional understandings of translation define it largely in terms of a mimesis, reflection, or
attempted correspondence to the "truth" of an original, one might just as easily
think of it in terms of a history of "instances," as Weber suggests, or of linguistic
negotiations occurring over time, each a poiesis, each establishing a new inscription and, with it, the possibility of new interpretation. The advent of media
technology in the last two centuries has already questioned the very notion of a
single "original." But seeing translation in more historical terms, focusing on its
role in perpetuating and transforming our cultural heritage, explains its ongoing
effectiveness as it accommodates our notions to changing media and the new
temporality they imply.

In light of considerations such as these, translation not only takes on the role
of a border concept between "cultural studies" and "literary theory."[18] It also
plays out its destiny as an essential genetic component of literary and cultural
histories. In so doing, it foregrounds its peculiar double bind, expressed in the
works of Derrida and Spivak, among others—a double bind with far-reaching

repercussions.[19] If we must translate in order to emancipate and preserve cultural pasts and to build linguistic bridges for present understandings and future thought, we must do so while attempting to respond ethically to each language's contexts, intertexts, and intrinsic alterity. This dual responsibility may well describe an ethics of translation or, more modestly, the ethical at work in translation. It can at least provide a moment of reflection in which an ethical relationship to others and to the self, to language and its international dissemination and transformation, might be conceived. Such reflections have, in fact, already led to new modes of literary and cultural analysis.

Recent genealogical inquiries into the linguistic, cultural, and historical contexts in which translation occurs, or into its purposes and relations to the future, often rely upon "thick descriptions" of conflictual historical and cultural hauntings inscribed in the text and its subsequent interpretations. As several of the essays insist, discussions along these lines, as well as along more strictly linguistic and theoretical lines, have also prompted a major rethinking of the aims and methods of comparative literature, the literary discipline that has defined itself from the first in terms of linguistic, national, and disciplinary border-crossings. Here, the questions raised by nation, language, and the ethics of translation have already begun to produce a more thoroughgoing interdisciplinarity, as well as a geo-linguistic decentering of major proportions, and intense self-reflection.

Yet these ethical issues have, I would suggest, still broader educational import. Though we have every reason to resist any reduction of literary texts to a set of "relevant" political or religious beliefs, the intertwined issues of nation, language, and translation argue forcefully for an ampler sense of this term. For little could be more relevant to the United States or to other nations in the contemporary world than the range of texts in need of translation and a heightened awareness of the complex negotiations among peoples and languages that translation, in its various modes, reveals. Indeed, without more refined and sensitive cultural/linguistic translations and, above all, without an education that draws attention to the very *act* of translation and to the interwoven, problematic otherness that it confronts, our global world will be less hospitable; in fact, it could founder.

An educational focus on our "translationality" would allow for a heightened attention to some of the most challenging issues facing us—as literary scholars and as world citizens. We might read literary texts as well as the daily news in a more informed and critical light. We might consider in different ways the intricate circulation of texts and its bearing upon nation and post-nation. More and better translations of non-English texts could, for instance, clearly help the Anglo-American reader to engage literary worlds and historical cultures that are not her own. Similar effects could be gained by more translations in other parts of the globe. A focus on translationality might even urge rethinking of globalization itself in more carefully defined, more humanistic terms.

Reflecting upon translation does not mean rejecting the rise in technology or the interwovenness of our cultures. But it does insist on seeing global society not only in the grand lines of financial, information, or military networks, but also in the interstices, the nodes, those endless, precarious junctures where translation between cultures and languages takes place. Be it in the workplace, in the newspaper, on television and films, on the Internet, in literary texts, there is an ever-increasing need to deal with more than one language—and therefore with translation. Here conflicting histories make their claims, with their stories of passions felt and decisions taken. Here lie the poems that make the surprising leap from culture to culture, but also the cliches of prejudice and superstition that, left unconsidered, can tragically undermine dialogue and compromise. In these junctures lie unheard, muted voices of past and present as well as possibilities for different, better-negotiated futures.

In such an imagined community, an education in translationality might well rely upon the close readings and thick descriptions characteristic of literary study. These offer models for denaturalizing a world that can be too tightly packaged and too simply described, and begin to provide space and time for words lost or forgotten. At every juncture where there is translation—in the law, military, news, finance, movies and television, information technology, and not least in literature—there is, along with problems of misunderstanding, deception, inequality, and linguistic oppression also hope for insight, reciprocity, and therefore creative negotiation, if never perfect resolution, between languages and peoples, between values, enmities and loves. There is, in short, an opportunity for the exercise of judgment and of a situated, ethical wisdom.

It is to such seldom theorized issues, and to such cautiously articulated hopes for a deepened understanding and more humane alternative to current conceptions of the globalizing present, or its views of the past, that these collected essays ultimately speak. They do not represent a unified linguistic, political, or literary view. But their various insights, drawn from specific contexts where cultures and languages meet, begin to limn alternative futures.

The four sections—"Translation as Medium and across Media," "The Ethics of Translation," "Translation and Difference," and "Beyond the Nation"—are each introduced separately and invite the reader to rethink the issues of nation, language, and translation in concrete, linguistically and culturally specific terms. Through such situated readings, a new and surprisingly different understanding of our world, its languages, and the individual cultural and historical perspectives so important to its flourishing, begins to unfold.

NOTES

1. See, for instance, Saskia Sassen, *The Global City: New York, London, Tokyo* (Princeton: Princeton University Press, 2001); also *Globalization and its Discontents* (New York: New Press, 1998).

2. Neal Sokol, "Translation and its Discontents: A Conversation with Ilan Stavans," *The Literary Review* 45 (3), spring 2002, p. 554.

3. Benedict Anderson, *Imagined Communities:Reflections on the Origin and Spread of Nationalism* (London: Verso, 1983); Timothy Brennan, *At Home in the World: Cosmopoli-*

tanism Now (Cambridge, MA: Harvard University Press, 1997); Partha Chatterjee, *National Thought and the Colonial World: A Derivative Discourse* (London: Zed Books, 1986), *The Nation and its Fragments: Colonial and Postcolonial Histories* (Princeton, NJ: Princeton University Press, 1993); Neil Lazarus, *Nationalism and Cultural Practice in the Postcolonial World* (Cambridge: Cambridge University Press, 1999); Bruce Robbins, *Feeling Global: Internationalism in Distress* (New York: New York University Press, 1999); Edward W. Said, *Orientalism: Western Representations of the Orient* (Harmondsworth: Penguin, 1978), *The World, The Text, and the Critic* (Cambridge MA: Harvard University Press, 1983), *Culture and Imperialism* (London: Chatto and Windus, 1993); Gayatri Chakravorty Spivak, *In Other Worlds: Essays in Cultural Politics* (New York: Methuen, 1987), *Outside in the Teaching Machine* (London: Routledge, 1993), *A Critique of Postcolonial Reason: Toward a History of the Vanishing Present* (Cambridge, MA: Harvard University Press, 1999); Gauri Viswanathan, *Outside the Fold* (Princeton, NJ: Princeton University Press, 1998); Robert J. C. Young, *White Mythologies: Writing History and the West* (London: Routledge, 1990), *Colonial Desire: Hybridity in Culture, Theory and Race* (London: Routledge, 1995), *Postcolonialism: An Historical Introduction* (Oxford: Blackwell, 2001).

4. Michel Foucault, *The Archaeology of Knowledge*, trans. A. M. Sheridan Smith (London: Tavistock, 1972), *The Order of Things*, trans. anonymous (London: Tavistock, 1970), *Discipline and Punish: The Birth of the Prison*, trans. Alan Sheridan (London: Allen Lane, 1977); *Language, Counter-Memory, Practice: Selected Essays and Interviews*, ed. Donald F. Bouchard, trans. Donald F. Bouchard and Sherry Simon (Ithaca, NY: Cornell University Press, 1977), *The History of Sexuality: Volume One: An Introduction*, trans. Robert Hurley (London: Allen Lane, 1978)

5. See J.H.H.Weiler, "To Be a European Citizen: Eros and Civilization," in *The Constitution of Europe: "Do the new clothes have an emperor?" and other essays on European integration* (Cambridge: Cambridge University Press, 1999), pp. 237–43, for a discussion of *demos* and nationality. Also Lawrence Venuti, "Local Contingencies: Translation and National Identities," included in this volume.

6. Young, *Postcolonialism*, pp. 6, 7–11. Throughout, Young underscores both the historical and theoretical complexity, as well as the emancipatory intentions, of postcolonial studies.

7. See Hans Ulrich Gumbrecht, "The Future of Literary Studies," in *The Future of Literary Studies*, ed. Hans Ulrich Gumbrecht and Walter Moser (Edmonton, CA: Canadian Comparative Literature Association, 2001), pp. 188–89. In fact, the issues raised in our volume reveal a productive interplay of the two, apparently separate "paradigms" of which Gumbrecht speaks.

8. See the essays to follow by Sylvia Molloy, Vilashini Cooppan, and Stathis Gourgouris.

9. See Andrew Benjamin, *Translation and the Nature of Philosophy: A New Theory of Words* (London: Routledge, 1989) for an elegant discussion of the relationship of philosophy to translation in twentieth-century thought.

10. *Merriam–Webster's Deluxe Dictionary*, Tenth Collegiate Edition, (Pleasantville: Reader's Digest Association, 1998), p. 1963.

11. Lawrence Venuti, *The Translator's Invisibility: A History of Translation* (London, New York: Routledge, 1995). Also his "Local Contingencies."

12. See Pierre Legrand, "Issues in the Translatability of Law," and Stanley Corngold, "Comparative Literature: The Delay in Translation" in this volume.

13. Walter Benjamin, "The Task of the Translator," in *Illuminations*, ed. Hannah

Arendt (New York: Schocken Books, 1968), p. 74; Ferdinand de Saussure, *Course in General Linguistics*, trans. and annotated by Roy Harris (London: Duckworth, 1983), p. 114.

14. Benjamin, "The Task," p. 78.

15. See Jacques Derrida, "Difference," in *Speech and Phenomena* (1973); also, his essays treating translation, "Living On. Border Lines," in *Deconstruction and Criticism*, eds. Harold Bloom, Paul De Man, Jacques Derrida, Geoffrey H. Hartman, J. Hillis Miller (New York: Seabury Press, 1979) pp. 75–176; "Des Tours de Babel," trans. Joseph F. Graham, in *Difference in Translation*, ed. Joseph F. Graham (Ithaca and London: Cornell University Press, 1985), pp. 165–248.

16. See Robert Eaglestone, "Levinas, Translation, and Ethics," in this book. Also Emmanuel Levinas, *Totality and Infinity: An Essay on Exteriority*, trans. Alphonso Lingis (Pittsburgh: Duquesne University Press, 1969), pp. 194–220.

17. Benjamin, pp. 71–72. See also Emily Apter, "Translation with No Original: Scandals of Textual Reproduction" in this volume.

18. Compare Gumbrecht, "The Future of Literary Studies."

19. See Andrew Benjamin on Derrida, in *Translation*.

PART ONE

Translation as Medium and Across Media

In the very last note of *Minima Moralia*, Adorno suggests that the only responsible philosophical answer to despair is "to contemplate all things as they would present themselves from the standpoint of redemption."[1] The essays in the first section of this book all situate themselves at some distance from despair, but they do consistently register difficulty, and they do have redemption firmly in mind. The essays concern the role of the intellectual as translator of what gets forgotten in the contemporary world, the possibility of translating law from culture to culture, the actual practice of simultaneous translation, the translatability and untranslatability of film as a medium, and the problematic but indispensable notion of "origin" in the theory of translation.

"For whom then does one write," Edward Said asks, "if it is difficult to specify the audience with any sort of precision?" The answer is that one writes for the audience one needs, the audience who must be there if we are not to despair. "The idea of an imagined community," Said continues, "has suddenly acquired a very literal, if virtual, dimension," and it is through our participation in this community, our willingness to imagine it into reality, that we can best serve those "less powerful interests threatened with frustration, silence, incorporation, or extinction by the powerful." If music for Adorno is a "silent witness to the inhumanity all around," then for Said the intellectual is the unsilenced translator, the person who lends voice to the unvoiced and half-voiced needs of the oppressed. He points out too that "film and photography, along with all the arts of writing, can be aspects of this activity."

Pierre Legrand argues eloquently against the "strategies of simplification" at work in the integrationist view of European law, which rests on the blunt or naive claim that "there is very little difference between European laws," that is, very little difference from culture to culture and nation to nation. This view is "irredeemably suburban," Legrand says, a violent refusal of "contextual knowledge," but all is not lost, and he himself shows us how to "redeem local knowledge," which is best described, he says, "in terms of its plasticity, pliability, diversity, and adaptability." Indeed, he suggests that justice itself can be redeemed if we respect the gaps between laws, just as literary translation respects the gaps between languages, a process that "inscribes alterity at the heart of identity through the new forms it creates," and reveals thereby, as Legrand subtly says, "the genuine nature of hospitality," which cannot exist without risks. We are close again to the imagined community of intellectuals.

Continuing this line of thought, but in an intensely practical context, Lynn Visson reminds us that "words which characterize the life, culture and historical development of any given country often have no precise equivalents in other languages." She offers a detailed list (often amusing) of elusive words and phrases in Russian, and describes in lucid detail the preferred rhetorical instruments of the simultaneous interpreter: "condensation, deliberate omission and addition, synecdoche and metonymy, antonymic constructions, grammatical inversion and the use of semantic equivalents," and other devices. Her crucial point, though, is that the interpreter is just that: a translator not only of language but of context, a person who, if she cannot redeem local knowledge, can give it all the depth that time allows. Visson too writes of difficulty and its overcoming. "Hardest of all is the search for *cultural* rather than for purely linguistic or semantic equivalents, for though these are often vastly different in the two languages, the role of an interpreter of culture is the interpreter's most important and most difficult function."

Samuel Weber makes an important distinction between "language" and "instance": "translation always involves not merely the movement from one *language* to another, but from one *instance*—a text already existing in one language—to another instance, that does not previously exist, but that is brought into being in the other language." This phrasing allows for translation of instances both within a single language and between different ones, and Weber has some subtle thoughts on these topics. His main project, however, is to display creation as it is described in *Genesis* as "almost a translation," because on close reading it appears as neither "an absolute beginning nor a pure performance"—only "almost a translation" because there is as yet only one place and only one language. Translation becomes "inevitable but also impossible" with the building and ruin of the Tower of Babel, and Weber now brilliantly glosses Walter Benjamin's conception of an origin as "the insistent but unachievable attempt to restore an anterior state." From the standpoint of redemption the attempt would still perhaps be unachievable but it would look toward the future rather than the past, toward the world it remains for us to imagine.

Michael Wood's essay seeks to understand, through a study of sound and silence in films from very different cultures, something of what translation can mean in the cinema: which images seem to travel without need of translation and which images do not, what visual translation looks like when it happens, how national film cultures separate and intersect, and what is the role of music in the language of film. We get a clear sense of the importance of translation in this medium when, prompted by Sergei Eisenstein,[2] we remember that what in English is called a close-up is in other languages called a shot in large scale. In both cases a visual perception is translated into words, but the implied story is very different. English-speaking cultures emphasize the mimetic effect of the technique, the apparent shortening of a distance. Other cultures stress the technical fact, the actual alteration in the size of the figures or objects in the frame. Many implications lurk in such a difference.

NOTES

1. Theodor W. Adorno, *Minima Moralia* (Frankfurt: Suhrhamp, 1951, 1993), p. 333; trans. E.F.N Jephcott (London: Verso, 1974, 1996), p. 247.

2. Sergei Eisenstein, *Film Form: Essays in Film Theory*, ed. and trans. Jan Leyda (New York: Harcourt Brace, 1949, 1977), pp. 237–38.

The Public Role of Writers and Intellectuals

EDWARD SAID

Twenty-one years ago, *The Nation* magazine convened a congress of writers in New York by putting out notices for the event and, as I understood the tactic, leaving open the question of who was a writer and why he or she qualified to attend. The result was that literally hundreds of people showed up, crowding the main ballroom of a midtown Manhattan hotel almost to the ceiling. The occasion itself was intended as a response by the intellectual and artistic communities to the immediate onset of the Reagan era. As I recall the proceedings, a debate raged for a long period of time over the definition of a writer in the hope that some of the people there would be selected out or, in plain English, forced to leave. The reason for that was twofold: first of all, to decide who had a vote and who did not, and second, to form a writer's union. Not much occurred in the way of reduced and manageable numbers; the hearteningly large mass of people simply remained immense and unwieldy, since it was quite clear that everyone who came as a writer who opposed Reaganism stayed on as a writer who opposed Reaganism.

I remember clearly that at one point someone sensibly suggested that we should adopt what was said to be the Soviet position on defining a writer, that is, a writer is someone who says that he or she is a writer. And, I think that is where matters seem to have rested, even though a National Writer's Union was formed but restricted its functions to technical professional matters like fairer standardized contracts between publishers and writers. An American Writer's Congress to deal with expressly political issues was also formed, but was derailed by people who in effect wanted it for one or another specific political agenda that could not get a consensus.

Since that time, an immense amount of change has taken place in the world of writers and intellectuals and, if anything, the definition of who or what a writer and intellectual is has become more confusing and difficult to pin down. I tried my hand at it in my 1993 Reith Lectures, but there have been major political and economic transformations since that time, and in writing this essay I have found myself revising a great deal and adding to some of my earlier views. Central to the changes has been the deepening of an unresolved tension as to whether writers and intellectuals can ever be what is called nonpolitical or not, and if so, how and in what measure. The difficulty of the tension for the individ-

A version of this essay appeared in *The Nation* in 2001; another in Edward Said, *Humanism and Democratic Criticism* (Columbia University Press), 2004.

ual writer and intellectual has been paradoxically that the realm of the political and public has expanded so much as to be virtually without borders. Consider that the bipolar world of the Cold War has been reconfigured and dissolved in several different ways, all of them first of all providing what seems to be an infinite number of variations on the location or position, physical and metaphorical, of the writer and, second of all, opening up the possibility of divergent roles for him or her to play if, that is, the notion of writer or intellectual itself can be said to have any coherent and definably separate meaning or existence at all. The role of the American writer in the post–9/11 period has certainly amplified the pertinence of what is written about "us" to an enormous degree.

Yet, despite the spate of books and articles saying that intellectuals no longer exist and that the end of the Cold War, the opening up of the mainly American university to legions of writers and intellectuals, the age of specialization, and the commercialization and commodification of everything in the newly globalized economy have simply done away with the old somewhat romantic-heroic notion of the solitary writer-intellectual (I shall provisionally connect the two terms for purposes of convenience here, then go on to explain my reasons for doing so in a moment), there still seems to be a great deal of life in the ideas and the practices of writer-intellectuals that touch on, and are very much a part of, the public realm. Their role most recently in opposing (as well, alas, as supporting the Anglo-American war in Iraq) is very much a case in point.

In the three or four quite distinct contemporary language cultures that I know something about, the importance of writers and intellectuals is eminently, indeed overwhelmingly, true in part because many people still feel the need to look at the writer-intellectual as someone who ought to be listened to as a guide to the confusing present, and also as a leader of a faction, tendency, or group vying for more power and influence. The Gramscian provenance of both these ideas about the role of an intellectual is evident.

Now in the Arab-Islamic world, the two words used for intellectual are *muthaqqaf*, or *mufakir*, the first derived from *thaqafa* or culture (hence, a man of culture), the second from *fikr* or thought (hence, a man of thought). In both instances the prestige of those meanings is enhanced and amplified by implied comparison with government, which is now widely regarded as without credibility and popularity, or culture and thought. So in the moral vacancy created, for example, by dynastic republican governments like those of Egypt, Iraq, Libya, or Syria, many people turn either to religious or secular intellectuals for the leadership no longer provided by political authority, even though governments have been adept at co-opting intellectuals as mouthpieces for them. But the search for authentic intellectuals goes on, as does the struggle.

In the French-speaking domains the word *intellectuel* unfailingly carries with it some residue of the public realm in which recently deceased figures like Sartre, Foucault, Bourdieu, and Aron debated and put forward their views for very large audiences indeed. By the early 1980s when most of the *maîtres penseurs* had disappeared, a certain gloating and relief accompanied their absence, as if the new redundancy gave a lot of little people a chance to have their say for the first time since Zola. Today, with what seems like a Sartre revival in evidence and with

Pierre Bourdieu or his ideas appearing almost to the day of his death in every other issue of *Le Monde* and *Libération*, a considerably aroused taste for public intellectuals has gripped many people, I think. From a distance, debate about social and economic policy seems pretty lively, and is not quite as one-sided as it is in the United States.

Raymond Williams's succinct presentation in *Keywords* of the force field of mostly negative connotations for the word "intellectual" is about as good a starting point for understanding the historical semantics of the word as we have for England.[1] Excellent subsequent work by Stefan Collini, John Carey, and others has considerably deepened and refined the field of practice where intellectuals and writers have been located. Williams himself has gone on to indicate that, after the mid-twentieth century, the word takes on a new somewhat wider set of associations, many of them having to do with ideology, cultural production, and the capacity for organized thought and learning. This suggests that English usage has expanded to take in some of the meanings and uses that have been quite common in the French, and generally European, contexts. But as in the French instance, intellectuals of Williams's generation have passed from the scene (the almost miraculously articulate and brilliant Eric Hobsbawm being a rare exception) and, to judge from some of his successors on the *New Left Review*, a new period of Left quietism may have set in, but especially since New Labour has so thoroughly renounced its own past and joined in the new American campaign to re-order the world, a renewal of the European writer's dissenting role has been enhanced. Neoliberal and Thatcherite intellectuals are pretty much where they have been (in the ascendancy), and have the advantage of many more pulpits in the press from which to speak, for example, to support or criticize the war in Iraq.

In the American setting, however, the word "intellectual" is less used than in the three other arenas of discourse and discussion that I've mentioned. One reason is that professionalism and specialization provide the norm for intellectual work much more than they do in Arabic, French, or British English. The cult of expertise has never ruled the world of discourse as much as it now does in the United States, where the policy intellectual can feel that he or she surveys the world. Another reason is that even though the United States is actually full of intellectuals hard at work filling the airwaves, print, and cyberspace with their effusions, the public realm is so taken up with questions of policy and government, as well as with considerations of power and authority that even the idea of an intellectual who is driven neither by a passion for office nor by the ambition to get the ear of someone in power is difficult to sustain for more than a second or two. Profit and celebrity are powerful stimulants. In far too many years of appearing on television or being interviewed by journalists, I have never *not* been asked the question, "What do you think the United States should do about such and such an issue?" I take this to be an index of how the notion of rule has been lodged at the very heart of intellectual practice outside the university. And may I add that it has been a point of principle for me not *ever* to reply to the question.

Yet it is also overwhelmingly true that in America there is no shortage in the public realm of partisan policy intellectuals who are organically linked to one or another political party, lobby, special interest, or foreign power. The world of the

Washington think tanks, the various television talk shows, innumerable radio programs, to say nothing of literally thousands of occasional papers, journals, and magazines—all this testifies amply to how densely saturated public discourse is with interests, authorities, and powers whose extent in the aggregate is literally unimaginable in scope and variety, except as that whole bears centrally on the acceptance of a neoliberal post–welfare state responsive neither to the citizenry nor to the natural environment, but to a vast structure of global corporations unrestricted by traditional barriers or sovereignties. The unparalleled global military reach of the United States adds to the new structure. With the various specialized systems and practices of the new economic situation, only very gradually and partially being disclosed, and with an administration whose idea of national security is preemptive war, we are beginning to discern an immense panorama of how these systems and practices (many of them new, many of them refashioned holdovers from the classical imperial system) assembled together to provide a geography whose purpose is slowly to crowd out and override human agency.[2] We must not be misled by the effusions of Thomas Friedman, Daniel Yergin, Joseph Stanislas, and the legions who have celebrated globalization into believing that the system itself is the best outcome for human history, nor in reaction should we fail to note what in a far less glamorous way globalization from below, as Richard Falk has called the post-Westphalian world system, can provide by way of human potential and innovation. There is now a fairly extensive network of NGOs created to address minority and human rights, women's and environmental issues, movements for democratic and cultural change, and while none of these can be a substitute for political action or mobilization, especially to protest and try to prevent illegal wars, many of them do embody resistance to the advancing global status quo.

Yet, as Dezelay and Garth have argued, given the funding of many of these international NGOs, they are co-optable as targets for what the two researchers have called the imperialism of virtue, functioning as annexes to the multinationals and great foundations like Ford, centers of civic virtue that forestall deeper kinds of change or critiques of longstanding assumptions.[3]

In the meantime, it is sobering and almost terrifying to contrast the world of academic intellectual discourse in its generally hermetic, jargon-ridden, unthreatening combativeness, with what the public realm all around has been doing. Masao Miyoshi has pioneered the study of this contrast, especially in its marginalization of the humanities.[4] The separation between the two realms, academic and public, is, I think, greater in the United States than anywhere else, although in Perry Anderson's dirge for the Left with which he announces his editorship of the *New Left Review* it is all too plain that in his opinion the British, American, and Continental pantheon of remaining heroes is, with one exception, resolutely, exclusively academic and almost entirely male and Eurocentric.[5] I found it extraordinary that he takes no account of nonacademic intellectuals like John Pilger and Alexander Cockburn, or major academic and political figures such as Chomsky, Zinn, the late Eqbal Ahmad, Germaine Greer, or such diverse figures as Mohammed Sid Ahmad, bell hooks, Angela Davis, Cornel West,

Henry Louis Gates, Miyoshi, Ranajit Guha, Partha Chatterjee, to say nothing of an impressive battery of Irish intellectuals that would include Seamus Deane, Luke Gibbons, Declan Kiberd plus many others, all of whom would certainly not accept the solemn lament intoned for what he calls the "the neo-liberal grand slam."

The great novelty alone of Ralph Nader's candidacy in the 2000 American presidential campaign was that a genuine adversarial intellectual was running for the most powerful elected office in the world using the rhetoric and tactics of demystification and disenchantment, in the process supplying a mostly disaffected electorate with alternative information buttressed with precise facts and figures. This went completely against the prevailing modes of vagueness, vapid slogans, mystification, and religious fervor sponsored by the two major party candidates, underwritten by the media, and paradoxically by virtue of its inaction, the humanistic academy. Nader's competitive stance was a sure sign of how far from over and defeated the oppositional tendencies in global society are; witness also the upsurge of reformism in Iran, the consolidation of democratic antiracism in various parts of Africa, and so on, leaving aside the November 1999 action in Seattle against the WTO, the liberation of South Lebanon, the unprecedented worldwide protests against war in Iraq, etcetera. The list would be a long one, and very different in tone (were it to be interpreted fully) from the consolatory accomodationism Anderson seems to recommend. In intention, Nader's campaign was also different from those of his opponents in that he aimed to arouse the citizenry's democratic awareness of the untapped potential for participation in the country's resources, not just greed or simple assent to what passes for politics.

Having summarily assimilated the words "intellectual" and "writer" to each other a moment ago, it is best for me now to show why and how they belong together, despite the writer's separate origin and history. In the language of everyday use, a writer in the languages and cultures that I am familiar with is a person who produces literature, that is, a novelist, a poet, a dramatist. I think it is generally true that in all cultures writers have a separate, perhaps even more honorific, place than do intellectuals; the aura of creativity and an almost sanctified capacity for originality (often vatic in its scope and quality) accrues to them as it does not at all to intellectuals, who with regard to literature belong to the slightly debased and parasitic class of critics. (There is a long history of attacks on critics as nasty niggling beasts incapable of little more than carping and pedantic wordmongering.) Yet during the last years of the twentieth century the writer took on more and more of the intellectual's adversarial attributes in such activities as speaking the truth to power, being a witness to persecution and suffering, and in supplying a dissenting voice in conflicts with authority. Signs of the amalgamation of one to the other would have to include the Salman Rushdie case in all its ramifications, the formation of numerous writers' parliaments and congresses devoted to such issues as intolerance, the dialogue of cultures, civil strife (as in Bosnia and Algeria), freedom of speech and censorship, truth and reconciliation (as in South Africa, Argentina, Ireland, and elsewhere), and the special symbolic role of the writer as an intellectual testifying to a country's or region's expe-

rience, thereby giving that experience a public identity forever inscribed in the
global discursive agenda. The easiest way of demonstrating that is simply to list
the names of some (but by no means all) recent Nobel Prize winners, then to
allow each name to trigger in the mind an emblematized region, which in turn
can be seen as a sort of platform or jumping-off point for that writer's subsequent
activity as an intervention in debates taking place very far from the world of literature. Thus, Nadine Gordimer, Kenzaburo Oe, Derek Walcott, Wole Soyinka,
Gabriel Garcia Marquez, Octavio Paz, Elie Wiesel, Bertrand Russell, Gunter
Grass, Rigoberta Menchu, among several others.

Now it is also true, as Pascale Casanova has brilliantly shown in her synoptic
book *La République mondiale des lettres*, that, fashioned over the past 150 years,
there now seems to be a global system of literature in place, complete with its
own order of literariness (*litterarité*), tempo, canon, internationalism, and market
values.[6] The efficiency of the system is that it seems to have generated the types
of writers that she discusses as belonging to such different categories as
assimilated, dissident, translated figures, all of them both individualized and clas-
sified in what she clearly shows is a highly efficient, globalized quasi-market system. The drift of her argument is in effect to show how this powerful and all-
pervasive system can even go as far as to stimulate a kind of independence from
it, in cases like those of Joyce and Beckett, writers whose language and orthogra-
phy do not submit to the laws either of State or of system.

Much as I admire it, however, the overall achievement of Casanova's book is
nevertheless contradictory. She seems to be saying that literature as globalized
system has a kind of integral autonomy to it that places it in large measure just
beyond the gross realities of political institutions and discourse, a notion that has
a certain theoretical plausibility to it when she puts it in the form of "un espace
littéraire internationale," with its own laws of interpretation, its own dialectic of
individual work and ensemble, its own problematics of nationalism and national
languages. But she doesn't go as far as Adorno in saying, as I would too (and plan
to return to briefly at the end), that one of the hallmarks of modernity is how at
a very deep level, the aesthetic and the social need to be kept in a state of irreconcilable tension. Nor does she spend enough time discussing the ways in which
the literary, or the writer, is still implicated, indeed frequently mobilized for use
in the great post–Cold War cultural contests provided by the altered political
configurations I spoke of earlier.

In that wider setting then, the basic distinction between writers and intellectuals need not therefore be made since, insofar as they both act in the new public sphere dominated by globalization (and assumed to exist even by adherents of
the Khomeini fatwa), their public role as writers and intellectuals can be discussed and analyzed together. Another way of putting it is to say that I shall be
concentrating on what writers and intellectuals have in common as they intervene in the public sphere. I do not at all want to give up the possibility that
there remains an area outside and untouched by the globalized one that I shall
be discussing here, but do not want to discuss until the end, since my main concern is with what the writer's role is squarely within the actually existing system.

Let me say something about the technical characteristics of intellectual intervention today. To get a dramatically vivid grasp of the speed to which communication has accelerated during the past decade I'd like to contrast Jonathan Swift's awareness of effective public intervention in the early eighteenth century with ours. Swift was surely the most devastating pamphleteer of his time, and during his campaign against the Duke of Marlborough from 1713 to 1714, he was able to get 15,000 copies of his pamphlet "The Conduct of the Allies" onto the streets in a few days. This brought down the Duke from his high eminence but nevertheless did not change Swift's pessimistic impression (dating back to *A Tale of a Tub*, 1694) that his writing was basically temporary, good only for the short time that it circulated. He had in mind of course the running quarrel between ancients and moderns in which venerable writers like Homer and Horace had the advantage of great longevity, even permanence, over modern figures like Dryden by virtue of their age and the authenticity of their views. In the age of electronic media, such considerations are mostly irrelevant, since anyone with a computer and decent Internet access is capable of reaching numbers of people quantum times more than Swift did, and can also look forward to the preservation of what is written beyond any conceivable measure. Our ideas today of archive and discourse must be radically modified, and can no longer be defined as Foucault painstakingly tried to describe them a mere two decades ago. Even if one writes for a newspaper or journal, the chances of multiplying reproduction and, notionally at least, an unlimited time of preservation have wrought havoc on even the idea of an actual, as opposed to a virtual, audience. These things have certainly limited the powers that regimes have to censor or ban writing that is considered dangerous, although, as I shall note presently, there are fairly crude means for stopping or curtailing the libertarian function of online print. Until only very recently, Saudi Arabia and Syria, for example, successfully banned the Internet and even satellite television. Both countries now tolerate limited access to Internet, although both have also installed sophisticated and, in the long run, prohibitively interdictory, processes to maintain their control.

As things stand, an article I might write in New York for a British newspaper has a good chance of reappearing on individual websites or via email on screens in the United States, Japan, Pakistan, Middle East, South Africa, as well as Australia. Authors and publishers have very little control over what is reprinted and recirculated. For whom then does one write, if it is difficult to specify the audience with any sort of precision? Most people, I think, focus on the actual outlet that has commissioned the piece, or on the putative readers we would like to address. The idea of an imagined community has suddenly acquired a very literal, if virtual, dimension. Certainly, as I experienced when I began ten years ago to write in an Arabic publication for an audience of Arabs, one attempts to create, shape, refer to a constituency, now much more than during Swift's time, when he could quite naturally assume that the persona he called a Church of England man was in fact his real, very stable, and quite small audience.

All of us should therefore operate today with some notion of very probably reaching much larger audiences than any we could have conceived of even a decade ago, although the chances of retaining that audience are by the same token quite chancy. This is not simply a matter of optimism of the will; it is in the very nature of writing today. This makes it very difficult for writers to take common assumptions between them and their audiences for granted, or to assume that references and allusions are going to be understood immediately. But, writing in this expanded new space strangely does have a further unusually risky consequence, which is to be encouraged to say things that are either completely opaque or completely transparent, and if one has any sense of the intellectual and political vocation (which I shall get to in a moment), it should of course be the latter rather than the former. But then, transparent, simple, clear prose presents its own challenges, since the ever present danger is that one can fall into the misleadingly simple neutrality of a journalistic World-English idiom that is indistinguishable from CNN or USA Today prose. The quandary is a real one, whether in the end to repel readers (and more dangerous, meddling editors), or to attempt to win readers over in a style that perhaps too closely resembles the mind-set one is trying to expose and dismiss. The thing to remember, I keep telling myself, is that there isn't another language at hand, that the language I use must be the same used by the State Department or the president when they say that they are for human rights and for fighting a war to "liberate" Iraq, and I must be able to use that very same language to recapture the subject, reclaim it, and reconnect it to the tremendously complicated realities these vastly overprivileged antagonists of mine have simplified, betrayed, and either diminished or dissolved. It should be obvious by now that for an intellectual who is not there simply to advance someone else's interest, there have to be opponents that are held responsible for the present state of affairs, antagonists with whom one must directly engage.

While it is true and even discouraging that all the main outlets are, however, controlled by the most powerful interests and consequently by the very antagonists one resists or attacks, it is also true that a relatively mobile intellectual energy can take advantage of and, in effect, multiply the kinds of platforms available for use. On one side, therefore, six enormous multinationals presided over by six men control most of the world's supply of images and news. On the other, there are the independent intellectuals who actually form an incipient community, physically separated from each other but connected variously to a great number of activist communities shunned by the main media, but who have at their actual disposal other kinds of what Swift sarcastically called "oratorical machines." Think of the impressive range of opportunities offered by the lecture platform, the pamphlet, radio, alternative journals, the interview form, the rally, church pulpit, and the Internet to name only a few. True, it is a considerable disadvantage to realize that one is unlikely to get asked on to PBS's *Newshour* or ABC's *Nightline*, or if one is in fact asked, only an isolated fugitive minute will be offered. But then, other occasions present themselves not in the sound-bite format, but rather in more extended stretches of time. So rapidity is a double-edged weapon. There is the rapidity of the sloganeeringly reductive style that is the main feature of expert discourse—to-the-point, fast, formulaic, pragmatic in appearance—and there is the rapidity of response and format that intellectuals and indeed most citizens can exploit in order to present fuller, more complete expressions of an alternative point of view. I am suggesting that by taking advantage of what is available in the form of numerous platforms (or "stages-itinerant," another Swiftian term) and an alert and creative willingness to exploit them by an intellectual (that is, platforms that either are not available to or are shunned by the television personality, expert, or political candidate), it is possible to initiate wider discussion.

The emancipatory potential—and the threats to it—of this new situation must not be underestimated. Let me give a very powerful, recent example of what I mean. There are about four million Palestinian refugees scattered all over the world, a significant number of whom live in large refugee camps in Lebanon (where the 1982 Sabra and Shatila massacres took place), Jordan, Syria, and in Gaza and the West Bank. In 1999 an enterprising group of young and educated refugees living in Deheisheh Camp, near Bethlehem on the West Bank, established the Ibdaa Center whose main feature was the Across Borders project; this was a revolutionary way through computer terminals of connecting refugees in most of the main camps—separated geographically and politically by impossible, difficult barriers—to each other. For the first time since their parents were dispersed in 1948, second-generation Palestinian refugees in Beirut or Amman could communicate with their counterparts inside Palestine. Some of what the participants in the project did was quite remarkable. Thus the Deheisheh residents went on visits to their former villages in Palestine, and then described their emotions and what they saw for the benefit of other refugees who had heard of, but could not have access to, these places. In a matter of weeks, a remarkable solidarity emerged at a time, it turned out, when the so-called final status negotiations between the PLO and Israel were beginning to take up the question of refugees and return, which along with the question of Jerusalem made up the intransigent core of the stalemated peace process. For some Palestinian refugees, therefore, their presence and political will was actualized for the first time, giving them a new status qualitatively different from the passive objecthood that had been their fate for half a century. On August 26, 2000, all the computers in Deheisheh were destroyed in an act of political vandalism that left no one in doubt that refugees were meant to remain as refugees, which is to say that they were not meant to disturb the status quo that had assumed their silence for so long. It would not be hard to list the possible suspects, but it is equally hard to imagine that anyone will either be named or apprehended. In any case, the Deheisheh camp-dwellers immediately set about trying to restore the Ibdaa' Center, and seem to some degree to have succeeded in so doing.

To answer the question "why" in this and other similar contexts, individuals and groups prefer writing and speaking to silence, is equivalent to specifying what in fact the intellectual and writer confront in the public sphere. What I mean is that the existence of individuals or groups seeking social justice and economic equality, and who understand (in Amartya Sen's formulation) that freedom must include the right to a whole range of choices affording cultural, political, intellectual, and economic development, ipso facto will lead one to a desire for articulation as opposed to silence. This is the functional idiom of the intellectual vocation. The intellectual therefore stands in a position to make possible and to further the formulation of these expectations and wishes.

Now every discursive intervention is, of course, specific to a particular occasion and assumes an existing consensus, paradigm, episteme, or praxis (we can all pick our favorite concept that denotes the prevailing accepted discursive norm), say, during the Anglo-American war against Iraq, during national elections in Egypt and the United States, about immigration practices in one or another country, or about the ecology of West Africa. In each of these and so many other situations, the hallmark of the era we live in is that there tends to be a mainstream-media-government orthodoxy against which it is very difficult indeed to go, even though the intellectual must assume that alternatives can clearly be shown to exist. Thus, to restate the obvious, that every situation should be interpreted according to its own givens, but (and I would argue that this is almost always the case) that every situation also contains a contest between a powerful system of interests on the one hand and, on the other, less powerful interests threatened with frustration, silence, incorporation, or extinction by the powerful. It almost goes without saying that for the American intellectual the responsibility is greater, the openings numerous, the challenge very difficult. The United States after all is the only global power; it intervenes nearly everywhere, and its resources for domination are very great, although very far from infinite.

The intellectual's role generally is dialectically, oppositionally to uncover and elucidate the contest I referred to earlier, to challenge and defeat both an imposed silence and the normalized quiet of unseen power wherever and whenever possible. For there is a social and intellectual equivalence between this mass of overbearing collective interests and the discourse used to justify, disguise, or mystify its workings while also preventing objections or challenges to it.

Pierre Bourdieu and his associates produced a collective work in 1993 entitled *La Misère du monde* (translated in 1999 as *The Weight of the World: Social Suffering in Contemporary Society*) whose aim was thereby to compel the politicians' attention to what, in French society, the misleading optimism of public discourse had hidden.[7] This kind of book, therefore, plays a sort of negative intellectual role, whose aim is, to quote Bourdieu, "to produce and disseminate instruments of defense against symbolic domination which increasingly relies on the authority of science," or expertise or appeals to national unity, pride, history, and tradition, to bludgeon people into submission. Obviously India and Brazil are different from Britain and the United States, but those often striking disparities in cultures and economies should not at all obscure the even more startling similarities that can be seen in some of the techniques and, very often, the aim of deprivation and repression that compel people to follow along meekly. I should also like to add that one need not always present an abstruse and detailed theory of justice to go to war intellectually against injustice, since there is now a well-stocked internationalist storehouse of conventions, protocols, resolutions, and charters for national authorities to comply with, if they are so inclined. And, in the same context, I reject the ultra-postmodern position (like that taken by Richard Rorty while shadowboxing with some vague thing he refers to contemptuously as "the academic Left"), which holds, when confronting ethnic cleansing, or genocide as was occurring in Iraq under the sanctions-regime, or any of the evils of torture, censorship, famine, ignorance (most of them constructed by humans not by acts of God), that human rights are cultural or grammatical things, and when they are violated, they do not really have the status accorded them by crude foundationalists, such as myself, for whom they are as real as anything we can encounter.

I think it is correct to say that depoliticized or aestheticized submission, along with all of the different forms of in some cases triumphalism and xenophobia, in others of apathy and defeat, has been principally required since the 1960s to allay whatever residual feelings of desire for democratic participation (also known as "a danger to stability") still existed. One can read this plainly enough in *The Crisis of Democracy,* coauthored at the behest of the Trilateral Commission a decade before the end of the Cold War.[8] There the argument is that too much democracy is bad for governability, which is that supply of passivity that makes it easier for oligarchies of technical or policy experts to push people into line. So if one is endlessly lectured by certified experts who explain that the freedom we all want demands deregulation and privatization or war and that the new world order is nothing less than the end of history, there is very little inclination to address this order with anything like individual or even collective demands. Chomsky has relentlessly addressed this paralyzing syndrome for several years.

Let me give an example from personal experience in the United States today of how formidable the challenges to the individual are, and how easy it is to slip into inaction. If you are seriously ill, you are suddenly plunged into the world of outrageously expensive pharmaceutical products, many of which are still experimental and require FDA approval. Even those that are not experimental and are not particularly new (like steroids and antibiotics) are life-savers, but their exorbitant expense is thought to be a small price to pay for their efficacy. The more one looks into the matter, the more one encounters the corporate rationale, which is that while the cost of manufacturing the drug may be small (it usually is tiny), the cost of research is enormous and must be recovered in subsequent sales. Then you discover that most of the research cost came to the corporation in the form of government grants, which in turn came from the taxes paid by every citizen. When you address the abuse of public money in the form of questions put to a promising, progressively minded candidate (e.g., Bill Bradley), you then quickly understand why such candidates never raise the question. They receive enormous campaign contributions from Merck and Bristol Meyers, and are most unlikely to challenge their supporters. So you go on paying and living, on the assumption that if you are lucky enough to have an insurance policy, the insurance company will pay out. Then you discover that insurance company accountants make the decisions on who gets a costly medication or test, what is allowed or disallowed, for how long and in what circumstances, and only then do you understand that such rudimentary protections as a patient's genuine bill of rights still cannot be passed in Congress, given that immensely profitable insurance corporations lobby there indefatigably.

In short, I find myself saying that even heroic attempts (such as Fredric Jameson's) to understand the system on a theoretical level or to formulate what Samir Amin has called delinking alternatives, are fatally undermined by their relative neglect of actual political intervention in the existential situations in which as citizens we find ourselves—intervention that is not just personal but is a significant part of a broad adversarial or oppositional movement. Obviously, as intellectuals, we all carry around some working understanding or sketch of the global system (in large measure thanks to world and regional historians like Immanuel Wallerstein, Anwar Abdel Malek, J. M. Blaut, Janet Abu-Lughod, Peter Gran, Ali Mazrui, William McNeill), but it is during the direct encounters with it in one or another specific geography, configuration, or problematic that the contests are waged and perhaps even winnable. There is an admirable chronicle of the kind of thing I mean in the various essays of Bruce Robbins's *Feeling Global: Internationalism in Distress*, Timothy Brennan's *At Home in the World: Cosmopolitanism Now*, and Neil Lazarus's *Nationalism and Cultural Practice in the Postcolonial World*, books whose self-consciously territorial and highly interwoven textures are in fact an adumbration of the critical (and combative) intellectual's sense of the world we live in today, taken as episodes or even fragments of a broader picture that their work as well as the work of others like them is in the process of compiling. What they suggest is a map of experiences that would have been indiscernible, perhaps invisible two decades ago, but which in the aftermath of the classical empires, the end of the Cold War, the crumbling of the socialist and nonaligned blocks, the emergent dialectics between North and South in the era of globalization, cannot be excluded either from cultural study or from the somewhat precincts of the humanistic disciplines.

I've mentioned a few names not just to indicate how significant I think their contributions have been, but also to use them in order to leapfrog directly into some concrete areas of collective concern where, to quote Bourdieu for the last time, there is the possibility of "collective invention." He continues by saying that

> the whole edifice of critical thought is thus in need of critical reconstruction. This work of reconstruction cannot be done, as some thought in the past, by a single great intellectual, a master-thinker endowed with the sole resources of his singular thought, or by the authorized spokesperson for a group or an institution presumed to speak in the name of those without voice, union, party, and so on. This is where the collective intellectual [Bourdieu's name for individuals the sum of whose research and participation on common subjects constitutes a sort of ad hoc collective] can play its irreplaceable role, by helping to create the social conditions for the collective production of realist utopias.

My reading of this is to stress the absence of any master plan or blueprint or grand theory for what intellectuals can do, and the absence now of any utopian teleology toward which human history can be described as moving. Therefore one *invents* goals abductively—in the literal use of the Latin word "*inventio*" employed by rhetoricians to stress finding again, or reassembling from past performances, as opposed to the romantic use of invention as something you create from scratch. That is, one hypothesizes a better situation from the known historical and social facts. So, in effect, this enables intellectual performances on many fronts, in many places, many styles that keep in play both the sense of opposition and the sense of engaged participation that I mentioned a moment ago. Hence, film, photography, and even music, along with all the arts of writing can be aspects of this activity. Part of what we do as intellectuals is not only to define the situation, but also to discern the possibilities for active intervention, whether we then perform them ourselves or acknowledge them in others who have either gone before or are already at work, the intellectual as lookout. Provincialism of the old kind—for example, I am a literary specialist whose field is early seventeenth-century England—rules itself out and, quite frankly, seems uninteresting and needlessly neutered. The assumption has to be that even though one cannot do or know about everything, it must always be possible not only to discern the elements of a struggle or tension or problem near at hand that can be elucidated dialectically, but also to sense that other people have a similar stake and work in a common project. I have found a brilliantly inspiring parallel for what I mean in Adam Phillips's recent book *Darwin's Worms* in which Darwin's lifelong attention to the lowly earthworm revealed its capacity for expressing nature's variability and design without necessarily seeing the whole of either one or the other, thereby, in his work on earthworms, replacing "a creation myth with a secular maintenance myth."[9]

Is there some nontrivial way of generalizing about where and in what form such struggles are taking place now? I shall limit myself to saying a little about only three of these struggles, all of which are profoundly amenable to intellectual intervention and elaboration. The first is to protect against and forestall the disappearance of the past, which in the rapidity of change, the reformulation of tradition, and the construction of simplified bowdlerizations of history, is at the very heart of the contest described by Benjamin Barber rather too sweepingly as Jihad versus McWorld. The intellectual's role is to present alternative narratives and other perspectives on history than those provided by combatants on behalf of official memory and national identity and mission. At least since Nietzsche, the writing of history and the accumulations of memory have been regarded in many ways as one of the essential foundations of power, guiding its strategies, charting its progress. Look, for example, at the appalling exploitation of past suffering described in their accounts of the uses of the Holocaust by Tom Segev, Peter Novick, and Norman Finkelstein or, just to stay within the area of historical restitution and reparation, the invidious disfiguring, dismembering, and disremembering of significant historical experiences that do not have powerful enough lobbies in the present and therefore merit dismissal or belittlement. The need now is for de-intoxicated, sober histories that make evident the multiplicity and complexity of history without allowing one to conclude that it moves forward impersonally according to laws determined either by the divine or by the powerful.

The second struggle is to construct fields of coexistence rather than fields of battle as the outcome of intellectual labor. There are great lessons to be learned from decolonization which are that, noble as its liberatory aims were, it did not often enough prevent the emergence of repressive nationalist replacements for colonial regimes, and that the process itself was almost immediately captured by the Cold War, despite the nonaligned movement's rhetorical efforts. What's more, it has been miniaturized and even trivialized by a small academic industry that has simply turned it into an ambiguous contest between ambivalent opponents. Benita Parry has addressed this matter in her recent work as a deformation of postcolonial studies.[10] In the various contests over justice and human rights that so many of us feel we have joined, there needs to be a component to our engagement that stresses the need for the redistribution of resources, and that advocates the theoretical imperative against the huge accumulations of power and capital that so distort human life.

Peace cannot exist without equality; this is an intellectual value desperately in need of reiteration, demonstration, and reinforcement. The seduction of the word itself—peace—is that it is surrounded by, indeed drenched in, the blandishments of approval, uncontroversial eulogizing, sentimental endorsement. The international media (as has been the case recently of the unsanctioned war in Iraq) uncritically amplifies, ornaments, unquestioningly transmits all this to vast audiences for whom peace and war are spectacles for delectation and immediate consumption. It takes a good deal more courage, work, and knowledge to dissolve words like "war" and "peace" into their elements, recovering what has been left out of peace processes that have been determined by the powerful, and then placing that missing actuality back in the center of things, than it does to write prescriptive articles for "liberals" à la Michael Ignatieff that urge more destruction and death for distant civilians under the banner of benign imperialism. The intellectual is perhaps a kind of counter-memory with its own counter-discourse that will not allow conscience to look away or fall asleep. The best corrective, as Dr. Johnson said, is to imagine the person whom you are discussing—in this case the person on whom the bombs will fall—reading you in your presence.

Still, just as history is never over or complete, it is also the case that some dialectical oppositions are not reconcilable, not transcendable, not really capable of being folded into a sort of higher, undoubtedly nobler synthesis. My third example, and the one closest to home for me, is the struggle over Palestine which, I have always believed, cannot really be simply resolved by a technical and ultimately janitorial rearrangement of geography allowing dispossessed Palestinians the right (such as it is) to live in about 20 percent of their land that would be encircled and totally dependent on Israel. Nor, on the other hand, would it be morally acceptable to demand that Israelis should retreat from the whole of former Palestine, now Israel, becoming refugees like Palestinians all over again. No matter how I have searched for a resolution to this impasse, I cannot find one, for this is not a facile case of right versus right. It cannot be right ever to deprive an entire people of their land and heritage. But the Jews too are what I have called a community of suffering and have brought with them a heritage of great tragedy. But unlike the Israeli sociologist Zeev Sternhell, I cannot agree that the conquest of Palestine was a necessary one. The notion offends the sense of real Palestinian pain, in its own way, also tragic.

Overlapping yet irreconcilable experiences demand from the intellectual the courage to say that *that* is what is before us, in almost exactly the way Adorno has throughout his work on music insisted that modern music can never be reconciled with the society that produced it, but in its intensely and often despairingly crafted form and content, music can act as a silent witness to the inhumanity all around. Any assimilation of individual musical work to its social setting is, says Adorno, false. I conclude with the thought that the intellectual's provisional home is the domain of an exigent, resistant, intransigent art into which, alas, one can neither retreat nor search for solutions. But only in that precarious exilic realm can one first truly grasp the difficulty of what cannot be grasped, and then go forth to try anyway.

NOTES

1. Raymond Williams, *Keywords: A Vocabulary of Culture and Society* (New York: Oxford University Press, 1976).

2. Yves Dézélay and Bryant G. Garth, *Dealing in Virtue: International Commercial Arbitration and the Construction of a Transnational Legal Order* (Chicago: University of Chicago Press, 1996).

3. Yves Dézélay and Bryant G. Garth, "L'impérialisme de la vertu," *Le Monde diplomatique*, May 2000.

4. Fredric Jameson and Masao Miyoshi, eds., *The Cultures of Globalization* (Durham, NC: Duke University Press, 1998); Masao Miyoshi and H D Harootunian, eds., *Learning Places: The Afterlives of Area Studies* (Durham, N.C.: Duke University Press, 2002).

5. Perry Anderson, 'Renewals,' *New Left Review*, second series, number 1, January–February 2000.

6. Pascale Casanova, *La République mondiale des lettres* (Paris: Editions du Seuil, 1999).

7. Pierre Bourdieu et al., *La Misère du monde* (Paris: Editions du Seuil, 1993); *The Weight of the World: Social Suffering in Contemporary Society*, trans. Priscilla Parkhurst Ferguson et al. (Cambridge: Polity Press, 1999).

8. Michel Crozier, Samuel P. Huntington, Joji Watanuki, *The Crisis of Democracy: Report on the Governability of Democracies to the Trilateral Commission* (New York: New York University Press, 1975).

9. Adam Phillips, *Darwin's Worms* (London: Faber, 1999) p. 58.

10. Keith Ansell-Pearson, Benita Parry, Judith Squires, eds., *Cultural Readings of Imperialism: Edward Said and the gravity of history* (London: Lawrence & Wishart, 1997); Laura Chrisma, Benita Parry, eds., *Postcolonial Theory and Criticism* (Cambridge: D.S. Brewer, 2000).

Issues in the Translatability of Law

PIERRE LEGRAND

For Casimir and Imogene, who live in translation.

Consider statutes and judicial decisions, two of the most common legal artifacts. If one accepts that statutes are not enacted by legislatures and that judicial decisions are not made by courts with a view to applying to foreign legal cultures, then legal borrowing across legal cultures is the practice of interrupting intention, which is a form of epistemic violence.[1] Statutes and judicial decisions nonetheless regularly find themselves being imported across legal cultures—that is, across cultures and languages—in order to underwrite local reforming agendas. In the process, these texts pass into new semiotic constellations. However, just as there cannot be equivalence of meaning between, say, a poem-in-translation and the original poem, given that the host language and the host culture attest to constructions of the world that are incommensurable with those propounded by the language and culture where the work originates,[2] there cannot be equivalence of meaning between the law-in-translation and the original law. A text—whether a poem or a law—requires an adaptive transformation in the course of transit in order to be made understandable elsewhere and to carry the kind of impact or appeal it did in its native environment. But the peregrine text is not alone in undergoing change, for its import enjoins alterations within the host language and host culture themselves. One recalls how Luther's translation of the Bible famously challenged the German language or, more recently, how Corbin's, Waelhens's, Martineau's, and Vezin's translations of Heidegger's *Sein und Zeit* have compelled the French language and French philosophy to undergo the kind of modification allowing for the narrativization of unfamiliar ideas. The adoption of a foreign law has the same transformative impact on the host law and host legal culture.

Against the background of these preliminary observations, this essay seeks to delve into the parallels between legal borrowing and literary translation and between comparatists-at-law (those who wrestle with legal borrowing) and literary

I have used original versions and supplied my own translations throughout except in two cases—Benjamin's *Die Aufgabe des Übersetzers* and Heidegger's *Sein und Zeit*—where the English texts have achieved such currency that it somehow appeared pedantic to ignore them. I owe Sandra Bermann and Nicholas Kasirer for their generous interest in my research and for numerous suggestions, which improved my argument. The usual disclaimer applies.

translators (those who wrestle with languages).[3] The argument begins with an overview of the legal scene, with specific reference to the contemporary European experience.

.   .   .

Since the late 1940s, economic considerations relating to the globalization of world markets have led an ever-larger group of Western European countries to unite in the quest for a supranational legal order, which, in time, generated the European Community. The Member States' early decision to promote economic integration through harmonization or unification has involved a process of relentless regulation in the guise of legislation or judicial decisions. This development was foreseeable: once the interaction amongst European legal cultures had acted as a catalyzer for the creation of a supra-culture, the need to achieve reciprocal compatibility between the infra-cultures and the supra-culture naturally fostered the advent of an extended network of interconnections (including legal links), which, as it was realized that the economy could not be neatly detached from other spheres of social action, eventually raised the question of further legal integration in the form of a common law of Europe.

Any proposal in favor of such a "European law" must, however, acknowledge the presence within the Community of legal traditions, that is, of epistemological clusters that have fashioned themselves over the very long term and that have conditioned epistemological approaches to law at the level of local legal cultures. I do not intend "tradition" in the static, linear, totalizing, atemporal, and idealized sense, which detraditionalists justifiably condemn. Specifically, I do not adopt the view of grounding in a causally self-sufficient source or subscribe to the doctrine of infant determinism or suggest that traditions are to be envisaged as windowless monads allowing neither for cross-cultural interaction nor for cultural overlap. Rather, I have in mind something like structures of attitude and reference having normative force for legal communities (even though operating beneath consciousness), both by empowering legal agents and by limiting their possibilities of experience in ways that attest to the fact that positionality or situatedness is never fully individual.[4] In brief, the notion of "legal tradition" is meant to embrace the idea of tacit knowledge as it defines a horizon of meanings and possibilities with respect to the theoretical and practical information that can be acquired and used within a legal culture. It refers to an idiosyncratic—and often unexplicitable—cosmology of *dispositions* (or, perhaps, *predilections*) allowing for an infinite array of world-defining responses and discriminations. This socially-generated and shared context of meaning, which renders action intelligible to those involved and delineates the boundaries of relevance and irrelevance within a legal culture, accounts for cognitive, intuitive, and emotional approaches to law, legal knowledge, the role of law in society, the way law is or should be learned, the place assumed by legislation in society, the function of the judge, and so forth.[5] As the comparatist considers the development of law in Europe since Roman times, it appears that there have emerged at least two discrepant conceptions of law, one where structures of attitude and ref-

erence relate insistently to enacted law and the other, very much in reaction to
the first, where structures of attitude and reference gesture primordially to the
drawing by the courts of factual isomorphs across judicial decisions. These
nomothetic and idiographic perspectives remain current. Most of the European
Community's legal cultures claim allegiance to the former historical configuration—what anglophones are fond of labeling the "civil-law" tradition. Two
"common-law" jurisdictions, the United Kingdom and Ireland, joined the Community in the 1970s.

Given the presence of these contrapuntal epistemological frameworks, one
might have expected that whatever scholarly initiatives were concerned with
legal integration in Europe would have wanted to address the law in its local,
specific context (whether historical, social, economic, or political) with a view
to promoting understanding across legal traditions and legal cultures. This kind
of project would have been concerned to show how law-in-context inevitably
differed across legal traditions and legal cultures, to explain why these differences made sense at local levels, and to examine to what extent they could or
should be circumscribed. But such endeavours have not materialized. Instead,
one has witnessed the mushrooming of instrumental initiatives purporting to
show that the problem of understanding is a false one, because, in effect, there is
very little difference between European laws. In other words, there has been no
attempt at implementing a strategy of complexification, which would have
aimed at explicative re-presentations of the various laws on their own terms,
which would have stressed that "the specific legal practices of a culture are simply dialects of a parent social speech," and which would have insisted that there
is no reason why a legal culture should be expected to "depart drastically from
the common stock of understanding in the surrounding culture."[6] This brand of
research would have attended to recurrently emergent, relatively stable, institutionally reinforced social practices and discursive modalities (a certain lexicon, a
certain range of intellectual or rhetorical themes, a certain set of logical or conceptual moves, a certain emotional register, and so forth) acquired by the members of a community through social interaction and experienced by them as generalized tendencies and educated expectations congruent with their conception
of justice.[7] Instead, one is faced with a whole range of strategies of simplification.
The point is no longer to ascribe meaning to a legal experience and to appreciate
why it has developed in a way that is historically, sociologically, economically, or
politically—that is to say, culturally—different from another, but to argue that
difference is simply not there or, at least, that it is not there in a meaningful way.
In thrall to the serviceable principle of parsimony, which prefers simple, coherent, and consistent solutions, such philistine tactics—whether seeking to unify
contract, torts, civil procedure, administrative law, criminal law, or trusts[8]—wish
to efface difference, to erase it. Difference is inconvenient. Worse, difference is a
curse.

Underlying all these initiatives is a formalist understanding of "law" whereby
the "legal" is, in substance, reduced to rules—which are usually not defined, but
are conventionally taken to mean legislative texts and, though less peremptorily,

judicial decisions. The governing idea is that law can somehow have an empirical existence that can be detached from the world of meanings that characterizes a legal culture and that it can, therefore, easily move from one legal culture to the next so as to foster the commonalities I have mentioned. One can, for instance, take the Belgian law as regards a specific question concerning consumer contracts and transport it to Ireland in pursuit of the ideal of uniformity in the conviction that it will operate over there in the self-same way it has over here. Or one can adopt an international text—such as a European Community directive—and assume that the rule embodied in, say, article 3 of the document, will be applied in a uniform manner in the various legal cultures implementing the accord. Change in the law, then, would be largely independent of the workings of any linguistic, cultural, historical, or social substratum; it would rather—and rather more simply—be a function of laws, of rules being imported from another legal culture. Indeed, it has been said that "the transplanting of legal rules is socially easy."[9] Clearly, such assumptions, which rapidly engender a frenetic and hasty search for commonalities-that-clearly-must-be-there-since-we-want-them-there, propound normalized schemes based on rational and (so-called) scientific principles showing small regard for context and none for contingency. They relegate the cognitive asymmetries between the civil-law and common-law worlds to ignorable differences, to the realm of epiphenomena, and show confusion between the legitimate desire to overcome barriers of communication across legal traditions and legal cultures, on the one hand, and the alleged need to elucidate presumed similarities, on the other. Basil Markesinis seems to have gone furthest by expressly condoning the "manipulation" of data in order to make laws look similar across Europe.[10]

Now, to focus on selected titbits of "black-letter" law without any consideration of the historical, social, economic, or political environment is to deceive on a massive scale by intimating that the superficial and brittle similarities regarding legislative texts or judicial outcomes matter more than the traditionary and cultural differences that dictate the epistemological framework within which a statute is enacted or a case is addressed (an approach evidently unconvincing to anyone who has studied and taught both in civil-law and common-law environments). Insensitivity to questions of cultural heterogeneity fails to do justice to the situated, local properties of knowledge, which are no less powerful because they may remain inchoate and uninstitutionalized. In the way it refuses to address plurijurality at the deep, cultural level, the rhetoric of commonality simply deprives itself of intercultural and epistemological validity. It deserts serious thought for earnest prostration before the instrumentalist sabotage of cognition.

Were lawyers to show greater sensitivity to the characteristic features of laws and experiences of law that are not theirs, they could be expected to address the limits within which any "convergence" agenda must operate and the constraints that, ultimately, must defeat it. The fact is that even though we live them simultaneously and manage to reconcile them in an obscure and private economy, civil law's nomothetism and common law's idiographism are irrevocably *irreconcilable*.[11] In my view, the realization that legal convergence can never fully transcend the manifestations of localism, including the historicity of law, is not to be regretted. No matter how insistently the bureaucratic ethos of technical/universal homogeneity promotes its centralizing and uniformizing ambitions, the reformulation of legal Europe cannot condone a disempowering of local histories in a context where the specificity of European legal discourse arguably lies precisely in its historicity. In an argument he devotes to the European experience, Jacques Derrida writes about "the *duty* to answer the call of European memory." He claims that that duty "dictates respect for difference, the idiomatic, the minority, the singular and commands to tolerate and respect everything that does not place itself under the authority of reason."[12] Elsewhere, Derrida observes that "this responsibility toward memory [ought to] regulat[e] the justice and the justness of our behaviour, of our theoretical, practical, and ethico-political decisions."[13]

As a comparatist-at-law, my goal is, accordingly, to redeem local knowledge, best described in terms of its plasticity, pliability, diversity, and adaptability. I wish to foster resistance to the trends toward the ever-increasing technological standardization of law and the ready political subordination of the lawyer (within or without the academy) to the comforting values of orthodoxy and reiteration. I advocate a militant approach, which argues for greater sensitivity to the characteristic features of laws and experiences of law that are not ours. Lawyers seeking to elicit epigrammatic answers from foreign laws must accept that, within the structural constraints set by the human interpretive apparatus, such understanding of a law or of an experience of law other than one's own as is possible can only arise from cultural contextualization.[14] What is required in an age of globalization, therefore, is not yet more illusory formalization of law on any given point. Rather, there is an urgent need to appreciate how various legal communities think about the law, why they think about the law as they do, why they would find it difficult to think about the law in any other way, and *how their thought differs from ours*. It is this kind of fundamental information about alterity-in-the-law that lawyers—and, in particular, comparatists-at-law—should be seeking to disseminate. I suggest that this goal can best be effectuated by securing pertinent anthropological, philosophical, and psychological insights. Indeed, I claim that lawyers can only account in a meaningful way for how the law is constructed in a foreign legal culture through an interdisciplinary investigation. The point, for instance, is that in enacting a *loi* for the reasons they do and in the way they do, as a product of the way they think, with the desires and ambitions they have, in enacting a specific *loi* (and not others), the French are not just doing *that*: they are also doing something typically French and are thus alluding to a modality of legal experience that is intrinsically theirs. In this sense, because it communicates the French sensibility to law, the *loi* can serve as a focus of inquiry into legal "Frenchness" and into Frenchness *tout court*. It need not be regarded only as a *loi* in terms of its effectivity as rule. There is more to *loi*ness than *loi*-as-rule. Indeed, *loi*-as-rule is a "cognitive intoxicant" bound to entail persistent misapprehension of the French experience of the legal.[15] A *loi* is necessarily an incorporative cultural form. As a compactly allusive accretion of cultural elements, of traditionary features that constitute individual autonomy and identity within a community, it is supported by impressive ideological formations. A *loi* is "encrusted, beyond lexical-grammatical definition, with phonetic, historical, social, idiomatic overtones and undertones. It carries with it connotations, associations, previous usages, and even graphic, pictorial values and suggestions (the look, the 'shape' of words)."[16] The part never states its own meaning, for it is an expression of the whole assumptive background: it conveys morally and politically resonant ascriptions. To borrow from Marcel Mauss, each manifestation of the law must be apprehended as a *"fait social total,"* a complete social fact (which is emphatically not to say that every manifestation of law within a culture is nothing but an example of that entire culture being acted out).[17] And it is precisely this ability to see the whole in the part, to move away from the underbrush of detail and lead to a clearing of responsive perception, that must define the interpretive competence of comparatists-at-law. In an era of globalization, their task is to appreciate the semantic field to which the rule belongs, to grasp the latent patterns of interest and struggle that shape the existence of postulated realities, the production of associations to which the rule is a clue.

To refute the view that legal rules are somehow modular and interchangeable entities unencumbered by linguistic, epistemological, or cultural baggage is to accept that a given rule cannot be equally at home everywhere in the world. Indeed, I claim that this is an important constitutive feature of law, not an inconvenient limitation. I argue that no form of words purporting to be a "rule" can find itself completely devoid of semantic content, for no rule can be without meaning. The meaning of the rule is an essential component of the rule; it partakes in the *ruleness* of the rule. The meaning of a rule, however, is not entirely supplied by the rule itself; a rule is never totally self-explanatory. To be sure, meaning emerges from the rule so that it must be assumed to exist, if virtually, within the rule itself even before the interpreter's interpretive apparatus is engaged. To this extent, the meaning of a rule is acontextual. But meaning is also—and perhaps mostly—a function of the application of the rule by its interpreter, of the concretization or instantiation of the rule in the events it is meant to govern.[18] This ascription of meaning is predisposed by the way the interpreter understands the context within which the rule arises and by the manner in which he frames his questions, this process being determined by who and where the interpreter is and, therefore, to an extent at least, by what the interpreter, in advance, wants and expects (unwittingly?) the answers to be. Hence, the meaning of the rule is a function of the interpreter's epistemological assumptions, which are themselves linguistically and historically, that is, culturally conditioned. These *pre-judices* (in the etymological sense of the term) are actively forged, for example through the schooling process in which law students are immersed and through which they become impressed with the values, beliefs, justifications, and the practical consciousness that allow them to consolidate a cultural code, to fashion their identities, and to become professionally socialized. Inevitably, therefore, a significant part of the very real emotional and intellectual investment that presides over the formulation of the meaning of a rule lies beneath consciousness, because the act of interpretation is embedded, in ways that the interpreter is often unable to appreciate empirically, in a morality, in a culture, and in a tradition, in sum, in a whole *ambience* that guides the experience of a concept—a process of embeddedness constituting what Hans-Georg Gadamer refers to as "pre-understanding."[19]

Lawyers must adopt a view of law as a polysemic signifier, which connotes *inter alia* traditionary and cultural referents. If one agrees that, in significant ways, a rule receives its meaning from without and if one accepts that such ascription of meaning by an interpretive community effectively partakes in the ruleness of the rule—indeed, in the *nucleus* of ruleness—it must follow that there could only occur a meaningful "legal transplant" when both the propositional statement as such *and* its ascribed meaning—which jointly constitute *the rule*—are transported from one legal culture to another. Given that the meaning ascribed to the rule is itself culture-specific, it is difficult to conceive, however, how this transfer could ever genuinely happen. In linguistic terms, one could say that the signified (meaning the idea content of the word) is never displaced since it always refers to an idiosyncratic semiotic situation. Rather, the propositional statement, as it finds itself technically integrated into another law, is understood differently by the host culture and is, on account of a process of semantic reconfiguration, ascribed a culture-specific meaning at variance with the earlier one (not least because the very appreciation of the notion of "rule" may itself differ): "one understands *differently, when one understands at all.*"[20] Accordingly, a crucial element of the ruleness of the rule—its meaning—does not survive the journey from one law to another. In other words, the act of communication involves the communication of *something* to *someone* and the tension between these two poles inevitably resolves itself in favor of the latter.

The relationship between the inscribed words that constitute the rule in its bare propositional form and the idea to which they are connected is largely arbitrary in the sense that it is culturally determined. Thus, there is nothing to show that the same inscribed words will necessarily generate the same idea in a different culture, a fortiori if the inscribed words are themselves different because they have been rendered in another language. As Walter Benjamin writes, "the word *Brot* means something different to a German than the word *pain* to a Frenchman."[21] And as José Ortega y Gasset observes in his *Miseria y esplendor de la traducción*, the Spanish "*bosque*" does not mean the German "*Wald.*"[22] In other terms, as words cross boundaries, a different rationality and a different morality intervene to underwrite and effectuate them: the host culture continues to articulate *its* moral inquiry (even at the level of the *mémoire involontaire*) according to standards of justification that are accepted and acceptable locally. Accordingly, the imported form of words is ascribed a different, local, *iconoclastic* meaning, which defeats the sui generis relation that the rule had instituted with language, culture, and tradition in its native environment and which makes the rule ipso facto a *different* rule. As the understanding of a rule changes, the meaning of the rule changes. And as the meaning of the rule changes, the rule itself changes. Meaning simply does not lend itself to transplantation; it is not negotiable internationally. Cross-cultural influences, rather than generate a kind of immanent rationalization across laws, lead to a local *métissage*, which, because the elements in the mix are specific to local circumstances, is itself idiosyncratic.[23]

Until the one universal, unassailable, and unassailed political truth is revealed in its univocally significant reality, every law remains an expression of the language, culture, and tradition that called it into being. There is always at work, if you like, an active agent of domestication, and that agent lives locally. At best, what can be displaced from one legal culture to another is, literally, a *meaning-less* form of words. To claim more is to claim too much. In any *meaning-ful* sense of the term, "legal transplants" cannot happen (the idea of "transplant," therefore, bespeaks far less the continued life of the plant than a displacement of its ground). As it crosses boundaries, the original rule necessarily undergoes a change that affects it qua rule. The disjunction between the bare propositional statement and its meaning prevents the displacement of the *rule* itself—a point which current anthropological research on cognition captures thus: "The fact that exactly the same word gets printed or uttered again and again does not mean that exactly the same meaning (which is half the word) spreads from minds to minds."[24] To quote from Eva Hoffman, "[y]ou can't transport human meanings whole from one culture to another any more than you can transliterate a text." This impossibility arises because, in the words of this writer again, "[i]n order to transport a single word without distortion, one would have to transport the entire language around it." There is more: "In order to translate a language, or a text, without changing its meaning, one would have to transport its audience as well."[25] In the way in which memory is not recuperation of past time but rather the figuration that time assumes in the moment of remembering, legal borrowing is less a repository for what is elsewhere than a modality of its (virtual?) *Darstellung*. But rather than point to an unproblematic reverberation, the kinship between the new and the original law generates their difference: on what basis could the new law claim to duplicate the original if no law, however original, in turn guarantees the objective reality of that which it names? (Indeed, how could the second performance replicate in all respects that of the opening night?) This means that the "logic" governing the circulation of legal rules is one of *connectedness* rather than identity, sameness, or mimesis: there is no *reprise*.[26] One is reminded of Benjamin's exposition of Romantic epistemology and of (some aspects at least of) his relational—and, hence, differentiating—motif of "*Zusammenhang*."[27]

What happens when a legal rule is formulated or reformulated in one legal culture on the basis of a legal rule prevailing in another is, indeed, closely analogous to the act of literary translation. In both instances, texts are intentional and relational. In both instances, the meaning of the original is assumed not to reside wholly within the original itself. In both instances, there are silences to be addressed.[28] In both instances, there is a certain "mutational" element occurring in every "copying" event. (In German, in fact, the language makes this link almost explicit: while "*über setzen*" conveys the idea of transportation to another shore—which could apply, at least metaphorically, to the adoption of legal rules across legal cultures—"*übersetzen*" means "to translate.") Just as the "transplant"

gives rise to the "untransplantability" of law and the idea of a "remainder," literary translation gives birth to the "untranslatability" of language and the idea of a
"remainder." The way in which literary translators are faced with the relationship between texts and culture, both in the guest and in the host languages, and
the way in which they bring to the act of translation, whether consciously or unconsciously, their theory of language, their ideas on words and meaning, their
cross-cultural knowledge, their sense of what is possible given specific cultural
frames, cultural regularities, and cultural key mechanisms, is akin to the manner
in which lawyers are required to approach legal borrowing across legal cultures.[29]

First, the literary translator must adapt the work-in-translation so as to facilitate understanding by the readership in the host language even though this strategy entails moving away from a strictly literal approach. Thus, in Gilbert Adair's
English translation of Georges Perec's famous lipogram, although the hero remains French and the action continues to be set in France, Anton Voyl becomes
Anton Vowl.[30] And while Perec has his main character proclaiming his admiration "*pour Cyrano*," the translator writes "for Rostand's Cyrano." Also, the translator substitutes adaptations of Shakespeare and Milton for those that Perec had
offered of Mallarmé and Hugo. Another well-known illustration of the accultur-
ation process I am contemplating is found in Pierre Leyris's French translation of
T. S. Eliot's "The Love Song of J. Alfred Prufrock," which seeks to reproduce the
poet's rhymic effect. Eliot has:

> In the room the women come and go
> Talking of Michelangelo.

The French text reads thus:

> *Dans la pièce les femmes vont et viennent*
> *En parlant des maîtres de Sienne.*[31]

There are, of course, many such examples—some of which have become familiar. I have in mind one of Robert Adams's favourites: in the Inuktikuk version of
the Bible, the "lamb of God" becomes the "seal of God."[32]

Second, the literary translator must adapt the host language in order to accommodate alterity—the point of translation being, of course, to allow a readership to partake in diversity, which cannot, therefore, be obliterated lest the idea
of translation itself be betrayed. In other words, the translator must accept that
the original presence of the guest language ought not to be effaced. Indeed, Gayatri Spivak writes of the need for the translator to "surrender" to language.[33] A
translation must not aim to look so "natural" within the host language as no
longer to appear like a translation. Otherwise, it denies the entitlement of alterity to exist as alterity and, ultimately, refuses to grant it hospitality. In the way it
purports to abandon the normal articulation of French sentences, Chateaubriand's translation of *Paradise Lost* offers a good example of an attempt to overcome ethnocentricity in the host language.[34] In 1836, as he was proceeding to
translate Milton, Chateaubriand stood as the unchallenged master of French
prose, which he had carried to a degree of sophistication that has since possibly

been surpassed only by Proust. Yet, in his observations on his translation strategy, Chateaubriand, crucially, wrote as follows: "I have not been afraid to change the regime of verbs whenever, had I remained more French, I would have made the original loose something of its precision, of its originality, or of its energy."[35] Chateaubriand himself illustrated this statement with an example, which he drew from Milton's description of Pandemonium, the palace of Satan:

> Many a row
> Of starry lamps
> Yielded light
> As from a sky [.]

> *Plusieurs rangs*
> *de lampes étoilées*
> *émanent la lumière*
> *comme un firmament [.]*

The translator offers the following explanation to justify the way in which he derogates from the canons of French syntax: "I know that *émaner* in French is not an active verb: a sky does not *émane* light, rather light *émane* from a sky; but if you translate like this, what becomes of the image? At least, the reader here enters into the genius of the English language; he learns about the difference that exists between the regimes of verbs in that language and in ours."[36] In this sense, Chateaubriand makes the French language hospitable to alterity through a rather sophisticated adaptive strategy—all the while showing how "fidelity" need not be subordinated to the notion of "communicative efficacy."[37]

Whether one is moving away from the literal rendition of the guest text or reworking the host language, one is engaged in an act of violence, which, however, must ultimately yield to the fact of untranslatability, that is, to the textness of the text's obstinate self-affirmation.[38] In this sense, failure inheres to the act of literary translation—a point captured by Chateaubriand in his allusion to the grief experienced by the translator.[39] But the failure is not complete, for translation inscribes alterity at the heart of identity through the new forms it creates "in the ductile matter of language."[40] Thus, the host language makes the work other-than-itself while the work offers the host language the opportunity to differ from itself. In this way, literary translation reveals the genuine nature of hospitality, which is that both the guest and the host should be exposed to a risk: the guest agrees to put herself in the hands of the host, the host agrees to change his ways in order to welcome the guest.[41] As this interaction takes place, emphasizing a shared condition of vulnerability,[42] there happens a displacement of the borders confining and ordering the existence of each language, a deterritorialization. Literary translation denationalizes language and inscribes it in a history, which does not reduce itself to that of its "native" speakers. Through translation, both the guest and the host languages make the point that they can potentially be at home "elsewhere" or "elsehow" and assert the possibility of acknowledging alterity through a movement of differentiation from oneself. They emphasize a phenomenon of disappropriation.[43] What is the case for literary translation applies also to legal borrowing, which, as I have observed, also inscribes alterity at the heart of identity by showing the adaptability of law, whether guest or host. Literary translation and legal borrowing allow the text to "ris[e] above itself, above its own linguistic enmeshments."[44] They encourage it to find fulfilment in something other than the original setting, they justify its transgression of boundaries, they favor its liberation from itself, they make possible its *redemption*. There is more, for translation can be apprehended as a (re)construction of the experiential continuity of the world in that it "express[es] the innermost relationship of languages,"[45] to the extent at least that all individual languages, although they differ in terms of words, sentences, and structures, intend to *disclose*. Likewise, one could say that legal borrowing expresses the innermost relationship of laws insofar as all laws intend to regulate.

In the same way as literary translators accept that words do not *just* travel across languages, lawyers must begin to appreciate that laws do not *just* travel across legal cultures. And in the same way as literary translators accept that translation requires modifications to the work-in-translation, lawyers must accept that legal borrowing requires modifications to the law-in-transit, if only as a condition of the acceptability of alterity by the interpretive community inhabiting the host law, as a condition of alterity *making sense* for that community. It is, therefore, simplistic to approach the matter of legal borrowing as if rules were interchangeable across space and time. Consider, by way of example, Alan Watson's assertion—one of many statements advanced by this author along the same lines: "Before the *Code civil* the Roman rules [on transfer of ownership and risk in sale] were generally accepted in France [. . .]. This was also the law accepted by the first modern European code, the Prussian *Allgemeines Landrecht für die Preußischen Staaten* of 1794."[46] Now, the fact is that the Roman "rules" were written in Latin and purported to regulate the dealings of citizens in sixth-century Constantinople. The French rules mentioned by the author were written in French and intended to govern citizens in pre-revolutionary France. And the Prussian rules to which the author refers were written in German and were concerned with legal relationships in what remained feudal Prussia. I argue that cultural constructions of reality and of law and of rules in the three settings would harbour certain distinctive characteristics, which would, therefore, affect the interpretation of the rule, that is, which would determine the ruleness of the rule according to the distinctive cultural logics of the native legal communities. These rules, therefore, are not the same rules. Any similarity stops at the bare form of words itself, for every form of words, because it emerges in a shared local context that is already meaningful locally and through which alone there can be any local understanding at all, can only get its meaning by fitting into and contributing to the local whole. Even then, this conclusion does not account for the fact that the inscribed words appear in three different languages with each language suggesting a specific relationship between the words and their signifying content (for example, "[n]o language divides time or space exactly as does any other [. . .]; no language has identical taboos with any other [. . .] ; no language dreams precisely like any other").[47] In this respect, Benjamin's observation may be usefully recalled: "Whereas content and language form a certain unity in the original, like a fruit and its skin, the language of the translation envelops its content like a royal robe with ample folds. For it signifies a more exalted language than its own and thus remains unsuited to its content, overpowering and alien."[48] Language—and the same could be said of culture—, whether having to do with poetry or law, acts as an operator of difference—not, to be sure, an absolute difference, not the kind of difference that would imply irrevocably divided realms, but the difference that Rodolphe Gasché calls, after Benjamin, a *caesura:* "difference is achieved in the fleeting touch of what is to be disregarded, in fidelity to what is to be abandoned."[49]

Arguments purporting to establish sameness of laws across legal cultures, which Watson's juxtaposition shows to rest on a comprehensive attitude *preceding* the facts that are supposed to call these claims forth, are necessarily based on a repression of differences located in the contextual matrix within which any manifestation of posited law is inevitably ensconced.[50] As against Watson's constitutive exclusions—which effectively remove legal relations from the field of direct experience of particular persons in their mutual involvement, force individuals to renounce their autonomy and assign them to the impersonal forces of the market in legal ideas, and replace a mode of engagement with a perfectly artificial and ideological mode of construction of axiomatic patterns established through strict reference to the formalized elements of law—the task of comparatists-at-law is to measure the gap or the *écart* between laws, not unlike the way in which literary translators constantly seek to apprehend the distance between languages. Comparative legal studies is best regarded as a phenomenological inquiry, that is, as the hermeneutic explication and mediation of plural and different forms of legal experience within a descriptive and critical meta-language—an important feature of this programme of disclosure being embodied in Paul Ricoeur's notion of a *hermeneutics of suspicion*.[51] Because insensitivity to questions of cultural heterogeneity does not do justice to the situated, local properties of knowledge, comparatists must never pretend to overlook the distance between self and other. Rather, they must allow the self to make the journey and see the other in the way she must be seen, that is, *as other*. Comparatists must permit the other to realize her vision of her world. Ultimately, comparative legal analysis must not have a unifying but a multiplying effect: it must aim to organize the diversity of discourses around different (cultural) forms and *counter* the tendency of the mind toward uniformization.[52] It must recognize the reproduction of distances at the very heart of the mechanisms of imitation. Comparative legal studies must grasp legal experience *diacritically*. Accordingly, comparatists-at-law must rebut any attempt at the universalization of singularity under the guise of ascribed similarity, such as is propounded by the positivistic defenders of the "legal transplants" thesis.

Law is part of the symbolic apparatus through which entire communities try to understand themselves better. Comparative legal studies can further one's understanding of other peoples by shedding light on how they understand their law. But unless comparatists-at-law can learn to think of law as a culturally-situated phenomenon and accept that the law lives in a profound way within a culture-specific—and, therefore, contingent—discourse, comparison rapidly becomes a pointless venture. I argue that the priority of alterity—best expressed through the consilience of individualizing and phenomenalistic elements—must act as a governing postulate for comparatists: even international conventions will not create legal uniformity given the inherently localized properties of language, culture, and tradition.

. . .

Just as there is no universal correspondence between words and world, such that literary translation is necessary, there is no universal correspondence between laws and world, such that legal borrowing is necessary. Whether one is considering literary translation or legal borrowing, only in deferring to the non-identical can the claim to *justice* be redeemed.[53] In the same way as literary translation cannot be subsumed under the governance of the same, legal borrowing must escape from the confines of reductive reproductibility. Literary translation is neither mere interpretation of the original text nor mere departure or license from the original. It does not purport to achieve unity and truth in language. Rather, it is that which repudiates the reflexivity of re-presentation—that which disrupts, decenters, and displaces re-presentation—through the multiplication and the constant renewal and the ultimate inexhaustibility of meanings and truths. Instead of falling within the logic of sameness, literary translation has sameness-resisting and difference-creating power.[54] It shares these key features with legal borrowing, which also exemplifies the openness of law to transformation and renewal and its inherent inexhaustibility. Any idea that law is reproducible and is, in fact, reproduced from one legal culture to the next forgets that here, too, the again is always the anew: *duo si idem dicunt, non est idem.* To borrow from Carol Jacobs writing about Benjamin's theory of literary translation: legal borrowing does not transform an original foreign law into one the importers may call their own, but rather renders radically foreign that law they envisage as being theirs.[55]

In French, one can refer to a *"parti pris"* and talk about *"prendre son parti."* Either formulation connotes three meanings that jointly capture three important facets of my argument. First, one can have a *"parti pris"* in the sense of showing purposefulness. For example, a French sentence can run thus: *"Chez lui, le parti pris de faire du bien se remarquait vite"* (In him, the determination to do good could easily be noticed). A variation on this sentence reads: *"Il avait pris le parti de faire du bien"* (He had determined to do good). Second, a *"parti pris"* refers to a prejudice as in the sentence, *"il y a trop de parti pris dans ses jugements"* (there is too much prejudice in his opinions). Third, *"prendre son parti"* can mean "to resign oneself." After one has lost an important vote, it can be said that *"il en a pris son parti,"* that "he has resigned himself to it." Purposefulness, prejudice, and resignation are three cardinal features of the brand of comparative legal studies I advocate. I argue that comparatists must *resign* themselves to the fact that law is a cultural phenomenon and that, therefore, differences across legal cultures can only ever be overcome imperfectly: not everything can be hygienically totalized.[56] Disclaiming any objectivity (and, therefore, bringing to bear their own *prejudices* as situated observers), they must *purposefully* privilege the identification of differences across the laws they compare lest they fail to address singularity with authenticity. For them, the challenge then becomes "how to restore to the singular, to the unexchangeable, to muteness, the attributes of power and, therefore, of health, of sovereignty—given that language, communication, exchange have attributed to *gregarious conformity* what is healthy, powerful, sovereign."[57] But academic proposals concerning the matter of European legal integration reveal the magnitude of the task. One of the integrationists' animating desires as they engage in their futile suburban enterprises is specifically to avoid gaining contextual knowledge and thick understanding, to ignore law's *facticity*, to *deworld* the law. Indeed, such cognitive deficit is constitutive of "doing law" for these individuals, which means that remedying one's ignorance by addressing the primordial questions that have been avoided heretofore can hardly be a genuine option as this would entail that one is no longer "doing law": "to be really good at 'doing law,' one has to have serious blind spots and a stunningly selective sense of curiosity."[58]

Nonetheless, only the pursuit of cultural understanding can engender an illuminating contrast to the comparatist's own assumptions, that is, can serve as an anchor for a renewed relation to lived experience, an improved self-understanding, and, ultimately, enhanced freedom—what Ortega y Gasset calls a new "in-oneselfness."[59] Ricoeur makes this point in the following terms: "It is the enlargement of one's own understanding of oneself that [the interpreter] seeks through the understanding of the other. Any hermeneutics is thus, explicitly or implicitly, the understanding of oneself through the detour of the understanding of the other."[60] The question to be asked is not What are they like?, but Why are they different from us?, and, therefore, What makes us what we are?. Comparison, like psychoanalysis, is a transferential process whereby one redefines oneself in the course of renegotiating one's relation with the other and, ultimately, with oneself—always bearing in mind, of course, that the other cannot be preconstituted in its otherness prior to the encounter, for otherness is a product of the encounter.[61] Through its inscription in something like Derrida's *écriture suspendue*, something like Maurice Blanchot's *entretien infini* thus generates something like Heidegger's *Erläuterung*. Here lies comparative legal studies's *emancipatory* interest. Here lies comparison-at-law's compelling affinity with translation,[62] aporetic experiences both on account of the fact that dealing with others-in-the-law or with others-in-language involves "the simple and necessary and yet so unattainable proposition that their way of being we, [is] not our way and that our way of being they, [is] not their way."[63]

NOTES

1. I understand the notion of "legal culture" to mean the framework of intangibles within which a legal community operates and that determines the identity of a legal community *as legal community*. The indeterminacy of "culture" or, if you will, the impossibility

of distinguishing between "culture" and "non-culture" in a way that would allow the identification of empirically verifiable causal relationships accounting for "cultural" explanations of legal behavior, has prompted many lawyers (within or without the academy) in search of mechanistic explications of experience to disqualify the notion altogether. To those who do not like the idea of "culture," I ask: What is your competing model of social cohesion? Or do you not like the idea of "social cohesion" either?

2. The fact that all significance is sayable does not detract from the further fact that sayability occurs within incommensurate lexicons. In other words, assertions do not determine truth conditions by virtue of their propositional content alone. Rather, true statements can only be made relative to a lexicon. For an influential thesis to this effect, see Friedrich Schleiermacher, *Ueber die verschiedenen Methoden des Uebersezens*, in *Sämmtliche Werke*, tome III, vol. 2 (Berlin: Reimer, 1838), p. 239: "Each language contains one system of concepts which, precisely because they touch, join, and complement each other in the same language, constitute a whole, the different parts of which do not correspond to any of those of the system of other languages" [(*Es) enthält jede Sprache (. . .) Ein System von Begriffen in sich, die eben dadurch daß sie sich in derselben Sprache berühren, verbinden, ergänzen, Ein Ganzes sind, dessen einzelnen Theilen aber keine aus dem System anderer Sprachen entsprechen*], 1813.

3. I deliberately do not address the matter of "legal translation" as such, that is, the actual translation of "legal texts." For an insightful overview of some of the crucial theoretical issues arising in this context, see, for example, Nicholas Kasirer, "François Gény's *libre recherche scientifique* as a Guide for Legal Translation," *Louisiana Law Review* 61(331), 2001. See also Janet E. Ainsworth, "Categories and Culture: On the 'Rectification of Names' in Comparative Law," *Cornell Law Review* 82(19), 1996; Peter Goodrich, *Law in the Courts of Love* (London: Routledge, 1996), pp. 204–9. This author develops his sophisticated argument further in "Europe in America: Grammatology, Legal Studies, and the Politics of Transmission," *Columbia Law Review* 101 (2003), 2001.

4. The notion of "tradition" is to be apprehended in terms of "antecedents" rather than "causes." My basic point is that "one cannot be a self on one's own": Charles Taylor, *Sources of the Self* (Cambridge, MA: Harvard University Press, 1989), p. 36. See also Alasdair MacIntyre, *After Virtue*, 2nd ed. (London: Duckworth, 1985), pp. 126–27, 130, 221–22, and passim. For a sensitive treatment of the idea of "tradition" allowing for agency and reflexivity, see Gerald L. Bruns, *Hermeneutics Ancient and Modern* (New Haven: Yale University Press, 1992), pp. 195–212. The notion of "structures of attitude and reference" to which I refer is a central motif in Edward W. Said, *Culture and Imperialism* (New York: Knopf, 1993). Although my argument focuses on translation from interlinguistic and intercultural perspectives, the idea of "tradition" also raises the matter of intralinguistic and intracultural translation given how members of any community must inevitably presentiate the past, which is always foreign and strange. For example, see Hans-Georg Gadamer, *Truth and Method*, 2nd, rev. ed., trans. Joel Weinsheimer and Donald G. Marshall (London: Sheed & Ward, 1989), p. 387: "The fact that a foreign language is being translated means that this is simply an extreme case of hermeneutical difficulty—i.e., of alienness and its conquest. In fact all the "objects" with which traditional hermeneutics is concerned are alien in the same unequivocally defined sense. The translator's task of recreation differs only in degree, not in kind, from the general hermeneutical task that any text presents," 1960. For the German text, see *Wahrheit und Methode*, 6th ed. (Tübingen: J.C.B. Mohr, 1990), p. 391: "*Die Fremdsprachlichkeit bedeutet nur einen gesteigerten Fall von hermeneutischer Schwierigkeit, d. h. von Fremdheit und Überwindung derselben. Fremd sind in dem gleichen, eindeutig bestimmten Sinne in Wahrheit alle "Gegenstände," mit denen es die tradi-*

tionelle Hermeneutik zu tun hat. Die Nachbildungsaufgabe des Übersetzers ist nicht qualitativ, son-
dern nur graduell von der allgemeinen hermeneutischen Aufgabe verschieden, die jeder Text stellt."

5. For historical aspects of the way in which civil law and common law have—and
have not—intersected, see, for example, Peter Goodrich, "Poor Illiterate Reason: History,
Nationalism and Common Law," *Social & Legal Studies* 1(7), 1992. A sophisticated differential analysis of relevant epistemological issues across these legal traditions is offered in
Geoffrey Samuel, *Epistemology and Method in Law* (Ashgate: Dartmouth, 2003).

6. Robert W. Gordon, "Critical Legal Histories," *Stanford Law Review* 36(57), 1984, p. 90.

7. I closely follow Barbara Herrnstein Smith, *Belief and Resistance* (Cambridge, MA:
Harvard University Press, 1997), p. 92.

8. See, for example, Hein Kötz and Axel Flessner, *European Contract Law*, tome I (by
Kötz): *Formation, Validity, and Content of Contracts; Contract and Third Parties*, trans. Tony
Weir (Oxford: Oxford University Press, 1997); Christian von Bar, *The Common European
Law of Torts*, tomes I and II (Oxford: Oxford University Press, 1998 and 2000); Walter
van Gerven, Jeremy Lever, and Pierre Larouche, *Tort Law* (Oxford: Hart, 2000); Commission on European Contract Law, *Principles of European Contract Law*, eds. Ole Lando and
Hugh Beale (Deventer: Kluwer, 2000); Marcel Storme, ed., *Rapprochement du droit judici-
aire de l'Union européenne / Approximation of Judiciary Law in the European Union* (Dordrecht: Martinus Nijhoff, 1994); Mauro Bussani and Ugo Mattei, "The Common Core Approach to European Private Law," *Columbia Journal of European Law* 3(339), 1997–98;
Jürgen Schwarze, ed., *Administrative Law Under European Influence* (London: Sweet &
Maxwell, 1996).

9. Alan Watson, *Legal Transplants*, 2d ed. (Athens, GA: University of Georgia Press,
1993), p. 95.

10. Basil Markesinis, "Why a Code is Not the Best Way to Advance the Cause of European Legal Unity," *European Review of Private Law* 5(519), 1997, p. 520.

11. I adopt and adapt Jacques Derrida, *L'écriture et la différence* (Paris: Le Seuil, 1967),
p. 427. See also *supra*, note 2.

12. Jacques Derrida *L'autre cap* (Paris: Minuit, 1991), pp. 75–77 [*le devoir de répondre à
l'appel de la mémoire européenne (. . .) dicte de respecter la différence, l'idiome, la minorité, la
singularité (. . . et) commande de tolérer et de respecter tout ce qui ne se place pas sous l'autorité
de la raison*], emphasis original.

13. Jacques Derrida, *Force de loi* (Paris: Galilée, 1994), p. 45 [*Cette responsabilité devant
la mémoire est une responsabilité devant le concept même de responsabilité qui règle la justice et
la justesse de nos comportements, de nos décisions théoriques, pratiques, éthico-politiques*].

14. See, for example, Paul W. Kahn, *The Cultural Study of Law* (Chicago: University of
Chicago Press, 1999).

15. Mark A. Schneider, *Culture and Enchantment* (Chicago: University of Chicago
Press, 1993), p. 40.

16. George Steiner, *Errata* (London: Weidenfeld & Nicolson, 1997), pp. 18–19.

17. Marcel Mauss, "Essai sur le don," in *Sociologie et anthropologie*, 6th ed. (Paris: Presses
Universitaires de France, 1995), pp. 274–75 and passim, 1925.

18. Paul Ricoeur observes that even "between the least contradicted rule and its application, there always remains a hiatus": *Philosophie de la volonté*, tome I: *Le volontaire et l'involontaire* (Paris: Aubier, 1950), p. 165 [*entre la règle la moins contredite et son application il
demeure toujours un hiatus*].

19. For Gadamer's notion of "pre-understanding," see his *Truth and Method*, *supra*, note
4, pp. 265–71 and 291–300. For the German text and the idea of "*Vorverständnis*," see
Wahrheit und Methode, *supra*, note 4, pp. 270–76 and 296–305. For Gadamer's considera-

tion of "prejudice," see *Truth and Method*, pp. 271–85. For the German text and the notion of "*Vorurteil*," see *Wahrheit und Methode*, pp. 276–90. The gist of Gadamer's claim appears from *Truth and Method*, pp. 276–77: "*the prejudices of the individual, far more than his judgments, constitute the historical reality of his being*", emphasis original. For the German text, see *Wahrheit und Methode*, p. 281: "die Vorurteile des einzelnen weit mehr als seine Urteile die geschichtliche Wirklichkeit seines Seins", emphasis original. This notion is indebted to the Heideggerian idea of "fore-conception" ("*Vorgriff*"). See Martin Heidegger, *Being and Time*, trans. John Macquarrie and Edward Robinson (Oxford: Blackwell, 1962), p. 191: "the interpretation has already decided for a definite way of conceiving [the entity we are interpreting], either with finality or with reservations; it is grounded in *something we grasp in advance*—in a *fore-conception*," 1926, emphasis original.

20. Gadamer, *Truth and Method, supra*, note 4, p. 297, emphasis original. For the German text, see *Wahrheit und Methode, supra*, note 4, p. 302: "*man anders versteht, wenn man überhaupt versteht*", emphasis original. An alternative way to make this point is to observe that it is precisely to the extent that *something* cannot let go of its source that communication fails. See Goodrich, *Courts of Love, supra*, note 3, p. 205. I should not be understood as claiming that communication across legal cultures is somehow made absolutely impossible. In fact, a legal culture can communicate its difference from other legal cultures to other legal cultures. But the existence of a taste for the foreign ("*die Lust am Fremden*"), of a sentiment of foreignness ("*das Gefühl des fremden*"), of a respect for foreignness ("*Achtung für das fremde*"), and of an inclination to translate ("*die Neigung zum Uebersezen*") permit a limited closing of the gap with alterity. The German formulae are from Schleiermacher, *Methoden, supra*, note 2, pp. 221, 215, 243, and 223.

21. Walter Benjamin, "The Task of the Translator," in *Selected Writings*, eds. Marcus Bullock and Michael W. Jennings and trans. Harry Zohn, tome I (Cambridge, MA: Harvard University Press, 1973), p. 257, 1923.

22. José Ortega y Gasset, *Obras completas*, tome V (Madrid: Alianza Editorial, 1994), p. 436, 1937. This point does not deny the existence of "regional modes and dialects" within a language: George Steiner, *After Babel*, 2nd. ed. (Oxford: Oxford University Press, 1992), p. 32.

23. The idea of "*métissage*," as it connotes fluidity, mutability, ambiguity, and enigmaticity—rather than syncretism, reconciliation, unity, or totality—is usefully thematized in François Laplantine and Alexis Nouss, eds., *Métissages* (Paris: Pauvert, 2001), pp. 7–16 and passim. Note, however, that despite the work that alterity performs within selfness, such that the other is not only the non-self but also helps to constitute the self's intimate meaning through an *othering* of the self, neither alterity nor selfness can be reduced to mere amalgamations, a process that would pay insufficient attention to the notion of "endogenous historicity": a Tupi who plays lute remains a Tupi. The quotation is from John Comaroff and Jean Comaroff, *Ethnography and the Historical Imagination* (Boulder: Westview, 1992), p. 27. My illustration is drawn from Serge Gruzinski, *La pensée métisse* (Paris: Fayard, 1999), passim, who refers to Brazilian verse—"*Sou um tupi tangendo um alaúde*"—linking local identity and a European musical instrument.

24. Dan Sperber, "Learning to Pay Attention," *The Times Literary Supplement*, December 27, 1996, p. 14, col. 3.

25. Eva Hoffman, *Lost in Translation* (London: Minerva, 1991), pp. 175, 272, and 273, respectively.

26. *Cf.* Jacques Derrida, *Marges de la philosophie* (Paris: Minuit, 1972), pp. 374–81, who links the idea of "repetition" with that of "differentiation" through his notion of "iterability"—a neologism which, etymologically, connotes at once "reiteration" and "alterity."

27. For Benjamin's notion of "*Zusammenhang*", see Anthony Phelan, "*Fortgang* and *Zusammenhang*: Walter Benjamin and the Romantic Novel," in Beatrice Hanssen and Andrew Benjamin, eds., *Walter Benjamin and Romanticism* (New York: Continuum, 2002), pp. 69–82.

28. Ortega y Gasset notes that "each language represents a different equation between manifestations and silences": *El hombre y la gente*, in *Obras completas*, tome VII (Madrid: Alianza Editorial, 1994), p. 250 [*cada lengua es una ecuación diferente entre manifestaciones y silencios*].

29. I am not suggesting that there are no differences arising between legal borrowing and literary translation. For example, any literary translator is indebted to the original in the sense that, although he intends to produce neither an original nor a copy of an original, he must give back what has been entrusted to him. There is no such duty on the part of the legal borrower. For the argument from indebtedness, see Jacques Derrida, *Psyché*, 2nd ed. (Paris: Galilée, 1998), pp. 211–12. The kindred notion of "restitution" is addressed in A. L. Becker, *Beyond Translation* (Ann Arbor: University of Michigan Press, 1995), pp. 18–20. Thoughtful theorizations of the ethical demands implied in the act of translation are offered in Anthony Pym, *Pour une éthique du traducteur* (Arras: Artois Presses Université, 1997); Lawrence Venuti, *The Scandals of Translation* (London: Routledge, 1998).

30. Georges Perec, A *Void*, trans. Gilbert Adair (London: Harvill, 1994).

31. T. S. Eliot, *Prufrock and Other Observations*, in *The Complete Poems and Plays* (London: Faber & Faber, 1969), p. 14, 1917; "La chanson d'amour de J. Alfred Prufrock," in *Poésie*, trans. Pierre Leyris (Paris: Le Seuil, 1994), p. 11, 1947.

32. Robert Adams, *Proteus, His Lies, His Truth* (New York: Norton, 1973), p. 7. Eugene Nida, to whom the paternity of this translation is often ascribed, calls the story "intriguing" but "without foundation in actual fact": Eugene A. Nida, *Bible Translating: An Analysis of Principles and Procedures with Special Reference to Aboriginal Languages* (New York: American Bible Society, 1947), p. 136.

33. Gayatri Chakravorty Spivak, *Outside in the Teaching Machine* (New York: Routledge, 1993), p. 183.

34. See Antoine Berman, *La traduction et la lettre ou l'auberge du lointain* (Paris: Le Seuil, 1999), pp. 97–114.

35. Chateaubriand, "*Remarques à propos de la traduction de Milton*," *Po&sie*, N° 23, 1982, pp. 113–14 [*je n'ai pas craint de changer le régime des verbes lorsqu'en restant plus français, j'aurais fait perdre à l'original quelque chose de sa précision, de son originalité ou de son énergie*], 1836. Cf. Paul Valéry, "Variations sur les *Bucoliques*," in *Oeuvres*, ed. Jean Hytier, tome I (Paris: Gallimard, 1957), p. 210, who observes that the translator favoring an exegetical approach "proses the way one coffins" [*met en prose comme on met en bière*].

36. Chateaubriand, "Remarques," note 35, p. 114 [*je sais qu'émaner, en français, n'est pas un verbe actif: un firmament n'émane pas de la lumière, la lumière émane d'un firmament; mais traduisez ainsi, que devient l'image? Du moins, le lecteur pénètre ici dans le génie de la langue anglaise; il apprend la différence qui existe entre les régimes des verbes dans cette langue et dans la nôtre*].

37. See Antoine Berman, *L'épreuve de l'étranger* (Paris: Gallimard, 1984), p. 17. Not insignificantly, a translation like Chateaubriand's can enhance the translator's status in the reader's eyes by allowing for an appreciation of the translator's authorship. See Lawrence Venuti, *The Translator's Invisibility* (London: Routledge, 1995), pp. 7–9 and passim.

38. Cf. Octavio Paz, *Sombras de obras* (Barcelona: Seix Barral, 1983), p. 31: "neither moral and aesthetic significations nor scientific and magical ones are entirely translatable

from one society to the other" [*ni los significados morales y estéticos ni los científicos y mágicos son enteramente traducibles de une sociedad a otra*].

39. Chateaubriand, "Remarques," *supra*, note 35, pp. 119–20. In "Die Aufgabe des Übersetzers," the original title of Benjamin's essay, "Task of the Translator," *supra*, note 21, the word "*Aufgabe*"connotes also the one who must renounce and thus alludes to the translator's defeat. See Paul de Man, *The Resistance to Theory* (Minneapolis: University of Minnesota Press, 1986), p. 80. I owe this reference to Simone Glanert.

40. Schleiermacher, *Methoden*, *supra* note 2, p. 213 [*in dem bildsamen Stoff der Sprache*].

41. The notion of "hospitality" is in Friedrich Schleiermacher, *Ueber Leibniz unausgeführt gebliebenen Gedanken einer allgemeinen philosophischen Sprache*, in *Sämmtliche Werke*, tome III, vol. 3 (Berlin: Reimer, 1835), p. 144 [*Gastfreiheit*], 1831.

42. Cf. Edward Shils, *Tradition* (Chicago: University of Chicago Press, 1981), pp. 10–11, who remarks on "the metaphysical dread of being encumbered by something alien to oneself."

43. Note that the initial fact of language appropriation is rather more limited than one might at first blush suspect, for when one refers to one's language using the possessive "my," one forgets—or hides—how much alienation this "appropriation" camouflages; in effect, a language is a law that comes from beyond the individual through education and socialization, to which, therefore, the individual is inevitably alienated—a point that explains how our own language is incomprehensible to us, as any francophone can verify by returning to Mallarmé. This is the central message of Jacques Derrida, *Le monolinguisme de l'autre* (Paris: Galilée, 1996).

44. Rodolphe Gasché, *Of Minimal Things* (Stanford: Stanford University Press, 1999), p. 68.

45. Benjamin, "Task of the Translator," *supra*, note 21, p. 255. See also pp. 256–57.

46. Watson, *Legal Transplants*, *supra*, note 9, p. 83.

47. George Steiner, *What is Comparative Literature?* (Oxford: Oxford University Press, 1995), p. 10. It seems pertinent to repeat that I should not be understood as arguing that communication across legal cultures is absolutely impossible.

48. Benjamin, "Task of the Translator," *supra*, note 21, p. 258. For an illuminating commentary on this metaphor, see Jacques Derrida, *Psyché*, 2nd. ed. (Paris: Galilée, 1998), p. 226.

49. Gasché, *Minimal Things*, *supra*, note 44, p. 78. For Benjamin's argument, see "Task of the Translator," *supra*, note 21, p. 261: "Just as a tangent touches a circle lightly and at but one point [. . .] a translation touches the original lightly and only at the infinitely small point of the sense." Cf. Clifford Geertz, *After the Fact* (Cambridge, MA: Harvard University Press, 1995), p. 28, who draws a helpful distinction between "difference" and "dichotomy": "[a difference] is a comparison and it relates; [a dichotomy] is a severance and it isolates." Of course, the question of "fidelity" plays itself out differently in the context of legal borrowing. See *supra*, note 29.

50. I am reminded of Lawrence Friedman's colorful language, which can usefully be quoted: he "took fields of living law, scalded their flesh, drained off their blood, and reduced them to bones": Lawrence M. Friedman, *A History of American Law*, 2nd ed. (New York: Simon & Schuster, 1985), p. 676.

51. Paul Ricoeur, *De l'interprétation* (Paris: Le Seuil, 1965), pp. 42–46 [*l'interprétation comme exercice du soupçon*].

52. See Giambattista Vico, *Principi di scienza nuova*, in *Opere* (Milan: Riccardo Ricciardi, 1953), bk. 1, ch. 47, p. 452: "the human mind naturally tends to take delight in what is uniform" [*La mente umana è naturalmente portata a dilettarsi dell'uniforme*], 1744.

53. See James Boyd White, *Justice as Translation* (Chicago: University of Chicago Press, 1990), pp. 257–69.

54. See Stephen D. Ross, "Translation as Transgression," in Dennis J. Schmidt, ed., *Hermeneutics and the Poetic Motion* (Binghamton: SUNY, 1990), pp. 25–42. I owe this reference to Simone Glanert. Indeed, Derrida perspicuously observes that "for the notion of translation, one will have to substitute a notion of *transformation*: the regulated transformation of a language by another, of a text by another." He adds: "We will never have been involved and never have been involved in fact in the 'transportation' of pure signifieds which the signifying instrument—or the 'vehicle'—would leave intact and untouched, from one language to another": Jacques Derrida, *Positions* (Paris: Minuit, 1972), p. 31 [*à la notion de traduction, il faudra substituer une notion de* transformation: *transformation réglée d'une langue par une autre, d'un texte par un autre. Nous n'aurons et n'avons en fait jamais eu affaire à quelque 'transport' de signifiés purs que l'instrument—ou le 'véhicule'—signifiant laisserait vierge et inentamé, d'une langue à l'autre*], emphasis original. This statement was made in the context of an interview with Julia Kristeva.

55. Carol Jacobs, *In the Language of Walter Benjamin* (Baltimore: Johns Hopkins University Press, 1999), p. 76.

56. See Homi K. Bhabha, *The Location of Culture* (London: Routledge, 1994), p. 12. Of course, to assert that difference lies beyond control does not mean that it lies beyond accommodation.

57. Pierre Klossowski, *Nietzsche et le cercle vicieux* (Paris: Mercure de France, 1969), p. 118 [*Comment restituer au singulier, à l'inéchangeable, au mutisme les attributs de la puissance donc de la santé, de la souveraineté—dès lors que le langage, la communication, l'échange ont attribué à la conformité grégaire ce qui est sain, puissant, souverain?*], emphasis original. Perhaps the most charitable way to assess such trivializing reductions is to observe that an understanding of what comparison means is itself a defining characteristic of any comparatist's being. Nonetheless, the contrast between this kind of snippety compilation acting as an epistemological barrier to knowledge and the thoughtful work on language and culture addressing the phenomenon of alterity in other disciplines is nothing short of shocking. For example, see Sanford Budick and Wolfgang Iser, eds., *The Translatability of Cultures* (Stanford: Stanford University Press, 1996); Paula G. Rubel and Abraham Rosman, eds., *Translating Cultures* (Oxford: Berg, 2003); Michael Cronin, *Translation and Globalization* (London: Routledge, 2003); Umberto Eco, *Experiences in Translation*, trans. Alastair McEwen (Toronto: University of Toronto Press, 2001).

58. Pierre Schlag, *The Enchantment of Reason* (Durham: Duke University Press, 1998), p. 140. For a textbook illustration of the ignorance strategy that Schlag stigmatizes, see Christian von Bar and Ole Lando, "Communication on European Contract Law: Joint Response of the Commission on European Contract Law and the Study Group on a European Civil Code," *European Review of Private Law* 10(183), 2002. For example, these authors' lack of even basic sociological and philosophical knowledge leads them to assert that "law is only that which is binding and [that] only a binding text will have profound practical impact" (p. 232) and to add that a common law of Europe can be "impartial" (p. 222), "dispassionate" (p. 222), and "neutral" (p. 228). An alternative view is developed, for instance, in Gunther Teubner, "Legal Irritants: Good Faith in British Law or How Unifying Law Ends Up in New Divergences," *Modern Law Review* 61(11), 1998. But this article, precisely because it adopts a sophisticated interdisciplinary perspective to illustrate the deficiencies of formalist thought, is ignored in Reinhard Zimmermann and Simon Whittaker, eds., *Good Faith in European Contract Law* (Cambridge: Cambridge University Press, 2000), a 750-page text purporting to offer a comprehensive study of its subject matter.

59. Ortega y Gasset, "*El hombre y la gente*," *supra*, note 28, pp. 79–98 [*ensimismamiento*], 1957.

60. Paul Ricoeur, *Le conflit des interprétations* (Paris: Le Seuil, 1969), p. 20 [*c'est (. . .) l'agrandissement de la propre compréhension de soi-même qu'il (l'exégète) poursuit à travers la compréhension de l'autre. Toute herméneutique est ainsi, explicitement ou implicitement, compréhension de soi-même par le détour de la compréhension de l'autre*]. Note that the other is not to be reduced to a simple vehicle for the recovery of the self, a mere occasion for self-consciousness, a variation on the theme of my "I-ness," an opportunity for the self-interested furtherance of self-reflective or monological identity, a maieutics: Egyptians do not owe their existence to Egyptologists. For a compelling introduction to the "hermeneutic motion" with specific reference to translation, see Steiner, *After Babel*, *supra*, note 22, pp. 312–435.

61. For an exploration of the connections between translation and psychoanalysis, see Andrew Benjamin, *Philosophy's Literature* (Manchester: Clinamen Press, 2001), pp. 45–70, who notes that Freud himself introduces the analyst as translator.

62. Interestingly, Ricoeur argues that translation involves the construction of comparables: Paul Ricoeur, *Sur la traduction* (Paris: Bayard, 2004), pp. 63–9.

63. Samuel Beckett, "The Capital of the Ruins," in *As the Story Was Told: Uncollected and Late Prose* (London: John Calder, 1990), p. 25, 1946.

Simultaneous Interpretation: Language and Cultural Difference

LYNN VISSON

Though modern simultaneous interpretation with its microphones, earphones, and sound equipment is a relatively new phenomenon, it certainly has ancient analogues.[1] In the first Letter to the Corinthians St. Paul orders, "If any man speak in an unknown tongue let it be by two, or at most by three . . . and let one interpret" (14:27). At various times interpreters have served as missionaries, liaison officers, military envoys, court interpreters, business couriers, and trade negotiators. The French drogmans (dragomans), who were trained in Oriental languages, were required not only to translate what was said but also to advise French officials as to the meaning of specific words or situations, to provide "cultural interpretation." Columbus sent young Indians from the New World to Spain to be trained as interpreters so that he could use them as go-betweens.

In nineteenth-century Europe there was little need for high-level interpretation, since French was the universal language of diplomacy and educated discourse. Consecutive interpretation was first used at the Paris peace conference of 1919, and simultaneous in 1928 at the Sixth Congress of the Comintern in the former Soviet Union. The first patent for simultaneous interpretation equipment was given in 1926 to Gordon Finley at IBM for his device based on an idea of Edward Filene's (founder of Boston's Filene's department store), and in 1933 booths were used at the plenum of the executive committee of the Communist International.[2] In Leningrad at the Fifteenth International Physiology Congress in 1935, academician Pavlov's introductory speech was translated from Russian into French, English, and German. In the 1920s the use of simultaneous interpretation expanded rapidly. At the Twentieth Party Congress interpretation was provided into six languages, and at the Twenty-first Party Congress into eighteen.[3] Simultaneous interpretation first emerged on the world scene in 1945 at the postwar Nuremberg trials. Many of the interpreters who worked there, emigrés and refugees with a knowledge of Russian, French, German, and English, later went on to become staff members at the United Nations. A Russian scholar gave the following description of the Americans who interpreted at Nuremberg:

Znachitel'nuiu chast' ikh sostavliali emigranty, prozhivshie mnogo let v Anglii i SShA, liudi, dlia kotorykh dva ili tri inostrannykh iazyka byli v ravnoi mere rodnymi. V roli perevodchikov podvizalis' i belye emigranty. Nekotorye iz nikh dolgoe vremia zhili vo Frantsii, a zatem emigrirovali v SShA i na protsesse perevodili s frantsuzskogo na angliiskii i obratno. Eti liudi, lishennye rodiny, razuchilis' govorit' po-russki. Ikh "russkii iazyk" pestrit bol'shim kolichestvom inostrannykh slov i arkhaizmov, iz-za sil'nogo aktsenta inogda dazhe trudno poniat', o chem oni govoriat.[4]

The need for interpreters became more urgent as international organizations and private conferences increasingly required their services. In 1948 the first school for interpreters was opened in Geneva, and Moscow's Thorez Institute began its interpreter training program in 1962. Today sophisticated and time-saving telecommunications networks, satellite technology, television space-bridges, and videoconferencing have opened up new opportunities for simultaneous interpretation.

How does the simultaneous interpreter work? Condensation, deliberate omission and addition, synecdoche and metonymy, antonymic constructions, grammatical inversion, and the use of semantic equivalents are a few of the tools that help do the job. As one professional noted, deliberate omission and condensation are quite different from omission errors resulting from noncomprehension:

> There are so many tiresome repetitions, such a great number of pyramided systems, that the interpreter feels it certainly will do no harm, maybe even help, if a few words are left out. How strong this temptation may be can well be appreciated by anyone who has sat through after-dinner speeches or other similar long-winded discourse and wished, in a rage that had to remain unspoken, that there were some way to amputate the wildly sprouting verbiage. The interpreter has that power.[5]

The very nature of simultaneous interpretation is predicated on a certain amount of judicious pruning. One study has shown that the average length of sentences in simultaneous interpretation is one to two words shorter than in written translation, and that syntax tends to be simpler.[6] If the Russian material, for example, is redundant, adds nothing to meaning, or if the speaker is racing along, the interpreter must resort to lexical or syntactical compression (*rechevaia kompressia*) to keep from falling too far behind or omitting important segments. He may drop one or more of a series of adjectives, or may engage in semantic condensation: *na mezhdunarodnom, natsional'nom i mestnom urovniakh* may become "on all levels" or "on several levels." Abbreviations such as UN for the United Nations or CPRF for the Communist Party of the Russian Federation may be useful timesavers.

The ability to condense is crucial to successful interpretation. A specialist in interpreter training has written that "an interpreter who cannot abstract is very much like a soldier who, once out of ammunition, doesn't know any better than to surrender."[7] A flair for editing is particularly important for Russian-English interpreters because both the length of the individual words and the grammatical constructions make for longer phrases in Russian. For example, *reshenie nachat' zabastovku* becomes "strike decision"; *programma kosmicheskikh issledovanii* can reduce to "space program."[8]

While key nouns and verbs must be translated, adjectival phrases and modifiers are prime candidates for condensation or omission. In simultaneous interpretation as opposed to written translation, "*chashche upotrebliaiut sushchest-vitel'nye, glagoly, prilagatel'nye i narechiia za schet umen'sheniia doli mestoimenii, chislitel'nykh, predlogov, soiuzov i chastits.*"[9] But here, too, context is the decisive factor: in some situations a noun or verb may have to go. *Gossekretar' predlozhil sozvat' konferentsiiu* can become "The secretary of state proposed a conference" (which is obviously going to convene and not to disband).[10] *Prosmotr sostoitsia 22-go sentiabria:* "The showing is on September 22" rather than "will take place on," an economy of several syllables. *My khoteli by s"ezdit' k vam v Kanadu* can shorten to "We would like to visit you" (or "your country") rather than the clumsy "We would like to come to you to your country," as one interpreter an-nounced. *Eto bylo opublikovano v gazete Niu-Iork Taims* sounds simply silly as "This was published in the newspaper the *New York Times*." "This appeared in the *New York Times*" is more idiomatic and saves syllables. If the publication is not well-known, however, the word "newspaper" should be retained.

Expressions such as *v oblasti*—for example, *v oblasti ekonomiki, v sviazi s chem, v chastnosti, kak izvestno, pri etom*, can also easily be dropped. *V oblasti ekonomiki* reduces to "in economics."[11] Connectives and superfluous interjections, along with such verbal *voda* as *nu, vidite, i tak* and other devices that allow the speaker to prepare the next utterance can safely be dropped. Adjectives such as *pred-stavlennyi, vysheupomianutyi,* or *sushchestvuiushchii* can often be safely dropped and replaced by the English definite article or by "this":

Predstavlennyi doklad poluchil podderzhku bol'shinstva delegatov.
[The/this/draft was supported/backed/by the majority of the delegates/]
Rassmatrivaemyi doklad soderzhit piat' glav.
[This report contains/has/five chapters/sections.]

With a very rapid speaker more drastic cuts may be needed:

V svoem poslanii vsem delegatam nashei konferentsii Prezident Soedinennyukh Shta-tov Bill Klinton skazal:
[In his message to us, President Clinton said:]

or

Peru, Argentina, Urugvai, Boliviia i mnogo drugie strany latinoamerikanskogo konti-nenta vystupili za . . .
[Many countries of Latin America favored . . .]

Natalya Strelkova used the following types of examples to teach her students at the former Maurice Thorez Institute how to turn literal translations into id-iomatic English. Though these sentences are intended for translators, inter-preters can "edit" orally, taking care not to drop important points.[12]
Russian text:

Etot vizit, podcherkivaetsia v kommiunike, iavliaetsia vazhnym vkladom v delo dal'neishego ukrepleniia i razvitiia druzhestvennykh otnoshenii i bratskogo sotrud-nichestva.

Literal translation:

The visit, stresses the communique, is an important contribution to the cause of further strengthening and developing friendly relations and fraternal cooperation.

Edited version:

The visit is an important contribution to friendly relations and (fraternal) cooperation, says the communique.

In the last sentence "fraternal" can be omitted to save time. Or the interpreter could begin the sentence thus: "The visit, states the communique, is an important contribution," etcetera.

Russian text:

Eti soglasheniia predusmatrivaiut sozdanie neobkhodimykh uslovii dlia dal'neishego razvitiia ekonomicheskogo sotrudnichestva i ispol'zovaniia preimushchestv mezhdunarodnogo razdeleniia truda.

Literal translation:

These agreements envisage the creation of the necessary conditions promoting the growth of economic cooperation and the utilization of the advantages offered by international division of labor.

Edited version:

These agreements will promote economic cooperation and make full use of the advantages offered by international division of labor.

Russian text:

Eti mery podchinili proizvodstvo interesam udovletvoreniia potrebnostei naroda.

Literal version:

These measures have subjected the interests of production to the interests of satisfaction of the needs of the people.

Edited version:

These measures have geared production to the needs of the people.

Though the interpreter does not have time for reflection and review and is less likely than the translator to risk major rearrangements of the components of a sentence, such oral editing is crucial for the generation of an idiomatic English sentence. While Russian-English interpretation tends to condense rather than to expand, English grammar and structure may require the addition of articles, auxiliaries, or modals in compound tenses (e.g., we shall have been doing this) or pronouns and possessives: *podniala ruku*—"She raised her hand."

Another technique involves metonymy and synecdoche, making the general specific and the specific general. When there is no equivalent in English for a general concept in Russian, or if the interpreter has missed a word, substitution of a more specific term is a good solution. *Nuzhno dobavit' zelen' v sup* could be rendered as "parsley and other herbs."[13] And a specific term can often be successfully used to replace a general one. The interpreter who fails to understand *aiva* in a list with *iabloki, grushi i persiki* would be quite safe in referring to "another fruit." "A bird" is better than saying nothing for *lastochka*, and translating *cheremukha* as a "flowering tree" is better than embarrassed silence if "bird cherry" does not spring to mind. "We've eaten" will do nicely for *my pozavtrakali* particularly if the interpreter is not sure whether the speaker has in mind breakfast or lunch, and the English "student" can cover *student, uchenik,* or *uchashchiisia*.

An approximate synonym can also cover an interpreter's sudden memory blank. If the speaker is going on about the need for *razriadka napriazhennosti v interesakh mira* and the interpreter has forgotten "detente," or "lessening of tensions," he or she can talk about the need to improve relations. Or if "as wise as Solomon" does not come to mind for *sem' piadei vo lbu* the interpreter can say "he paid him a compliment." The ultimate degree of such descriptive avoidance of specific items occurs when the interpreter simply has no idea of what the speaker has said. Following a delegate's statement, "A seichas ia budu govorit' o———" if "———" is incomprehensible, short of shutting off the microphone and bursting into tears, a solution is, "There is another point I would like to raise," or "There is something else I wish to say." More often than not in the next sentence the speaker will go into detail and clarify the thought.

Antonymic inversion, changing positives to negatives and vice versa, is a very useful device for avoiding literal translation. *Ia vse pomniu* can be rendered as "I haven't forgotten anything," or *Vy dolzhny molchat'* as "You mustn't say anything" rather than the more literal and awkward "You must be silent." *Tam bylo ochen' neplokho* can be "It was great there" or "Things were fine."[14] Such flips, of course, depend on context, and there is often no reason to reverse a positive or negative statement. This is a matter of idiomatic usage. Take the Russian *Ia ikh ponimaiu*. "I understand them" would be perfectly acceptable for explaining why people did something fairly neutral—decided to study English or moved to a bigger apartment. But if these people were being criticized for their apparently rational actions, then "I for one/myself/ personally don't blame them" comes closer to the real meaning. Or *Eto neredko byvaet* implies "This happens often."[15]

Grammatical inversion and the switching of grammatical categories, translating a verb by a noun, a noun by a verb, or an adjective by an adverb is another way of avoiding *mot-à-mot* interpretation. For example:[16]

Podniat'sia okazalos' legche, chem on ozhidal.
[The climb was easier than he had expected.]

I v promyshlennom, i v voennom otnoshenii, eti plany nashei strany . . .
[Militarily and industrially, our country's plans . . .]

Ikh bylo bol'she.
[They prevailed.]

On chelovek nachisto lishennyi moral'nykh tsennostei.
[He has no moral values at all/whatsoever.]

Etot forum mog by kvalifitsirovanno i s neobkhodimoi glubinoi rassmotret' vsiu sovpokupnost' voprosov razoruzheniia.
[This forum could engage in/provide competent and in-depth consideration/analysis of the whole/entire/full range of disarmament questions.]

My s ponimaniem otnosimsia k ikh stremleniiam.
[We feel for/empathize with/side with/support their desires/wishes/aspirations.]

The use of semantic equivalents and the search for expressions that avoid mot-à-mot renderings are vitally important to sounding idiomatic. Russians are *gluboko ubezhdeny*, but Americans are firmly—rather than deeply—convinced. A *soderzhatel'nyi* report is "informative" to an English speaker. *Idti komu-to na vstrechu* is to accommodate someone. *Ne kazhetsia li* does not necessarily require the verb "seem"; "Isn't it likely?" will get the point across. *Sluchainye liudi v politike* are not random individuals but laymen or outsiders in politics; *belye piatna* in our knowledge are "gaps." *Politicheskoe litso mira* can be rendered as the political realities, situation, or configuration in today's world. A few more examples:[17]

Zloveshchie plany [sinister prospect(s)]
On snial trubku [he answered the phone]

Syntactic and/or semantic equivalents can provide an idiomatic English rendering of the Russian:[18]

On skazal ei svoe mnenie o nikh.
[He told her what he thought of them.]

Poslali za vrachom.
[The doctor has been summoned/called/sent for.]

Vasha zhena prekrasno gotovit.
[Your wife is an excellent cook.]

Here nouns replace verbs (*gotovit*/cook), syntax and active and passive moods are reversed (*poslali za*/has been summoned), and a noun replaces a verb (*mnenie*—thought). Fixed formulaic phrases can be rendered through carefully chosen equivalents:[19]

Ob"iavliaiu zasedanie otkrytym.	I call the meeting to order.
Ne veshaite trubku.	Hold on/Just a minute.
Ia vas slushaiiu.	Hello (if on the phone)/What can I do for you?/I'll take your order (if in a restaurant).

These Russian and English idioms are so different that literal translation would sound comic. Hardest of all is the search for cultural rather than for purely linguistic or semantic equivalents, for though these are often vastly different in the two languages, the role of cultural interpretation is the interpreter's most important and most difficult function.

The specific nature and structure of a language determine the way its speakers view the world, and serve as an organizing principle of culture. As Whorf has posited, "Facts are unlike to speakers whose language background provides for unlike formulation of them."[20] Of crucial importance to the interpreter is the fact that "the grammatical pattern of a language (as opposed to its lexical stock) determines those aspects of each experience that must be expressed in the given language."[21] For example, the Russian sentence *Ia nanial rabotnitsu* conveys immediate information concerning the sex of the employer and the sex of the employee, which are lacking in the English statement "I hired a worker." The effect of grammatical categories on the semantic impact of such a Russian sentence is enormous and, as Jakobson has pointed out, "naturally the attention of native speakers and listeners will be focused on such items as are compulsory in their verbal code."[22] An excellent example of the problems grammar imposes on semantics—and on the interpreter—is the sentence, "*Ty otkuda prishla, s verkhu, iz Nizhnego, da ne prishla, po vode-to ne khodiat*" from Gorky's *Detstvo*. Gender, aspect, motion verbs, and the play on upper-lower *verkh-Nizhnii* create a chain of translation problems.[23] The absence—or existence—of entire categories of words in one or another language creates a major problem for the interpreter. Russian lacks articles and a complex tense system. English does not have aspect, case endings, or the Russian system of prefixation. The article may be indicated by words such as *odin* or *tot*:

Tot muzhchina, kotoryi tol'ko chto voshel—ee brat.
[*The* man who just came in is her brother.]

Odin ego drug skazal mne eto.
[*A* friend of his told me that.]

Words that characterize the life, culture, and historical development of any given country often have no precise equivalents in other languages. It has even been argued that only proper names, geographic, scientific, and technical terms, days of the week, months, and numerals have full lexical correspondence in several languages.[24] *Obed* translated as "lunch" may suggest a sandwich and a cup of coffee to an American but oily chunks of beet and carrot, a watery soup, a slab of meat and fried potatoes to a Russian. The taste and texture of *kotlety* are closer to American meat loaf than to "cutlets" or even to hamburgers. This difficulty of cross-cultural equivalents has been beautifully illustrated by the translator Richard Lourie:

The translator's heart sinks at the sight of words like *kommunalka* which he knows he must render as "communal apartment." He is willing to lose all the coloration of the original—the slightly foreign *kommun*, as in *kommunizm*, made Russian by the kiss of the diminutive suffix *ka*, here expressing a sort of rueful affection. The English term conjures up an image of a Berkeley, California kitchen, where hippies with headbands are cooking brown rice, whereas the Russian term evokes a series of vast brown rooms with a family living in each, sharing a small kitchen where the atmosphere is dense with everything that cannot be said and the memory of everything that shouldn't have been said, but was.[25]

This problem of cross-cultural communication was nicely demonstrated by a Japanese-speaking American professor who assumed at the end of a faculty meeting he had chaired on a strike-torn Japanese campus that the group had finally reached agreement, since all the professors had spoken in favor of the item under discussion. "All this may be true," his Japanese colleague remarked at the end of the meeting, "but you are still mistaken. The meeting arrived at the opposite conclusion. You understood all the words correctly, but you did not understand the silences between them."[26]

Cultural communication was particularly complex in Soviet-American contacts, and is still an issue in Russian-American relations today. Edmund Glenn gives an excellent example in his brilliant essay, "Semantic Difficulties in International Communication":

> It is too often assumed that the problem of submitting the ideas of one nation or cultural group to members of another national or cultural group is principally a problem of language. . . . Soviet diplomats often qualify the position taken by their Western counterparts as "incorrect" *nepravil'noe*. In doing so, they do not accuse their opponents of falsifying facts, but merely of not interpreting them "correctly." This attitude is explicable only if viewed in the context of the Marxist-Hegelian pattern of thought, according to which historical situations evolve in a unique and predetermined manner. Thus an attitude not in accordance with theory is not in accordance with truth either; it is as incorrect as the false solution to a mathematical problem. Conversely, representatives of our side tend to promote compromise or transactional solutions. Margaret Mead writes that this attitude merely bewilders many representatives of the other side, and leads them to accuse us of hypocrisy, because it does not embody any ideological position recognizable to them. The idea that "there are two sides to every question" is an embodiment of nominalistic philosophy, and it is hard to understand for those unfamiliar with this philosophy or its influence.[27]

This heavy use of *nepravil'noe* led many Western diplomats to see the Soviet side as stubborn and dogmatic, while Soviets perceived the American insistence on looking at both sides of the question either as deliberate attempts to avoid taking a position or as a way of covering up a stand. Unless the interpreter had time to explain Hegelian theory to Western listeners, he could say "we disagree" or simply "no," instead of "that's wrong" or "that's incorrect," thus rephrasing the Soviet position in Western linguistic-cultural terms. Soviet references to *opredelennaia stadiia* of a historical process or a meeting could mean "this particular stage," "another stage," or nothing more than "some stage." The words "definite" or "determined"—all too frequent translations of *opredelennyi*—sound odd and dogmatic to a Western listener. "It fits in with the Marxist interpretation of history according to which evolution proceeds necessarily from one 'well-determined phase' to another," writes Glenn.[28] In Marxist political writing *opredelennyi* does and can convey a notion of determinism, but in ordinary speech the word is semantically quite neutral and should be translated as such: *opredelennye idei*— "certain ideas," *opredelennye liudi*—"some people." Here a problem arises when a text (or term) oriented toward the bearer of one culture is aimed at a foreign receiver. A Soviet listener would have had no problem with *nepravil'no* or *opredelennaia stadiia*.[29] It is ironic that so many texts aimed at foreign audiences—for example, *Moscow News, Soviet Life,* speeches delivered abroad—were written using a terminology intended for Soviet readers and listeners.

The question of linguistic and cultural identification is particularly relevant for compound and coordinate bilinguals.[30] While compound bilinguals have acquired their two languages from childhood, they are not generally familiar with the culture of one of the languages—for example, an American who learned Russian entirely in the United States in a Russian-speaking home but had little or no contact with Russian life. Coordinate bilinguals acquire the second language somewhat later than the first, associate words with empirical referents, and maintain two distinct linguistic systems—for example, an American of Russian background from a family with a strong interest in Russian culture, who, even if Russian was not spoken a great deal at home, has spent much time in Russia. Theoretically, the coordinate bilinguals will produce interpretation with greater equivalency than the compound group because of their separate referent systems for the two cultures.[31] To a compound Russian-English bilingual the word *restoran* as used for an eatery in Soviet Russia may conjure up the image of a place where people gather to eat and drink, while a coordinate will see the huge smoke-filled room, dance floor, orchestra, din, and lengthy meals that were part of Soviet dining out. Both groups may be subject to role strain if for intellectual, emotional, or psychological reasons they identify more strongly with one of the cultures and try—consciously or unconsciously—to tilt the outcome of negotiations in that side's favor.

A Russian-English interpreter must have an excellent knowledge of *realii*, the phenomena of daily life, politics and culture in Russia and the United States. Such Russian realii have been defined as "words that stand for realities that do not exist in the West and have no ready verbal equivalent in English (e.g., *predsedatel' kolkhozam, subbotnik,* or "those words that, though they do exist in English, mean something else, and . . . are used in a different context (*pafos sozidaniia*)."[32] *Idealizm* used by a Soviet speaker referred to a philosophical trend of thought opposed to materialism, while for an American the word means the advocacy of lofty ideals over practical considerations. Some such *realii* may need fleshing out in English for clarification:

> Dnem oni poshli s druz'iami v ZAGS, a vecherom svad'bu spravili v restorane "Arbat." [In the afternoon they went to sign the marriage registry, and in the evening they had a reception in the Arbat restaurant.]

The cultural context of realii must be maintained in the English translation. Just as a Chinese-English interpreter would not turn rice into bread, the Russian-

English interpreter should not turn Russian *limonad* (fruit-flavored soda) into American lemonade, or the Komsomol into the Boy Scouts. For a Russian, *ob-shchestvennaia zhizn'* means various kinds of civic and public activities, including volunteer or community work, while, as a Russian commentator noted in the United States, "'social life' *oznachaet vsiakoe otnoshenie s liud'mi, vkliuchaia pose-shchenie platnykh kursov, teatrov i restoranov.*" Nor does Russian *obshchestvennaia rabota* with its political and educational connotations have much in common with English "social work," which "*oznachaet, v osnovnom, pomoshch' bedniakam, obychno oplachivaemuiu mestnymi vlastiami.*"[33] Today, however, as Western concepts and words intrude into Russian life and language an enormous number of English-language *realii* require translation into Russian, but aside from recognizing them in order to translate them from Russian back into English this is not our subject here. Many of these English words have already taken firm root in Russian, for example, *brifing, imidzh, kholdingovaia kompaniia, displei, pleier.*

The sentence *My dolgo stoiali v ocheredi na kvartiru* was once translated by an interpreter as "We stood on line for a long time for an apartment," creating the impression that one could obtain housing by patiently standing in the street. What is meant is "For a long time we were on a waiting list." The interpreter must both know *realii* and be able to recode quickly. A woman saying, "*U nas dve komnaty i obshchaia kukhnia s sosediami*" is not referring to a "common kitchen,"—a phrase with a possible double meaning. She means "We share the kitchen with the other people in our communal apartment." *Sosedi* is a *lozhnyi drug perevodchika,* for to the American ear "neighbors" imply only the people in the next apartment, not in one's own. Or take a complaint about the *nizkaia kul'tura protivochatochnykh sredstv u nas.* The "culture of contraceptives" sounds bizarre indeed. The speaker is referring to the poor quality of, and lack of knowledge concerning, birth control devices. "Our problems with birth control devices" would cover both categories.

Another word that often causes misunderstandings is "friend," for here the literal translation and cultural connotations are worlds apart. For an American a friend can be an old college roommate one sees every five years, a business associate with whom one plays golf every week, or someone who attends the same church. Americans tend to see friends as people with whom they engage in activities, such as tennis or going out to dinner. For a Russian a friend is a soul mate, a trusted confidant, a bulwark against the outside world. It is not a word used lightly. There are separate words in Russian for a casual acquaintance (*znakomyi*), a closer acquaintance or friend (*priatel'*), and a real friend (*drug*). Americans take minutes to make friends. Russians take months or years.

A word such as *kollektiv* needs explanation. *Nash shkol'nyi kollektiv* might refer to a class or a sports team, depending on context, while *kollektiv nashego instituta* is the staff and *kollektiv nashego zavoda* the employees. The word could mean group, personnel, staff, colleagues, coworkers, associates, or all those who work at X.[34] The eminent Russian interpreter G.V. Chernov has suggested descriptive translations for a series of such *realii*:[35]

stazh	seniority, period of service
medalist	honor student
vrednaia professiia	hazardous occupation
ZAGS	civil registry office
kursy povysheniia kvalifikatsii	refresher courses, advanced training courses
subbotnik	an unpaid weekend/stint/volunteer effort/ community effort/donation of a day's work.[36]

This list could be continued indefinitely. L. A. Cherniakhovskaia, a Russian specialist on Russian and English syntax, gives several good examples of translation-explanations of realii:

Oni nadeiutsia, chto nedalek tot den,' kogda v strane budut otkryty krupnye zalezhi.
[They hope that large deposits will soon be discovered in Kazakhstan.][37]

We know from context that Kazakhstan is the particular republic referred to, and the name is much less confusing than "the country." *Nedalek tot den'* could, of course, be rendered literally—"the day is not far off when"—but English usage tends to bring this kind of lofty Russian prose down to earth. Cherniakhovskaia suggests "they hope eventually to discover," but "soon" is shorter and closer to the original *nedalek*. Or:

22 iuniia on ushel dobrovol'tsem na front.
[On June 22, the day Nazi Germany attacked, he went to/volunteered for the front.]

The interpreter's decision here must be based on the audience. For an audience of historians, adding "On the day Nazi Germany attacked" would be insulting, but to say only "On June 22" to a group of American farmers might be confusing.

The interpreter may also change Soviet historical terms to those used in the West, for example, rendering *Velikaia Otechestvennaia Voina* as "World War II." Contemporary realii as well as historical references may require such cultural conversion of terms. For example:

Nashi kurorty funktsioniruiut kruglyi god.
[Our health resorts are/stay open all year round/year round.][38]

The literal rendering, "Our resorts function the whole year," does not work. Or:

Eti tri goda dali nam glavnoe, chto neobkhodimoe dlia molodykh liudei—pole dlia aktivnoi deiatel'nosti.
[These three years gave us what (the) young people needed most/what was most important for young people, a chance to do big/important/great things/to build the country/to make full use of their abilities/gave young people a chance to work and grow.]

The literal rendering, "a field for active activity" is comically repetitive. While to a native speaker a Russian fixed expression may sound quite normal, to the English listener it may seem pompous or odd. Recoding can even out such stylistic differences.

The dangers of cross-cultural mot-à-mot rendition are particularly clear for those cognates that are *lozhnye druz'ia perevodchika*. Here are a few examples of such words that can—and do—regularly entrap interpreters:

adresnyi	targeted, specific (adresnye rekomendatsii, sanktsii)
aktual'nyi	topical, pressing, relevant, immediate, important
argument	reasons, convictions (not disagreement)
artist	any performing artist
avantiura	a shady or risky undertaking
dekada	ten days, not ten years
dekoratsii	stage sets
diversiia	military diversionary tactic, subversion, sabotage
ekonomnyi	thrifty, frugal, practical
fal'shivyi	artificial, forged, imitation, counterfeit
kharakter	nature, disposition (a character in a work of literature is a personazh)
kharakteristika	description, a letter of recommendation
konkretnyi	actual, specific, positive, definite
kur'eznyi	amusing, odd, intriguing, funny
manifestatsiia	public mass demonstration
miting	mass public demonstration, rally (never a get-together of a few people)
moment	period of time, element, point, aspect (odin iz momentov ego vystupleniia)
normal'no	well, properly (on vel sebia normal'no)
operativnyi	effective, quick, practical, current, timely
pafos	excitement, inspiration, enthusiasm, emotion, thrill
personazh	character in a literary work
perspektivnyi	promising, future, long-range
poema	a long epic poem, not short verses (stikhi) metaphorically—something wonderful: Etot tort—poema
pretendovat'	lay claim to, have pretensions to: On pretendoval na imushchestvo svoego soseda
simpatichnyi	nice, pleasant, sweet
titul	title for the nobility (e.g., duke, count)
tsinichnyi	crude, shameless, ruthless, amoral[39]

Many of these cognates are clearly very far apart in meaning, but this distance is one precise measure of cultural difference.

In interpreting language and culture the interpreter is constantly seeking the middle ground of understanding, trying to convey the speaker's meaning through a rendering that takes cultural context into account. At the same time, even when shifting and condensing, the interpreter must not replace the original with something the speaker never said. When a speaker's phrases bounce off the mirror of cultural differences, it is the interpreter with a thorough knowledge of both language and culture, with experience gained over time and through trial and error, who can provide a sparkling reflection rather than a warped distortion of the meaning behind those words.

NOTES

1. For the history of simultaneous interpretation see G. V. Chernov, *Teoriia i praktika sinkhronnogo perevoda* (Moskva: Mezhdunarodnye otnosheniia, 1978), pp. 3–8; E. Gofman, "K istorii sinkhronnogo perevoda," *Tetradi perevodchika*, 1, 1963, pp. 21–26; Jean Herbert, "How Conference Intepreting Grew," in *Language Interpretation and Communication*, eds. David Gerber and H. Wallace Sinaiko (New York and London: Plenum Press, 1977), pp. 5–10; Henry Van Hoof, *Théorie et pratique de l'interprétation* (München: Max Hueber Verlag, 1962), pp. 9–23; Patricia E. Longley, *Conference Interpreting* (London: Pitman, 1968), pp. 1–5.

2. Gofman, p. 20.

3. Chernov, p. 5, and N. D. Cheburashkin, *Tekhnicheskii perevod v shkole*, izd. 4-e (Moskva: Prosveshchenie, 1983), pp. 154–55. See also Vadim Grebenshchikov, "Traductions, théories et traducteurs en URSS," *Meta* 12(1), 1967, pp. 3–8.

4. Gofman, p. 22. "A significant proportion of them were emigrants who had lived in England and America for many years, who spoke two or three languages with native fluency. 'White' emigrants also worked as translators. Several of these lived in France for a long time, and then emigrated to the US, and as a result were able to translate from French to English and vice-versa. These people, deprived of their homeland, unlearned their language. Their 'Russian' is dotted with a large quantity of foreign words and archaisms, and because of their strong accent, it was sometimes even hard to understand what they were talking about."

5. Ekvall, Robert, *Faithful Echo* (New York: Twayne, 1960), p. 104.

6. A. F. Shiriaev, *Perevod i lingvistika* (Moskva: Voennizdat, 1973), p. 126.

7. Sergio Viaggio, "Teaching Beginners the Blessings of Abstracting (and how to save a few lives in the process)," unpublished paper, ATA 1989 Conference, Washington, D.C.

8. T. G. Seidova, "Vybor ekvivalenta semanticheski nepolnykh atributnykh slovosochetanii pri perevode s angliiskogo iazyka na russkii," *Tetradi perevodchika*, 11, 1974, pp. 59–61.

9. A. F. Shiriaev, "O nekotorykh lingvisticheskikh osobennostiakh funktsional'noi sistemy sinkhronnogo perevoda," *Tetradi perevodchika*, 19, 1982, pp. 73–85. [Nouns, verbs, adjectives and adverbs are used more often at the expense of pronouns, numerals, prepositions, conjunctions, and particles.]

10. L. S. Barkhudarov, *Iazyk i perevod* (Moskva: Mezhdunarodnye otnosheniia, 1975), p. 222.

11. See S. Ia. Shmakov, "Iazyk sovetskikh gazet glazami anglichan (po povodu uchebnogo posobiia R. Genri i K. Iang)," *Tetradi perevodchika*, 23, 1989, pp. 172–73.

12. N. S. Strelkova, *Uchebnoe posobie po prakticheskoi stilistike angliiskogo iazyka i stilisticheskomu redaktirovaniiu perevoda* (Moskva: MGPIIIA), 1984), pp. 19–21.

13. See R. K. Min'iar-Beloruchev, *Obshchaia teoriia perevoda i ustnyi perevod* (Moskva: Voenizdat, 1980), p. 105.

14. Ibid, p. 106.

15. Barkhudarov, *Iazyk i perevod*, p. 214.

16. *Translation: Theory and Practice* (Tashkent: Ukituvchi, 1989), pp. 20–21; V. N.

Komissarov, Ia. I. Retsker, V. I. Tarkhov, *Posobie po perevodu s angliiskogo iazyka na russkii.* Ch. I (Moskva: Izdatel'stvo literatury na inostrannykh iazykakh, 1960), pp. 34–47; G. G. Yudina, *Improve Interpreting Skills* (Mosvka: Mezhdunarodnye otnosheniia, 1976), pp. 95–96; A. D. Shveitser, *Teoriia perevoda.* Status/problemy/aspekty (Moskva: Nauka, 1988), pp. 134–35.

17. Shveitser, *Teoriia perevoda*, pp. 85–86, 125–26; *Translation: Theory and Practice*, p. 29.

18. Ibid., pp. 82–84.

19. Ibid, p. 129.

20. Quoted by Roman Jakobson, "On Linguistic Aspects of Translation," in *On Translation*, ed. Reuben A. Brower (New York: Oxford University Press, 1966), p. 234.

21. Ibid., pp. 235–46.

22. Ibid., p. 236.

23. See J. C. Catford, *A Linguistic Theory of Translation* (Oxford: Oxford University Press, 1965), pp. 96–98.

24. See C. I. Vlakhov, *Neperevodimoe v Perevode* (Moskva: Mezhdunarodnye otnosheniia, 1980), p. 55.

25. Richard Lourie and Aleksei Mikhailov, "Why You'll never Have Fun in Russian," *The New York Times Book Review*, June 18, 1989, p. 38.

26. Helmut Morsbuch, "Words Are Not Enough: Reading Through the Lines in Japanese Communication," *Japan Society Newsletter*, 36(6), March 1989, p. 3.

27. Edmund S. Glenn, "Semantic Difficulties in International Communication," in *The Use and Misuse of Language*, ed. S. I. Hayakawa (Greenwich, CT: Fawcett Publications, 1962), pp. 47–48.

28. Ibid., p. 63.

29. See A. D. Shveitser, "Sotsiologicheskie osnovy teorii perevoda," *Voprosy iazykoznaniia* 5, 1985, pp. 18–20.

30. See Bruce W. Anderson, "Perspectives on the Role of Interpreter," in *Translation: Application and Research*, ed. Richard W. Brislin (New York: Gardner Press, 1976), pp. 208–27, and Georganne Weller, "Bilingualism and Interpretation: An Under-Exploited field of Study for Research," in *Languages at Crossroads: Proceedings of the 29th Annual Conference*, ATA, 1988, pp. 407–13.

31. Anderson, "Perspectives," p. 215.

32. N. S. Strelkova, *Prakticheskaia stilistika angliiskogo iazyka i stilisticheskoe redaktirovanie perevodov*, Ch. 3 (Moskva: MGPIIIA, 1982), p. 33.

33. L. T. Mikulin, "Zametki o kal'kirovanii s russkogo iazyka na angliiskii," *Tetradi perevodchika*, 15, 1978, p. 63.

34. Strelkova, *Prakticheskaya stilistika*, p. 44.

35. G. V. Chernov, "Voprosy perevoda russkoi bezikvivalentnoi leksiki ("sovetskikh realii") na angliiskii iazyk na materialakh perevodov sovetskoi publitsistiki." Kandidatskaia dissertatsiia (Moskva: MGPIIIA, 1958).

36. Strelkova, *Prakticheskaya stilistika*, p. 51.

37. L. A. Cherniakhovskaia, *Perevod i smyslovaiia struktura* (Moskva: Mezhdunarodnye otnosheniia, 1976), pp. 241–48.

38. Ibid., pp. 241–48. Translations mine.

39. Examples are from *Anglo-russkii and russko-angliiskii slovar' "Lozhnykh druzei perevodchika,"* ed. V. V. Akulenko (Moskva: Sovetskaiia entsiklopediia, 1969); E. K. Popova, *Tekhnika perevoda s angliiskogo iazyka na russkii* (Leningrad: LGU, 1959); S. K. Shmakov, "Iazyk sovetskikh gazet glazami anglichan (po povodu uchebnogo posobiia R. Genri i K. Iang)," *Tetradi perevodchika*, 23, 1989, p. 174; and the author's personal experience.

A Touch of Translation: On Walter Benjamin's "Task of the Translator"

SAMUEL WEBER

Translating "Translation" in an Age of Globalization

If one were to search today for a way of reflecting on the destiny of language and literature in an age dominated increasingly by electronic media, there is probably no better place to start—and perhaps even to end—than with the question of translation. This might seem a somewhat surprising assertion to make, given the widespread tendency to associate the rise of electronic media with what is usually called the "audiovisual," as distinct from the linguistic, discursive, or textual. Such an association is, of course, by no means simply arbitrary. In 1999, the dollar value produced by the sales of video games, considered on a global scale, for the first time surpassed that of computers—and to be sure, sales of printed matter were not even close to either. Given such developments, how is it possible to claim that the question of translation can serve as a valuable index of the changing signification of language and literature in an age of electronic media?

The answer to this apparent paradox cannot be simple, of course. Translation as such covers a wide variety of activities, most of which are aimed at making texts accessible to people who do not know the language in which the text is written. Thus, for most translation activities in this sense, what is decisive is the goal of rendering a text written in one language understandable in another language. Meaning is thus the informing goal, a meaning generally held to transcend individual languages the way universality transcends particularity. There are, however, other kinds of translation—poetic, literary, philosophical—in which the transmission of meaning cannot be separated from the way that meaning is articulated or signified. And although this sort of translation may be statistically and economically far less important than the first kind, it may also in many ways be more revealing of the relationship between the linguistic medium and other media.

At any rate, my initial assertion is concerned with this latter type of translation, in which the "what" cannot be separated from the "how." The *what*—that is, meaning—may be conceived as existing *apart* from its specific linguistic local-

This work was previously published in *Estudos De Tradução em Portugal, Novos Contributos para a História da Literatura Portuguesa, Colóquio realizado na Universidade Católica Portuguesa em 14 e 15 Dezembro de 2000*, Organização Teresa Seruya, Universidade Católica Editora, Lisboa 2001, pp. 9–24.

ization; the *how* is not. Its transmission, transport, or translation thus inevitably raises the question of how one moves from one relatively restricted linguistic system to another. Usually, the linguistic systems between which translations move are designated as "natural" or "national" languages. However, these terms are anything but precise or satisfactory. "Portuguese," for instance, although named for a specific nation, is no more a "national" language than is "English," "French," "German" or "Spanish." Yet, to call these languages "natural" is perhaps even more unsatisfactory than to designate them as "national." The imprecision of such terms is in direct proportion to the linguistic diversity they seek to subsume. To be sure, such diversity does not exclude the fact that individual language systems exist and are distinct from one another. But such distinctions and the language systems they differentiate, are by no means as homogeneous as their names might tend to suggest. The difficulty of finding a generic term that would accurately designate the class to which individual languages belong is indicative of the larger problem of determining the principles that give those languages their relative unity or coherence—assuming, that is, that such principles really exist.

The fact that the names of individual language systems are not generally considered to be problematic is indicative not of the absence of such problems but rather of an established but largely unconscious decision not to acknowledge them in everyday practice. This decision is destabilized, potentially at least, whenever anything like "translation" is attempted. Such destabilization has to do with the fact, already mentioned, that translation always involves not merely the movement from one *language* to another, but from one *instance*—a text already existing in one language—to another instance, that does not previously exist, but that is brought into being in the other language. The tension between the generality of the language systems and the singularity of the individual texts is reflected, but also *concealed,* by the ambiguity of the very word "translation" itself, which designates both *a general process*, involving a change of place, and *a singular result* of that process: *translating* in general, and (a) translation in particular. The tension between the general process and the individual product tends to be obscured by an attitude that regards translation as an instrument in the service of the "communication" of meaning or of a message. This attitude privileges the generality of the process at the expense of its singularity.

Such a tendency is reinforced today by the spread of what is known as "globalization." The figure of the *globe* suggests an all-encompassing immanence in which singular differences are absorbed into a generalized whole. Nevertheless, precisely because of its homogenizing tendencies, "globalization" also exacerbates the need for differentiation. In facilitating circulation, transmission and contact, globalization brings the most remote and diverse areas and languages into contact with one another. Such contact, while clearly increasing the need for translation, does it in a way that is no less ambivalent than globalization itself. The following remarks seek to explore certain aspects of the ambivalent contact of languages that is never very far from the surface when they are *touched* by translation.

The history of translation is marked by a tension between two inseparable and yet incompatible motifs: fidelity and betrayal. Both result from the split relationship of translation to its own history, which is to say, to its "origin." Translation, *translatio*, does not merely signify carrying-across, transporting, transferring *in general*: it also entails a specific, singular relation of texts to one another, and more particularly, of a text to that which it transports, its origin or *original*. The status of this *terminus ab quo*, the *original*, has been radically transformed by the spread of electronic media, and in particular, by the development of digital modes of presentation and transmission. The very notion of "medium" is changed by this extension of digitalization. Aristotle, for instance, defined a medium (metaxos) as a *diaphanous* interval that allows a certain transmission to take place.[1] The *medium* was thus construed as an intermediary *between* two places. Movement through the medium was—and in most people's minds still is—defined through the implicit reference to and contrast with the *fixity* of the *places between* which it moves.

This, then, becomes the model of what is known as the "senses" and their "perception." The classical example cited by Aristotle in the passage quoted is that of an ant in the sky being visible only by virtue of the action of the intervening medium, which allows light to pass through.

The discussion of the medium is thus associated, from the very beginnings of Western philosophy, with sense-impressions in general, and with the sense of sight in particular. That continuing power of this association is reflected even today in the widespread use of a term such as "television" to designate a process that involves audition as much as vision. This privileging of the visual can also be observed in the current tendency to equate "multimedia" with "audiovisual."

With the development of media technology over the past half century, the traditional conception of the medium as an interval both separating and linking a subject to an object via the physical senses has become increasingly problematic.[2] Correlatively, the notion of "origin" and of "original" has also been affected. The ramifications of this change, however, can only be correctly evaluated by contrast with that which it is altering: the traditional notion of origin. Doubtless the most influential articulation of this notion for the cultural tradition of the "West" is to be found in the first book of Genesis, where origin is understood as creation. I propose therefore to reread briefly a few passages from this text, in order to discern certain traits that will continue, until today, to leave their imprint on what we call "translation."

I begin, therefore, with "the beginning," in the King James Version:

> In the beginning, God created the heaven and the earth, and the
> earth was without form, and void; and darkness was upon the face
> of the deep. And the Spirit of God moved upon the face of the
> waters. (I.1)

Creation, in the biblical account, operates above all through a series of dichotomies, beginning with the distinction between unbounded space ("heaven") and limited place ("earth"). At first, the limitation of place, "earth," is purely abstract, establishing the minimal dichotomy necessary for a distinction, but one that is otherwise wholly indeterminate, "without form and void" and hence totally obscure. Only in a second phase, as it were, is the abstract dichotomy of heaven and earth defined through a series of oppositions that progressively differentiate the *place* called earth. In addition to this general tendency to describe the creation of the world through a series of dichotomies, there is another aspect that does not exactly fit in, but that will turn out to be quite significant. The second sentence of Genesis I.1, recounts how, after the initial creation of heaven and earth, "the spirit (*ruach:* breath) of God moved upon the face of the waters." This kind of movement is very different from that implied by the oppositions that otherwise predominate: it suggests a quasi-tactile moment, in which Creator and Creation no longer are clearly distinguished or separated from one another. Rather, there is a certain convergence and contact between the two, without any sort of merging or fusion taking place. This unusual event is quickly submerged, as it were, by the introduction of temporal succession as the medium through which the creation moves toward its completion. This temporal progression culminates, on the Sixth Day, with the creation of man:

> God said, Let us make man in our image, after our likeness . . . So
> God created man in his own image, in the image of God created he
> him; male and female created he them. (I.26–27)

The biblical account of the creation of "man" introduces two conditions that will be of particular significance for the problem of translation. Taken separately, each is familiar enough by itself, but their interaction has perhaps not been sufficiently considered. First, in contrast to all other living beings, "man" is made in the "image" of God, a relationship that is interpreted, in the King James Version at least, as "likeness." In more contemporary terms, one could say that the ruling role of man in the Creation is a consequence of his "analogical" relation to his divine origin.

This, however, is only half of the story. For there is a second trait that distinguishes human beings from other animate beings in the biblical account, gender: "Male and female created he them." To be sure, the distinction of gender can be judged as already implied in the creation of other living beings, insofar as they are admonished by the Creator to be "fruitful and multiply." The fact remains, however, that it is only with respect to man that gender is mentioned explicitly.

That the gendered creation of human beings is anything but self-evident is suggested in the biblical text by the somewhat awkward addition of a second, more elaborate version of the creation of man, in chapter 2 of Book 1. In this expanded account, man is created not directly by the word of God, but indirectly, formed out of "the dust of the ground." The association of man with earth and "dust" anticipates the Fall, the expulsion from Eden, and the advent of human mortality. At the same time, however, this second version of the creation links man's destiny to his origin, now understood not to be purely divine, but as also earthly and hence, bound up with a *place*. To be earthbound is above all to be determined by one's *location*.

This topographical aspect of the second story of the creation of man is reinforced by the geographical details and place-names that now proliferate in the ensuing account. Man is "put" into a "garden" that is "planted . . . eastward in

Eden." Through this garden flows a river that subsequently divides "into four heads." Each of these four rivers receives a proper name linked to the name of a country or region. In this second account of man's creation, woman is created from a rib "taken from man," in short, as the result of a bodily mutilation.

All of this complicates the initially "analogical" relationship of man as the image and likeness of the creator. It introduces an unbridgeable distance and difference that clashes with the relationship of man to God implied by the notion of "image" as "likeness." Man and woman are no longer created ex nihilo, as in the first chapter of Genesis, but rather out of already existing matter: dust and rib, earth and body. Creation, in this second version, is a process of transformation. It no longer implies an absolute beginning or a pure performance, but rather almost a translation—almost, but not quite. It is not *yet* a translation for two, interrelated reasons. First, because there is still no place available that would make a traversal—the "trans-" of translation—either necessary or even thinkable. Despite the growing sense of separation of the created from the Creator, the only place inhabited by man is still the Garden of Eden. Second and correlatively, just as there is still only one place, so there is still only one language: the language of the Creator is the language of man.

This situation changes radically, of course, with the expulsion from the Garden of Eden. Of this momentous event, I want here to point out only one or two traits that are pertinent for our discussion. First, when Eve, having been accosted by the serpent, responds, she repeats the words of the Creator prohibiting her and Adam from eating of the Tree of Knowledge. But when she recites the divine prohibition, which modern biblical translations usually render as a direct citation, she adds something not found in the "original" version of God's words:

> And the woman said unto the serpent, We may eat of the fruit of
> the trees of the garden: But of the fruit of the tree which is in the
> midst of the garden, God hath said, Ye shall not eat of it, *neither
> shall ye touch it,* lest ye die. (I.3:3, my emphasis)

Here is the original account:

> But of the tree of the knowledge of good and evil, thou shalt not
> eat of it: for in the day that thou eatest thereof thou shalt surely die.
> (I.2:17)

What Eve, herself the product of a bodily transformation, adds in her ostensible citation of the words of God, is the apparently anodyne detail of *touch:* "Ye shall not eat of it, neither shall ye touch it, lest ye die." Could this be the first case, in the Western tradition at least, of the famous formula, *traduttore–tradditore?* Yes and no. No, insofar as Eve's quotation is not "properly" a translation, insofar as the repetition takes place *within* a single language rather *between* different ones. Yes, insofar as her rendering of the words of God involves a change of place, even if that place is still the Garden of Eden.[3]

In short, the divine prohibition, as recited by Eve at least, involves not just *eating* from the tree of knowledge, but *touching* it as well. A second instance of touching, which like the first we will leave suspended, but not for very long.

Shortly thereafter, when God has discovered that Adam and Eve have eaten from the tree of knowledge, he responds as follows:

> And the Lord God said, Behold, the man is become as one of us, to
> know good and evil: and now, *lest he put forth his hand, and take*
> also of the tree of life, and eat, and live for ever: Therefore the
> Lord God sent him forth from the garden of Eden. (3:22–23)

Adam and Eve are banished from the Garden of Eden not just as a punishment for what they have done, but as a way of preventing them from doing what Eve precisely had already acknowledged in her response to the serpent: *touching* and not simply *eating*.

However, this is a very different kind of "touching" from that encountered at the beginning of the creation, when the "spirit of God moved upon the face of the waters." For the "touching" of the Tree of Life is a means of *taking possession*, and thereby of becoming "as one of us." Touching here, then, becomes a form of taking, turning *likeness* into *sameness*.[4] It is also associated with a certain form of knowledge: the dichotomous-hierarchical knowledge that distinguishes between Good and Evil. This sort of knowledge turns touching into taking, thus collapsing analogy into equality, likeness into sameness, difference into identity, and it is this that causes God to intervene once again, in the process redefining what is involved in *touching*:

> And the Lord God said unto the serpent, Because thou hast done
> this, thou art cursed above all cattle, and above every beast of the
> field; upon thy belly shalt thou go, and dust shalt thou eat all the
> days of thy life. (I.3:14)

The serpent will thus "crawl on its belly and eat dust" (New Jerusalem Bible), *touching* the earth but *not taking* it. Similarly, man will no longer touch the earth in order to possess it, but rather be touched and taken by it, back to the formless form of *dust*:[5]

> In the sweat of thy face shalt thou eat bread, till thou return unto
> the ground; for out of it wast thou taken: for dust thou art, and unto
> dust shalt thou return. (I.3:19)

Conflict and struggle thus seem to be programmed by the biblical story of the creation. On the one hand, man is said to be created in the image of God, or at least as his likeness. On the other, however *like* the Creator he may be, man is still part of the creation and hence irrevocably different from its Author. The first chapters of Genesis tell the story of man's efforts to reduce the differences that separate the human from the divine, and the ensuing reinforcement of that separation. In the process, the first of *two* necessary conditions for translation emerges: a certain *distance*. Yet a second condition is still required, and this brings us to the second biblical event commonly associated with translation: the

Tower of Babel. In the perspective just elaborated, however, we will discover that in a certain sense it is a replay of the Fall:

> And the whole earth was of one language, and of one speech.
> And it came to pass, as they journeyed from the east, that they found a plain in the land of Shinar; and they dwelt there. . . .
> And they said, Go to, let us build us a city and a tower, whose top may reach unto heaven; and let us make us a name, lest we be scattered abroad upon the face of the whole earth.
> And the Lord came down to see the city and the tower, which the children of men builded.
> And the Lord said, Behold, the people is one, and they have all one language; and this they begin to do: and now nothing will be restrained from them, which they have imagined to do.
> Go to, let us go down, and there confound their language, that they may not understand one another's speech.
> So the Lord scattered them abroad from thence upon the face of all the earth: and they left off to build the city.
> Therefore is the name of it called Babel; because the Lord did there confound the language of all the earth; and from thence did the Lord scatter them abroad upon the face of all the earth. (Gen. 11:1–9)

If the original Fall befell "man" and "woman" *as such*, its repetition now affects fallen *men* and *women* as members of a community or group. Their project now is not to touch and eat from the Tree of Knowledge, but rather to build both a "city" and a "tower, whose top may reach unto heaven." This effort here is to re-create a place that will be as perfectly self-sufficient as that from which they have been banned. Once again, then, they seek to be like God, who is One, only this time as a "people." To be united, however, a "people" must possess a proper place, a city, but also a "name, lest we be scattered abroad." One people, one city, one name, and one tower reaching to the Heavens. And above all, one language. It is this ambition that provokes the second intervention of God, after the expulsion from the Garden of Eden, but with a similar result. The result is another expulsion, "scattering" the people "abroad," all over the "face of the earth." However, such scattering is the result not of brute force, as it were, but of the "confounding" of what up to then was the single language of man. The institution of *languages*, in the plural, is thus tied to the dispersion of the community. No longer do they dwell in one place but in many. No longer do they bear one name, but many; no longer do they speak one language, but different languages. It is this splintering of human unity, which at once entails a dispersal of political unity, that marks the origin not of "language" in the singular, but of languages in the plural.

It is only from this point on that *translation* will become an inevitable, but also *impossible*—that is, never perfectly achievable—condition of human existence. This, however, in turn means that "human" existence is no longer simply "human" because it has no single proper name. "Man" is now one name among

many, ambiguously designating diversity, particularity, singularity—of peoples
and communities and groups as much as of individuals.

This significance of "Babel" and of its consequences can be gauged in terms of
the transformations it imposes upon the "name." The initial project aims at constructing a city and a tower that would reach to—which is to say, *touch*—the
skies. In this respect, it recalls the transgression committed in the Garden of
Eden, that of touching of the Tree of Knowledge. To touch is to reduce the distance and difference between human and divine, created and creator, to the
barest minimum. Such touching is thus the effacing of the most decisive and
constitutive of all limits—that between mortals and immortal, as the latter recognizes: "They have all one language; and this they begin to do: and now nothing will be restrained from them, which they have imagined to do." To touch the
skies means to surmount diversity and acquire the attribute reserved to the One
God: unity. It also means to have the power to make a name that is proper. The
divine response, therefore, is to "confound" all names and languages, thereby instituting a medium in which *touching* will never simply be a means of *taking* (*possession*). This transformation begins with the name of Babel itself, which means
both confusion, imposed by God upon language, and "gate of the god."[6] In this
name, meanings touch one another but do not fuse into unity. Rather, they stand
in tension to one another. The gate of the god is thus marked by the confusion of
names, and languages. It is a gate that does not lead back to the single language
of Eden, but rather that opens onto the impossible and henceforth ineluctable
task of translation. In view of this history, the task of translation can be described as that of *touching* without *taking*.

The phrase, "task of translation" touches on the last text to be discussed in
this paper. In a certain sense, this essay has already informed much of the previous discussion, without being named or quoted directly. "The Task of the Translator" is of course the title of an essay written by Walter Benjamin in 1921, to accompany his translation of Baudelaire's *Tableaux parisiens*. Were there space
enough and time, I would have liked to introduce this essay via another, somewhat later text of Benjamin's, in which he elaborates a notion of "origin" that is
very helpful in understanding the way he construes the relation of translation to
the "original." Instead, however, I will simply quote a short passage that hopefully will suggest the rather unusual way in which Benjamin construes the notion
of origin. This passage is found in the "epistemo-critical Preface" to his ill-fated
study of German Baroque Theater, written in 1924. In this passage, Benjamin insists that the notion of origin must be understood *historically*. What he means by
"history" however turns out to be quite different from the way that word is commonly understood:

Origin, although an historical category through and through, has nevertheless nothing
in common with emergence [*Entstehen*]. In origin what is meant is not the becoming of
something that has sprung forth [*das Werden des Entsprungenen*], but rather the springing-forth that emerges out of coming-to-be and passing away [*dem Werden und Vergehen
Entspringendes*]. Origin stands in the flow of becoming as a maelstrom [*Strudel*] that irre-

sistibly tears (*reißt*) the stuff of emergence into its rhythm. In the bare manifestation of the factual, the original is never discernible, and its rhythm is accessible only to a dual insight. It is recognizable on the one hand as restoration, as reinstatement, and on the other, precisely therein as incomplete, unfinished.[7]

The notion of *origin* that Benjamin articulates in this passage contrasts sharply with the *creatio ex nihilo*—or more precisely, creation out of formlessness—that informs the biblical text of Genesis. By contrast, in the passage just quoted the notion of origin—and hence, the notion of the original—is construed not as an absolute beginning, nor as the passage from formlessness to form, nor as the result of anything like the intervention of a divine logos. It is also not conceived as a function of *becoming* (*Werden*) or of its dialectical counterpart, passing away (*Vergehen*).

As something that neither "comes to be" nor "passes away," which Benjamin designates with a participial noun as "*Entspringendes*,"[8] the origin is an *event* involving both singularity and repetition. This paradoxical combination is never to be found in the merely "factual," Benjamin asserts, since what it entails is less a self-contained phenomenon than a complex *relationship* that is described as a "rhythm," thus emphasizing both its repetitive and temporal aspect. This rhythm of the origin, he states, in what can only be a deliberate mixing of metaphors (and senses), is accessible

"only to a dual insight. It is recognizable on the one hand as restoration, as reinstatement, and precisely in this, as on the other hand, incomplete, unfinished."[9]

An "origin" is historical in that it seeks to repeat, restore, reinstate something anterior to it. In so doing, however, it never succeeds and therefore remains "incomplete, unfinished." Yet it is precisely such *incompleteness* that renders origin *historical*. Its historicality resides not so much in its ability to give rise to a progressive, teleological movement, but rather in its power to return incessantly to the past and through the rhythm of its ever-changing repetitions set the pace for the future.

By thus determining "origin" as the insistent but unachievable attempt to restore an anterior state, Benjamin's 1924 text suggests that something like "translation" is already at work in the "rhythm" of the original, insofar as it is historical. This account of origin thus illuminates, retroactively, the discussion of translation he had undertaken three years earlier, in the "Task of the Translator." The necessarily incomplete attempt to restore and reinstate what has been, which defines the original, indicates how and why translation can never attain an existence that would be independent of its origin. Since the original defines itself historically through the ever-incomplete attempt to restore and reinstate itself, it is from the start, as it were, caught up in a process of repetition that involves alteration and transformation, dislocation and displacement.

This conception of the original explains why Benjamin should approach "The Task of the Translator" not in terms of translation, understood as a self-contained process or structure, but in terms of what he calls the "translatability" of "the original." Translatability is not simply a property of the original work, but rather a *potentiality* that can be simply realized or achieved, and that therefore has less to do with the enduring life usually attributed to the work than with what Benjamin calls its "after-life" or its "survival" (*Nachleben, Fortleben, Über-leben*). With respect to this afterlife, the original is already irrevocably departed and is thus not directly affected by the factual history of its translations. Its historical significance, however, is inseparable from its translatability. This is because translatability is never the property of an *entity*, such as a *work*, but rather of a *relation*. And relations, Benjamin warns, should not necessarily be judged in exclusively human terms, such as the needs of actual human beings to understand works written in a foreign language:

> Only superficial thinking could declare both for essentially the same. . . . Against such a conception it must be pointed out that certain relational concepts (*Relationsbegriffe*) receive their good, indeed best meaning when they are not a priori and exclusively applied to human beings. . . . Correspondingly, the translatability of linguistic structures (*Gebilde*) would still deserve consideration even if these were untranslatable for human beings. (*Origin*, 254)

If, then, "translatability" is to be understood as a "relational concept," but not as one that cannot be "a priori and exclusively applied to human beings," how is it to be thought? To what does translatability *relate?*

Benjamin's response is double. First, he argues, languages relate to one another. Second, they relate not to human needs, which is to say, to meanings or messages, but to what Benjamin calls "pure language." Contrary to what one might suppose, pure language is not prelapsarian language, not the unified and performative language of the Creative Logos. Pure language emerges out of the interplay of what Benjamin, invoking a scholastic term, calls "way (or mode) of signifying" (*Art des Meinens*). Languages are distinguished, he argues, not by their referents but by the way they refer to them, by their mode of signifying. It is the differential interplay of these diverse ways of signifying that constitutes the medium of translation, and the "task of the translator" is to render this interplay legible by revealing how *each self-contained unit of meaning* is always exceeded by the *way* it is *meant:*

> There remains in all language and its manifest structures (*Gebilden*) apart from that which is communicable something incommunicable, which, always according to the (specific) context in which it occurs can be either Symbolizing or Symbolized. Symbolizing merely in the finite structures of languages; symbolized, however, in the becoming of the languages themselves. And that which strives to expose itself, indeed to produce itself (*sich darzustellen, ja herzustellen sucht*) in the becoming of languages is the nucleus of pure language itself. . . . If that ultimate essence, that is, pure language itself, is in language bound only to language and its transformations, in works it is charged with heavy and alien meaning. To free it from this charge, *to make the Symbolizing into the Symbolized* itself, to reconquer pure language in structured form (*gestaltet*) for the move-

ment of language–this is the powerful and singular ability (*Vermögen*) of translation. (*Origin*, 261, my emphasis)

Although it cannot be demonstrated here, the distinction Benjamin draws, between the "movement of language" as signification on the one hand, and the resulting work as a repository of meaning on the other, continues a line of thinking that he developed first in his thesis on German Romanticism and continued in his study of German Baroque Theater. In both cases, Benjamin sought to uncover the dynamics hidden within the ostensibly stable status of the self-contained, meaningful work—whether as the work of art or as the "good works" of redemption. At the same time, he never mistook the necessity of some sort of instantiation or *taking place*. This is why translation, or rather translatability, functions in his writings as a kind of paradigm indicating the necessity of defining a work or construct that would *not* be self-contained or lasting, but rather only the stopping place of an ongoing movement.

The passage under discussion is obviously extremely enigmatic and dense, and would require much more time and space to unpack than is available here. Instead, I will simply present my interpretation of its main gist, by reducing it to the formula, "make the Symbolizing into the Symbolized." What translation does is not communicate meaning but point to—signify—the movement of symbolization itself, as it is at work already in the original, and then more obviously between the original and its displacement, repetition, and dislocation by and as translation. Translatability is the never realizable potential of a meaning and as such constitutes a *way*—*way of signifying*—rather than a *what*.

But if it is a way, if it makes its way, where is it headed? Not simply back to the original or to the origin, but rather *away* from it. In moving away from the original, translation unfolds *the ways* of meaning by moving words *away* from the meanings habitually attached to them, and which are generally construed as points of arrival rather than of departure. Meaning is generally conceived as a self-contained, self-standing universally valid entity, one that precedes the words that express it. Translation's way to go, by contrast, leads in the direction of other words and other meanings, exposing a complex and multidimensional network of signification in which word occurrences are inevitably inscribed. The ways of meaning that emerge in and as translation assign a determining function to *syntax* over *semantics*. Benjamin's formula for this decisive aspect of translation—one that despite its speculative character has eminently practical implications—is "literalness (wordliness) of syntax":

> It is therefore . . . not the highest praise of a translation to read like an original in its language. . . . True translation is translucent (*durchscheinend*), it does not cover up the original, does not stand in its light, but rather allows pure language, as though strengthened by its own medium, to fall all the more fully upon the original. This is accomplished above all by literalness (*Wörtlichkeit*: literally, "wordliness") in the rendition (*Übertragung*) of syntax and it is this that reveals the word, not the sentence, to be the primary element of the translator. For the sentence is the wall before the language of the original, wordliness the arcade. (S. 18, "Task of the Translator," 261)

Benjamin's notion of the word, although it echoes the celebrated beginning of the Gospel of St. John, "In the Beginning was the Word," is anything but traditionally theological. For the word to which Benjamin here refers, is not the Creative Word of God but a word that *gestures toward other words* and that is therefore defined not by its semantic content but by its syntactic position.

The syntactical literalness of the interlinear translation is his model. The interlinear translation comes close to its original, almost touching it, and yet it remains irreducibly distant from it. For the repetition of syntax excludes semantic resemblance. It results not in an analogical relation of translation to original, based upon shared meanings, but rather in a positioning that inevitably strains the grammatical coherence of the translation. This relation of words to one another results in a relation of translation to original that Benjamin describes with a remarkable figure, one that sums up much of our previous discussion:

> The pure language that is banned in the foreign tongue—to redeem it in one's own . . . that is the task of the translator. For its sake he breaks the brittle limits of his own language: Luther, Voss, Hölderlin, George have extended the limits of German.—What remains of this for the relation of translation and original can be formulated in a figure. *As the tangent fleetingly touches* (flüchtig berührt) *the circle only in one point and as it is this touching* (Berührung), *not the point, that governs its trajectory into the infinite, so the translation touches the original fleetingly and only in the infinitely minute point of its meaning, in order to pursue its own course* (Bahn) *following the law of fidelity, in the freedom of the movement of language.* (my emphasis)[10]

Practically speaking this does not mean that translation simply ignores the meaning of the original, something that would be hard to imagine. It means precisely what Benjamin states that it means: namely, that the translation that follows "syntactical literalness" pursues a course that leads it to fleetingly touch—glancing off—the meaning of the original and then to follow the trajectory that results. The angle of that trajectory is determined by the tangential encounter of two different languages *at a specific historical time and place*. The vector that results from this tangential encounter involves the interplay of the different possible meanings of the original text and of the translation. That interplay results not in a single meaning but rather in a *difference of meanings* that, like a difference of opinion, signifies precisely through its disunity.

Since this remains rather abstract, it may be helpful to close with an example. In the previous discussion, I have translated Benjamin's German word, "*Berührung*" variously as "touching" and "glancing." But in German, it can also signify, paradoxically, the "state of being moved," as by an emotion. In his essay, Benjamin links his remarks on "way of meaning" to what is called an "emotional tone" (*Gefühlston*, p. 17). The glancing movement of translation moves whatever it touches, but above all, it moves the language in which it takes place and those who depend on it.

And yet, translation "moves" only by arresting movement. By reproducing the syntactic arrangement of words from one language to another according to the precept of "syntactic literalness," the movement of translation disrupts the grammatical rules that create meaning and institutes in their stead a sequence that does not add up to a whole. Translation thus grazes the original, touches it without taking hold, like the interlinear translation that runs parallel to the original text without ever merging or resembling it. What it resembles, by reassembling it, is the spacing of the words, a certain positioning. By reassembling and dispersing the original, the translation touches a chord in it that causes it to resonate, "like an Aeolian harp is touched by the wind of language" ("Task of the Translator," 21). Or like that wind, *ruach*, "sweeping over the waters" (New Jerusalem Bible) before the creation of the world.

Translation thus suggests a conception of medium that would be very different from that of the transparent interval between two fixed points. Instead of diaphanous transmission and transparency, translation brushes up against a past and in so doing opens itself to the future. Any attempt to interpret the media today would do well to reckon with the draft that such an encounter can produce.

Notes

1. In his text, *On the Soul*, Aristotle writes: "Democritus misrepresents the facts when he expresses the opinion that if the interspace [*to metaxou:* the medium as interval, that which is in between] were empty, one could distinctly see an ant on the vault of the sky; that is an impossibility. Seeing is due to an affection or change of what has the perceptive faculty and it cannot be affected by the seen color itself; it remains that it must be affected by what comes between. Hence it is indispensable that there be *something* in between—if there were nothing, so far from seeing with greater distinctness, we should see nothing at all." *The Complete Works of Aristotle*, ed. Jonathan Barnes, vol. 1 (Princeton: Princeton University Press, 1984), p. 667; 419a 15–21.

2. Marshall McLuhan's equation of "medium" with "message" marked a first contemporary assault upon this tradition. McLuhan, *Understanding Media: The Extensions of Man* (Cambridge: MIT Press, 1994).

3. The Word of God that creates the world, man, and the Garden of Eden, is not "placed" within it as are Adam and Eve.

4. The editors of *The New Jerusalem Bible* note that the word for "likeness" already introduces a distancing from the more intimate relation implied by "image" (*The New Jerusalem Bible*, Garden City: Doubleday, 1985, p. 19). Note: "'likeness' appears to weaken the force of image by excluding the idea of equality.").

5. Benjamin's description of the "dusty fata morgana" that covers the glass ceilings of the Winter Garden, can be read in this context: "dust" appears as the material manifestation of temporal transience (W. Benjamin, "Das Passagenwerk," *Gesammelte Schriften*, vol. 1, Frankfurt am Main: Suhrkamp, 1982, p. 217; F 3, 2).

6. See *The New Jerusalem Bible*, op. cit., Genesis I. 11, p. 15, note.

7. Walter Benjamin, *Ursprung des deutschen Trauerspiels* (Frankfurt: Suhrkamp, 1963), p. 30; English translation by John Osborne (London: Verso Books, 1977), p. 45 (my translation).

8. Benjamin's word echoes Hölderlin's description of the Rhine, in his poem of the same name, as *"Reinentsprungenes"*—except that he significantly replaces the past with the present participle ("Der Rhein," *Hymns and Fragments*, intro. and trans. Richard Sieburth (Princeton: Princeton University Press, 1984), p. 70.

9. Walter Benjamin, *Origin of the German Mourning Play*, trans. John Osborne, (London and New York: Verso Books, 1977), p. 45.

10. Benjamin, "The Task of the Translator," p. 20.

The Languages of Cinema

MICHAEL WOOD

> "Just think: a Soviet film director conceived the production of an
> English play while flying to Japan."
>
> —Grigori Kozintsev, *King Lear: the Space of Tragedy*

What is the language of a Russian film? Of a Japanese film? The question sounds like a trick or a riddle, a children's joke, along the lines of "Who wrote Beethoven's Eroica Symphony?," or "What was the date of the 1848 revolutions?" And there is an obvious answer, of course. The language of the film, in the most literal sense, is Russian or Japanese. But if we say this we need to note at once how much we have smuggled into, or taken for granted about, the meaning of the word "film." We are probably thinking of sound films, although if we are being cautious we shall remember the title cards in silent films. And we are almost certainly thinking of representational images rather than abstract designs, or the dancing cartoons of Disney's *Fantasia*, for example; of a pictured world in which humans or animals speak, and therefore speak a national language of some sort, whether they are heard in the film or not. There are many other kinds of film.

But there is another, less literal sense in which the language of these films is still Russian or Japanese, and we can usefully think, with Christian Metz, of the language of cinema, and wonder to what extent that nonverbal language is already national.[1] As my title suggests, I do want to prolong that question, but mainly I want to consider the issue of translation in film: what is being translated onto film; how viewers translate among the different sign-systems they are seeing on a screen (and hearing on a sound track); how and when national cultures count and do not count. But we need some examples.

The credits are in Russian, and just before they end we hear a human voice chanting, also in Russian. Then comes a series of noises calling out for interpretation or naming. They sound like, and turn out to be, the creaking of a crude wooden-wheeled cart being pushed over rough ground, and the limping, irregular footsteps of a man walking with a stick on the same terrain. The images appear. They are black and white, and shot mostly from a middle distance, that is, neither in close-up nor in long shot. A group of poorly dressed people, men and women, many of them cripples, make their way with difficulty over a hillside dotted with stones like monoliths. It is hard to place them in time or space by their ragged clothes, but we may think of some undefined period in Europe some-

where between the Middle Ages and the Enlightenment. They look like whatever the European poor are supposed to look like when we allow them into the
historical picture. One of them pauses, and blows a signal on a primitive horn:
an announcement of some kind. Orchestral music starts up in the sound track.
Now we do get a long shot, and a clearer sense of the hillside. Beyond it is a val-
ley, into which these people—there must be a hundred or more of them—are
peering. We suddenly see some horsemen in a row, their tall lances erect beside
them. We cannot locate them in relation to the gathering mass of people because they have only sky behind them. But then suddenly we in are a particular
place, where different, much better-dressed people are waiting, and two poised
and wealthy-looking gentlemen walk down a wooden stairway leading from the
battlements of a castle. The castle looks medieval, the two gentlemen and the
waiting assembly seem to belong to a generic European Renaissance. The men
speak, in Russian, the opening lines of *King Lear:*

> I thought the King had more affected the Duke of Albany than Cornwall.
>
> It did always seem so to us, but now, in the division of the
> kingdom, it appears not which of the dukes he values most, for
> equalities are so weighed, that curiosity in neither can make choice
> of either's moiety.

The division of the kingdoms. That, presumably, is what the blast of the horn
announced, that is what the cripples and the poor are assembling to hear about,
however remotely. That is what the gentry are attending to more closely.

We are looking at the beginning of Grigori Kozintsev's film of *King Lear*
(1971). The Russian words we hear are those of Boris Pasternak, author of this
translation, and the discreetly sounding music is by Dmitri Shostakovich. But
the words we see on the screen, if we are viewing a print with English subtitles,
are not a translation of what we hear. They are the text of *King Lear,* the source
of the speeches, not their rendering in English. We are hearing Pasternak's translation, but reading untranslated Shakespeare. This unusually complicated relation of Russian to English, and of screen speech to screen text, opens up a whole
range of questions about language and translation in film, although the questions
take on their full force only when we remember the larger context of the presentation: printed credits, chanting voice, noises off, black and white moving images, sound of horn, music in the sound track, difficulty of correlating images,
hillside and castle, crowd and horsemen, speech in Russian, text in English.

And who are these people on the hillside, for whom Shakespeare's text seems
to give no warrant, since it opens with the words I have just quoted? They inhabit "a cruel stone world," in Kozintsev's words, they and the landscape are "the
ends of a civilization": "the road to Lear's castle, a way through the ravages of
epochs, a stone chronicle."[2] But they do in fact respond to a textual cue. They
are the "wretches" whom Lear, like most productions of the play, has forgotten
and whom he remembers only in extreme destitution and distress. They are the
people of the kingdom he has given away, and to whom he belatedly thinks a
ruler should "shake the superflux"—as if he or any other ruler would ever think

the superfluous was superfluous while they had it. Kozintsev does not make his Lear speak of any superflux, but he does bring these people—rhetorically present in Shakespeare's "wretches, wheresoe'er you are"—physically to the screen. They cluster on the hillside at the start of the film, and they or their counterparts return when Lear enters a hovel on a heath, a huddled heap of faces and limbs, a vision of a human tangle borrowed, perhaps, from the crowded ship's quarters of Eisenstein's *Battleship Potemkin* (1925). Lear addresses them not as a memory of injustice but as a present mass of human suffering:

> Poor naked wretches . . .
> That bide the pelting of this pitiless night [the subtitle has storm],
> How shall your houseless heads, and unfed sides,
> Your loop'd and window'd raggedness, defend you
> From seasons such as these? O, I have ta'en
> Too little care of this![3]

Houseless, unfed, and ragged, they are the world of the governed, "the people without rights,"[4] as Kozintsev calls them, the hapless human contents of the portions into which Lear has divided up his kingdom, and the film places them at its opening in order to remind us that a kingdom is more than land, and that a land anyone wants to rule almost always has people on it.

Another hillside, more horsemen. But the hills are vast and grassy, and we see long vistas of them, a green landscape of rounded summits and deep valleys. The horsemen sit waiting, in groups of four or three or two, the only visible movement the twitching of their horses' tails. There is faint, high violin music in the sound track. The credits on the side of the screen are in Japanese, so we can guess where we are. A closer look at the horsemen reveals them to have the beards and costumes of ancient Japanese warriors, longbows in their hands, quivers of arrows strapped to their backs. Suddenly a boar appears in close-up, and we know why the horsemen are waiting. The boar hears a sound, and starts to run. The hunting warriors appear behind him in hot pursuit. Other boars appear and the chase is on, boars and mounted huntsmen racing through the long grass. We see the oldest of the huntsmen draw his bow, still riding fast as he does so. The music now features a high-pitched flute, and the screen suddenly shows the film's title, two large red characters, which look almost as if they have been painted in blood: *Ran*, meaning chaos.

After the title the huntsmen sit in a canvas enclosure discussing their day. The oldest one, Lord Hidetora, falls asleep, and awakens to announce a strange dream. Then Hidetora says the time has come for peace, and he is stepping down, leaving his hard-won territories and his first castle to his eldest son; his second and third castles and corresponding lands to his second and third sons. He will retain only a thirty-man escort and the title of Great Lord. He plans to visit each of his son's castles in turn. The first two sons make obsequious speeches, saying all the right things, and the third son calls his father senile and crazy. The third son is blunt and harshly outspoken, not merely honest, but we begin to recognize the structure. The third son is Cordelia, he cannot lie, and he understands that his father fails to understand himself. More important, he understands, and clearly says, that their whole world is one of strife and chaos, that one cannot step down from a history of violence, and that an imperious, warlike father is not likely to have raised docile and unambitious sons. Like Cordelia, the third son is banished, and the story follows the pattern of King Lear—with the significant difference, of course, that English daughters have been transformed into Japanese sons. The film is Akira Kurosawa's Ran (1985).

The hunting scene corresponds in more than one way to that of the gathering crowd in Kozintsev's King Lear. The huntsmen, like the crowd, are waiting, and until we see the boar, we do not know what they are waiting for: an enemy, perhaps, a raid, or the onset of a battle. And although we soon learn the men are gathered for a sporting occasion, the occasion itself, the fast-riding, armed horsemen, and the ensuing conversation, are full of memories of war. More discursively, Kurosawa, like Kozintsev, is giving us, in imagery, a deep story that Shakespeare's text only hints at. In place of "the people without rights" and their stony terrain, we have a culture of vigilance and discipline and the struggle for survival. "I've tried to give Lear a history," Kurosawa said. "I try to make it clear that his power must rest upon a lifetime of bloodthirsty savagery."[5] He makes it more than clear in the abdication scene I've just described, but all kinds of hints of this history lie in the opening images, with their complicated mixture of beauty and menace.

In both Kozintsev's and Kurosawa's films something more than a production of Shakespeare is taking place: the cinema is not just a modern stage. In effect, we are witnessing a double translation: from culture to culture and from medium to medium. The cultural translation is easy enough to track, and translation seems close enough to the right word. Shakespeare's ancient England becomes Kozintsev's Renaissance Russia; Lear's time becomes Shakespeare's time. In the early stages of planning his film, Kozintsev visited Lear's "places" in England: "Newcastle-upon-Tyne, a ninth-century cathedral, castles, Anglo-Saxon monuments . . ." He reports, "I did not yet know what surroundings Lear was to have. Only not these; the action could not take place here." Later he says his scene was to be "the world of history without external historical characteristics; a world which is absolutely real (filmed on location), without existing in nature, constructed out of a montage which will last for two hours."[6] Much film theory is compressed into this lucid and paradoxical sentence, and we have seen the practice that results: the construction not of an illusion but of an emblematic reality. Kurosawa's translation of England into Japan, here as in his earlier film, Throne of Blood (1957), based on Macbeth, comes eerily close not so much to Shakespeare as to what we imagine the world of Shakespeare's sources to be like: violent and unforgiving, less courtly and Christian than he has managed to make it, even if his characters (in King Lear) do repeatedly invoke pagan gods. And the translation of three daughters into three sons is, I think, more than a response to cultural difference. It is true that Shakespeare's audience would have had no difficulty in imagining powerful women, since their country had been ruled by two shrewd and ruthless queens for all of the fifty years before Shakespeare wrote King Lear, and that there is no Japanese equivalent for such public authority being given to women. But even if the shift of gender starts in historical plausibility, it ends somewhere else: in an implied question about the difference gender makes in struggles for power. This is too large a subject to tackle here, but it is worth saying briefly that *Ran* seems both to insist on the difference, and to make it, after we have registered all the obvious effects of dress and language and means of action, rather hard to find, since the most lethal and captivating figure in the film is not the king or any of this three sons, but the first son's wife (and second son's mistress), Lady Kaede.

The translation from medium to medium is harder to describe correctly, since literally we are seeing the realization in one medium of a text designed for another: a virtual translation, let's say, or a real translation of the virtual text composed of various stage productions of the play, remembered, reconstructed, or imagined. It is not clear that translation is exactly the right word here; not clear either that there is a better one, since the phantom of a stage production of a famous play must haunt all film versions. One of the things these films must necessarily be, apart from films, is not-the-play. We think of live bodies, physical space, real time, and the triumphs and failures of stage illusion—that unmistakable, never precisely repeated gesture, that terrible makeup. A film has none of this, and in films based on Shakespeare we remember this absence. In fact, the difference between good and bad Shakespeare films often has to do with this absence. The trick is not to make us forget it, but to persuade us to do something with our memory. Kozintsev and Kurosawa remind us constantly that their films are films, and it is for this reason that the notion of translation will not go away—even though it can usually quite easily be made to go away in the cinema. Both films turn a literal absence of fleshly life, a sequence of shadows on a screen, into a series of questions about the end or absence of life, about mortality and the shadowiness even of much actual existence. Think again of Kozintsev's notion of a setting that is real but does not exist in nature and is made out of montage. A film world is always remade, put together out of pieces. Both of these films ask us to think about the pieces and the putting together. And beyond that, since the translation is double (from medium to medium and from culture to culture) they ask us to think of the national origins of two sets of pieces, and of the national styles involved in putting them together—assuming that even the most talented individual directors do not work entirely outside of any tradition.

What is a national film style? Is there an international film style? I do not think there are narrowly national styles of any great interest, and of course it's true that good directors work as much against their traditions as with them. I do not think there is an international style of any great interest either, unless we take the well-made Hollywood film as having become an international model, through a sort of imperialism of expressive means. But there are distinct traditions, and Kozintsev, for example, for all his interest in Japan and Kurosawa, and all forms of inventive filmmaking from Dreyer to Welles and Buñuel and Fellini, remains a director in the tradition of Eisenstein, and there are clear family resemblances between his *King Lear* and Eisenstein's *Ivan the Terrible* (1942, 1945), as well as the previously mentioned *Battleship Potemkin*. Kozintsev gets less hieratic and less symbolic performances out of his actors, but they still look as if they are ready to step into a brilliant archive of gesture and posture, and we would not confuse them with characters in a British or Italian or French film, even if the costumes were more or less the same. Similar things can be said of Kurosawa, the most international of all Japanese directors, and a man long scorned in Japan because of that very reputation. The very silences in Kurosawa sound Japanese, and are unlikely to be found even in the most silent moments of Western film.

But style is not the same as language, and it is worth recalling the elements of film language we have glanced at so far: noises, voices, music, black and white images, images in color, pictures of humans, of animals, of landscapes, of castles, of tents; dialogues about rule and division, changing faces, sudden gestures. Many of these elements are going to be national in particular cases, but in principle, and described as generally as I have just described them, they are international. Gesture as a locally interpretable language will always belong to a specifiable culture, but the idea of gesture as language belongs to culture at large. Each individual king will govern (or not) a particular country, but kingship is found in many places. We might think of this relation between the general and the particular as the relation between a word and a referent, or a word and a name: between the word "pointing," for instance, and the act of pointing at this; between the word "king" and the name Lear. But then we shall need to complicate our picture at once, because Lear functions both as a word (the man with the three daughters or sons, the man who divides his kingdom, the man to whom the whole story of Lear happens) and a name (this actor, this particular incarnation, this face, this hair, this set of highly individualized motions). This is true on stage, of course, and true more generally of literature, since every reader must actualize a version of the characters he or she reads about. That is why Henry Fielding could say, in one of his slyest jokes, that it was a mistake for Cervantes to set *Don Quixote* in Spain—since one could see its characters in London any day.[7] But the force of the referent or the name is especially compelling in film, where we see an unavoidable range of stark particulars, and often can reach the general, or the translatable, only after a considerable interpretative struggle. In photography, still or moving, "the referent adheres," Roland Barthes says, the object or person remains stubbornly an object or a person, will not quite turn into a sign.[8] This was not always entirely true, and whatever truth the claim had has vanished with the advent of digital photography. A digital image may resemble an object or a person, and we usually understand it through that resemblance. It is not a purely conventional sign like a word. But it reconstructs rather than registers an illusion, and the same is true of digital sound. These are not traces of objects or persons, as photographs and recordings once were; like footprints or a fingerprints. And Barthes' claim about photography tells us something important about the cinema—that is, about the history and theory of moving images prior to the digital age. In the cinema the referent (often) adheres not only because of what we know about the technology that produces the images but because the screen and the sound track are full of referents, of signs that have not made it all the way into "signhood." If we think again of any of the instances I have evoked so far, we shall see we are caught up in a curious kind of semantic travel, from the irreducible creak or tap or horse or armor to a relay of implied meanings. We turn the sounds and images into words or at least into candidates for words: cart, lameness, hunt, warriors. Then we make another move and turn these notions into larger suggestions on the verge of allegory: poverty, rightlessness, vigilance, violence. But then we look again and all the generalities have vanished. All there is is the creak and the tap and the horse and the armor, nothing else. And the travel starts again.

To Barthes' claim that the referent adheres to the photograph, we could add Benjamin's idea that photography refuses or evades art because "the beholder feels an irresistible urge to search . . . a picture for the tiny spark of contingency, of the Here and Now, with which reality has so to speak seared the subject."[9] This is a fantasy about photography, but a fantasy with a long historical life. It suggests not that the camera cannot lie, but that it cannot shake off the world.

Of course the camera can shake off the world in all kinds of ways. Every act of framing a shot excludes something. And blanking out wrinkles from a finished photo, retouching waistlines, or airbrushing out whole casts of characters, are all ways of refusing aspects of actuality. But the fantasy, forgetting these things, remembers something else: that a camera can be pictured as perfectly lacking in intelligence, and therefore unable to scrutinize or alter what it sees.

The fantasy is not about the camera always doing this; no one thinks the posed studio photograph is anything other than a posed studio photograph. The fantasy is about the chance, once in a while, of catching mere contingency, and especially in a moving film. Near the beginning of the story "A Scandal in Bohemia," Sherlock Holmes is called an "observing-machine," and a little later makes a famous distinction between seeing and observing. "When I hear you give your reasons," Watson remarks, 'the thing always appears to me to be so ridiculously simple that I could easily do it myself, though at each successive instance of your reasoning I am baffled until you explain your process. And yet I believe that my eyes are as good as yours." "Quite so," Holmes says. "You see, but you do not observe. The distinction is clear. For example, you have frequently seen the steps which lead up from the hall to his room." Watson says he has.

> "How often?"
> "Well, some hundreds of times."
> "Then how many are there?"
> "How many? I don't know."
> "Quite so! You have not observed. And yet you have seen. That is just my point. Now, I know that there are seventeen steps, because I have both seen and observed."[10]

"Observing" is not reflection or intelligence, it is just better seeing. The observing-machine will always have counted the steps, or rather will not even need to count them, because it will register the seventeen steps every time. It does not have to remember because it does not have a means of forgetting. What the machine represents in such an interpretation is not so much a modern technology as the mind so close to perception it can scarcely think.

There is an extraordinary moment in *A la Recherche du temps perdu* that catches the mind in just such a phase, and evokes it through a recourse to the image of just this technology. The camera, Proust suggests, defamiliarizes the world and reveals our tricks of perception to us. But it also reveals the world itself and our loved ones to us, especially when we have wrapped them up in all kinds of protective familiarities. This is an intricate and painful affair, because the camera tells the very truth that human agencies are conspiring to deny. When Proust's narrator writes of "film" in this passage (*a la façon des pellicules*), I do not know whether he means the film you put in a camera or the film you see in a cinema. Probably the second, since early films are full of stories of what a camera will see when it is inadvertently left running, when the world stumbles into its view, so to speak. As if the camera were a kind of spy without a job—who need only to wait to become employed. There are many things to be said about this passage, but let me for the moment mention only the delicacy of its multiple perspectives, marked by words like affectionate, cruel, intelligent, devoted, loving, and deceptive, and by the intense desire not to see what is so sadly to be seen, along with the faithful reporting of seeing it. I'd like to note too that the real narrator is a ghost and the real grandmother a sort of photographic hallucination: when so-called reality returns it means the cover-up is back in place, and the film, what Proust elsewhere calls mere "cinematic procession," is over. The narrator enters a room where his grandmother is reading:

> I was there in the room, but in another way I was not yet there because she was ignorant of the fact, and, like a woman who has been caught unawares at some piece of needlework that she will hide away if anyone comes in, she was absorbed in thoughts which she had always kept hidden in my presence. The only part of myself that was present—in that privileged moment which does not last and in which, during the brief space of a return, we suddenly find ourselves able to perceive our own absence—was the witness, the observer, in travelling coat and hat, the stranger to the house, the photographer who has called to take a photograph of places that will never be seen again. What my eyes did, automatically, in the moment I caught sight of my grandmother, was take a photograph. We never see those who are dear to us except in the animated workings, the perpetual motion of our incessant love for them, which, before allowing the images their faces represent to reach us, draws them into its vortex, flings them back on to the idea of them we have always had, makes them adhere to it, coincide with it. . . . But if, instead of our eyes, it should happen to be a purely material lens, a photographic plate, that has been watching things, then what we see, in the courtyard of the Institute, for example, instead of an Academician emerging into the street to hail a cab, will be his tottering attempts to avoid falling on his back, the parabola of his fall, as though he were drunk or the ground covered in ice. Similarly, some cruel trick of chance may prevent the intelligent devotion of our affection from rushing forward in time to hide from our eyes what they ought never to linger upon, and, outstripped by

chance, they get there first with the field to themselves and start to function mechanically like photographic film, showing us, not the beloved figure who has long ceased to exist and whose death our affection has never wanted to reveal, but the new person it has clothed, hundreds of times each day, in a lovingly deceptive likeness. . . . I, for whom my grandmother was still myself, I who had only ever seen her with my soul, always at the same point of the past, through the transparency of contiguous and overlapping memories, suddenly, in our drawing-room which had become part of a new world, the world of Time, inhabited by the strangers we describe as "aging well," for the first time and for a mere second, since she vanished almost immediately, I saw, sitting there on the sofa beneath the lamp, red-faced, heavy and vulgar, ill, her mind in a daze, the slightly crazed eyes wandering over a book, a crushed old woman whom I did not know.[11]

This is not the place to distinguish minutely between still and moving photography. It will be enough to say that still photography often returns to "art" while movies before the digital age frequently work best when they claim not quite to have been there. This is an art too, of course, but an art that announces its insufficiency, its dependence on a merely material, untransformed world. Its realm is the real that is not natural, as Kozintsev says; a place of incomplete signs, in Barthes' sense; of contingency, in Benjamin's; of (almost) unthought, unedited perceptions, as in Proust's narrator's glimpse of his grandmother.

It is often said that the arrival of sound altered the cinema drastically, and in one sense it did. But only because films, and especially North American films, came to depend so massively on talk. Films not only spoke, they became garrulous, turned to dialogue for all their story lines, jokes, and the mapping of emotions. This in turn generated dubbing for overseas audiences, and the use of subtitles—which need to be clearly distinguished from the title-cards of silent films, themselves part of a film-text, not translations into the print of one language of the spoken sounds of another. These talkative films became markedly national, not just because they spoke a national language, but because they spoke so much and had such need of speech.

There are other relations of sound and image, and we have only to think of the celebrated seven minute "silent" sequence in *Ran* to see what they may be. This sequence is silent in the sense that it has no dialogue or sound effects, only slow, haunting Mahler-influenced orchestral music (by Toru Takemitsu). But the silence is sudden, and the absence of noise is felt throughout the sequence. Lord Hidetora is being attacked by his two elder sons, we hear horses neighing, soldiers shouting, and see his abrupt alarm. One of his soldiers, several arrows in his body, collapses and dies, but not before saying they are in hell. Then the music rises, and everything else goes totally silent: arrows hit the castle walls, guns are fired, soldiers fall, Hidetora's concubines commit suicide, men are yelling, flames appear, clouds billow—all inaudible. Then Hidetora's eldest son Taro rides into the castle courtyard. The battle is over, apparently. The slow music continues, and so does the silence of the represented world. Then sound returns loudly as a gunshot kills Taro—one of his brother's men has murdered him. Kurosawa's metaphors are both visual and aural: a scene of carnage and sounds both heard and unheard. Death and betrayal are hell, and hell is silence, the dream-like muffling of the noises of the world, a place where even extreme violence cannot make itself heard.

This sequence, like the most memorable moments in many films, presents us with a finely articulated instance of the complexity of our question about translation. Here are countless elements that are local and untranslatable; local and translatable; not local at all but not translated; or translated into the most enduring, cosmic terms. We see persons and a world both clothed and unclothed in interpretation, in Proust's terms, dressed in the brilliant colors of ancient courtly Japan, but also showing glimpses of Lear's "thing itself," "unaccommodated man."[12] And as we listen to the civilized music of the Western concert hall we try in vain to hear the sounds of an Eastern world that has died.

NOTES

1. Cf. Christian Metz, *Film Language: a Semiotics of the Cinema*, trans. Michael Taylor (Chicago: Chicago University Press, 1991).

2. Grigori Kozintsev, *King Lear: The Space of Tragedy*, trans. Mary Mackintosh (Berkeley and Los Angeles: University of California Press, 1977), pp. 83, 130.

3. William Shakespeare, *King Lear*, Act III, Scene Four. London: J M Dent, 1935, p. 54.

4. Kozintsev, *King Lear*, p. 36.

5. Stuart Galbraith IV, *The Emperor and the Wolf: The Lives and Films of Akira Kurosawa and Toshiro Mifune* (New York and London: Faber and Faber, 2001), p. 578.

6. Kozintsev, *King Lear*, pp. 21, 81.

7. Henry Fielding, *Tom Jones* (New York: Signet, 1961), p.160. "The facts we deliver may be relied on, though we often mistake the age and country wherein they happened: for though it may be worth the examination of critics whether the shepherd Chrysostom, who, as Cervantes informs us, died for love of the fair Marcella, who hated him, was ever in Spain, will any one doubt but that such a silly fellow hath really existed?"

8. Roland Barthes, *La Chambre claire* (Paris: Gallimard Seuil), 1980, p. 18.

9. Walter Benjamin, "A Small History of Photography," in *One-Way Street*, trans. Edmund Jephcott and Kingsley Shorter (London: Verso Books, 1985), p. 243.

10. Arthur Conan Doyle, "A Scandal in Bohemia," in *Sherlock Holmes: The Complete Novels and Stories, Volume 1* (New York: Bantam, 1986), p. 211.

11. Marcel Proust, *The Guermantes Way*, trans. Mark Treharne (London: Penguin Books, 2002), pp. 137–38.

12. Shakespeare, *King Lear*, Act III, Scene Four, p. 56.

PART TWO

The Ethics of Translation

Though all the essays in this volume deal with the ethics of translation, those included in this section make it their primary theoretical focus. Several address the ethical double bind in any act of translation—the impossibility of fully rendering another's voice or meaning, and yet the necessity of making the attempt. Other essays focus on the question of the "original," a topic raised by Weber in part I, that returns as a leitmotif throughout the volume.

As the first four essays underscore, much responsibility for creating an ethical translation lies with the translator. If translation has always been a "conflict more than an achieved task," Gayatri Chakravorty Spivak reminds us that it carries added responsibilities today, especially when translating non-European texts into English. In a market eager for quick translations of all sorts, the writer must proceed with humility, attempting to inscribe the "trace of the other, the trace of history, and even cultural traces." "Trace," as a "marker of anterior presence," is the operative concept here, as Spivak brilliantly translates and explicates Bengali texts from Farhad Mazhar's *Ashoumoyer Noteboi—Untimely Notebooks*, walking her reader carefully through the historical, linguistic, and religious presuppositions of their author, "translating the poet translating his language through the history of nation-states and internationality toward the transcendental." In the final section of her essay, Spivak returns to a chief concern, translation as reading, and to the Bengali poet Benoy Majumdar, who, years earlier, wrote a book dedicated to Gayatri Chakravorty. Striving to "other the characters" of this seductive text, she begins to explore its protocols, where "her youthful proper name is obliterated in the concerns of general readers" and where she must remember that the poet's "presuppositions have a history and a geography, and that," as she writes, "I am a translator into English."

In Spivak's essay, the responsibility of the translator walks hand in hand with that larger responsibility to human otherness, a responsibility famously articulated by Emmanuel Levinas. Though many commentators have described the central role that translation holds in Levinas's work—especially the translation between what he calls "Hebrew" and "Greek"—Robert Eaglestone wisely sounds a cautionary note, pointing out that to see Levinas's work this way is "to offer a limited view both of his achievement and of the nature of translation." If linguistic otherness reminds us of all we cannot comprehend, including our "pre-ontological" ethical responsibility to those whom we do not, and cannot, ever fully know, translation (in the usual sense) can be seen only as a "comprehension," a taking of power, and a reduction of otherness. According to Eaglestone, it is rather language's ultimate *untranslatability*, its "foreignness," that makes it important to Levinas. Does this mean we should not translate? No, but as this essay eloquently argues, it means we have ethical grounds to be suspicious of the idea of translation, especially as it relates to communities, and their tendency to reduce otherness to sameness.

Questions of cultural translation and radical otherness form the background for Henry Staten's discussion of the "native informant," or "aboriginal," in the work of Gayatri Spivak. At the farthest point from a Western "metropolitan" subject, the aboriginal takes the role of the worldly other that is least knowable in a Western globalizing world. Staten astutely notes a structural relation between Spivak's "tracking of the native informant" and her account of ethical translation: In each case, the task is to know the "other" as intimately as possible, yet also to acknowledge its complex modes of inaccessibility. Though such related projects could lead a critic into either a simple nostalgia for the pure immediacy of a native culture or language, or an equally simple awareness that there is no pure originary presence, Spivak's "deconstructive tracing . . . of the presuppositions behind Eurocentrism" preserves her from both. It also preserves her from that particular mis-translation of the non-Western that Staten terms "civilizationism," in which "civilization is normed by the species 'Europe.'" At the close of an essay that effectively critiques a number of ethnographic and literary strategies, Staten reminds us that the ethics of translation Spivak defines also discloses the ethics of reading a literary text. Here "'our own' culture is as unknowable as is that of 'the other' and the ethics of cultural translation is the ethics of reading."

Approaching issues of reading and translation from a somewhat different perspective, Stanley Corngold discusses the salutary "delay" in translation exemplified in the discipline of comparative literature. Arguing against the view that translation offers a good analogy for the work of comparative literature, he insists that the two must, in fact, be carefully distinguished. In comparative literature, readers do not pass quickly to the translation of texts, noting similarities and differences, but rather hold original language texts together in the mind, even "being, for one moment, without a language." On the ethical level, "this holding two pieces together in the mind is a warrant against the violence of premature analogy, against improper associations." As Corngold eloquently argues, the internal silence and "dislocation" that occurs in comparative reading provides room for the ethical movement toward cultural otherness, even the otherness of Spivak's "subaltern, impoverished, woman of color," and a future understanding of the "common human grain."

If these first four essays alert us to the responsibilities of the translator and the reader, the final two examine more closely the status of the "original." What do we mean when we speak of the original language text and its relation to the translation? Must these be seen as a hierarchy, with the original as the ethical and epistemological reference point for evaluating subsequent renditions? As the essays by Jonathan Abel and Emily Apter show, instances in literary history clearly undermine this common assumption as they point to new and different conceptions.

Jonathan Abel argues, for instance, that translated and translation ought to be viewed as part of what Jean-Luc Nancy would call a community, a single ontological order, in which any assumption of a "sacred" original is eliminated. This is especially important in considering a work such as *Genji monogatari* with its complex textual history. Here, scholars do not have only one original, but rather several. Moreover, Abel effectively shows that Murasaki's classical Japanese enjoys a range of very different translations into modern Japanese, "in which style is always foregrounded, in which change is assured and in which the original text is far from sacred." With its historically multiple "origin" and its varied subsequent renditions, translation and translated are best viewed as a "being in common," a "literacy communism" inviting a careful analysis of similarities and differences.

Similarly questioning the status of the original, Emily Apter insists that all translations are in some sense "forgeries," since they pretend to a contract of fidelity they never keep. True, pseudotranslations, such as those by Pierre Louÿs and Kenneth Rexroth, put the original dramatically into question since these poems never even try to transcribe an original, but only pretend to do so. Yet as Apter brilliantly shows, such examples are not just exceptions to a more general rule. Viewing them as effects of "textual cloning" allows her to broach broader ethical issues surrounding textual reproduction. She claims, in fact, that such apparent "forgeries" reveal a "technology of literary replication that engenders textual afterlife without recourse to a genetic origin." They thereby substantiate Benjamin's understanding of translation as that which "usurps the place of the original while ensuring its afterlife." In this sense, the final essays in this section articulate the importance of translation not only as a means to promote cultural understanding and ethical self-reflection. They also bear witness to its temporal quality, whose effects orient us toward the present and future as much as to the past.

Translating into English

GAYATRI CHAKRAVORTY SPIVAK

I'd like to begin with what should to be an obvious point. That the translator should make an attempt to grasp the writer's presuppositions. Translation is not just the stringing together of the most accurate synonyms by the most proximate syntax. Kant's "Religion Within the Boundaries of Mere Reason" is written with the presupposition that mere (rather than pure) reason is a programmed structure, with in-built possibilities of misfiring, and nothing but calculation as a way of setting right.[1] Since the eighteenth century, English translators, not resonating with Kant's philosophical presuppositions, have psychologized every noun, making Kant sound like a rational-choice, bourgeois Christian gentleman.[2] Kant's insight could have taken on board today's major problem—Can there be a secularism without an intuition of the transcendental, of something that is inscrutable because it cannot be accessed by mere reasoning? Kant's project, to protect the calculus of reason by way of the transcendental as one parergon among four, was counterintuitive to his English translators.[3]

I will add three more examples here to show the generality of the problem. In these, the lack of translators' sympathy stalled a possible use for each text, a use that relates to the limits of rational choice. This brings the examples into my chief concern: the responsibility of the translator into English. I hope some readers will care to follow the trajectory suggested by each.

When Marx wrote about the commensurability of all things, that it was "contentless and simple" (*inhaltslos und einfach*) he was speaking as a materialist speaks of form.[4] Not as *form*, but as a thing without content. Generations of empiricist English translators have missed the point, not resonating with Marx's philosophical presuppositions, translated *inhaltslos* as "slight in content," and thus made nonsense out of the entire discussion of value. Marx's insight could have taken on board today's transformation of all things into data—telecommunication rendering information indistinguishable from capital. Marx's presuppositions, to control the inevitability of intelligible formalism in a materialist interest, were counterintuitive to his English translators.

In his seminar on the gaze or glance, the eminent French psychoanalyst Jacques Lacan presents the scopic or apparently objectivizing sweeping glance as

This work was first presented as a keynote on January 17, 2001, at the Sahitya Akadami (The National Academy of Letters), at a conference of translators. Since India has at least twenty-two languages, the internal translators were not all knowledgeable about Derrida, Foucault, and Lacan, though Kant was known to some, and Marx, of course, to all.

something like a symptom. To show his students this, Lacan cannot use proof. It is the very production of proof in the patient that Lacan is opening up. He therefore uses the interesting coinage *apologue*—apology, excuse, but also something that is just a little off the side of the *logos*. "I will tell you a little apologue," he says (*Je vais vous raconter une petite apologue*).[5] The naturalizing translator, thinking Lacan is just talking about people looking, translates this important sentence as "I will tell you a little story."

When the French historian Michel Foucault described the ground floor of power as set up with "irreducible over-againsts" (*irréductible vis à vis*), he was trying to avoid transcendentalizing the empirical.[6] Humanist English translators, unable to resonate with Foucault's philosophical presuppositions, have translated "vis-à-vis" as "opposite," given content to a nonformalist intuition of form, and turned the argument into the micropolitics of power, understood as ordinary language.

Grasping the writer's presuppositions as they inform his or her use of language, as they develop into a kind of singular code, is what Jacques Derrida, the French philosopher who has taught me a great deal, calls entering the protocols of a text—not the general laws of the language, but the laws specific to this text. And this is why it is my sense that translation is the most intimate act of reading.

I begin this way because I am a translator *into* English, not just *from* specific languages. Because of the growing power of English as a global lingua franca, the responsibility of the translator into English is increasingly complicated. And, although I chose my four opening examples in order to avoid cultural nationalism, it is of course true that the responsibility becomes altogether more grave when the original is not written in one of the languages of northwestern Europe.

For a variety of reasons, the market for quick translations from such languages is steadily on the rise. Since the mid-1970s, it has been enhanced by a spurious and hyperbolic admiration not unrelated to the growing strength of the so-called international civil society.[7] In the 1970s, extra-state collective action in Europe, Latin America, Asia, and Africa concerned itself with issues such as health, the environment, literacy, and the like. Although their relationship with the nation-state was conflictual, there was still a relationship. Gradually, with the advance of capitalist globalization, this emergent force was appropriated into the dominant. These earlier extra-state collectivities, which were basically nongovernmental entities, often with international solidarity, were now used to undermine the constitutionality (however precarious or utopian) of the state. Powerful international NGOs (nongovernmental organizations) now control these extra-state circuits globally. Indigenous NGOs typically have a large component of foreign aid. This self-styled international civil society (since it is extra-state) has a large cultural component, especially directed toward gender issues. It is here that the demand for translation—especially literary translation, a quick way to "know a culture"—has been on the rise. At this point, we translators into English should operate with great caution and humility.

Yet the opposite is often the case. Meenakshi Mukherjee, the well-known feminist Bengali scholar of English literature, has spoken to me of a person—she did not mention the name—who has recently turned her or his hand to translating from the Bengali. Upon repeated questioning about her or his proficiency in Bengali, this would-be translator has given the same answer: "*bangla porte jani*" (I can read Bengali). We all know of such cases.

It is time now to mention the other obvious point—the translator must not only make an attempt to grasp the presuppositions of an author but also, and of course, inhabit, even if on loan, the many mansions, and many levels of the host language. *Bangla porte jani* is only to have gained entry into the outer room, right by the front gate.

I am at the moment engaged in translating Mahasweta Devi's novel *Chotti Munda ebong tar tir* (Chotti Munda and his Arrow) published in 1980.[8] In the last paragraph that I translated I made a choice of level when I came across the phrase *mohajoner kachhe hat pa bandha*. "Arms and legs in hock to the moneylender," I wrote. "In hock" is more in the global lingua franca than in the English that is one of the Indian languages. Sujit Mukherjee, the brilliant Indian translator from Bengali into English, and I, had a running conversation about such choices. But "mortgaged" would have been, in my judgement, an error of level, and would have missed the pun, "being tied up or trussed," present in the original. Not that "in hock" catches the pun. But "hock" is sufficiently confusing in its etymology to carry the promise of nuances. The translator must play such games.

Lower down in the paragraph, I'm less satisfied with my treatment of the phrase *hoker kotha bollo na Chotti?* as "Didn't Chotti speak of 'rights'?" *Hok*, in Bengali, a *totshomo* or identical loan from the Arabic *al haq*, is not rights alone but a peculiar mix of rights and responsibilities that goes beyond the individual. Anyone who has read the opening of Mahasweta's novel knows that the text carries this presupposition. I have failed in this detail. Translation is as much a problem as a solution. I hope the book will be taught by someone who has enough sense of the language to mark this unavoidable failure.[9]

This for me is an important task of translation, especially from languages that are dying, some fast, some slow, for want of attention. In our particular circumstances, we translators from the languages of the global South should prepare our texts as metropolitan teaching texts because that, for better or for worse, is their destiny. Of course, this would make us unpopular, because the implicit assumption is that all that "third world" texts need is a glossary. I myself prepare my translations in the distant and unlikely hope that my texts will fall into the hands of a teacher who knows Bengali well enough to love it, so that the students will know that the best way to read this text is to push through to the original. Of course not everyone will learn the language, but one might, or two! And the problem will be felt. I should add here that I have the same feeling for Aristotle and classical Greek, Hrotswitha von Gandersheim and Latin, Dante and Italian—and, of course, Kant and Marx and German, Lacan and Foucault and French. It is just that these latter texts have plenty of teaching editions and the languages are not ignored. I received a contemptuous notice, I think, if memory serves, from *Kirkus Reviews*, some years ago, for preparing a volume of fiction by Mahasweta Devi with a preface and an afterword.[10] Literature and philosophy do, of course, belong to different slots on a publisher's list, but I contrast this with the abundant praise I have received over the last twenty-seven years all over the world for providing just that apparatus for a volume of philosophical criticism by Jacques Derrida.[11]

In this spirit I will turn now to *Ashomoyer Noteboi—Untimely Notebook* by Farhad Mazhar, the activist-poet from Bangladesh.[12] *Ashomoy* is an interesting word. *Dushhomoy* would be "bad times" of course. But Nietzsche's use of *Unzeitmäßig*, typically translated as "untimely," as in *Untimely Meditations*, gave me a way out.[13] And a notebook is a place where meditations are jotted down.

Mazhar thinks of himself as "untimely" quite as Nietzsche does, indeed quite as Nietzsche believes genuine cultural figures must be: "Virtue . . . always swims against the tide of history, whether by combating its passions as the most proximate stupid factuality of its existence or by dedicating itself to being honorable while the lie spins its glittering web around it."[14] He offers no alternatives: "The untimely thinker, which is how Nietzsche viewed himself, does not work directly towards the establishment of another culture, in which his arguments might become 'timely'; rather, he is working 'against my age, and thereby influencing my age, and hopefully for the benefit of a future age.'"[15]

As Foucault suggests in "Nietzsche, Genealogy, History":

> If genealogy in its turn poses the question of the land that saw our birth, of the language that we speak, or of the laws that govern us, it is to make visible the heterogeneous systems which, under the mask of our "we," forbids us all identity . . . [Another] use of history . . . uncovers the violence of a position taken: taken against ignorant happiness, against the vigorous illusions by which humanity protects itself, taken in favor of all that is dangerous in research and disturbing in discoveries.[16]

In pursuit of heterogeneity, Mazhar goes clear out of culture into nature, undertaking impossible translations from the animal world in a recognizably Nietzschean mode. We recall that this is precisely where Derrida locates Nietzsche as philosopher of life:[17]

> Now then notebook, will you get the Philip's
> > Prize this time?
> Try hard, try hard, by Allah's grace.
>
> > Caution
> I'm copying down how the grass crawls
> I'm copying down how the jaguar grabs
> I'm slipping, my foot's missed its hold
> I'm copying down the problems on the way
> > along with the foot's heel
> Caution caution
> Earlier you had to fight standing
> > on the other side of the barbed wire
> Now on both sides: Right and left, top and
> > bottom, in water and on land . . .

Go get your teeth fixed by the alligator
From the snake a rubber spine
Go suckle the breasts of the bat
Hey my untimely notebook, the times are bad
                                                        chum
Must walk with eyes peeled on all sides my
                                                    friend

            Be careful!!
            Caution!!!

In the previous stanza, he speaks of the woman Nurjahan who was stoned to
death because she was supposed to have slept with someone other than her husband. I can commend Mazhar's feminism and work out his spiritual link with the
anything-but-feminist Nietzsche but I cannot work out the words *murtad* and
dorra in lines 2 and 3:

Untimely notebook, I'm giving a fatwa,
            you're murtad
I'll dorra you a hundred and one times
            you're shameless
I'll fix you in a hole and stone you to death
            In front of the whole village
            You to Chhatakchhara, to Kalikapur
Must go, this time to die
Seek out a torn sari or a pitcher
Shariat witness, Allah has bred girls
            For the village elders and the world's rich men
Shariat witness, the task of imam and mollah
            is to fulfill's Allah's will
Go faith go money go reaction go progress go
Go Jamayate Islami go imperialism go Subal
            go Sudam[18]
Go hand in hand twin brothers let's watch and
                                    be delighted . . .

I am unable to access *murtad* and *dorra* because they are *tatshomo* words from
Arabic. I add an explanation of this word and the companion word *tadbhabo*,
words that were known to every Bengali schoolchild when I went to high school
in the early fifties. I am not a Bengalist, merely a translator in love with the language. What I am about to give you is a generalist's sense of things.

   Tat in these two words signifies "that" or "it," and refers to Sanskrit, one of the
classical languages of India, claimed by the Hindu majority. They are descriptive
of two different kinds of words. *Tadbhabo* means "born of it." *Tatshomo* means
"just like it." I am using these two words by shifting the shifter *tat*—that or it—to
refer to Arabic as an important loan-source.

   Through the centuries of the Mughal empire in India (1526–1857) and the corresponding Nawabate in Bengal, Bengali was enriched by many Arabic and especially Persian loan-words. Of course Bengali is derived from Sanskrit, which was by then "dead," so the relationship is altogether different. But learned and worldly Bengali gentlemen were proficient in Arabic, and especially Persian—the languages of the court and the law. The important entry of the British into India was by way of Bengal. It is at least the generalist's assumption that the British played the Bengali Hindus with promises of liberation from the Muslim empire. William Jones's discovery that Sanskrit, Greek, and Latin were related languages even gave the Hindus and the English a common claim to Aryanism, a claim to intertranslatability, as it were.[19] And, from the end of the eighteenth century, the fashioners of the new Bengali prose purged the language of the Arabic-Persian content until, in Michael Madhusudan Dutt's (1824–73) great blank verse poetry, and the *Bangadarshan* (1872–76) magazine edited by the immensely influential novelist Bankim Chandra Chattopadhyaya (1838–94), a grand and fully Sanskritized Bengali emerged. Its Arabic and Persian components became no more than local color. This was the language that became the vehicle of Bengali nationalism and subsequently of that brand of Indian nationalism that was expressed in Bengali. The medium was simplified, expanded, and diversified into the contemporary Bengali prose that is the refined edge of my mother tongue, which I learned in school, and which did not allow me to translate *murtad* and *dorra*.

A corresponding movement of purging the national language Hindi of its Arabic and Persian elements has been under way since independence in 1947. Such political dismemberments of language have become part of Partition Studies—as Serbian separates from Croatian, Czech from Slovak, and Cantonese is dismissed as a mere dialect of Han. The political production of internal translation requires a different type of analysis, which I will touch upon in my conclusion.

If the Arabic and Persian elements were purged out of Bengali, how do I encounter them as a translator today? I encounter them as part of a general movement in Bangladesh to restore these components. This is not to be confused with an Islamicization of the language, since there can be no question of transforming the Sanskrit base of Bengali. Indeed, Mazhar uses the Sanskrit-based vocabulary of Bengali with considerable flair. One may call this an attempt persistently to mend the breach of a partition that started—as I have indicated in my generalist tale—long before the named Partition of India in 1947. It is to restore a word-hoard that went underground.

What was created as East Pakistan in 1947 became independent as Bangladesh in 1971. Although there was an important political and military conflict that brought this about, it would not be incorrect to say that one strong factor of the mobilization of what was to become Bangladesh was the issue of language.[20] And indeed the naming of the new nation as Bangladesh was to shrink an older cartography. Bangladesh (Banglaland) is the name of the entire land area whose people use Bangla, or Bengali; or Bangla is the name of the language of the entire people of the land or desh called Bangladesh. Before the independence-partition of 1947, this would have been the entire British province of Bengal, in-

cluding today's Indian state of West Bengal and the modern nation-state of
Bangladesh, whose geographical descriptive could be East Bengal—in Bengali
Paschim and Purbo Banga. Banga is the ancient name of a tract of land somewhat larger than the British province of Bengal. Thus the proper name of a premodern area and kingdom, displaced into the name of a Nawabship, translated
into the colonial proper name of a province, expanded beyond a language area
into the governmental abstraction of a presidency—is now modernized to designate, not a language-area but a bounded nation-state metonymically claiming
the whole.

This may be seen as the celebration of partition, however benign. Since 1947,
the Indian state of West Bengal (or Paschim Bango) is the western part of a
place that does not exist. Unlike those who propose solutions such as calling it
merely Bango, so that it too can claim the whole, by a more ancient name, I propose no nominative solution. Such a solution would finalize partition by making
official the historically asymmetrical name of the whole for each geographically
asymmetrical half. Even that could be undone, of course; for each half could say
we are each the whole, in different ways. In the long run, it would not matter a
great deal, for named places do not, strictly speaking, exist as such, since there
are re-namings. If there is history, there is the re-naming of place. In this case as
elsewhere, I am interested in the political mode of production of the collectively
accepted existence of named places, whose "other names" linger on as archaic or
residual, emergent as local alternative or opposition, always ready to emerge.[21]

If the establishment of a place named Bangladesh in a certain sense endorses
the partition of 1947—the language policy of the state, strangely enough, honors
that other partition—the gradual banishment of the Arabic and Persian elements of the language that took place in the previous century—and thus paradoxically undoes the difference from West Bengal. The official language of the
state of Bangladesh, 99 percent Muslim, is as ferociously Sanskritized as anything
to be found in Indian Bengali.

It is over against and all entwined in this tangle that the movement to restore
the Arabic and Persian element of Bengali, away from its century-old ethnic
cleansing, does its work. And it is because I grew up inside the tangle that, in
spite of my love of Bengali, I could not translate *murtad* and *dorra*—though I
could crack *ashamoyer* with Nietzsche.

I am only a translator, not a Bengalist. I can cite only two names in this movement: Akhtaruzzaman Ilias (1943–1998), the author of *Chilekothar Sardar* and the
fantastic *Khoab-Nama*; and Farhad Mazhar, whose poem I was about to translate
when I launched into this lengthy digression.[22] It may be claimed that these writers do a double bluff on the Sanskritized linguistic nationalism of Bangladesh.

At the meeting of the Sahitya Akadami I was immediately sidetracked into a
translation of the word *huda* (about which more later), as an Arabic-origin Urdu
word foreign to Bengali; and a learned etymologico-philosophical disquisition (a
pale imitation of which I would be able to provide for Sanskrit-origin Bengali
words) from a distinguished professor of Urdu from Kashmir. None of the Indian
Bengalis could offer a translation.

Murtad and *dorra* can be translated as "apostate" and "whiplash." *Huda* so overwhelmed the discussion that they remained un-Englished at the Akademi meeting. I have withheld this information for so long because, as I was moving through various European and Asian countries, revising, I kept wondering how I would get to find the English equivalents! A chance encounter—someone reading Bengali web in Bangkok airport, must be Bangladeshi!—provided them at last.

It is my belief that unless the paleonymy of the language is felt in some rough historical or etymological way, the translator is unequal to her task. Strangely enough, I got this lesson at St. John's Diocesan Girls' High School in Calcutta, from Miss Nilima Pyne, a young Christian woman (we thought her ancient, of course) who had learned Sanskrit with heart and soul. She had quoted at us, when I was no more than eleven or twelve, that famous pair of Sanskrit tags, both meaning "there's a dry branch in the way." See if you can sense the complete dissonance in the two sets of sounds; be sure to mark the greater length of the vowels in the second example. I have not followed accepted phonetic transliteration, but given the closest Englishing of the Sanskrit sounds:

  a. shushkum kashthum tishthattugrey
  b. neerasa taruvara poorata bhaati

Can you sense the completely different ring of the two sentences? If you don't have a sense of Sanskrit, which is rather different from "knowing" Sanskrit, you cannot, of course. Sound and sense play together to show that translation is not merely transfer of sense, for the two lines "mean the same thing." Sanskrit is not just a moment in Benveniste.[23]

This was not a lesson in translation. But it was such instruction that allowed us to understand, three or four years later, Shakespeare's play with "the same meaning," once in Latinate and once in "Anglo-Saxon" English, metaphorizing enormity in the enormousness of the encompassing ocean:

> This my hand,
> Will the multitudinous seas incarnadine,
> Making the green one red.

We transfer content because we must, knowing it cannot be done, in translation as in all communication, yet differently. We transpose level and texture of language, because we must, knowing that idiom does not go over. It is this double bind that the best and most scrupulous translation hints at, by chance, perhaps. *Mimesis* hits *poiesis* by *tuchè*.[24] Translators from the languages of the global South into English have lost this striving. The loss is incalculable. Responsible translators from the languages of the global South into English therefore often translate in the shadow of the imminent death of the host language as they know it, in which they are nurtured.

Translating these two words in Mazhar, I was also suggesting that the burden of history and paleonymy are added to this double bind. Arrived here I often hear, Not everybody can be so well prepared! Is there ever such a refusal of craftspersonly expertise for European-language translation? I suggest we pay no attention to such excuses and proceed to the next poem, where another kind of history is invoked.

This poem refers us not to Bengali in the history of the nation-state but in the internationality of Islam. As already mentioned, Bengali is not of Arabic/Persian origin. It is not taken seriously as a language of Islam. During the war that established Bangladesh, soldiers of the then West Pakistan regularly taunted East Pakistani soldiers and civilians as not "real" Muslims, no more than the force-converted dregs of Hinduism. (It may be worth mentioning here that Assia Djebar is most unusual in acknowledging Bengali among the non-Arabic Islamic languages: "Arabic sounds—Iranian, Afghan, Berber, or Bengali.")[25] In this frame, Mazhar addresses Allah, as follows:

BANGLA IS NOT YOURS

You've built the Bangla language with the crown of
    my head and the roof of my mouth
My epiglottis plays with the "ah" and the long "ee"
Breath by breath I test the "om" and my chest's
                beat
Heartstrings ring in the enchanted expanse of the
                con-sonant

Oh I like it so, lord, I like the Bangla language so
                much
I lick it clean, greedy, as if paradise fruit.
Are you envious? For in this tongue you never
Proclaimed yourself! Yet, all day I keep at it
Hammer and tongs so Queen Bangla in her own
Light and power stays ahead of each and all, my dearest lord.

Some ask today, So, Bangla, are you divine as well?
You too primordial? Allah's alphabet?

I'm glad Bangla's not yours, for if it were—
Her glory'd raise your price, for no reason at all.

Let us look at the last line. *Dānt* is one of those particularly untranslatable idiomatic words: airs and graces, swelled head, hype—you see the choice I've made: "raise your price." What is interesting is that this word has been coupled with *behuda*, another Arabic *tatshamo* word that I have translated "unreasonably." Let me first say that there is a common Sanskrit-origin word—*ajotha* (Sansk. *ayathā*)—that would fit snugly here. *Behuda* points at itself, incomprehensible to "the common reader." I believe now that the word is in general use in Bangladesh. As I have already mentioned, I received a lecture on the Arabic word *huda* from my learned colleague from Kashmir. I could best grasp his meaning by turning it into the English familiar. "Reason" in "for no reason at all" is an ordinary language word. Yet "reason" is also a word of great philosophical weight. *Huda* has a comparable range. What reason is being invoked here to claim a language connected to Revelation by imagination rather than letter? This is a different argument from the right to worship in the vernacular, where, incidentally, content transfer must be taken for granted. I go everywhere in search of the "secular." I will come back to this later. Here is a hint that expanding religion beyond mere reason may bring with it a question of translating rather than recording the transcendental.

Attempting to make the reader walk with the translator translating the poet translating his language through the history of nation-states and of internationality toward the transcendental, I will cite three poems here with brief introductions.

First, "Lady Shalikh."

The *shalikh* is a household bird, with no claim to beauty or musical skill. Mazhar is invoking the simplicity of the malnourished rural Bangladeshi woman, not the famed beauties of Bengal. Mazhar is a feminist poet. (I cannot unpack this difficult sentence here.) What does it mean to make the common woman cry out to Allah, in desperate humility, as the poet had, in pride of language?

> In the garden of paradise a body-brown Shalikh
> Calls. O my life, did you hear on paradise branch
> Our kindhearted Shalikh calls with life and soul
> Calling her own words at Allah's Durbar.
>
> Can you hear, can you see, our Lord,
> Holding the knee of her yellow gam straight
>   On gandam branch
> Hacking her throat with her humble beak in weak
> Abject low tones our Begum Shalikh calls?
>
> What have we asked, dear Lord, our hopes are
>   small
> Let our life's bird reside in paradise
> Even if a darkskinned girl, snub-nosed,
>   bandy-legged
>
> Eyes sunk with body's work, yet in Bengal
> A well-loved daughter, without her paradise
>   lost—
>
> Bird call, call with life and soul, even Allah's
>   heart does melt.

The next poem refers to Rabindranath Tagore, who has already been mentioned as a master fashioner of modern ethnically cleansed Bengali, a language that slides easily into English. Mazhar cannot disclaim his pervasive influence, but . . .

THE TAGORE KID

Our sir Rabi is a huge big poet, white folks
Gave him the Nobel prize to vet his literary might
Just right. His dad and gramps
Ran after the Brits and gathered in the loot
Became landowners by own claim
But family faults ne'er stopped
His verse—he's now the whole world's poet.

I salaam him, welcome him heartfelt.
Yet my soul, dear lord, is not inclined
To him. Rabindra had faults. His pen
Remembered many a lucky sage, saint, renouncer, and great man,
But never in wildest dream did the name of
Prophet Muhammad come in shape or hint
To his pen's point, so I can never forgive.

But dear lord of grace, you please forgive that boy, from Tagore clan.

In the last poem that I will cite, the poet addresses a figure within the Hindu tradition who was open to all others. Sri Rama Krishna Paramahansa (1836–86) as he was known, was also a poet of the transcendental, although his medium was not literary verbality. He was not an intellectual and therefore could not alter the course of public language. But if *poiesis* is a making of the other that goes past *mimesis*, Rama Krishna must be called a poet in the general sense. Islam took its place among his imaginings and his iterations of the self. Because these moves acknowledged the irreducibility of the imperative to translate rather than its denial for the sake of identity, here Mazhar responds as part of that which is translated, not an "original," but an other. Here translation surprises the poet as no displacement at all, perhaps; the mode is not declarative and introduces a picture of the poet dancing in the othered mode: "Have I moved, then?"

In Rama Krishna's name Mazhar undertakes yet another translation or transfer into the transcendental, a messenger from the human mystic to God himself—the most easily recognizable name of the transcendental as such. And yet it is a translation: the poet articulates a plea for polytheist worship (a hibiscus for Kali) to achieve felicity in Allah's acceptance. He daringly offers to transport the Hindu hibiscus to the austere Allah of Islam. In the present of the poem, the transfer is forever performed.

SRI RAM PARAMHANSA

Have you seen the red hibiscus? You told that flower
to bloom, in Bengal
So it does hang and bloom
Blood red—*haemoglobin* of blood
In petals perhaps, it glows in wood and plot.

I a hibiscus flower in your honor my lord
Will give into the hands of th' blessed one,
Sri Rama Krishna Paramhansadeb.
He'll give his little chuckle, gap-tooth glowing in
                              laugh
And say "O my Sheikh's Boy, here you are, you've come?"

Have I moved, then? Nope, I didn't move
If going, I go the same way everywhere.
Entranced the lord of love dances in state
The sheikh boy dances equal, loving this lord.

By way of Kali when Paramhansa sends
Hibiscus to you lord, accept with love.

Ground level countertheological Islam has managed such exchanges, perhaps not so spectacularly, wherever Islam has flourished. Today, when the great tradition of Islamic secularism is tarnished, it seems particularly important to allow poetry such as this to launch us on an imaginative journey that can be risked if reader and translator venture beyond the sanctioned ignorance that guards translation from the languages of the global South into English. The literature of Bangladesh does not appear prominently on the roster. Rokeya Sakhawat Hussain's *Sultana's Dream* and *The Secluded Ones* are resuscitated from time to time in an indifferent translation from the Feminist Press.[26] Otherwise it is the fashioners of that other Bengali and their descendants who get Englished. It is of course different with development material, but that is another story.

As writers like Mazhar attempt to enter the detheologized "religious," they question the premises of a superficial secularism. They are, in turn, incorrectly perceived as providing fuel for fundamentalists.

I started this essay with a reference to "Religion Within the Boundaries of Mere Reason." I mentioned that a problem of translation does not allow us to see that in that text Kant considers with scrupulous honesty if secularism is possible without the possibility of thinking the transcendental. This task is absolutely crucial today. Those sanitized secularists who are hysterical at the mention of religion are quite out of touch with the world's peoples, and have buried their heads in the sand. Class-production has allowed them to rationalize and privatize the transcendental and they see this as the welcome telos of everybody everywhere. There is no time here to connect this with the enforcement of rights, and the policing of education by the self-selected moral entrepreneurs of the self-styled international civil society—with no social contract and no democratic accountability. I can only assert here that the connection can and must be made. I hope I have been able at least to suggest that this state of the world has something to do with a failure of responsible translation, in the general and the narrow sense.

I have walked you through the hybridity of a single language. I want now to make a comment on the notion of hybridity that is the migrant's wish-fulfillment:

irreducible cultural translation in any claim to identity. I wish translation could be so irreducibly taken for granted. The impossibility of translation is what puts its necessity in a double bind. It is an active site of conflict, not an irreducible guarantee. If we are thinking definitions, I should suggest the thinking of trace rather than of achieved translation: trace of the other, trace of history, even cultural traces—although heaven knows, culture continues to be a screen for ignoring discussions of class. If translation is a necessary impossibility, the thought of a trace looks like the possibility of an anterior presence, without guarantees. It is not a sign but a mark and therefore cannot signify an "original," as a translation presumably can, especially when assumed as definitively irreducible. I contrast a comfortable notion of a permissive hybridity to the thought of the trace because the former is associated, sometimes precisely by the assurance of cultural translation, with the sanitized secularism of a global enforcement politics. This permissive hybridity can also foster an unexamined culturalism that can indeed give support to fundamentalisms here and there. That bit of the migrant population that faces a repressive state as well as dominant racism becomes a confused metonym for this other, separate global face of hybridity as translation.

If the European context brought us to the sense of problems in the global public sphere, the context of Bangladesh brought us to the question of secularism. In my last section I come back to what has always been one my chief concerns: translation as reading. I examine here the problems of entering the protocols of a text, when the text seems to give way. I move to a singular example where the aporia of exemplarity—that the singular example loses singularity by entering the category "example"—is cleanly resolved by the poet himself into no more than a reader's choice:

> This book of poems, focused on a girlfriend, and dealing only with a plea for love is indeed a diary. . . . If you think only of me, this poetry is only a plea for love. . . . Yet, because any one part is applicable to many situations connected to love, social theory, politics, science and many other topics, therefore one should be able to find a successful realization of any kind of situation in the lives of any sort of reader, male or female.[27]

This book of poetry was first published in 1961 and then republished in 1962 under the title *Phire Esho Chaka* (*Come Back Wheel*). The book was dedicated to Gayatri Chakravorty. (The Sanskrit *chakra* of the surname means wheel and is transformed into *chaka* is modern Bengali. A cunning translation.)[28] Chakravorty did not know the poet, although she had noticed the intensity of his gaze. She left Kolkata for the United States in 1961. She did not read the poems, although she knew of the book's fame, and that it was dedicated to her. Many of the poems lament her absence, his loneliness without a response. It is not clear that such lamentations, included in poetry, require "response" in the ordinary way. Must the lost object not remain lost for the poems to retain their exact verbal contour? If reading is a species of translation, here was a rather singular double bind of translation, for a singular reader, with a specific proper name. Gayatri Chakravorty, not having read the poems, did not have to live this double bind.

In 2002, some forty years after the publication of the book, a facsimile edition of the manuscript was published. This book, in the poet's impeccable hand, is entitled *Gayatrike* (*To Gayatri*). I was shown a review of this text by a colleague, and a woman in the family bought me a copy. I have now read these brilliant poems. There is no question of response, other than what you read here.

A face and body, a figure, is a cipher, to be deciphered, read. The figure cannot read itself. The poet's uncanny eye has deciphered Gayatri Chakravorty, prefigured predicaments that she would like to think she averted in ways that he had counseled in those unread poems. At a certain point, the poet advises a different way of living:

> Not success outside,
> But a selfsame flowering as unstiff as the body's sleep
> Is what lovers want. . . .
> Go on, try opening by yourself, like a shell would,
> Fail, yet that bit of sand, the little sand that finds its way just in,
> Will little by little be pearl, the proper success,
> > Of movement.
> If you want a life as easy and all nature, like the sleeper's pose,
> Try breathing in the heart's interior fragrance. (8)

This reader would like to think that the prayer to be haunted by the ethical is kin to that advice.

Benoy Majumdar has been in and out of mental hospitals for the last forty years. What is it for such a man to write: "I will now be mad, at last by insane claws / Will prise out the angel's home address, the door" (30)? There are poems that delicately hint how "madness" must be managed, and poems that ask: "O time, where, at whose door shall I appear / With my armored charms, my naked ways" (85)?

There is no question of response. The occasion of these poems has been translated into the transcendental. The facsimile edition ends with poems marked "not to be included in the printed version." I do not know if they are to be found in the printed versions. The last one of them is the only straightforward narrative poem in the sequence. The others are written "according to the psychological process by which we dream (setting together scene after scene)" (Foreword). Indeed, Gayatri Chakravorty is called "Dream-Girl" a number of times.

It is not possible to write about these poems briefly. There is spare praise of auto-eroticism, praise of the austere comforts of poetry, despair at loss of skill, a tremendous effort to imagine the smallest creatures, and the uncaringness of star and sky, to frame human frailty and loss, and a brilliantly heterogeneous collection of addressees. Sometimes the imagery is a rarefied dream lexicon: nail, cave, delta, rain. I hope they will not be translated soon. At last I would like to translate them.

There are repeated references to oneself as a letter lying on the wrong threshold, destined to err, a plea to be called if some "social need" should arise:

> Come and pick me up like torn bits of a letter
> Put 'em together for curiosity's sake, read once and leave
> As if to disappear, leaving them like a slant look. (16)

There are reprimands to the frivolous girl, references to the future laughing at her sudden death (36), cryptic judgments such as the following, where nothing in the poems allows us to decide if Dream-Girl is among the exceptions or the rule: "In very few women is there a supplement placed" (3). I have been unable to catch the specificity of *ramani*—one of a handful of common words for woman—that carries the charge of *ramana*—the joy of sex. I have also been unable to catch the pun in *krorepatra* (translated "supplement")—literally "lap-leaf." What does the pun mean? This poet is uncharitable to women who merely breed and copulate.

It is this particular ambivalence in the poems that seems exciting for this translator to access, as she makes the mistake of thinking the named subject is she. Thus the ambivalence seems to offer a codicil to that bit in Coetzee's *Waiting for the Barbarians* that she had so liked: How does the other see me? Identity's last secret. Coetzee describes the Magistrate describing his deciphering effort thus: "So I continue to swoop and circle around the irreducible figure of the girl, casting one net of meaning after another over her. . . . What does she see? The protecting wings of a guardian albatross or the black shape of a coward crow afraid to strike while its prey yet breathes?"[29]

I am the figure of the girl, the translator thinks, making that easy mistake, and this book offers what the poet sees as he casts his net. I come up both ways, albatross and crow. This is a lesson: to enter the protocols of a text one must other its characters.

In the last poem in the facsimile edition, in and out of the book, since it is not meant to be included in the printed version, Gayatri Chakravorty or "my divine mistress" is translated into a declarative narrative of transcendental alterity. Response stops here, in the representation of response without end:

> I've grasped it surely, life on earth is done;
> I'm straight in heaven's kingdom, earth's body's shed.
> These heavenly kingdoms are indeed our home, and we
> Are just two spirits—Dream-Girl and I—this pair
> Divinely live in heaven's kingdom now. I see,
> That she's still that familiar youthful form,
> And stands with a greeting smile upon her lips.
> My divine mistress. I too have by desire kept a body,
> Even in heaven—healthful, like Dream-Girl's,
> As tall as she, no glasses, eyesight good,
> I am to her taste, a goodlooking young man.
> Smiling she speaks up—You're done, you've come at last,
> Now for the bliss of peace, fulfillment, thrill
> In body and mind, in deep immeasurable kind,
> Everything just so, as we would like it. Come.
> Next, in a clasp so deep, and deeper still a kiss,
> She promises that she will spend with me,
> An eternity of shared conjugal life. (85)

What is it to be an "original" of a translation? This is what teaches me again the lesson of the trace. For a name is not a signifier but a mark, on the way to a trace. Benoy Majumdar makes Gayatri Chakravorty a hybrid, but not by the assurance of some irreducible cultural translation. The name as mark is caught between the place under erasure—crossed out but visible—on the handwritten title page—and its generalization as "my divine mistress"—*amar ishwari*.[30]

On the flyleaf of this book I find notice of something that no critic has spoken of so far, a prose book, presumably, entitled *Ishwarir Swarachita Nibandha*—*An Essay* or *Essays Composed by the Divine Mistress Herself*. The book was out of print, I heard, but about to be printed again. How shall I be encountered by myself in that text, where I think the poet has attempted to access Gayatri Chakravorty's thinking? Here is an allegory of translation, turned inside out.

This task remains. And it remains to try that second way of reading, impersonal or diverse situations connected to social theory, politics, science. I am back where I began. I must get around the seduction of a text that seems to be addressed to myself, more than most texts, and enter the author's presuppositions, where my youthful proper name is obliterated in the concerns of general readers, equally welcome.[31] As I do so, I must of course remember that those presuppositions have a history and a geography, and that I am a translator into English.

NOTES

1. Immanuel Kant, "Religion Within the Boundaries of Mere Reason," in *Religion and Rational Theology*, eds. Allen W. Wood and George di Giovanni (Cambridge: Cambridge University Press, 1996), pp. 39–215.

2. It is not that translators since the eighteenth century have not been aware that problems exist. The best-known is the *Willkür-Wille* distinction, which the great translator T. K. Abbott translated as "elective will" and "will" respectively, thus coming close to the sense of the mere mechanical ability to select one thing rather than the other, preserved in the ordinary language associations of "whim" or "willfullness" attached to *Willkür*. This is why, as John R. Silber notes, Kant associates *Willkur* with heteronomy rather than autonomy. Silber seems to me to be correct in suggesting that "[t]he discovery and formulation of meanings for these terms was . . . one of Kant's foremost achievements in the *Religion* and in the *Metaphysic of Morals*. . . . The evolving complexity of Kant's theory of the will is missed by the English reader unless they can know when Kant is using 'Wille' and when he is using 'Willkür'" ("Introduction," in Kant, *Religion Within the Limits of Reason Alone*, trans. Theodore M. Greene and Hoyt H. Hudson [New York: Harper, 1960], p. lxxxiv).

3. "Parergon" is Kant's word, describing a task that is outside the limits of the work undertaken ("Mere Reason," in Ibid., p. 96 and passim. It is to be noticed that these parerga belong not only to the work of mere reason but that of pure reason as well. To discuss this detail is beyond the scope of this essay.

4. Karl Marx, "Preface to the First Edition," *Capital: A Critique of Political Economy*, Vol. 1, trans. Ben Fowkes (New York: Vintage, 1977), p. 90.

5. Jacques Lacan, "The Line and Light," *The Four Fundamental Concepts of Psychoanalysis*, trans. Alan Sheridan (New York: W.W. Norton, 1978), p. 95.

6. Michel Foucault, *History of Sexuality*, Vol. 1, trans. Robert Hurley (New York: Vintage, 1980), vol. 1, p. 96.

7. For an assessment of the limits of the international civil society, see Satendra Prasad, "Limits and Possibilities for Civil Society Led Redemocratization," *Prime* (2000), pp. 3–28; for a somewhat unexamined encomium, see Homi K. Bhabha, "Democracy De-realized," in *Documenta 11, Platform 1: Democracy Unrealized*, ed. Okwui Enwezor (Ostfildern-Ruit: Hatje Cantz, 2002), pp. 346–64.

8. The translation appeared in 2002. Mahasweta Devi, *Chotti Munda ebong tar tir* (Kolkata: Seagull; Oxford: Blackwell).

9. I have discussed the ambivalence of *al haq* in Spivak, *Imperatives to Re-Imagine the Planet* (Vienna: Passagen, 1999). Patrick Wolfe has an interesting comment about "hock" and "haq," an unwitting coupling on my part: "I have nothing to base this on, but I can't help feeling that your text isn't the first place that these words have met up. In English, 'hock' has to do with ransoming—opposing groups (men and women, tenants and landlords, etc) mock-kidnapped each other (tying up and trussing were involved) at Easter time and dues had to be paid for their return. A fair amount of ransoming went on during the Crusades. A practice associated with Saracens, hence the Arabic loan-word? Wild and woolly, I may well be suffering from a William Jones complex, but no doubt there's a philologist somewhere who'd know" (private communication).

10. Mahasweta Devi, *Imaginary Maps*, trans. Spivak (New York: Routledge, 1993).

11. Jacques Derrida, *Of Grammatology*, trans. Spivak (Baltimore: Johns Hopkins University Press, 1976).

12. Farhad Mazhar, *Ashomoyer Noteboi* (Dhaka: Protipokkho, 1994), p. 42; translation mine). I have discussed this poem in another context in Spivak, *A Critique of Postcolonial Reason* (Cambridge: Harvard University Press, 1999), pp. 362–3n. I have underlined the words in English in the original.

13. Friedrich Nietzsche, *Untimely Meditations*, trans. R. J. Hollingdale (Cambridge: Cambridge University Press, 1983).

14. Ibid., p. 106; translation modified. See also pp. 22, 55, 60, 95, 146, 206, 251.

15. Gianni Vattimo, *Nietzsche: An Introduction*, trans. Nicholas Martin (London: Athlone, 2002), pp. 31–32.

16. Michel Foucault, "Nietzsche, Genealogy, History," in *Language, Counter-Memory, Practice: Selected Essays and Interviews*, trans. Donald F. Bouchard and Sherry Simon (Ithaca: Cornell University Press, 1977), pp. 162–63; translation modified.

17. Jacques Derrida, *Of Spirit: Heidegger and the Question*, trans. Geoffrey Bennington and Rachel Bowlby (Chicago: University of Chicago Press, 1989), p. 54, and p. 57, note 3.

18. Friends of the Hindu god Krishna. Mazhar typically mingles the Hindu and Muslim elements of Bengali culture. More about this in the text.

19. I have discussed this at greater length in *Critique of Postcolonial Reason*. Homi Bhabha misses this important and substantive religion/caste point when he quotes Alexander Duff as relating English and the Brahmins as proof of the merely formal irreducibility of hybridity (Bhabha, "Commitment to Theory," *Location of Culture* [New York: Routledge, 1994], p. 33).

20. For discussions of the Bangladeshi language movement, see *Chinta* 22–23 (Mar 15, 2000), pp. 20–25.

21. I have discussed this in terms of the name "Asia" in "Our Asias," in Spivak, *Other Asias*, forthcoming from Blackwell.

22. Akhtaruzzaman Ilias, *Chilekothar Sepai* (Dhaka: University Press, 1995); *Khoabnama* (Dhaka: Maola Brothers, 1996).

23. Emile Benveniste, *Indo-European Language and Society*, trans. Elizabeth Palmer (London: Faber, 1973).

24. Aristotle, *Poetics*, trans. Stephen Halliewell (Cambridge: Loeb Classical edition, 1995), p. 29.

25. Assia Djebar, "Overture," *Women of Algiers in Their Apartment*, trans. Marjolin de Jaeger (Charlottesville: University of Virginia Press, 1992).

26. Rokeya Sakhawat Hussain, *Sultana's Dream and Selections from the Secluded Ones*, trans. Roushan Jahan (New York: Feminist Press, 1988).

27. Benoy Majumdar, *Gayatrike* (Kolkata: Protibhash, 2002), "Foreword." Hereafter cited in text with page numbers.

28. I have just read Jacques Derrida, *Voyous: deux essais sur la raison* (Paris: Galilée, 2003). His luminous and anguished words on the wheel ("La roue libre," pp. 25–39) add greater poignancy to this singular narrative.

29. Cited in Spivak, *Death of A Discipline* (New York: Columbia University Press, 2003).

30. I am using Derridian language here. The editor of the facsimile edition thinks there is some connection between Benoy's perceptive glance and my "spreading Derrida," as she puts it (Kankabati Dutta, "À Propos,"). Perhaps there's something there, but she has got her dates wrong. I started teaching Derrida (and Lacan, and Foucault) in the 1960s, not the 1980s.

31. I was in Kolkata for two nights recently, after this essay was submitted to the editors. It was the time of the justly celebrated Calcutta Book Fair. There seemed to be a Benoy Majumdar revival. I acquired the slim *Complete Works*. I read this, written in 1992, thirty-one years after book publication, in a letter: "Gayatri Chakravorty was a student at Presidency College, and came First Class First in English in her B.A., in 1960 or 1961 A.D. [actually 1959], thinking that she alone would understand my poems the book *To Gayatri* was addressed to her, and therefore I called the book *To Gayatri*, and I wrote in the book what I had to say to her" ("Patraboli," *Ishwareer Swarachito Nibandha o Anyanya* [Kolkata: Pratibhash, 1995], p. 3). But also this, in 1986, in an interview, twenty-five-years later:

> I wanted to ask [says the interviewer]—Were you in love with Gayatri?
>
> Hey, no—I only knew her for two or three days–she was a famously beautiful student of English literature at Presidency College—then she went off somewhere—to America or some place, I'm not sure.
>
> Then why write poems about her?
>
> One must write about someone, after all. Can one write forever about mango trees, jackfruit trees, and tuberoses? ("Phire Esho Chakar Nam Paribartan Shommondhe," *Kabyoshamogro* [Kolkata: Pratibhash, 1993], vol. 1, p. 162).

Benoy had in fact never exchanged a word with Gayatri. Translator's note: the three items in the last sentence seem exotic in English. They are the Bengali equivalent of: "apples and pears and red, red roses," let us say. I include these passages here in the interest of bibliographical detail. To think through their implications will take time.

Tracking the "Native Informant": Cultural Translation as the Horizon of Literary Translation

HENRY STATEN

Within or, at the boundaries of, literary studies, the most radical extension of the contemporary reflection on the "ethics of translation" is unquestionably that of Gayatri Spivak, with its relentless pursuit of inaccessible cultural otherness. What makes this pursuit so difficult to follow, as some critics have complained, is the accompanying metacritical reflection, adhering simultaneously to Marxism, radical feminism, and deconstruction, on the positionality of the theorizing Metropolitan eye in all its varieties, especially those most closely related to Spivak's own perspective: the Metropolitan first-world feminist and the "diasporic" intellectual who has come from the Third World to ply her trade in the West. Metracritical reflection is of course the characteristic mark of poststructuralist, and especially deconstructive, writing in general; but Spivak goes beyond any other theorist in her attempt to give a historically and culturally specific content to each moment of her reflection. Unlike, say de Man, for whom the abyssal obscurity of subjectivity emerges from a general problematic of language, and is, so to speak, an *empty* abyss, the tortuousness of Spivak's account results from a sort of inaccessible overfullness of the context within which subjectivity must in each case be located;[1] there is always too much history, too much human reality beyond what language can adequately represent.

The evocation of an inaccessible overfullness throws us from the "classical" deconstruction of *Of Grammatology*, with its suspicion of fullnesses of all kinds, inaccessible ones in particular, into the terrain of Derrida's later "affirmative" deconstruction, with its valuation of the "experience of the impossible" that is prior to all calculation, including the calculation of *differance*.[2] However, even experienced readers of Derrida and Spivak can have trouble understanding how the new overfullness of affirmative deconstruction is to be distinguished from the transcendental fullnesses of ontotheology, or of more homely forms of "nostalgia for presence" such as Rousseauian primitivism. Thus, for instance, when Spivak says in her magnum opus, A *Critique of Postcolonial Reason,* that "knowledge of the other subject is theoretically impossible"[3] she must mean other subjects in general, including Western subjects; yet it is the non-Western other, and at the limit the "Aboriginal," who is for Spivak the supreme figure of the unspeakable excess of postcolonial reason, the human who comes *before the subject* and is thus the most "wholly other" to whom she feels responsible:[4]

The figure of the New Immigrant has a radical limit: those who have stayed in place for more than thirty thousand years. We need not value this limit in itself, but we must take it into account. Is there an alternative vision of the human here? The tempo of learning to learn from this immensely slow temporizing will not only take us clear out of diasporas, but will also yield no answers or conclusions readily. Let this stand as the name of the other of the question of diaspora. (402)

How is this thought of the aboriginal related to the idea of the "Native Informant" that Spivak tells us it was her original aim to track in this book (ix)? The native informant, variously referred to by Spivak as a "figure" (ix), an "unacknowledged moment" (4), "a name for that mark of expulsion from the name 'Man'" (6), and an "(im)possible perspective" (9), is not any actual person or group but an artifact of colonialist ideology; with the term "aboriginal," by contrast, Spivak gestures at the complex reality of the historical peoples who have remained invisible behind this ideological construct. Yet Spivak says that in the classic ethnological and philosophical texts of the Western tradition the native informant is "needed and foreclosed" (6), implying the existence of a real, if inaccessible, subject position behind the concocted ideological figure. Thus, for example, Spivak speaks of the effacement of the native informant as "the foreclosure of the subject whose lack of access to the position of narrator is the condition of possibility of the consolidation of Kant's position" (9), and in a "casual rhetorical gesture" (30) that Spivak excavates from the Third Critique this limit of the human is named as the "New Hollander [Australian aborigines] or the inhabitants of Tierra del Fuego" (26–27). Spivak uses the figure of the native informant to trace the complex way in which certain Western texts both open and seal off a certain space of alterity, and this space, while it is not identical with real aboriginality, communicates with it in some way.[5] Is there then some thought of nativeness or aboriginality at the root of both the colonialist foreclosure and Spivak's validation of alterity? There is no readily available answer to this question. Spivak is testing the limits of contemporary deconstructive thinking, and the reader must attempt to think along with her and, if possible, to develop new lines of thought of his own.

I will structure my own attempt around two questions that I pose here as naively as possible. First, How can Spivak posit a limit idea of subjectivity deemed aboriginal or native and still be following a deconstructive itinerary? And second, Supposing I could show that this was still deconstruction—why would such a demonstration matter? Why is it necessary for the postcolonial theorist to practice deconstruction?

Postcolonial studies of all stripes share in common the goal of validating the non-Western other so far as possible in her own terms, terms that often do not exist in any readily available form, if at all. The literate, institutionally empowered critic or theorist seeks to articulate in writing the heretofore unheard experience, perspective, and interests located at subject positions that have not previously had access to such articulation; and the pursuit of this articulation, while it has obvious political overtones, is fundamentally an ethical task. Spivak has called this task "translation in general" or "cultural translation," and has situated the task of literary translation within its encompassing horizon.[6]

Cultural translation was always implicitly the horizon of literary translation, but this background problem could be underplayed so long as translation theory focused primarily on translation across languages belonging to the European tradition. Because ethnology studied cultures outside this tradition, its development, as Derrida noted in his most famous essay, marked the beginnings of the rupture of "centered" Eurocentric thought. Yet, as Derrida also noted, the discourse of ethnology continued to inhabit the interior of the system of concepts it began to supersede. The final collapse of the ethnographer's confidence in the possibility of *knowing* the other in its otherness began around the time "Structure, Sign, and Play" was written, and was influentially declared a done deal in 1986 in the Clifford and Marcus anthology *Writing Culture*.[7]

The new ethnography struggled with the problem that the attempt to know the cultural other would either treat this other as an object, thereby stripping her of her subjectivity or, in attempting to represent the interiority of another culture, treat it as the mirror of our own. From a pragmatic ethnological standpoint, however, this problem meant only that improved, more flexible and self-aware methods of investigation and what Mary Louise Pratt called a richer "discursive repertoire" (49) were called for. In Michael Fischer's formulation, "anthropological cultural criticism" ought to be "a dialectical or two-directional journey examining the realities of both sides of cultural differences so that they may mutually question each other, and thereby generate a realistic image of human possibilities and a self-confidence for the explorer grounded in comparative understanding rather than ethnocentrism" (217). There was still a controlled lucidity and epistemological optimism in the approaches to otherness espoused in this volume that belied the almost impenetrable obscurity of the question that it opened, the question of an otherness that would escape the purview of even the most scrupulous ethnological method. The poststructuralist mindset discerned beyond the lucidity of the "writing culture" admonition—"cultural otherness is more other than was previously realized; we must be attentive to the lenses through which we refract our view of the other"—the abyss of an ethical task, and hence of a trans-ethnological discursive space that, for a number of writers, including Derrida, called for the turn to Levinas.

The task then became to know the other in a way that respects the constraint of radical or absolute otherness; a paradoxical conception that necessitates giving up the conceit of knowledge altogether, whether objective, subjective, or any fusion of the two. If there is a relation to the other as other, Levinas taught, it cannot be one of knowledge; it can only be an ethical relation, one that comes prior to any epistemological or even ontological question or presupposition.

Levinas's meditation on the other was philosophical rather than ethnological, as indeed, in its underpinnings at least, was the poststructuralist reflection in general. Concepts that could be held relatively stable by theorists of ethnography were for poststructuralism sites of what threatened to become endlessly reflexive critique. Fischer's "dialectical or two-directional journey" implied not only the stability, each within its own boundaries, of subject and other, but of the discursive dialectical rules that would govern such an equal exchange—an implicitly Habermasian picture whose shortcomings have subsequently been detailed by feminist and poststructuralist critiques of Habermas. Clifford evokes both Nietzsche and Derrida as essential contributors to the new idea of ethnographic writing, but prunes his references to a handy size: Nietzsche gives us perspectival historicism (7), Derrida contributes the idea that speech is already writing (118). Clifford does not mention Nietzsche's critique of the value of all values, or Derrida's deconstruction of presence.

It is entirely proper that the authors represented in *Writing Culture,* given their discursive aims, should have drawn the limits of their reflections where they did. Trying to think cultural translation in the context of globalizing modernity, while simultaneously plumbing the depths of the critique of the Western episteme, and then to write in a way that at every moment registers the totality of one's awareness, is a nearly impossible task; yet it is the task Spivak has taken upon herself. She speaks of the encounter with the other in terms that, mediated through Derrida, are almost Levinasian: translation is a "surrender" to the other's text; we are responsible to a most intimate, secret encounter with the other that is nevertheless "theoretically impossible." The site of the other is for Levinas pre-ontological; to evoke the "(im)possible perspective" of the other in Spivak's terms as either that of "the native informant" or the aboriginal, by contrast, evokes an "ontic"—worldly or historical—site, which is however to be investigated against the backdrop of the impossible encounter of ethics.

Meditating on the complexly stratified space of otherness deemed native or aboriginal that Spivak's text variously evokes, I detect or invent a relation, beyond Spivak's letter, between her account of the ethics of literary translation, with its emphasis on knowing the target language *intimately,* and the question of nativeness or aboriginality. Is it by a merely casual ambiguity that the most intimate knowledge of a language is said to be *native?* The secret that is in some measure broached in the intimate surrender to a text is not the secret of ultimate ethical encounter, which as such is in principle impossible. But the experience of this surrender seems to serve as at least an *intimation* of the encounter that can itself, as such, never be. And the door to this possibility is opened by the translator's acquisition of something approximating *native knowledge* of the language. Every culture, no matter how civilized or advanced, is constituted at its most elemental human level as a space of nativeness in a strong sense, as a space of knowledge and relation that must in principle remain largely implicit, by definition unknowable from any perspective of universality; the native speaker is the one who uses a language with the knowledge of this context "in her bones."[8] Spivak names this translinguistic cultural dimension of language, this "silence between and around words," *rhetoric,* arguing that rhetoric in this sense disrupts the translatable "logic" of language ("Politics of Translation," 180–81). The translator has access to the rhetoric of the text only if her familiarity with the language being translated is such that "one sometimes preferred to speak in it about intimate things" (183). Of course translation theory, even in an intra-European context, has always recognized the nonlinguistic specificity of cultural situations with which the language of texts is suffused, and the necessity for something approaching "native" knowledge of the language that is translated. It is also true that European peoples have numerous prejudices against each other, and there is a status hierarchy among them; but there is a quantum leap in the difficulty of literary/cultural translation when it becomes a case of Europe's others.[9] For the translator attempting to render into a hegemonic language a language from the Third World, everything becomes more problematic, more intensely "political," than in anything envisioned by pre-postcolonial translation theory.

I discern a structural relation, unremarked and perhaps unintended by Spivak, between her problematic of translation and her tracking of the native informant. Certainly there is no aboriginal on the other end of this impossible encounter; when Spivak translates Ram Proshad Sen or Mahasweta Devi, the subject in question is literate, author of written texts, and, as a caste Hindu, far removed from the Indian "tribals." This author is however still a native in the crudest, most unreconstructed Eurocentric sense of the term, as a member of the human species who has not been (sufficiently) Europeanized. We should not ignore this sense of nativeness; it allows us to see the continuity with each other of concepts that would otherwise seem unrelated, and to map the spectrum of meanings along which the notion of nativeness, not without contradiction, slides.

The Third World writer is thus a native in the sense that almost everyone in any culture is, as intimate with the silence of the "mother tongue," and in addition a native in the sense that her mother tongue is embedded in the silence of a non-European culture. In the latter sense, Spivak's attempt to render into English the original voice of Sen or Devi is an attempt to bring a "native informant" out from under her occlusion or foreclosure.[10] Spivak more than any other theorist has taught us that there is no single lived experience even within the culture to which one is "native," that the subject is marked by a multitude of striations of which race-class-gender are only the most readily nameable; the space of nativeness is never going to be "an undifferentiated transcendental preoriginary space" (286). And yet the privilege she gives to *knowing the language intimately*, for example Bengali, as "the language in which the other woman learned to recognize reality at her mother's knee" (191), indicates a certain quasi-homogeneity of the culturally specific, "Bengali" dimension of language-transcending silence. To know the language intimately will not by itself guarantee faithful translation of a given text, since the subject position of the writer will inevitably be more or less heterogeneous to the translator's; and the real test of the translator's cultural/linguistic knowledge is the ability to make value discriminations among the texts in the target language (189–90); but intimate knowledge of the language opens at least the possibility of "surrender" to that culturally specific heterogeneity, the surrender that would make something like translation possible.

Where is the Aboriginal in all this? The Aboriginal would be native in both the first two senses and then one more, as the one *most* alien to European culture, the one most securely expelled from the name "Man." The figure par excellence occluded by that of the native would be the most native of natives, apparently a (female) member of a Paleolithic culture, the culture furthest removed from the overlay of colonialism, hence representing "the inaccessible intimacy of the least sophisticated, least self-conscious way of being" (238).[11] Although one cannot take literally the notion of people who have "stayed in place for more than thirty thousand years," there have been until quite recently a few small groups, for example in New Guinea, that at least approximated this definition; practically speaking, however, as Spivak is well aware, the cultures of most of the groups that can still meaningfully be called "tribal" or "indigenous" around the world have been long since penetrated in greater or lesser degree not only by more "advanced" or "civilized" cultures, as for example the tribal peoples of India by the culture of the caste Hindus, but by European culture itself. Practically speaking, the native is always already more or less a colonial subject; and Spivak goes to great lengths to keep the prior contamination of categories always explicitly in view.

Spivak has always stressed the inaccessibility *under the most favorable conditions* of otherness in general; as I read it, the invocation of Paleolithic culture names the worldly vanishing point of all the varieties of inaccessibility that turn up everywhere in her investigations. This vanishing point also serves as a check on the presumptive nativeness of any given native informant, so that if the "New Immigrant" must be measured against the "radical limit" of Paleolithic woman, so would Spivak's Rani of Sirmur. For if the Rani is a woman and subjected by both Hindu patriarchalism and British imperialist paternalism, she is also a caste Hindu, therefore structurally superior to the Indian "tribals" (a fact that, Spivak points out, the British were quick to recognize and turn to their advantage [228]) and heir to an ancient literate "high" culture. Even though she has left no written trace of herself, "in trying to locate the Rani we may be groping in the margins of official Western history, but we are not among marginal women in their context" (239). Similarly, in the case of the Gypsy-Greek woman Hanife Ali: Spivak calls her "the gendered subaltern as native informant," yet, at home in Komitini, Ali was "the cusp-person of the Gypsy community, the one who translated for the visiting American" (407). For the Americans at the workshop in New York, she takes on the vague outlines of "subaltern/native informant"; but in her own village, she might be a woman of rank, education, and, relatively, superior social and economic class.

Oriented toward the "radical limit" of aboriginality, we remain alert to the fact that Ali is somewhere on a spectrum of possibilities of nativeness: she functions as native informant but the native informant does not exist. If there were a true native informant it would be the aboriginal, but by definition the aboriginal qua aboriginal, as inhabiting "the inaccessible intimacy of the least. . . . self-conscious way of life," cannot function as an informant for the Western observer.

If there is today no empirically existing pure other of Western civilization, there is a scale of degrees of closeness to and distance from the fully constituted "metropolitan subject." On my reading, Spivak's notion of the aboriginal marks the furthest point of this scale and calibrates all the other forms of nativeness and native informant. The transcendental or quasi-transcendental notion of radical alterity is the most severe constraint on our notions of ethical encounter, which Spivak conceives on this basis as both imperative and impossibility; *this notion, however, is meta-ethical and does not by itself provide us with any political point of application.* Spivak needs the notion of the aboriginal in order to link radical alterity to the problematic of Westernizing, capitalist globalization; the aboriginal is not the transcendental but worldhistorical other of globalization. On Spivak's radical analysis, even Marx did not think this otherness on its own terms, even to the degree that that is possible.

This furthest point is evoked most strikingly in "Politics of Translation" when she touches on the Caribbean bone flute, made of human bone, discussed by Wilson Harris. "Consuming our biases and prejudices in ourselves," Harris writes, "we can let the bone flute help us open ourselves. . . . The link of music with cannibalism is a sublime paradox" (quoted in *Outside*, 196).[12] Spivak shrewdly observes that this remarkable passage presents a striking contrast with Hegel's famous account of the bone, in the form of the skull, as the limit of representation, glossed by Zizek as "the inertia of a non-language object"; one might add that the cannibalism that is associated with the bone flute is for the West the limit of primitivity, of other-than-civilization, the most barbarous of barbaric customs. Against Hegel and Zizek's reading of this moment in Hegel, Spivak, following Harris, reads the bone flute as a figure of "the obligation of the translator to be able to juggle the rhetorical silences" between two languages. Spivak complains that for Hegel the passage between spirit and bone would be "mere logic," thereby ignoring the silence, the intimacy, of the rhetorical dimension of language that the bone flute evokes and to which the translator must submit. Spivak does not, as the hasty reader might think, succumb here to the melocentrism that, in carrying the power of expression beyond the limits of articulate language, expresses the nostalgic core of logocentrism;[13] her musical bone does not pipe "unheard melodies sweeter yet"; it arrests the reader in a moment of pure affection by an almost entirely inaccessible otherness of which only some trace of a trace remains, in the mode of a vanished, inaccessible, yet strictly *historical* time, the traumatic resonance of which still registers on the present day "natives" of the Caribbean. Similarly, in the example from Toni Morrison that precedes Spivak's discussion of the bone flute, the effaced trace of the history of slavery in the United States marks the limits of language, a dimension of silence that not only cannot be, but ought not be, transgressed; yet the effacement of the trace, the silence, to which Spivak calls attention is not the terminus of her discourse. *There is always a historical signification* to the effaced marks on which Spivak focuses: no matter which culture or which historical moment it comes from, it always signifies the silencing, traumatizing effect of dominating power on those it has historically dominated, and above all but not only—for Spivak always insists on the lines of domination-subjection that fissure from within the colonialized cultures for which she speaks—the effects of European imperialism and colonialism. Thus the limit of language, "rhetoric" that "points at absolute contingency," sends Spivak, and many who have followed her lead, off to the historical archive, and produces an efflorescence of "logic," of historical analysis that is fully articulated even if the human reality toward which it turns our gaze is not.

Spivak's project must be clearly distinguished from two positions that would be equally uncritical and equally inadequate. The first would be the nostalgic pursuit of the pure immediacy of a native culture that Western modernity has covered over; the second would be the simple rejection of the first on the basis of a demystified awareness that there is no pure originary presence, that the subject is always already decentered, and that speech is always already writing. The latter set of propositions, true as far it goes, by itself yields only a new universal structure of subjectivity-as-*differance*; it is a set of critical guidelines that the rigorous translator must keep always in mind but which by themselves can teach us nothing about the specificity of any given cultural translation and blocks off any possibility of validating some genuinely other cultural perspective, what Spivak calls "an alternate vision of the human," on the basis of which we could make a judgment on the ethical foundations of our own culture.

Spivak's meditation on the native informant and the aboriginal suggests that the 'primitive' must be distinguished from the 'civilized' and then valorized *in a certain, very precisely controlled way* if we are not always covertly to reintroduce a precritical valorization of "civilization" into our most enlightened attempts to criticize Eurocentric thinking. This *civilizationist* prejudice turns up most frequently, and most disastrously, in discourses that affirm the dignity of *some, not all* non-Western cultures by awarding them the honorific of 'civilization' which on the sternest Eurocentric view belongs only to the West. Since the genus 'civilization' in these discourses continues to be normed by the species "Europe," the valorization of some of Europe's others by this honorific covertly maintains that very privilege of the West that is explicitly being challenged. Civilizationist thinking too readily assimilates the virtues of the non-Western civilized to our own, and in so doing passes an implicit judgment on those cultures that are not at the level of these presumed virtues. I will give three notable examples of civilizationism in postcolonial theory.

First, Rey Chow's recent attack on Derrida's account of the Chinese ideogram in *Of Grammatology*.[14] Derrida's account of the ideogram is part of his analysis of Western logo-phonocentrism, which privileges so-called "phonetic" writing over other, more "primitive" writing systems—the very analysis cited by Clifford as Derrida's crucial contribution to the critique of Eurocentrism. Derrida's deconstructive critique of logocentrism yielded a generalized concept of writing according to which it was no longer possible to draw a simple boundary of essence between cultures with and cultures without writing, or between cultures with *true*, fully achieved, phonetic writing, and cultures with *imperfect*, hence more or less primitive writing systems made up of nonphonetic ideograms, hieroglyphs, pictographs, mnemonic markings, or the like.

Now, the question of writing is not one question among others in the definition of what will count as civilization, or, given a hierarchy of civilizations, what rank a given civilization will be accorded in that hierarchy. No doubt writing begins as a system of marks with commercial and administrative functions; for the ideology of civilizationism, however, the telos of writing is the pure self-transparency of spirit, and only in phonetic writing is this transparency fully possible. Only in phonetic writing can literature, philosophy, and theology find their fulfilled form and civilization accede to the realm of the properly moral or ethical. Here we arrive at the pinnacle of the pyramid formed by this ensemble of civilizationist themes: the civilized "man" is defined pre-eminently as the one who is *properly moral or ethical*. I am getting a little ahead of myself here, but the question of phonetic writing must be grasped from the outset in the context of the teleology that gives it its importance, a teleology that is inescapably, consciously or, more often, unconsciously, Hegelian.

Chow, apparently oblivious to Derrida's deconstructive critique, notices only one thing: that Derrida treats the Chinese written mark as an *ideogram*, and Chinese writing therefore as for the most part nonphonetic. The civilizationist axiomatics on the basis of which Chow reads dictate her conclusions in an entirely predictable way: Derrida's denial that Chinese writing has the same character as Western writing must mean that he is demeaning China, indulging in cultural stereotypes, "hallucinating China" (70); for Chow, to value Chinese civilization justly one must recognize that, just like Europe, it has reached the telos of phoneticization.

Chow uncritically relies on the logo-phonocentric norm as a value and remains indifferent to the questioning of this norm in the book she claims to be criticizing—and this while positioning herself as *more critically anti-Eurocentric than Derrida*, as revealing in Derrida's epochal critique of Eurocentrism a spot of Eurocentric blindness. Chow's blunder shows that the critique of Eurocentrism requires more than sharp intelligence and a desire to vindicate the other against Eurocentric slurs (she hurls the word "stereotype" at Derrida at least a dozen times in this short piece); it requires a deconstructive tracing of the dialectical crossings and returns of the entire system of presuppositions behind Eurocentrism.

There are of course empirical questions regarding Chinese writing that, in principle at least, have nothing to do with civilizationism or its deconstruction. Scholars have debated the nature of the Chinese ideogram for generations, and nothing guarantees that the account to which Derrida subscribes will ultimately gain universal acceptance.[15] What is clear, however—although this too goes unnoticed by Chow—is that even the scholar of Chinese writing on whose authority she rests her case against Derrida operates under the compulsion of the logocentric axiomatics. Chow's authority, John DeFrancis, does indeed conclude, on the basis of very extensive analysis of Chinese writing, that it is "basically" phonetic.[16] But if Chinese is phonetic, if this is the telos in terms of which it is to be judged, not as an externally imposed norm but as intrinsic to its nature, this is the judgment that logically follows for DeFrancis: Chinese writing is a "mess" (262), an "abysmally" bad example of a phonetic scheme (129) comprising an "outsized, haphazard, inefficient, and only partially reliable syllabary"[17] that lay about as a "disorderly conglomeration" until "Western scholars" reduced it to some sort of order (*Chinese Language*, 93) because "the Chinese seem to have almost a penchant for avoiding simplification and standardization" (119).

Chow's attempt to vindicate Chinese writing in the face of Derrida's purported Eurocentrism thus, in the absence of deconstructive vigilance, turns out to have the opposite sense from what she intends. A meager acceptance of Chinese as basically phonetic—an acceptance that is moreover valuable only on the basis of European logocentrism—is bought at the price of an alternate stereotype.

Detectable in DeFrancis's judgments is the following, familiar schema of civilizationist thinking: a culture, or some aspect of a culture, might be deemed outside the essence of the properly civilized, hence as "barbaric" or "savage," or it might be included within the circle of essence, but at some distance, and perhaps, as in the case of DeFrancis's judgment of Chinese writing, the greatest possible distance, still within the circle of essence, from the center or fullness of that essence. Primitiveness is measured along a discontinuous scale; the truly primitive is the other-than-civilized; but within civilization there are degrees of primitivity.

This schema is important for understanding my second example: Edward Said's 1999 presidential address to the MLA, which was, like Chow's essay, published in PMLA.[18] The lure of pure spirit as telos of civilizationist thinking is clearly evident in Said's remarks, where the name of the civilizationist telos is "humanism," defined as "recovering . . . the topics of mind from the 'uncontrollable mystery on the bestial floor,'" by the action of an isolated, "heroic" individual, "pen in hand, manuscript or book on the table," whose "positive, convinced, self-reliant action of thinking" attempts to "impose credibility on the vast background acreage of human possibility that has not yet been organized" (289).

Said does not specify just what he understands by the unorganized "background acreage" of human possibility but, as the area of human life not under the command of the pen, the book, and the mind, its scope would be vast indeed, both within any given individual insofar as he is more or other than the "topics of mind," within a given culture, insofar as not everyone in it has become a heroic, literate humanist, and, massively, in those quarters of the world where erudite humanism has not yet, or just barely, arrived. This massive exclusion is only implied; in the foreground is the inclusivist gesture typical of civilizationist anti-Eurocentrism; Said wants to bring under the aegis of humanism the "Islamic schools" of the Middle Ages, as well as certain "Indian and Chinese humanists" of the premodern period. These non-Westerners "prefigured" what in the West is called "humanism"; they "were doing what we think of rather quaintly as Western things well before the West was capable of either knowing about or doing them itself" (288).

Said is quite rightly contemptuous of the historical ignorance or amnesia of those who do not recognize the magnitude of the Islamic contribution to what is thought of as European culture; but he seems unaware of anything at all problematic about finding the value of Islamic, Indian, and Chinese civilization in what they *prefigure* of the Western achievement. The irony in the tag, "what we think of rather quaintly as," signals Said's belief that these things are not in fact properly called "Western"; and yet what Said says about the things in question (the "topics of mind," the literate man's battle against—note the startling reversal of the sense in which Yeats uses the phrase!—the "uncontrollable mystery on the bestial floor")[19] confirms everything, except for their Western origin, that we as unreconstructed Westerners already think about them. Said wants only to note the belatedness of the West in arriving at this telos called humanism—a telos that is apparently the same always and everywhere, and therefore equally discoverable by any culture no matter how other to the West.

Said's validation of Muslim civilization in this address, and in many other places, has something in common with the strategy of a certain type of identitarianism that has flourished in the United States, notably the Aztlanist movement among Chicanistas (which linked Chicano identity to Aztec civilization)[20] and various forms of Afrocentrism among African Americans (for example the type influenced by Martin Bernal's *Black Athena,* which claims Egypt as the ancestral Black African civilization). Because Europeans have historically been reluctant to grant that other cultures had genuine civilizations, these identitarians presume that there is some essential point of pride and dignity to be made by linking their people to a historical culture recognized as possessing at least some of the qualities that the European tradition has valorized.

Suppose what is not at all clear, that the relation to a past civilization could, in principle, be "inherited" in some biological, cultural, or transcendental way, or, if not inherited, somehow "strategically" laid claim to or appropriated. The question remains: why should we accept the idea that civilization is ennobling in the first place, that my cultural identity is somehow validated by the civilization connection? Does the notion of such validation not imply a view of culture, and of humanity, that is essentially of a social-evolutionist and ultimately of a Hegelian type? If I take pride in the notion that I am related to the Aztecs or the Egyptians, does this not entail a corresponding depreciation of the tribes the Mexicans call the "bárbaros del norte" or of the hunter-gatherers of subequatorial Africa? If we are somehow raised in the scale of value by our link to civilization, what are we to say of those vast segments of humanity who cannot lay any such plausible claim, those who have, as Spivak hyperbolically says, "stayed in place for over thirty thousand years"? Are they merely "a vast background acreage of human possibility"?

Without a demystifying analysis of the value of civilization that it invokes, the strategic move of identifying one's group with Aztec or Egyptian or Indo-Aryan or Medieval Islamic culture carries encoded within it the same crypto-Eurocentric value that it opposes. And it is not clear what, in the wake of such analysis, would remain of the strategy. For is not civilization, be it as humanist as you like, inherently imperialist? As Benjamin's famous formula has it, "every document of civilization is a document of barbarism," or, as Nietzsche earlier and more vividly put it, "we might compare dominant culture to a victor who reeks of blood, who drags the vanquished along as slaves in his triumphant procession." Civilizations are created by overcoming the autonomy of the smaller, originally "tribal"—and in practice often *more democratic*—organizations in which human beings live at an earlier stage of history; the ideological concept of civilization as it exists in the West interprets this conquest as the triumph of a more highly evolved and articulated form of the human spirit over the dim light of primitivity.

My third example is at once the clearest instance of civilizationist prejudice and also the point at which the moving ground beneath the deconstructive inquiry begins entirely to give way. Achebe's *Things Fall Apart*[21] has been subjected by a multitude of critics, both Western and African, to an ethical normativity that is, as Michael Valdez Moses has noted, transparently Hegelian in its presuppositions, most often with the laudable intention of justifying the apparently "primitive" ethical fabric of Umuofia by showing that its customs, myths, and institutions are ethically enlightened in a way that we can approve and even admire—prefigurations, one might say, of civilized morality. The protagonist Okonkwo, however, is deemed not to live up to what Bu-Buakei Jabbi calls the "more or less rounded system of values" of Igbo society, with its complex balance of masculine and feminine that Okonkwo subverts by his one-sided adherence to the code of violent masculine heroism. According to critics of this tendency, implicit within Igbo society as a whole are our own highest values of respect for the other and of critical reflection on traditional norms, and Okonkwo is not an adequate representative of the ethical wisdom of his culture.[22] Nevertheless, having granted the recognition it deserves to the sophistication of the Igbo ethical world, the contemporary critic must confront the fact that, even though Okonkwo does not represent Igbo society at what from our sociohistorical perspective we judge to be its best, nevertheless he does truly reflect quite fundamental aspects of Igbo culture: its high valuation of war and the warrior, its contempt for unmasculine men, its customs of human sacrifice and exposure of newborn twins. Okonkwo has killed five men in battle and taken their heads as trophies, and on ceremonial occasions he drinks his wine from the skull of his first victim; and he is respected and admired for this. It remains true, then, as Jabbi says, that Okonkwo's "inadequacies exemplify to some extent the clan's own central cultural malaise; that is, those cruel customs of ignorance perpetuated by them."[23] When Christianity comes, preaching lovingkindness and egalitarianism, it answers to what Solomon Iyasere calls a "pre-existing need" felt by certain people in Umuofia who, already before the coming of Christianity, were troubled by the cruel side of Igbo culture (75–76).

These critics and others who make similar arguments are alive to the problems of Eurocentric distortion of African realities, and critical of colonialism; yet they end up rendering a judgment on Okonkwo and his culture that coincides with the most ordinary liberal-Eurocentric view of the matter. There is some universal, humane set of values that recognizes and respects the dignity of every individual regardless of what sort of character or achievements this person might have, and it is in the European tradition that these values came to mature expression. Umuofia, by contrast, even at its best reflects the highest ethical values only as in a cracked mirror; there is some ethical telos of human culture to which primitive Africa needed to find its way. In the event, it was Europe that showed the path; ideally the Africans would have gotten there on their own, but in any case the telos would have been the same. Hence Biodun Jeyifo ends his Marxist reading of the novel with these reflections:

> What if the colonizers had not come? Was the precolonial social order so static that its internal dialectic could not have found its own synthesis, its own resolution? That is, would people like Ikemefuna and Nwoye, the women subjected to the harsh patriarchal order or forced to cast away their twin children, or the despised *osu* have received restitution without colonialism? If we accept Amilcar Cabral's revolutionary dictum that postcolonial societies "must return to the upward path of their own culture," what such paths are indicated in the dialectic of Achebe's narrative?[24]

Okonkwo, and that aspect of Igbo culture that he epitomizes, seem indefensible not only by the standards of traditional European morality but even more by those of the most advanced contemporary anti-Eurocentric humanism with its strong feminist tendency. What would Spivak say about this cultural otherness? When she discusses the Caribbean bone flute she does not dwell on the implications of its cannibalistic origins, the warrior cannibal of whom there is a reminiscence in Okonkwo's habit of drinking from a human skull. When we look back to the pre-civilized for "an alternative vision of the human," at what point, and in what form, does it become necessary to invoke the telos implied by Cabral's notion of the "upward path"? Is Hegel always right, in the end? The enlightened contemporary critic can laugh at *The Philosophy of History* much more easily than he can escape the system of its philosophical presuppositions. It is not at all clear that we can answer the question, "What is the value of civilization?," without recourse to notions of the refinement or elevation or superior ordering power of the human spirit whose force depends on the contrast with states of human being that are defined as characteristic of earlier "stages of development" of human society. Perhaps, beyond the prejudices in favor of phonetic writing or erudite humanist literacy, we might be able to discern some realm of humane ethical consciousness and practice that is the essential core of the values we confusedly think of as "civilized," such that we could then, without civilizationist prejudice, locate the presence of this core in this or that "pre-civilized" society; but the case of *Things Fall Apart* suggests that we do not yet know how to separate this essential core of value from the full reality of a historical culture without at least implicitly confirming the civilizationist judgment on barbarism.

My own feeling is that, while I cannot simply reject the values they invoke, Okonkwo's critics have moved too fast to judgment. It is not a matter of defending him against their charges, or justifying the cruelties of Umuofia—although I am certain that the contemporary liberal notion, popularized by Richard Rorty, that "cruelty is the worst thing there is" begs all the crucial questions. It is a matter of shifting the ground of the debate in such a way that we do not immediately fall into the either/or of barbarism and enlightenment. This rush to judgment always forecloses deconstructive reflection on the civilizationist prejudice. We are well aware that our own civilization is not perfect; we think it embodies the ethical telos, yet, paradoxically, cruelty and inhumanity exist under the aegis of Westernizing globalization on a scale that, given the numbers of human beings involved, arguably exceeds the inhumanities of any previous age. Is this merely a contingent misfortune, leaving untouched the purity of the ethical principles themselves, and of our hearts insofar as we subscribe to these principles? What if ethical principle, be it as humane as you like, and historical reality are bound together so indissolubly that the purity of ethical principle will always turn out to be a deluded idealization? At the limit, the deconstructive reflection reaches Nietzsche's abyssal question regarding the value of all previously existing (European, humanist, civilizationist) moral values. But Nietzsche looked back only as far as the archaic warrior nobilities for his alternative vision of the human; perhaps we need, with Spivak, to look even further back. And then Umuofia, which is very far from a Paleolithic culture, could be thought about not from the perspective of some future to which it has not yet attained, but from the past that it shares with all other cultures, a past in which, if we are to believe Marshall Sahlins, scarcity had not yet been instituted, economic man not yet invented, nor the corresponding large concentrations of power and hierarchical distinction that are so characteristic of civilization and are already present in a fairly developed form in Okonkwo's Igboland.[25]

Yet we also need to approach with an attitude of greater respect precisely those aspects of Things Fall Apart that we find most indigestible, because in such an approach we can learn something about cultural difference that our ordinary goodhearted openness will not accommodate—and not only something about cultural difference but about literary representation as well. For the enigma of literary representation lies very close to that of cultural difference. Literary works, even when they emanate from our own culture, are subject to the same type of undeconstructed moralization to which Things Fall Apart has been subjected. The tension between our everyday humane values and the integrity of the literary work is isomorphic with the tension between these values and the integrity of another culture. As a literary representation of another culture, Things Fall Apart presents us with both of these tensions at once; but, at the limit, "our own" culture is as unknowable as is that of "the other" and the ethics of cultural translation is the ethics of reading.[26]

NOTES

1. As in "Politics of Translation," discussed below.

2. Spivak gives an important summary account of this turn in Derrida's thought in Critique, pp. 423–31 (see esp. 426–27).

3. Ibid., p. 283.

4. Speaking of the question, famously posed in the name of an anthology, "who comes after the subject?," Spivak comments: "I have indeed thought of who will have come after the subject, if we set to work, in the name of who came before, so to speak. Here is the simple answer . . . : the Aboriginal." Critique, p. 27n.

5. See also p. 352, where Spivak invokes the "(im)possible perspective of the Native Informant" and turns in the paragraph immediately following to "Japanese indigenous minorities" and, once again, the Australian aborigines.

6. Spivak, "The Politics of Translation," pp. 179–200.

7. James Clifford and George E. Marcus eds., *Writing Culture: The Poetics and Politics of Ethnography* (Berkeley: University of California Press, 1986).

8. Cf. Mary Douglas's important reflections on the "restricted code" of the space of nativeness in her book (mostly neglected by literary theorists), *Natural Symbols: Explorations in Cosmology* (New York: Pantheon Books, 1982).

9. Who may, of course, be located within the borders of Europe that are visible on a map.

10. Spivak however draws a strict distinction between surrendering to a text and surrendering to the author as "intending subject" ("Politics of Translation," 190). The essential question of exactly where, and how, the intending subject comes into Spivak's problematic of otherness is one that I cannot explore here.

11. Within the limits of this essay, I have not been able to do justice to the fact that the problematic of gender is always central to Spivak's thought. I realize this is a severe limitation.

12. Gayatri Spivak, *Outside in the Teaching Machine* (New York: Routledge, 1993).

13. On the transformation of logocentrism into melocentrism in Rousseau, see *Of Grammatology*, trans. Gayatri Spivak (Baltimore: Johns Hopkins University Press, 1976), pp. 196–201 and esp. 248–49.

14. Rey Chow, "How (the) Inscrutable Chinese led to Globalized Theory," *PMLA* 116(1), Jan. 2001, pp. 69–74.

15. Derrida's analysis does, however, draw powerful independent confirmation from an article by Chad Hansen, "Chinese Ideographs and Western Ideas," *Journal of Asian Studies* 52(2), May, 1993, pp. 373–99. Hansen, a scholar of traditional Chinese thought, through a sophisticated philosophical analysis based on Wittgenstein arrives at the same conclusion reached by Derrida: that the notion of the ideogram is merely confused if it posits a self-interpreting mental semantic entity, but makes good sense if conceived as a conventional sign, made of a mixture of elements, some originally pictorial, some phonetic, that has meaning by virtue of syntax and historical convention alone.

16. John DeFrancis, *The Chinese Language: fact and fantasy* (Honolulu: University of Hawaii Press, 1984).

17. John DeFrancis, *Visible Speech: the diverse oneness of writing systems* (Honolulu: University of Hawaii Press, 1989).

18. Edward W. Said, "Presidential Address 1999: Humanism and Heroism." *PMLA* 115(3), May 2000, pp. 285–91.

19. The quotation is from "The Magi," whom Yeats describes as *searching for* the mystery on the "bestial floor" because they are "unsatisfied" by "Calvary's turbulence."

20. I have commented on the internal tensions of Aztlanism and Chicanismo in general in "Ethnic Authenticity, Class, and Autobiography: the Case of *Hunger of Memory*," *PMLA* (January, 1998), pp. 103–16.

21. Chinua Achebe, *Things Fall Apart* (London: Heinemann, [1958] 1962).

22. Cf. what Spivak calls the "race-divisive" distinction made by the British in the nineteenth century between the "bestial Hindu" and the "noble Hindu" (*Critique*, p. 236).

23. Simon O. Iyasere ed., *Understanding* Things Fall Apart: *Selected Essays and Criticism* (New York: Whitston Publishing Co., 1998), p. 138.

24. Biodun Jeyifo, "The Problem of Realism in *Things Fall Apart*: A Marxist Exegesis," in *Approaches to Teaching Achebe's* Things Fall Apart, ed. Bernth Lindfors (New York: MLA, 1991), pp. 112–17; quotation from 117.

25. Marshall Sahlins, *Stone Age Economics* (New York: de Gruyter, 1972). This im-

mensely important book, which has been, like Mary Douglas's cited above, surprisingly ignored by literary theorists, uses exhaustive quantitative and statistical data to make its
case for the nature of economic life among the most "primitive" human groups.

26. The question that opens out as I am forced to bring this essay to a close is the following: Does the attempt to read Okonkwo with respect not, perhaps, reveal a fundamental fracture that would run through culture, text, and translation/reading alike, a fracture
between literature as faithful representation of the savage core of culture (where "savage"
does not necessarily mean "primitive") and literature as serving an ever more humane vision of humanity?

Levinas, Translation, and Ethics

ROBERT EAGLESTONE

Many commentators have suggested that translation is central to the ethical philosophy of Emmanuel Levinas. Not, clearly, translation from one language to another, in the sense of translating, say, German into French, nor translation in the sense of introducing intellectual developments from one national tradition into another, although Levinas is widely credited with introducing phenomenological thought into France in 1930. The commentators suggest that Levinas offers translation in a wider sense between what he calls "Hebrew" and "Greek," where the names for the languages stand in for much wider frameworks or worldviews. However, although this is a constructive approach that offers much insight into his work, and has no little backing from his own remarks, I will suggest that to see his work in this way is to offer a limited view both of his achievement and of the nature of translation. More than this, I will suggest that his own thought runs against this way of understanding it: instead, I will argue that Levinas's work offers an understanding of ethics that suggests the impossibility of translation.

What hangs on this question—which seems at first to be one limited to "Levinas scholarship" or obscure phenomenological debates—is a set of questions about the nature of what it is to be human, what it is to be part of a community and a world, and how the West should engage with other cultures. All of these, too, of course, are issues of translation.

TRANSLATING THE GREEKS AND THE BIBLE

Levinas argues that there are two fundamental discourses that both orient and form the horizon for Western thought: the language of the Bible and the language of the Greeks. Seeing things in these terms is not new, of course. It was a staple of nineteenth-century intellectual life: For example, Arnold wrote that Heine

> had in him both the spirit of Greece and the spirit of Judaea; both these spirits reach the infinite, which is the true goal of all poetry and all art—the Greek spirit of beauty, the Hebrew spirit of sublimity. By his perfection of literary form, by his love of cleanness, by his love of beauty, Heine is Greek; by his intensity, by his untamableness, by his "longing that cannot be uttered" he is Hebrew. (Arnold 127–28)

Moreover, putting these two together is not a new project either: Maimonides in the Jewish tradition, for example, and Aquinas in the Christian both attempted to reconcile faith with philosophy. In the Islamic tradition, too, Avicenna and al-Farabi tried to bring the Koran together with philosophy. However, Levinas is slightly different: "I have never aimed to 'harmonise' or 'conciliate' both traditions. If they happen to be in harmony it is probably because every philosophical thought rests on pre-philosophical experiences and because for me reading the Bible has belonged to these founding experiences" (Levinas, *Ethics and Infinity* 24). For many commentators, Levinas's work is not one of compilation, but of translation.

Levinas discusses what he means by "Greek" in a particularly illuminating interview. He says that the

> essential character of philosophy is a certain, specifically Greek way of thinking and speaking. . . . Philosophy employs a series of terms and concepts such as *morphe* (form), *ousia* (substance), *nous* (reason), Logos (thought) or *telos* (goal) etc which constitute a specifically Greek lexicon of intelligibility. French and German and indeed all Western Philosophy is entirely shot through with this specific language; it is a token of the genius of Greece to have been able to thus deposit its language in the basket of Europe. (Kearney 54–55)

This need not be seen simply as a Heideggerian insight, although it clearly is for Levinas. Wittgenstein, for example, remarks:

> We keep hearing the remark that philosophy does not really progress, that we are still occupied with the same philosophical problems as were the Greeks. Those who say this, however, don't understand why this is so. It is because our language has remained the same and keeps seducing us into asking the same questions. As long as there is a verb "to be" that looks as though it functions in the same way as "to eat" or "to drink," as long as we still have the adjectives "identical," "true," "false," "possible," as long as we talk of a river of time and an expanse of space etc etc, people will keep stumbling over the same cryptic differences and staring at something that no explanation seems capable of clearing up. (Wittgenstein 22e)

Here, it is not only the formal language of philosophy that is shot through with "deposits of Greek," but ordinary language: "to be," "true," "false," "possible," rivers of time and an expanses of space. What is new is the awareness of the significance of this. "This is the Copernican revolution that the thought of our time has inherited from nihilism," writes Agamben: "We are the first human beings who have become completely conscious of language" (Agamben 45). Levinas's relation to this language, to the "Greaco-European adventure" (Derrida, *Writing and Difference* 82) of the West is one of tension, caught between an awareness of its insight and a suspicion of its power, and changed over his career.[1] To summarize briefly: on the one hand, Levinas knows that this language, "the language of the university such as it should be," (Levinas, *In the Time of Nations* 53) is one that allows "comparison . . . judgement" (Wright, Hughes, Ainley, "The Paradox of Morality" 174–75) and so communal interaction, or politics: reason makes society possible. But, he writes, "a society whose members would only be reason would vanish as a society" (Levinas, *Totality and Infinity* 119). The discourse of the Greeks is not complete: "its unbiased intelligence risks sometimes remaining naïve" and "something may be lacking in its 'clear and distinct ideas'" (Levinas, *In the Time of Nations* 52). What it is lacking is a way of understanding, or responding to the ethical: Greek philosophy cannot answer the question, Why should I be good?

In a key passage in *Otherwise than Being*, Levinas asks this key ethical question in three different ways: "Why does the other concern me? What is Hecuba to me? Am I my brother's keeper?" (117). His answer is not straightforward but it does explain why "Greek" cannot answer the question. "These questions have meaning only if one has already supposed that the ego is concerned only with itself, is only a concern for itself" (117)—an echo of Heidegger's definition of *dasein*, that being for which its own being is an issue. "In this hypothesis" Levinas writes, that is, in Greek, "it indeed remains incomprehensible that the absolute outside-of-me, the other, would concern me" (117). There seems to be no way of justifying ethics inside this system of thought, in this language. However, "in the 'prehistory' of the ego posited for itself speaks a responsibility. The self is through and through a hostage, older than the ego, prior to principles. What is at stake for the self, in its being, is not to be. Beyond egoism and altruism is the religiosity of the self" (117). "'Hebracism' has frequently been identified as one of the two counter-critiques by which Western civilisation has been kept vigorous and alive. Precisely what Hebracism is, however, has rarely been recognised" (Hartman and Budick ix): For many commentators on Levinas, it is this "religiosity" that represents "hebracism," which is why many readers of his readers argue that Levinas is translating the Bible into Greek. It is only in "Hebrew" that this can be articulated. However, I suggest that this reading of Levinas relies on a faulty understanding of translation. It has, for example, many risks.

RISKS OF TRANSLATION: THE EXAMPLE OF "ATHENS AND JERUSALEM"

"'Athens and Jerusalem,' "religious philosophy"—these expressions are practically identical: they have almost the same meaning. One is as mysterious as the other, and they irritate modern thought to the same degree by the inner contradiction they contain. Would it not be more proper to pose the dilemma as: Athens *or* Jerusalem, Religion *or* Philosophy?" (Shestov 47).

One of the most serious risks or temptations that argue that Levinas is translating—in this large sense—the Bible into Greek, translating Jerusalem into Athens, is highlighted, probably unwittingly, by Levinas himself: "I often say, although it is a dangerous thing to say publicly, that humanity consists of the Bible and the Greeks. All the rest can be translated: all the rest—all the exotic—is dance" (Mortley 18). Here, Levinas has taken the grounds of possibility of the translation between these two discourses—their centrality in Western thought—and has presupposed that they are the only two discourses. The re-

mark is racist because "humanity"—however it is understood—draws on much
wider traditions than only the Bible and the Greeks and is Eurocentric because
only those in the European tradition might think that "we" (whoever we are) do
not. It might be possible to defend this remark: one might suggest that it was
made, off the cuff, in a interview and not a long-deliberated written essay, or that
Levinas is foregrounding the way in which the category of the "human" is, or has
been, a Western category, through and through a construction of a certain metaphysics that does indeed have its roots in the Bible and the Greeks ("When I
search for Man in the technique and style of Europe," Fanon wrote, "I see only a
succession of negations of man, and an avalanche of murders" (Fanon 252). But
these defenses and excuses would be disingenuous. It is more honest, it seems to
me, to admit that this remark is both racist and Eurocentric and to admit that
there may be "a racist logic intrinsic to European philosophy" (Critchley 128)
uncovered here by thinking about translation and community: but more, to suggest that Levinas's thought nearly always runs against such a remark, which I will
aim to show here.

   Levinas's thought is about an openness to the other at the expense of the self.
This is the meaning of his recurrent use of the term "persecution": the other
"persecutes" the self, leaves no room for escape or evasion of responsibility. Or, as
Derrida puts it, Levinas's first major work, "*Totality and Infinity* bequeaths to us an
immense treatise *of hospitality*" (Derrida, *Adieu* 21). To be hospitable means to
welcome the other, the stranger and in no small part, this involves recognizing
the otherness of the stranger precisely as otherness, not as some version of one's
own thought.

   The opposition or relation between Athens and Jerusalem is a recognizable
part of Western thinking, and is the trope that Levinas picks up on. Athens, the
cradle of philosophy and reason, is opposed to Jerusalem, the city of faith: a very
binary opposition. Tertullian, in an attempt to de-Hellenize the early Christian
church, wrote "What has Athens to do with Jerusalem?." Lev Shestov's monu-
mental Athens and Jerusalem is an example of the use of these cities in the
twentieth century, and they have played a role in more recent work by, for example Martin Jay, Gillian Rose, and Susan Handleman.[2] However, these two
names, as metonyms, are very revealing about the discourses that use them.
Athens and Jerusalem are not the only cities, not the only traditions. It might be
possible to contrast them with cities that stand for other traditions: Mecca, or
the Forbidden City, or Zimbabwe. More than this, it might be possible to contrast them not to cities but to other places that embody traditions: the Ganges,
Mt. Fuji, Ayers Rock. But these comparisons all work on the assumption that "as
Athens is to the tradition of Western Philosophy, so (say) the Ganges is to Hinduism." This is a faulty assumption that masks the "otherness" of other communities, and reveals that Western thought takes for granted—at least in this
limited context—an idea of the polis, the city/community. It is as if each community, defined as much by its thought and traditions as by its location—its nature as imagined community—has to become a recognizable Western "polis" before it can be recognized as a community or as a people by the Western thought

that stems from and recognizes Athens and Jerusalem. Unless each community (understood in its widest sense) has an Athens, it is not recognized by Western thought. It is as if being a Western-style community or polis is the grounds for the possibility of translation. If a community does not speak a language that relies on a Western-style polis, it will not be recognized. It is not surprising that this idea has entered, at a deep level, Western thought.

And it is this idea that Levinas criticizes. He takes Heidegger as the paramount example of this theme in Western thought and writes that "Heidegger with the whole of Western history takes the relation with the other as enacted in the destiny of sedentary peoples, the possessors and builders of the earth. Possession is pre-eminently the form in which the other becomes the same" (Levinas, *Totality and Infinity* 46). This "leads inevitably," he writes "to another power, to imperialist domination, to tyranny" (46–47). His thought of hospitality aims to run counter precisely to this. Even the metonym of Athens and Jerusalem is inhospitable and exclusive. It would turn other cultures (that draw on neither the Bible nor the Greeks) into the poorer versions of European culture, or simply refuse to recognize them. In the light of Levinas's own thought, this remark made in an interview looks out of place and mistaken. However, it does highlight the dangers of translation if it is understood in this way.

"WHOLE VESSELS": UNDERSTANDING TRANSLATION AFTER BENJAMIN

These dangers may be bypassed if we understand translation differently. As Walter Benjamin argues, a translation "instead of resembling the meaning of the original, must lovingly and in detail incorporate the original's mode of signification, thus making both the original and the translation recognisable as fragments of a greater language, just as fragments are part of a vessel" (Benjamin 79). Over all, Benjamin argues that "the act of translation negotiated not so much between language x and language y as between the forbidden idea of the absolute, original language and its pale reflections in human language—the language of God and the language of Man" (Steinberg 17–18). The whole vessel, for Benjamin, is the language of God.

Levinas uses something akin to this model by maintaining the same structure: languages (Greek, the Bible) can be translated because they refer to a third and all encompassing category, a whole vessel. However, although Levinas is often seen as a religious thinker, he does not rely on the idea of the "language of God." His position is, as Robert Gibbs points out, closer to that of Rosenzweig (an influence on Levinas so great that it is too "present . . . to be cited" (Levinas, *Totality and Infinity* 28). Rosenzweig argues that revelation "reveals its truth in human words, leading us towards the original speech of humanity. This historical speech is not an historical claim about an adamic speech but rather a reference to the experience of social conversation" (Gibbs, *Why Ethics?* 289). For Benjamin, the claim is that "languages are not strangers to each other, but are, *a priori* and apart from all historical relationships, interrelated in what they want to express" (Benjamin 73)—the divine language of which they are pale shadows. But Levinas goes further, and is even more "Greek": He argues that the "whole vessel" arises "within experience" (Levinas, *Totality and Infinity* 23). That is, he argues that the ethics—the relation with the other—is grounds of the possibility of experiencing the world in the first place, the ur-experience and that the discourse of philosophy has not yet found a way to explore, explain or justify this. His work, then, as Derrida writes, "seeks to be understood from within a recourse to experience itself. Experience and that which is most irreducible within experience: the passage and departure toward the other; the other itself as what is most irreducibly other within it: Others" (Derrida, *Writing and Difference* 83). Levinas, in this respect, is a good phenomenologist, and seeks to make his case by recourse to reflection on experience alone. This is why his books move through detailed phenomenological readings ("a thicket of difficulties," Levinas, *Totality and Infinity* 29) that all come from human experience. John Llewelyn compares *Totality and Infinity* to *Mediations on First Philosophy* or *Phenomenology of Spirit* since, like those works, it follows a narrative and a "chronological order" of "stages of the analysis of the self" (Llewelyn 200) beginning with experience.

If Levinas is translating, then, what for him serves as the language of God, the "whole vessel" is not—contra those who argue for it—simply a question of a religious tradition: it is experience itself that is shared by every "human being" (before the term "human being" and all that this implies—the UN declaration of human rights, for example—has even been applied to them). However, that aspect of experience in which he is most interested—ethics—is best revealed not by Greek reason that cannot explain it. Rather, it is that aspect of experience that a religious tradition reveals, or reveals best. When Levinas writes that beyond "egoism and altruism is the religiosity of the self" (Levinas, *Otherwise* 117) by "religiosity" he does not mean being religious in the sense of being Jewish, Christian, Muslim, Hindu, or so on. He understands the essence of religion etymologically: the things that bind. "We propose to call 'religion' the bond that is established between the same and the other without constituting a totality" (Levinas, *Totality and Infinity* 40). Texts that are religious—the Bible and the Talmud are Levinas's texts—are those in which this "religiosity" is explored most explicitly, and it is to these that Levinas turns in all his "confessional" writings. However, and significantly, this religiosity of the self, its putting into question by and responsibility for the other does not only come from religious texts. It appears

> at the summit of philosophies . . . the beyond-being of Plato, the entry through the door of the agent intellect in Aristotle; it is the idea of God in us, surpassing our capacity as finite beings [Descartes] . . . the exaltation of theoretical reason in Kant's practical reason . . . the study of recognition by the Other in Hegel himself . . . the sobering of lucid reason in Heidegger. (Levinas, "Philosophy and Awakening" 215)

Indeed, some of Levinas's work aims to show precisely how this appears in the work of other thinkers. As Tamra Wright argues, "Levinas finds indication of the 'ethical relation' and the 'beyond being' both in the Bible and in the . . .

western philosophical canon" (Wright 169). (More than this: Derrida's whole project can be seen as a Levinasian one. Derrida's readings are searches for the "exorbitant" in philosophical texts, that which is outside the orbit or orb (as in "eye") of Western thought: "the point of a certain exteriority to the totality of the age of logocentrism" (Derrida, *Of Grammatology* 161–62). He does this precisely for "ethical" reasons and this putting into question of that tradition in thought is clearly similar to Levinas's aims). But, for Levinas, ethics can only appear as a subject for philosophical discourse because it arises from pre-philosophical experience.

Pre-Philosophical Experience?

This is all very well, but it raises a difficult question of what a pre-philosophical experience might be. Levinas, in general, seems to suggest that the languages of "the Bible" and "the Greeks" supplement each other: each revealing blindspots in the other and filling them, to some degree. The blindspots are caused by their failure to match up with experience (or, one might add, how we reflect on experience—the experience of experience, as it were). However, are these "outside philosophy?" For Levinas, to some degree they are: he writes that "Not to philosophise would not be 'to philosophise still'" (Levinas, *Collected Philosophical Papers* 172). In contrast—and this is the crux of their disagreement—Derrida writes that "the attempt to achieve an opening toward the beyond of philosophical discourse, by means of philosophical discourse, which can never be shaken off completely, cannot possibly succeed *within language*" (Derrida, *Writing and Difference* 110). To speak—in Greek—is to speak philosophically. But more than this, the power of Greek is such that the "meaning of the non-theoretical as such (for example, ethics or the metaphysical in Levinas' sense)" is only made clear by "theoretical knowledge" (Derrida, *Writing and Difference* 122). That is, that which is not Greek is only understood in relation to the Greek language of philosophy. For Derrida, there is no area of (Western) existence that is not infiltrated by Greek philosophical thinking. It is impossible to escape both the technical language of philosophy (*morphe, ousia, nous, Logos, telos*, etc.) when we are "doing philosophy" (in the seminar room, for example) but also in our everyday discussions and business ("identical," "true," "false," "possible," "a river of time," "an expanse of space"). To appeal to experience is, as Derrida argues, an empiricism that is only a "dream" that "must vanish at daybreak, as soon as language awakens" (Derrida, *Writing and Difference* 151).

To put this another way: Is there a universal human experience to which Levinas can refer and that could serve as the "unbroken vessel"? When Levinas offers analyses of "bare life," of shelter, of isolation, which in turn lead to an uncovering of the "religiosity of the self," its unavoidable relation to and responsibility for the other, are these phenomenological analyses applicable universally? Or do they rely, as he says for his case, on the "pre-philosophical experience" of reading the Bible.

The anthropologist Clifford Geertz offers a way of exploring this by contrasting two ways of understanding the human being, the "stratigraphic" with the "synthetic." The stratigraphic version comes from the Enlightenment and suggests that there is "a human nature as regularly organised, as thoroughly invariant, and as marvellously simple as Newton's universe. Perhaps some of its laws are different, but there are laws; perhaps some of its immutability is obscured by the trappings of local fashion, but it is immutable . . . men are men under whatever guise and against whatever backdrop" (Geertz 34). This belief goes on to suggest that one can "strip off the motley forms of culture" from an individual like layers of an onion and find the "structural and functional regularities of social organisation"; beneath these the "underlying psychological factors and—at the bottom—the "biological foundations" (Geertz 38). In a way, this is what Levinas appears to be doing in his phenomenological analyses.

Geertz criticizes this as "an illusion": "what man is may be so entangled with where he is, who he is and what he believes that it is inseparable from them" (35). Indeed, he argues that modern anthropology asserts that "men unmodified by the customs of particular places do not in fact exist, have never existed and most important, could not in the very nature of the case exist" (35). Simply, there is no universal human being: no woman and man, only particular men and women (one might go so far as to say "men" and "women"). Geertz argues this by showing how attempts to draw links between so-called "underlying needs"—the urge to reproduce, for example—and the many different so-called cultural strategies to fulfill them—"marriage"—flounder both because of the huge range of very different practices and the inability to "construct genuine functional interconnections between cultural and non cultural factors": instead there are "only more or less persuasive analogies, parallelisms, suggestions and affinities" (43). In contrast, Geertz suggests we replace the stratigraphic view of the human being with a "synthetic one . . . in which biological, psychological, sociological and cultural factors can be treated within a unitary system of analysis" (44). This view does not seek to "peel the layers off"—indeed, there are no layers to peel—but rather to take the whole complex of body, culture, and identity together. Geertz writes that

> extreme generality, diffuseness, and variability of man's innate response capacities mean that the particular pattern his behaviour takes is guided by predominantly cultural rather than genetic templates, the latter setting the overall psychophysical context within which the precise activity sequences are organised by the former . . . [thus] it is through the constructions of ideologies, schematic images of social order, that man makes himself for better or worse a political animal. (217–18)

These images of social order in turn are what "render otherwise incomprehensible social situations meaningful, to so construe them as to make it possible to act purposefully within them": this accounts for their "highly figurative nature and for the intensity with which, once accepted, they are held" (220). These "cultural templates" can be seen as the "deposits of Greek" in our technical language or in our ordinary language (a verb "to be" that looks as though it functions in the same way as "to eat" or "to drink") or, by the same token, the deposits of "Hebrew," too: the "longing that cannot be uttered," the "religiosity of the self."

From this point of view—from the philosophical view that there is nothing comprehended that does not rely at some level on a basic philosophical vocabulary, from the anthropological view that behavior and thought are guided by "predominantly cultural" ideas—a third space that could encompass this all, Benjamin's "whole vessel" or the language of God, looks impossible or even imperialistic.

This seems to leave us with two possibilities, to generalize. Either we can affirm with Levinas and Benjamin that there is something to be understood metaphorically as universal human experience (perhaps in the very basic form of "bare life," those things every human organism might be said to have in common), the language of God, "the unbroken vessel." Or we can affirm with Geertz and Derrida that there is no such vessel and that we are enmeshed in a highly complex weave of culture and beliefs held so deeply that we no longer recognize them as beliefs or even as ideas.[3] With the first, we might translate "Die Aufgabe des Übersetzers" as "The Task of the Translator": with the second, after de Man as "The Defeat of the Translator" ("If you enter the Tour de France and you give up, that is the Aufgabe—"er hat aufgegeben," he doesn't continue the race any more" (de Man 80). How might one decide between these two possibilities?

The Limits of Community

However, as with the example of Athens and Jerusalem, it might be possible to find a way to exceed this opposition in Levinas's own work. This opposition relies on a sense of "who we are," what language we speak: a sense of community. In his essay on Benjamin's "The Task of the Translator," Paul de Man suggests that translation "implies . . . the suffering of what one thinks of as one's own—the suffering of the original language. . . . We think we are at ease in our own language, we feel a cosiness, a familiarity, a shelter in the language we call our own, in which we think that we are not alienated. What translation reveals is that this alienation is at its strongest in our relation to our own language" (de Man 84). For de Man, this suffering is not pain or pathos, nor even individual suffering: it is "specifically linguistic" (86):

> The way in which I can try to mean is dependant upon linguistic properties that are not only [not] made by me, because I depend on the language as it exists for the devices which I will be using, it is not made by us as historical beings, it is perhaps not made by humans at all. . . . To equate language with humanity . . . is in question. If language is not necessarily human—if we obey the law, if we function within language, and purely in terms of language—there can be no intent. (87)

Intention and agency are removed and "[W]hat I mean is upset by the way I mean" (87). However, what I want to concentrate on here is not the way that language reduces agency and seems to defer meaning rather than guarantee it—

that staple of literary deconstruction—but the sense that translation reveals our own alienation in our own language: once the possibility of translation—that is, the appearance of other languages—exists, one language does not appear to be enough. This seems particularly devastating to those languages that have claimed—or seem to have claimed—that they are enough: the Bible, the Greeks.

However, I would suggest, after Levinas, that it is precisely this "failure to be enough," that disrupts our cosiness in our communities which makes these languages ethically significant. Benjamin praises Pannwitz, and cites him: "'Our translations, even the best ones, proceed from the wrong premise. They want to turn Hindi, Greek, English into German instead of turning German into Hindi, Greek English'" (de Man 81). However, even the second (better, for Pannwitz) of these still takes the latter language away. No matter how much the language is abrogated by shifts in vocabulary, grammar, allusion, register switching, vernacular transcription, neologisms (to make "German like Hindi," say) it is still "German." No matter how much other discourses may try to resist, the discourse of the Greeks and the Bible will still consume other discourses as they assume that they are comprehensible in the languages of Europe: Greek and the Bible. However, if the point for Levinas's philosophy is that the self suffers an infinite persecution and an infinite demand for hospitality, based on the assumption that the other is other and not like one's self, then it is precisely the untranslatability, the otherness, of another language that makes it important. Levinas writes that "the other is a neighbour . . . before being an individuation of the genus man" (Levinas, *Otherwise* 59) and again that the "unity of the human race is in fact posterior to fraternity" (166) where fraternity means the unmediated relation with the other. In a wider context, translation can be seen as what I have called elsewhere the "metaphysics of comprehension": knowing the other is most often a comprehension, a "taking power." Comprehension works by understanding, by grasping, the other by reducing the other into a third, neutral term. These terms vary: Socratic Reason, "Hegel's universal, Durkheim's social, the statistical laws that govern our freedom, Freud's unconscious" (Levinas, *Totality and Infinity* 272) and Heideggerian "Being" are all ways to turn the other into a category understood by the same. I suggest that the possibility of translation—if it is understood as relying on a "whole vessel," the "language of god" or a "universal human experience"—is also one of these terms. To translate the neighbor is to turn him/her/it into a category of our own language and so to deny him/her/its otherness. It is only by approaching the neighbor, the other, as that which we cannot understand or comprehend, or translate, that we act ethically: "I posit myself deposed of my sovereignty. Paradoxically it is qua *alienus*—foreigner and other—that man is not alienated" (Levinas, *Otherwise* 59). This means that the Western question of the relation between language, polis, and the human is bypassed by the neighbor.

This is only to argue, really, that ethics (how should I behave?) precedes and underlies epistemology (how do I know what sort of thing this is?). It is to argue that the "cosiness" and security found in communities seems to mitigate against ethics in the Levinasian sense. Levinas's thought is about translation—but that movement is heading out from the community to the other, precisely where translation is impossible. Levinas argues for an unending (and so infinite) ethical responsibility incumbent on each of us. The counterintuitive conclusion is that we are each responsible for those we do not, cannot, and could not understand. This conclusion has particular force in the era of hybridization, globalization, and global terrorism, where those from communities we (whoever "we" are) in the West do not understand are not far from "us" and "our" everyday lives. Does this mean that we should not translate? No. But it does mean that we have ethical grounds to be even more suspicious of the idea of translation and the way in which it relates to communities: "what I translate is upset by the way I translate."

NOTES

1. Two studies by Robert Gibbs go into these changes and this relationship in detail. Moreover, it is to his most recent book, *Why Ethics?*, and to a very stimulating paper that he gave at the "Jewish Textualities" Seminar at the School of Advanced Studies of the University of London, in Summer 2001, that this paper is indebted and is, in part, a response: that he would disagree with much of what I have to say I do not doubt, but I write it in a Levinasian spirit.

2. See, for examples, in addition to Shestov, in particular: Martin Jay, *Downcast Eyes: The Denigration of Vision in Twentieth Century French Thought* (London: University of California Press) (esp. pp. 23–24, p. 33); Gillian Rose, *Judaism and Modernity: Philosophical Essays* (Oxford: Blackwell, 1993); Susan A. Handelman, *Fragments of Redemption* (Bloomington: Indiana University Press, 1991); Susan A. Handelman, *The Slayers of Moses* (Albany: SUNY Press, 1982); Geoffrey Hartman and Sanford Budick, *Midrash and Literature* (London: Yale University Press, 1986).

3. Although this is not to say, for example, that Derrida does not recognize the benefits of such a universalism or what Paul Gilroy, after Fanon, calls "planetary humanism." Indeed, his book *The Politics of Friendship* seems to suggest that it is this or something like it for which we should be aiming and trying to shape: thus "messianic telepoesis." Gilroy writes, in a similar vein, that our "challenge should now be to bring even more powerful visions of planetary humanity from the future into the present and to reconnect them with democratic and cosmopolitan traditions" (Gilroy 356).

WORKS CITED

Agamben, Giorgio, *Potentialities*, trans. Daniel Heller-Roazen (London: Stanford University Press, 1999).

Arnold, Matthew, *Lectures and Essays in Criticism: Complete Prose Works*, Vol. 3, ed. R. H. Super (Ann Arbor: University of Michigan Press, 1962).

Benjamin, Walter, *Illuminations*, trans. Harry Zohn (London: Pimlico, 1999).

Critchley, Simon, *Ethics-Politics-Subjectivity* (London: Verso, 1999).

de Man, Paul, *The Resistance to Theory* (Manchester: Manchester University Press, 1986).

Derrida, Jacques, *Of Grammatology*, trans. Gayatri Chakravorty Spivak (London: Johns Hopkins University Press, 1976).

———, *Writing and Difference*, trans. Alan Bass (London: Routledge and Kegan Paul, 1978).

———, *The Politics of Friendship*, trans. George Collins (London: Verso, 1997)

———, *Adieu to Emmanuel Levinas*, trans. Pascale-Anne Brault and Michel Naas (Stanford: Stanford University Press, 1999).

Fanon, Franz, *The Wretched of the Earth*, trans. Constance Farrington (Harmondsworth: Penguin, 1990).

Geertz, Clifford, *The Interpretation of Cultures* (London: Fontana, 1993).

Gibbs, Robert, *Correlations in Rosenzweig and Levinas* (Princeton: Princeton University Press, 1992).

——— *Why Ethics? Signs of Responsibilites* (Princeton: Princeton University Press, 2000).

Gilroy, Paul, *Between Camps* (London: Allen Lane, 2000).

Hartman, Geoffrey and Sanford Budick, eds., *Midrash And Literature* (London: Yale University Press, 1986).

Kearney, Richard, *Dialogues with Contemporary Continental Thinkers: The Phenomenological Heritage* (Manchester: Manchester University Press, 1984).

Levinas, Emmanuel, *Otherwise than Being: or, Beyond Essence*, trans. Alphonso Lingis (The Hague: Martinus Nijhoff, 1981).

———, *Ethics and Infinity: Conversations with Phillipe Nemo*, trans. R. A. Cohen (Pittsburg: Duquesne University Press, 1985).

———, *Collected Philosophical Papers*, trans. Alphonso Lingis (Dordrecht: Kluwer Academic Publishers, 1987).

———, *In the Time of Nations*, trans. Michael B. Smith (Bloomington: Indiana Univerity Press, 1994).

———, *Totality and Infinity: An Essay on Exteriority*, trans. Alphonso Lingis (London: Kluwer Academic Publishers, 1991), p. 28.

———, "Philosophy and Awakening," trans. Mary Quaintance in *Who Comes after the Subject?*, eds. Eduardo Cadava, Peter Connor, Jean-luc Nancy (London: Routledge, 1991), pp. 206–16.

John Llewelyn, *The Hypocritical Imagination: Between Kant and Levinas* (London: Routledge, 2000).

Mortley, Raoul, *French Philosophers in Conversation* (London: Routledge, 1991).

Shestov, Lev, *Athens and Jerusalem*, trans. Bernard Martin (Athens: Ohio University Press, 1966).

Steinberg, Michael P., introduction, in *Walter Benjamin and the Demands of History*, ed. Michael P. Steinberg (London: Cornell University Press, 1996), pp. 1–23.

Wittgenstein, Ludwig, *Culture and Value*, rev. ed., eds. G. H. von Wright and Alois Pichler, trans. Peter Winch (Oxford: Blackwell, 1994).

Wright, Tamara, *The Twilight of Jewish Philosophy: Emmanuel Levinas' Ethical Hermeneutics* (Amsterdam: Harwood Academic Publishers, 1999).

Wright, Tamara, Peter Hughes, and Alison Ainley, "The Paradox of Morality: an Interview with Emmanuel Levinas," in *The Provocation of Levinas*, eds., Robert Bernasconi and David Woods (London: Routledge, 1988).

Comparative Literature: The Delay in Translation

STANLEY CORNGOLD

It is often claimed today that comparative literature is a kind of translation and, being a practice less transparent than translation, should take translation as its model. This claim feels avant-garde: it resonates with the "linguistic turn" that informed most of the humanistic disciplines during the last quarter of the last century and vividly survives today in neighboring disciplines, like English, foreign languages, history, and anthropology, with their concerns for globalization, the media, and the mentalities of postcolonialism. But whether the translation model for comparative literature is to be a step forward, a step back, or the source of a sort of productive delay very much depends on how translation is understood. What sort of understanding of translation is presupposed when comparative literature is compared with it?

Now, each translation has a way of producing its own theory of what it is about; this is unavoidable, since acts of translation may be seen as radically singular, involving, as is commonly agreed on, a certain surd irrationality as the "thing" that is always left out, the thing that is untranslatable in the representation of one particular piece of one particular language in another. And where the defining characteristic of each particular act of translation is always ineffable, one cannot say whether or not or to what extent this translation resembles any other. Nonetheless, in the effort to produce a general theory of translation, one type of metaphor persistently crops up, and that is the prosopopeia meant to picture the relation of the source text to the target text—the relation of "fidelity." One translation must be as faithful as the next in the manner, let us say, that spouses, lovers, or friends are held to be.

Consider Walter Benjamin's radical essay "The Task of the Translator" (*Die Aufgabe des Übersetzers*), which actually disrupts the two-text model in describing translation as a relation between two *languages*, the goal of which is to bring to light a third language—"pure language" [*reine Sprache*]. In this enterprise the translator's task is least of all the salvaging of an original meaning through "accurate communication" (*genaue Mitteilung*), for "all information, all sense, and all intention finally encounter a stratum in which they are destined to be extinguished. This very stratum furnishes a new and higher justification for free translation; this justification does not derive from the sense of what is to be conveyed, for the emancipation from the sense is the task of fidelity."[1] This thesis is striking as much for the way it dislodges the customary translation paradigm of text-unto-text as for its employment of the kind of metaphor I have said is recurrent in theories of translation—figures of ethical intersubjective relation (here, again: "fidelity" [Treue]). The appearance of this metaphor in even so "inhuman" a description as Benjamin's suggests the operations of the propadeutic identified by Goethe in his advertisement to his novel *Elective Affinities* (*Die Wahlverwandtschaften*): "The author . . . might have noticed that in the natural sciences ethical analogies are very often used to make things that are far remote from the circle of human knowledge more accessible."[2] Consider, too, a more recent example—George Steiner's reflections in *After Babel* on "translatability" as the enabling feature of cultural communication. For him the "far remote" character of translation lies less in its literal distance from human affairs than in the inscrutable ubiquity of its embeddedness: it cannot be directly identified because it always already indwells each attempt to understand it.[3] Steiner puts the governing "postulate" of his work as follows: "Translation is formally and pragmatically implicit in *every* act of communication, in the emission and reception of each and every mode of meaning, be it in the widest semiotic sense or in more specifically verbal exchanges."[4] Interestingly, Steiner's wide sense of the concept also includes the illuminations of "inadequate" moments of translation supplied by writers who "articulate the conventions of masked or failed understanding which have obtained between men and women, between women and men, in the lineaments of dialogue we call love or hatred."[5] Here, once again, translation falls under the head of intersubjective relation: "love or hatred." If we include uninhibited sexuality under the head of such relations, then Goethe's famous apothegm settles the matter: translators are those "industrious pimps who, in extolling the adorable charms of a partly-clothed beauty, excite in us an irresistible desire for the original."[6]

Now, if comparative literature has come to be treated of late as the proper disciplinary context for discussions of translation—an association so seemingly natural that the discipline has itself been likened to translation itself—this privileged relation has, I believe, been strengthened by the subliminal view on translation as an affair of the communication of subjectivities. In this case the "linguistic turn" is also an "inward turn," a "journey into the interior." The view that the translator must above all maintain his or her "fidelity" to the other text would indeed prove attractive to a discipline whose self-conception has been indebted to models of dialogue, "influence," colloquy—an affair not of the relation of languages but of characters and voices.

And yet, with all these provisions, translation can at the same time, though in a privative and cautionary sense, remain a model for comparative literature, on the logic of the Prison Chaplain in Kafka's *The Trial*, who declares: "The correct understanding of a matter and misunderstanding the matter are not mutually exclusive."[7] To clarify this latter point of logic, one could also go to Paul de Man, writing on Martin Heidegger's view of the great German poet Friedrich Hölderlin as a witness to the experience of Being. De Man declares that Heidegger writes on Hölderlin just because "Hölderlin says exactly the opposite of what Heidegger makes him say," a statement that reads, for our purposes, as follows: I come to this question of translation as a model for comparative literature because "comparative literature" says exactly the opposite of what the claim to the efficacy of the translation model makes it say. But I should not like to be misunderstood. "Such an assertion"—so de Man continues—"is paradoxical only in appearance." For "at this level of thought, it is difficult to distinguish between a proposition and that which constitutes its opposite. In fact, to state the opposite is still to talk of the same thing although in an opposite sense; and to have the two interlocutors ['comparative literature,' on the one hand, and 'the translation model' on the other] manage to speak of the same thing in a dialogue of this sort is already a major achievement."[8]

I say that comparative literature is not translation because translation means carrying over a piece of foreign language into one's native or "near-native" language—the target language. But the act that I call "comparison," means, in fact, being, for one moment, without a language; it means being, not lost *in* translation but lost *for* translation: being at a place of thought where the target language is absent.

Doing comparative literature means studying works written in different languages without the benefit of translation. It means not needing to translate, on the claimed strength of being able to translate. So what we project as the specific competence of the comparativist is his or her ability to put in immediate relation things conjured by the words of different languages.

I hold together in my mind a piece of Kafka and a piece of Flaubert, and I think about them. Never has the "I think" been stranger. If I have been accustomed to say, "I think in English," it is clear that for at least one nanosecond I am without English, and yet I am thinking or getting ready to think. I am not translating. I understand (I think) the German, and I understand (I think) the French—and if I am understanding, am I not thinking? I would seem to be, in French and in German: but when I compare these texts, intuiting the basis for comparison, what language, then, am I thinking in?

In what medium are such pieces compared? Each belongs to a different language; what language contains them both? Are we on the verge, the other verge of that "pure language" toward which, according to Walter Benjamin, all particular translations strive, yet only when they shun "communication or the imparting of information"?[9]

Whatever zone of being contains, suspends, enfolds the configurations of different languages, and moreover in its space produces the aftershocks of recognition, which for a tremulous instant stay ungathered into any single language, is sponsored, authorized, upheld by the discipline of comparative literature. This means: we will authorize a model of translation on the basis of "comparison" but not the other way around.

Comparative literature is not a matter of detecting analogies between literary objects, because configurations in different languages are never analogous; they may stand in "relationship," which is an affair for investigation, for reason, and for law. But the law of their relationship is not readable on the surface; following Benjamin, that law is hidden "among [the] alien tongues in which that pure language is exiled"; and then again it is hidden in the unknown place in conscious-ness where comparison repeats this relationship.[10]

Comparative literature registers the products of a textual collision—a necessary embarrassment, for these products are without habitation and a name: they have no reference except as the mind abandons them for unsuitable analogies—as it sooner or later must. (The name of this abandonment is "translation.") But for readers accustomed to assume the adequacy of correlations for literary entities in the mind, under the spell of hermeneutics, there is here a salutary arrest of the referencing function, for comparative literature brings about a higher order of indetermination (the relationship between disparate pieces of "literary" language); and any blockage of the referencing function—the uprush of clichés—is bound to do some good. There is complex pleasure in an attunement without conceptual clarification—there is even revelatory pleasure; here we are in the aesthetic-ethical universe of Kant's *Third Critique*.

This play of languages issues forth into languagelessness and a patient abiding in the place where language-is-about-to-be. Comparison reacquaints us, might reacquaint us with the sense of the *Ursprung* or "origin" of articulated thought (about which we may not be too celebratory since "Ursprung" simultaneously means an "Ur-*Sprung*"—a rip or tear—in the texture of language). But this adventuresome place might also be the promise of a bliss, the advent of that happiness, perhaps, that Adorno mentions in *Aesthetic Theory*. This is not a hedonism, he declares. "Aesthetic hedonism," I quote, "is to be confronted with the passage from Kant's doctrine of the sublime, which he timidly excluded from art: Happiness in artworks would be the feeling they instill of standing firm."[11]

Comparative literature asks you, too, to stand firm in the delay of translation. This holding two pieces together in the mind is a warrant against the violence of premature analogy, against improper association. Midwifing their conjunction, establishing the copula, calls for a patience exceeding even the greatest tact.

These disparate pieces are alike (in some nonsensuous way) and they are unlike, deeply, immeasurably unlike, because if there is something alike in the things they are about (they have a thematic similarity), they are profoundly, immeasurably unlike in the way they mean what they mean, what Benjamin calls their "Art des Meinens," a "way" that traverses the whole of the discrete language in which they are at home.

The way they mean cannot be got at as what these texts commonly "express." To paraphrase Benjamin on the relation of the phenomenal appearance—the shining semblance [*Schein*]—and truth in art—: their relation is determined by "the expressionless," "that which arrests this shining semblance [of mere beauty], spellbinds the movement, and interrupts the harmony."[12] The orders of truth and semblance are unlike, yet they belong together; they cannot be separated, and yet they cannot mingle. Benjamin gives the example of such a caesura, such interruption, in the falling star that shoots over the heads of the lovers in Goethe's *Elective Affinities*.[13] Is it possible that the very operation of this "expressionless" in individual works is sustained, induced in the force field of the delay in translation? What you then get is something like Novalis's "geistige Elektrizität," an astral-electrical mood of intelligibility.[14]

The moment I am trying to define has its structural counterpart—in the opposite sense!—in the nonbeing that de Man famously concluded from his reading of Shelley's "The Triumph of Life": "[The Triumph] . . . warns us that nothing, whether deed, word, thought, or text, ever happens in relation, positive or negative, to anything that precedes, follows, or exists elsewhere, but only as a random event whose power, like the power of death, is due to the randomness of its occurrence."[15] I could accept only one of these features for the structural moment of comparison I want to define, for mine has more in common with Benjamin's "expressionless" than de Man's "lifeless." I want, most decidedly, a moment of relation, of "nonseparation" (Benjamin: shining and essence in art are not separate) in the comparison of nonequivalent texts, while granting that this moment cannot be mingled with the "deed, word, thought or text" that finally follows. But this movement, I believe, is not random (you can see that we are still very fundamentally in the conceptual universe of Kant's *Third Critique*); it is necessarily produced from the collision of two pieces of "literary" language in the mind of the schooled comparer. "All are welcome," but training is necessary.

Aside from Benjamin, models of the relationship of these two (or more) disparate pieces of literature exist: Kant gives us more than one. In the sense that they are incommensurable (*unangemessen*), we are at the precincts of the sublime. The pleasure of their conjunction includes the pain [*negative Lust*] of our "embarrassment [*Verlegenheit*]." How else except as negative pleasure are we to have the intimations of that pure language to which all discrete languages aspire, since it shuns communication? The moment has its siblings, as we will see, in (1) the silence in books; (2) the silence that lurks behind language; and (3) the silence that's like a language. Proust criticized Ruskin's "fetishistic respect for books" (*respect fétichiste pour les livres*), "an idolatry [in the words of Kevin McLauglin] that substantializes literary value and imagines it as comparable to 'a material thing deposited between the leaves of books.' "By contrast," McLaughlin continues, "Proust insists that the conserving action of reading concentrates on 'interstices': 'not only the sentences [of a text] . . . [but] between the sentences . . . in the interval separating them, there still remains today as in an inviolate burial chamber, filling the interstices, a silence centuries old.'"[16] I think one is more nearly certain to detect that silence in the interstices between pieces of different languages.

In 1937 Samuel Beckett spoke of wanting "to bore one hole after another into it [language], until what lurks behind it—be it something or nothing—begins to seep through." Mark Harman notes: "Beckett's goal in ripping apart the veil of language is [quote] 'to feel a whisper of that final music or that silence that underlies all.'"[17]

"A whisper of the silence?" I cite Törless, the adolescent aesthete-hero of Musil's turn-of-the-century novella *Perplexities of the Pupil Törless*, who, in conversation with his poisonous friend, the mystic Beineberg, invokes the "sudden silence that's like a language we can't hear."[18]

Comparative literature is the discipline of this mystic thing—like language, underlying language, in between language pieces—accounted audible and silent, archaic and new. Comparative literature is a disciplined mysticism.

How now—as I conclude—to connect this moment to futurity, to the future of comparative literature and indeed of the humanities? The moment I describe is packed with futurity, it is a moment of pure possibility. The "translation" I have in mind that one now makes is more nearly the leap from one field to another entirely unlike it, for the latter is the accustomed field of the target language, but here we are speaking of salvaging a moment of pure thought—the intuition of relationship. How could we? The moment is audible (whispered), and unheard, centuries old and an origin.

The situation is odd, shapeless, even "monstrous" in the nicest sense of the word. I am thinking of Kafka's question: "What is literature? Where does it come from? What use is it? What questionable things! Add to this questionableness the further questionableness of what you say, and what you get is a monstrosity."[19]

If literature is monstrous—and its questionableness, its way of provoking questions about its nature, is monstrous—then the questions it provokes will seem to have the same nature as the thing questioned—as literature: so what today we call theory is deeply part of the monstrosity. This monstrosity is the sign of the future—the future of comparative literature ("of" as genitive, "of" as ablative); and, indeed, of every such future we have heard another thinker, Derrida, say that it appears "only under the species of the nonspecies, in the formless, mute, infant and terrifying form of monstrosity."[20] It is exactly this monster—comparative, untranslatable—that we should wish to protect.

I have written about a moment that has to take place if comparative literature is to have any effect whatsoever, including empirical effects on cities and nations and "the globe" and also conceptual effects on the project of bringing such terms into correlation. So I do not finally wish to stop at this mystic, "inside"-sounding moment, place, or thing.

How could we then move out from it—temporally, toward a future— spatially, toward another place, to other geographies, with persons in it without the leisure or the skill to compare literary texts. Take the radical case: this other person who has been named in many oral presentations by Gayatri Spivak, in the radical form of her human "otherness"—the subaltern, impoverished, woman of color whom we need to know and whom it is strange and difficult to know.

How should we begin to know such a person—and we must—otherwise than by becoming acquainted with dislocation, our own dislocation, outside language, outside competence? What room is there for this difficult strangeness, if we have not learned to stand firm in the midst of it, abiding a moment of inexpressibility, an incommunicable sense of otherness, of intimacy with a common human grain.

This is an attitude of scrupulous neutrality, an *Augenblick* of silence. Communication should not be figured as occurring only at the level of imparting information. The *Augenblick* of such silence is generally imputable. It does not exclude community. This moment that bespeaks a common human grain moves along the grain of its silence.

NOTES

1. Walter Benjamin, "The Task of the Translator," trans. Harry Zohn, in *Selected Works*, ed. Michael Jennings and Marcus Bullock (Cambridge: Harvard University Press, 1997), 1:261

2. Johann Wolfgang von Goethe, *Sämtliche Werke* (Münchner Ausgabe, Band 9, Munich: Hanser, 1987), p. 285.

3. George Steiner, *After Babel: Aspects of Language and Translation*, 2nd ed. (Oxford, New York: Oxford University Press, 1992).

4. Ibid., p. xii.

5. Ibid.

6. J.W.V. Goethe, *Maximen und Reflexionen. Nach den Handschriften des Goethe- und Schiller Archivs*, ed. Max Hecker (Weimar 1907), Nr. p. 299.

7. Franz Kafka, *The Trial*, trans. Breon Mitchell (New York: Schocken, 1998), p. 219.

8. Paul de Man, *Blindness and Insight: Essays in the Rhetoric of Contemporary Criticism*, 2d ed., rev. (Minneapolis: University of Minnesota Press, 1983), p. 255.

9. Benjamin, "Task of the Translator," 261, pp. 253.

10. Ibid., p. 261.

11. Theodor Adorno, *Aesthetic Theory*, eds. Gretel Adorno and Rolf Tiedemann, newly trans., ed., and with a trans. introduction by Robert Hullot-Kentor (Minnesota: University of Minnesota Press, 1997), p. 15.

12. "Goethe's Elective Affinities," trans. Stanley Corngold, in Benjamin, *Selected Works*, p. 340.

13. Ibid., p. 355.

14. "Geistige Elektrizität," for which "solid bodies [*feste Körper*] are necessary." Novalis, *Schriften*, eds. F. Schlegel and L. Tieck (Berlin, 1802), p. 67. Cited under the entry "Witz" in Grimm's *Deutsches Wörterbuch* (Leipzig: Hirzel, 1960), 14/2:874.

15. Paul de Man, *The Rhetoric of Romanticism* (New York: Columbia University Press, 1984), p. 122.

16. Proust, "Journées de lecture," *Contre Saint-Beuve*, Bilbiothèque de la Pléiade (Paris: Gallimard, 1971), pp. 183, 180, and 193; "On Reading," *On Reading Ruskin*, trans. Jean Autet and William Burford (New Haven: Yale University Press, 1987), pp. 120, 118, and 128. Cited in Kevin McLaughlin, "The Coming of Paper: Aesthetic Value from Ruskin to Benjamin," *Modern Language Notes* 114(5), Dec. 1999, p. 970.

17. Mark Harman, "Beckett and Kafka," *The Partisan Review* 66(4), 1999, p. 576.

18. *Young Törless*, an English translation of Robert Musil's *Die Verwirrungen des Zöglings Törless*, trans. Eithne Wilkins and Ernst Kaiser (New York: Pantheon, 1955), p. 26.

19. Franz Kafka, *Dearest Father*, trans. Ernst Kaiser and Eithne Wilkins (New York: Schocken, 1954), p. 246.

20. Jacques Derrida, "Structure, Sign and Play in the Discourse of the Human Sciences," in *Critical Theory Since Plato*, ed. Hazard Adams (New York: Harcourt Brace, 1992), p. 1126.

Translation as Community: The Opacity of Modernizations of *Genji monogatari*

JONATHAN E. ABEL

[W]hat sort of social relation is translation in the first place?[1]

[H]ow do we communicate? But this question can be asked seriously only if we dismiss all "theories of communication," which begin by positing the necessity or the desire for a consensus, a continuity and a transfer of messages. It is not a question of establishing rules for communication, it is a question of understanding before all else that in "communication" what takes place is an *exposition*: finite existence exposed to finite existence, co-appearing before it and with it.[2]

One of the ways to get around the confines of one's "identity" as one produces expository prose is to work at someone else's title, as one works with a language that belongs to many others. This, after all, is one of the seductions of translating. It is a simple miming of the responsibility to the trace of the other in the self.[3]

Several recent studies focus on translations in order to deconstruct notions of the other and, thereby, to reveal the foreign originary light filtered through the domesticating (here read colonizing, racist, sexist, etc.) lenses of a translating self. Such studies that rigorously locate translations in the moments and places of their translation (rather than in some translatable essence) may expose some general presumptions of lay readers who overlook the translated-ness of a translation. In doing so, however, they obviate the possibility of not only translation, but also reading. That is to say, in finding difference, in explicating the ways in which translators "mutilate" and "abuse" the "sacred" text, these arguments fail to acknowledge dynamics of meaning-making inherent in reading processes and ignore key relationships posited by the act of translation—the community of author, translator, and reader of texts and translated texts. In his *La communauté désoeuvrée* (*The Inoperative Community*), Jean-Luc Nancy describes community based not on a "common being" wherein singularities give themselves up to a whole, but rather on a "being in common" in which singularities stand in relation, in which self and other are each one of two. Discussing translation in terms of Nancy's community foregrounds both similarities and differences between text and other text, while maintaining the integrity of both.

Wrought from historical conditions that conflict with notions of an original, *Genji monogatari* 源氏物語 (*Tales of Genji*) continues to provide critics and authors a site for identity formation. Translations from an archaic, supposedly *onna-de* 女手 (woman's hand) Heian-period style into various post-*genbun'itchi* 言文一致[4] twentieth-century prose modes reiterate this theme of identity. While providing a new approach to *Genji*, reading modern Japanese translations as existing in a community with earlier versions revises and refines not only notions of what *Genji* is, but also recent theoretical approaches to translation and Nancy's notions of community.

Translation as Community: Countering the Ethics of Difference

Beginning where Stuart Hall and Homi Bhabha,[5] amongst others, leave off in their declarations of the infinitely appropriable nature of texts, Anthony Pym, Antoine Berman, and Lawrence Venuti[6] celebrate the difference of translation from the translated and the agency of the translator. In particular, Venuti thrills at the possibility of Benjamin's foreignizing[7] translation: "The ethical stance I advocate urges that translations be written, read, and evaluated with greater respect for linguistic and cultural differences."[8] If this important difference of translation from translated, a difference that deconstructs "transparency," is taken to an extreme, then translation and reading become impossible. If texts are only always already located in, prisoners of their moments of production, then to translate or read would be a hopeless attempt to recover origins. Moreover, as we shall see, transparency is not a universal, transhistorical assumption about translation and, thus, only needs deconstructing in particular cultural moments.

In the spirit of Hall and Bhabha, it is useful to reiterate that any text is infinitely able to be appropriated, articulated, or translated; furthermore, no such appropriations are any more necessary or correct than any others. Contrary to those who would promote a universal ethics of translation, I begin with the potentially reductive and relativist assumption that there is no transhistorically good translation; there are only notions of translation as manifested differently in varied times and spaces. When and where a text is considered to be translation, it is translation. A translation does not reside in a necessarily subservient place below a canonical translated original.

Some recent translation scholars seem to concur that translation is possible; yet they praise the tacit references to the foreign within a translation that simultaneously proclaim translated-ness and conversely deny the possibility of translation and even reading. In other words, a translation that contains ungrammatical sentences, that includes words from the foreign text, that, in short, is uncomfortable for the reader of the target language, evokes both awareness of its own translated-ness and the impossibility of translation.

Aware of this conundrum, David Bellos proposes that, "translatability is the only imaginable guarantee of meaning. In that sense it offers a commonsensical and irrefutable definition of what a language is: a language that is impossible to translate is not a language; a text that is impossible to translate is not written in a language."[9] Everything written in language is translatable. Naoki Sakai's fixation on heterogeneity of language echoes Bellos's claim that translation is never impossible, but possible within language may be revised. Sakai writes: "every translation calls for a countertranslation, and in this sort of address it is clearly evident that within the framework of communication, translation must be endless. Thus, in the heterolingual address, the addressee must translate any delivery, whether in speech or writing, in order for that delivery to actually be received."[10] Communication necessitates translation from heterogeneous linguistic space into another heterogeneous linguistic space. Though they differ from the others by openly recognizing the necessity and possibility of translation, Bellos and Sakai share with Pym, Berman, and Venuti an overvaluation of translation as the communication of a message or meaning.

Though he does not openly relate his ideas to issues of translation, Nancy argues for a different notion of communication: "what communication writes, what writing communicates, is in no way a truth possessed, appropriated or transmitted—even though it is, absolutely, the truth of being-in-common."[11] In this sense, communication is not the transference of a message, but rather the existence of identities standing in relation to one another. Differences and similarities, selves and others, texts and intertexts, commune in ways that never allow for the speaking of one without the other; they exist, are identifiable only in relation:

> We are alike because each one of us is exposed to the outside that *we are for ourselves*. The like is not the same (*le semblable n'est pas le pareil*). I do not rediscover *myself*, nor do I recognize *myself* in the other: I experience the other's alterity, or I experience alterity in the other together with the alteration that "in me" sets my singularity outside me and infinitely delimits it. Community is that singular ontological order in which the other and the same are alike (*sont le semblable*): that is to say, in the sharing of identity.[12]

Though Nancy does not explicitly mention translation, his thoughts readily apply to the relationship of trans-lator/lation to translated: The translator (and the translation) experiences the translated's alterity; and at this limit of identity one text exposes itself to another. Community is that singular ontological order in which the translated and the translation are alike. Contrary to notions that normatively judge translations in terms of similarities and differences with an original, viewing translation as community reveals how both similarities and differences constitute the singular identities of the translated and the translation. These identities stand in a relationship, not as a dominant, original influencer and subordinate, derivative influenced, not even as in a dialogue, but rather as entities equally and infinitely interpretable, appropriable, articulatable, and translatable. Through these acts of meaning-making, that is, through these readings, identities form in relation to each other. Being in common, the community, appears most clearly in constellations of texts that go by the same title, modern language translations.

GENDAIGOYAKU AS TRANSLATION: ORIGINALS, DRIVE, SIMPATICO, AND ORIGINALITY

translate. to turn from one language into another; to change into another language retaining the sense; to render; also, to express in other words, to paraphrase.[13] (OED)

やく 【訳】 ある言語表現を体系の異なった別の言語で言いかえて、意味を通じさせること。「翻—」「通—」「—文」[14] (Kōjien)

A modernization of a classic into a contemporary form of "the same language" might seem very different from a translation.[15] The gendaigoyaku chosen here, however, represent a unique mode of translation for at least two reasons: first, an assumption of translation as transparent is largely a non-issue with these works; second, the vast discontinuities and gaps between *gendaigo* 現代語 (modern language) and *bungo* 文語 (classical, literary language) engender significant variety within the heterolingual space now called "Japanese." In an ancient culture in which reading, writing, and speaking were one and in a modern, cosmopolitan culture that is continually adopting and adapting, there can be little ado about the sacredness of the original. Though the name of the text is canonical, its contents are appropriable, excisable, and translatable with little outrage except among a few pedantic critics. This represents a significant situation overlooked by recent translation theorists, a situation featuring famous writers singing their individuality, rather than obscure scholars hiding in marginalia. Despite the absence of characteristics that some might assume to be inherent in translation, gendaigoyaku may be considered translations. The gap between classical *onna-de* discursive style and contemporary forms of post-*genbun'itchi* Japanese prose presents a situation necessitating and calling for translation;[16] in other words, *Genji* is so much an other to modern readers and authors that it requires a redefinition of self. Contemporary commentaries on modern language translations attest to the difference of the Heian discourse from modern understanding/language and the subsequent desire to translate (or, as Berman, in somewhat Freudian terminology, refers to it, "the translation drive").

From Heian "Originals" to Cartoon Genjis

The Heian reading and composing environment, the early textual variants, and the many post-Heian appropriations of *Genji* disallow presumptions about translation that posit the translated as superior, sacred, and original. In much contemporary scholarship on *Genji*, a palpable slip between rhetoric and subject reveals logical problems in critical arguments; in their complicated tales of textual variants from no fewer than three lineages, some critics' words expose their own assumptions about authorial power, the integrity of the entire text, and an originary source. After discussing the multitude of variant extant classical texts, Haruo Shirane writes: "It is thus impossible to know *the* original *Genji*. The text that this study is based upon is an edited version of the *Aobyōshi* (Blue-Cover) recension that is probably close to *the* original but that, in the final analysis, represents only one version of this masterpiece"[17] (emphasis added). The desire for an original Genji contradicts general truths not only of composition at any moment in history, but also of the cultural situation of texts in Heian, and of how those texts have been taken by the non-scholarly community since—namely, that there is never such an entity as an original and that such desire for an origin opposes how *Genji* means at various historical junctures.

The scant knowledge available about ancient writing and reading practices suggests a situation rather foreign to the common contemporary modes of keyboards and silence. In the inner world of the salon, Heian court ladies probably read aloud, looked at pictures, and copied texts in groups. The texts themselves may have acted as prompters (rather than scripts) to speakers who would embellish and omit as the occasion demanded. For these reasons, the various *Genji monogatari* are most likely the products of joint participation of writer/speaker and listener/copier.[18] But these terms themselves are problematic and provisional: the writer/speaker also likely listened to reactions of the listener/copier; and, after all, is not the copier also a writer? In addition, the collection of "chapters" now known as *Genji* was likely composed in a very different order than modern annotated versions propound.[19] The tales themselves also have various origins in literary and historical figures popular throughout the period.[20] Furthermore, it is evident that the tales were read/told and reread/retold in different settings in front of various audiences. Under such circumstances, producers and receivers, texts and intertexts are inseparable. And it is precisely the multifarious production effort that denies the notion of monumentality[21] of the text or a unified original moment or person responsible for text production. The texts produced had to be in constant flux, changeable as the situation was due or even upon the whim of a listener/reader/writer/copier/speaker.

The notion of an original to be translated is further complicated by the numerous textual lineages. Even before the search for extant *Genji* texts during the Kamakura period (1192–1333), several versions circulated in Murasaki's lifetime, at least one of which was not authoritative.[22] Since Teika (1162–1241) and Mitsuyuki (1163–1244), scholars have unsuccessfully endeavored to produce an authoritative original *Genji*.[23] Though scholars have long sought an original with which to prove their adversaries wrong, the desire to maintain the sacred place of an original seems to have been less of a concern for later producers of cultural material. *Genji* has been a favorite playground for witty satirists and literature-savvy dilettantes since at least the Edo period (1600–1868). One of the more famous *gesaku* (low-brow) versions, Tanehiko Ryūtei's *The Phony Murasaki and the Redneck Genji* (*Nise-Murasaki inaka-Genji*, 1829–42) provided a plucky summary of the Genji stories—a version that, according to some, proves that, "*Genji monogatari* was read, without exception, as a wholly lustful book (もっぱら好色本)."[24] While it is true that this kind of satire could only occur/exist in a period when *Genji* maintained cultural capital as a topos, *Redneck Genji* counters the notion of a sacred text. This kind of free play drawing on both the canonical status and the infinite appropriability of *Genji* continued in several

Edo *e-maki* (picture book) versions and no fewer than three *manga* (comic book) versions in the twentieth century.[25]

Difficulty

Y: The international value of *Genji monogatari* is on the rise, and even within Japan it has become a widely familiar work through the *gendaigoyaku* starting with Yosano Akiko's, then Tanizaki's, Enchi's, and Funabashi's and such. How and why has this familiarity been cultivated? In short, where is the charm in *Genji*.

A: Well, to make reading the classical *Genji* a subject of research is not interesting at all. It's a pain! (Laugh)[26]

In Yutaka Yamanaka's interview with renowned literary scholar Akio Abe, the subject turns briefly from the inherent "charm of *Genji*" to the particular charm of *Genji* in translation. After Yamanaka suggests that the translations have some causal relationship with the recent, burgeoning charm, Abe concurs, noting the difficulty of the classical versions. Indeed, it is this difficulty, difference, alterity, otherness, and "pain" of the Heian texts that demands their translation. The difficulty is attested to by the contemporary nuance of the phrase *Suma kaeri* (returning from Suma) referring not to Genji's, the character's, return from Suma, the geographic locale, but to perplexed readers who go back and begin reading the story again with the hope of renewed understanding when they reach the end of "Suma," the locale of the twelfth of fifty-four chapters.[27]

The discourse on this difficulty ranges from commentators on to producers of the gendaigoyaku, among whom are some of the most well-known Japanese scholars and writers of the twentieth century. In a roundtable discussion with Harumi, a.k.a. Jakuchō, Seto'uchi (several years prior to her own *gendaigoyaku* of *Genji*), Yukio Mishima, himself known for his nuanced readings and appropriations of premodern language, noted: "There is a problem of *gendaigoyaku*. I am definitely against modernizations of the classics in principle. . . . But if it's *Genji monogatari*, well, that's a bit of an exception, because it's so difficult. Right?"[28] For a virtuoso of Mishima's stature to admit the difficulty of the text is *not* the exception, but the rule. Ivan Morris notes that "some, including as prominent a literary man as Hakuchō Masamune, find Arthur Waley's (English language) translation more comprehensible than the original text"(parenthetical added).[29]

In commentary on each of the three gendaigoyaku to be considered here, this expression of the difficulty of the classical texts surfaces. Ōgai Mori (writing as Rintarō Mori) wrote in his preface to the first edition of Akiko Yosano's *Shinyaku Genji monogatari* (1911–13): "When I read *Genji*, I am always overcome by resistance (抵抗に打ぺ条つた) and I feel like I can not develop the meanings from the words."[30] Expressing similar views, Yoshio Yamada, the scholar who acted as a supervisor and consultant on Jun'ichirō Tanizaki's first two gendaigoyaku and whose name appears along side Tanizaki's on those title pages, wrote "Mr. Tanizaki and *Genji monogatari*: The Words of a Supervisor," an article published in *Chūō kōron* (1939) concurrently with the publication of the Tanizaki's wartime gendaigoyaku. According to Yamada, the difficulty of the original barred modern readers from understanding the flow of the entirety of the Genji stories. He saw the gendaigoyaku as allowing readers to sense this for the first time.[31] Finally, in her 1974 preface, Fumiko Enchi equated writing her gendaigoyaku to climbing Mount Everest; the desire to climb and write both stemming from a "because it's there" attitude.[32]

Drive From Monogatari to Shōsetsu

> In as unproblematic words (気難しくない言葉) as possible, I wanted to tell the *Genji* I read in my heart to the modern reader. . . . To read [*Genji*] like a regular novel (並みの小説), that is the feeling I wanted readers to have as they turn the pages.[33]

For modern translators, the difficult challenge presented by translation of *monogatari* is countered by a "translation drive" that combines both a domesticating impulse and an "innate antagonism toward the translator's native tongue."[34] What Yamada claims to be a desire to "revitalize (再生) it in the form of a modern novel (現代の小説),"[35] clearly manifests itself in the subtle conversion of the *monogatari* (tale) form to that of the *shōsetsu* (novel). For Takuya Tamagami, scholar of Heian reading practice, this transformation represents only a loss: "Almost imperceptibly, the number of people who think of *monogatari* as *shōsetsu* has grown. They think that by regarding *monogatari* as *shōsetsu* the value of *monogatari* will increase."[36] However, the "anti-*monogatari*-ness" (反物語性)[37] of the *gendaigoyaku* both extinguishes aspects of monogatari and gives birth to new notions of novel. At once, this process of translation elides aspects of monogatari and disrupts shōsetsu conventions.

Author's Role in Cultivating New Originality

> Of course gendaigoyaku are nothing more than spin-offs of the original that pass through the interior of the translator. As for this translation, it is meant to naturally touch off awakening to the differing meanings (異趣) of the original, but regarding the original's system of expression one should look for guidance in the multifaceted notes whereby the unfolding world into which the self is cast, the reader and their daily activities are separate, and don't they become a people living in another world?[38]

Writing on the scholarly gendaigoyaku accompanying the classical text in the recent Shōgakkan edition of *Genji*, Ken Akiyama argues for the necessity of modernizations for bringing the Heian world to the reader ("その世界が私たべの前に引き寄せられる"[39]), but is in no way convinced that the translations are transparent renderings. For Akiyama the translations begin to open the world of Heian, but are secondary and derivative "spin-offs" 副産物. Compared with these marginal glossing translations, intended not as transparent mirrors·

but as scholarly guides to the texts at hand, the difference from the classical texts of the gendaigoyaku written by major authors is tremendous. What concerns the argument at hand is less Akiyama's normative language than the recognition of this alterity stemming from the "interior of the translator." Where readers have to search the text to find the names of writers of the scholarly marginal translations, the popular translations scream the names of their translators on the covers and title pages. Perhaps surprisingly for those who would deconstruct the transparency of translations, in the case of Yosano's, Tanizaki's, and Enchi's gendaigoyaku, the name of the putative author, Murasaki Shikibu, is nowhere to be found on covers or title pages. These are not translations of Murasaki Shikibu's tale, but rather translations of *Genji* according to Yosano, Tanizaki, and Enchi. The subjectivity of the new author/translator is always opaque.

These writers of gendaigoyaku hold no illusion of transparency with their urge to bring the difficult translated to a wider audience. Though, to varying degrees, translators tend to note their own sympathies for and understandings of the "original text" (原文), an originary author (Murasaki Shikibu), or the Heian court, all are aware of the manipulations, embellishments, and elisions their translations inscribe. In short, though *simpatico* is overtly stated as justification for the right to translate, none are so bold as to suggest that their versions equal the classic. And here, though it would seem to argue for the perception of a derivative inferiority of translation, gendaigoyaku, precisely in their stated difference from the classics, gain individual identity. Authors admit the "damage" done to the original and, in so doing, construct the being of the translation, a being that is not partial, derivative, or subordinate, but as whole, independent, and self-contained as any other text.

Though in the end Venuti negates the importance of simpatico as a criteria of translation, he recognizes the seductive temptation of the belief in sameness: "The translator works better when he and the author are *simpatico*, . . . (meaning) not just 'agreeable' or 'congenial,' . . . but also 'possessing an underlying sympathy.' The translator should not merely get along with the author, not merely find him likeable; there should also be an identity between them."[40] Here Venuti raises the myth of the common identity, the common being that Nancy calls "fascist" and "non-communitarian." Despite the fact that all such common identities are dangerous fictions that can erase individuality and freedom, identity politician Gayatri Spivak, too argues for a similar notion of simpatico: "Unless the translator has *earned the right* to become the intimate reader, she cannot surrender to the text, cannot respond to the special call of the text."[41] While Spivak would argue that Tanizaki had never truly earned the right, the logical extreme to her brand of identity politics would end in his presumptuous proclamation: "I feel that we cannot easily forgive (Genji's) contrivances with other women and the sweet words exchanged. I am a feminist (フェミニスト) so I feel this even more."[42] This declaration, though dubious, perhaps, results from the belief in shared common being. While this kind of belief exemplified also in both Akiko Yosano's and Fumiko Enchi's comments,[43] may provide added motivation and incentive during the painstaking process of translation, it does not necessarily have the effect of producing translations that exhibit a common being, but rather ones that share a being in common with the Heian texts. That is, rather than producing texts that are derivative ancestors of some tradition, this belief has the end of producing unique texts with identities of their own, which, because of the agency inherent in such identity, can then share in a literary community with the Heian text. This community of individual texts is most apparent in the comments on gendaigoyaku that speak of their different and unique styles.

Here we shall find no assumption of the anonymity of the translator, but rather continual praise of the particular personality of the translator. On the publication of Akiko Yosano's first of three gendaigoyaku, both Bin Ueda and Ōgai Mori fixate on the suitableness of Yosano to the job; Ueda writes, "When I heard that a modern spoken word translation (現代口語訳) of Genji monogatari was being published from the hand of Ms. Yosano, I celebrated the fact that for this work they've hit on the most suitable person."[44] Later in the same preface, Ueda praises the loss of honorifics in her version. Here it is not that Yosano is best suited because of her ability to transparently render the original in modern Japanese, but rather that she has a modern style well suited to rewrite Genji for the modern age. Mishima similarly draws attention *not* to the relative transparency of different gendaigoyaku, but rather to their individual style. Lamenting Tanizaki's lack of *kango* 漢語 (Sinified words), Mishima comments, "Now Tanizaki's is really very characteristic, but Yosano's, well, that is the one I really like. It's so chic (ハイカラ). It's got the feel of a woman's Blue Stocking novel from Meiji."[45] Though critical of the *kango* style of Mishima, Yosano, and Ōgai, Tanizaki concurs, declaring the matter to be one of style: "A long time ago, Mr. Ōgai said something like Genji is one kind of bad style (一種悪文) but thinking about it, Genji's sentences are not at all suited to the personality of Mr. Ōgai by their very nature. One might say that Mr. Ōgai's deeply thought-out, word-by-word, clear style without excess is exactly the opposite of Genji's."[46] Whatever writers may state the "essence" of *the* classical Genji to be, such "essence" always relates to issues of style for translators and readers alike; furthermore, in the wealth of writing about their work, translators continually show a consciousness of choosing a new style and manner. Aware of her own agency in her translation, Enchi writes:

> [T]he concise (streamlined 流線型) beauty of the expert, *kana* hand that wrote the sentences in Genji cannot possibly be communicated in modern Japanese; while doing this trial run of a translation I felt keenly that if you force the communicating you end up with the exact opposite result. So, daringly, I took the concise beauty that combines strength and softness and threw it out in the modern sentences.[47]

Though Enchi calls herself "daring" while attempting to avoid doing the "opposite" of the classic, she later recognizes that changes are inevitable: "It is a natural fact that, when we read the original from our viewpoint of 1970's Japan, the light and echoes through which our reality will creep will necessarily differ from those Genji readers in the dawn of Heian."[48] In an interview after the release of his memoirs on translating Genji, Osamu Hashimoto goes even further than Enchi, declaring his sovereignty as an author while expressing his desire to "torment" the icon, Murasaki Shikibu: "'Torment' means, of course, taking Murasaki's subject matter and doing something else with it (題材に何か別のことをやること). . . . As for me, if Murasaki Shikibu read both *Genji's Requiem* (Hashimoto's memoirs, *Genji kuyō* 源氏供養) and *Half-Baked Genji* (his translation, *Yōhen Genji monogatari* 窯変源氏物語) and went into a jealous frenzy and ripped them up, I'd be happy."[49] Though perhaps overstated here, that the gendaigoyaku "tramples" the "original" is rarely forgotten by translators and readers alike.

Though the gendaigoyaku is a translation, it represents a form of translation rarely encountered in current North American discussions of translation—a form in which style is always foregrounded, in which change is assumed, and in which the original text is far from sacred. Takehiko Noguchi writes:

> The language of literature is recycled in the language of the next literature. . . . In the vernacular (俗語) translations of classical works, the language is not just the accumulation of various individual meta-languages (メタ言語). Even for those who claim an unabridged translation is derivative (secondary, 二次的), the language must be consistent with itself. For instance, Akiko Yosanov, Jun'ichirō Tanizaki and lately Fumiko Enchi's modernizations of *Genji monogatari* must be independent creations (自立した作品).[50]

This independence of gendaigoyaku is necessary for them to be translations. If they merely repeat the text in wholly transparent form, then they may end with the extreme translation in Borges's "Pierre Menard, Author of the Quixote," one that is so precise it repeats the original word for word.[51]

Merely seeking the difference of these texts, merely locating them in their biographical, political, social, and historical discursive moments would insufficiently address the identities of these gendaigoyaku. Though such studies may return agency to the translator in cultures where transparency is assumed, they tend to deny the relationship among texts in order to do so. Translations do share something with the translated, but this sharing is not the communicating of one text's message to another, the erasing of one by another, the domineering of one over another, or the embellishment of one text at the expense of the other. This sharing is the being-in-common, the standing-in-relation between two texts. How such texts (gendaigoyaku) stand in relation to other texts (intertexts) can only be sought through a careful analysis of differences *and* similarities, and, thereby, of consideration of what difference and similarity mean. As a reflection on how certain kinds of translations exist in certain moments, this essay is only a first step in a process of highlighting the functioning of a literary communism, the risk and promise of which would depend on the careful delineation of the similarities and differences between several versions of gendaigoyaku.

NOTES

1. Naoki Sakai, *Translation and Subjectivity: On Japan and Cultural Nationalism*, (Minneapolis: University of Minnesota Press, 1997), p. 3.

2. Jean-Luc Nancy, *The Inoperative Community*, trans. Peter Connor, Theory and History of Literature, vol. 76 (Minneapolis: University of Minnesota Press, 1991), p. xl.

3. Gayatri Chakravorty Spivak, "The Politics of Translation," in *Destabilizing Theory: Contemporary Feminist Debates*, eds. Michèle Barrett and Anne Phillips, (Stanford: Stanford University Press, 1992), p. 178.

4. The late nineteenth century movement to "unify" written and spoken forms, that is to make written, literary Japanese more like spoken Japanese. Arguments for *genbun'itchi* tend to revolve around the as-it-is quality of spoken form and the need for similar transparency in written language.

5. See Hall and Bhabha on articulations and appropriations. Stuart Hall, "On Postmodernism and Articulation," in *Stuart Hall: Critical Dialogues in Cultural Studies*, eds. David Morley and Kuan-Hsing Chen (New York: Routledge, 1996); Homi K. Bhabha, "Signs Taken For Wonders: Questions of Ambivalence and Authority Under a Tree Outside Delhi, May 1817," *The Location of Culture* (New York: Routledge, 1994), passim.

6. Anthony Pym, *Translation and Text Transfer: an Essay on the Principles of Intercultural Communication* (Frankfurt am Main: Peter Lang, 1992); Antoine Berman, *The Experience of the Foreign: Culture and Translation in Romantic Germany* (Albany: State University of New York Press, 1992); Venuti, *The Translator's Invisibility*; Venuti, *Scandals*.

7. By "foreignizing," I mean here a translation that interrupts the grammar of the target language. Walter Benjamin, "Task of the Translator." Here we might also note that Luise von Flotow-Evans has argued for translations that actively confront, change, and improve their text. She concentrates on feminist retranslations of the Bible. Luise von Flotow-Evans, *Translation and Gender: Translating in the "Era of Feminism,"* Translation Theories Explained, ed. Anthony Pym, vol. 2 (Ottawa: University of Ottawa Press, 1997), passim.

8. Venuti, *Scandals*, 6.

9. David Bellos, "Translation, Imitation, Appropriation: On Working With Impossible Texts," in *On Translating French Literature and Film*, ed. Harris, Rodopi (Atlanta: Rodopi, 1996), p. 12. For Bellos, the only text impossible to translate is written with "pragmatic, pictorial, numerical or other non-lexical, non-grammatical, non-linguistic features of the signified"(13). This is a claim that is substantiated by the number of translations of seemingly impossible texts. In addition to Bellos's translations of Perec, one might add the Japanese translations of James Joyce's *Ulysses*, or the numerous foreign language translations of *Genji monogatari*.

10. Sakai, *Translation and Subjectivity*, p. 9.

11. Nancy, *The Inoperative Community*, p. 40.

12. Ibid. pp. 33–34.

13. "Translate," *The Oxford English Dictionary*, eds. J. A. Simpson and E.S.C. Weiner, 2d ed., vol. 20 (New York: Oxford University Press, 1989).

14. "*Yaku*: to take linguistic expressions and systematically change them into another language, the passing on of meaning. See *hon'yaku* [translation] *tsūyaku* [interpret] and *yakubun* [version]." From "Yaku," *Kōjien*, ed. Izuru Shinmura, Dai 4-han. (Tōkyō: Iwanami Shoten, 1991)

15. Modernizations of Middle English texts like Chaucer or even Shakespeare abound, but rarely are used beyond the high school level. However, Seamus Heaney's recent modernization of the Old English *Beowulf* will probably be more widely read than the original. This is comparable to the case of modernizations by famous authors of classical Japanese, with the notable difference that where there are few classics of Old English, many of the canonical works of Japanese literature stem from within one hundred years of *Genji*; yet it is the language and story of *Genji* that has appealed to scores of writers throughout the

twentieth century to a greater degree than other Heian literature. (Most notably, only *Genji* and *Heike* have been translated into modern Japanese by famous writers in the last few years.)

16. It is not insignificant that one of the early essays in the *genbun'itchi* debates ended in attempt at *gendaigoyaku*, that is in rewriting several sentences from classical texts in a *genbun'itchi* style. Takami Mozume, "Gembun'itchi," *Meiji bunka zenshū*, vol. 20 (Tōkyō: Nihon Hyōronsha, 1967).

17. Haruo Shirane, *The Bridge of Dreams: A Poetics of the Tale of Genji.* (Stanford: Stanford University Press, 1987), p. 226.

18. Takuya Tamagami, "Monogatari ondokuron josetu—*Genji monogatari* no honsei (sono ichi)—," *Genji monōgatari hyōshaku*, ed. Takuya Tamagami, vol. 13 (Tōkyō: Kadokawa Shoten, 1964–1969), passim.

19. Aileen Gatten, "The Order of the Early Chapters in the *Genji monogatari*," *Harvard Journal of Asiatic Studies* 41(1), 1981, passim.

20. See Okada, Bowring, and Shirane, passim. Richard Okada, *Figures of Resistance: Language, Poetry, and Narrating in The Tale of Genji and Other Mid-Heian Texts*, Post-Contemporary Interventions (Durham: Duke University Press, 1991); Richard John Bowring, *Murasaki Shikibu, The Tale of Genji*, Landmarks of World Literature (New York: Cambridge University Press, 1988).

21. Michael Riffaterre, *Semiotics of Poetry* (Bloomington: Indiana University Press, 1978), pp. 20–22.

22. Bowring, *Murasaka Shikibu*, p. 81.

23. Okada, *Figures of Resistence*, p. 20. Teika lamented, "As there was not an authoritative text, I inquired about in an attempt to obtain one. I compared various texts, but all were in the worst state of disorder, fraught with omissions and obscurities" (Bowring, p. 84).

24. Takehiko Noguchi, *"Genji monogatari" o Edo kara yomu* (Tōkyō: Kōdansha, 1985), p. 90.

25. Masashi Nishizawa, *Genji monogatari o shiru jiten*, (Tōkyō: Tōkyōdō Shuppan, 1998), p. 233. See also Uesaka Nobuo on several television versions. Nobuo Uesaka, *Genji monogatari no shii. Josetsu* (Tōkyō: Yūbun Shoin, 1982), p. 390.

26. Akio Abe and Yutaka Yamanaka, "*Genji monogatari* no miryoku," in *Genji monogatari no shiteki kenkyū*, ed. Yutaka Yamanaka (Tōkyō: Shibunkaku, 1997), p. 425.

27. Nishizawa, *Genji monogatari o shiru jiten*, p. 230.

28. Yukio Mishima and Harumi Setouchi, "*Genji monogatari* to gendai," in *Hihyō shūsei Genji monogatari*, ed. Akiyama Ken, vol. 3 (Tōkyō: Yumani Shoten, 1999), p. 177.

29. Ivan I. Morris, *The World of the Shining Prince; Court Life in Ancient Japan*, (New York: Knopf, 1964), p. 279.

30. Rintarō (Ōgai) Mori, "*Shinyaku Genji monogatari* jo," in *Hihyō shūsei Genji monogatari*, p. 92.

31. "And for *Genji* there are many writings that shorten and clarify the plot. But even if you know the interpretations and the plot outline, it doesn't mean that you will necessarily enjoy the entirety of the work." Yoshio Yamada, "Tanizaki-shi to *Genji monogatari*— kōetsusha no kotoba," in *Hihyō shūsei Genji monogatari*, p. 282. This concept is also expressed in Ueda Bin's introduction to Yosano's gendaigoyaku twenty years earlier. "In order to enjoy the voluptuous beauty of the entirety, generally, people will inevitably desire a modernization. I think that this is the *raison d'etre* of Yosano Akiko's modernization." Bin Ueda, "*Shinyaku Genji monogatari* jo," in *Hihyō shūsei Genji monogatari*, p. 96.

32. Fumiko Enchi and Shikibu Murasaki, *Genji monogatari*, Shinchō bunko, vol. 1, 6

vols. (Tōkyō: Shinchōsha, 1979), pp. 3–4. She also recalls the experience as one of going through a "steep, long mountain tunnel."

33. Ibid.

34. Julie Candler Hayes, "Look but don't read: Chinese characters and the translating drive from John Wilkins to Peter Greenaway," *Modern Language Quarterly*, September 1999, p. 354.

35. Yamada, "Tanizaki-shi to *Genji monogatari*—kōetsusha no kotoba," p. 281.

36. Takuya Tamagami, "Keigo no bungakuteki kōsatsu—*Genji monogatari* no honsei (sono ni)," in *Genji monogatari hyōshaku*, ed. Takuya Tamagami, vol. 13 (Tōkyō: Kadokawa Shoten, 1964–1969), p. 143.

37. Musubana Kitamura, "*Genji monogatari* no henyō—gendaigoyakuron—1," *Kindai* 65(12), 1988, p. 77.

38. Ken Akiyama, "Mirai wo hiraku chie no hōten," in *Genji monogatari*, eds. A. Abe, Ken Akiyama, G. Imai and H. Suzuki, vol. 20, Nihon koten bungaku zenshū (Tōkyō: Shogakkan, 1994), p. 3.

39. Ibid.

40. Venuti, *The Translator's Invisibility*, p. 273.

41. Spivak, "The Politics of Translation," p. 181.

42. Jun'ichirō Tanizaki, "Nikumare kuchi," in *Hihyō shūsei Genji monogatari*, p. 135.

43. See G. G. Rowley, "Textual malfeasance in Yosano Akiko's *Shin'yaku Genji monogatari*," *Harvard Journal of Asiatic Studies* 58(1), 1998, and Fumiko Enchi, *Genji monogatari shiken*, Shinchō bunko (Tōkyō: Shinchōsha, 1974) passim.

44. Ueda, "*Shinyaku Genji monogatari* jo," 94. Ōgai follows suit, "If you ask who among our generation is a person suitable for translating *Genji monogatari* the people, there is probably no one but Yosano Akiko." (Mori, "*Shinyaku Genji monogatari* jo," p. 92).

45. Mishima and Setouchi, "*Genji monogatari* to gendai," p. 177.

46. Tanizaki, "Nikumare kuchi," p. 137.

47. Enchi, *Genji monogatari*, p. 6.

48. Ibid., p. 7.

49. Naoko Okada, "'Genji kuyō' jōge maki—Hashimoto Osamu: Watashi no kaita hon—Intabyū," *Fujin kōron* 79(5), 1994, pp. 358–9.

50. Noguchi, "*Genji monogatari*" o Edo kara yomu, p. 206.

51. Jorge Luis Borges, "Pierre Menard, Author of the Quixote," *Labyrinths* (New York: New Directions, 1962), passim.

Translation with No Original: Scandals of Textual Reproduction

EMILY APTER

In a short story titled "The Dialect of the Tribe" by the American Oulipo writer Harry Mathews, the narrator ponders an academic article authored by an Australian anthropologist of the 1890s by the name of Ernest Botherby. The article is of interest because it offers the example of a mysterious technique, "used by the Pagolak-speaking tribe to translate their tongue into the dialects of their neighbors. 'What was remarkable about this method was that while it produced translations that foreign listeners could understand and accept, it also concealed from them the original meaning of every statement made.'"[1] The narrator is immediately intrigued: "To translate successfully and not reveal one's meaning—what could be more paradoxical? What could be more relevant?. . . . What could be more extraordinary than a method that would allow words to be 'understood' by outsiders without having their substance given away?" (HC 8–9). "You and I might know," the narrator confides with smug Eurocentrism to the reader, "that translation may, precisely, exorcise the illusion that substantive content exists at all—but what led a remote New Guinean tribe to such a discovery?" (HC 10). These ironic questions tap into primal truisms of translation: to wit: something is always lost in translation; unless one knows the language of the original, the exact nature and substance of what is lost will be always impossible to ascertain; even if one has access to the language of the original, there remains an x-factor of untranslatability that renders every translation an impossible world or faux regime of semantic and phonic equivalence. What makes Mathews's story so clever, in the manner, say, of Jorge Luis Borges's short story "Tlön, Uqbar, Orbis Tertius" (in which the place-name "Uqbar," presumed to be a variant on the name of the country of Iraq, is suspected of being an "undocumented country . . . deliberately invented . . . to substantiate a phrase"), is that it reveals the way in which translations are always trying to disguise the impossibility of fidelity to the original tongue.[2] In the Mathews story, it is the delusional belief that a possible world of translatability exists that induces the narrator to defect from his own language into a Pagolak-speaking world. Translation is thus revealed to be a special case of literature "hors de ce monde"—"Any where out of the world!"—to borrow Baudelaire's famous phrase; that is to say, a literary world that is possible, indeed even plausible, only insofar as it actualizes a parallel universe in and on its own terms.

The narrator's election to enter a possible world of translatability brings to mind the contention of the language philosopher David Lewis that a plurality of worlds must be posited hypothetically, to exist, if the rules of the language allow for it. Lewis's truth-conditional theory of semantics is concerned to determine the conditions under which a sentence is true. Language, he has asserted, needs to be able to talk about things that may not exist, as in the sentence, "Someone seeks a unicorn." We know that the creature doesn't exist but the sentence can be understood. If the meaning of p is posited as true, by necessity, then Lp is true in given worlds in which p is.[3] This grammar of necessity, positing the hypothetical grounds of linguistic and literary possible worlds, may well yield what Umberto Eco has referred to as "lunatic linguistics." Eco traces this language lunacy back to Gabriel Foigny's invention of a self-translating "austral" grammar, in his 1676 work *La Terre australe connue*, but one finds numerous examples closer to the contemporary period in those writers cherished by Deleuze and Foucault who created their own private worlds of syntactic and lexical "shizanalyse": J-C Brisset, Raymond Roussel, and Louis Wolfson.[4] What these writers have in common is the ability to make standard language strange to itself—superimposing their own private grammatical logics and laws of homonymic and syllabic substitution onto the vehicular tongue, such that it remains quasi-intelligible; in a state, if you will, of semi-translation. For a recent example of this process, consider Jonathan Safran Foer's 2002 best-seller, *Everything is Illuminated*, narrated by a young Russian translator whose stilted English is riddled with malapropisms and American pop-cultural lingo. Here, the reader is entered into a possible world that could be characterized as the language limbo of the non-native speaker.[5] In such cases of "lunatic linguistics" we discover an order of language that is not pure babel, but something between a discrete or standard language and a translation; a language-in-a-state-of-translation, that becomes "possible" according to the criteria of modal realism and counterfactual logic used by David Lewis to define the conditions of possibility.

What interests me here is not so much the argument, albeit a fascinating one, over whether possible world theory is useful to the analysis of self-translating private languages (languages that are cybernetic in their capacity to generate new grammatical logics for each new possible linguistic world), but rather, the ethical problem that arises when there is, strictly speaking, no "original" language or text on which the translation is based. The reader is either placed in a netherworld of "translatese" that floats between original and translation, or confronted with a situation in which the translation mislays the original, absconding to some other world of textuality that retains the original only as fictive pretext. In both instances, the identity of what a translation *is* is tested; for if a translation is not a form of textual predicate, indexically pointing to a primary text, then what is it? Can a literary technology of reproduction that has sublated its origin still be considered a translation? Or should it be considered the premier illustration of translational ontology, insofar as it reveals the extent to which all translations are unreliable transmitters of the original, a regime, that is, of extreme untruth?

Translation studies typically frame the ethics of textual infidelity in terms of a translation's infelicitous rendering of an original (measured as lack of accuracy, formal and grammatical similitude, literary flair or poetic feeling), or in terms of the target text's dubious connection to its source; its status as pseudo or fictitious translation. As part of a larger effort to rethink the critical premises of translation studies,[6] I will be concentrating on the latter case, taking up issues of how to interpret celebrated examples of texts that have turned out to be translations with no originals. My purpose is not to visit the scandal of pseudotranslation for its own sake, but to explore the broader ethical issues surrounding textual reproduction that such scandals bring into theoretical focus.

Douglas Robinson (following Anton Popopvic) defines pseudotranslation as "not only a text pretending, or purporting, or frequently taken to be a translation, but also . . . a translation that is frequently taken to be an original work." As Robinson sees it, any work "whose status as 'original' or 'derivative' is, for whatever social or textual reason, problematic" qualifies as pseudotranslation.[7] This broad definition creates as many problems as it solves by inviting controversy over which kind of texts should qualify as pseudotranslation. James MacPherson's 1760 "translation" of "Ossianic" poems, *Fragments of ancient poetry translated from the Gaelic or Erse language*, clearly warrant designation as such, but other examples—Longfellow's *Hiawatha* (putatively based on a Finnish scholar's transposition of Chippewa legends), or medieval glosses of Roman texts—inhabit a fuzzy zone between translation and transcription and become harder to classify as pseudo.

Pseudotranslation, as Robinson's definition suggests, invites emphasis on the exposure of fraudulent translations, with the critic's efforts concentrated on rectifying mistaken attributions in literary history, on drawing generic distinctions between model and imitation, or on refining criteria used in authenticating the status and value of an original work of literature. The literary scandals and accusations of forgery opened up by allegations of pseudotranslation are not unlike the connoisseur wars raging around the de-attribution of pricey masterpieces in prestigious museums and private collections worldwide. The drama of revelation—of fakery and forgery laid bare—is what drives this kind of interpretation thematically. By contrast, if the issue of textual fidelity to the original is defined in terms of a theory of textual reproduction, the focus shifts from questions of textual veracity and sham to the conditions of the original's reproducibility. The problem of authorial counterfeit is thus displaced by consideration of whether a translation is born not from a "real" original (an authenticated work by a given author), but from a kind of test tube text of simulated originality; a text, if you will, that is unnaturally or artificially birthed and successfully replicated. The idea of textual cloning—emphasizing, in a metaphorical way, literary analogues to genic coding, copying, and blueprinting—problematizes "the work of art in the age of genetic reproduction" in a way that brings Walter Benjamin's famous essay on "The Work of Art in the Age of Mechanical Reproduction" (1936) into colloquy with controversies over the status of original identity in the age of the genome project.[8] As a code of codes (a kind of HTML or master-code used in machine translation), translation becomes definable as a cloning mechanism of textual transference or reproducibility rather than as a discrete form of secondary textuality predicated on an auratic original. Benjamin's equally famous essay "The Task of the Translator" (1923) also returns in another guise. His identification of translation as that which usurps the place of the original while ensuring its after-life, may be used to associate textual cloning with the idea of a reproductively en-gineered original, (comparable, say, to the replication of RNA molecules in a test tube), or with a translation that grows itself anew from the cells of a morbid or long-lost original. Under these circumstances, it is increasingly difficult to distin-guish between original and cloned embryonic forms; indeed the whole category of originality—as an essentialist life-form—becomes subject to dispute.

Pseudotranslation versus textual cloning: two paradigms that address problem-atic originality in the field of translation studies, two paradigms that are concep-tually related, but emphasize distinctly different problems and questions. My par-ticular interest here will be in exploring what the concept of textual cloning might bring to the age-old discussion of textual fidelity in translation studies; how it shifts the terms of translation studies, from original and translation, to clone and code.

Pseudotranslation

There are few more flagrant cases of pseudotranslation than Pierre Louÿs's *Les Chansons de Bilitis* [Songs of Bilitis], published in 1894 with the subtitle *traduites du grec pour la première fois par P.L.* [translated from the Greek for the first time by P.L.] and marketed as the translation of works by a sixth-century half Greek/half Turkish poetess. Louÿs, as his biographer Jean-Paul Goujon notes, was educated in the manner of the great nineteenth-century philologists and historians: Michelet, Quinet, Renan, Mommsen, Taine, Littré, and Gaston Paris among others. Philological dogma was frequently marshaled in the service of translation. Leconte de Lisle, a mentor to Louÿs, was, from 1861 on, dedicating his energies to translations of Theocritus, Homer, Aeschylus, and Euripides.[9] Claiming archeological as well as poetic value, the studies of antiquity that emerged in the second half of the nineteenth century inspired Louÿs to follow suit: first, because he believed he could do better in restaging the past; second, because he suspected erotic censorship on the part of academic classicists; and third, because he was a proponent of Greek decadence, promoting Alexandrian Greek literature (deemed barbaric or obscene) over and against the privileged literature of fifth-century Athens (PL 92). Lucan, Meleager, Theocritus, and Sappho, each orientalized, homosexualized, and sensualized to the maximum, formed the canon of Louÿs's "other Hellenism" according to Goujon. Bilitis was billed as a writer of Turkish Greek origin, and Louÿs's translation of Meleager was acclaimed for its invention of a "hellenized Orient" or Syrianized Greece (PL 92).

When *Les Chansons de Bilitis* was initially published, Rémy de Gourmont be-stowed fulsome praise: "A personal manner, that is to say, a new way of experiencing an old form of Greek poetry full of ideas and images that have passed into the public domain, restores to this poetry a beauty that it had lost or had relinquished when it was translated by a mediocre professor."[10] It was just such a "mediocre professor," however, who ostensibly discovered the original manuscript of Bilitis's poems and served as their first translator. When Louÿs published *Les Chansons* he included notes on the text's provenance, claiming that the erotic prose poems were discovered by a German philologist by the name of G. Heim in the course of an archeological excavation in Cypress. When Louÿs delivered the manuscript to his editor Bailly, he maintained that it was a French translation of Heim's German translation from the Greek. Despite allegations of error in his previous translations of Meleager and Lucan's *Scenes from the Lives of Courtesans*, Louÿs's reputation as a classicist passed muster and contributed to the favorable reception of *Les Chansons* when it was first published.

Initially, Louÿs confided the secret of the text's true author only to his brother George Louis, but a number of friends detected the ruse, including Gide, Valéry, Debussy, and Hérédia. Gide may have unwittingly helped the hoax along by introducing Louÿs to the Algerian courtesan Meryem bent-Ali, thought to have been the live model for the figure of the Greek courtesan. Several critics suspected that the text had a fictitious origin, among them Camille Mauclair, who lauded the book as a "livre d'art" rather than as a translation, and Henri de Régnier, who wrote: "I do not know if Bilitis ever existed, but certainly she lives fully in these little poems that M. Louÿs has collected, and engraved on the walls of her pungent, imaginary tomb" (CB 327). Other readers, however, seem to fall into the trap; one sent Louÿs some "variants on the translation," and the respected classicist, Gustave Fougère, to whom Louÿs had sent copies of both *Les Chansons* and his Meleager translation, wrote back: "Bilitis and Meleager were not unknown to me, for a long time I have considered them personal friends" (CB 322). Working closely with poems by Sapphic epigones, and putting literary sleuths off the scent by acknowledging his poetic license (especially in the most decadent sections of the song cycle), Louÿs took special precautions to guarantee that this paleographic mock-up would be received as an authentic translation. He suppressed his initial temptation to oversimulate the look of a scholarly edition by reducing the plethora of notes, providing a scaled-down yet plausible "Life" of Bilitis, and including an addendum of so-called untranslated verse. In the book's preface Louÿs wrote:

> I wanted this story to be Bilitis's, because in translating the *Songs* I myself fell in love with this lover of Mnasidika. Her life was undoubtedly as marvelous as it seems. I only regret that the classical authors did not speak of her more, and that the records that survived were not so meager in providing information about her life. Philodemus, who ransacked her work twice, does not even mention her name.[11] (CB 25)

The success of Louÿs's *supercherie* (even though it only lasted until 1898 when the text was "outed" coincident with the release of the second edition), was helped along by the vogue of Greek revivalism in fin-de-siècle erotic literature. The work's reception was buoyed by the reading public's keen appetite for

Baudelairean Lesbos and Parnassian pastoral love poetry. The same appetite was responsible for the later popularity of Natalie Clifford Barney's 1902 *Cinq Petits Dialogues grecs* [Five Short Greek Dialogues] and Renée Vivien's free translations of Sappho that appeared in 1903. Anticipating Rémy de Gourmont and Natalie Clifford Barney's reinvestment of the Amazon myth, and André Gide's appropriation of Platonic dialogue for gay polemic in *Corydon*, Louÿs placed utopian sexual politics at the heart of his agenda in using Greek conceits to express feminine same-sex love. In a letter to his brother he declared his intention to liberate the expression of lesbian desire from the shackles of the femme fatale stereotype, and he "respectfully" dedicated the *Chansons* "to the young women of future society."[12] Louÿs confided to his brother that he thought of lesbian love as a "deformation" not of love but of maternal instinct. Expressive of the essence of femininity unencumbered by Christian morality, lesbianism affords an ideal sexual paradigm of fecundity without biological reproduction. In "Hymn to Astarté," we find this idea of contraceptive reproducibility affixed to a figure of the sui generis Mother: "Mother, inexhaustible, incorruptible, creator, born first, engendered by yourself, conceived by yourself, issue of yourself alone, you, who pleasures herself, Astarté/O perpetually fecund, o virgin and universal wet-nurse" (CB 137). The apparent oxymoron of fertile sterility resurfaces in other poems in the cycle descriptive of lesbian love-making. "Les Seins de Mnasidika" for example, features Mnasidika making an offering of her breasts to Bilitis in lieu of offspring: "Love them well, she tells me; I love them so! They are dear ones, little children" (CB 101). Bilitis conflates maternal and erotic associations as she vows to play with the little breasts, to wash them with milk and put them to bed in wool blankets. Mnasidika enjoins her lover to become a wet-nurse to her breasts: "Since they are so far from my mouth, kiss them for me," she orders Bilitis (CB 101).

In attempting to pass as the translator of erotic verse by a woman writer, Louÿs, one could argue, was to fin-de-siècle France what Kenneth Rexroth was to postwar America. In much the same way as his decadent forbear, Rexroth, the proto-beat poet, introduced the voice of a Japanese woman author by the name of Marichiko in an anthology that he edited, titled *One Hundred More Poems from the Japanese* (1974). Rexroth was active as a translator from the earliest stages of his literary career until the end, publishing collections of translations that included: *100 Poems from the Chinese*; *Love and the Turning Year: 100 More Poems from the Chinese*; *The Orchid Boat: the Women Poets of China* (with Ling Chung); *Poems from the Greek Anthology*; *100 Poems from the Japanese*; *100 More Poems from the Japanese*; *30 Spanish Poems of Love and Exile*; and *Selected Poems of Pierre Reverdy*. He apparently had serviceable knowledge of Chinese and Japanese, and worked in close collaboration with native speakers whose technical renderings provided the grist for his own compositional arrangements.

When it came to publishing these collaboratively produced translations under his own name, Rexroth seems to have evinced no qualms. In a preface to the first anthology of Japanese poems, he gave the impression that he was the sole translator: "In my own translations I have tried to interfere as little as possible with the simplicity of the Japanese text. . . . Some of my versions manage with considerably fewer syllables than the originals. On the other hand, I have not sacrificed certain Japanese ornaments which some have considered nonsense or decorative excrescences."[13] Characterizing his translations as literal, in the manner of Arthur Waley, Rexroth assures the reader that his respect for the poems has allowed him to preserve the integrity of the original Japanese in American English. Of course, there was nothing particularly unusual, especially at the time, for a poet-translator to take full credit for a translation that was only partly his or her own. But what makes such credit-grabbing stand out in hindsight is that it attests to a cavalier attitude toward authorship that was later confirmed by Rexroth's publication of his own "translations" under Marichiko's phantom imprimatur.

Rexroth's biographer Linda Hamalian treats the Marichiko hoax as a career curiosity rather than as a scandal of authorial counterfeit:

> In the last decades of his life, Rexroth did a very curious thing: he published a book of his own poems but identified them as translations from the work of Marichiko, "the pen name of a contemporary young woman who lives near the temple of Marishi-ben in Kyoto." Marishi-ben is patron goddess of geisha, prostitutes, women in childbirth, and lovers. At first, he tried to fool his readers, his publishers and his friends into believing the writer actually existed. In the Marichiko poems, he explored every aspect of what he imagined to be one woman's psyche in order to come to terms with how he as a man who had professed great love for women, could at last acquire a rudimentary understanding of woman's nature.[14]

In his monograph, *Revolutionary Rexroth: Poet of East-West Wisdom*, Morgan Gibson glides over the question of the unacknowledged "invention," preferring to frame the Marichiko poems as Rexroth's way of paying tribute to Yosano Akiko (1878–1942), famous for her sexually daring love poetry and often deemed to be "the greatest woman poet of modern Japan."[15] Noting the narrative parallels in the Marichiko cycle to "a Tantric parable of contemplative ecstacy, in which the goddess Marishiben unites with Buddha," Gibson reads the Marichiko poems as Rexroth's most successful representation of feminine "erotic enlightenment" (RR 84).

It remains to be seen whether Rexroth's "feminist" justification for his specious translation is particularly convincing. Some would say he used feminism opportunistically as cover for the expropriation of feminine literary voice, or as a means of eluding the radar of erotic censorship. Certainly Rexroth's performance of gender ventriloquism has been construed by his critics as a self-serving effort to whitewash his reputation as a predator on female students and admirers. However Rexroth's motivations are hypothetically construed, it is striking that he and Louÿs, both identified with two of the most flagrant cases of pseudotranslation, would adopt the genre of feminine erotic verse for their exercises in literary travesty.

Detection of Rexroth's forgery becomes easier the more closely the poems are examined. Superficial similarities can be found between a Yosano Akiko and a Marichiko poem: a shared hair motif, for example, allows parallels to be drawn between Akiko's "Hair unbound, in this / Hothouse of lovemaking, / Perfumed with lilies, / I dread the oncoming of / The pale rose of the end of night," and Marichiko's "I cannot forget / The perfumed dusk inside the / Tent of my black hair, / As we awoke to make love / After a long night of love," which Rexroth writes disingenuously in a footnote "echoes Yosano Akiko."[16] Further consideration, however, reveals the sexual realism of the Marichiko texts to be more graphic, more prone to Orientalist kitsch. Marichiko's verse XXXII grafts the decorative imagery of *japonisme* (flowers, boats) onto an explicit sex scene: "I hold your head tight between / My thighs, and press against your / Mouth and float away / Forever, in an orchid / Boat on the River of Heaven" (FWH 123). By contrast, an Akiko poem favors metaphorical reticence: "Press my breasts, / Part the veil of mystery, / A flower blooms there, / Crimson and fragrant" (OHM 16). Akiko's poems draw a distinct line around the autonomous object, as in this stripped-down image of a deserted boat symbolizing an abandoned woman: "Left on the beach / Full of water, / A worn out boat / Reflects the white sky / Of early autumn" (OHM 11). Rexroth's pastiche breaks down the isolationism of the lyrical "I," introducing pronominal games with gender and identity, that, knowing what we do now about the false identity of Marichiko, read like embedded clues:

> Who is there? Me.
> Me who? I am me, you are you.
> But you take my pronoun,
> And we are us. (FWH 116)

On close scrutiny the Marichiko poems fall apart as credible simulations of Japanese women's writing. But why should this matter if the Marichiko texts stand up as aesthetic artifacts in their own right? What difference does it make whether the Marichiko texts are received as genuine translations or as pseudo-translations that successfully advance the creative use of literary *japonisme* in western literature, and which place Rexroth in a continuum of distinguished writers—Mallarmé, Arthur Waley, Victor Segalen, Lafcadio Hearn, Ernest Fenellosa, Ezra Pound, W. B. Yeats, Henri Michaud, and Wallace Stevens—all of whom used literary Orientalism as a springboard to modernism and wrenched japonisme from the clutches of bad translation? (In a lecture on "The Influence of Classical Poetry on Modern American Poetry," Rexroth placed the brunt of blame for this tradition of infelicitous Japanese translation on the poet Sadakichi Hartmann, who may have been "a bohemian of bohemians," and a "wise and witty man," but who was ultimately responsible for "a long tradition of vulgarization and sentimentalization of Japanese classical poetry in translation.")[17]

Rexroth loyalists have located him squarely in this modernist tradition as a transitional figure between the early twentieth century modernists and the Beats. The Marichiko poems may fail the authenticity test but, so this version of the story goes, they are acquitted by virtue of their adherence to Rexroth's iconoclastic philosophy of translation. A good translation, he held, should not be hobbled by fidelity to the original, but rather, motivated by "advocacy": "The ideal translator, he wrote in "The Poet as Translator," "is not engaged in matching the words of a text with the words of his own language. He is hardly even a proxy, but rather an all-out advocate. His job is one of special pleading. So the prime criterion of successful poetic translation is assimilability. Does it get across to the jury?"[18] This idea of a translation as a reception-driven "case" to be made in court is complemented by a principle of translational vivacity. H.D.'s poem "Heliodora" is exemplary, because instead of "being" translation, it is, rather, "of" translation, demonstrating "the poignancy of that feeling of possession and the glamour of the beautiful Greek words as they come alive in one's very own English" (PT 22 and 26). For Rexroth, how the text communicates translational aliveness is far more important than whether or not the text accurately translates from Meleager's Greek original. Truth value is supplanted by performative value. Having shifted the ethical imperatives of translation in this way, Rexroth inadvertently clears the way for authorizing the Marichiko poems as examples of alive translation.

Of course, reading the Marichiko poems on Rexroth's terms sidesteps the larger issue of what it means for a translator to pass as a native speaker. Was Rexroth covertly sending up the reader's transferential relation to cultural affect, concentrated in a fetishism of the aesthetic codes of japonisme (haiku-esque brevity, blank spaces, ellipsis, understatement, imagism)? Was he using this exercise in textual counterfeit to reveal the reader's profound investment in conquering the other's language without actually having to learn it? However one might choose to answer these questions, the hoax illuminates the extent to which translation caters to the fantasy of having access to the foreignness of a language without the labor of the language lab.

The revelation of translational false coin leaves the reader aware of the dimension of epistemological scam or faked-up alterity inherent in all translation. The translation business is geared to keeping this scam from view, for it wants to convince readers that when it markets an author in translation, the translated text will be a truly serviceable stand-in for the original; affording a genuine translinguistic encounter with a foreign literature in the language of self-same. But cases of pseudotranslation reveal the fundamental unreliability of a translation's claim to approximating the original in another tongue.

According to this reading, the Rexroth case is scandalous not just by dint of its cultural appropriationism or caricatural Orientalism, but because it reveals the extent to which all translations qualify as a form of linguistic forgery. The implied ethics of translation presupposes a contract holding between reader and translator whereby the former assumes the good faith effort of the latter to deliver an authentic copy of the original. In breaching that contract, Louÿs and Rexroth exposed the ways in which all translators are to some extent counterfeit artists, experts at forgeries of voice and style.

TRANSLATION AS TEXTUAL CLONING

The Rexroth hoax, on first reading, highlights the case of translation as cultural forgery. But the forgery model—drawing on analogies to the connoisseurial practice of authentication—tends to reduce complex conceptual distinctions between plagiarism, counterfeit, and copy to a familiar discussion of "autographic" authenticity. According to Nelson Goodman, "a work of art is defined as 'autographic' if and only if even the most exact duplication of it does not thereby count as genuine."[19] In the Rexroth case, where there is an "autographic" reproduction of an *absent original,* the forgery model breaks down. What might be substituted in its stead is a genetic model of textual reproducibility that defines the translation as the clone of a clone (or clone of a code), that has effectively severed its primordial connection to an original subjective signature. At issue here is the way in which the notion of originality is complicated by what scientists have referred to as replication parameters. These become clear in questions around whether a program that reproduces daughter programs (as in the case of the Tierra program, "born" of the "Ancestor" computer code 85), should be considered a form of life, or whether the notion of original life should be strictly reserved for metabolizing cells whose DNA is replicated in the clone. In fabricating a text out of the codes of "Japanese-ness"-in-translation, Rexroth, I would submit, experimented with the literary equivalent of cloning from code.

Reading the Marichiko poems as models of genetic reproduction without origin points to the way in which Rexroth's very notion of poetic creation was entwined with theories of eschatology, parthenogenesis, metempsychosis, and reincarnation. During the early 1940s Rexroth immersed himself in the writings of Meister Eckehart, English mystics of the late Middle Ages, St. John of the Cross, Ouspensky, Madame Blavatsky, and Jacob Boehme's *The Signature of All Things* (the title of which Rexroth took over for one of his own collections of poetry). According to Linda Hamalian: "Since childhood Rexroth had experienced 'occasional moments of vision . . . momentary flashes of communion with others' where time and space did not exist" (H 125). This passion for Western mysticism provided a natural transition to Zen Buddhism. Rexroth discovered Arthur Waley's *The Way and Its Power,* Chinese Taosim, Tantric Buddhism, hatha and kundalini yoga (H 125). The title poem of *The Phoenix and the Tortoise*—the culminating masterwork of this period—is imbued with hybrid mysticism: the poetic subject acts as a conduit channeling the spirits of "ruined polities," from ancient Greece to the shores of California, where the body of a dead Japanese sailor has washed up, confirming fears of what will happen in the internment camps that were set up in California in the wake of Pearl Harbor. The corpse seems to make eye contact with the poet, and as he watches with "open hard eyes," the poet experiences a shock of self-identification: "Me—who stand here on the edge of death, / Seeking the continuity, / The germ plasm, of history, / The epic's lyric absolute."[20]

Genetic models of textual reproduction might seem far-fetched if it were not for the fact that Rexroth's own way of describing the creative process were not so eerily compatible with them. In his preamble to *The Phoenix and the Tortoise* he wrote: "I have tried to embody in verse the belief that the only valid conservation of value lies in the assumption of unlimited liability, the supernatural identification of the self with the tragic unity of the creative process. I hope I have made it clear that I do not believe that the Self does this by an act of Will, by sheer assertion. He who would save his life must lose it" (PT 9). The self-

perpetuating force of *bios* is introduced in a literal way as synonymous with poetic reproduction. Rexroth's evocative notion of "unlimited liability" suggests an
ethics of responsibility to the future, with poetry operating as agent and guaran-
tor of the work of art's reproducibility. And the phrase "he who would save his
life must lose it," while obviously a kind of *tao*, also brings out that aspect of
cloning that carries the megalomaniac dream of infinite self-preservation at the
expense of an originary, signature identity. Consider, in this regard, an extract
from Rexroth's epic poem, *The Phoenix and the Tortoise*, that defines "the person"
as a condition of uniqueness, embodied in perfect surrogacy: "The fulfillment of
uniqueness / In perfect identification, / In ideal representation, / As the usurping
attorney, / The real and effective surrogate" (PT 19). The mystic self, infinitely
iterated through history, is defined here as an original form of futural being
whose signature is preserved in a copy or clone, itself characterized legalistically
as a "usurping attorney"; a guardian, if you will, of the original trust. In this sense
the clone succeeds in leasing rather than appropriating or fully embodying an
original subject.

In the introduction to *The Phoenix and the Tortoise*, Rexroth also claimed that
the poem "proceeds genetically or historically" (PT 9). But the textual genetics
described by Rexroth is less like developmental evolution or hereditary transmission, and more like what we might now, in a digital era, call sampling. Rexroth
sifts through the classical archive, paraphrasing and pastiching Hellenistic,
Byzantine, and Latin Roman sources. Sometimes he draws directly from Martial,
at other moments he avowedly treats his source material more freely, inserting
paraphrases from antiquity inside larger poems, and allowing the citation pieces
to, in a sense, reprogram the new cell into which they have been placed. (As
Gina Kolata reminds us: "In cloning, scientists slip a cell from an adult into an
egg with its genetic material removed. The egg then reprograms the adult cell's
genes so that they are ready to direct the development of an embryo, then a
fetus, then a newborn that is genetically identical to the adult whose cell was
used to start the process. No one knows how the egg reprograms an adult cell's
genes.")[21] This reprogrammed work, depending on where one stands on the
ethics of cloning, could either be condemned as a tissue of plagiarized fragments,[22] or hailed as a new translational form that, following Walter Benjamin's
ascription, ensures the original's glorious afterlife.

Benjamin's theory suggests that the genetic paradigm extends the view of
translation as literary testate or inheritance to a philosophy of writing that defines translation as a mechanism of textual reproducibility. In this scheme, the
significance of origins and originality cedes to grander concerns over the work of
art's messianic perpetuity. Rexroth's faux Japanese translations, might, in these
terms, seem more legitimate: their inauthentic originality deemed the price
worth paying for a form of japonisme that bequeathed new life to American poetry. According to this reading, Robert Creeley, Gary Snyder, Philip Whalen,
and Cid Corman—all of whom credited Rexroth's Buddhist psesudotranslations
as a source of inspiration—spawned the regional/ecological/spiritual aesthetic of
California Beat poetry.

The diminished status of originality (long a fixture of avant-garde doctrine or modernist credos of authorial impersonality), finds a limit case in examples of pseudotranslation in which readers are, in effect, urged to accept the clone of a code as a replacement for the original, or to give up conventional, essentialist notions of what the original "is." As far as the ethics of translation is concerned, this demotion of originality accords the translator such license that he or she is authorized to invent an extramural or imaginary source. In this way, just as Rexroth ethically sanctioned his transcription of Japanese verse by a poet who never was, so the late James Merrill and his partner David Jackson, dedicated themselves to channeling the voices of those no longer there: Plato, Proust, Auden, Maya Deren, Maria Callas, Rimbaud, and Yeats. Alison Lurie's *Familiar Spirits: A Memoir of James Merrill and David Jackson* describes the strange, life-long fascination of the pair with the spiritist messages of the Ouija board.[23] Merrill's magnum opus *The Changing Light at Sandover* (1980) was, in the poet's own estimation, not a work of self-inspired imaginative lyric, but the most *outré* form of prosopoeia, an address from the dead transcribed "en direct." Lurie characterizes the way in which the poem "came" to Merrill and Jackson like a set of instructions in code that demanded transcription rather than an act of imaginative translation. For Lurie, this amounts to a downgrading of the poetic, a submission to the prosaic quality of code and a tragic sacrifice of lyrical talent on Merrill's part.

Merrill's *The Changing Light at Sandover* constitutes an extreme case of translation without an original; an example of translation as language code transmitted from the beyond, of instructions express-mailed from an untenable source written as master-code or program. The text is rendered through the artificial assistance of the poet, now cast as the genetic engineer or technician whose primary challenge consists in transporting the work to its afterlife (Rimbaud will be re-birthed in T. S. Eliot in the phrase: "YET RIMBAUD? IN HIS GENES WAS A V WORK CUT OFF BY LIFE. . . . Rimbaud ghostwrote 'The Waste Land'"),[24] or in preventing the garbling of instructions. Not unlike the processes of machine translation or digitally created sound; the text code is recorded, unscrambled, and recombined. Consider this excerpt from Mirabell: Book 2:

> 741 now dictates D's and my
> Vastly simplified *Basic Formulas:*
> JM: 268/I:I,000,000/5.5/741
> DJ: 289/I: 650,000/5.9/741.1 (S 143)

The poet of *Sandover* duly transcribes and decodes these numerological formulas: "Number of previous lives; then ratio / Of animal to human densities." "At 5.1 Rubenstein, 5.2; Eleanor / Roosevelt, 5.3; and so on. The Sixes are / LINDBERGH PLITSETSKAYA PEOPLE OF PHYSICAL PROWESS / & LEGENDARY HEROES / Characters from fiction and full-fledged / Abstractions came to Victor Hugo's tables" (S 143). If Victor Hugo is here transcoded as a kind of literary DNA, elsewhere in the Book of Mirabell, textual cloning is an explicit trope: "Is DNA, that sinuous molecule, / The serpent in your version of the myth?" (S 119) or "I AM A MERE MIXING AGENT WITH MY SUPERIORS" (S 155) or "CAN IT BE? DO WE FORETELL THE

CLONE?" (S 184). Cloning, in this instance, may be identified as a translational technology that banally reproduces poetic voice (repeating and unscrambling the codes by which it communicates) while providing the latter-day version of aesthetic reincarnation.

In "Task of the Translator," Benjamin defines translatability as "an essential quality of certain works." Certain originals have it—the Bible, Heine, Baudelaire—and others do not. Merrill's *Sandover*, according to Benjaminian criteria, would probably fall well below the bar of a text intrinsically worthy of translational afterlife. But what is perhaps most relevant to the ethics of translation is the way in which Benjamin implicitly devalues the original; suborning the source text (and its privileged status as *primum mobile*) to the translation (now elevated to the position of midwife in the obstetrics of translatability):

> It is plausible that no translation, however good it may be, can have any significance as regards the original. Yet, by virtue of its translatability the original is closely connected with the translation; in fact, this connection is all the closer since it is no longer of importance to the original. We may call this connection a natural one, or, more specifically, a vital connection. Just as the manifestations of life are intimately connected with the phenomenon of life without being of importance to it, a translation issues from the original—not so much from its life as from its afterlife. For a translation comes later than the original, and since the important works of world literature never find their chosen translators at the time of their origin, their translation marks their stage of continued life.[25]

Here, it would seem, translation reproduces not an original text, but an afterlife cloned from the (lost) life of the original. In shifting the ethics of translation away from questions of fiability and fidelity (crucial to determinations of pseudotranslation), and toward debates over the conditions of textual reproducibility, Benjamin provides the groundwork for defining translation in its most scandalous form: that is, as a technology of literary replication that engineers textual afterlife without recourse to a genetic origin.[26]

NOTES

1. Harry Mathews, "The Dialect of the Tribe," in *The Human Country: New and Collected Stories* (Chicago: Dalkey Archive Press, 2002), p. 8. Further references to this collection will appear in the text abbreviated HC.

2. Jorge Luis Borges, "Tlön, Uqbar, Orbis Tertius," trans. Alastair Reid, in *Ficciones* (New York: Grove Press, 1962), p. 18.

3. David Lewis, *On the Plurality of Worlds* (Oxford: Blackwell, 1986).

4. Umberto Eco, *Serendipities. Language and Lunacy*, trans. William Weaver (New York: Columbia University Press, 1998), pp. 80–81.

5. Jonathan Safran Foer, *Everything is Illuminated* (New York: Houghton Mifflin, 2002). The parts of the novel written in "translatese" are both weird and funny. English takes on the quality of a language learned word by word out of the dictionary rather than holistically. The narrator's diction, when not in flagrant violation of good grammar, opens up a

world of linguistic possibility precisely because it is off. "In Russian, he writes, my ideas are asserted abnormally well, but my second tongue is not so premium. I undertaked to input the things you counseled me to, and I fatigued the thesaurus you presented me, as you counseled me to, when my words appeared too petite or not befitting. If you are not happy with what I have performed, I command you to return it back to me. I will persevere to toil on it until you are appeased" (p. 23).

6. The work of rethinking the terms of translation studies is, of course, well underway. The ethical considerations I am raising here are indebted to Lawrence Venuti's work, particularly his book *The Scandals of Translation*.

7. Douglas Robinson, *Routledge Encyclopedia of Translation Studies*, ed. Mona Baker (New York: Routledge, 1998), p. 183.

8. Gayatri Chakravorty Spivak has also drawn out the category of translation as a "life" code. In *Death of a Discipline* (New York: Columbia University Press, 2003), she refers to the "irreducible work of translation, not from language to language but from body to ethical semiosis, that incessant shuttle is a 'life.'" In an earlier essay, "Translation as Culture," quoted in *Death of a Discipline*, she uses psychoanalysis—specifically Melanie Klein's theory of the good and bad object—as the basis for a theory of translation that in turn affords a digital model of conscience:

> The human infant grabs on to some one thing and then things. This grabbing (*begreifen* as in *das Begriff* or concept) of an outside indistinguishable from an inside constitutes an inside, going back and forth and coding everything into a sign-system by the thing(s) grasped. One can call this crude coding a "translation." In this never-ending shuttle, violence translates into conscience and vice versa. From birth to death this "natural" machine, programming the mind perhaps as genetic instructions program the body (where does body stop and mind begin?) is partly metapsychological and therefore outside the grasp of the mind. (pp. 13–14)

9. Jean-Paul Goujon, *Pierre Louÿs, Une vie secrète (1870–1925)* (Paris: Editions Seghers, 1988), p. 90. All further references to this work will appear in the text abbreviated PL.

10. Rémy de Gourmont, in a letter to Louys of January 7, 1899, as cited by Jean-Paul Goujon in his edition of *Les Chansons de Bilitis* (*Avec divers textes inédits* [Paris: Gallimard, 1990], p. 332). Further references to this work will appear in the text abbreviated CB. The original French reads: "Une manière personelle c'est-à-dire nouvelle de sentir une vieille poésie grecque pleine même d'idées et d'images passées dans le domaine commun peut donner à cette poésie une beauté qu'elle n'avait plus et qu'elle n'as pas quand elle est sentie et traduite par un médiocre professeur."

11. "Je voudrais que cette histoire fût celle de Bilitis, car, en traduisant ses *Chansons*, je me suis mis à aimer l'amie de Mnasidika. Sans doute sa vie fut toute aussi merveilleuse. Je regrette seulement qu'on n'en ait pas parlé davantage et que les auteurs anciens, ceux du moins qui ont survécu, soient si pauvre de renseignements sur sa personne. Philodème, qui l'a pillée deux fois, ne mentionne pas même son nom" (CB 35).

12. In a letter of December 22, 1897 Louÿs wrote: "jusqu'ici les lesbiennes étaient toujours représentées comme des femmes fatales." As cited by Jean-Paul Goujon in his preface to *Les Chansons de Bilitis*, p. 14.

13. Kenneth Rexroth, ed. and trans., *One Hundred Poems from the Japanese* (New York: New Directions, 1955), p. x.

14. Linda Hamalian, *A Life of Kenneth Rexroth* (New York: W.W. Norton & Co., 1991), p. 252. Further references to this work will appear in the text abbreviated H.

15. Morgan Gibson, *Revolutionary Rexroth: Poet of East-West Wisdom* (Hamden, CT: Archon Books, 1986), p. 82. Further references to this work will appear in the text abbreviated RR.

16. Kenneth Rexroth, *One Hundred More Poems from the Japanese* (New York: New Directions Books, 1974), p. 9, and Kenneth Rexroth, *Flower Wreath Hill: Later Poems* (New York: New Directions Books, 1974), pp. 124 and 143. Further references to these works will appear in the text abbreviated OHM and FWH, respectively.

17. Kenneth Rexroth, "The Influence of Classical Japanese Poetry on Modern American Poetry" (1973), in *The World Outside the Window*, ed. Bradford Morrow (New York: New Directions Books, 1987), p. 268. Rexroth wrote:

> The translations and imitations of Yone Noguchi and Lafcadio Hearn, and of E. Powys Mathers, from the French, were considerably better, yet no better than the best sentimental verse of the first years of the twentieth century. They established Japan in the literary imagination as a reverse image of America, a society whose system of values had been moved through the fourth dimension so that left was right and up was down. Japan became a dream world in the metaphorical sense—a world of exquisite sensibility, elaborate courtesy, self-sacrificing love, and utterly anti-materialistic religion, but a dream world in the literal sense, too, a nightside life where the inadequacies and frustrations of the American way of life were overcome, the represssions were liberated and the distortions were healed. This isn't Japan any more than materialist, money-crazy America is America, but like all stereotypes some of the truth can be fitted into it. (p. 268)

18. Kenneth Rexroth, "The Poet as Translator," in *Assays* (New York: New Directions Books, 1961), p. 19.

19. Richard Wollheim, "Nelson Goodman's *Languages of Art*," in *On Art and the Mind* (Cambridge, MA: Harvard University Press, 1974), p. 291.

20. Kenneth Rexroth, *The Phoenix and the Tortoise* (Norfolk, CT: New Directions, 1944), p. 14. Further references to this work will appear in the text abbreviated PT.

21. Gina Kolata, "Researchers Find Big Risk of Defect in Cloning Animals," *The New York Times* (March 25, 2001), p. 1.

22. In a 1948 letter to James Laughlin, his editor at New Directions: "I am working on the Chinese & Japanese poetry book—I think we will have an incomparably better book than anyone else. I plan to translate from [Judith] Gautier (use [Stuart] Merrill for her) and to translate from French versions of IndoChinese poetry. . . . You have some sort of block re the orient. You have no idea of how popular such subjects are in universities now." This remark to Laughlin is interesting not just because it identifies the cultural provincialism and distinct lack of interest in non-Western literature that prevailed in American letters in 1948, but also because it provides rather concrete evidence of what we are associating with textual cloning. For this letter comes accompanied by an editorial note citing Laughlin's "discovery" "of the source of KR's first Japanese and Chinese translations, rather to his chagrin." Laughlin, according to his own account, noticed marked similarities between Rexroth's Chinese and Japanese translations and French translations from the 1890s that were included in Judith Gautier's *Livre de Jade*, and later carried over into Stuart Merrill's anthology *Pastels in Prose*. *Kenneth Rexroth and James Laughlin: Selected Letters*, ed. Lee Bartlett (New York: W.W. Norton, 1991), p. 121.

23. Alison Lurie, *Familiar Spirits: A Memoir of James Merrill and David Jackson* (New York: Viking, 2001).

24. James Merrill, *The Changing Light at Sandover* (New York: Knopf, 2000), p. 217. Further references to this work will appear in the text abbreviated S.

25. Benjamin, "Task of the Translator," p. 71.

26. Jacques Derrida's famous reading of Benjamin's translation theory, titled "Des Tours de Babel" engages the problem of afterlife as "sur-vie," a problem to which he returns in depth in an essay titled "Living On," devoted to Blanchot's "Arrêt de Mort" ("Death Sentence." See, Derrida, "Des Tours de Babel," in *Difference in Translation*, ed. Joseph F. Graham (Ithaca: Cornell University Press, 1985), pp. 209–48).

PART THREE

Translation and Difference

Social groups both fear and need difference, and three of the essays in this section are linked by this double preoccupation. The other essays explore difference from a slightly different angle: within the very concepts of translation and naming, and across the line, if there is such a line, which divides lived history from memory.

Translation, paradoxically, has often been used to build national identity by means of organized borrowing from different languages and cultures. In this "specular process," as Lawrence Venuti aptly calls it, one becomes more one's self by selectively becoming another. Or rather by openly trying and secretly failing in the attempt. Venuti's essay lucidly lays out the theory of this project, and offers precise case studies. There are forms of nationalism, he suggests, where "the national status of a language and culture is simultaneously presupposed and created through translation," and Schleiermacher's argument about German and Germany is precisely this: "Our language can thrive in all its freshness and completely develop its own power only by means of the most many-sided contacts with what is foreign." Yopie Prins shows how a whole generation of scholars, poets, and educators in Britain tried to become more truly English by becoming more Greek than the Greeks. Matthew Arnold, Prins says, thought "modernity was the demand for the right measure and . . . England was a nation in need of measure," and the Homeric hexameter offered itself as the haunting and implausible solution to a problem both of poetry and culture. The hexameter, Prins shrewdly adds "was invoked by Arnold as a metrical imaginary," a way of getting the "native genius" of English to speak in tones that mere native forms did not allow. It measured, as she says, "the distance between culture and anarchy"—always a little further than Arnold wanted to think.

Azade Seyhan also notes, in her study of German exiles in Turkey during World War II, "the coexistence of an extensive practice of translation with a passionately articulated uniqueness and moral superiority of Turkish nation and national identity." The paradox returns, and looks less paradoxical each time. Her essay is a study in what she calls "cultural geography," the formation of "cities of refuge," places where exiled modes of thought and teaching could both be preserved for their own future and rather different life and have a very large effect on the local culture. "In a certain sense," she writes, "the best intentions of the Enlightenment paradigm survived in a self-reflexive, reinterpreted or reimagined mode in pockets and margins of exile."

"Globalization has taken our tongues from us," Jacques Lezra's essay begins, but the process started much earlier than we most often assume. For Lezra the common modern concept of the nation, associated with Renan, is a matter of a people's will, or more precisely a settled relation between will and language. But there is an earlier idea, which troubles just this relation, and Lezra subtly explores its manifestations in Renaissance grammarians, translators, and theorists of translation. In Covarrubias's dictionary, for example, to translate is both to take something from one place to another and to set something on the road—the first a complete action, a transaction between nations, the second a sort of unfinished adventure, a step into a space beyond the nation of departure. What Lezra calls an "insecure subjectivity" develops, and "upon this torn lexical ground, this broken, translated culture, early modern internationalism flourishes, like sown dragon's teeth."

"This torn spot is where a particular social freedom can be located," Lezra says, a thought echoed by Stathis Gourgouris's reading of Don DeLillo's novel *The Names* as an exploration of "the transgressive legacy of the Tower of Babel." "Our second chance at Babel," Gourgouris writes, "is to recognize . . . the force that enables societies to dare imagine themselves otherwise, beyond the Name." Beyond the name and beyond the nation, we might say. Language, no longer the instrument of a domineering policy or purpose, no longer single-minded enough to command or receive commands, becomes the place where we slip away from the tyranny of the will.

Everywhere beneath these complex project and antiprojects, these large schemes for translating the world into various models of desire, lurks the notion of experience, which is the central focus of Sandra Bermann's essay on René Char. If we can translate within a language as well as from language to language, we can also translate from what Bermann calls the "lived historical event" to the legible trace of that event, and from starkly present experience to the spectral permanence of memory. No one understood the difficulty of this task better than Char, and through Bermann's delicate essay we understand precisely what is lost and gained in the writing and reading of these luminous fragments.

Local Contingencies: Translation and National Identities

LAWRENCE VENUTI

PRELIMINARY DISTINCTIONS

> When you offer a translation to a nation, that nation will almost
> always look on the translation as an act of violence against itself.
> Bourgeois taste tends to resist the universal spirit.
> To translate a foreign writer is to add to your own national poetry;
> such a widening of the horizon does not please those who profit
> from it, at least not in the beginning. The first reaction is one of rebellion.
>
> —André Lefevere, *Translation/History/Culture*

These comments are drawn from Victor Hugo's 1865 preface to his son François-Victor's version of Shakespeare's works. They are worth examining, not simply because Hugo uses translation as the basis for a critique of nationalism, but because his critique at once exposes and is itself riddled with contradictions that have characterized the relations between translation and national identities, regardless of the language and culture in which the translating is performed. Formulating the contradictory implications of Hugo's comments, then, will be a useful way to introduce my reflections on nationalist agendas in translation.

Translation can be described as an act of violence against a nation only because nationalist thinking tends to be premised on a metaphysical concept of identity as a homogeneous essence, usually given a biological grounding in an ethnicity or race and seen as manifested in a particular language and culture.

For Catalan materials and discussions of Catalan translation, I am grateful to Montserrat Bacardí, Universitat Autònoma de Barcelona; Pilar Godayol, Universitat de Vic; Marcel Ortín, Universitat Pompeu Fabra; Francesc Parcerisas, Departament de Cultura, Generalitat de Catalunya; and Martha Tennent. Susan Bernofsky of Bard College patiently answered my questions concerning the history of German translation. Susanna Basso and Rossella Bernascone were helpful informants on Italian questions. None of these scholars and translators can be held responsible for what I have made of their generous assistance. Unattributed translations in this essay are mine. Earlier drafts were presented at conferences held by the American Comparative Literature Association and the International Association of Translation and Intercultural Studies. For these opportunities, I thank David Damrosch and Theo Hermans.

Since translation works on the linguistic and cultural differences of a foreign text, it can communicate those differences and thereby threaten the assumed integrity of the national language and culture, the essentialist homogeneity of the national identity. As an example Hugo cites Voltaire's attack on the Shakespearean translator Pierre Letourneur, who is said to "sacrifice every French writer without exception to his idol (Shakespeare)" and "does not deign even to mention Corneille and Racine," an omission deplored as an "offense that he gives to France" (Hugo 456). Nationalism, Hugo suggests, goes hand in hand with a literary xenophobia, a fear that foreign literatures might contaminate native traditions, an attitude that he tellingly phrases in biological terms: "Who could ever dare think of infusing the substance of another people into its own very life-blood?" (Lefevere 1992, 18).

This attitude, however, is contradicted by the fact that nations do indeed "profit" from translation. Nationalist movements have frequently enlisted translation in the development of national languages and cultures, especially national literatures. A language, Hugo remarks, "will later be strengthened" by translation, even if "while waiting it is indignant" (Hugo 455). The forms taken by such translation agendas vary with the social situations in which they are deployed, and their varying approaches to foreign texts and cultures may be diametrically opposed, seeking either to preserve or to erase linguistic and cultural differences. Yet in both cases the differences of the foreign texts are exploited to construct a national identity that is assumed to pre-exist the translation process. As Jacques Derrida explains, nationalist thinking rests on a circular logic: the nation, imagined to be a homogeneous essence, must be constructed, but the construction is understood as "a recourse, a re-source, a circular return to the source" (Derrida 1992, 12). Nationalist translation agendas depend on the same circularity: the national status of a language and culture is simultaneously presupposed and created through translation. Insofar as such agendas implicitly reveal the incompleteness of the nation, translation is a scandal to nationalist thinking, providing yet another motive for indignation and offense, for perceiving a translated text as an international act of violence.

The concept of nation, moreover, can be regarded as democratic, at least in principle, subsuming social divisions beneath a collective identity. The term that Hugo uses in his critique is "le peuple" (the people), an undifferentiated population united here in its resistance to a translation. Yet the arbiters of a national culture, even the theorists who articulate the very idea of a nation, may well belong to an elite minority. Hence, Hugo implicitly equates the cultural values of one class, "bourgeois taste," with the collective culture that resists translation. Nationalist translation agendas have often been initiated by cultural elites who aim to impose their linguistic and literary values on an entire population. The success of these agendas shows, however, that nationalisms cannot be viewed simply as forms of class dominance: translations must be accepted by a mass audience to be effective in constructing national languages, cultures, identities (cf. Easthope 6–8).

Do Hugo's comments, although critical of nationalism, take a clear stand on nationalist translation agendas? Here too contradictions emerge. On the one hand, he acknowledges that translation traffics in linguistic and cultural differences that threaten nationalisms even while enriching national literatures. On the other hand, he suppresses the constructive hybridizing effects of these differences by positing the existence of a "universal spirit," an essentialist concept of humanity that transcends the boundaries of class and nation. In a posthumously published commentary on translation, similarly, he asserts that translators "transfuse the human spirit from one people to another," but when he addresses the languages that mediate this transfusion, his thinking again issues into contradiction: "The human spirit is greater than every idiom. Languages do not all express the same quantity of it" (Hugo 631). Even though translation is seen as the practice that overcomes the boundaries between national languages and cultures to communicate the universal spirit, we must still ask what linguistic and cultural differences shape the translator's work on another literature and complicate the communicative process. At every turn, Hugo must confront the question of which nation at once gives rise to and is affected by a particular translation practice.

His universalism actually reveals the close relationship between his thinking and nationalism. Derrida points out that "nationalism does not present itself as a retrenchment onto an empirical particularity, but as the assigning to a nation of a universalistic, essentialist representation" (Derrida 1992, 19). Considered from the vantage point of an individual social agent, then, nationalism is not the empirical fact of national citizenship, but an identification with or self-recognition in a particular discourse of nation. Thus, despite the fact that Letourneur was a French citizen, his translation of Shakespeare might still cause offense to Voltaire's nationalistic investment in French literature, might still be perceived as an insult to France. The English playwright seems a "monster" and "a barbarous actor" to Voltaire because he identifies with an essentialist image of French culture that assumes it is the seat of two universal principles: human nature and civilization (Hugo 456). Hugo, in effect, attributes to humanity what Voltaire attributes to France. Universalism can be useful in criticizing the exclusionary effects of nationalism, but by suppressing linguistic and cultural differences it pre-empts the articulation of theoretical concepts to understand how national identities are formed and what role translation might play in their formation.

To work toward such an understanding, I shall set out from Antony Easthope's productive synthesis of poststructuralism and psychoanalysis in which human subjectivity is seen as constructed in language, in the subject's identification with a self-image reflected by an other's language use (Easthope 3–57). This language-based process of identification at once elicits desire and—since that desire originates in an external object—defers its satisfaction, producing an irremediable lack in the subject. A national identity is constructed when the external object is both a particular discourse of nation and a social group, so that a double process of identification is enacted and housed in social institutions designed to reproduce the national culture and the nation-state. Yet neither culture nor state can guarantee the unity of the nation: not only are they disjunctive, characterized by incommensurate institutions and practices that may be in conflict (such as when a national cultural agency exacerbates political divisions), but they are each in their turn heterogeneous, since citizenship can be granted to foreigners and foreign values can be assimilated into the domestic culture. These incommensurabilities and heterogeneities, in the presence of such other conditions as the modern displacement of traditionally close-knit communities by impersonal social relations and the domination of a colonial or hegemonic power, evoke within individuals the desire for a national collective and sustain the process of national identity formation. As Easthope observes, "the disjunction in nation between state and culture (as well as the heterogeneity of each) is disavowed through fantasy identification with a unified identity, state and culture together" (46).

Translation can support the formation of national identities through both the selection of foreign texts and the development of discursive strategies to translate them. A foreign text may be chosen because the social situation in which it was produced is seen as analogous to that of the translating culture and thus as illuminating of the problems that a nation must confront in its emergence. A foreign text may also be chosen because its form and theme contribute to the creation of a specific discourse of nation in the translating culture. Similarly, a foreign text may be translated with a discursive strategy that has come to be regarded as a distinguishing characteristic of the nation because that strategy has long dominated translation traditions and practices in the translating culture. A translation strategy may also be affiliated with a national discourse because it employs a dialect that has gained acceptance as the standard dialect or the national language. Such translation practices form national identities through a specular process in which the subject identifies with cultural materials that are defined as national and thereby enable a self-recognition in a national collective. The fact that the materials at issue may include forms and themes, texts and cultures that are irreducibly foreign is repressed in a fantastic identification with an apparently homogeneous national identity. The irreducible foreignness of these materials may actually result in an intensification of national desire: in this instance, whatever linguistic and cultural differences may be communicated by a translation elicit a desire for a unified nation that the translation cannot fulfill by virtue of those very differences.

INTENTIONALITY AND THE TRANSLATOR'S UNCONSCIOUS

Although translation nationalisms are usually deliberate, driven by specific cultural and political goals, neither translators nor their audiences need be aware of the social effects produced by translated texts. The formation of national identities can remain unconscious because it occurs in language that originates elsewhere, in the subject's relations to others, but that the subject perceives as his or her own self-expression. In Easthope's words, nation is "an identity that can speak us even when we may think we are speaking for ourselves" (5). A translation, then, might serve a nationalist agenda without the translator's conscious intention. Hugo remarks that "Letourneur did not translate Shakespeare; he parodied him, ingenuously, without wishing it, unknowingly obedient to the hostile taste of his epoch" (Hugo 457). Letourneur's decision to translate Shakespeare deviated from contemporary French literary canons, but his discursive strategy unconsciously conformed to them. This conformity could only highlight Shakespeare's deviation, simultaneously intensifying and offending Voltaire's nationalistic investment in French literature.

The translator's unconscious formation of national identities can be developed further if we examine a specific case more closely. Consider the American translator William Weaver's 1968 version of Italo Calvino's scientific fantasies, *Cosmicomics*. On a few occasions, Calvino uses "ricotta" as an analogy to describe imaginary features of the moon and interstellar matter. The word refers to a soft, mild Italian cheese made from the whey of cow's or sheep's milk. Weaver repeatedly replaces it with English words that do not maintain a semantic equivalence with the Italian:

> Il latte lunare era molto denso, come una specie di ricotta.
> [Moon-milk was very thick, like a kind of cream cheese.]
>
> La ricotta volava
> [The cheese flew]
>
> adesso s'erano trovati prigionieri d'una specie di ricotta spugnosa
> [now they were imprisoned in a kind of spongy cream]
> (Calvino 6, 7, 27; Weaver 5, 6, 24)

In each instance, Weaver suppresses the cultural specificity of "ricotta" by using words that are more familiar to English-language readers. His choices include "cheese," which generalizes the Italian word; "cream," which diverges from the very notion of cheese; and "cream cheese," which for many readers would refer to a distinctively American cheese made from cream and milk, sometimes associated with a brand name, Philadelphia Cream Cheese, but in any case very different from Italian ricotta. These renderings constitute lexical shifts that assimilate the Italian text to English-language cultural terms, a tendency that recurs in the translation:

> La Galassia si voltata come una frittata nella sua padella infuocata, essa stessa padella friggente e dorato pesceduovo
> [The Galaxy turned like an omelet in its heated pan, itself both frying pan and golden egg]
>
> cosa volete che ce ne facessimo, del tempo, stando lì pigiati come acciughe?
> [what use did we have for time, packed in there like sardines?]
>
> Attraversai una metropoli nuragica tutta torri di pietra
> [I crossed a piled-up metropolis of stones]
>
> —Ragazzi, avessi un po' di spazio, come mi piacerebbe farvi le tagliatelle!—
> ["Oh, if I only had some room, how I'd like to make some noodles for you boys!"]
> (Calvino 41, 45, 49, 57; Weaver 38, 43, 46, 56)

In each case, the translation adheres closely to the Italian passages until a culturally specific term appears, at which point a lexical choice reveals a discursive
strategy that can be called Anglocentric. The word *pesceduovo*, or "fish [made] of
egg," refers to an omlette that has been folded to form an elongated, fish-shaped
roll. Weaver not only simplifies the word for English-language readers, but strips
it of its peculiarly Italian significance. With the Italian phrase *pigiati come
acciughe*, or "pressed like anchovies," he removes "anchovies," a staple of Italian
rather than British or American cuisine, and reverts to an analogy that has long
been a cliché in English: "packed like sardines." The Italian word *nuragica*, a
technical term that refers to the prehistoric conical monuments found in Sar-
dinia, is similarly replaced by a simpler yet somewhat unclear rendering, "piled-
up." And the Italian word *tagliatelle*, referring to a long, ribbon-like pasta, gives
way to the generic "noodles."

These Anglocentric renderings belong to an overall strategy in which the
translator's choices are evidently made to enhance intelligibility for a broad
English-language readership. The translation is primarily written in the current
standard dialect of English, devoid of any typically British or American markings. It also draws on fairly common colloquialisms. Thus, *Ignoranti . . . Ignoran-
toni* (Ignoramuses . . . The big ignoramuses) is translated as "Bunch of ignorant
louts . . . Know-nothings"; *la forte miscela* (the strong mixture) becomes "the
heady blend"; *la partita è nulla* (the game is invalid) becomes "the game's null and
void"; *poteva avere torto marcio* (he could be totally wrong) becomes "he could be
dead wrong"; *l'avreste capita* (you would have understood) becomes "to catch
on"; *non mi sarei cambiato* (I would not have changed) becomes "I wouldn't have
traded places"; *sbranarla* (tear her to pieces) becomes "tear her from limb to
limb" (Calvino 30, 58, 67, 74, 83, 99; Weaver 27, 57, 66, 73, 82, 98). These examples show that Weaver consistently favors the colloquial word or phrase, the
cliché-like idiom, the informal contraction, even where Calvino uses standard
Italian. As a result, the translation is extremely fluent, immediately recognizable
to English-language readers and therefore easily readable.

This discursive strategy allows the translation to produce several potentially
nationalistic effects. The easy readability fosters an illusion of transparency
whereby the second-order status of the translation is effaced and the reader
comes to feel as if he or she were reading, not a translation, but the original,
Calvino's Italian text. Through this illusionism, the translation validates the
most widely used forms of English by seemingly demonstrating their power to
express the truth of Calvino's writing. Here the experience of reading Weaver's
translation coincides with the formation of a national identity. Whether the
nationality is British or American (or linked to some other English-speaking
country) depends on the reader to a significant extent because Weaver's English is not regional, not geographically marked. Yet the identity should be
considered national because it is grounded in a validation of a national language, the standard dialect and the most familiar colloquialisms, and reinforced through Anglocentric cultural terms. The very illusion of transparency,
furthermore, is characteristic of Anglo-American cultural traditions: not only

has it dominated English-language translation at least since the seventeenth century, but in implying that language use can give unmediated access to truth or reality, it is closely linked to the empiricist epistemologies that have long distinguished British and American philosophies (Venuti 1995; Easthope). The transparency of Weaver's translation invites a British or American reader to identify with a particular discourse of nation, a British or American national culture, defined as empirical, common-sensical, and pragmatic insofar as the translator's work was governed by an Anglocentric norm of acceptability. The fact that Weaver's version of *Cosmicomics* might effectively form a national identity was confirmed in 1969, a year after publication, when it won the National Book Award for translation, a prize given by a consortium of American publishers who judged it, not according to standards of accuracy or adequacy to the foreign text, but according to literary standards that they also applied to contemporary American writing.

Nonetheless, the translator was—and remains—entirely unaware of the potential cultural and political effects of his translation. In a 1980 interview, Weaver's response to the question, "Should translations sound foreign?," contradicted the Anglocentric strategy he employed with Calvino's *Cosmicomics*:

> "Yes, I think sometimes they should. I don't think they should sound American. I don't think Italian characters should say 'gee whiz' to each other or 'gosh' or whatever, and I don't think if they're eating pizza you should translate it into peanut butter sandwiches or anything like that. And I think occasionally you can leave a word in Italian . . . because it can't otherwise be translated. Or sometimes I leave it in Italian and add a very tiny apposition, explaining what it is." (Venuti 1982, 19)

Calvino's text is fantasy, of course, and the characters are not presented as specifically Italian, but rather as personifications of scientific concepts and phenomena. Still, Calvino was undoubtedly writing in Italian for an Italian audience, and the retention of such words as *ricotta* and *tagliatelle* would help to signal the Italian origin of the text to English-language readers. Yet they are replaced by words such as "cream cheese" and "noodles," which do indeed "sound American." In a more recent interview, when asked why he avoided the word "ricotta," Weaver explained that it fit the context of a cheese-coated moon: "I used 'cheese' because we used to say, 'the moon is made of green cheese.' But also thirty years ago nobody in the US knew what ricotta was" (phone conversation: November 10, 2001). This comment reveals the translator's Anglocentric strategy, his effort to bring English-language cultural traditions to bear on his translating (the comparison between the moon and green cheese actually dates back to the sixteenth century) and to avoid communicating any sense of foreignness to the English-language reader by, for instance, retaining the foreign word and adding an explanatory phrase in apposition. In fact, when asked why he rendered *tagliatelle* as "noodles," Weaver responded, "Well, they *are* noodles," demonstrating that his investment in transparent translating continues to be so deep as to suppress the linguistic and cultural differences of the foreign text. A translator too can identify unconsciously with a national cultural discourse, here with the empiricist privileging of transparency that has long prevailed in British and American thinking about language.

A translation intended to serve a nationalist agenda might similarly have unanticipated effects that conflict with the translator's intention, whether in serving the interests of one social group instead of a national collective or even in undermining those group interests. Consider Sir Thomas Hoby's 1561 translation of Baldassare Castiglione's courtesy book, *The Courtyer*. Hoby, like other Elizabethan translators, presents his work as a contribution to an English national culture (see Ebel). "Englishemen," he argues in his dedicatory preface, "are muche inferiour to well most all other Nations" in their unwillingness to translate foreign literary, philosophical and scientific texts, and so they fail to render "a commune benefite to profite others as well as themselves" (Hoby 8). Hoby wishes to reverse this tendency, not only because Castiglione's work possesses such moral value that it ought "to be in estimation with all degrees of men" in England, but also because the practice of translation can develop the English language:

> As I therefore have to my smal skil bestowed some labour about this piece of woorke, even so coulde I wishe with al my hart, profounde learned men in the Greeke and Latin shoulde make the lyke proofe, and everye manne store the tunge accordinge to hys knowledge and delite above other men, in some piece of learnynge, that we alone of the worlde maye not bee styll counted barbarous in oure tunge, as in time out of minde we have bene in our manners. (9)

Yet despite Hoby's repeated insistence that his work aims to benefit the nation, his very decision to translate a courtly text makes clear that his primary concern is the aristocracy. Thus, in dedicating the translation to Lord Henry Hastings, Hoby asserts that "none, but a noble yonge Gentleman, and trayned up all his life time in Court, and of worthie qualities, is meete to receive and enterteine so worthy a Courtier" as Castiglione describes in his book; and when Hoby turns to list the "degrees" or social classes that he imagines as his readership, he includes only "Princes and Greate men," "yonge Gentlemen," and "Ladyes and Gentlewomen" (6–7). Such remarks assume an ideological representation of absolute monarchy wherein the royal court governs the nation, not merely through its political authority, but through its exemplary morality. Within absolutist ideology, Hoby's address to the aristocracy is consistent with his nationalist agenda, so that his nationalism takes the form of a class dominance. The wide circulation of his translation suggests that it was instrumental in forming courtly identities, regardless of the social position occupied by his readers. During the Elizabethan period alone, it was reprinted three times, in 1577, 1588, and 1603.

Hoby's discursive strategy, even though it can be considered Anglocentric in sixteenth-century terms, further complicates his nationalist agenda. He follows the example set by the humanist Sir John Cheke, who in a prefatory letter to the translation urges English writers to avoid foreign borrowings and use primarily Anglo-Saxon words:

our own tung shold be written cleane and pure, unmixt and unmangeled with borowing of other tunges, wherin if we take not heed by tijm, ever borowing and never
payeng, she shall be fain to keep her house as bankrupt. For then doth our tung natu-
rallie and praisablie utter her meaning, when she bouroweth no counterfeitness of
other tunges to attire her self withall, but useth plainlie her own, with such shift, as nature, craft, experiens and folowing of other excellent doth lead her unto . . . (Hoby 12)

Cheke's purist recommendation constitutes a vernacular nationalism in which
words derived from Anglo-Saxon are assumed to express an essential Englishness, the truth of an English "self" that would be obscured by the "counterfeitness" of foreign borrowings. In Hoby's translation, this Anglo-Saxonism leads to
a remarkable rendering of the key Italian term "*sprezzatura*":

vendo io già più volte pensato meco onde nasca questa grazia, lasciando quelli che dalle
stelle l'hanno, trovo una regula universalissima, la qual mi par valer circa questo in tutte
le cose umane che si facciano o dicano più che alcuna altra, e ciò è fuggir quanto più si
po, e come un asperissimo e pericoloso scoglio, la affettazione; e, per dir forse una nova
parola, usar in ogni cosa una certa sprezzatura, che nasconda l'arte e dimostri ciò che si
fa e dice venir fatto senza fatica e quasi senza pensarvi. (Castiglione 61–62)

[I, imagynyng with my self oftentymes how this grace commeth, leaving a part such as
have it from above, fynd one rule that is most general whych in thys part (me thynk)
taketh place in al thynges belongyng to man in worde and deede above all other. And
that is to eschew as much as a man may, and as a sharp and daungerous rock, Affecta-
tion or curiosity and (to speak a new word) to use in every thyng a certain Recklesness,
to cover art withall, and seeme whatsoever he doth and sayeth to do it wythout pain,
and (as it were) not myndyng it.] (Hoby 59)

The Italian "sprezzatura" is a neologism that Castiglione devises to signify the ef-
fortless grace that distinguishes the ideal courtier's actions. Hoby, who knew
French, might have used a French loan word, namely "nonchalance," but in his
adherence to Cheke's vernacular nationalism he instead chose "Recklesness," a
word derived from the Anglo-Saxon *recceléas*. Hoby clearly intended the word
to communicate a sense of natural, spontaneous action, seemingly without
thought or deliberation, without "reck" or care. Yet in the sixteenth century, as
today, "Recklesness" denoted neglect, carelessness, irresponsibility, meanings
that worry Hoby's etymological rendering and transform it into a moral criticism
of courtly behavior that subverts the nationalist agenda he imagined for his
translation. A similar effect occurs in his rendering of Castiglione's assertion that
the courtier can acquire his skills from *ottimi maestri* or *bon maestri* (excellent
teachers, good teachers): In both instances, Hoby uses "cunning men," another
Anglo-Saxonism that carries negative connotations in Elizabethan English,
since "cunning" might signify not only skillful, expert, learned, but also crafty,
guileful, sly (Castiglione 60–61; Hoby 57–58). At such points, the different national discourses that inform Hoby's translation, absolutist as well as humanist,
issue into contradictions of which he was obviously unaware.

Although ethnocentric discursive strategies may endow a translation with a nationalistic effect, they can never entirely remove the foreignness of a foreign text. Cultural differences will still be communicated on other textual levels, both formal and thematic, insofar as they deviate noticeably from cultural works and traditions in the receiving language. Any such differences, in conjunction with the translator's strongly assimilative work on the language of the foreign text, can acquire a nationalistic value in reception. More precisely, they can intensify a reader's sense of belonging to a national collective and may even elicit an unconscious desire for a unified nation distinct from the foreign nation that the text is taken to represent. These possibilities are suggested by D. J. Enright's admiring response to Weaver's version of Calvino's *Cosmicomics* in the *New York Review of Books*: "The opening story, which makes the film *2001* look about as imaginative as a spilled bucket of distemper, tells of the time when the moon was so close to the earth that Qfwfq and his companions could row out in a boat and scramble up on it to collect Moon-milk, which was 'very thick, like a kind of cream cheese'" (Enright 23). Here not only is Calvino's story treated as uniquely "imaginative," but it serves to remind this British reviewer of an Anglo-American work that he had found disappointing, Stanley Kubrick's recently released film *2001: A Space Odyssey*. The contrast in aesthetic value tacitly rests on a national distinction that involves Enright's own culture, the Italian writer versus the American director resident in England. And Calvino's narrative premise of a moon coated with "cream cheese" is cited to illustrate the imagination that determines the cultural difference of his story. Nonetheless, Weaver's Anglocentric rendering, "cream cheese," is evidently as transparent to Enright as the Britishism "distemper" (where an American writer might use "whitewash"), demonstrating that his own identity as a reader is inextricably bound to a national language, the British dialect of English—which he assumes will be immediately intelligible to the predominantly American audience of a New York-based periodical. When confronted with an Italian work of fiction, Enright seems to feel all the more strongly his investment in English linguistic and cultural forms, notwithstanding—or because of—the hybridity of the language and the imaginative weakness he perceives in the film.

Translation and Nationalist Cultural Politics

Nationalist translation agendas have been devised to intervene into specific social situations, but they do possess a number of common features. While taking into account significant historical differences, I want now to present a critical taxonomy of these features, considering how translation theories and practices have been used to shape a concept of nation and what cultural and social effects have resulted from this use. I will focus on two especially revealing cases: Prussia during the Napoleonic Wars and China under the late Qing dynasty.

In both of these cases, translation was enlisted in a defensive nationalist movement that was designed to build a national culture so as to counter foreign aggression. During the eighteenth century, the Prussian aristocracy had fallen under French cultural domination so that, as the theologian and philosopher Friedrich Schleiermacher complained, even King Frederick II "was incapable of producing in German the literature and philosophy he produced in French" (Lefevere 1977, 83). After 1806, when Napoleon defeated Prussia, Schleiermacher's sermons not only called on congregations to resist the French occupation, but articulated a concept of the German nation. With a victory, he told them, "we shall be able to preserve for ourselves our own distinctive character, our laws, our constitution and our culture" (Schleiermacher 73). A key factor in this nationalist agenda was the German language, which Schleiermacher felt might be best improved through translation: "Our language," he argued in a lecture delivered in 1813, "can thrive in all its freshness and completely develop its own power only by means of the most many-sided contacts with what is foreign" (Lefevere 1977, 88).

Later in the nineteenth century China faced a somewhat different adversarial situation, characterized by foreign commercial and military invasion. Defeated in the war against Britain over the opium trade (1839–42), China was forced to grant economic and political concessions to several Western nations who established colonies in various ports and, after the Chinese lost the first Sino-Japanese War (1894–95), divided the country into spheres of interest. Just as the Boxer uprising against the foreign presence was repressed by an international force (1898–1900), translators such as Lin Shu and Yan Fu began introducing Western ideas to reform the Chinese nation and enable it to struggle against the invaders. Lin Shu's preface to his version of Rider Haggard's novel *The Spirit of Bambatse* suggests that such Western literary texts are valuable because "they encourage the white man's spirit of exploration" and can instill a similar "spirit" in his Chinese readers: "The blueprint has already been drawn by Columbus and Robinson Crusoe. In order to seek almost unobtainable material interests in the barbarian regions, white men are willing to brave a hundred deaths. But our nation, on the contrary, disregards its own interests and yields them to foreigners" (Lee 54). Similarly Yan Fu, who had studied in England during the 1870s, chose to render works on evolutionary theory by T. H. Huxley and Herbert Spencer precisely because he believed them to be useful to the "self-strengthening and the preservation of the race" (Schwartz 100).

As the translators' comments indicate, they intended their translations to form national identities by soliciting their readers' identification with a particular national discourse that was articulated in relation to the hegemonic foreign nations. This relational identity, always fundamentally differential, shaped through a distinction from the other on which the identity is nonetheless based, might be either exclusionary or receptive. German translators defined the German nation as incorporating a respect for the foreign that led them to reject French cultural practices that did not show this respect. They valued a foreignizing method of translation, described by Schleiermacher as one in which "the translator leaves the author in peace, as much as possible, and moves the reader towards him," a literalism imprinted with the foreignness of the foreign text, whereas the French were seen as advocating a domesticating method, in which the translator "leaves the reader in peace, as much as possible, and moves the author towards him," a much freer rewriting of the foreign text according to the intelligibilities and interests of the receiving culture (Lefevere 1977, 74). French translation, from the German point of view, even went to the extremes of paraphrase and adaptation, both of which were to be lamented. In a satiric dialogue from 1798, August Wilhelm Schlegel, whose own versions of Shakespeare's plays exemplified the foreignizing method, demonstrated how different translation practices might be taken as representative of opposed national identities:

FRENCHMAN: The Germans translate every literary Tom, Dick, and Harry. We either do not translate at all, or else we translate according to our own taste.
GERMAN: Which is to say, you paraphrase and you disguise.
FRENCHMAN: We look on a foreign author as a stranger in our company, who has to dress and behave according to our customs, if he desires to please.
GERMAN: How narrow-minded of you to be pleased only by what is native.
FRENCHMAN: Such is our nature and our education. Did the Greeks not hellenize everything?
GERMAN: In your case it goes back to a narrow-minded nature and a conventional education. In ours education is our nature.
(Lefevere 1977, 50)

Chinese translators, in contrast, sought to form a national identity by accepting Western values. They particularly prized the individualism and aggressiveness that seemed to them so important in motivating Western imperialism in China. For Lin Shu, the emulation of these values required that they be assimilated to Chinese cultural traditions that were consequently revised or in certain instances abandoned. Hence, his criticism of the Confucian virtue of "yielding" or deference:

The Westerners' consciousness of shame and advocacy of force do not stem entirely from their own nature but are also an accumulated custom. . . . In China, this is not so. Suffering humiliation is regarded as yielding; saving one's own life is called wisdom. Thus after thousands of years of encroachments by foreign races, we still do not feel ashamed. Could it also be called our national character? (Lee 54)

Chinese notions of deference and self-preservation ran counter to the collective "consciousness of shame" that might accompany the recognition of one's self as belonging to a nation under seige. Lin Shu's reference to a Chinese "national character" was itself a cultural import from the West.

In using translation to form national identities, the translators expose the contradictory conditions of their nationalist agendas. Terms such as "nature" and "race" point to a concept of nation as an unchanging biological essence that pre-exists the translation process and so reveals the circular logic of nationalism: the translating can only return to the identity that it is said to create. Yet terms such as "education" and "custom," along with the very use of a cultural practice like translation, implies that identity is constructed in a discursive formation and therefore can be changed and developed, precisely to intervene against the embattled social situations where the German and Chinese translators were working. The essentialistic strain in their thinking, furthermore, coincides with a universalism. The national identity that translation is summoned to form in each case embodies universalistic traits. For Schleiermacher, what distinguishes the German nation is its capacity to mediate all other national cultures, making it the historical culmination of "translation in general":

> Our nation may be destined, because of its respect for what is foreign and its mediating nature, to carry all the treasures of foreign arts and scholarship, together with its own, in its language, to unite them into a great historical whole, so to speak, which would be preserved in the centre and heart of Europe, so that with the help of our language, whatever beauty the most different times have brought forth can be enjoyed by all people, as purely and perfectly as is possible for a foreigner. This appears indeed to be the real historical aim of translation in general, as we are used to it now. (Lefevere 1977, 88)

Here German culture, created through translation, achieves global domination, and the "respect for what is foreign" that is characteristic of the German "nature" ultimately suppresses the cultural differences of other nations by forcing the "foreigner" to appreciate the canon of world literature in German. A. W. Schlegel similarly argued that the practice of translation is synonymous with German culture: Because "poetic translation is a difficult art," he asserted, "its invention was reserved for German fidelity and perseverance" (Lefevere 1992, 78–79). In Lin Shu's thinking, the universalism took the form of assuming the global validity of Chinese cultural traditions, notably Confucianism. Thus, he read the most diverse British novels as exempla of the Confucian reverence for filial piety, an interpretation that he made explicit in his habit of retitling the English texts. His version of Dickens's *The Old Curiosity Shop* became *The Story of the Filial Daughter Nell* (Lee 47).

Nationalist agendas in translation involve the conceptual violence that occurs whenever the unity of a nation is proclaimed, whether at its founding moment or subsequently in its cultural and political institutions. An assertion of national unity fictively creates that unity in the very process of asserting it by repressing the differences among the heterogeneous groupings and interests that comprise any social collective. As Derrida remarks, "the properly *performative* act must produce (proclaim) what in the form of a *constative* act it merely claims, declares, assures it is describing" (Derrida 1987, 18). Translation nationalisms are based on performative acts of this sort because they assert a homogeneous language, culture, or identity where none is shared by the diverse population that constitutes the nation. Such agendas in translation necessarily entail various exclusions, not only in drawing distinctions between the nation and its foreign others, but in privileging certain cultural forms, practices, and constituencies within the supposedly unified nation. Foreign texts are chosen because they fall into particular genres and address particular themes while excluding other genres and themes that are seen as unimportant for the formation of a national identity; translation strategies draw on particular dialects, registers, and styles while excluding others that are also in use; and translators target particular audiences with their work, excluding other constituencies.

Thus, the German translators at the turn of the nineteenth century aimed to build a national language and culture, but they actually belonged to an elite bourgeois minority whose taste dictated both the selection of foreign texts for translation and the development of discursive strategies to translate them. The translators focused on canonical works of European literature and philosophy. Johann Heinrich Voss rendered Homer, Schleiermacher Plato, and A. W. Schlegel Shakespeare, to cite a few representative examples, whereas the great majority of German-language readers preferred translations of French and English novels by such authors as Choderlos de Laclos and Samuel Richardson (see Ward). The foreignizing method of translation, although relying on the standard dialect (High German), avoided familiar, conversational forms: "The indispensable requirement of this method," in Schleiermacher's words, "is a feeling for language that is not only not colloquial but also causes us to suspect that it has not grown in total freedom but rather has been bent towards a foreign likeness" (Lefevere 1977, 78–79). And although the German translators wished their translations to be read by every member of the German nation, the foreignizing method was guided by an appeal to an elite segment of the national audience; "any reader," states Schleirmacher, "educated in such a way that we call him, in the better sense of the word, the lover and the expert" (76). The identity formed by the resulting translations was less national than learned and bourgeois.

The Chinese translators, in rendering Western literary, philosophical, and scientific texts, unavoidably displaced native cultural traditions, but they also tended to neglect foreign texts that in their view were not conducive to the creation of a resistant national identity. Because their political goal was reformist, intended to strengthen an imperial culture that had lost authority amid foreign invasion, they adopted a domesticating method of translation that resulted in diverse forms of cultural and social exclusion. Thus, Lin Shu and Yan Fu not only translated into the classical literary language (*wenyan*) to appeal to an academic and official elite, but in some cases they revised Western texts so as to assimilate them to Chinese values and make their nationalist agenda more acceptable to their readers. Lin Shu's 1899 version of Alexandre Dumas fils's *La Dame aux camélias* renders the French *ange* (angel) with the Chinese *xian* (fairy maiden), which evokes ancient Chinese mythology in place of the Judeo-Christian tradition (Wong 213). Similarly, when in the novel a man greets a woman by kissing her hand, Lin Shu inserted an explanatory note to anticipate the Chinese reader's surprise at this Western practice. The identity formed by such translations could only be hybrid, not simply national, but imperial, not simply classical Chinese, but also modern and Western to some extent.

To produce significant cultural and political effects, however, nationalist movements must win the spontaneous support of a broad cross-section of the population, even if this very breadth simultaneously puts into question the notion of a unified nation. Translation nationalisms likewise cannot be restricted to the cultural elite who is most likely to devise and execute them; the translations that are designed to form a national identity must circulate widely among the diverse constituencies that comprise the nation so as to produce a nationalistic effect that might result in social change. From this point of view, the German translators' impact was inevitably limited. Although they initiated a translation tradition that stretched into the twentieth century, inspiring such theorists as Nietzsche and Walter Benjamin, in their own historical moment their foreignizing translations of canonical texts were most powerful in forming a national identity among readers who, like them, were not just scholarly in their interests, but acquainted with previous German translations as well as German literary developments. Thus, in 1814, Goethe argued for the usefulness of a prose translation of Homer "in the first stages of education," observing that "If you want to influence the masses a simple translation is always best. Critical translations vying with the original really are of use only for conversations the learned conduct among themselves" (Lefevere 1992, 75). Wilhelm von Humboldt's preface to his 1816 version of Aeschylus' *Agamemnon* took an opposing view, although the nationalistic tenor of his remarks shows that he was engaging in precisely the sort of learned conversation that Goethe had in mind:

> What strides has the German language not made, to give but one example, since it began to imitate the meters of Greek, and what developments have not taken place in the nation, not just among the learned, but also among the masses, even down to women and children since the Greeks really did become the nation's reading matter in their true and unadulterated shape? Words fail to express how much the German nation owes to Klopstock with his first successful treatment of antique meters, and how much more it owes to Voss, who may be said to have introduced classical antiquity into the German language. A more powerful and beneficial influence on a national culture can hardly be imagined in an already highly sophisticated time, and that influence is his alone. (137)

Given the fact that in successive editions Voss brought the German of his Homeric translations closer to the Greek and so increased the difficulty of reading them, one must doubt Humboldt's enthusiastic assessment of their mass readership. Schleiermacher, in fact, seems to have felt that Voss's foreignizing version was too extreme to be pleasurably readable (see Bernofsky). In Humboldt's case, the linguistic differences of the Greek poems intensified his own national identity even as they deepened his appreciation for Voss's translation, as well as the dramatist Friedrich Klopstock's imitation of classical prosody.

The social impact of the Chinese translators' work was much more consequential because it was extremely popular, extending beyond the academic and official elite that was their immediate audience to encompass independent intellectuals and both secondary-school and university students. Among this wide readership, to be sure, Lin Shu's version of Dumas fils's sentimental novel did not consistently elicit the same patriotic response that he voiced in drawing an analogy between the courtesan Marguerite and two Chinese ministers renowned for their devotion to the emperor. Here the cultural differences of *La Dame aux camélias* strengthened his nationalistic identification with imperial culture: "Strong are the women of this world, more so than our scholar-officials, among whom only the extremely devoted ones such as Long Jiang and Bi Gan could compare with Marguerite, those who would die a hundred deaths rather than deviate from their devotion. Because the way Marguerite served Armand is the same way Long and Bi served their emperors Jie and Zhou" (Hu Ying 1995: 71). Nonetheless, the nationalist agenda of the late Qing translators established a model for a later, more radical generation. Lu Xun, the modernist innovator in Chinese fiction, read their versions of Haggard and Huxley and decided to translate science fiction because he believed that Western popularizations of science might "move the Chinese masses forward" (Semanov 14). By 1909, however, he had rejected the strongly Sinicizing approach of his predecessors while retaining their project of building a national identity so as to alter China's subordinate position in geopolitical relations. He wrote foreignizing translations of fiction from Russia and Eastern European countries that occupied a similar position, but whose literatures subsequently gained international recognition (for a detailed account, see Venuti 1998, 183–86). Yan Fu's translations, especially his version of Huxley's *Evolution and Ethics*, had a much more direct influence on Chinese identity. A contemporary observer noted that "after China's frequent military reversals, particularly after the humiliation of the Boxer years, the slogan 'Survival of the Fittest' (lit., 'superior victorious, inferior defeated, the fit survive') became a kind of clarion call" (Schwartz 259, n.14).

TRANSLATION NATIONALISMS IN TIME: CATALUNYA

Although translation nationalisms turn to essentialistic concepts to articulate a discourse of nation, such agendas are fundamentally determined by the local contingencies into which they intervene. The communicative effectiveness of any translation in fact depends on its capacity to engage with the intelligibilities and interests that define the social situation where the translator is working. Nationalist agendas that seek not just to communicate the meanings of foreign texts, but to use those texts in constructing national identities, must tactically take into account the linguistic forms, cultural values, and social groups that are arrayed, always hierarchically, in their historical moment. And this accounting inevitably shapes the translating as well as the kind of national identity that the translator aims to establish, challenging any essentialism. I want to develop these points further by considering translation nationalisms within the same culture at two different moments. My site is Catalunya during the twentieth century; my cases are two influential Catalan translators, Josep Carner (1884–1970) and Joan Sales (1912–83).

Catalan nationalism emerged during the nineteenth century with the recovery of Catalan as a literary language in opposition to Castilian, the language of the hegemonic Spanish state. By the turn of the century, the formation of a language-based Catalan identity stimulated the pursuit of political autonomy from Madrid, resulting in the establishment of a regional commonwealth or Mancommunitat in 1914 (Balcells 25–27, 67–72). Enric Prat de la Riba, the elected president, had previously addressed the issue of Catalan "nationality" in a work that relied heavily on Johann Gottfried Herder's notion of *Volksgeist* or the spirit of a people, revealing the contradictions typical of nationalist thinking:

> La societat que dóna als homes tots aquests elements de cultura, que els lliga, i forma de tots una unitat superior, un ésser col.lectiu informat per un mateix esperit, aquesta societat natural és la *nacionalitat*. Resultat de tot això és que la nacionalitat és una unitat de cultura o de civilització; tots els elements d'aquesta mena, l'art, la ciència, els costums, el Dret . . . tenen llurs arrels en la nacionalitat. (Prat de la Riba 1906: 66)

> [The society that gives to men all these elements of culture, that binds them together, and forms from them all a higher unity, a collective being informed by a selfsame spirit, this natural society is *nationality*. The result of all this is that nationality is a unity of culture or of civilization; all the elements of this kind, art, science, customs, Law . . . have their roots in nationality.]

On the one hand, nationality is a socially determined form of "collective being" that is manifested in diverse cultural practices; on the other hand, it is the "natural" form of a homogeneous "spirit" that transcends social determinations (cf. Llobera 345–46). The passage shifts seamlessly between these contradictory concepts, the first materialist, the second idealist, finally treating national identity as a biological essence indistinguishable from the soil in which the national culture is said to take root.

The questionable logic of Prat de la Riba's thinking did not discredit it as an intellectual force in the defensive nationalism that drove the Catalan bid for self-government. On the contrary, the very contradictions were more likely to have stimulated the desire for a unified nation by putting into question its possibility. And in fact his work was extremely effective in rationalizing the cultural and social projects that were initiated during the *Mancommunitat*, including the standardization of the Catalan language. "La llengua," he wrote, "és la manifestació més perfecta de l'esperit nacional i l'instrument més poderós de la nacionalització i, per tant, de la conservació i la vida de la nacionalitat" (84). [Language is the most perfect manifestation of the national spirit and the most powerful instrument of nationalization and therefore of the preservation and life of nationality.] Although in 1923 the Spanish state intervened to impose an anti-Catalan dictatorship on Catalunya, the elections of 1931 resulted in the establishment of a Catalan republic or Generalitat that broadened the range of cultural and social initiatives. Under the Generalitat, Catalan joined Castilian in becoming an official language in political institutions, the educational system was reorganized to prepare for the introduction of Catalan, and both the Catalan periodical press and book industry underwent a significant expansion (96–100).

These historical developments motivated Josep Carner's work as a translator even as he contributed to them. A prolific prose writer as well as a poet, he belonged to the modernist literary movement known as *Noucentisme*, which collaborated closely with the Manicommunitat in promoting a standardized language. In his 1913 article "La dignitat literària," he echoed Prat de la Riba in asserting that "la paraula és la pàtria. La seva dignitat és una dignitat nacional" (the word is the fatherland. Its dignity is a national dignity [Carner 1986, 132]). Carner, like other Noucentist writers, considered the translation of canonical literary works as a means of developing the Catalan language and literature so as to construct a national identity. In 1907, at the start of his career as a translator, he sketched this project in an article that celebrates the translation of Shakespeare's plays into Catalan:

> Perquè el català esdevingui abundós, complexe, elàstic, elegant, és necessari que els mestres de totes les èpoques i tots els països siguin honorats amb versions a la nostra llengua i, agraïts, la dotin de totes les qualitats d'expressió i diferenciació que li calen. Perqué la literatura catalana es faci completa, essencial, illustre, cal que el nostre esperit s'enriqueixi amb totes les creacions fonamentals. Com podria ésser sumptuós un palau, sense els hostes! (56)

> [In order for Catalan to become abundant, complex, flexible, elegant, it is necessary that the masters of every period and every country be honored with versions in our language and, in gratitude, endow it with every quality of expression and differentiation that it needs. In order to make Catalan literature complete, essential, illustrious, our spirit must be enriched with every fundamental creation. How could a palace be sumptuous without guests (hostes)!]

Here too Carner adopted Prat de la Riba's essentialistic lexicon in referring to the Catalan "spirit." Yet unlike the Catalanist ideologue, Carner took a more materialist approach. Neither the language nor its literature is adequate or self-sufficient in its expressive power, and neither can be developed solely on the basis of the Catalan "spirit," which itself "must be enriched" through literary translation. For Prat de la Riba, Catalan identity, the "Iberian ethnos," transcends its linguistic and cultural conditions, predating and persisting through the Roman conquest of the peninsula:

> Aqueix fet, aqueixa transformació de la civilització llatina en civilització catalana, és un fet que per ell sol, sense necessitat de cap altre, demostra l'existència de l'esperit nacional català. Encara que després d'engendrar la llengua catalana no hagués produït res més, l'ànima del nostre poble ens hauria ja revelat les ratlles fonamentals de la seva fesomia, estampades en la fesomia de la seva llengua. (Prat de la Riba 89)

> [This fact, this transformation of Latin civilization into Catalan civilization, is a fact that by itself, without any need for others, demonstrates the existence of the Catalan national spirit. Even if after the Catalan language was begotten it had not produced anything more, the soul of our people would have already revealed to us the basic lines of its physiognomy, engraved in the physiognomy of its language.]

Whereas in Prat de la Riba's thinking Catalan identity pre-exists the language that constitutes its transparent expression, in Carner's this identity is largely a linguistic construction that requires translation to be viable, the importation of foreign cultural materials that complicate any such notion of transparency. Indeed, because the Catalan word *hostes* is ambiguous, capable of signifying both "guests" and "hosts," Carner's metaphor of the palace suggests that Catalan literature lacks not only the productive influence of foreign writing, but more sophisticated Catalan writers. The palace of Catalan literature can be sumptuous only if it is inhabited by hosts who are imaginatively enriched by translation.

Carner's cultural politics was not simply nationalist, but implicitly critical of Catalan traditions and practices that did not seem consistent with his agenda. Hence, his nationalism involved an explicit utopian projection grounded on an estimation of Catalan deficiencies. In his 1908 article "De l'acció dels poetes a Catalunya," where the word *acció* signifies not so much action as military or political engagement, he again resorted to a telling architectural metaphor to describe the work that Catalan poets must perform on their language and literature:

> Nosaltres els poetes som els constructors dels pobles, i avui que tenim encara tanta feina a fer en el casal projectat de la civilització catalana, no sentim, en amidar tot ço que encara ens manca, en veure aqueixos forats per on entra el sol, una impressió de descoratjament i de pessimisme, sinó una ànsia de creació que és benaventurada perquè ha de ser fecunda. (Carner 1986, 95)

> [We poets are constructors of peoples, and now that we still have so much work to do in the house planned for Catalan civilization, we do not feel, in surveying all that we still lack, in seeing those holes through which the sunlight enters, any sense of discouragement and pessimism, but a yearning for creation that is fortunate because it must be fertile.]

Carner seems to have been aware that the "yearning" or desire for a national literature was based on lack that, however, could never be eradicated because it was supplied through the translation of foreign literatures, through the introduction of linguistic and cultural differences that sustained creativity.

His translating aimed to form a national identity that was based on two exclusions: hegemonic Spanish culture, or in his words "el monopoli castellà dels destins d'Espanya" (the Castilian monopoly on the destinies of Spain [Carner 1986, 77]), and limited Catalan literary traditions. This relational identity is evident, first, in his selection of foreign texts for translation. Although typical of twentieth-century Catalan writers he possessed a native proficiency in both Spanish and Catalan, he avoided Spanish literature and placed the greatest emphasis on French and English traditions. Moreover, he chose to translate texts that were distinguished by fantasy and ironic humor and therefore ran counter to the realism that dominated nineteenth-century Catalan fiction, what Marcel Ortín has described as "the naturalists' limitation to the documentable real" (Ortín 1996, 112). Between 1908 and 1934, Carner published 33 translations, including one or more texts by such writers as Shakespeare and Molière, La Fontaine and Hans Christian Andersen, Dickens and Lewis Carroll, Twain and Robert Louis Stevenson, Erckmann-Chatrian and Villiers de l'Isle-Adam (105–07). Carner was particularly interested in the identity-forming power of children's literature because, as he prefaced his 1918 version of Andersen's tales, "el gradual reviscolament de la imaginació catalana és el primer fonament per a fer pròsperes i inven-cibles les empreses de l'art i la política, de la cultura i el diner" (the gradual revival of the Catalan imagination is the first foundation for insuring that the enterprises of art and politics, culture and money prosper and become invincible, 43).

To advance his nationalist agenda, Carner wrote translations that were enjoy-ably readable, but that contained noticeable departures from current usage. Al-though at the beginning of his translating career the process of linguistic stan-dardization had not yet begun and Catalan usage displayed variations at every level, it is still possible to see that he devised innovative strategies that resulted in a richly heterogeneous Catalan. His lexicon deliberately mixed archaisms, learned diction, dialectalisms, and neologisms, at times deviating from the regis-ters and styles of the foreign texts, at others resorting to literalisms or calques of foreign words and phrases (Busquets; Sellent Arús 25; Pericay and Toutain 266–67; cf. Ortín 2001). Thus, in his preface to his 1908 version of Shake-speare's *A Midsummer Night's Dream*, he noted his decision to assign "neolo-gismes i arcaismes a personatges qui són en l'espai i el temps tan allunyats de nos-altres" (neologisms and archaisms to characters who are so remote from us in time and space [Carner 1986, 102]). Carner's agenda might also lead to more ag-gressive translation moves, such as the insertion of allusions to the Catalan cul-tural and political situation. In his version of *Alice in Wonderland*, published in 1927 during the Madrid-imposed dictatorship, the Cheshire cat became *el gat castellà* (the Castilian cat), and the King and Queen of Hearts became *el Rei i la Reina d'Espases* (the King and Queen of Swords), referring not just to the Span-ish deck of playing cards, but to the military repression enacted by the Spanish state, a monarchy (Carner 1927, 93, 88).

The identity formed by such translations could only be hybrid, cast in the Catalan language yet an amalgam of linguistic and cultural differences that did not conform to the homogeneous essence imagined by Prat de la Riba. Nonethe-less, Carner's translations undoubtedly enabled his readers to recognize them-selves as Catalans. This becomes clear in a 1921 review in which the Barcelona-based poet and translator Carles Riba admired how Carner handled La Fontaine's fables in a very different cultural situation. The French writer's irony, Riba argued, combines

una malícia xampanyesa i una restricció mundana, sovint amb llurs formularis mateixos. Les condicions socials de Catalunya, del català per tant, havien forçosament d'afeblir la mundanitat i engruixudir la plasticitat camperola. Però la meravella de la traducció de Josep Carner consisteix a fondre l'una i l'altra en una bonhomia burgesa, tota barcelonina, amb la seva fraseologia feta i tot. (Riba 170–71)

[a wickedness characteristic of Champagne and a worldly restraint, often with the same forms. The social conditions of Catalunya, and therefore of Catalan, inevitably had to weaken the worldliness and thicken the rural plasticity. Yet the wonder of Josep Carner's translation consists in joining both in a bourgeois bonhomie that is entirely Barcelonian, complete with its own phraseology.]

For Riba, Carner's translation communicates the distinctiveness of the French text in a compelling way that reinvents a familiar Catalan identity—although obviously that identity was strongly inflected by bourgeois values.

The Spanish Civil War abruptly suspended the nationalistic effects produced by the work of Noucentist translators like Carner. During the war the authority of the Generalitat was increasingly weakened both by internal political divisions and by the beleaguered Spanish state, and after 1939 many Catalan politicians and intellectuals went into exile. Franco's regime enforced a harsh repression of Catalan identity that lasted for more than two decades (Balcells 127, 143–44). Public use of the Catalan language was prohibited, as was publication of Catalan books and periodicals; teachers suspected of being Catalanist sympathizers were dismissed or transferred to other Spanish regions; and Catalan culture and history were excluded from curricula. Near the end of the 1950s, however, the Francoist repression began to ease. Catalan publishing, which had continued outside of Catalunya, witnessed an increase despite the continuing threat of censorship, and the ban that had been specifically placed on translations into Catalan was lifted (147–48). Whereas in 1960 Catalan publishers issued 193 books, 10 of which were translations, 1966 saw the publication of 655 books including 207 translations, figures that represent a return to book output levels during the 1920s and 1930s (Vallverdú 102–3).

Joan Sales's work as a publisher, novelist, and translator constituted an important intervention into this cultural and political situation. During the 1940s he joined a group of Catalan writers in Mexico, where he published the journal *Quaderns de l'Exili* (Notebooks from Exile). Their nationalism was based on Prat de la Riba's essentialist notion of an "Iberian ethnos," which they joined to Catholicism and to the patriotic romanticism of the nineteenth-century Catalan movement known as the *Renaixença,* producing an ensemble of ideological concepts that were militant in opposing Franco's repressive dictatorship, populist in promoting the egalitarianian view that *La Nació és el Poble* (the nation is the people), and anti-intellectual in rejecting Noucentisme (Casacuberta 1989). The first issue in 1943 ran a policy statement that made clear the editors' approach to culture:

> Defensem la cultura basada en els caràcters nacionals i posada al servei de l'home. Rebutgem l'intellectualisme, la deshumanitizació i la supèrbia de tota manifestació que s'anomeni cultural a si mateixa, però que pretengui sobrepassar o menystenir l'Home. Rebutgem una cultura sense contingut i que es nodria infinitament dels seu propis residus. Entenem que l'home val més que el seu rostre, el contingut més que la continent, el pensament més que la forma. Ambicionem un estil directe, senzill i digne, subordinat a l'obra. (quoted in ibid., 99–100)

> [We uphold culture grounded in national characters and put in the service of man. We reject intellectualism, dehumanization and the arrogance of every expression that calls itself cultural, but that seeks to go beyond or undervalue Man. We reject a culture without content which is infinitely nourished by its own residue. We take man to be

worth more than his face, the content more than the container, the thought more than the form. We aspire to a style that is direct, natural and appropriate, subordinated to the work.]

In their frank humanism, in their idealist assumption that "Man" exists apart from and is transparently expressed in language, these values are opposed to the materialist position of a writer like Carner for whom stylistic innovation was necessary to construct human identity. It was in fact these values that informed Sales's editorial activities upon his return to Catalunya in 1947: Despite the prohibitions of Franco's regime, Sales sought to popularize canonical works of Catalan literature in adaptations that were cast in current usage and designed especially for young readers (Bacardí 27–28).

Sales's most consequential work as a publisher and translator began after 1959, when he assumed the directorship of the Catalan press El Club dels Novel.listes. His editorial policy was decidedly nationalist, but also populist. He focused on one literary genre, the novel, as he later said, "perquè precisament els franquistes ho volien impedir i perquè era l'unica manera de fer una literatura contemporània nacional" (because precisely the Franquistas wished to stop it and because the novel was the only way to create a contemporary national literature [Ibarz 15]). Since he aimed to expand the Catalan readership, he published only accessible realistic narratives, rejecting those that were difficult to read because they lacked a coherent plot or required a specialized knowledge of literature. Thus, he published Catalan versions of such novels as Giuseppe Tomasi de Lampedusa's *The Leopard* (1962), Alan Paton's *Cry the Beloved Country* (1964) and J. D. Salinger's *The Catcher in the Rye* (1965). Sales himself translated three novels for the press, including Kazantzakis's *The Last Temptation of Christ* (1959) and Dostoevsky's *The Brothers Karamazov* (1961). To insure that the translations effectively produced the realist illusion, Sales insisted that the language closely follow current usage with an emphasis on oral forms, what he called the *llenguatge vivent* (living language) in the preface to his own novel, *Incerta glòria* (1956). This discursive strategy enhanced verisimilitude, but it also effaced the translated status of the texts. As Sales explained in introducing his version of Dostoevsky's novel:

> El Club dels Novel.listes cregué que el que importava per damunt de tot era que el traductor s'identifiqués amb l'esperit i l'estil de l'obra, que se la fes seva, que sabés posar en boca dels seus personatges un català tan viu com ho és el rus de l'original, fins al punt que el lector, llegint-la, arribés a oblidar que llegia una traducció. (Sales 1961, 8–9)

> [El Club dels Novel.listes believed that above all it was important that the translator identify with the spirit and style of the work, that he make it his, that he know how to put in his characters' mouths a Catalan as alive as the Russian of the original, to such an extent that the reader, while reading it, might come to forget that he is reading a translation.]

In the sheer invisibility of Sales's translating, Catalan readers might also overlook the deep contradictions in his nationalist agenda. He wished to create a national identity based on two exclusions: on the one hand, a resistance against the

Franquista pressure that Catalans abandon their language and speak Castilian and, on the other, a refusal of the standardized Catalan supported by Noucentist intellectuals, the *exercicis de grammàtica* (grammatical exercise) that he saw opposed to the "living language" (Sales 1956, 10). Yet not only did he translate Flaubert's *Madame Bovary* and *Salammbô* into Castilian, but his reliance on current usage in his Catalan translations as well as his novel resulted in a style filled with Castilianisms (Bacardí 30–31; Vallverdù 142–46). Sales questioned the Noucentist emphasis on French literary texts and rather chose to work with foreign literatures that were associated with relatively minor cultures whose subordinate position resembled that of Catalunya: Lampedusa's Sicily, Paton's South Africa, or the Provence of Loís Delluc whose Provençal novel *El garrell* he translated into Catalan in 1963 (Bacardí 32–33, 36–37). Yet in advocating a discursive strategy that produced the illusion of transparency, Sales was soliciting his reader's identification with the religious values that he himself perceived in foreign texts, even *The Brothers Karamazov*, which he described as "l'obra màxima de la novel.la cristiana universal" (the greatest work of the universal Christian novel [Sales 1961, 7–8]). There is, finally, the question of the foreign "spirit and style" with which he and his readers identified in his translations of Kazantzakis and Dostoevsky: since he knew no Greek or Russian, he queried specialists and based his Catalan text on several other versions of the novels, including Castilian and French (Sales 1961, 9). The linguistic and cultural differences that constituted Sales's translations might do no more than create a hybrid Catalan identity, stimulating the reader's desire for a unified nation that they simultaneously withheld.

Carner and Sales represent two nationalist agendas in translation driven by different theories and practices and reflecting different historical moments. In both cases, their defensive nationalisms sought to construct collective identities based on Catalan, and their translations can be seen as a linguistic ecology, a means of protecting and developing a language that was not simply marginal in relation to the dominant Spanish culture, but threatened with suppression. Yet important distinctions can be drawn between their work. Carner cultivated an experimentalism that took advantage of the variations in Catalan before standardization. His translations registered the foreignness of the foreign texts even as they formed a recognizably Catalan identity. Thus, they can be described as foreignizing, employing a strategy that, as Schleiermacher observed, "cannot thrive equally well in all languages, but only in those which are not the captives of too strict a bond of classical expression outside of which all is reprehensible" (Lefevere 1977, 79–80). Sales's translating, in contrast, was much more conservative, at once consolidating current usage and validating its expressive possibilities during a period when the very viability of Catalan had been weakened by Franco's regime, when "diglossia had established a foothold even in the educated classes and the quality of the spoken language was steadily deteriorating" (Balcells 144). Sales's translations were thus domesticating, written in the most familiar forms of Catalan, creating an image in which the reader could experience a self-recognition as a Catalan, however much hybridized by the diversity of the language and the foreign texts.

Carner and Sales also wrote translations that mystified—in their respective ways—the contradictions in their nationalist agendas. Both announced their intentions to translate for a national collective, but both belonged to elite literary groups who comprised their primary readerships. Carles Riba's review is a reminder that Carner's cosmopolitanism was closely linked to the taste of the Barcelona bourgeoisie. And despite Sales's adherence to popular taste his directorship of El Club dels Novel.listes made it truly a literary "club" or circle, as Montserrat Bacardí has indicated, by creating "an authentic forum that would permit Catalan writers to comment on and discuss their works, given the absence of communicative media that addressed Catalan literature" (Bacardí 31).

Perhaps the most instructive distinction between these two translators is the place of essentialism in their nationalistic thinking. Although both were influenced by Prat de la Riba's notion of a transcendental Catalan identity, Carner's openness to linguistic and cultural differences, partly because of his modernist inclination toward stylistic innovation and partly because of the variations in Catalan usage, led him to adopt a materialist approach to translation that assumed human identity was constructed in discursive formations. The sheer repressiveness of Sales's later period, however, encouraged the adoption of various conceptual defenses, all essentialistic, whether the universalist humanism of *Quaderns de l'Exili* or the egalitarian populism of the "living language."

These cases show that it would be reductive to attempt any ethical or political evaluation of translation nationalisms without considering the historical moments in which they emerged. Translation can be motivated by an essentialism that conceals the constitutive differences of the cultural identity it is deployed to form. But such an essentialism may be strategic, as Gayatri Spivak has noted, used "in a scrupulously visible political interest" (Spivak 214), with the self-critical awareness that in different historical circumstances it might harden into a conceptual repression just as strong as the political force it is intended to combat. Neither Carner nor Sales could develop this awareness in their defensive cultural situations. But in studying their examples later Catalan translators might, admitting variations in current usage that deviate from standardized forms so as to signal the foreignness of foreign texts—and make a productive difference in Catalan identities.

Works Cited

Bacardí, Montserrat, "Joan Sales i els criteris de traducció," *Quaderns: Revista de Traducció* 1, 1998, 27–38.

Balcells, Albert, *Catalan Nationalism: Past and Present*, ed. Geoffrey J. Walker, trans. Jacqueline Hall (New York: St. Martin's Press, 1996).

Bernofsky, Susan, "Schleiermacher's Translation Theory and Varieties of Foreignization: August Wilhelm Schlegel vs. Johann Heinrich Voss." *The Translator* 3, 1997, pp. 175–92.

Busquets, Loreto, *Aportació lèxica de Josep Carner a la llengua literària catalana* (Barcelona: Fundació Salvador Vives Casajuana, 1977).

Calvino, Italo, *Le Cosmicomiche* (Milano: Mondadori, 1993 [1965]).

Carner, Josep, *El reialme de la poesia*, eds. Núria Nardi and Iolanda Pelegrí (Barcelona: Edicions 62, 1986).

———— trans., *Alícia en terra de maravelles* (Barcelona: Editorial Joventut, 1987 [1927]).

Castiglione, Baldassare, *Il libro del Cortegiano*, ed. Ettore Bonora (Milano: Mursia, 1972).

Casacuberta, Margarida, "*Quaderns de l'Exili* (Mèxic 1943–1947), una revista d'agitació nacional," *Els Marges* 40, 1989, pp. 87–105.

Derrida, Jacques, "The Laws of Reflection: Nelson Mandela, In Admiration," trans. Mary Ann Caws and Isabelle Lorenz, in *For Nelson Mandela* (New York: Seaver Books, 1987), pp. 13–42.

———— "Onto-Theology of National-Humanism (Prolegomena to a Hypothesis)," *Oxford Literary Review* 14(1–2), 1992, pp. 3–23.

Easthope, Antony, *Englishness and National Culture* (London and New York: Routledge, 1999).

Ebel, Julia G, "Translation and Cultural Nationalism in the Reign of Elizabeth," *Journal of the History of Ideas* 30, 1969, pp. 593–602.

Enright, D. J., "Effrontery and Charm," *New York Review of Books* (November 21, 1968), pp. 22–24.

Hoby, Sir Thomas, trans. Baldassare Castligione, *The Book of the Courtier*, ed. Walter Raleigh (New York: AMS Press, 1967 [1900]).

Hugo, Victor, *Œuvres Complètes: Critiqué*, ed. Jean-Pierre Reynaud (Paris: Laffont, 1985), vol. 11.

Hu Ying, "The Translator Transfigured: Lin Shu and the Cultural Logic of Writing in the Late Qing," *Positions* 3, 1995, pp. 69–96.

Ibarz, Mercé, "El pensament fermat de Joan Sales," *L'Avenç* 67, 1984, p. 15.

Lee, Leo Ou-fan, *The Romantic Generation of Modern Chinese Writers* (Cambridge: Harvard University Press, 1973).

Lefevere, André, ed. and trans., *Translating Literature: The German Tradition from Luther to Rosenzweig* (Assen: Van Gorcum, 1977).

———— ed. and trans., *Translation/History/Culture: A Sourcebook* (London and New York: Routledge, 1992).

Llobera, Josep R., "The Idea of the *Volksgeist* in the Formation of Catalan Nationalist Ideology," *Ethnic and Racial Studies* 6, 1983, pp. 332–50.

Ortín, Marcel, *La prosa literària de Josep Carner* (Barcelona: Quaderns Crema, 1996).

———— "Els Dickens de Josep Carner i els seus crítics," *Quaderns: Revista de Traducció* 7, 2001.

Pericay, Xavier and Ferran Toutain, *El malentès del Noucentisme: Tradició i plagi a la prosa catalana moderna* (Barcelona: Proa, 1996).

Prat de la Riba, Enric, *La nacionalitat catalana* (Barcelona: Edicions 62, 1998 [1906]).

Riba, Carles, *Clàssics i moderns*, ed. Joaquim Molas (Barcelona: Edicions 62, 1979).

Sales, Joan, *Incerta glòria* (Barcelona: Club Editor, 1956).

———— trans., "Nota dels editors catalans," in Fiodor Dostoievski, *Els germans Karamàzov* (Barcelona: Club Editor, 1961).

Schleiermacher, Friedrich, *Selected Sermons*, ed. and trans. M. F. Wilson (New York: Funk and Wagnalls, 1890).

Schwartz, Benjamin, *In Search of Wealth and Power: Yan Fu and the West* (Cambridge: Harvard University Press, 1964).

Sellent Arús, Joan, "La traducció literària en català al segle XX: alguns títols representatius," *Quaderns: Revista de Traducció* 2, 1998, pp. 23–32.

Semanov, V. I. *Lu Hsün and His Predecessors*, trans. C. Alber (White Plains, New York: M.E. Sharp, 1980).

Spivak, Gayatri, "Subaltern Studies: Deconstructing Historiography," in *The Spivak Reader*, eds. Donna Landry and Gerald MacLean (New York and London: Routledge, 1985), pp. 203–36.

Vallverdú, Francesc, *L'escriptor català i el problema de la llengua* (Barcelona: Edicions 62, 1968).

Venuti, Lawrence, "The Art of Literary Translation: An Interview with William Weaver," *Denver Quarterly* 17(2), 1982, pp. 16–26.

———— *The Translator's Invisibility: A History of Translation* (London and New York: Routledge, 1995).

———— *The Scandals of Translation: Towards an Ethics of Difference* (London and New York: Routledge, 1998).

Ward, Albert, *Book Production, Fiction and the German Reading Public, 1740–1800* (Oxford: Oxford University Press, 1974).

Weaver, William, trans., Italo Calvino, *Cosmicomics* (San Diego and New York: Harcourt Brace, 1968).

Wong, Laurence, "Lin Shu's Story-retelling as Shown in His Chinese Translation of *La Dame aux camellias*," *Babel* 44, 1998, 208–33.

Nationum Origo

JACQUES LEZRA

> [W]hat needeth a Dictionarie? Naie, if I offer service but to them that need it, with what face seek I a place with your excellent Ladiship (my most-most honored, because best-best adorned Madame) who by conceited industrie; or industrious conceite, in Italian as in French, in French as in Spanish, in all as in English, understand what you reade, write as you reade, and speake as you write; yet rather charge your minde with matter, then your memorie with words? And if this présent presènt so small profit, I must confesse it brings much lesse delight: for, what pleasure in a plot of simples, *O non viste, o mal note, o mal gradate*, Or not seene, or ill knowne, or ill accepted?
>
> —John Florio, *A Worlde of Wordes*

> *The Manifesto, says The Manifesto* in German, will be published in English, French, German, Italian, Flemish and Danish. Ghosts also speak different languages, national languages, like the money from which they are, as we shall see, inseparable. As circulating currency, money bears local and political character, it "uses different national languages and wears different national uniforms."
>
> —Jacques Derrida, *Specters of Marx*[1]

Globalization has taken our tongues from us—local, autochthonous, idiomatic, ancestral tongues. Its clamorous internationalism hangs critics on a mute peg, with no common voice or general vocabulary on which to string alternative inter- or transnational forms of work, thought, and organization. And so the disarmed, heteroglot opposition takes shelter in various weak utopianisms, in weakly regulative images generally and understandably drawn from increasingly abstract domains (from reinvigorated notions of the "human" and of "humanism," for instance or, most recently, from the sketchy descriptions of an antihegemonic *Europe* that Jürgen Habermas and Derrida erect against the depredations of the United States in Iraq and elsewhere). Consider for example these words from Michael Hardt and Antonio Negri's *Empire*, in which an active and complex ethic of circumstantial *translation* serves this sheltering, utopian function:

[T]here is no common language of struggles that could "translate" the particular language of each into a cosmopolitan language. Struggles in other parts of the world and even our own struggles seem to be written in an incomprehensible foreign language. This too points toward an important political task: to construct a new common language that facilitates communication, as the languages of anti-imperialism and proletarian internationalism did for the struggles of a previous era. Perhaps this needs to be a new type of communication that functions not on the basis of resemblances but on the basis of differences: a communication of singularities.[2]

Not a little *pathos* inflects these lines, in which Negri and Hardt seek to recast the grammar of organic, critical, intellectual discourse in the wake of the collapse of state socialism. Their acknowledgment that the global vocabularies of more or less orthodox, internationalist Marxisms disastrously ignored every struggle's particularities quickly becomes a way of reflecting upon the increasing fragmentation of current critical idioms. For Negri and Hardt, the peculiarity of one or another circumstance requires—the injunction is distinctly an ethico-political one—an act of translation into a "new common language," imagined here as a "communication of singularities" in both senses furnished by the genitive: communication between radically particular, circumstantial "struggles," and the communication of that particularity across national, linguistic, political, and other frontiers. (The massive, coincident global protests against the war in Iraq surely furnish a vivid example of this double translation.)

Set aside the claims of novelty (the "new common language," the "new type of communication" that Negri and Hardt describe). A part of the appeal of *Empire* (and of many of the most effective, weak-utopian critiques of globalization) is surely due to the odd *familiarity* of its prescriptions. Thus the concept that Empire seeks to furnish for weak-utopian "translation," a vehicle for the "communication of singularities," has the unmistakable shape of the general equivalent or index commodity value.[3] (*Empire* shifts the equivalent's indexing function from the general economic domain, to the critico-descriptive one.) So also the figure of the critic, whose new, singular "translations" retain the roughly Gramscian gusto for reasoned *sabotage* that Negri's early writing provocatively displays. Even the notion of oppositional internationalism itself, one might argue, arises alongside the earliest understandings of the nation form, as Europe reached in the course of the sixteenth century for a cultural, economic, and political modernity whose defining description would not arrive until much later.

Say then that we seek useful, consequential discursive alternatives to globalization—a "tongue," a cosmopolitan epistemology, a new international. We ask in this context what might be the *genealogy* of the recent turn to "translation," of its "new" characterization as a communication of singularities, of its deployment as a weak-utopian concept on which a critique of economic and cultural globalization can be mounted. We understand these questions to be prefatory but necessary to considering the ethico-political demand made for contemporary intellectuals in works like *Empire*, or by critics like Edward Said, Homi Bhabha, Derrida, Habermas, and others. Even posing these roughly genealogical questions requires of us a peculiar set of historical translations among the contemporary moment, the defining and familiar nineteenth-century historiographic devices that continue to inform our postmodern vocabularies, and the early modern historical moment when technological, demographic, and other shifts bring the twin knots of incipient nationalization and linguistic translation to the fore, and into explicit contact with each other.[4] So let's open this wavy, genealogical avenue by observing that Ernest Renan's own, famous question of 1882, "Qu'est-ce qu'une nation?" is already determined and over-determined by a fantastical voluntarism built about and against an earlier understanding of linguistic identity that is troublingly fluid, or fractious, or heteroglot. In a word, against an early modern form of collective and individual identity that cannot be *translated* into "national" or protonational collectivities. But as he moves famously toward his definition of the nation as "a soul, a spiritual principle," Renan appears untroubled. He considers and sets aside the concept's traditional vehicles: race, "ownership in common of a rich legacy of memories," religion, common interests, and geography.[5] Only when he takes up "le langage" will Renan's most searching claim clearly emerge: "There is in man something superior to language: and that is the will" [Il y a dans l'homme quelque chose de supérieur à la langue: c'est la volonté].[6] *La volonté*. For Renan, the notion braids together in time and act the juridical and the psychosocial domains, tidily gathered in this grammatical triplet: "current consent, a desire to live together, and the will to value the undivided heritage that one has received" [le consentement actuel, le désir de vivre ensemble, la volonté de continuer à faire valoir l'héritage qu'on a reçu indivis]. Note the distinctly pre-Nietzschean priority granted to the will over historical accidents, as well as the almost scholastic certainty "Qu'est-ce qu'une nation?" expresses that the faculty can be cleanly separated from contiguous faculties and concepts (memory, desire, interest). Renan's earlier remarks "Des services rendus aux sciences historiques par la philologie" (1878) make the point again, starkly: "the nation is for us something absolutely separate from language" (chose absolument séparée de la langue). "There is something that we place above language and above race," Renan continues, "and that is respect for man, understood as a moral being," a "being" whose moral autonomy is manifested characteristically, as in Kant and in the ethico-political tradition that flows from the second *Critique*, as a "will to continue living together" (volonté de continuer à vivre ensemble).[7]

For Renan, as for his contemporary Jakob Burckhardt, the highest *political* example of the superceding of linguistic particularism is Switzerland; the highest historical examples of the autonomous acts of will that constitute the decision "to continue to live together" are to be found among the "great men of the Renaissance, who were neither French, nor Italian, nor German. They had rediscovered, by means of their traffic with antiquity, the secret of the human mind's true education" [Ils avaient retrouvé, par leur commerce avec l'antiquité, le secret de l'éducation véritable de l'esprit humain].[8] Both the location and the period are unsurprising choices. We know that England, Spain, and Italy saw a remarkable burst of published translations from the classical languages by the last quarter of the sixteenth century, but the emergence of what can fairly be called a *European* humanist lexical culture dates perhaps to the appearance of Nebrija's influential 1499 *Gramática*, or to the publication in 1502 of Ambrosius Calepinus's *Cornucopiæ* (later re-edited and better known as the *Dictionarium* or as the *Calepino*).[9] By "lexical culture" I mean the loose subgroup of practices and ideologies that surround and concern the writing, copying, printing, and transmission of lexicons, grammars, hard-word books, and dictionaries, both monolingual and multilingual, in the new print culture of the European elite.[10] What better evidence that language is imagined to serve the will, than that provided by these various texts, intended as linguistic instruments for teaching oneself, or others, different languages? And I intend the double stress on "Europe" and on the "human." *Pari passu* with recognizable *local* or even (proto-)*national* forms of identification (you and I identify with each other as speakers of this or that distinct and historically discrete language, or as subject to the same autochthonous political and economic regimes), the Renaissance's traveling books and manuscripts about words, *calepinos*, *trésors*, *florilegia*, *gramáticas*, primers on translation, and assorted other metalinguistic texts furnish spectacularly deterritorialized, polyglot identities.[11] This for instance is from Sebastián de Covarrubias's 1611 definition of *lengua*, "tongue"; remark the suturing work that the term "human," *humano*, performs, as well as the characteristic stress on the *pedagogical* scene:

> La noticia de muchas lenguas se puede tener por gran felicidad en la tierra, pues con ellas comunica el hombre diversas naciones, y suele ser de mucho fruto en casos de necessidad, refrenando el furor del enemigo, que hablándole en su propia lengua se reporta y concibe una cierta afinidad de parentesco que le obliga a ser humano y clemente. . . . Yo también me contentaría con que los professores de qualquiera facultad supiessen y aprendiessen juntamente con la lengua Latina la lengua Griega; pues para toda diciplina sería de grandíssima importancia.

> [Knowledge of many tongues can be a matter of great happiness on earth, for with them man can communicate with diverse nations, which can be of great profit in case of need, as it dampens the fury of the enemy, for, speaking to him in his own tongue, he moderates himself and conceives a certain familial affinity that obliges him to be human and merciful. . . . And I too would be satisfied if teachers of any subject knew and learned the Greek language alongside Latin, for this would be of great importance for all disciplines.][12]

For the historiography of the late Enlightenment, then, the Humanistic *internationalism* one glimpses here is both an effect and the primary source of early modern, European lexical culture. The knotted, fiercely overdetermined concept takes shape in association with the loose origins of modern disciplinarity, in hand with the work of (linguistic, cultural, and historical) translation, inseparably from post-Tridentine philosophico-religious debates concerning the nature and attributes of the *will*, and braided with an ethico-organic "conception of familial affinity" among "humans" from which flow distinctly *political* forms of identity, association, and obligation. Recall, too, in this sketch of the discursive *thicket* embrambling lexical culture with protonational identification in early modern Europe, and in its defining historiographies, the double work that Renan's term "commerce" carries out. The emergence of protonational formations coincides not just with the rise of a speculative class of "grands hommes" belonging properly to no particular nation ("ils n'étaient ni français, ni italiens, ni allemands," writes Renan), but also with the consolidation of a *commercial*, merchant class equipped (financially, technically, culturally) to negotiate the diverse requirements of different trading circumstances. More forcefully: the circulations of lexical culture and the earliest construction of an international commercial regime (inter-European, pan-Mediterranean, or trans-Atlantic) cannot be separated from each other. Internationalist, lexical humanism arises with, conditions and enables (is conditioned and enabled by) commercial flows based in and profiting from increasingly differentiated commodity and labor markets—hence the peculiar ambivalence of all recent appeals to a "humanist" alternative to the encroachment of globalization under information-capitalism.[13]

Or put it like this. After Renan, Burckhardt, and Marx, after the aesthetico-political concepts of the "nation" and the "civilization of the Renaissance" assume their well-known organizing function in the historical epistemologies of the middle nineteenth century, as the notion that a "new mercantilism" characterizing European trade from between 1570 and 1620 comes to form the basis of "modern," labor-based economics, we are free to derive from texts like Covarrubias's the determining image of a network of "grands hommes" and great educators linked in a reciprocal commerce with antiquity when not with each other, a baggy network of scholars, merchants, and courtiers trading texts, commodities, and ideas across and against the grain of religious, linguistic, and protonational differences. This translating figure (it can be many-headed: think of Pico, Erasmus, Covarrubias, Marguerite de Navarre, More, and others) represents the shadow-form of a conciliar orthodoxy with equally internationalist reach and desires: indeed, the institutional history of the Counter-Reformation Church after Trent cannot be understood except in light of the uncomfortable propinquity between conciliar ecumenicism and humanist internationalism.

Think again of the heroic shape that the ethico-political demand takes in Negri and Hardt's *Empire*. For them, as for the great nineteenth-century historiographies that they seek to renew, the modern subject's movement beyond a local, native language, beyond a received *legs de souvenirs* or a limiting autochthony, is achieved just as the genuine "spirit of a nation" must be for Renan: as a communitarian form of identification deliberately and repeatedly elected. The humanist internationalism that their work recalls thus preserves as a core, determining value the labor of deliberate and informed choice: The archaic function of the will, in its articulation with language and education, is the *minimum* that differentiates it from conciliar, corporatist internationalism, both in early modernity and in the mediatized postmodernity we inhabit. But the articulation of pedagogy, will and translation at the heart of humanist internationalism considerably precedes the formation of modern "nations" that Renan's stress on the Renaissance's "grands hommes" helped to diagnose and to codify. And in certain respects, the translating figure we derive in light of modern historiographies, from Renan to *Empire*, considerably misconstrues the much more fluid

shape that lexical culture furnishes to early modern humanism. The print industry in the time of the *grands hommes* is still not consolidated, ideologically or
technically; easier communication has not yet meant a standardized pedagogy or
a conventional "commerce" with antiquity or with religious protocol; the definition of the will's freedom or servitude in the pedagogical, doctrinal and philosophical domains is sharply and explicitly divided). Impressed decisively into the
academic resistance to the ideologies of economic liberalization, the contemporary construction of Humanist internationalism obscures a characteristic troubling of the relation between "will" and "language" to be found at work in the
lexical culture of early modern Europe—may, indeed, arise so as to displace or
evade it. One might risk a new, rather different return to the "grands hommes de
la Renaissance," to the *weakest*, that is, to the least "grand" aspects of their
thought. In the hesitant translations, in the linguistic troubles we encounter in
the work of Covarrubias, Ascham, Minsheu, Verstegan—to say nothing of
Machiavelli, Bruno, or Shakespeare—we come across the rough concept for a
"common language" for communicating singularities and for "electing" thereby
to identify with one or another communicative commonality. The cost we pay
for learning this language, for trading in this rough concept, will be high, for in
the lexical culture of Early Modern Europe the "will" is invested elsewhere than
in individuals: in accidents, contingencies, and "cases" both linguistic and historical. The "communication of singularities" on which early modern lexical culture turns blocks the articulation of individualism, the close cousin (to stay
within Covarrubias's familial metaphor) of humanist internationalism, with will
that comes to support the ethico-political project of the Enlightenment.

Here are two useful ways of approaching the matter. The first comes from the
series of definitions that Covarrubias provides for the term "translation" in his
Tesoro de la lengua castellana. Glossing the hoary etymology that links traducción
and "translation" to the Latin *trans-* and *ducere*, to carry over or across, the Spanish lexicographer and seeming translator writes: "lleuar de vn lugar a otro alguna
cosa, o encaminarla . . . el boluer la sentencia de vna lengua en otra, como
traduzir de Italiano, o de Francés algún libro en Castellano" [To take something
from one place to another, or to set it on a path . . . to change the phrase from
one language into another, as when one translates a book from Italian, or
French, into Castilian"].[14] The geographical vehicle is traditional: linguistic
translation—*traducción*—resembles for Covarrubias merely carrying or returning, *llevar* or *bolver alguna cosa* (a national language or idiom, say), from one spot
to another. That this *alguna cosa* remains the same from one language to another
simply reflects the underlying ontological stability of things, irrespective of the
various names they may carry (a stone is a stone, whether it is called *piedra* or
pierre: only our certainty that this is so allows us to identify "pierre" as a translation of "piedra," and either as a suitable version of "stone"). The *speakers* of these
different languages borrow from the logically necessary stability of the referent a
companion sense that they too are at heart the same—very much, in other words,
as one's capacity to speak another language suggests to an enemy "a certain familial affinity that obliges him to be human." But linguistic translation *also* re-

sembles, as the definition's odd, pseudoappositive shape suggests, just setting something (an idiom, language, *cosa*) on the road, *en* and *caminar*—with no sense that one follows that road oneself, or concerns oneself to ensure that *alguna cosa* safely reaches the end of the road, or has any stake in how, after all, *alguna cosa* (a national language, again) might "move" along this or any other road. One might make the point more forcefully by stressing the disjunctive aspect of Covarrubias's definition: translation is *either* a way for a subject to carry a particular, identifiable thing from one location in which it has one name, to another in which it has a different one; *or* it is the gesture of releasing a thing from its name, placing it as it were underway, upon the road, for any one to take. The stakes of this rather recondite grammatical point become clearer if we recall the explicitly *political* function of the conjunction "o" in the title of Covarrubias's dictionary: *Tesoro de la lengua castellana, o española*. The project of national centralization initiated in Spain under the Hapsburgs, as well as the history of local and regional resistance to that project, might be said to hang on the status of this slight "o," disagreements over different efforts to make *lo castellano* synonymous with rather than alternative to *lo español* showing no signs of abating to this day.

Or we might simply read on in the *Tesoro*'s definition of translation, where it becomes increasingly clear that Covarrubias isn't quite sure which road a *translation* actually "takes," or who or what, for that matter, is taking that road:

> TRADVCION . . . Si esto no se haze con primor y prudencia, sabiendo igualmente las dos lenguas, y trasladando en algunas partes, no conforme a la letra, pero según el sentido sería lo que dixo vn hombre sabio y crítico, que aquello era verter, tomándolo en sinificación de derramar y echar a perder. Esto aduirtió bien Horacio en su *Arte poética* diziendo, "Nec verbum verbo curabis reddere fidus Interpres."[15]

> [TRANSLATION . . . If it is not carried out with care and prudence, knowing both languages equally, and translating in some places, not as the letter demands, but according to the sense, it would be what a wise and acute man once said, that this was to spill, meaning by this to overturn, or waste or spoil something. Horace noted this clearly in his *Ars poetica* when he wrote: "Nec verbum verbo curabis reddere fidus Interpres."] (As a true translator you will take care not to translate word for word.)

This seems in most respects perfectly anodyne, even hackneyed. Just what it is that gets "spilled" or "wasted" or "spoiled" when one translates "as the letter demands" remains unclear, however: is it the original's "sense," *sentido*? Manifestly, though not quite, for it is hard to say just what sense Covarrubias intends to give the term *sentido* in this brief definition, in which the "sense" of "translation" is translated as "overturning" or "knocking something over," but only if one "means by these" latter terms some "sense" stipulated by the faithful interpreter. "To overturn" or "knock over," *verter*, can be rendered as both "to spill," *derramar*, and "to waste or to spoil," *echar a perder*": but are "spilling" and "wasting" quite the same? Are they equally good translations of *verter*? (They are at least not synonyms: things go to waste without being spilled, and vice versa.) The "sense" even of a "wise man's" phrases requires a gloss, a faithful interpreter, a very inward of the "wise man," an adviser who already knows the "sense" of his "sense," the meaning of his meaning. It is not unreasonable to imagine the Spanish lexicographer and pedagogue stepping into this consular role, not just here, where he translates the "sense" of another's "translation" for his readers, but throughout his *Tesoro . . .*, whose definitions set the sense of the Castilian tongue for its users, native and not. And say that we accept the adviser's gloss, his sense of how the "wise man" *intended* to render the translation of "translation" as "spilling" or "spoiling," *verter* as *derramar* or *echar a perder*. Matters get tricky again as we reflect more closely on the three-fold means that Covarrubias suggests for avoiding this wasteful "spillage" (of sense, in whichever sense we take it). In order to translate truly or faithfully, he writes, we must know both languages equally, proceed with prudence and care, and at moments translate "according to the sense" rather than "as the letter demands." Here the crossing of Horatian poetics with a Pauline hermeneutics (the letters of Mosaic law giving way to the sense or spirit of the new law, as mere obedience gives way to faith) proves less than stable. For just as the "sense" of *sentido* and of *verter* turns muddy just where it should be clearest, where it bears the greatest weight, so too does the "faith" or "faithfulness" that guides the *interpres* lose its sole sense just where it should least require interpreting. The translator's faithfulness to the original, whether of the plodding, word-for-word sort or of the more delicately interpretive kind, flows not only from his great and equal acquaintance with the languages in translation, but also from his enjoying two distinct affective dispositions (*primor* and *prudencia*). These dispositions, Covarrubias's text makes clear, turn out to be almost incompatible sociologically, and they are aligned throughout the *Tesoro* with two quite different class positions. "Primor," which the *Tesoro* uses (under *primo*) to describe artisans who do work expertly, is again not only a partial synonym, but also a contrastive term to *prudencia*, a term associated with "wise and acute or critical" hierophants, and that will notoriously come to characterize no less a figure than Philip II (remembered to this day as *el rey prudente*). Recall for instance how the distinction between craft and art in treatments of Velázquez's work supports descriptions, ranging from the psychological to the materialist, of the painter's ambitions at court (his painting "Las hilanderas," for example, has appeared to many an allegory of the relation between the material *craft* of tapestry-making, and the higher *art* of dramatic representation that true painting strives to capture): in the *Tesoro*, we might conclude, the translator, both craftsman and "prudent" man, also works both as *lengua*, Covarrubias's term for a primarily *spoken*, mechanical "intervention" ("lengua, el intérprete que declara una lengua con otra, interviniendo entre dos de diferentes lenguas") and as the *intérprete*, who works characteristically in writing, with the "alusiones y términos metafóricos" of diverse languages (Covarrubias's example of bad *interpretación* is a droll mistranslation from the Spanish of *La Celestina* into overly literal Italian). But Covarrrubias's brief descriptions of the work of translation cannot proceed with the schematic hygiene one would expect, given all that seems to hang upon the term. "Care and prudence," we understand, are needed not only in carrying-over the sense of a phrase, whether "according to the letter" or following the sense of the sentence, but also in distinguishing those moments when one needs to vary from conformity to the letter in the first place. We are not free, in short, to align plain, workaday translation (*conforme a la letra*) with an inflexible commitment to the letter or the old Law of the text, and the looser, "prudential" translation *según el sentido* with a new, Pauline attention to its spirit. Merely knowing two languages is not enough; to achieve the *intérprete's* prudential understanding of the "sense" of a text, and in order to distinguish when its translation is to be carried out *conforme a la letra* or *según el sentido*, is a matter of education, of faith, and of the will.

Now consider how Roger Ascham's very different *Schole-Master* (1570) treats the articulation of translation and education in the production of what we are calling lexical culture. Ascham's concern in *The Schole-Master* is how best to teach "children, to understand, write, and speake, the Latin tong, but specially purposed for the private bringing up of youth in Ientlemen and Noble mens houses."[16] The *Schole-Master's* argument against wholesale "beating" has been a staple of progressive educational theory, in particular these lines that bear on the formation of the child's will: "Beate a child, if he daunce not well, & cherish him, though he learne not well, ye shall have him unwilling to go to daunce, & glad to go to his booke . . . And thus, will in children, wisely wrought withal, may easely be wonne to be very well willing to learne. And witte in children, by nature, namely memory, the onely key and keeper of all lerning, is rediest to receive, and surest to keepe, any maner of thing, that is learned when we were yong" (10v–11r). Ascham further warns that the schoolmaster must be gentle in order "wisely" to work the young scholar's will toward learning, and offers as the practical means and best example of this gentle work what he refers to, classically, as double translation. This is how Ascham puts it:

> Translate [some portion of Tullie] you yourself, into plaine naturall Englishe, and then geve it him to translate into Latin againe: allowing him good space and time to do it, both with diligent heede, & good visement. Here his witte shall be new set on worke: his iudgement, for right choice, trewlie tried: his memorie, for sure retaining, better exercised, than by learning any thing without the booke: and here, how much he hath profited, shall plainlie appeare. When he bringeth it translated unto you, bring forth the place of Tullie: lay them together: compare the one with the other: commend his good choice, & right placing of wordes: shew his faultes iently, but blame them not over sharply: for, of such missings, ientlie admonished of, procedeth glad & good heed taking: of good heed taking, springeth chiefly knowledge. (31v–32r)

Ascham's strategy is a particularly humane one (note the palliative expressions: "good space and time," "commend his good choice, & right placing," show faults "iently," do not blame "sharply," admonish again "iently"), though it turns on a rather problematical pivot: the supposition that the schoolmaster's first translation—into "plaine naturall English"—will as it were vanish into Tully's text on being translated (back) into Latin. The schoolmaster's "comparison," "commending," "showing" and so on depend upon his furnishing a "plaine naturall English" version of the original from which the student can fairly derive an

approximate re-translation, an ideal circuit closely reminiscent of the closed geographies we first found in Covarrubias (*lleuar de vn lugar a otro alguna cosa, o encaminarla*, [to take something from one place to another]). As to the possibility
that the schoolmaster may have lost his way, or that his translation may merely
have set the Latin text as it were under way, *en camino*, or that he may have sacrificed sense or "right placing" of words in his desire to produce "plaine naturall
English": in brief, as to the possibility that the *first* translation should also be the
subject of "comparison" with the original (and with the student's *second* translation), that the humane authority of the pedagogue, *lengua*, or *intérprete* hangs in
the balance here as well, Ascham's work is entirely silent.

It would be anachronistic, not to say absurd, to expect a pedagogy of the oppressed from Ascham, however "progressive" or modern his tone may appear to
us. My point is a different one. Note the genuinely remarkable lines with which
Ascham closes his description of the pedagogy of double translation: "of such
missings, ientlie admonished of, procedeth glad & good heed taking: of good
heed taking, springeth chiefly knowledge." Here Ascham proceeds with great
subtlety, combining registers that stress on the one hand the schoolmaster's disciplinary and monitory role (he "compares," he "admonishes"), while on the
other hand they acknowledge that the pupil's knowledge itself "springs" from
other, mediating and consequent habits that the schoolmaster may have encouraged, but does not directly control. Just as the schoolmaster's "plaine naturall
English" vanishes in the circuit of double translation, so too does Ascham's pedagogy itself seem to fade from an active, monitory role, becoming merely the occasion for the springing-forth of the pupil's knowledge. One is inclined to approve this almost Rousseauian account—with the sharp reservation that this
double vanishing, of the translation and the translator, lesson and teacher, into
the apparent knowledge and the spontaneous will of the pupil finally shelters the
schoolmaster (and *The Schole-Master*) from "comparison," from "blame," from
admonishment, and from judgments, however gentle, concerning his and the
work's "faultes" and "missings." In the humane scene in which the pupil's knowledge and will are fashioned, the technique of double translation vanishingly es-
tablishes and then protectively erases from view the school's mastery and its invisible persistence *as the will and very language* of the pupil.

My purpose is not to make Ascham and Covarrubias out as precursors of Al-
thusser on ideological apparatuses (a grotesque but appealing thought), but to
suggest the nature of the overdeterminations that the concept of translation suffers in early modern articulations of identity. Covarrubias and Ascham embed in
their different, complementary descriptions of the translator and of the techniques and purposes of translation local anxieties concerning the translator's so-
cioeconomic status, concerning the stability of the translated work and the original, the legitimacy of the pedagogical enterprise to which translation seems
intimately tied, concerning finally the "freedom" of a will constituted in and by
means of this pedagogical-linguistic enterprise. It lies much beyond the scope of
this essay to convey a full sense of the economic, ethico-political registers in
which these "local anxieties" operate in early modern Europe. We might produc-

tively complicate matters, though, by considering briefly two roughly complementary, roughly contemporaneous works, John Minsheu's 1599 A *Dictionarie in
Spanish and English*, adapted from Richard Perceval's 1591 dictionary, and Richard
Verstegan's odd and influential A *Restitution of Decayed Intelligence in Antiquities;
concerning the most noble and renowmed English nation* (1605), that more directly
link the figure of translation to the consolidation of national identities and trading regimes.

The *Restitution* opens with a dedication to King James I, followed by an "Epistle to our Nation" in which Verstegan, after noting "the very naturall affection
which generally is in all men to heare of the woorthynesse of their anceters" and
"seeing how divers nations did labor to revyve the old honour and glorie of their
own beginings and anceters, and how in so dooing they shewed themselves the
moste kynd lovers of their naturall friends and countrimen," deplores the prevailing confusion among both "our English wryters" and "divers forreyn writers"
(Jean Bodin is Verstegan's example) between "the antiquities of the Britans" and
the "offsprings and descents" of the English.[17] The balance of the *Restitution* . . .
will be devoted to recovering the "true originall and honorable antiquitie" of the
English nation, a project animated in seemingly equal parts by the wish to set
"the reverend antiquaries" of England straight and by "the greatnes of my Love,"
Verstegan says, "unto my most noble nation; most deere unto mee of any nation
in the world, and which with all my best endevours I desire to gratify." It is rather
difficult to assess the value that these fulsome expressions of national pride and
nostalgia might have had at the time of the work's publication. The dedication
to James, whose Scots and Catholic roots placed him aslant of the dominant
British tradition and in particular of Elizabeth's harshly repressive measures
against English recusants, suggests Verstegan's quite understandable effort to en-
list to his cause a monarch whose background seemed briefly to promise much to
Catholics. The extent of Verstegan's own interest in recusant politics, both
within and without England, is still obscure—though it was by no means negligi-
ble.[18] Verstegan was the agent in Antwerp of the exiled English Jesuit leader,
Robert Person [Parsons], and was charged by Person with translating and publishing Person's important *Responsio ad Edictum* of 1592; animated no doubt by a
zeal no less commercial than religious, Verstegan also wrote two pamphlets serving in some measure to preface and advertise the *Responsio* or *Philopater*, as it
came to be known (after Person's pseudonym: Andreas Philopater). The *Philopater* represented the most vigorous and consequential Jesuit response to the 1591
proclamation of Jesuit "sedition," and more generally to the religious politics of
Elizabeth I's treasurer, Lord William Cecil.[19] Verstegan's two pamphlets, published anonymously in Antwerp in 1591 and 1592, came in the shape first
of a *Declaration* . . . and then of An *Advertisement written to a Secretarie of my
L. Treasurers of Ingland, by an Inglishe Intelligencer as he passed through Germanie
towards Italie.*

Verstegan illustrates the opening page of the *Restitution* with an emblem of his
own devising, showing the tower of Babel and the dispersal of its builders into
different linguistic nations. The emblem's *lemma* reads "*Nationum origo.*"

Nationum Origo.

Image from the opening page of the *Restitution*, showing the Tower of Babel. *Nationum origio*, the title vignette from Richard Verstagan's *A restitution of decayed intelligence* (London: Iohn Bill, 1628). Reproduced courtesy of the Department of Special Collections, General Library System, University of Wisconsin-Madison.

At the time, and reflecting the influence of Josephus's interpretation of Genesis 11, the story of Babel was understood as a parable of hubris, and as the origin of linguistic variation from a common tongue.[20] The choice of image is of considerable interest, the emblem of Babel conceivably serving in 1605 as a sort of double warning to the new King—against provoking divisiveness within his kingdom, but also, perhaps more interestingly, as a comment on the policies of his predecessor Elizabeth, represented compactly both by the aspiring and quarreling masses hubristically raising the tower of Anglicanism against the Roman church, and as the source of European and national division, of the edicts that provoke England's division into different (religious and linguistic) "nations." It is not I think farfetched to imagine the distinctly physiognomic composition of the woodcut (a nasal, phallicoid tower, distant armies resolving into eyes and brows, a cluster of foregrounded squadrons in the triangular formation of a mouth and

two cheeks) as a sort of landscaped portrait of the King, a looking-glass emblem
of James in the manner of the various chorographic portraits of Elizabeth associating her with her kingdom. Nor can it be discounted, given the peculiarly personal turn that the "Epistle to our nation" takes, that this Babel-faced fron-
tispiece also serves, fascinatingly, as Verstegan's effort at a self-portrait. Here is
how the "Epistle" continues:

> For albeit my grandfather *Theodore Rowland Verstegan* was borne in the duchie of *Gel-
> dres* (and there descended of an ancient and woorshipful familie) whence by reason of
> the warres and losse of his freindes hee (beeing a young man) came into *England* about
> the end of the raign of king *Henry the seaventh*, and there maried, & soone after dyed;
> leaving my father at his death but nyne monethes old, which gave cause of making his
> fortune meaner than els it might have bin: yet can I accompt my self of no other but of
> the English nation, aswel for that *England* hath bin my sweet birth-place, as also for
> that I needs must pas in the self descent and ofspring of that thryce noble nation; unto
> the which with all dutifull respect and kynd affection I present this my labor.

Victor Houliston has suggested that both Verstegan and Person conceive of the
Elizabethan repression of the Jesuit order (and of related events, like the foundation of the Jesuit colleges in Valladolid) on two competing models, a Providential and a consequentialist one (Providential, because divinely sanctioned, motivated and understood; consequentialist, because flowing from freely chosen
human actions).[21] Houliston has in mind Person and Verstegan's pamphlets in
response to the 1591 edict of expulsion, but a similar hesitation between historiographic models is at work in the *Restitution . . .* as well. Here, the story of the
origin of nations that Verstegan tells accounts for linguistic variation, and for
subsequent scholarly and doctrinal disagreements concerning that variation, by
making the unexpected destruction of the original language parallel *both* to a
form of cultural forgetting (nations and national languages drift apart "naturally," forgetting an original tongue into which they can no longer translate their
words); *and* to the effect of persuasion (by means of untruths, violence, coercion:
nations and natural languages are separated by an act or acts of will, divine or
human, from each other and from their common tongue). Verstegan's exile, we
infer, is both a bit of Providence and a deplorable human act; he both can and
cannot hold Elizabeth (and then James) to account for the repudiation of the Jesuits and for his own circumstances; nations originate in a catastrophic *decision*,
or grow apart gradually, consequentially, without the direct intervention of any
human or other agency. The "Epistle's" autobiographical turn, as well as the odd
compounding (if that is what it is) of the figures of James, Verstegan, the Biblical
landscape and Verstegan's "sweet birth-place," England, would seem to sit un-
easily upon this double stool. And perhaps necessarily so: for the *Restitution* envi-
sions a mythico-religious model of linguistic and national identity characterized
by the very exilic insecurity that Babel inaugurates and that Elizabeth later imposes, a model of individual and collective agency built upon the same unresolved hesitation between Providential and consequential accounts of an event's
origins (and of a person's: Verstegan's own genealogy, for instance, syntactically

atwitch between "albeit" and "and yet," the two grammatical horns of the providentialist and consequentialist dilemma). The practice, history and theory of translation are for Verstegan the record of this insecure subjectivity.

Minsheu's situation is on its face much different from Verstegan's. A teacher of languages in London, he is not directly associated with the Catholic cause. There is some evidence that he was of Jewish origin (a significant detail, Jesuits and Jews being in different ways marginal populations under Elizabeth and James, and more than many others interested for obvious reasons in the economics and cultural-religious politics of translation). Minsheu seems to have led a rather hard-scrabble life, moving at one point to Cambridge so as to finish work on his 1599 *Dictionarie* . . . For so minor a figure he is not uncontroversial: the scale and audacity of his scholarly borrowings were such that to this day he is routinely referred to as an arch-plagiarist (Ben Jonson succinctly calls him a "rogue"), though one with a famously enterprising and famously persistent side.[22] Finding it hard to scare up a publisher for his *Ductor in linguas* (1617), Minsheu sold subscriptions to the volume, which he then published himself—the first subscription publication in England; nonetheless, he is remembered by Edward Phillips, in the *New World of English Words* of 1658, as "Mr. *Minshaw* that spent his life and estate in scrutinizing into Languages, still remaines obnoxious to the misconstructions of many . . . invading censurers."[23] His *Dictionarie* and more obviously still his later and much better known *Ductor in linguas*, seem oriented toward a coherent articulation of the social sphere, based (like the project of subscription and the enterprise of teaching languages) on the tricky juncture between commercial and linguistic interests.[24]

Minsheu's Spanish-English lexicon appeared bound together with a collection of "Pleasant and delightfull dialogues in Spanish and English," which became strikingly popular on their own, were re-edited by Minsheu in 1623, and translated into French (by César Oudin) and edited separately in Spain as the *Diálogos apacibles*. . . .[25] The seven "dialogues" bound with the *Dictionarie* (Oudin adds an eighth, which then becomes part of the tradition of these stories' reception) are models of language pedagogy, and take their form from Noel de Barlement's [Berlaimont] *Colloquia cum dictonariolo linguarum* of 1536, a compendium of polyglot dialogues arranged in parallel columns.[26] A sort of precursor to Berlitz's dialogues, Minsheu's little exchanges are set in different useful venues: a *hidalgo* wakes and calls to his waiting-man for his clothes, sword, and dress; yet another hidalgo and his wife shop for silver and jewels; five gentlemen dine together, comment on their food and drink, then play at cards; two travelers, a muleteer and an innkeeper keep company and discuss travel and lodging in Spain; three pages meet after a trip to Court and tell tales; four friends, two English and two Spanish, meet and contrast the customs and language of their countries; and a Sergeant and a soldier discuss the qualities that make a good soldier. The motives of the didactic enterprise are clear, and appear, on the surface, distinctly different from the purpose that Roger Ascham's Schole-master advanced, some fifty years earlier, for learning Latin: for Minsheu, one learns English or Spanish in order to facilitate economic and social exchange, and his works' readership is drawn from a merchant or a military class newly able to trade internationally, seeking every advancement in its trade with Holland, Spain, France, Italy, and the Turkish empire and the Mahgrebi monarchies.

It comes as no surprise to us that Minsheu's dialogues all concern sites of exchange and merchandising, for in his dialogues what Covarrubias calls "La noticia de muchas lenguas" (knowledge of many tongues), not only facilitates travel, the exchange of goods, and social mobility; it is also understood to be a commodity itself, both the means for facilitating exchange and an "object" with value to be exchanged. The duplicity of the language in translation thus makes these dialogues peculiarly reflexive, perhaps even allegorical: Minsheu teaches translation in dialogues that are in part about translation; that make of translation a place-holder for economic value and for economic exchange; and that thus reflect throughout on the economics of translation (its value, its costs, its materials). Take the first two of the "Pleasant and delightfull dialogues." The first opens domestically; ostensive designations abound as the characters call for the odds and ends to hand in any house. The scene then moves outdoors. In the second dialogue, a hidalgo and his wife go to purchase plate ("In nothing I spend money with a better will than in plate," opines Thomas, the hidalgo; "That which is laid out in plate is not wasted, but to change small peeces for great peeces," answers Margaret, his wife) and then jewels ("Now let us go to the place where they sell Iewells," suggests Margaret. "This is a way that I goe unwillingly," says Thomas. "What is the reason?" "Because these Iewels are as maidens, that while they are maids, and kept in, they are of much value, and in taking them abroad they loose all, and are worth nothing"). Both the vocabulary and the nature of the objects named has changed. Minsheu's readers are no longer learning the names of things familiar from the domestic setting, the highly instrumental objects described in the first dialogue—the clothes, shoes, hats, chairs, and other useful matter of day-to-day trade. Between the first and second dialogue, and between the scene in the silversmith's shop and the scene in the jeweler's shop, the squire and his wife move not only geographically, as it were, but also in increasing order of economic and linguistic complexity, calling for this or that instrument representing (as even in Augustine) the first order of linguistic acquisition, trading in substitutes (one bit of plate for another, just different sizes) representing a second order of linguistic complexity (in which words retain a substantial, material identity with each other), and trading in jewels representing a third, dangerously public, uprooted and exposed order of linguistic complexity (like a maiden's worth, the value of a jewel depends, as Thomas wrily notes, on another bauble, reputation). The risks of the market are here the risks to which the new speaker of another tongue also exposes himself: a loss of value, of sense, dignity, "maidenhood," and of a private, linguistic, and domestic domain in which to "keep" them safe. It is no surprise that one requires a guide, a pedagogue or a *ductor*, as one ventures into the exile of the streets, of the market, of another language. The pedagogical value of Minsheu's lesson is largely established in the content of his dialogues, which set on stage not just the benefits of language acquisition, but also and as critically the *risks* it entails, and thus make clear (as in

Ascham and in Covarrubias) the value of the school master, lexicographer, *fidus interpres* or pedagogue in guiding the exposed pupil through these shoals.

Or so it would appear. For Minsheu's first dialogue expresses rather more hesitation about the socioeconomics of value (and about the value of the pedagogy of translation) than we might expect. The dialogue concludes with this exchange between the two servants, in which the virtue of knowledge finds a kind of check:

ALONSO: O quanto polvo tiene esta capa!

AMA: Sacude la primero con una vara.

ALONSO: Ama, más que vien hechos están estos calçones.

AMA: Tan bien entiendo yo de esso, como puerca de freno.

ALONSO: Pues qué entiende?

AMA: A lo que a mí me importa si tu preguntáras por una basquiña, una sáya entera, una ropa, un manto o un cuerpo, una gorguera, de una toca y cosas semejantes, supiérate yo responder.

ALONSO: De manera que no sabe léer, mas de por el libro de su aldea.

AMA: Quieres tu, que sea yo, como el ymbidióso, que su ciudado es en lo que no le va ni le viéne.

ALONSO: Siempre es virtúd savér, aunque sean cósas que parece que no nos ympórtan.

AMA: Bien sé yo, que tu sabrás hazér una bellaquería, y ésta no es virtúd. . . . A ora hermano dexate de retóricas y has lo que tu ámo te mandó.

ALONSO: Sí haré aunque bien créo que no por esso me tengo de asentár con el a la mesa.

[ALONSO: Oh what a deale of dust hath this cloke?

Nurse. Beat it out first with a wand.

A. Nurse, how exceeding well are these breeches made.

N. I have as good knowledge therein as a sow in a bridle.

A. What have you knowledge in then?

N. In what belongeth unto me, if thou hadst asked of a peticoate, a womans cassocke, a womans gowne, a mantell, a paire of bodies, a gorget, or a womans bead attire, and like matter, I could have answered thee.

A. So then the Priest cannot say Masse but in his owne booke.

N. Wilt thou, that I should be as the envious person which setteth his mind on that which belongs not unto him.

A. Yet alwaies is it a vertue to know, although they be things which seeme not to appertaine unto us.

N. I know well, that thou knowest well how to play the knave, and that I am sure is no vertue. . . . Now Brother, leave your Rhetoricke, and doe that thy Master commanded thee.

A. So will I doe, although I beleeve, for all that I am not to sit at table with him.]

The dialogue's brief turn at the end, the wry observation on the part of Alonso that he will not sit at the table with his master, has the effect of placing in question much of the value that the dialogue has rested on the transportability of knowledge—what the Spanish renders as "sabe leer, por el libro de su aldea," and the English, rather more polemically, as "the Priest, cannot say Masse but in his own booke." Doing what the master commands will not bring one to the table, Minsheu's character says—but perhaps, we are left to think, a little bit of "envy" will manage to do so.

What is the nature of this "envy"? And why does envy, rather than any of the cardinal virtues, prove to be the ground for social mobility? In what ways are envy and *translation* related? Set these questions aside for the moment. Minsheu seems to have been entirely aware of the provoking duplicity of his dialogues; indeed, he seems to take a particular pleasure in showing how translations suddenly acquire quite searching ethico-political implications. Take his Spanish dedication to the suspiciously Shandean figure of Don Eduardo Hobby.[27] The queer mixture of bombast and flattery veils, none too thickly, a fable moralized politically, and bearing on a topic much in the air as Elizabeth's reign drew to a close, and in the months following the deaths of her Spanish rival and near-consort, Philip II. It is, precisely, an argument *against* the social function of *envy*, a passion excited but also regulated by the artist. Minsheu opens his dedication relating a well-known story about Apelles,

> que aviendo acabado de pintar una hermosa tabla, teniendola colgada en parte publica, inumerable gente de todas suertes combidada de la lindeza della . . . entre los de mas, se acerto a llegar un rustico labrador, y como todos alabassen grandemente el ingenio del artificio, iuntamente con la pintura: el villano, con boz roonca y mal compuesta, dixo, una gran falta tiene esta tabla; lo qual como oyesse Apeles, le pregunto qual fuesse esta? El respondio, aquella espiga sobre la qual esta aquel paxaro sentado, deviera estar mas inclinada, porque conforme al peso que presuppone el paxaro y la flaqueza de la caña, no podia sustentarle sin doblarse mas, oydo esto por el pintor, vio que tenia razon el villano; y tomando el pincel, emendo luego alla falta, siguiendo su parecer; soberbio pues el rústico con ver que se uviesse tomado su voto, passó mas adelante, y dixo, aquellos çapatos que aquella figura tiene no estám nuennos, a esto le respondió Apeles, Hermano, cura de tu arte, y dexa a cada uno el suyo. Esta figura, muy ilustre señor, he querido traer, por dezir, que si todos los hombres se conformassen con lo que saven y que su ingenio alcança, no quisiessen passar adelante, a saber lo que no es de su profession ny les toca, ni ellos quedarian corridos, como este villano, ni el labrador se entremeterría a tratar de la guerra, ny el mercader de la cavallería . . . sino que tratando cada uno aquello a que su capacidad se estiende, y no mas, seria un concierto maravilloso, que resultaria en grande utilidad de toda la republica, y para esto devriamos tomar ejemplo de las cosas naturales, las quales perpetuamente guardan su orden y concierto, sin entremeterse las unas a hazer el oficio de las otras. . . . Pues aviendose de guardar éste concierto y órden, a v.m. conviene y toca el juzgar de esta mi obra . . .

> [[Apelles] who, having completed a lovely painting, hung it in a public spot, where numberless people flocked, attracted by its beauty . . . among these, a rustic peasant happened by, and as all those present were praising greatly the ingenuity of the artifice, as well as the painting: the villain, with a hoarse and ill-formed voice, said: this piece has a great flaw. When Apelles heard this he asked what the flaw was. The peasant answered, that sprig of wheat on which that bird is sitting, should be bent further, because

if one takes into account the weight of the bird and the thinness of the stalk, it could not hold the bird without bending further. When Apelles heard this he realized that the villain was right; and taking up his brush, he corrected the mistake, as he saw fit. The peasant, swollen with pride because his advice had been taken, went a step further, and said, those shose that that figure is wearing are not [correct]. Apelles answered him, Brother, stick to your art [*arte*], and let each mind his own. I have adduced this figure, most illustrious sire, so as to say, that if all men confined themselves to what they know and to the reach of their native wit [*ingenio*], they would not want to go beyond, and seek to know what is not of their profession [*professión*] and doesn't concern them, and they wouldn't be offended, as this peasant was, nor would the peasant intrude with opinions concerning the war, nor would the merchant opine about cavalry . . . but rather as each would treat only that matter to which his capacity extends, and none other, a marvelous concert or harmony would ensue, which would be of the greatest utility for the whole republic, and to this end we should take our example from natural things, which keep their order and arrangement perfectly, and none of them interrupts another seeking to do the other's job. . . . And since this order and harmony must be maintained, it is your honor's part to judge this my work . . .]

The anecdote finds its way to Minsheu from Pliny, and by the time the English lexicographer and cultural entrepreneur employs it the proverb embedded within the anecdote–*Ne sutor supra crepidam*, roughly "let not the cobbler aspire above his last," or in Spanish *Zapatero a tus zapatos*—has acquired a most respectable Humanist pedigree, having been collected and moralized in Erasmus's *Adagia* and largely glossed by his followers. The "Dialogues" follow a variant reading that if anything tightens the slight conceptual knot in the scene.[28] What Minsheu's dedication refers to as "concierto," something like social harmony, effectively excludes the figure of Apelles himself (he conceals himself, provokes comment in the street, functions as a sort of permanent threat of duplicity and surveillance—a whiff of Platonic indignation at the social role of art seems patent). This exclusion assumes a nearly paradoxical shape, however, when the dedication's device is unpacked according to Minsheu's loose prescription: Minsheu, the work's hidden Apelles, presents his *tableau* to the patron, his judge ("And since this order and harmony must be maintained, it is your honor's part to judge this my work"), who is now under Pliny (and Minsheu's) warning not to overstep his competency. The entire edifice of social "order and harmony" hangs upon the appropriateness, one might say, of the patron's experience and past knowledge to his current judgment: *Ne sutor supra crepidam*. The dedication appears in this way to anticipate the conclusion to Minsheu's first dialogue, in which the Ama's satisfaction with her own (social and other) limitations serves to contain the rather more subversive "envy" expressed by Alonso, the page.

Two aspects of the scene disturb its sense of "concert." Would one need to warn one's patron, as it were to prompt him not to stray above his shoes, if there were no danger that his judgment might not, after all, quite fit with his experience? Or say that one accepts this aesthetic "concert" as a model of social and economic harmony, status and experience in perfect accord, the soothing fantasy of an entirely saturated, transparent polity whose "parts" marry organically, working each with each. (One thinks here of Hardt and Negri's "communication of singularities," or of a Habermasian ideal-speech situation a bit *avant la lettre*.) Where in this aristocratic fantasy would the marginal, scrabbly figure of the pedagogue, of the translator, of the enterprising salesman of subscriptions belong? More particularly, What would didactic texts like the "Pleasant and delightfull dialogues" and the *Ductor in linguas* actually *teach*? The *linguistic economy* of Minsheu's dictionaries and dialogues turns on an altogether different sense of the relation between experience, knowledge, class, and judgment than his "Dedication" advances—and they furnish a radically different account of the mobile, "envious" political economy of the early market. From its very opening, then, the work accosts the reader. *Either* the dialogues have no didactic function, or have only the function of conveying the exact translation of an existing state of affairs (the rustic voice of the laborer remains just that, unimproved by works he cannot judge, or understand); and the figure that Minsheu brings to bear in the "Dedication" only "teaches" Edward Hobby to recognize himself (in the warned figure of a "judge" who must not stray outside what he already knows); and the "Pleasant and delightfull dialogues in Spanish and English" themselves "please" and "delight" without in any way facilitating social, commercial, or international mobility (of the sort that would allow a "villein" to become a "shoemaker," or a shoemaker to "set[ ] his mind on that which belongs not unto him," move beyond a local market, change his tongue, export his wares, eventually aspire to "sit at the table" of an Edward Hobby). *Or else* the "figure" that Minsheu employs in his dedication is entirely improper to the "Dialogues," slily open to correction, calling for a figure—a humanist, a trader in cultural translations, a figure with a mobility of intelligence and experience to match the political-economic instability and *disconcerting* he will come to represent—able to understand the bent or veiled critique of aristocratic functionalism that the appeal to Sir Edward Hobby embeds.

Nothing in Minsheu's work serves to *teach us* which of these characterizations of his project, and of his readers, Minsheu advocates. But neither are his readers expected to experience the absence of this lesson *as a painful lack*. Quite the opposite. The stories that the "Pleasant and delightfull dialogues" tell embed scenes in which mistranslation and rhetorical misunderstanding flowing from the absence of criteria for making judgments do not result in disaster of one or another monitory sort. They are prized and enjoyed instead, and work as alternatives to "doing what thy M[aster] commands thee": the "pleasantness" and "delightfulness" of the dialogues, in short, comes into conflict with their explicit pedagogical role. I've mentioned in brief Alonso's resistance, in the first dialogue, to the Nurse's fulsome praise of knowledge. By the time that the seven dialogues conclude, what seemed a monitory hesitation has become hinged explicitly with the dialogues' pedagogical and linguistic project—as though the subtle articulation of reading with the priest's saying Mass, that occurs in the commerce between the Spanish and the English texts, has become the structuring principle of the dialogues. One learns from these "Dialogues" *because of* their errors (in and about translation)—but *what* one learns can no longer in the same way be learned; one cannot, for instance, "learn" from them whether one should aspire to occupy the position of Edward Hobby, of Apelles, or of the sly Alonso, the new figure for mercantilist, envious mobility. To put it more polemically than a brief description can support: what one learns from the "Dialogues'" "errors" and paradoxes is no longer the object of the reader's, or of the writer's, will.

Like Richard Verstegan, Minsheu thus lights upon a highly unstable account of social and economic "concert," from which the aristocratic figure of *judgment* emerges dramatically changed. For Minsheu's project is not only, and not primarily a *critical* one (he has many projects, after all). The English lexicographer, translator, and pedagogue is also modestly a political philosopher with an affirmative program to complement a sharply critical one. Minsheu's radical pedagogy of translation washes the Enlightenment's fantastical construction of the early modern subject's political *will* in revealing acids: the irreducibility of *envy*; the noncorrespondence between judgment, "taste," and experience; the provocative vulnerability of one's linguistic "home" or "nation" as one's language steps translated into the market. One can get a slightly clearer sense of the disconcerting political philosophy that emerges from early modern lexical culture by returning very briefly to another scene of origins, where "letters," "ground," "culture" and their various translations mythically meet. When Covarrubias defines the word "letter" he reminds us that:

> Otros sienten auerse dicho à *lite*, porque de las letras como de los primeros elementos se forman las sílabas, y las dicciones: y para juntarse entre si tienen vna manera de contienda hiriéndose vnas a otras. Y esta es la común moralidad en que se fundó la fábula de Cadmo, que auiendo muerto la serpiente, Minerua le mandó sembrar los dientes della: y dellos nacieron hombres armados, que peleando entre sí se mataron, hasta quedar en cinco. Estas se entienden las letras vocales, que son el origen y vida de las demás, y assi le dan por autor de las letras.

> [Others believe it to come from *lite*, because syllables and statements are formed from letters, as from primary elements: and in order to assemble amongst themselves they have a sort of battle, wounding one another. And on this common moral the fable of Cadmus is based. When he killed the serpent, Minerva ordered him to sow its teeth, and from those teeth were born armed men, who fought amongst themelves and killed each other off, until only five remained. These are taken to be the vowels, which are the life and origin of all others, and hence Cadmus is taken to be the author of all the letters.]

This depiction of a primal battle set in the very cradle of the letter also "kills off" the genteel claims of lexical humanism that Covarrubias advances in defining "tongue," *lengua*: the hidden claim that the stability of the referent guarantees the "humanity" shared by speakers of different languages, and the consequent claim that speaking in another tongue "dampens the fury of the enemy, for, speaking to him in his own tongue, he moderates himself and conceives a certain familial affinity that obliges him to be human and merciful." At the heart of the word, embedded in the letter itself, lies not the "concert" and aristocratic harmony of rhyming "judgment," "experience," "familial affinity," self-identity, and the sort of mutual obligation that turns upon the restraint of the will, but fratricidal conflict, envy, murder, warfare. Not natural *law*, but the claim of *jus naturale* or natural *right*, to turn to Hobbes's crucial and polemical distinction, makes up the matter of linguistic exchange.[29] Not national fantasies, or the *deliberate* assumption of culturally sanctioned, fantasmatic, and *aristocratic* genealogies (such as Verstegan and Minsheu's works glancingly provide their authors and readers), but quarreling, envious, inconstant forms of partial and conflicted *linguistic*—lexical—identification make up the matter of early modern communitarian, *political* thought. The *fidus interpres*, the pedagogue, the lexicographer, all charged seemingly with regulating the "world of wordes," to evoke John Florio's lovely title, succeed only in telling over Cadmus's story; their words, syllables or statements (in different languages) about words (that is to say, dictionaries, hardword books, translation guides, *calepinos*, *florilegia*, various "tesoros") sow serpents' teeth. Upon this torn lexical ground, this broken, translated culture, competing early modern internationalisms flourish.

Or put it like this: Minsheu and Verstegan (and Covarrubias in Spain) share an understanding of the relation between "will" and "language" that places them closer to Nietzsche and Hobbes than to Renan: for them, translation marks the spot where language paradoxically least lends itself to the will's use. And in both cases, as in Covarrubias's enigmatic *Tesoro*, this torn spot is where a particular social freedom can be located: for Verstegan, the freedom of a certain kind of recusancy, of an exilic, compensatory and riven identity; for Minsheu, a political-economic freedom derived from the disharmony between economic and epistemological interest. In a broader sense, the politico-historiographic tradition that so lionizes the Renaissance's "grands hommes," so compellingly holds them up as the models of a modern, Machiavellian, individual autonomy—this tradition arises so as to bypass these two arenas of social freedom—precisely because these "freedoms" cannot be squared with the model of Kantian autonomy on which Renan's and Burckhardt's thought rests, and on which the discipline of modern Renaissance studies depends. Likewise, the utopian moment of intellectual internationalism that structures recent work as distant in spirit and argument as that of Derrida, or Negri and Hardt, or Bhabha, or Balibar cannot today be understood without reference to its hidden link with this reactive definition of early modern humanist internationalism. For at the moment of the emergence of the nation form, the lexical culture of translation designates a specifically nonsubjectivist form of cultural (self) resistance with consequences so radical as to have generated a whole subdiscipline dedicated to evading it, and a contemporary weak utopianism dedicated to reproducing it.

NOTES

1. My epigraphs are from John Florio, A *Worlde of Wordes* (better known, in its second, 1611 edition, as *Queen Anna's New Worlde of Wordes*), printed in London, by Arnold

Hatfield for Edw. Blount, 1598 (n.p.); and from Jacques Derrida, *Specters of Marx: The State of the Debt, the Work of Mourning, & the New International*, trans. Peggy Kamuf (London: Routledge, 1994), 104. Derrida is citing from Marx's *Contribution to the Critique of Political Economy*, trans. by S. W. Ryazanskaya, ed. Maurice Dobb (New York: International Publishers, 1970), p. 107. Except where indicated, the translations throughout this essay are mine. I'd like to express my gratitude to Jason Cohen for his careful help and keen advice at every stage in the preparation of this essay.

2. Michael Hardt and Antonio Negri, *Empire* (Cambridge, MA: Harvard University Press, 2000), p. 57.

3. The same is achieved, to some extent, by Ernesto Laclau's call for a "constructed universal." See Ernesto Laclau, "Constructing Universality," in *Contingency, Hegemony, Universality: Contemporary Dialogues on the Left*, Judith Butler, Ernesto Laclau, and Slavoj Žižek (London and New York: Verso, 2000).

4. Much of the recent, fine work discussing the formation of "national" identity in early English modernity draws from Richard Helgerson's careful and searching *Forms of Nationhood: The Elizabethan Writing of England* (Chicago: University of Chicago Press, 1992). I have also found especially intriguing Peter Sahlins's studies of border communities, especially his *Boundaries: The Making of France and Spain in the Pyrenees* (Berkeley: University of California Press, 1989). I hope that my debt to the work of Ben Anderson, Homi Bhabha, and others will be clear throughout.

5. Renan, "Qu'est-ce qu'une nation?" (*Conference faite en Sorbonne 11 Mars, 1882*), in Ernest Renan, *Œuvres complètes*, ed. Henriette Psichari (Paris: Corbeil Press, Calmann-Levy, 1947), vol. 1, p. 903.

6. Ibid., p. 899.

7. Renan, "Des services rendus aux sciences historiques par la philologie," in Renan, *Œuvres complètes*, vol. 8, pp. 1231–32.

8. Renan, "Qu'est-ce qu'une nation?", pp. 899–900.

9. One might also list the dictionaries of Estienne (in the 1530s), Plantin (beginning in the 1560s), Florio (1598 and 1611), Perceval, Cawdrey (1604), and Covarrubias (1611 and 1613).

10. Jürgen Schäfer has written of the "insecurity of many speakers" at this time, and of the "socio-linguistic" problem posed in England "at the beginning of the seventeenth century [by] the influx of new words derived from Latin and the Romance languages." He maintains that "at this critical juncture in the development of the English language a new genre of books . . . began to appear, the lists of hard words" (in his "The Hard Word Dictionaries: A Re-Assessment," *Leeds Studies in English* n.s. 4, 1970, p. 31). This assessment of the lexical "insecurity" prevalent in early modern Europe, and in England in particular, has a different valence in Noel Osselton's *Branded Words in English Dictionaries before Johnson*: "To the purist's protest that the ale-wife cannot know Latin, the dictionary provides the answer: she need not—she need only have access to a dictionary, and then she may understand and speak as finely powdered a language as any" (9). And: "In the early dictionaries . . . this intention is clearly an educational one first and foremost. The object was to instruct those who did not understand. . . . Up to 1656 the dictionary was undoubtedly intended for the guidance of those people who were in difficulties among the host of new words; and these included—notably—foreigners, the ladies and the young." In Noel E. Osselton, *Branded Words in English Dictionaries before Johnson* (Groningen: J. B. Wolters, 1958), pp. 11–13.

11. In the middle to late sixteenth century the study of the "antiquities" of England—Saxon customs, artifacts and language—was used to assert that the English Reformation

was nothing less than a return to earlier forms of Christian worship, a triple articulation of linguistic, "nationalist," and religious idioms that effectively delegitimates the importation of "foreign" or "Popish" translations of the Gospel. In an early article, Rosemond Tuve linked this well-known historical thesis to contemporary, twentieth-century protocols of research and critical professionalization, briefly opening a fascinating line of inquiry that circumstances—mobilization for a European and American war—soon closed down. See her "Ancients, Moderns, and Saxons," ELH 6(3), 1939, 165–90. Tuve remembers that William L'Isle calls "'the Saxons a people most devout' who have left us not only all these monasteries and churches but also 'in our Libraries so goodly monuments of reverend antiquitie, divine handwritings" (169–70), and she dates the articulation of "nationalist," religious, and lexical idioms to John Bale and John Leland's *The Laboryouse Journey & serche of John Leylande, for Englands Antiquitees . . . with declaracyons enlarged, by Iohan Bale* (London, 1549). She cites these remarkable lines from the *Laboryouse Journey*. Addressing the "cyties of Englande," Bale-Leland cries: "steppe you fourth . . . and shewe your naturall noble hartes to your nacyon. As ye fynde a notable Antyquyte . . . lete them anon be imprented . . . both to their and your owne perpetuall fame" (C^v–C2^r).

12. Sebastián de Covarrubias Horozco, *Tesoro de la lengua castellana, o española* (Madrid: Luis Sánchez, 1611). I have lightly modernized the text.

13. This "increasing differentiation" refers not only to increased technical specialization (on the manufacturing side), or to progressively more specific demands (on the side of consumption), but also to the waning of what Marx calls (but only "approximatively"!) the mythic, early modern "co-operative form" of the capitalist mode of production, the "handicraft-like beginnings of manufacture" [*handwerksmäßigen Anfängen der Manufaktur*]; see *Capital* I, 4, ch. 13–14, trans. Samuel Moore and Edward Aveling (New York: International Publishers, 1967), pp. 317–18. For the tradition associating *translation* with economic value, see Doug Robinson's "Translation and the Repayment of Debt," Delos 7(1–2), April 1997, pp. 10–22; and Anthony Pym's work, especially "Translation as a Transaction Cost," Meta 40(4), 1995, pp. 594–605.

14. A *seeming* translator, or perhaps better, a translator barely *manqué*: at the end of his life Covarrubias was completing a translation into Spanish of Horace's *Odes*; the Royal license to print "un libro intitulado *Las Sátiras, Epístolas y Arte poético de Quinto Oracio Flaco*" was granted a month after the lexicographer's death.

15. Covarrubias is remembering these lines attributed to Horace: "Publica materies privati iuris erit, si / non circa vilem patulumque moraberis orbem; / nec verbum verbo curabis reddere fidus / interpres, nec desilies imitator in artum, / unde pedem proferre pudor vetet aut operis lex." Ben Jonson's 1640 translation, in *Q. Horatius Flaccus: his Art of poetry. Englished by Ben Jonson. With other workes of the author, never printed before* (London: Printed by I. Okes, for Iohn Benson, 1640, p. 10; reprinted in Edward Blakeney, ed., *Horace on the Art of Poetry* (Freeport, NY: Books for Libraries Press, 1970, p. 114), reads as follows: "For, being a Poet, thou maist feigne, create, / Not care, as thou wouldst faithfully translate, / To render word for word . . ."

16. Roger Ascham, *The Schole-Master* (London), printed by John Daye, 1570 [–71], n.p.

17. Richard Verstegan [a.k.a Verstegen], *A Restitution of Decayed Intelligence: In antiquities. Concerning the most noble and renowmed English nation. By the studie and travaile of R.V. Dedicated unto the Kings most excellent Maiestie.* Printed at Antwerp by Robert Bruney, 1605; And to be sold at London in Paules-Churchyard, by Iohn Norton and Iohn Bull.

18. For a recent account of Verstegan's role in the pamphlet debacle that followed the 1591 edict, see Victor Houliston, "The Lord Treasurer and the Jesuit: Robert Person's

Satirical *Responsio* to the 1591 Proclamation," *Sixteenth Century Journal* 32(2), 2001, pp. 383–401, especially 384–93. Anthony G. Petti's "Richard Verstegan and Catholic Martyrologies of the later Elizabethan Period," *Recusant History* 5(2), 1959–60, pp. 64–90, has a fuller account of Verstegan's role in publicizing the persecution of Catholic dissenters under Elizabeth, in works like Verstegan's *Briefve Description des diverses Cruautez que les Catholiques endurent en Angleterre pour la foy* (Paris, 1584) and most importantly in the *Theatrum crudelitatum haereticorum nostri temporis* (Anvers, 1587). A full account of the impact of Verstegan's *Theater of cruelties* may be found in Frank Lestringant's edition of the work's first French translation, *Le Théâtre des cruautés des hérétiques de nostre temps* (Anvers, 1588; Paris: Éditions Chandeigne, 1995).

19. And to his *linguistic* policies as well: note that Randall Cotgrave, like Ascham before him, dedicates his 1611 *Dictionarie of the French and English Tongues* (London: Printed by Adam Islip, 1611) to Cecil; clearly Cecil's circle perceived that the wars of "sedition" were carried out in the domain of the lexical as well. Cotgrave's *Dictionarie* addresses to Cecil the following, rather heavily veiled complaint: "My desires have aimed at more substantial markes [than "so meane a Peece" as the *Dictionarie*]; but mine eyes failed them, and forced me to spend much of their vigour on this Bundle of words; which though it may be unworthie of your Lordships great patience, and perhaps ill sorted to the expectation of others, yet is it the best I can at this time make it, and were, how perfect soever, no more then due to your Lordship, to whom I owe, for what I have beene many yeres, whatsoever I am now, or looke to be hereafter."

20. This is how Hobbes puts it: "But all this language gotten, and augmented by *Adam* and his posterity, was again lost at the Tower of *Babel*, when by the hand of God, every man was stricken for his Rebellion with an oblivion of his former Language. And being hereby forced to disperse themselves into several parts of the world, it must needs be, that the diversity of Tongues that now is, proceeded by degrees from them, in such manner, as need (the mother of all inventions) taught them; in tract of time grew everywhere more copious." In Thomas Hobbes, *Leviathan, or, The matter, form, and power of a common-wealth ecclesiastical and civil* (London: Printed for Andrew Crooke, 1651), Bk. I, ch. 4, p. 12.

21. See Houliston, "The Lord Treasurer and the Jesuit," pp. 399–401.

22. Accusations of plagiarism were not uncommon in the small world of writers of dictionaries, for obvious reasons. John Rider, author of what comes to be known as *Riders Dictionarie* (1589), was also accused of plagiarism; Thomas Thomas's heirs brought charges against him for filching material from Thomas's own dictionary.

23. Edward Phillips, *The New World of English Words, or a Generall Dictionary* (London: Printed for Nath Brooke at the Angell in Cornhill, 1658), n.p.

24. The *Ductor in linguas* is explicitly intended for the use of "merchants." John Minsheu, *Ductor in linguas and Vocabularium hispanicolatinum* (*A most copoius Spanish dictionary*) (London: at John Brown's shop, 1617). Facsimile edition, with an introduction by Jürgen Schäfer (Delmar, NY: Scholar's Facsimiles & Reprints), 1978. Schäfer's introduction helpfully distinguishes Minsheu's project from that of scholars interested in "elucidating Latin texts for an international audience." *Ductor in linguas* is instead "a practical guide for merchants," a work that aims to help "the native speaker of English to express himself in a foreign language" (vii). This is consistent with the practice at the time. Compare these prefatory words by John Rider [Ryder] to his *Bibliotheca Scholastica. A Double Dictionarie*, printed by Joseph Barnes, Printer to the Universitie of Oxford, 1589. The "double dictionary," Rider writes, is "penned for all those that would have within short space the use of the Latin tongue, either to speake, or write. Verie profitable and necessarie for Scholers, Courtiers, Lawyers and their Clarkes, Apprentices of London, Trave-

liers, Factors for Marchants, and briefly for all Discontinuers within her Maiesties Realmes of England and Ireland" (cited in DeWitt T. Starnes, *Renaissance Dictionaries: English-Latin and Latin-English* [Austin: University of Texas Press, 1954]).

25. For an account of Minsheu's sources and of his lavish use of Percyvall's *A Dictionarie in Spanish, English, and Latine* (bound as part II in the *Bibliotheca hispanica* of 1591 [London: John Jackson for Richard Watkins]), see the description of Minsheu's 1599 *Dictionarie in Spanish and English* (as well as its 1623 edition, and a description of the 1617 *Ductor in linguas*) in Roger J. Steiner, *Two Centuries of Spanish and English Lexicography* (Mouton: The Hague, 1970), pp. 38–57. Steiner's "Appendix C" (pp. 113–14) enlarges his discussion on pp. 40–42 of Minsheu's "difficulties as far as borrowing and copyright were concerned." Titled "Intrigue in the 16th-Century English Book Trade," the appendix imagines Percyvall and his co-author Thomas Doyley (or D'Oylie) "swinging into action in an effort to stop Minsheu's edition of their work" (113). More recently, see Daniel W. Noland, "The Sources and Methods of John Minsheu's *A Dictionary of Spanish and English* (1599)" in *Dictionaries: Journal of the Dictionary Society of North America* 11, 1989, pp. 41–52; Daniel M. Sáez Rivera, "Vida y obra de Francisco Sobrino," *Introducción a Francisco Sobrino. Anexos Revista LEMIR*, 18–21. Sáez reviews much of the biographical material on Minsheu, mentioning his Jewish roots, nodding also to the controversy over the authorship of the "Pleasant and delightfull dialogues" (attributed by Steven Ungerer to Alonso de Baeza, and by José Antonio Cid to the Erasmist scholar Antonio del Corro). Consult as well the edition of Minsheu's *A Dictionarie in Spanish and English*, prepared by Gloria Guerrero Ramos and Fernando Pérez Lagos (Málaga: Servicio de Publicaciones de la Universidad de Málaga, 2000), pp. 5–22.

26. The title of Barlement's work varies almost as much as his own name does: *Vocabulaer, Vocabulaire*, etc. For a vivid sense of his influence in England, see the "Chronological list of the relevant works" that Gabriele Stein provides in *The English Dictionary before Cawdrey* (Tübingen: Max Niemeyer Verlag, 1985), pp. 410–31: Stein lists thirty-three editions of the *Dictionariolo* between 1567 and 1623. Minsheu may also have had access to *The Spanishe Schoolemaster conteyninge 7 Dialogues, according to everie daie in the weeke . . .* by William Stepney (London, 1591). For the tradition of didactic dialogues, see Werner Hüllen, *English Dictionaries 800–1700: The Topical Tradition* (Oxford; Clarendon Press, 1999), pp. 104–32.

27. William Camden's *Rerum Anglicarum et Hibernicarum Annales, regnante Elizabetha* mentions that Edward Hobby (a.k.a. Hoby) was the ensign-bearer for the 1596 incursion against Spain, at which Lord Thomas Howard, Sir Wiliam Paget, Sir Walter Raleigh, Sir Robert Southwell, Richard Levison, Philip Woodhouse, and Robert Mansfield also fought; by 1603 Hoby is mentioned as a member of parliament, and in March 1603 is being considered for the position of Speaker (the DNB reports that Hoby was Speaker in 1586, but this is probably an error). See *The historie of the life and reigne of the most renowmed [sic] and victorious Princesse Elizabeth, late Queene of England . . . composed by way of annals, by the most learned Mr. William Camden; and faithfully translated into English* (London: Printed for Benjamin Fisher), 1630, Bk. 4, pp. 92–93, a translation of Camden's *Annales Rerum Gestarum Angliae et Hiberniae Regnante Elizabetha* of 1615–1625. For Hoby's role in parliament, see the *Journal of the House of Commons* (Great Britain: House of Commons), Journals 1 (1547–1628), pp. 140–41 and 933–45. For our purposes, it's particularly worth noting that Hoby's uncle Philip was Henry VIII's ambassador to the Spanish court of Charles V, and that Edward Hoby himself translated from the Spanish a *Theorique and practise of warre. Written to Don Philip Prince of Castil, by Don Bernardino de Mendoza. Translated out of the Castilian tonge into Englishe, by Sr. Edwarde Hoby*

Knight. Directed to Sr. George Carew Knight (Middelburg: Printed by Richard Schilders), 1597.

28. In Pliny, according to Holland's 1601 translation,

His [Apelles's] order was when he had finished a peece of worke or painted table, and laid it out of his hand, to set it forth in some open gallerie or thorow fare to be seene of folke that passed by, and himselfe would lie close behind it to hearken what faults were found therewith; preferring the judgment of the common people before his owne, and imagining they would spie more narrowly and ensure his doings sooner than himselfe: and ass the tale is told, it fell out upon a time, that a shoemaker as he went by seemed to controule his workemanship about the shoe or pantophle that he had made to a picture, and namely, that there was one latchet fewer than there should bee: *Apelles* acknowledging that the man said true indeed, mended that fault by the next morning, and set forth his table as his manner was. The same shomaker coming again the morrow after, and finding the want supplied which he noted the day before, tooke some pride unto himselfe, that his former admonition had sped so well, and was so bold as to cavil at somewhat about the legs: *Apelles* could not endure that, but putting forth his head from behind the painted table, and scorning thus to be checked and reproved, Sirrha (quoth he) remember you are but a shoemaker, and therefore meddle no higher I advise you, than with shoes: which word also of his came afterwards to bee a common proverbe, *Ne sutor supra crepidam.*

In *Historie of the World*, Pliny the Elder, trans. Philemon Holland (London: Printed by Adam Islip, 1601), Bk. 35, ch. X, p. 538. The Latin reads: "Apelli fuit alioqui perpetua consuetudo numquam tam occupatum diem agendi, ut non lineam ducendo exerceret artem, quod ab eo in proverbium venit. idem perfecta opera proponebat in pergula transeuntibus atque, ipse post tabulam latens, vitia quae notarentur auscultabat, vulgum diligentiorem iudicem quam se praeferens; feruntque reprehensum a sutore, quod in crepidis una pauciores intus fecisset ansas, eodem postero die superbo emendatione pristinae admonitionis cavillante circa crus, indignatum prospexisse denuntiantem, ne supra crepidam sutor iudicaret, quod et ipsum in proverbium abiit." Caius Plinius Secondus (Pliny the Elder), *Historia Naturalis* (Leipzig: Teubner, 1897), bk. XXXV, section 36, pgph. 85–86.

29. This is *Leviathan*, Bk. I, ch. 14, p. 64:

"THE Right of Nature, which Writers commonly call *Jus Naturale*, is the Liberty each man hath to use his own power as he will himself for the preservation of his own Nature; that is to say, of his own Life; and consequently, of doing anything which, in his own Judgement and Reason, he shall conceive to be the aptest means thereunto. By LIBERTY is understood, according to the proper signification of the word, the absence of external Impediments; which Impediments may oft take away part of a man's power to do what he would, but cannot hinder him from using the power left him according as his judgement and reason shall dictate to him."

Metrical Translation:
Nineteenth-Century Homers and the Hexameter Mania

YOPIE PRINS

The question of metrical translation—its history, theory, and practice—is not often posed in current translation studies, except perhaps by translators who confront "a choice between rhyme and reason," as Nabokov asked himself in translating Pushkin: "Can a translation while rendering with absolute fidelity the whole text, and nothing but the text, keep the form of the original, its rhythm and its rhyme?"[1] Like swearing an oath to tell the whole truth and nothing but the truth before going on trial, the translator who vows to be true to "the whole text, and nothing but the text" must be faithful to its form as well as its content. Of course, because every translation falls somewhere between rhyme and reason, the vow of absolute fidelity will be broken, and the translator pronounced guilty. But what happens when the translator tries to do justice to a text by finding another way to tell rhyme's reason, by re-telling the truth of its rhythm and its rhyme in another form? What happens when meter itself is being translated? Rather than assuming a transhistorical definition of meter as a fixed form that can be transported from source language to target language, we might look for the historical transformation of metrical forms through translation, and so bring into view the cultural function of metrical translation as a complex mediation and recirculation of literary forms at a particular moment within a particular culture.

I offer a case study by looking at various translations of Homer in Victorian England, where debates about translating dactylic hexameter—the metrical form associated with classical epic—were closely linked to the formation of a national literary culture. These hexameter debates went to great lengths to pronounce or denounce English imitations of Classical meter. Not only was this a trial of different systems of versification, ruled by "stress" vs. "length" and arbitrated by poetic justice; it was also a political effort to legislate an English literary idiom that would enable the sort of national identification described by Ernest Gellner in *Nations and Nationalism*. With the rise of the British empire, as England was struggling to accommodate foreignness both within and beyond its national borders, the consolidation of a common language out of heterogeneous elements seemed especially urgent. One example of this urgency was Matthew Arnold's plea for hexameter translation in his famous lectures *On Translating Homer* (1861–62). In urging poets to translate Homer into English hexameters

for the cultivation of English poetry and the future of English culture, Arnold anticipated the ideals of criticism and culture articulated in "The Function of Criticism at the Present Time" (1864) and "Culture and Anarchy" (1869). Indeed, as
Arnold tried to persuade his contemporaries, the function of hexameter at the
present time would be to measure the distance between culture and anarchy.

Arnold's turn to English hexameters was not a return to the measures of antiquity, but an attempt to create a new measure for modernity that would give order
to modern life in the modern nation. In *England and Englishness*, John Lucas follows Gellner in demonstrating how, as a nation develops, "it becomes increasingly necessary to produce a culture which, in its realization through a formalized
common language, seeks to homogenize all members of the nation."[2] According
to Lucas, Arnold in particular emphasized the role of poets in formalizing such a
language: "Arnold had a very definite sense of what England ought to be, and it
did not include the right to utterance by a wide variety of voices," since he regarded "heteroglossia as a form of anarchy, the clamour of the barbarians at the
gates" (9). But even while Arnold prescribed hexameters to hold off the barbarians at the gates, he also opened the gates to various metrical experiments that
seemed "barbarous" to the very readers whose Englishness he sought to cultivate.
As we shall see, the various hexameter translations that began to circulate in the
decade after Arnold's lectures point to contradictory patterns of reading voice:
rather than imagining a unified voice for a unified nation, these English hexameters allowed different forms of Englishness to be performed more equivocally.

The central role played by poets in forming ideas about nation and empire in
Victorian England has been elaborated by recent critics, including Matthew
Reynolds in *The Realms of Verse, 1830–1870: English Poetry in a Time of Nation-
Building*. The idea (or ideal) of a national literary culture emerged not only
through the novel and the newspaper, as Benedict Anderson has argued in *Imagined Communities*,[3] but through the circulation of poetry in print. Reynolds extends Anderson's argument to show how Victorian poets worked to identify and
address a community of English readers: their poems "explore consonances between aesthetic and political forms, so that readers who enter into their realms
of verse experience restraints and liberties, and patterns of cohesion and disintegration."[4] Through various kinds of formal analysis, often metrical, Reynolds
suggests that such poems recreated the difficulty of creating a coherent English
nation, as a composite form with different parts, sometimes coming together and
sometimes falling apart. Focusing more specifically on metrical translation, I
argue that hexameter translations of Homer also allowed readers to enter into a
realm of verse defined by patterns of cohesion and disintegration, and thus to experience forms of continuity and interruption associated with the modern nation. Like other print media, meter served as a medium for the creation of a national literature that could be called English, and although English hexameters
may not have produced a homogeneous community of readers (quite the contrary), nevertheless the debates around hexameter served to produce a powerful
metrical imaginary in Victorian England. For Arnold and his contemporaries,
the nation was a form that might be transformed by acts of metrical translation,

and the meter that allowed nineteenth-century poets, scholars, translators, critics, and readers to prescribe this idea of an English national literature was hexameter. Therefore much was at stake in the English hexameter mania: who would be able to legislate a perfect hexameter?

Arnold's Measure for the Present Time

In "The Modern Element in Literature," his inaugural lecture for the Poetry Chair at Oxford in 1857, the newly appointed Professor Matthew Arnold professed the importance of "literatures which in their day and for their own nation have adequately comprehended, have adequately represented, the spectacle before them."[5] As Arnold defined it, the modern element in all literatures, past or present, is the ability to take the measure of their own time, and thus to give a comprehensive and adequate representation of the present "in their day and for their own nation." Even ancient literatures have this modern element, especially ancient Greek poetry, for "in the poetry of that age we have a literature commensurate with its epoch" (31). The question for Arnold was, how might English literature achieve such commensurability, in its own day and for its own nation? "Our present age has around it a copious and complex present, and behind it a copious and complex past," according to Arnold, and "it exhibits to the individual man who contemplates it the spectacle of a vast multitude of facts awaiting and inviting his comprehension" (20). The individual man—say, Arnold— needs a general law to comprehend this complex temporality and give order to the multitude of mental impressions "which we feel in presence of an immense, moving, confused spectacle." But what kind of law would this be?

A few years later Arnold turned to metrical law, again via the example of Greek literature. In the meters of Homer (whose epic poetry was composed in dactylic hexameter, a line running rapidly in six feet, mostly dactyls), he discerned a movement that might adequately represent and comprehend the multiplicity of the modern age. His lectures On Translating Homer, delivered at Oxford in 1860–61, prescribed hexameter not only for future translators of Homer but also for the future of English poetry. "The hexameter, whether alone or with the pentameter, possesses a movement, an expression, which no metre hitherto in common use amongst us possesses, and which I am convinced English poetry, as our mental wants multiply, will not always be content to forego" (148). If, as Arnold implied, modernity was the demand for the right measure and if, as Arnold believed, England was a nation in need of measure, then perhaps, as Arnold hoped, hexameter would be a way to measure up to these modern times. Indeed English hexameter might even work to displace iambic pentameter with noniambic measures, and so invent a new national meter. Mediating between continuity and contemporaneity, between the complex past and the complex present, hexameter became Arnold's measure of, and for, the present time.

Arnold's turn to hexameter was controversial by definition, returning to ancient Greek versification yet also turning it into modern English verse. His three

lectures provoked a wide range of reactions, inspiring some translators and infu-
riating others, prompting scholarly articles and critical parodies, and fanning the
flames of Victorian hexameter debates. What kind of hexameter was Arnold pre-
scribing for English poetry? Quantitative meter, measured by length of syllables,
like the dactylic hexameter of Homer or the stately measures of Virgil? Accentual meter, numbered in stressed syllables, like the (too) popular hexameters of
Longfellow? Some combination or modification of the two? How would the new
English hexameter be written, and by whom? How would it be read, and by
whom? And what would it sound like?

In response to skeptics, Arnold gave a fourth lecture to defend the idea of
metrical translation, and to define his ideal of hexameter. In "Last Words,"
delivered November 30, 1861, he explained how hexameter translations of
Homer might work to improve current English hexameters, and train the English ear to hear new rhythms: "In the task of translation, the hexameter may
gradually be made familiar to the ear of the English public; at the same time
that there arises, out of all these efforts, an improved type of this rhythm"
(202). Step by step, placing one foot before the other, English poetry would
gradually move toward a new and improved hexameter, conceived by Arnold
and born through the labors of poets and translators. And this labor would not
be in vain, according to Arnold, as it would give birth to the future of English
poetry: "I am inclined to believe that all this travail will actually take place, because I believe that modern poetry is actually in want of such an instrument as
the hexameter" (202).

In fact English poets were less "in want" of hexameter than Arnold implied;
he was more interested in telling them what kind of hexameter they would, or
should, want. If anything, there were already too many English hexameters
circulating in nineteenth-century England. In George Saintsbury's *History of English Prosody*, for example, we find an entire chapter dedicated to "The Later
English Hexameter and Discussions On It." Surveying the "battle of the hexameter" that dominated Victorian metrical theory, Saintsbury called it "the hexameter mania."[6] Within this unruly proliferation of hexameters, Arnold's call for
new translations of Homer was an attempt to regulate the form of English hexameter, and transform it into an ordering principle for modern poetry. The rapid
movement of Homeric hexameter, as Arnold understood it, would thus be
"translated" into an English meter commensurate with modern times, not as nostalgia for the time of the ancients but as a way of comprehending the temporality
of modernity and the modern nation.

In the decade immediately following Arnold's *Lectures on Translating Homer*,
there was a proliferation of English hexameter translations.[7] Although these Victorian experiments in metrical translation may seem antiquated to us now—a
dead end for modern prosody—nevertheless it is worth exhuming some of the
hexameter debates that proved so lively in the nineteenth century. Victorian
hexameters often sound like a failure, enforcing an awkward pronunciation. This
awkwardness is inscribed in the subtitle of my essay, which might be scanned as a
line in hexameter as follows:

/   /   I / x x I /   / I I/   x   x I / x x I /x x
Nineteenth-century Homers and the Hexameter Mania

With a caesura after the third foot (where it never should fall) and a final foot that is not quite a spondee (unless "mania" is elided into two syllables), this line falls short of an ideal hexameter. Its movement is interrupted: the first three feet seem to limp along lamely in spondee, dactyl, spondee, and the last three feet gather dactylic momentum only if we stress "and": "nineteenth-century Homers AND the hexameter mania." Nevertheless I wish to stress the conjunction, not only to make the line scan but to mark a link between Victorian versions of Homer and the development of English hexameter. Instead of stressing what is lost in translation, we might see what is gained through metrical translation as a reversal of the relation between form and content: what is translated is not a "content" but the performance of form itself, and the possibility of its transformation.

These Victorian hexameter translations have been mostly forgotten, amidst the many versions of Homer circulating in England by the end of the nineteenth century.[8] However in *The Translator's Invisibility*, Lawrence Venuti argues that the Arnoldian approach to translating Homer has continued well into the twentieth century, demonstrating "Arnold's continuing power in Anglo-American literary culture" and "the dominant tradition of English-language translation, fluent domestication."[9] Arnold's "domesticating method," as Venuti defines it, was "to produce familiar, fluent verse that respected bourgeois moral values" for the English nation, in contrast to the "foreignizing method" of Newman, who translated Homer into an archaic ballad form that Venuti associates with a more popular and democratic concept of English culture (130–31). Venuti's chapter on "Nation" focuses on these different ideologies of translation in the Arnold-Newman debate and, according to Venuti, Arnold "won": the idea of Homer in Arnold's lectures served to consolidate a national ideal, enforced by a strategy of translation that sought to domesticate the foreign text. But while Venuti argues for the importance of making the material and historical conditions of translation visible, the material and historical form of hexameter translations remains invisible in his argument; he does not read the form itself to make its strangeness visible. Within the context of nineteenth-century hexameter debates it is difficult to read Arnold's call for hexameter translations simply as a triumph of fluent domestication. Although Arnold admired the rapid flow of Homer, the work of translation that Arnold prescribed to invent "such an instrument as the hexameter" was slow, laborious, and strange; even while familiarizing the English ear, hexameter was also an instrument of defamiliarization, and anything but transparent.

TRUE TO THE ANCIENT FLOW

The viability of writing verse in classical meters was an obsession among poets and prosodists throughout the Victorian period, and what obsessed them most of all was the revival of hexameter. In addition to counting the number of accents and syllables in a line (as in the tradition of English accentual-syllabic verse), they tried to measure the length or duration of syllables by following the rules of quantity in classical Greek and Latin poetry. Not since the sixteenth century had there been as much interest in quantitative meter as a model for reading and writing English poetry. Elizabethan verse in classical meters was influenced by Latin prosody in grammar schools, where schoolboys learned to scan by marking the long and short syllables of the Latin text, dividing the lines into feet, and then reading this aloud according to the rules they had memorized. As Derek Attridge argues in *Well-Weighed Syllables*, such techniques of scansion emphasized the apprehension of durational patterns through the written rather than the spoken word, and led to a conception of meter removed from the rhythms of the vernacular.[10] Elizabethan experiments in quantitative verse proved a failure, as iambic versification became increasingly normalized and indeed naturalized for English poetry as it was written, heard, and spoken. By the nineteenth century, however, poets were turning with renewed enthusiasm to experiments in classical meters, to explore alternatives to iambic pentameter and extend the idea of "English" verse in new directions.[11]

But if sixteenth-century quantitative experiments were attempts to classicize English verse by removing it from the rhythms of the vernacular, nineteenth-century experiments tried to naturalize classical verse by drawing it closer to the vernacular: its meter was scanned in written form, yet its rhythm was supposed to "flow" like the spoken word. In contrast to Elizabethan quantitative verse modeled primarily on Latin, Victorian prosody increasingly turned to ancient Greek as its ideal, as schoolboys were taught to memorize Homer in particular, and to admire the rhythmic flow of Homeric hexameter through oral recitation.[12] Learning to read Homer out loud led to various controversies about the proper pronunciation of Greek, and in particular the problem of pronouncing quantitative verse, as it was easy to confuse, or conflate, Greek quantities with English accents. Eager to revive a dead language no longer spoken, classical scholars in England became preoccupied with the sound of Greek and although no one really knew how it sounded, they devised elaborate systems of accentuation in order to imagine its resonance.

Trying to understand the two languages—Greek and English, ancient and modern, dead and living—in relation to each other was a preoccupation for poets throughout the nineteenth century as well, already in the early work of Samuel Taylor Coleridge. Reviewing a scholarly pamphlet, "On the Prosodies of the Greek and Latin Languages," Coleridge agreed with the concern of classical scholars that "we indeed of this country read the Greek and Latin as we read the English" and thereby cause "metrical havoc."[13] Because English accentuation tended to distort the length of syllables in classical verse, it caused mispronunciation in the very attempt to pronounce Greek and Latin. Coleridge's recommendation was "to reform this barbarous mode of reading, and to teach the way of giving accent, so as to be not destructive of quantity," and he envisioned an educational system where recitation of Greek poetry would teach better pronunciation of English as well: "To read regularly a few lines of some Greek . . . would form . . . an amusing and useful exercise for the higher classes in our great school. The young men would at least acquire by it the habit of distinct pronunciation, so important in public speaking, but which so few of our public speakers possess." Like many nineteenth-century men of letters, Coleridge (who had acquired a good "ear" for Greek during his early education at Christ's Hospital) believed that reading Homer would create better English speakers, and perhaps even great orators.

Homeric hexameter thus emerged as an idea of sound, circulating in a written form that readers were taught to hear. In his various meditations on hexameter—in notebooks, letters, reviews, and his own metrical experiments—Coleridge tried to reconstruct the sound of quantitative verse in Greek, and to describe its audible effect in English.[14] His poetic imitation of hexameter, "Described and Exemplified," was one attempt to recreate the experience of reading Homer's Greek:

> /   x x l/   x   x l/ / l / x   x l/ x x l   / /
> Strongly it bears us along in swelling and limitless billows,
> /   x   x l/ / l /   x   x l/   x x l / x   x l/ /
> Nothing before and nothing behind but the sky and the ocean.

Here the Homeric epithet for "the many-sounding sea" is recycled to describe and exemplify the movement of the verse itself, as "strongly it bears us along" in the rise and fall of wave after wave.[15] We are carried by this rhythmic cadence to an infinite horizon of sound, "nothing before and nothing behind" except the "limitless billows" of hexameter lines. Coleridge represented hexameter as a force of nature in another imitation of classical meter as well, an elegiac couplet (alternating lines in dactylic hexameter and pentameter):

> /   x   x l/ x x l /x   x l   / /   l / x x l/ /
> In the hexameter rises: the fountain's silvery column,
> /   x   x l/ x   x l /ll / x   x l /x x l /
> In the pentameter aye: falling in melody back.

Coleridge taught his reader to read the flow of the verse as a rising hexameter and a falling pentameter, seeming to overflow the caesura in the first line, while the second line pauses at the caesura in a momentary interruption of the melody. Like the endless waves of the sea or a fountain forever ascending, hexameter is associated with the perpetual flow of Homer's verse: a metrical lesson taught to generation after generation of Victorian schoolboys.

Coleridge's lesson was learned by his nephew Henry Nelson Coleridge, who turned it into a principle of pedagogy in *Introduction to the Study of the Greek Classic Poets, Designed Principally for the Use of Young Persons at School and College* (1830). This popular schoolbook explained that young persons must be taught to read hexameter according to the rules, but they must also feel the rhythm that moves beneath and beyond the rules of the meter: "The verse of the Iliad seems the musical efflux of a minstrel whose unpremeditated songs are borne on the breeze-like tunings of a lyre. It is idle to attempt to lay down rules for the rhythm of the Iliad; those who have read the poem, know and feel, though cannot understand or imitate, its incomparable melody."[16] The fluency of this rhythm influenced the reading of hexameter throughout the century as an idealized and naturalized metrical form, frequently compared to the influx of water in streams and oceans or the efflux of air in breezes and human breath. Indeed, because Homeric hexameter was no longer spoken it could be imagined by both of the Coleridges and their Victorian successors as more resonant, more melodious, and more flowing than their own spoken language. The "incomparable melody" of Greek could only be felt, and never fully heard or understood in English, let alone imitated.

Nevertheless various efforts to imitate hexameter were collected in an influential 1847 anthology, *English Hexameter Translations*, prefaced by elegiac couplets that asked the "lover of Song" to read these hexameters as if they appealed naturally to the listening ear:

> /   x   x| /x x| /   / | /   x   x| / x x| /   /
> Art thou a lover of Song? Would'st fain have an utterance found it
> /   x   x| / / | / | || / x x| /   x x| /
> True to the ancient flow, true to the tones of the heart,
> /   x   x| /   x   x| /   / | / x x |/   x x | /   /
> Free from the fashions of speech which tinsel the lines of our rhymesters?
> / x x | / x x |/ || / x x |/ x x | /
> Lend us thy listening ear: lend us thy favouring voice.[17]

In a curious reversal of vernacular and classical languages, the contemporary language that is spoken is figured as "lines" to be read, while the ancient language that is written is figured as a song to be heard: the "ancient flow" of hexameters conveys "the tones of the heart" more musically than the "lines of our rhymesters." Rather than attending to the passing "fashions of speech" inscribed in the rhyming lines of English verse, the reader's "ear" and "voice" must be attuned to a song that flows over time in another kind of line: the meter of this elegiac couplet, as it alternates between full and abbreviated lines in dactylic hexameter. The (over)flow of this rhythm is measured by the enjambment between the first and second line ("found it / true") and in the reiteration of "true" across the caesura in the second line: "true to the ancient flow, // true to the tones of the heart." And in the fourth line, we cross the caesura again in a musical movement from "ear" to "voice," as if the melody survives uninterrupted in our hearing and then our voicing of the meter: "Lend us thy listening ear; // lend us thy favouring voice."

One reader who did indeed lend his "listening ear" and his "favouring voice" to these imitations was Matthew Arnold. In his lectures, *On Translating Homer*, delivered a decade after the publication of *English Hexameter Translations*, he mentioned this book as example of what might be achieved in hexameter. "The most successful attempt hitherto made at rendering Homer into English, the at-

tempt in which Homer's general effect has been best retained, is an attempt
made in the hexameter measure," Arnold wrote in praise of one of the translators, "the accomplished Provost of Eton, Dr. Hawtrey" (149). Hawtrey had published a passage from the *Iliad* in a section of *English Hexameter Translations*, entitled "From Homer," where the poet is introduced as "Time-Honour'd Bard" who
"roll'st into ages to come the sounding strain of the Epos / Here may its echo revive, here on Cimmerian shores!"[18] This introductory verse, followed by Hawtrey's
translation, implied that English hexameters are at best an echo of the original:
when the waves of Homeric hexameter wash up on English shores, what we hear
is not Homer's "sounding strain" but its resonance: the revival of an echo as an
effect of reading.

Arnold's ear was attuned to this difference. While he praised Hawtrey's
Homer because "it reproduces for me the original effect of Homer: it is the best,
and it is in hexameters" (150), he did not claim that Hawtrey had actually reproduced the original sound of Homer; rather, the Provost of Eton had reproduced
the "effect" of Homer, the experience of reading Greek as it was taught at
schools like Eton (or in Arnold's case, Rugby) and at the universities. In calling
for more hexameter translations of Homer, Arnold was not advocating a revival
of this meter as it was heard in ancient Greece, but remembering how it was read
in modern England. Arnold made this point emphatically throughout his lectures *On Translating Homer*, which began by acknowledging that "we cannot possibly tell how the *Iliad* affected its natural hearers" (98), and insisting repeatedly
that the task of the translator was not to recreate the sound of Homeric hexameter but rather to imitate its effect upon the reader: "All we are here concerned
with is the imitation, by the English hexameter, of the ancient hexameter *in its
effect upon us moderns*" (195) and again, "the modern hexameter is merely an attempt to imitate the effect of the ancient hexameter, as read by us moderns"
(198). Turning himself into an example of "us moderns," Arnold famously went
on to define the four features of Homer's "grand style" in terms of "what is the
general effect which Homer makes upon me,—that of a most rapidly moving
poet, that of a poet most plain and direct in his style, that of a poet most plain
and direct in his ideas, that of a poet eminently noble" (119).

Arnold's definition of the "grand style"—hovering between prescription (how
Homer should impress everyone) and description (the impression of Homer
"upon me")—was an early articulation of his aesthetic theory, increasingly concerned with poetry's effects on its audience.[19] What the translator had to recreate was the "effect" of the Greek text, to show how "Homer's rapidity is a flowing
rapidity," as Arnold repeatedly insisted (136): "Homer's movement, I have said
again and again, is a flowing, rapid movement. . . . In reading Homer you never
lose the sense of flowing and abounding ease" (145). But he understood this
movement to be produced by the modern mind in *reading* Homer, and reproduced by the translator to achieve a similar rapidity in English. For this reason
he criticized translations that seemed antiquated, such as a recent version by
Charles Ichabod Wright in the Miltonic manner of Cowper, "entirely alien to
the flowing rapidity of Homer," and a version by William Sotheby in "Pope's lit-

erary artificial manner" (103), or antiquarian, such as the "slip-shod" or "jog-trot and humdrum" ballad-manner in versions by William Maginn and, most notoriously Francis Newman (124, 128). Moving either too slow or too fast, these translations had not found a way to recreate the flowing ease of Homer as experienced by a modern reader in modern times.

To be "true to the ancient flow" English translators would have to modernize hexameter, perhaps along the lines of a modern poet like Arthur Hugh Clough, who had left classical scholarship at Oxford and turned to poetry and politics. According to Arnold, "Mr. Clough's hexameters are excessively, needlessly rough; still, owing to the native rapidity of this measure . . . his composition produces a sense in the reader which Homer's composition also produces, and which Homer's translator ought to *re*produce" (151). Clough had made hexameter "current" in both senses: a contemporary, rapid form that reproduced the effect of ancient Greek on the English reader. Although Clough's meter was "rough" at times, interrupting the flow of the reading, Arnold considered his poetry the best example of hexameter in English. He finished the last of his lectures with a eulogy for his friend, whose hexameters "come back now to my ear with the true Homeric ring" (216): not the original sound, but a resounding echo that reproduced "a sense in the reader which Homer's composition also produces."

Of course the poet who had contributed most to the currency of hexameter in the nineteenth century was Henry Wadsworth Longfellow, but Arnold went out of his way in his lectures to emphasize that the translator "must not follow the model offered by Mr. Longfellow in his pleasing and popular poem of *Evangeline*" (151). He considered these hexameters "much too dactylic," a debasement of English hexameter by an American poet who had been parodied in the press as "Professor Long-and-short-fellow."[20] Arnold was ambivalent about the success of *Evangeline*, simultaneously admiring and criticizing its popular appeal: "If a version of the *Iliad* in English hexameters were made by a poet who, like Mr. Longfellow, has that indefinable quality which renders him popular . . . it would have great success among the general public," he admitted, but not without qualification: "Yet a version of Homer in hexameters of the *Evangeline* type would not satisfy the judicious, nor is the definite establishment of this type to be desired" (202). Arnold as much as warned Longfellow not to take up the task of translating Homer: "One would regret that Mr. Longfellow should, even to popularize the hexameter, give the immense labour required for a translation of Homer, when one could not wish his work to stand." An American Homer would and should not influence the future of English hexameters, or so Arnold believed.

In addition to marking a distinction between English and American hexameters, Arnold was anxious to distinguish English from German hexameters as well. Although English poets had been influenced by German hexameter experiments, and although German poets might have been more successful in achieving the effects of quantitative verse, Arnold insisted that the English language was better suited to recreating the "rapidity" of Homer. Even the most successful translator of Homer in nineteenth-century Germany was at a disadvantage, according to Arnold, because that language seemed so slow and ponderous in comparison to English: "In Voss's well-known translation of Homer, it is precisely the qualities of his German language itself, something heavy and trailing both in the structure of its sentences and in the words of which it is composed, which prevent his translation, in spite of the hexameters, in spite of the fidelity, from creating in us the impression created by the Greek" (101). Arnold believed that the transformation of quantitative into accentual hexameter by English poets was unique to England, because "by this hexameter the English ear, the genius of the English language, have, in their own way, adopted, have *translated* for themselves the Homeric hexameter" (196). The native genius of the English language could be made manifest by translating hexameter into a form quite distinct from other languages, both ancient and modern.

After surveying the long history of translating Homer in various English verse forms (fourteen-syllable lines, blank verse, heroic couplets, Spenserian stanzas, ballad measure), Arnold therefore predicted that "the task of translating Homer into English verse both will be re-attempted, and may be re-attempted successfully" (167) by "a poetical translator so gifted and so trained" (168) as to produce perfect hexameters in English. More than one meter among many, hexameter was invoked by Arnold as a metrical imaginary, an ideal form that he tried to illustrate with his own translation of selected passages from Homer into hexameter. However he was quick to admit that his attempts—"somewhat too strenuous and severe, by comparison with that lovely ease" of Homer (167)—fell short of his own ideal. In his rather stilted translations, he found it difficult to follow "the fundamental rule for English hexameters,—that they be such as to *read themselves* without necessitating, on the reader's part, any non-natural putting-on or taking-off of accent" (197). It would take "some man of genius" (202) to find a middle ground between the rough hexameters of Clough and the too-smooth dactyls of Professor Long-and-short-fellow, so instead of ending with his own translations, Arnold's lectures were ultimately addressed to "the future translator of Homer" (213). "It is for the future translator that one must work" (215), he concluded: someone who could mediate between ancient quantities and modern accents to create hexameters that would naturally "*read themselves.*" Like the second coming, "our old friend, the coming translator of Homer" (170) might redeem the confusion of the present time by making hexameter into an English form, and a perfect form of Englishness.

NESTOR'S ELOQUENCE

Not long after the publication of Arnold's lectures, hexameter translations of Homer sprang up like native plants in English soil. Among the scholarly poets and poetic scholars who turned to translating Homer was C. B. Cayley. In an article entitled "Remarks and Experiments On English Hexameters" (1862), Cayley agreed with Arnold that hexameter has "pleased cultivated nations through many generations" and might be cultivated to grow naturally in England as well:

"each literature has its own accustomed measures: but from time to time many such are found to bear transplantation into foreign languages."[21] Since hexameters had been successfully transplanted from Greek to Latin verse, Cayley wondered, "is there not a chance of their being adapted to a language of intermediate cadence, like the English, which has many words accented after the Greek model . . . and many, of course, after the Latin model?" (75). He believed the English language, being composite, could combine different accentual structures with some sense of duration in syllables; he pointed out the persistence of primary and secondary accents in English and, while "the Greeks no doubt, had elocutional habits more lively than ours" (79), he argued that it was indeed possible for English poets to recreate some of the complex accents and cadences of classical hexameter, especially around the caesura: "as in English we certainly have weak syllables and primary accents and secondary, so in an hexameter formed on classical principles, one caesura, at least—and if possible, one of the principal caesuras should be preceded by a weak syllable, or at worst by a secondary accent, or if there is such a thing in English, by a circumflexed syllable" (78). Even if quantities of syllables ("circumflexed" or otherwise) could not be consistently measured in English, nevertheless English hexameters could achieve a musical cadence by manipulating stronger and weaker syllables.

Rallying around Arnold's call for hexameters, Cayley offered a more detailed explanation of how this meter might be made to work in English. He began his article by disclaiming what "is commonly said that modern versification depends on accent only, as the ancient depended on quantity," and proclaiming instead that "we cannot banish all the feeling of time even from the modern cadences" (67). And to illustrate his "suggested method in hexameters" (84), he ended his article with a sample translation from Book I of the *Iliad*: a speech by made Nestor, who exercises authority over generations of heroes through the power of persuasive speech. The role of Nestor in Homeric epic is to weigh his words carefully and teach others to do the same, as he says in Cayley's English translation: "Yet did they meditate my words, they obey'd my counsels" (85). This line is also carefully weighed to teach Cayley's method in hexameters, with a caesura after "meditate" (preceded by a weak syllable, as Cayley prescribed) and another caesura after "words," to create a pause for meditation on the cadence of these words. Placed at the end of Cayley's long explanation of hexameters, his translation turns the content of Nestor's speech into a performance of its form, as if Cayley were instructing other translators to meditate on this example and (if they obey'd his counsels) turn it into a model for English hexameters.

As Homer's veteran orator and master of performative speech, Nestor was a strategic choice for such a self-reflexive rhetorical performance. In *The Language of Heroes*, Richard Martin shows how Nestor is a heroic performer of words who has mastered the genre of memory speeches, recalling the past in order to authorize himself in the present.[22] Nestor's ability to remember and remind is embedded in the etymology of his name (connected to *mnestis*, memory), and closely linked to the power of epic narrative (inspired by Mnemosyne, the muse of memory); indeed the Homeric epithet used for Nestor "refers to divine speech within Greek archaic poetry," according to Martin: *heduepes*, "having sweet words" (102). Nestor's speech in Book I of the *Iliad* is introduced by two lines in Greek that describe how "sweet-speaking Nestor, the clear-voiced orator from Pylos arose, from whose tongue flowed speech sweeter than honey":

    __ x x /__ x x | __ x x | __ x x | __ x x | __ __

ἡδυεπὴς ἀνόρουσε, λιγὺς Πυλίων ἀγορητής

    __ x x | __ __ | __ x x | __ x x | __ x x | __ __

τοῦ καὶ ἀπὸ γλώσσης μέλιτος γλυκίων ῥέεν αὐδή (11.248–49).

Nestor is a "sweet" and "clear" speaker, whose words stream (ῥέεν, from the verb "to flow") like honey from his tongue. This description of Nestor's eloquence appealed to many nineteenth-century readers, including Samuel Taylor Coleridge who meditated on *"the flowing Line* of the epic" in one of his notebooks by quoting the same line about Nestor: "'Ῥῆμα. ῥέω, fluo. Stream of words. Flow of eloquence. Hence perhaps the German, *ich rede*, the old English, *I areed*, & our Read it to me, doubtless first used by those who could not read. = Make it *flow* for me. τοῦ καὶ ἀπὸ γλώσσης μέλιτος γλυκίων ῥέεν αὐδή."[23] Coleridge associated the ancient flow of Homeric epic with Nestor's flowing speech, and (by speculative etymologizing) used the example of Nestor to imagine how a literary culture might be formed around this idea of an oral tradition.

Cayley had a similar purpose in ending his article with the example of Nestor, as the embodiment of an oral tradition perpetuated in written form; through Nestor's stream of words, readers might be taught to "hear" the flow of hexameters in English. For his complete version of the *Iliad*, published in 1877, Cayley framed his earlier translation of Nestor's speech with a description of "Soft-spoken Nestor, Pylos's clear-toned haranguer, / Whose mouth of parlance honey-sweet was a fountain abateless."[24] The adjectives "soft-spoken" and "clear-toned" used to describe Nestor's address to his audience might also serve to address the reader of this translation, in accents softly spoken and quantities clear in tone: a combination of accentual and quantitative verse, with primary and secondary accents and carefully-timed caesuras, as prescribed by Cayley in his article. But it is difficult to scan this line as hexameter, since by English pronunciation it falls into five feet:

    /   x   x| / / ll/   xx| /   x   x|/   /

    Soft-spoken Nestor, Pylos's clear-toned haranguer,

Only if we scan "soft-spoken Nestor" rather awkwardly into spondees (lengthening the vowels because they are followed by double consonants, according to classical rules of quantity) can we prolong the line into hexameter. And although the next line does fall into six feet, the tendency for an English reader to start scanning in iambs must be overruled by stressing (again rather awkwardly) the long vowel in the first syllable to produce a dactyl:

    /   x   x| /   / | / / | /   x x| /   x   x| /   /

    Whose mouth of parlance honey-sweet was a fountain abateless.

Although Cayley's hexameters did not exactly "*read themselves*" as Arnold might have wished, nevertheless they found in the "parlance honey-sweet" of Nestor a "fountain abateless" of inspiration for the English translator: the orator as figure for the perfection of metrical translation, and embodiment of its persuasive effects.

Indeed, when Cayley finished his translation of Homer, it was dedicated to one of the great orators of the Victorian period: *The Iliad of Homer, Homometrically Translated, With Permission Dedicated to the Right Honourable Gladstone* (1877). With this dedication, Cayley associated the eloquence of Nestor and other Homeric orators with William Ewart Gladstone, an eloquent politician, British prime minister, and scholar of Homer. In his 1857 essay "On the Place of Homer in Classical Education and Historical Inquiry," Gladstone had emphasized the need for boys and men to learn about "the faculty of high oratory" by reading Homer,[25] and in *Studies on Homer and the Homeric Age* (1858) Gladstone wrote at length about the variety of orators and orations in Homer, in order to demonstrate "how and why it was, that the great Bard of that time has also placed himself in the foremost rank of oratory for all time."[26] In Achilles and Odysseus he found "specimens of transcendent eloquence which have never been surpassed" (107), and he mentioned Nestor as another specimen: "Then we have Nestor the soft and silvery, whose tones of happy and benevolent egotism flowed sweeter than a stream of honey" (105). This sentence is virtually a translation of Homer's description of Nestor: the movement of the poetry is transferred to Gladstone's dactylic prose, whose "tones" come close to recreating the effects of Homeric hexameter. The same lines from Homer are paraphrased by Gladstone again later in his *Studies on Homer,* when he alludes to the famous description that "the Poet has given of the elocution of Nestor": "To Nestor (Il. I. 248,9) he seems to assign a soft continuous flow indefinitely prolonged" (III, 240–341). Here too the "continuous flow" of Nestor, "indefinitely prolonged" by Gladstone, seems to have influenced his own style of writing.

Gladstone's fascination with the power of Homeric oratory was reflected not only in his writing, but even more in his speaking. He had been quick to learn Greek as a schoolboy at Eton, where his knack for versifying and speechifying on classical models drew the attention of Dr. Hawtrey himself (who later became headmaster of Eton and the translator of Homer, singled out by Arnold for praise). Richard Shannon's biography notes that Gladstone's classical education at Eton was important in "providing him with a forum for expression in speech and print," and in giving him a sense of vocation through studies in Homer that inspired him at the university and for the rest of his life. His vocation as a politician was quite literally the discovery of a voice for Gladstone, who was celebrated as a great debator at Oxford and throughout his long political career. His contemporaries remarked that he had "a very fine voice" and "the deepest-toned voice I ever heard,"[27] and Carlyle famously called Gladstone "the man with immeasurable power of vocables."[28] But it was through Homer in particular that Gladstone made this claim to voice, as he wrote in a letter: "Most of my time is taken up with Homer and Homeric literature, in which I am immersed with great delight up to my ears."[29] He represented his virtuosity in speaking as an effect of reading Homer, an appeal to the English ear that he had learned because of his immersion in ancient Greek. He engaged in conversations about Homer at every opportunity, including more than one occasion with Tennyson who did his best to find Gladstone "very pleasant and very interesting . . . even when he discoursed on Homer, where most people think him a little hobby-horsical."[30]

It was not surprising, then, that Cayley's translation associated Gladstone with Homer (and perhaps with the long-winded Nestor in particular). The fluency of Gladstone's speeches was another way to imagine the cadences of Homeric epic in English, reviving the ancient flow of Homer in a modern tongue. Like Nestor he was a heroic performer of words, recalling the past in order to speak to the present and perhaps even to the future, as Gladstone was chosen by Edison to record his voice on wax cylinder. When Gladstone's contemporaries heard this recording they were amazed by "the marvellous carrying-power of the most eloquent voice of our time . . . with all its compass of persuasive intonation," and indeed from the 1888 recording it is possible to imagine the smooth metrical flow of his speech, as Gladstone almost seems to speak in dactyls:

> I lament to say that the voice which I transmit to you is only the relic of an organ, the employment of which has been overstrained. Yet I offer you as much as I possess and so much as old age has left me, with the utmost satisfaction as being, at least, a testimony to the instruction and delight that I have received from your marvelous invention.[31]

In the recording this voice is indeed a relic of a past age, "overstrained" by old age and difficult to hear. Yet this voice also speaks to future ages, by giving testimony to the means of its own transmission through a "marvelous invention" that would preserve it for posterity, not unlike the marvelous invention of English hexameter that would preserve the voice of Homeric epic in Victorian England. Gladstone was the modern version of an ancient orator, who could be heard (and read) as the voice of his age, especially in retrospect. In the monumentalizing biography published in 1903 by John Morley, for example, the life of Gladstone is narrated in an epic strain (sometimes even in dactylic rhythm, like Gladstone's prose) that recalls the beginning of Homer's *Iliad* or *Odyssey*: "how can we tell the story of his works and days without reference . . . to the course of events, over whose unrolling he presided, and out of which he made history?"[32] Because he made history through his speeches in particular, Gladstone gave shape to the unruly course of events during "an agitated and expectant age" according to Morley (4), who presented Gladstone as heroic representative figure for the Victorian period and the very embodiment of its historical rhythm.

Arnold also associated Gladstone with Homer, especially at a time when the place of Homer in the classics curriculum and the purpose of Greek studies in general were being debated at schools and universities.[33] In his lecture "On the Modern Element in Literature" Arnold referred to Gladstone as "a distinguished person, who has lately been occupying himself with Homer" (31) and his lectures *On Translating Homer* followed on the heel of Gladstone's *Studies on Homer and the Homeric Age*. For both men this turn to Homer was a response to times of rapid change in Victorian England, and an attempt to shape the temporal experience of modernity. Gladstone was not so sure, however, that hexameter would be the best modern form for translating Homer or that it could serve to carry the reader into the future of English poetry. He wrote a letter to Arnold after his lectures, confessing "when asked to believe that Homer can . . . be rendered into English hexameters, I stop short."[34] Gladstone's experiments in translating Homer were mostly trochaic, in alternating tetrameter and trimeter lines that slowed down the rapid movement of Homer as Arnold imagined it. In contrast to his flowing eloquence as an orator, Gladstone's translations moved in stops and starts that fell short of Homeric hexameter. Despite the dedication of Cayley's Homer "homometrically translated" to Gladstone, Gladstone's own version of Homer did not quite achieve this epic effect: Gladstone was famous for his prose, not his prosody.[35]

Even among the prosodists there was no clear consensus about the sound of hexameters in Victorian England. Translators who tried to write in English hexameter, as prescribed by Arnold, struggled and failed. In the preface to *Homer's Iliad, Translated from the Original Greek into English Hexameters*, published in 1865, the translator Edwin Simcox wrote apologetically about his attempt to "place before the English reader a close, and, as it were, a photographic view of the poem, so far as the English language, in his humble hands, can produce this result; but it must be remembered that the Greek surpasses the English, *in sound*, as far as the organ does the pianoforte."[36] According to Simcox, the best a translator could give his reader was a "photographic view" derived from a negative image of the original: a graphic representation of sound in writing that faded away (like notes struck on a pianoforte) and could not be sustained (like the tones played on an organ). Rather than prolonging the duration of syllables, Simcox depended on the percussive effects of accentual verse, as performed in his translation of Homer's description of Nestor:

```
 /      x  x l /   x x l /   x l    /   x xl  /x x l  / x
Sweet-spoken Nestor arose, the wise rhetorician of Pulos,
 /    x     x l / x l /      x l /   x  l / x   x l / x
He, from whose skilful tongue, the words fell sweeter than honey. (8)
```

As a self-reflexive performance of metrical translation, these lines were skillfully arranged by Simcox into dactylic hexameter, but without trying to recreate classical quantities as Cayley had recommended. Simcox readily substituted trochees for spondees, allowing the second syllable of a foot to be read simply as an unaccentuated syllable, and the caesuras in the first line (after "Nestor arose") and the second line (after "skilful tongue") allowed the hexameters to be read almost as double trimeters in English. Thus the words that "fell" from Nestor's tongue also served to demonstrate the cadence of English hexameters, falling away from the sound of Greek.

Other translations attempted in response to Arnold's call for hexameters included: *The Iliad of Homer in English Hexameter Verse*, by J. Henry Dart (1865); *Homer's Iliad, Translated into English Hexameters*, by James Inglis Cochrane (1867); and *The Iliad of Homer, Translated into English Accentuated Hexameters*, by John F.

W. Herschel (1866). Dart had previously published the first half of his translation in 1862, praised by Arnold as a "meritorious version" but also criticized for the "blemish" of forcing accents; according to Arnold, his rule that hexameters must "*read themselves*" in English was occasionally violated by Dart.[37] When Dart completed his translations three years later, he agreed with Arnold that certain kinds of accentuation (especially the Greek pronunciation of proper names) might be "unpleasing to an English ear" and that "further consideration, aided by the light of criticism" had prompted him to eliminate this blemish from his translation.[38] But in final consideration of "the vexed question of metre," Dart saw "no reason to regret having selected the Hexameter," as he believed along with Arnold that "in it, and in it alone, is it possible . . . to combine adequate fidelity to the original, with that vigor and rapidity of movement." He further argued, like Arnold, that "very many of those who now entertain a sense of dislike to the metre, would feel differently if their ears were but habituated to its use" (vii–viii). An apt example of Dart's approach to metrical translation is, again, the description of Nestor:

> /   x   x | / xx | /   x   x| / x x |/x x | /   /
> Up rose the Pylian king, the melodious orator, Nestor.
> /   x   x| /   x   x| / x x | / x x | / x x | /   /
> Soft o'er his lips ran mellifluous words, as the running of honey. (10)

Dart's interest in recreating Homer's "rapidity of movement" is exemplified in the verbs "ran" and "running" (his translation of the Greek verb "to flow"), and in the momentum of uninterrupted dactyls, moving almost too rapidly for Arnold's taste: Dart's version came close to the relentless dactyls of Longfellow, depending perhaps too much on the American poet for the habituation of the English ear to the use of hexameter.

The translation of the *Iliad* by Cochrane also turned to foreign models in the effort to define English hexameter. Like other translators, he used the preface to justify his method of translation, explaining that "he prepared himself for the task by translating from the German ten or twelve thousand verses; for, although he was always of opinion that the measure was quite as well adapted as any other to the English language, yet, there were so many conflicting opinions on the subject, that he had in a considerable degree to grope his way, and ascertain for himself what the English language was capable of."[39] Cochrane emphasized that poets were still looking for a clear articulation of English metrical law: "Every hexameter writer had his own particular theory, and there were no definite and acknowledged rules to guide one." But this irregularity proved in some respects an advantage for Cochrane, who combined different theories of hexameter to achieve greater variation in his hexameter lines. Thus, in his translation of Nestor, we find a combination of accentual and quantitative verse:

> / x   x | /   / | /xx |/x x| / x x | /   x
> Nestor, the sweet-ton'd Pylian orator, rose to address them;
> /   x   x | /   /   / | |/   x x | / x x | / x   x| / x
> He from whose tongue flow'd sweeter than honey the words which he utter'd. (15)

While "sweet-ton'd" and "tongue flow'd" can be scanned as spondees according to classical rules of quantity, the final feet of both lines are closer to trochees according to the principles of English accentuation. Indeed Cochrane suggested that Nestor's speech is heard in accents, as his translation went on to describe Nestor, "counseling wisely, in these kind accents he spake, and address'd them." The utterance of Nestor could thus be read simultaneously in quantities and accents, but without a "particular theory" or "acknowledged rules" for integrating the two systems of versification as Cayley had proposed.

Another translator who embraced accents even more fully was Herschel, as announced by the title of his *Homer, Translated in English Accentuated Hexameters*. The translator's preface (again a strategic piece of rhetoric) defended Herschel's decision to translate quantitative into accentual verse, and appealed to readers to give it a "fair hearing":

> The Hexameter metre is on its trial in this country. It is therefore entitled at all events to a fair hearing. It may at least claim to be read as any other of our received metres is read; with no deliberate intention to caricature it, or to spoil it in the reading: without sing-song or affectation, and according to the ordinary usages of English pronunciation. So tried, if it fail to please and to make its way, it stands condemned. But in the perusal of so long a poem it must be borne in mind, in common candour, that all our ordinary forms of verse have a certain elasticity,—admit a certain latitude of accommodation between the accent proper to the verse—its dead form—and that which constitutes its living spirit and interprets its melody to the hearer.[40]

Herschel asked readers to conflate legal and aesthetic judgment—to give this trial of hexameters a "fair hearing" and also in "hearing" to find them "fair"—and in their exercise of English metrical law, to decide by the rules "in this country" and according to "usages of English pronunciation." However he added some special pleading: the readers who judged his translation would have to be sufficiently lenient to "admit a certain latitude of accommodation" between the "dead form" of the verse and its "living spirit." To breathe new life into Homeric hexameter and revive its spirit would take an act of inspiration, a translator who could "interpret the melody to the hearer" by giving it a living form. Herschel was inspired to interpret the melody of Nestor's speech as "harmonious accents" in his translation:

> / x x l/ xx l/   x l / x x l /   x x l / x
> Nestor, the Pylian sage, whose eloquence, clear and persuasive
> / x x l / x x l / xx l / x l l / x x l / x
> Flowed from his lips in harmonious accents, sweeter than honey. (10)

Rather than attempting quantitative verse (as in Cayley's "clear-toned" or Cochrane's "sweet-ton'd" versions of Nestor), Herschel presented the speech of Nestor in accentuated hexameter, freely alternating dactyls and trochees. To emphasize the harmonious flow of his translation, the verb "to flow" has been placed at the beginning of a line, and the placement of caesuras at variable points within each line creates a sense of overflow rather than interruption. Thus Nestor is made to speak, "clear and persuasive," in English accents.

BARBAROUS HEXAMETERS

As Poet Laureate, Tennyson did not think much of the hexameter experiments inspired by Arnold's *Lectures on Translating Homer*. In 1863 Tennyson criticized attempts by Herschel and others to revive a dead form and interpret its melody: "Some, and among these one at least of our best and greatest, have endeavoured to give us the Iliad in English hexameters, and by what appears to me their failure, have gone far to prove the impossibility of the task."[41] To go even further in proving the impossibility of the task, Tennyson's skeptical headnote introduced a parody of hexameter, written by himself in elegiac couplets and entitled, "On Translations of Homer. Hexameters and Pentameters":

/ / l/ x xl/ / l/   x xl / x x l / /
These lame hexameters the strong-winged music of Homer!
/   x x l / / l/   ll / x x l / x x l/
No, but a most burlesque, barbarous experiment,
/   x xl / / l / x xl / / l / x x l / /
When was a harsher sound ever heard, ye Muses, in England?
/   x xl / / l/ ll / x xl / x xl /
When did a frog coarser croak upon our Helicon?
/ x x l / / l /   / l/ / l/ x x   /
Hexameters no worse than daring Germany gave us:
/ x x l/x x l / ll / x x l / x xl/
Barbarous experiment, barbarous hexameters.

Tennyson's verse is deliberately awkward, prompting us to read "these lame hexameters" not only as a description of Homeric translations but as a performance of its own mock-versification. The parody begins lamely with a spondee, ironically contrasting "these lame" feet in English with the "strong-winged music of Homer," getting stronger in dactyls but disrupted by the dissonance in the following line: "No, but a most burlesque, barbarous experiment." The harsh sound of plosives in "but," "burlesque," and "barbarous" is amplified into the "harsher sound" of croaking, in a line that is made more difficult to pronounce by forcing the accentuation of an unaccented syllable; "When did a frog coar*ser* croak?" The penultimate line makes a mockery of German hexameters by lengthening the feet into ponderous spondees and (as if to illustrate the failure of the meter) falling short of a beat at the end: what "daring Germany gave" requires an extra syllable and is nothing but an empty form.

Thus any attempt to recreate the music of Homer in English hexameters was made to sound like a "barbarous experiment," a strenuous combination of stresses repeated twice by Tennyson for comic effect, in the second line and again at the end. To add insult to injury, the scansion of the last phrase is so ridiculous that it sounds almost like *barbarous hexameters* are written by "barbarous hexamateurs." Translators of Homer, we might conclude, are amateur poets who threatened to turn English into the language of barbarians, according to the Greek etymology of the word: in trying to recreate Greek hexameters, English syllables are reduced to the meaningless iteration of "barbar . . . barbar," like the stuttering repetition of "barbarous" in the final line. Furthermore, the caesura between "barbarous experiment // barbarous hexameters" draws another double bar, disrupting the flow of Homeric rhythm. Instead of melodious song, we hear harsher sounds that are measured by their own interruption and disruption. Derived from a dead language that is neither heard nor spoken by the Muses in England, these hexameters are abstracted into a series of metrical bars that barbarize English and make it sound foreign.

In his *History of English Prosody,* Saintsbury's diatribe against "the hexameter mania" came to a similar conclusion. Quoting Tennyson's parody, he commented on the final line that "the syllables must be forced into improper pronunciation to make the quantities audible . . . you have to pronounce, in a quite unnatural way, 'experimennnnnnt,' 'hexameterrrrr'" (III.421). Of course the poetic success of Tennyson's hexameters was measured precisely by that failure of pronunciation, but Saintsbury took Tennyson at his word. His chapter on "The Later English Hexameter" became a tirade against "English Quantity-Mongers" (411) and "classicalisers" (422) who introduced quantities difficult to measure or hear in English: "With the self-styled quantitative hexameter you must either have a new pronunciation, or a mere ruinous and *arrhythmic* heap of words," Saintsbury concluded (400). He worried that the spoken language would be regulated (or rather, deregulated) by rules that make English unpronounceable: far from melodious, the ideal of Homeric rhythm might have the contrary effect of making English poetry "arrhythmic." He therefore dismissed the prescription of classical rules for English hexameter as an experiment "reinforcing lack of ear" and "foredoomed to failure" (415).

Cayley's translation of Homer was singled out by Saintsbury as a particularly ruinous and arrhythmic heap of words. In a prefatory verse to his *Iliad,* Cayley had asked readers to listen carefully to the length of the syllables in his "homometric" hexameters, without simply counting the accents:

/ /I/ x xI/ x xI / / I/ x xI / /
Dons, undergraduates, essayists, and public, I ask you
/ / II/ x xI/ /I / /I / x xI / /
Are these hexameters true-tim'd, or Klopstockish uproar?

Although the pronunciation of these lines might seem odd at first, Cayley claimed his translation was nothing like the noisy German hexameters of Klopstock, but a more subtle appeal to the English ear in "true-tim'd" quantitative verse. Saintsbury made a mockery of Cayley's "homometric" hexameters. To emphasize that scanning ancient Greek was not the same as reading English verse, Saintsbury tried to scan "dons, undergraduates" in Cayley's couplet and pointed out the difficulty of pronouncing "underrrgraduayte" according to antiquated rules of quantity—an instructive academic exercise for dons and undergraduates, perhaps, but too artificial for English readers ready to graduate from pedantic metrical instruction. "Our business is with English," Saintsbury insisted, "And I repeat that, *in English*, there are practically no metrical fictions, and that metre follows, though it may sometimes slightly force, pronunciation" (435).

But since, as Saintsbury conceded, pronunciation may (and even must) be forced by the meter "sometimes," the new wave of hexameter translations in the wake of Arnold's lectures tried to show how a metrical fiction might be naturalized and nationalized in English poetry. The next chapter in this metrical fiction was written by James Spedding, who argued that English hexameter should resist accent altogether.[42] Arnold distanced himself from Spedding's radical theories: in "Last Words" he worried that Spedding "proposes radically to subvert the constitution of this hexameter," and instead Arnold proposed an approach to the form more conservative than Spedding, who "can comprehend revolution in this metre, but not reform" (197). Nevertheless by the end of the century, the revolution was well underway in the work of prosodists like William Johnson Stone and Robert Bridges, who were experimenting with quantitative hexameter to change the history of English versification and redefine English national meter. For example Stone's pamphlet "On the Use of Classical Metres in English" (first published in 1899 and reprinted by Bridges) concluded that "accentuated verse" had become "too easy and too monotonous" and it was time to displace traditional blank verse with English verse in classical meters.[43] To illustrate his theory of hexameter, Stone included his metrical translation of a passage from Homer's *Odyssey*, beginning with the lines: "When they came to the fair-flowing river and to the places / Where stood pools in plenty prepared, and water abundant, / Gushed up, a cure for things manifold uncleanly . . ." These lines redirected the ancient flow of Homer into a "fair-flowing river" of verse that might cure, cleanse, and purify English poetry, and lead it to new places, perhaps in the next century.

Given the ongoing controversies about many possible forms of English hexameter, the Arnoldian legacy in metrical translation is (clearly) not as transparent a discourse as Venuti would claim. Even in the late twentieth century, in *Rhyme's Reason: A Guide to English Verse*, John Hollander poses the problem of "putatively 'quantitative' dactylic hexameters" in a self-reflexive metrical performance that cannot answer its own question:

> All such syllables arrang'd in the classical order
> Can't be audible to English ears that are tun'd to an accent
> Mark'd by a pattern of stress, not by a quantitative scrawl.

As Hollander remarks on (and in) his poem, "these lines 'scan' only if we show that the pattern of 'long' and 'short' syllables falls into the classical 'feet,' or musical measures."[44] The inaudibility of this music makes classical hexameter a graphic effect rather than a vocal phenomenon, something seen and not heard, something read and not spoken. The difference between the poem in the eye and the poem in the ear is further explored in *Vision and Resonance: Two Senses of Poetic Form*, where Hollander devotes a chapter to experiments in quantitative meter as "a written code" haunted by our desire to hear it spoken. Looking beyond Elizabethan and Victorian experiments he discerns "the last ghost of quantitative hankering in English and American poetry" where "specters continue to appear" (70) to confuse our two senses of poetic form in a weird extrasensory perception, as if eyes could hear, and ears see. Hollander is skeptical (as Tennyson was, and Saintsbury too) of "the rebarbative air of the crank," by which he means, "the quantitative crank, someone with Classical training who for complex reasons fancies he hears true quantity in English."[45]

Yet for Arnold, hexameter was not rebarbative; to the contrary, it exemplified the civilizing measures of meter and a measured response to modern times. In the decade leading up to his lectures, Arnold had already been calling for such measures to give order to the chaos of the present. In the 1853 preface to his *Poems* he wrote that "commerce with the ancients" such as Homer would produce "in those who constantly practise it, a steadying and composing effect" (493), and he explained why he turned to Greek models in his own poems: "I seemed to myself to find the only sure guidance, the only solid footing, among the ancients" (494). Although in 1853 Arnold had not yet discovered a "steadying effect" and "solid footing" in the feet of dactylic hexameter, he took the next step as Professor of Poetry at Oxford, when he recommended hexameter translation for the future of English poetry and the orderly progression of English national culture. But even as Arnold called upon English hexameters as a form of and for national identification, he also detached meter from the traditions of versification identified as "English." In *The Powers of Distance*, Anderson dedicates a chapter to "the range of forms of detachment to be found in Arnold's work," and in his critical writing from the 1850s and 1860s she observes a tendency toward "transcendence of constraining *Englishness*" and "an implicit ideal of cosmopolitan cultivation."[46] Hexameter, I would add, served as another form of detachment for Arnold, precisely because it could cultivated *as* a form. In "Culture and Anarchy" Arnold stressed the need for the English critic to "dwell much on foreign thought" and imagine how "the ideas of Europe steal gradually and amicably in, and mingle, though in infinitesimally small quantities at a time, with our own notions."[47] To define national identity through hexameter, Arnold also had to identify its international origins. Dwelling on the "foreign" thought of Homer, Arnold hoped that English forms could be transformed, "small quantities at a time," by the ideas of Europe.

Contrary to his hopes, Arnold did not find consensus in England. In *The Saturday Review* he was accused of turning to foreign models to define "what is no English metre at all," and readers were informed that Arnold's hexameter translations were too strange, too distant, too remote from English utterance: "We hold it to be an utter mistake to try to reproduce the Greek hexameter . . . in a language like English."[48] The reviewer emphasized that Homer's poetry was removed from speech even in Greek ("It was such Greek as nobody spoke," [96]) and therefore its literary effect would always be an estrangement of the common language. Ultimately the article was an ad hominem attack on Arnold, as the embodiment of a professor alienated from the culture to which he wanted to give form. "The whole of the lectures are one constant I—I—I—*Dass grosse ich* reigns from one end to the other. . . . But it is not the mere number of I's in Mr. Arnold's lectures, it is the way in which 'I' always comes in—an authoritative, oracular way, something akin, we venture to guess, to 'the grand style' " (96). Arnold's oratory was conflated with the style of Homer, as a written form that was no longer spoken, and therefore must remain strange—perhaps even barbarous—to English audiences.

Arnold's grand style was also lampooned by Charles Ichabod Wright (whose translation of Homer in blank verse had been curtly dismissed by Arnold's lectures). In a pamphlet, Wright took revenge on the "Poetry-Professor" who had led a generation of translators into oblivion: "By the sanction of his name as the representative of Poetry, Professor Arnold has led on a number of men to pursue a phantom, in the hope that they might nationalize the Hexameter." But Wright insisted, "our language is incapable of giving a naturalization to a metre in which rules of quantity are indispensable."[49] Wright believed that English could not be quantified, and so, in a wicked parody of bad hexameter verse, he imagined "the Professor" professing the rise and fall of his aspirations. "It perhaps may be allowed me to imagine the feelings which animated the Professor on the occasion, and to express them in verses somewhat akin to his own famed hexameters," he wrote, ventriloquising Arnold:

> 'Aye, surely are vanished the host of Translators of Homer!
> My spear—it hath swept them like leaves of the forest in Autumn.
> I only remain. My glory it never shall perish;
> And Oxford shall triumph in me her redoubted Professor.'

Although Arnold seems to be reveling here in the triumph of his hexameter mania, none of the lines achieve full hexameter: they are missing a syllable in the first foot, turning the initial word of each line into an anacrusis or "upbeat" for the dactyls that follow. This is especially dramatic in "I only remain," where the stress on "I" virtually reduces the pronoun to a metrical mark (not unlike the I—I—I of *dass grosse ich*). All that remains, in other words, is a failed metrical form.

Arnold's triumph turns out to be failure, as Wright went on to imagine Arnold in despair: "Allow me once more to indulge my fancy in an imaginary soliloquy, reminding us of the reverses incident to humanity, from which even a Professor is not exempt." In the following verse, Arnold apostrophizes his own hexameters as a dead and deadly form, unable to reanimate the poetry of Homer:

> O cursed Hexameters—ye, upon whom I once counted
> To wake up immortal, unique Translator of Homer,
> I would ye had never been cherished and nursed in my bosom!
> Ye vipers, ye sting me! Disgraced is the chair that I sit in;
> And Oxford laments that her Muses have lost their protector.

In the transition from the first verse (celebratory) to the second verse (elegiac), Arnold seemed to suffer the "reverses" of poetic fate: in the attempt to re-verse the relationship between form and content, to find content in the performance of the form itself, his versification proved a failure.

Nevertheless if we linger long enough in this dead end of Victorian prosody, we might see how the pursuit of a phantom—the revival of Homeric hexameter as an empty form—haunts modernity. Rather than regulating the unruly time of national culture, Arnold's call for English hexameters was already an articulation of the temporal disjunction upon which the modern nation is predicated: a double temporality that is an equivocal movement, a present that is both continuous and discontinuous with the past, simultaneously historical and contemporaneous, progressive and repetitive. Metrical translations of Homer failed to achieve the fluency to which they aspired, as their flow was disrupted by misplaced accents and displaced caesuras. But this fluency defined by interruption was prefigured and indeed prescribed by Arnold's reading of Homer; it was the caesura of the modern, played out in the metrical form of the double bar of those barbarous hexameters.

NOTES

1. Vladimir Nabokov, "Problems in Translation: 'Onegin' in English," *Partisan Review* 22, 1955: 496–512. Reprinted in *The Translation Studies Reader*, ed. Lawrence Venuti (London: Routledge, 2000), p. 77.

2. John Lucas, *England and Englishness: Ideas of Nationhood in English Poetry, 1688–1900* (Iowa City: University of Iowa Press, 1990), p. 184.

3. Benedict Anderson, *Imagined Communities: Reflections on the Origin and Spread of Nationalism* (London: Verso, 1983 and 1991), pp. 24–25.

4. Matthew Reynolds, *The Realms of Verse 1830–1870: English Poetry in a Time of Nation-Building* (Oxford: Oxford University Press, 2001), p. 274.

5. Matthew Arnold, *On the Classical Tradition*, ed. R. H. Super (Ann Arbor: University of Michigan Press, 1960), p. 21. Unless otherwise noted, all references to Arnold will be cited in the main text from this edition.

6. George Saintsbury, *A History of English Prosody, from the Twelfth Century to the Present Day*, first edition 1906–1910. Page numbers (cited in the main text) are from vol. III of the 2d ed. (London: Macmillan, 1923).

7. In the 1860s at least six hexameter translations were published in England by C. B. Cailey (1862), J.T.B. Landon (1862), J. Dart (1862), James Inglis Cochrane (1867), Edwin Simcox (1865), and John F. W. Herschel (1866). In America, William Cullen Bryan experimented with hexameter before publishing his translation of *The Odyssey* in blank verse (1872); see also the American response to Arnold in *The North American Review* (1862).

8. From between 1860–1900 more than fifty British and American translations of Homer appeared, as listed by F.M.K. Foster in *English Translations from the Greek, A Bibiographical Survey* (New York: Columbia University Press, 1918), pp. 67–76. Various English translations (including excerpts from Victorian versions) are collected in *Homer in English*, edited by George Steiner with Aminadav Dykman (London: Penguin Books,

1996). On nineteenth-century ideas about Homer, see James Porter, "Homer: The Very Idea," *Arion*, 10.2 (Fall 2002), 57–86.

9. Venuti, *The Translator's Invisibility*, pp. 144–45.

10. In *Well-Weighed Syllables: Elizabethan Verse in Classical Metres* (Cambridge: Cambridge University Press, 1974), Derek Attridge shows how Elizabethan experiments in quantitative verse moved "away from any conception of metre as a rhythmic succession of sounds, akin to the beat of the ballad-monger or the thumping of a drum" and toward an abstract, mathematized order "where words are anatomised and charted with a precision and a certainty unknown in the crude vernacular" (pp. 77–78). I am grateful to Derek Attridge for his feedback on metrical experiments in the Victorian period.

11. On the proliferation of metrical forms toward the end of the nineteenth century, see Yopie Prins, "Victorian Meters," in *The Cambridge Companion to Victorian Poetry*, ed. Joseph Bristow (Cambridge: Cambridge University Press, 2000). On nineteenth-century experiments with hexameter in particular, see also Kenneth Haynes, *English Literature and Ancient Languages* (Oxford: Oxford University Press, 2003), pp. 131–33; Erik Gray, "Clough and His Discontents: *Amours de Voyage* and the English Hexameter," in *Literary Imagination: The Review of the Association of Literary Scholars and Critics* 6(2) 2004, pp. 195–210; Christopher Matthews, "A Relation, Oh Bliss! unto Others": Heterosexuality and the Ordered Liberties of The Bothie of Toper-Na-Fuosich," *Nineteenth-Century Literature* 58.4 (March 2004), pp. 474–505.

12. See for example popular accounts in Victorian school stories of boys learning to read Homer (as in Thomas Hughes's *Tom Brown's Schooldays* from 1857) and having the lesson (rhythmically) beaten into them (as in F. W. Farrar's *Eric, or, Little by Little* from 1857 and *St. Winifred's* from 1862). The practice of memorizing Homer was part of Victorian metrical education.

13. George Whalley, "Coleridge on Classical Prosody: an Unidentified Review of 1797," *Review of English Studies* 2(7), 1951, p. 244. Whalley reprints S. T. Coleridge's anonymous review of Samuel Horsley, *On the Prosodies of the Greek and Latin Languages* (1796), and notes that Coleridge also refers to John Foster, *An Essay On the Different Nature of Accent and Quantity With Their Use and Application in the English, Latin, and Greek Languages* (1763), and Henry Gally, *A Dissertation against pronouncing the Greek Language according to accents* (1754). Whalley further notes that Coleridge's review coincided with yet another pamphlet published by Dr. Warner in 1797, *Metronariston: or a new pleasure recommended, in a dissertation upon a part of greek and latin prosody* (1797), but does not speculate further" what had aroused this sudden interest in Greek prosody and pronunciation" (p. 241).

14. In *Romanticism at the End of History* (Baltimore: Johns Hopkins University Press, 2000), Jerome Christensen describes how the notebooks of Coleridge dedicated many pages to "notations of a staggering array of poetic meters, clouds of diacritical marks combined and arranged into the phantom of verse" (p. 99). According to Christenson, Coleridge discovered in his analysis of German and English hexameter how "each language falls afoul of the Homeric antecedent in its own way," and therefore in his own experiments with English hexameter Coleridge "concentrated on the cadence, the modulation or fall of voice that accents poetic language." See also Ernest Bernhardt-Kabisch, "'When Klopstock England Defied': Coleridge, Southey and the German/English Hexamter," in *Comparative Literature* 55(2), Spring 2003, pp. 130–63.

15. The comparison of Homer's verse to the sea has a long history that continues in "Dactylic Meter: A Many-Sounding Sea," a recent essay by Annie Finch who claims "the dactylic meter has rolled through Western literature like a 'polyphlosboiou thalassa'

(many-sounding sea), to use a phrase of Homer's." In *An Exaltation of Forms: Contemporary Poets Celebrate the Diversity of their Art*, eds. Annie Finch and Kathrine Varnes (Ann Arbor: University of Michigan Press, 2002), p. 66.

16. Henry Nelson Coleridge, *Introduction to the Study of the Greek Classic Poets, Designed Principally for the Use of Young Persons at School and College*, Part I (1st ed. 1830; 2nd ed., London: John Murray, 1834). Coleridge writes, "In noticing the Versification of the Iliad, it may be truly said that its Meter is the best, and its Rhythm the least, understood of any in use amongst the ancients . . . not one ever maintained, for twenty lines together, the Homeric modulation of the Hexameter. . . . The variety of the rhythm of the Homeric Hexameter is endless . . . and all the learning in the world on the subject of Caesura and Arsis has no more enabled posterity to approach to the Homeric flow (American edition, Boston: James Munroe, 1842), p. 125.

17. Preface, *English Hexameter Translations from Schiller, Goethe, Homer, Callimachus, and Meleager*, by J.F.W. Herschel, W. W. Lewell, J. C. Hobhouse, E. C. Hawtrey, J.G.L. Lockhart (London: John Murray, 1847).

18. In *English Hexameter Translation*, the section "From Homer" includes translations from the *Iliad* by Hawtrey and Lockhard, and is introduced by another epigram in elegiac couplets: "Time-Honour'd Bard, all hail! That on eagle's pinions sailing / Mark'st with their rhythmical sweep measures of loftiest song, / Roll'st into ages to come the sounding strain of the Epos, / Here may its echo revive, here on Cimmerian shores!"

19. In her discussion of Arnold's preface, for example, Dorothy Mermin notes that "poetry is defined almost exclusively in terms of its effect on the audience . . . a poem should make a 'total impression,'" *The Audience in the Poem: Five Victorian Poets* (New Brunswick: Rutgers University Press, 1983), p. 101. Isobel Armstrong also notes that Arnold's "grand style *is* the aesthetic. It enacts the aesthetic state, the end product, the work of art's results, rather than working on the experiences which produce that result. Hence its concern with effects. . . . It is effectively a psychological theory of art as calm, as therapeutic composure and unity," *Victorian Poetry: Poetry, Poetics and Politics* (London: Routledge, 1993), p. 211.

20. Albert Smith, "Syringaline: by Professor Long-and-short-fellow," *The Month* (September 1851), pp. 192–96.

21. C. B. Cayley,"Remarks and Experiments On English Hexameters," in *Transactions of the Philological Society* (Berlin: A. Asher) 1862–63, pp. 71–72.

22. Richard Martin focuses on speech genres in the *Iliad* that are named *muthoi*; the performance of a memory is a particular speech act or *muthos* associated with Nestor in particular. Nestor's ability to command through feats of memory is exemplified in his first speech in the *Iliad*. Nestor's line in Cayley's translation ("yet did they meditate my words, they obey'd my counsels") is translated by Martin as follows: "And they understood my counsels and obeyed the muthos." *The Language of Heroes: Speech and Performance in the Iliad* (Ithaca: Cornell University Press, 1989), p. 80.

23. *The Notebooks of Samuel Taylor Coleridge*, eds. Kathleen Coburn and Merton Christensen (Princeton: Princeton University Press, 1990), vol. 4 part 1, 4832,f60. According to Coburn, Coleridge probably derived this note from his reading of Creuzer: "Finally *rhema*, from *rheo* flow, actually signifies words flowing from the mouth, a relationship which the natural artist Homer so happily expresses in the description of Nestor's speech" (*The Notebooks of Samuel Taylor Coleridge*, vol. 4 part 2).

24. From C. B. Cayley, *The Iliad of Homer, Homometrically Translated, With Permission Dedicated to the Right Honourable Gladstone* (London: Longmans, 1877), p. 7.

25. William E. Gladstone, "On the Place of Homer in Classical Education and in Historical Inquiry," *Oxford Essays* (1857), p. 17.

26. William E. Gladstone, *Studies on Homer and the Homeric Age* (Oxford, 1858), III, p. 104.

27. Quoted by Richard Shannon, *Gladstone*, vol. I: 1809–1865 (London: Hamish Hamilton, 1982). Shannon also notes "the copiousness of the flow of Gladstone's words" (p. 93).

28. Tennyson's *Memoir* 2(236). Quoted by Cornelia Pearsall, who offers an excellent account of Tennyson and Gladstone on Homer and Homeric eloquence in *Tennyson's Rapture: Civic Transformation in the Victorian Dramatic Monologue* (Oxford, 2005). On the "Homeric competition" between Tennyson and Gladstone, see also Gerhard Joseph, *Tennyson and the Text: The Weaver's Shuttle* (Cambridge: Cambridge University Press, 1992), pp. 130–40.

29. Quoted by John Morley, *The Life of William Ewart Gladstone* (London: Macmillan, 1903), vol. 1, p. 549.

30. Quoted by Shannon, *Gladstone*, vol. I, p. 458.

31. I quote the transcription of Gladstone's recording, and the enthusiastic response of James Russell Lowell, from John Picker, *Victorian Soundscapes* (Oxford: Oxford University Press, 2003), pp. 121–22. Gladstone's "Congratulation to Edison" was recorded in London in 1888, and a transcript published in "Mr. Gladstone and Mr. Edison" in the London *Times*, January 11, 1889, p. 5.

32. John Morley, *The Life of William Ewart Gladstone* (London: Macmillan, 1903), vol. 1, p. 3.

33. On Gladstone's contribution to Victorian debates about classical education, see Christopher Stray, *Classics Transformed: Schools University, and Society in England, 1830–1960* (Oxford: Oxford University Press, 1998). On the place of Arnold and Gladstone in the politics of "knowing Greek" in the 1860's, see Simon Goldhill, *Who Needs Greek? Contests in the Cultural History of Hellenism* (Cambridge: Cambridge University Press, 2002), chapter 4.

34. Gladstone to Arnold, February 11, 1861. Quoted by Shannon, *Gladstone*, p. 431.

35. Gladstone acknowledged the limits in his own "faculty of poetry, which was very defective" and described his faculty in prose by analogy to Carlyle: "I remember asking Tennyson whether he did not consider Carlyle to be a true poet. He answered, 'Certainly: he is a Poet to whom Nature has denied the faculty of verse,'" *The Gladstone Papers* (London: Cassell, 1930), p. 35.

36. Edwin Simcox, *Homer's Iliad, Translated from the Original Greek into English Hexameters* (London: Jackson, Walford and Hodder, 1865).

37. In a long footnote to "Last Words," his final lecture on translating Homer, Arnold mentioned "Mr. Dart['s] recent meritorious version of the Iliad" but with reservations about its similarity to "the current English hexameters" of Longfellow (197).

38. J. Henry Dart, preface to *The Iliad of Homer in English Hexameter Verse* (London: Longmans, 1865), p. vi.

39. James Inglis Cochrane, *Homer's Iliad, Translated into English Hexameters* (Edinburgh: printed for private circulation, 1867), p. v. The preface was reprinted from his translation of Book I, first published in 1862.

40. John F. W. Herschel, *The Iliad of Homer, Translated into English Accentuated Hexameters* (London: Macmillan, 1866), p. xiv.

41. "On Translations of Homer. Hexameters and Pentameters," *Cornhill Magazine* (De-

cember 1863). Reprinted in ed. Christopher Ricks, *The Poems of Tennyson* (Essex: Longman, 1987), vol. 2, p. 654. See also A. A. Markley, "Barbarous Hexameters and Dainty Meters: Tennyson's Uses of Classical Versification," in *Studies in Philology* 95(4) Fall 1998, pp. 456–86.

42. James Spedding reviewed Arnold's *Lectures* in *Fraser* (June 1861), and further elaborated his theory of quantitative hexameter in *Reviews and Discussions*, 1879.

43. William Johnson Stone, "On the Use of Classical Metres in English" (London: Oxford University Press, 1899), pp. 50–51. According to Stone, the monotony of blank verse could only be counteracted by "exceeding to the utmost limit" so that it became "an art essentially without limit . . . ametron, asumetron" (a-metrical and a-symmetrical), p. 51.

44. John Hollander, *Rhyme's Reason: A Guide to English Verse* (New Haven: Yale University Press, 1981), p. 35.

45. John Hollander, *Vision and Resonance: Two Senses of Poetic Form* (New Haven: Yale University Press, 1975), pp. 59, 60.

46. Amanda Anderson, *The Powers of Distance: Cosmopolitanism and the Cultivation of Detachment* (Princeton: Princeton University Press, 2001), p. 94.

47. Matthew Arnold, "Culture and Anarchy," quoted by Anderson, ibid., pp. 93–94.

48. "Homeric Translators and Critics," *The Saturday Review* (July 27, 1861), p. 95.

49. Ichabod Charles Wright, "A Letter to the Dean of Canterbury, On the Homeric Lectures of Matthew Arnold, Professor of Poetry in the University of Oxford" (London: Macmillan, 1864).

Translating History

SANDRA BERMANN

> Just as the manifestations of life are intimately connected with the phenomenon
> of life without being of importance to it, a translation issues from the original—
> not so much from its life as from its afterlife. . . . In the final analysis, the range
> of life must be determined by history rather than by nature, least of all by such
> tenuous factors as sensation and soul. The philosopher's task consists in
> comprehending all of natural life through the more encompassing life of history.
>
> —Walter Benjamin, *"The Task of the Translator"*

René Char's "Feuillets d'Hypnos" brings before us the lived history of the French resistance, joining traumatic memory with hopes for a future of freedom and human dialogue. Closely intertwined with Char's own actions as captain on the maquis, the collection of prose poems offers a rare engagement with historical experience in poetic form, both a tragic affirmation of life and, in its own right, a means of resistance. But I also argue here that this example of historical poetry illustrates some important connections between the writing of lived historical event and translation. Both are linguistic acts dedicated to the "survival" of an "original," a survival, which as Derrida suggests in a reading of Benjamin's "Task of the Translator," has a double sense—both a continuity, or "living on" of the original (Benjamin's *fortleben*) and also a "life after death," (Benjamin's *überleben*).[1] But what makes Char's text such a telling example is that it is not only a historical inscription that allows the past to "survive," but also an "original" in its own right, a highly self-conscious poetic text capable of generating a literary afterlife of its own. By considering Char's translation of historical event into poetry and its own claim to an interpretive afterlife in the years that follow, I mean to underscore Benjamin's fundamental insight that cultural "life," like the greater empirical life of which it is a part, can best be seen in its temporal or historical trajectory, and that "translation," variously understood, plays a vital role in this.

I would like to thank the Jacques Doucet library, the Columbia University Insitute for Scholars at Reid Hall, and especially Marie-Claude Char, without whose generous assistance this work could not have been completed. I am also grateful to Michael Wood and Mihaela Bacou for their helpful comments and suggestions. Parts of this essay appear in French translation in *René Char et ses alliés substantiels:artistes du XXe siècle* (Association Campredon Art et Culture: "Maison René Char," 2003).

When France entered World War II in 1939, the poet was thirty-two years old. He was by this time known as one of the younger surrealists, having joined the group nine years earlier. Collaborating with Eluard, Aragon, Breton, as well as with Picasso, Buñuel, and Dalí, and often emphasizing violence and revolt, he had already registered his opposition not only to bourgeois cultural norms, but also to Franco in Spain, to the Colonial Exposition, the Indochina colonization and especially to the rise of Nazism.[2]

But Char's entrance into historical action, like that of many of his contemporaries, was not premeditated. It was abrupt and even surprising. He was mobilized in Nîmes in 1939 and sent to fight in the battle of Alsace, in the 173rd regiment of heavy artillery. Demobilized in 1940, he returned to his home at L'Isle-sur-la-Sorgue, but only briefly, since he was soon denounced there as a militant of the extreme left. Thanks to a friendly warning, he escaped, traveling East and North to Céreste. There, while other French poets, including his friend André Breton, waited in Marseille for American visas, Char began creating links with local resistants in Céreste, L'Isle-sur-la-Sorgue, Aix, Avignon, and Digne.

By 1941, Char's armed opposition had begun. Military history tells the rest.[3] From between 1941 and 1942 he was part of the Armée Secrête (AS), acting as head of the section Durance-Sud under the code name of Capitaine Alexandre, the name he kept until the end of the war. By 1943, he was leading partisan groups of the FFC (Forces Françaises Combattantes) in the Alpes de Provence and serving as departmental chief of seven regions of the maquis for parachute landings of arms and munitions (S.A. P.-R2) in the Basses Alpes. Eventually, he acted as joint regional chief in preparation for the Allied landing in Provence in 1944, and traveled to Algiers to advise the Supreme Allied Headquarters. After the war, he was decorated for bravery and leadership by both France and the United States.

It is well known that throughout the long years of Char's military resistance, he wrote prolifically. Yet unlike most other "Resistance poets," Char did not publish any of his work between 1940 and 1945, not even in clandestine journals. Not only was he skeptical about the political and personal motives of much resistance poetry, he also did not want to support any appearance of normalcy during the "Hitlerian night." Yet with the postwar publication of his wartime poetry, first "Seuls demeurent" (1945), then extracts of "Feuillets d'Hypnos" (1945), and eventually the entire text of the "journal" in Camus' series, "L'espoir" (1946), and in his own collection from the war years, Fureur et Mystère (also 1946), his reputation grew enormously. He would always claim that this period and the poetry he wrote during it fundamentally changed both his life and his writing. The prose poetry of "Feuillets d'Hypnos," reflecting upon the years 1943–44 is, in many ways, a central document in this transformation.

Though Char never wrote much about interlingual translation as such, except in letters to those translating him during his lifetime, he did describe poets as great "trans-porteurs," who transport meaning through metaphor and imagery, "mais qui doivent d'abord déguster jusqu'au bout les cataclysmes du réel" (but who first must savor to the fullest the cataclysms of reality).[4] A reading of Char's

"Feuillets" confirms this intense engagement with lived experience. If some poets use language to signal their attempt to leave the material world for something more transcendental, Char instead strives to recall it, grappling with the memory of the maquis in a language at least as keenly trained on the historical events it transcribes as on its multiple semantic potential as poetry. For this reason, perhaps, the word "translation" seems particularly apt. In Char's poetic response to the traumatic events of the maquis, we see the poet's often mournful gesture toward an original impossible to transcribe, and at the same time, his paradoxical insistence that this lost original must live on, if differently, in its new linguistic site.[5] A deep meditation on historical experience, Char's text casts new light on the mourning of the original that haunts the writing of history as it does, in a different but related way, the writing of translation. But it also sets into relief the "new beginning" that language, and especially poetic language, permits.

MEMORY, MOURNING, TRANSLATION

Written in the bleakest years of the war (1943–44), Char's wartime journal, "Feuillets d'Hypnos," began as a notebook kept on the maquis. He describes its material history in a letter to Gilbert Lély, "J'ai été heureux pour retrouver récemment ce journal que je tenais à Céreste, enfoui à mon départ pour Alger dans un trou de mur. C'est ce journal que je vais publier (une sorte de Marc-Aurèle!)" (I was pleased recently to recover this journal that I used to keep in Céreste, buried in a hole of a wall when I left for Algiers. It's this journal that I am going to publish [a sort of Marcus Aurelius!]).[6] Supplementing this between 1945 and 1946 with a number of other poems similarly reflecting upon the experience of the war, Char underscores its material connection with the historical events it records—and his reaction to them—in his introduction to the published collection:

> Ces notes n'empruntent rien à l'amour de soi, à la nouvelle, à la maxime ou au roman. Un feu d'herbes sèches eût tout aussi bien été leur éditeur. La vue du sang supplicié en a fait une fois perdre le fil, a réduit à néant leur importance. Elles furent écrites dans la tension, la colère, la peur, l'émulation, le dégoût, la ruse, le recueillement furtif, l'illusion de l'avenir, l'amitié, l'amour. C'est dire combien elles sont affectées par l'événement.

> [These notes owe nothing to love of self, to chronicle, to the maxim or the novel. A fire of dry grass might just as well have been their publisher. The sight of tortured blood once made me lose their thread, reduced their importance to nothing. They were written in tension, anger, fear, emulation, disgust, guile, furtive contemplation, the illusion of a future, friendship, love. Which is to say how much they are affected by event . . .][7]

Situated between the reality of the empirical experience and its recollection in the prose poems to follow, this preface prepares the reader well for the text as a whole. The contingent event—the grass fire that could have served as editor, the spilled blood that caused him to lose the thread—sparks the reactions of the author who writes. These individual texts, short poems in themselves, in no way claim to be transparent windows to the "original" acts taken or suffered. They are a dense poetic "living on" of events inscribed in memory and suffused with human affect. Like other histories of traumatic events, they emerge from a past no longer directly accessible, and at the same time reach toward a future where a cultural survival is sought.

As poetic memories, Char's poems preserve a significant number of referential details. Of the 237 entries that together make up the "Feuillets d'Hypnos," a number reflect upon particular historical incidents or persons. Some of the most notable include Char's careful list of orders for his lieutenant, Leon Zingermann (#87); Roger Bernard's execution by the Nazi SS (#138); the torture and death of a farmer near Vacheres (#99); the aerial dropping of munitions (#97) and men (#148); the forest fire that once ensues (#53); the SS's search for Char himself in the village of Céreste (#128) and his eight-meter fall and injury while on a nocturnal mission near German guards (#149); the mourning for Francis Curel's capture and deportation (#11); the remembered murder of friends and fellow resistants such as Emile Cavagni, Roger Chaudon, Gustave Lefèvre (#157, #231, #94).

Such references testify repeatedly to the history of the French Resistance, specifying the uniqueness of the moments witnessed and the role that poet and reader have in their afterlife. They thereby accentuate the complexity entailed both in remembering lived experience and in "translating" it into a poetic language that is able to bear witness. Char's are "haunted" texts, haunted by event, by the poet's own affect, and by other texts in this collection. Several announce themselves as acts of mourning and clearly reveal the subjectivity, complexity, and strange temporality that characterize them. Take, for example, the remembered execution of Roger Bernard (#138):

> Horrible journée! J'ai assisté, distant de quelques mètres, à l'exécution de B. Je n'avais qu'à presser la détente du fusil-mitrailleur et il pouvait être sauvé! Nous étions sur les hauteurs dominant Céreste, des armes à faire craquer les buissons et au moins égaux en nombre aux SS. Eux ignoraient que nous étions là. Aux yeux qui imploraient partout autour de moi le signal d'ouvrir le feu, j'ai répondu non de la tête . . . Le soleil de juin glissait un froid polaire dans mes os.
>
> Il est tombé comme s'il ne distinguait pas ses bourreaux et si léger, il m'a semblé, que le moindre souffle de vent eût dû le soulever de terre.
>
> Je n'ai pas donné le signal parce que ce village devait être épargné à tout prix. Qu'est-ce qu'un village? Un village pareil à un autre? Peut-être l'a-t-il su, lui, à cet ultime instant?

> [Horrible Day! I was witness, some hundred meters away, to the execution of B. I had only to press the trigger of my Bren gun and he could have been saved! We were on the heights overlooking Céreste, arms enough to make the bushes creak and at least equal in number to the SS. They unaware we were there. To the eyes around me everywhere begging for the signal to open fire I answered no with my head . . . The June sun slipped a polar chill into my bones.

He fell as if he didn't make out his executioners and so light, it seems to me, that the least breath of wind could have lifted him from earth.

I didn't give the signal because this village had to be spared at *any price*. What is a village? A village like any other? Did he perhaps know at that ultimate instant?]

Playing on the themes of what can be "seen" and what lies beyond any individual's physical sight or memory of it, the three short paragraphs describe the final moments of the historical Roger Bernard, Char's young friend, partisan and poet, as witnessed by the resistants. Imagery of the natural world, at odds with itself in the antithesis "soleil de juin—froid polaire," depicts a moment of contradiction, desperately out of joint, while references to B's lightness and the "souffle de vent" that almost lifts him point to the mystery and to the "almost resurrection" implicit in the terrible events described. The final lines provide the "explanation" of the poet-witness: the execution, otherwise preventable, could not be interrupted, since the village had to be saved. But they end with questions to the reader: What is the value of the village, this or any other, compared with a single life? And had Bernard somehow understood his sacrifice at the "ultime instant"? The questions must remain unanswered, poised in the anguish of the speaker's responsibility, the mysterious complexity of memory, and the appeal to the reader to continue the meditation. Such questions, related with the profound lightness attributed to B's fall, and scattered in the leaves of Char's text, transform the experience of the maquis into an intense dialogue engaging both poet and reader.

As I suggest above and as this brief prose poem emphasizes, the "Feuillets" provide a record that, while witnessing a traumatic historical event, draws the reader, like a cinematic lens, into the realm of individual memory. Here we find exclamations and a first-person perspective, dramatized in passion, recollection, and rumination. The effect is heightened by an omission of the simple past, the tense reserved for history, in favor of the passé composé and imperfect, that tie each remembrance to the linguistic present. Moving in the end to address the reader in explanation and questions, a dialogue between poet and reader holds to the zone of *discours* rather than *récit*. Char thus recalls a lived moment and engages the reader as directly as possible in this effort to "pass on" a traumatic experience.

Such deliberately subjective and dialogical diction is hardly limited to #138, cited above. It accumulates throughout the collection where events, though pointing to the referential world of the past, are rendered in discours and often, in phrases without verbs at all, for which the reader must provide the temporal framework.[8]

Each moment is itself a zone of intense complexity, and necessary interpretation. The subjective lens of Char's prose poems discloses some of this complexity, indeed the mystery and plurality, of poetic memory. We find, for instance, that references to Bernard's passing recur elsewhere in Char's oeuvre, suggesting the need to repeat, in therapeutic fashion, the traumatic memory of a death and a decision. But even the single text quoted above emphasizes the multiple perspectives from which any given event is seen and remembered: the SS sees Bernard but not the partisans surrounding them; the partisans have their sights on Bernard, but also on the SS and their leader, the poet as witness; Bernard appears not to see the SS ("comme s'il ne distinguait ses bourreaux") but perhaps, the last line suggests, focuses on an interior vision; the witnessing poet physically sees not only the SS, his men, and Bernard, but also mentally "sees" the nearby village, and speculates upon Bernard's inner vision; he also "sees" in the important section two, that Bernard is almost transported, or that he ought to have been, transported; in the final questions, the reader is asked to view these various layers. In this hallucinating play of perspectives, one "sees" a tragic historical event but, equally important, one "sees" the difficulty of seeing, and the limits of interpreting.

For what is the reader given to observe? The event narrated is as absent as present. Inscribed as a painful metonymy in which the cause is suppressed in favor of the result, the one thing the poet does *not* describe, and that the reader cannot see, is the execution itself, which remains hidden in the blank of the page separating the first paragraph from the second. The "original" from which the poet works is a memory refracted through several perspectives. Recalled explicitly and in some detail, the event emerges as both multiple and opaque, incomplete even when so brilliantly etched. Nor is Bernard monumentalized through the fullness of his name. Though his complete name is provided in other texts, here we find only the initial "B.," the mere synecdoche of the referential anchor normally afforded by the proper name.

As is evident from this one example, the poet's words do not pretend to lift an integral and cognizable past into language. Rather, they disseminate an awareness of the human complexity of events witnessed, while tracing the keenness of loss and intensity of an instant's decision. As the body of Bernard was almost, but never quite, transported by a "breath" of wind, the human breath of the poet's own words do not in fact transport the past "original" into poetic history. Any such complete transposition is impossible—and ultimately unsought. His words do figure a "translation," but a poetic and therefore not fully "relevant" one, in the usual sense of the word.[9] A subjective mourning, a memory transcribed in the present, it lives on in the different, more exemplary "materiality" of poetry where it survives "otherwise," able to affect the future. A later poem in the collection (#228), referring to this and the deaths of many others, describes this afterlife in words that echo the passage on Roger Bernard: "La grandeur réside dans le départ qui oblige. Les êtres exemplaires sont de vapeur et de vent" (Greatness resides in the departure that is binding. Exemplary beings are of vapor and wind).

In these ways, Char's "Feuillets d'Hypnos" creates a haunting paradigm of an important aspect of translation, even interlingual translation. Impossible yet necessary, translation inevitably entails a loss as well as a gain. Loss is nowhere more evident than in translation's nostalgia for an original it can never fully render, nostalgia, that is, for a singular textual body it can never appropriate or recreate. A translation can at best inscribe a subsequent understanding, detailed in a new language that can never repeat the original but, at the most, touch it from the point of a tangent, allowing it to live into the future along a new and different line.[10]

Though this may well be the condition of all translation, or even, if we follow a certain line of reasoning, of all linguistic meaning, Char's "translation" of traumatic experience into the medium of language lays bare this more general yearning and loss. Here, the original toward which language yearns is not only inaccessible because it is in another language (assuming that memory is another language); here the original is inaccessible because it refers to an irretrievable past, even as memory. Like the death it attempts to describe, the past this text "translates" lies beyond any tactile or visible certainties. A text translating the lived experience of the past can only be produced out of new and different cloth, woven in the airy uncertainties of memory, affect and language. Char's "Feuillets d'Hypnos" shows the difficulty of this—the suffering, the mourning, and the complexity that are part of any such poetic trans-port, any such use of language. But as I will attempt to outline briefly, it also shows its necessity and the linguistic "gain" that brings with it a difficult but clearly affirmative hope.

It is a loss and a gain that is best gauged by looking not only to individual poems, but also to the collection as a whole. For here it becomes evident that Char writes both of individual loss and also of a more general loss, or disillusionment. Opening the "Feuillets d'Hypnos," one immediately sees each entry standing alone, a poetic particular, juxtaposed rather than logically connected to other poetic descriptions, exhortations, self-reflections. Though all are numbered, they follow no usual chronological or logical order. In this notebook, deeply inscribed by event but seemingly untouched by traditional beliefs in Providence, far from the Hegelian dialectic, and beyond—or before—usual realistic, linear "plotlines" or historical mythologies, we see a world of constant change and unpredictable reversals. It is a text with close ties to Nietzsche and Heraclitus, riven with a tragic pessimism that comes not only from the shock of horrific events but also from the loss of more general historical certainties. Nowhere in the collection does Char envision specific positive outcomes, or even a telos, a point of closure that would offer an end and therefore meaning to the individual entries. Quite the contrary. He asks at one point, "La vie commencerait par une explosion et finirait par un concordat? C'est absurde" (Life should begin with an explosion and end with a concordat? It's absurd.) (140). Even more specific to his own time and frighteningly prescient of our own is entry #7:

Cette guerre se prolongera au delà des armistices.platoniques. L'implantation des concepts politiques se poursuivra contradictoirement, dans les convulsions et sous le couvert d'une hypocrisie sûre de ses droits. Ne souriez pas. Écartez le scepticisme et la résignation et préparez votre âme mortelle en vue d'affronter intra-muros des démons glacés analogues aux génies microbiens.

[This war will prolong itself beyond platonic armistices. The implanting of political concepts will be conflictingly pursued in convulsions and under cover of an hypocrisy certain of its rights. Don't smile. Thrust aside skepticism and resignation and prepare your mortal soul for the intramural confrontation with icy demons analogous to mircrobial spirits.]

There is no foreseeable end to the agon Char describes, or even an easily vanquished enemy. The journal, though heroic in some of the acts it relays and in its persistence in relaying them, engages not at all in "patriotic" rhetoric. There is surprisingly little discussion here of Germans or French militia as enemy. Even the Resistance appears through a veil of irony and transience. In this poetic rendition of wartime, a time described without the usual mystifications or nationalisms, we note Char's refusal of simple dichotomies of good and evil, heroes and enemies, or of a dialectics of trauma and revenge, to embrace instead what Nietzsche might call the "tragic," a keen awareness of the fearful contingency, changefulness, and inevitable conflict at the heart of existence. This is certainly an important aspect of this journal, and one of its most honest and courageous themes. If it is essential to take arms against oppression and cruelty, an oppression and cruelty Char knew at close range, such war, even such oppression, is anything but a simple matter. It does not have a single face or a predictable end. Endemic to his time, perhaps to all time, it is ultimately fought against internal, intransigent, demons.

In this temporal context without anchors in historical patterns from the past or in clear expectations for the future, life is lived—and here portrayed—as so many individual, unpredictable, often harrowing moments. As in the entry on Bernard, which ends so provocatively with the word "instant," Char emphasizes the war's way of whittling experience down to the second: "On donnait jadis un nom aux diverses tranches de la durée: ceci était un jour, cela un mois, cette église vide, une année. Nous voici abordant la seconde où la mort est la plus violente et la vie la mieux définie" (They used to give names to the different portions of duration: this was a day, that a month, this empty church a year. Here we are approaching the second when death is most violent and life best defined.) (#90). It is in the individual, seemingly disconnected moment, that life and death precariously vie. Like so many clicks of the camera, each marking one event, one insight, one action, one instruction, Char's entries attempt to give us time without myth, without the framing narrative, without the explanatory logic, without the distilling and distancing lens of history's usual "realist" perspective. Etched instead in the "real time" of poetic enunciation, the "Feuillets" attempt to evoke the unadorned particularity that, ascribed to history since Aristotle, is ultimately its most haunting and most eagerly disguised quality.

Yet as Hannah Arendt eloquently notes in her preface to *Between Past and Future*, the time Char describes at this historical juncture was not only a site of radical disillusionment or courageous acceptance of the tragic. It was also a site of active conflict and of thoughtful action.[11] In this space/time where past and future meet, a site no longer prepared by philosophical or political thought as also no longer channeled by a continuity of tradition, or its most cherished historical myths, human action could—and did—choose to mark out new and unexpected meanings. In a time "out of joint," yet in the only time there was, the physical and intellectual struggle of the resistance went on, outside the official government, outside its official history, in day-to-day—indeed in moment to moment—acts, always unpredictable, requiring discriminating decisions that held life and death in the balance.

In this context, Char claims that poetry itself has an important role to play: "la part imaginaire qui, elle aussi, est susceptible d'action" (the imaginary part which, also, is susceptible of action.) (#18). And it is in this poetic "action" that the "gain" to be found in Char's translation of history is most clearly seen. If Char's "Feuillets" provides a powerful "living on" of traumatic memory (*fortleben*) in some of the ways outlined above, it also acts in the "now" of language to offer a life after death, (*überleben*), a moment of renewal, a new beginning.

AN "AFTER LIFE" IN HISTORY

Char clearly saw poetry not only as memorial or mimetic, but also as an act of signification, one that, by its very nature, gives birth to the future and to hope. Like the physical resistance, his poetry offers no answer, no specific truth, certainly no new government or political system. Yet it does act to foster change, to enter into lived history and offer an inaugural moment, a new beginning. "Être du bond," writes Char, "N'être pas du festin, son épilogue" (To be of the leap. Not to be of the feast, its epilogue, (#197). Erupting within the ruins of mortality, the death and guilt so poignantly described in the recollection of Bernard, such poetic action allows for a continual nascency. Action for Char (as for Arendt), is defined precisely by its opening to the future, by its indeterminability, the uncharted effects it will have in times to come.[12] This relation to the future, not as telos but as site of the unknown, as a zone of rebirth or renewal, is evident throughout Char's poetic translation of the past. Such awareness of incompleteness, existing not only because the past can never be recovered, but also because the future is itself filled with mystery, with the living possibility for new action and interpretation, makes Char's text "translatable," in Benjamin's sense of the term. Through its acts of signification, it becomes an "original" that calls to the future for its own continuity and its interpretive afterlife.

Char's call to the future pervades the collection in many ways. It does so, for instance, through its profound and ever-vigilant sense not only of risk but also of beauty: "Dans nos ténèbres, il n'y a pas une place pour la Beauté. Toute la place est pour la Beauté" (In the depths of our darkness there is no one place for Beauty. The whole place is for Beauty.) (#237). It also appears in a surprising reapprehension of the specific images of the everyday that demand gratitude—and interpretation: "Le silence du matin. L'appréhension des couleurs. La *chance* de l'épervier" (The morning silence. The apprehension of colors. The *chance* of the sparrowhawk.) (#152) or, "Toute la masse d'arôme de ces fleurs pour rendre

sereine la nuit qui tombe sur nos larmes" (All the massed fragrance of these flowers to pacify the night that falls upon our tears) (#109), or "Vous tendez une
allumette à votre lampe et ce qui s'allume n'éclaire pas. C'est loin, très loin
de vous, que le cercle illumine" (You hold a match to your lamp and what is
lit provides no light. It is far, far away from you, that the circle illuminates)
(#120).

But often Char's orientation toward semantic transformations and to the interpretive work of his readers is yet more evident. It can emerge, for instance,
through the energetic and surprising aphorism. An admirer of Heraclitus, he describes his aphoristic powers this way: "Héraclite possède ce souverain pouvoir
ascensionnel qui frappe d'ouverture et doue de mouvement le langage . . ." (Heraclitus possesses this sovereign ascensional power that strikes in opening and endows language with movement.)[13] In Char's own use of this short, pithy form,
examples of which are frequent in the "Feuillets" (as the entries cited above
begin to illustrate), ordinary grammar gives way to disjunctive splicings of verbs
and nouns, while metaphor bears the burden of poetic trans-portation. Nour-
ished by the reading of Heraclitus, Rimbaud, and Baudelaire, Char's metaphoric
images are neither ornamental nor mimetic. They are themselves surprising journeys of emotion and thought—beyond referential anchors into a zone of new
possibility. Essential to their quality is a force of contradiction and complexity
that resists any sense of knowledge possessed. Often the aphorism is born of the
verb, the linguistic matrix of action and transformation. Consider, for instance,
"Conduire le réel jusqu'à l'action comme une fleur glissée à la bouche acide des
petits enfants. Connaissance ineffable du diamant désespéré (la vie)" (Bring the
real to the point of action like a flower slipped into the acid mouth of little children. Ineffable knowledge of the desperate diamond [life]) (#3). Fusing a general
directive with the particular and surprising instance, this is a poem driven by the
energy of transformation, or translation: reality into action, flowers into the
acidic mouth of children. It addresses its readers through an infinitive that takes
an imperative tone, and looks to them to lead its juxtaposed images to some, albeit incomplete, resolution.

Through their linguistic action, such aphorisms speak to the future inhabiting
interpretation as it inhabits all human deeds, whose consequences can never be
determined at the moment they occur. As Char states in #187, "L'action qui a un
sens pour les vivants n'a de valeur que pour les morts, d'achèvement que dans les
consciences qui en héritent et la questionnent" (The action that has a sense for
the living has value only for the dead, conclusion only in the consciences that
inherit and question it). Actions themselves, be they physical or linguistic, give
birth to future dialogues that only in time may hope to create their meanings.

But if Char's subtle meditations and energetic aphorisms engage the reader's
interpretive efforts, they can also challenge and defy, resisting imprisoning myths
that came before.[14] They can transform religious imagery, humanizing it. For instance, Char's use of the term "Ange" translates divine expectations to the
earthly ("Ange, ce qui, à l'intérieure de l'homme, tient à l'écart du compromis
réligieux . . . Connaît le sang, ignore le céleste. Ange: la bougie qui se penche au

nord du Coeur," (Angel, what, within man, holds aloof from religious compromise. . . . Knows the blood, is ignorant of the celestial. Angel: the candle that inclines to the heart's north.) (#16). The theological term *Verbe* becomes Char's word for the language of poetry. One of the most notable mythic reversals concerns Hypnos, the almost forgotten Greek god of sleep, now firey and transformative, who leaves his signature on the collection as a whole and whose name becomes synonymous with poetry and hope: "Résistance n'est qu'espérance. Telle la lune d'Hypnos, pleine cette nuit de tous ses quartiers, demain vision sur le passage des poèmes" (Resistance is only hope. Like the moon of Hypnos full tonight in all its quarters, tomorrow vision upon the passage of poems) (#168).

In ways such as this, the "Feuillets" perform their own intervention in the world, acting to reject prescribed mythic patterns (all the more palpable in the era of Nazi mythology), as well as language's accustomed syntax and lexicon. This strategy alone allows for a loosening of everyday conventions, an opening for the new to appear—for interpretation, for hope, and even for freedom. "A tous les repas pris en commun, nous invitons la liberté à s'asseoir. La place demeure vide mais le couvert reste mis," (At all the meals taken in common, we invite freedom to have a seat. Its place remains empty, but it stays set.) (#131) writes Char. It is poetry's action that helps prepare this place.

But at one point in the collection, the poetic "gain" of Char's translation of the historical becomes especially explicit. Striking in its reference both to the historical past and to the hope offered by linguistic action is Char's well-known meditation on "Le Prisonnier," by Georges de la Tour (#178):

> La reproduction en couleurs du "Prisonnier" de Georges de la Tour, que j'ai piquée sur le mur de chaux de la pièce où je travaille, semble, avec le temps, réfléchir son sens dans notre condition. Elle serre le coeur mais combien désaltère! Depuis deux ans, pas un réfractaire qui n'ait, passant la porte, brulé ses yeux aux preuves de cette chandelle. La femme explique, l'emmuré écoute. Les mots qui tombent de cette terrestre silhouette d'ange rouge sont des mots essentiels, des mots qui portent immédiatement secours. Au fond du cachot, les minutes de suif de la clarté tirent et diluent les traits de l'homme assis. Sa maigreur d'ortie sèche, je ne vois pas un souvenir pour la faire frissonner. L'écuelle est une ruine. Mais la robe gonflée emplit soudain tout le cachot. *Le Verbe de la femme donne naissance a l'inespéré mieux que n'importe quelle aurore.* Reconnaissance à Georges de la Tour qui maitrisa les ténèbres hitlériennes avec un dialogue d'êtres humains. (emphasis mine)

> [The color reproduction of the "Prisoner" by Georges de la Tour, which I've stuck on the whitewashed wall of the room in which I work, seems, with time, to reflect its sense upon our condition. It wrings the heart but how it quenches thirst! For two years, not one partisan who, coming through the door, hasn't burnt his eyes at the proofs of this candle. The woman explains, the immured listens. The words that fall from this earthbound silhouette of a red angel are essential words, words that immediately bring help. In the dark of the dungeon, the tallow minutes of clarity draw out and dilute the features of the seated man. Scrawny as a dry nettle there isn't a memory comes to my mind to make him shiver. The bowl is a ruin. But the swollen robe suddenly fills the

whole dungeon. *The Word of the woman gives birth to the unhoped-for better than any dawn whatever.*

Gratefulness to Georges de la Tour who subdued the Hitlerian darkness with a dialogue of human beings.]

Claiming a new beginning ("une naissance") through the act of language, this text returns us to issues of translation and history in a number of ways. Most clearly, the poem provides a miniature, or *mise en abyme* of the historical situation of the resistance, and one with which Char clearly identified.[15] At the same time, it is a fragment that resumes a number of images scattered throughout the "Feuillets." Here is the "Ange," presented as human, dressed in red (Ange, ce qui ... connaît le sang, ignore le céleste," #16); here is the "chandelle," like the "lampe," associated by Char with the resistance itself, the light provided by human action, not nature, and able to extend its rays beyond the immediate "ténèbres" (#5, #174).

On another level, the fragment might well be called an intermedial translation—an ecphrasis that "translates" the visual arts into poetry. Not surprisingly, Char's words translate in such a way as to reveal the specific interaction of art object with the referential and the real. The painting, described in some detail, is a reproduction, taken from its "original" historical context, and now placed within his workroom where, the poet explains, it reflects its "sense upon our condition." The painting is seen in direct relation with the specific historical situation. Indeed, not unlike the later Benjamin in his insistence on the "dialectical image," the poet here acts to seize an image from the past and reveal its resonance for "now."[16] And in Char's poem, as in Benjamin's momentary junctures of past and present, the "now" is a present in which the "unhoped for" future is able to appear.

Written in the first person, with exclamations that anchor it in the emotional response of the writer's memory, this entry depicts a painting that is, according to Char, ultimately about language itself, the words a terrestrial "Angel" speaks to a prisoner. Her presence in the cell, her candle, but above all her words (the poetic "Verbe"), give birth to the "unhoped-for" and do so better, Char claims, than any (merely natural) dawn. The final line, with its antithetical echoes "ténèbres hitlériennes" and "êtres humains," and its definitive and otherwise rare use of the passé simple, praises the painter, Georges de la Tour, for having mastered the "hitlerian shadows" with the liberating act of dialogue.

In examples such as this, we begin to see that Char's texts are haunted by the past and by the future as well. Whether the afterlife of "Les Feuillets" is generated through the subtle use of imagery, the "commotion" of unresolved aphorisms, the defiant redefinitions of myth, the allegorical readings of Georges de la Tour, or the poignant questions that end #138 on Roger Bernard, it creates an interpretive future that is as much a part of Char's text as the historical memory it perpetuates.

In one of his rare statements about translation, Char writes, "Traduction, si j'ose dire, comme re-création du souffle et des mots; les mots sont une forme d'action, la perpétuité concrétisée de cette Action fugitive" (Translation, if I

may say so, is like the re-creation of breath and of words: words are a form of action, the concretized eternity of this transitory Action).[17] The historical translator's words set into motion an attempt to re-create the "souffle" of what is past,
but also a present and ongoing action whose consequences usher in a future as
yet unknown. Through the dialogue it initiates, this action will persist as long as
readers read. It will allow a "living on" of the remembered action of the past
(Benjamin's *fortleben*) but also an active participation in its "life after death"
(*überleben*). With it comes an opening to reflection upon times "out of joint,"
both those of the past and our own, but also upon freedom and hope. It is precisely this dual reach, toward a future as well as a past, that animates Char's
translation of history in "Feuillets d'Hypnos," and has allowed it to live on over
the years, in France and abroad.

The Vigil

Benjamin tells us that the "the task of the translator consists in finding that intended effect [*Intention*] upon the language into which he is translating which
produces in it the echo of the original."[18] The translation ought not, that is, aim
for a literal rendition of meaning, the mere "what" of the text, but rather for its
distinctive "how," which he calls its mode of intention.[19] If this can be achieved,
the translation, calling toward the language of the original, will create an echo
effect in its own that evokes the original text, allows us to "hear" it again,
through the words of its translator. As Benjamin reminds us at various points in
his essay, such translation is a temporal as well as a geo-linguistic or spatial affair.
The translator elicits the echo not only of a *different* but also of a *previous* language in his or her own: "For translation comes later than the original, and since
the important works of world literature never find their chosen translators at the
time of their origins, their translation marks their stage of continued life. . . . The
life of the original attains in them [the translations] to its ever-renewed latest
and most abundant flowering."[20]

In the sixty years since Char wrote the "Feuillets d'Hypnos," it has been translated many times and into many languages. Several have, I believe, contributed
to what Benjamin would call its historical "flowering." The best–known Anglo-
American translation appears in the 1956 collection *Hypnos Waking: Poems and
Prose by René Char*, selected and translated by Jackson Matthews with the collaboration of William Carlos Williams, Richard Wilbur, William Jay Smith, Barbara Howes, W. S. Merwin, and James Wright.[21] Another version, to which
Char contributed suggestions, is the 1976 *Leaves of Hypnos* by Cid Corman used
in the translations above.[22] But to explore further the afterlife of Char's journal, I
will turn briefly to a brilliant text by Adrienne Rich, another, more recent, "resistance poet." Her poem, entitled "Char," published in the 1999 collection *Midnight Salvage*,[23] interprets portions of "Feuillets d'Hypnos" through the lens of her
own textual memory: "Hermetic guide to resistance I've found you and lost you
several times in my life." Part translation, part poetic interpretation, and part

overt dialogue, it evokes in its different language and from its own historical perspective a number of themes already discussed. It reminds us, for instance, of interlingual translation's investment in historical memory—the mourning, the nostalgia for the body of the "original" text. But it also provides an intriguing example of the ongoing "afterlife" of the original. Like Char's writing of lived history, Rich's poem allows the past to "live on," but also to acquire an active "life after death" as it speaks to its Anglo-American audience.

In its relatively brief span, some fifty-eight lines divided into three numbered sections, Rich refers to a number of Char's fragments, eliciting and re-"activating" episodes. In part #1, she evokes Char's text primarily through poetic paraphrase or impersonation: "There is the bracken, there is the mulberry," she writes, taking on the poet's stance as witness to everyday sights and sounds on the maquis. Without attempting full translations, her pointed references, articulated through a series of deictics that highlight action in the here and now, begin to catch the echo of the original: "there is the moon ablaze in every quarter," "there is the table set at every meal/for freedom whose chair stays vacant."

Only in the last six lines of the opening section does translation, in the usual sense of the term, appear. It is a fragmentary translation—selected, shaped, and set into italics, like an artwork or collage—that deliberately transports shards of memory into a new linguistic site. Yet as Rich's footnote makes clear, these translations themselves entail a complex, historically rich, and clearly perspectival "living on" of the original: "I have drawn on both Jackson Matthews and Cid Corman's translations of Char's journal in integrating his words into my poem." Like Char's own memories, refracted through conflicting viewpoints, the poetic memory that translation permits is mediated here through a linguistic archive, emphasizing the "impossibility," as well as the continual renewal, implied by translation.

Which texts are translated in the few lines of Rich's poem? Though several appear, two dominate. One is the episode of Bernard's assassination. Shades of Char's #138 thread their way through the first two sections of the poem, sometimes in actual translation ("*A horrible day. . . . Perhaps he knew, at the final instant? / The village had to be spared at any price*"), sometimes in Rich's imitation ("All eyes on him in the woods crammed with maquisards ex- / Pecting him to signal to fire and save their comrade / Shook his head and watched Bernard's execution."). In this way, her description of Bernard's passing recalls its repetitive, fragmentary mode of survival in the "Feuillets." If anything, it is yet more ghostly now. Through history-laden English translations, themselves indirect citations of Char, Matthews, and Corman, the complex perspectives of traumatic memory persist, with their inability to repeat or recapture the past they nonetheless relate.

But Rich's text, like Char's original, calls to the future as well. It does so thematically, by foregrounding a complete translation of #7 of the Feuillets (the only entry translated in full), echoing in contemporary English Char's earlier disillusionment and dire prediction. Situated at the head of section two, creating a framework for references to Bernard, it asks today's reader to hear once again what was written between 1943 and 1944 and to judge its pertinence for now: "The war will prolong itself beyond any platonic armistice. The implanting of political concepts will go on amid upheavals and under cover of self-confident hypocrisy. Don't smile. Thrust aside both skepticism and resignation and prepare your soul to face an intramural confrontation with demons as cold-blooded as microbes."

The choice of text and its dramatic positioning underscore Rich's own role as fellow "poet-resistant," a role reinforced in section #3. Here the poet suddenly addresses Char directly, an "I" speaking to a "you," over the rift of time and death: "Insoluble riverrain conscience echo of the future / I keep vigil for you here by the reeds of Elkhorn Slough." Though connections of place frame the two figures, two internal phrases bind them yet more closely. The first is "echo of the future." If Char's poetry is, in its sentiments as well as in its linguistic action, a text that not only haunts the future but looks to it for interpretation, Rich's text acts to respond. Through her choice of incidents, her image-filled mode of writing, her "historicized" translation, and the pervasive fragmentariness of her sections #1 and #2, she calls Char's past into the poetic present. But in the overall unfolding of her poem, and especially in its progression from impersonation, to translation, and finally to dialogue in part #3, we see that her own text, not unlike Char's dialectical illumination of present and past in his description of "Le Prisonnier," has cited/translated Char's poetry from the past at least in part in order to allow it to reflect its "sense into our condition." Speaking to our war-torn planet at the turn-of-the century through the poetic memories of World War II, it asks us to pause, to reflect. In the process, Char's work, this "echo of the future" acquires new vitality.

The second phrase, "I keep vigil for you," repeated at the beginning and end of Rich's last section, underscores the point. Does the term "vigil" look to the past, suggesting a rite in memory of the dead? Or does it look to the future, signifying the watch kept on the eve of a festival or holy day? Standing between past and future, like so many of Char's own words, it seems to insist, above all, on a purposeful wakefulness. As Rich herself tells us, "the poem is the vigil."[24] Its "now" entails that particular wakefulness that poetic language can provide: a resistance to expected myths or fixed meanings, a sharpened sense of semantic possibilities, and a call to readerly engagement.

In its strange, fragmented form, Rich's poem thus creates a complex "dialogue d'êtres humains." It speaks to the ghost of Char—and Char's ghostly figure Bernard, presenting the poet's historical action against injustice and his hope through tragic awareness. It speaks to the voices of previous translations. It also reminds us of something that Char—like Rich herself—believes: that poetry can, and perhaps must, be a part of action and a taste of life: "[Y]ou / held poetry at your lips a piece of wild thyme ripped / from a burning meadow a mimosa twig / from still unravaged country. You kept your senses about you like that and like this I keep vigil for you." Using metaphor to bridge poetry and historical reality, English and French, Rich's vigil offers its active wakefulness in remembrance, and as a contemprorary model of resistance and hope. In the process, her text extends its dialogue to twenty-first century Anglo-American readers. As she writes in a recent essay, "To read, to listen, to write, to feel, to fear, to draw courage from others, to take risks, to wrestle with contradictions, to engage with others—this is, indeed, the verb without tenses, the conversation without an end."[25]

Through these readings, I have attempted to draw out some of Benjamin's insights into the way translation contributes to the "more encompassing life of history." While focusing primarily on Char's poetry of World War II, I have also considered more briefly Rich's compelling "vigil," the 1999 poem entitled "Char." Both, I would argue, are linguistic acts that relay historical experience with all the power of that "temporal imagination" so evident in writers who matured through the violent upheavals of the twentieth century. In different ways, each creates a verbal echo of the past that resonates in the consciences—and words—of those who, as Char puts it, "inherit and question." Translating history, they remind us that translation is a temporal art, one that can contribute to the action of history itself, and to the ongoing "conversation" that gives it a meaning and a future.

NOTES

1. Jacques Derrida, "What is a 'Relevant' Translation?" *Critical Inquiry* 27(2), pp. 174–200. Also Jacques Derrida, "Des Tours de Babel," in *Difference in Translation*, ed. Joseph F. Graham (Ithaca: Cornell University Press, 1985), pp. 209–49.

2. See René Char, *Oeuvres complètes* (Paris: Gallimard, 1983), pp. LXVI–LXXII; Marie-Claude Char, ed., *René Char: Dans l'atelier du poète* (Paris: Gallimard, 1996), pp. 96–319; Mary Ann Caws, *René Char* (Boston: Twayne Publishers, 1977), pp. 13–34; also Laurent Greilsamer, *L'éclair au front: la vie de René Char* (Paris: Fayard, 2004) pp. 47–133.

3. See testimonies collected in *René Char: Cahier de l'Herne* (Paris: Edition de l'Herne, n.d.), pp. 14–15; 191–209. Also Greilsamer, *L'éclair*, pp. 137–224.

4. Paul Veyne, *René Char en ses poèmes* (Paris: Gallimard, 1990), p. 419. (Translation mine)

5. On the topic of trauma and the need for the "unspeakable" confession, see Shoshana Felman and Dori Laub, M.D., *Testimony: Crises of Witnessing in Literature, Psychoanalysis and History* (New York: Routledge, 1992); Cathy Caruth, ed., *Trauma: Explorations in Memory* (Baltimore: Johns Hopkins University Press, 1995); Caruth, *Unclaimed Experience: Trauma, Narration and History* (Baltimore: Johns Hopkins University Press, 1996).

6. Letter of René Char to Gilbert Lély, July 17, 1945. Cited by Jean-Claude Matthieu, *La poésie de René Char II* (Paris: José Corti, 1985), p. 211. Translation mine.

7. René Char, *Feuillets d'Hypnos* in *Oeuvres complètes* (Paris: Gallimard, 1983), p. 173. Further references to individual numbered texts will be included parenthetically. Unless otherwise noted, this and all subsequent translations of *Feuillets d'Hypnos* are drawn from René Char, *Leaves of Hypnos*, trans. Cid Corman (New York: Grossman, 1973).

8. See, for instance, #23, "Présent crénelé," ("Crenellated present"), or #101, "Imagination, mon enfant" ("Imagination, my child.")

9. Derrida, "What is," pp. 179–83. See, by contrast, pp. 199–200.

10. Walter Benjamin, "The Task of the Translator," p. 80.

11. Hannah Arendt, *Between Past and Future* (New York: Penguin Books, 1993), pp. 3–15.

12. Hannah Arendt, *The Human Condition* (Chicago: University of Chicago Press, 1958), pp. 175–247.

13. René Char, "Héraclite d'Éphèse," in *René Char: Dans l'Atelier du poète*, ed. Marie Claude Char (Paris: Gallimard, 1996), p. 547. Translation mine.

14. See, for instance, Char's fragment #153 with its words, "L'homme s'éloigne à regret de son labyrinthe. Les Mythes millénaires le pressent de ne pas partir" (Man withdraws reluctantly from his labyrinth. The millennial myths urge him not to go).

15. Bertrand Marchal, "Le tableau pulvérisé: le prisonnier, la lampe, l'ange. René Char et Georges de la Tour," *L'Information littéraire*, 41 année, no. 5, pp. 14–19. See the article for further details on motifs mentioned here. It cites, for instance, a letter from Char a G. Lely, du 10 avril, 1944: "La poésie représente 'la liberté' c'est vers elle que se tendent mes bras du prisonnier intense (J'ai devant les yeux la reproduction que tu connais de l'admirable peinture de Georges de la Tour où tout au fond d'un cachot lointain, inatteignable, une femme éclaire verticalement, d'une bougie dense comme la racine du jour, un homme assis plus nu et decharné que le limon des origines: me voici)." (Poetry represents "liberty"; it is toward her that my arms, those of a desolate prisoner, reach out [I have before my eyes the reproduction that you know of the wonderful painting by Georges de la Tour where, in the depths of a remote, unreachable dungeon, a standing woman gives light, from a candle thick as the root of day, to a seated man more naked and emaciated than the dust from which we came: this is me]).

16. Benjamin, "Theses on the Philosophy of History," in *Illuminations*, p. 263. Though Benjamin's article on translation preceded his "Theses on History" by more than fifteen years, it is clear that his ideas about translation and his later description of history are closely linked. In each case, the past becomes redeemed in the present and in a way that allows a "future" to appear. Past lived experience, or past language acquires new meaning in the "now" of the translator's language in a way that allows it to live actively in the present as it opens to the future of unformulated interpretation.

17. Letter of René Char to Vittorio Sereni, December 21, 1969, courtesy of Marie-Claude Char. Translation mine.

18. Benjamin, "The Task," p.76.

19. See essay by Samuel Weber, part I of this volume.

20. Benjamin, "The Task," pp. 71–72.

21. René Char, *Hypnos Waking: Poems and Prose by René Char*, selected and trans. by Jackson Matthews, with the collaboration of William Carlos Williams, Richard Wilbur, William Jay Smith, Barbara Howes, W. S. Merwin and James Wright (New York: Random House, 1956).

22. René Char, *Leaves*, trans. Cid Corman.

23. Adrienne Rich, *Midnight Salvage* (New York: Norton, 1999), pp. 16–18, and 71. For Rich's essays on poetry and politics, see her *What Is Found There* (New York & London: W. W. Norton, 2003).

24. Adrienne Rich, *Arts of the Possible* (New York: Norton, 2000), p. 132.

25. Rich, *What*, p. XVIII.

German Academic Exiles in Istanbul: Translation as the *Bildung* of the Other

AZADE SEYHAN

Alexander Rüstow, a classicist by training and a Socialist by calling who was the administrative director of the German Machine Manufacturing Association (*Verein deutscher Maschinenbauanstalten*) and *Dozent* at the Berlin Trade Institute (*Berliner Handelshochschule*) made a narrow escape to Istanbul, when his efforts to form a coalition government to keep Hitler out of power failed. Political activist, cultural sociologist, economist, and philosopher, Rüstow taught economics, economic geography, and philosophy at the University of Istanbul between 1933 and 1949. He was also active in the anti-Nazi movement of the German refugees in Istanbul and acted as liaison between the OSS (Office of Strategic Services, a U.S. wartime intelligence agency) and the German resistance. Rüstow's many areas of scholarly expertise constituted a prototype of the interdisciplinary field of cultural studies. However, his unwavering commitment to political action and the contiguity of his theory with practice make Raymond Williams's version of cultural studies look like ivory tower scholarship. Rüstow's doctoral dissertation, entitled, *Der Lügner: Theorie, Geschichte, und Auflösung* (The Liar: Theory, History, and Solution), was an analysis of the classical Greek paradox of the liar: "Epimedines the Cretan says, All Cretans always lie: True of False" (Dankwart A. Rustow xiv). The Nazi reign of terror that sent Rüstow into a long-term exile forced German culture to experience its most fateful paradoxes. Theodor Adorno and Max Horkheimer, Rüstow's fellow exiles during Hitler's reign, made the radical observation that the paradox of the Enlightenment led to the demise of its own humanistic ideals and resulted in the darkness of an age arguably unparalleled in its barbarism.

The premise of Adorno and Horkheimer's *Dialektik der Aufklärung* (Dialectic of Enlightenment) is that the Enlightenment, which was initially a critique of the mythical world, became in time fossilized, resistant to self-questioning, and ultimately resembled that which it sought to replace—the ancient myth. Adorno and Horkheimer see this transformation as the inevitability of a dialec-

I would like to thank Professor Jeffrey Peck, Director of the Canadian Center for German and European Studies for inviting me to Toronto to present an earlier version of this essay at the Special Session on German/European Cosmopolitanism at the Annual Meeting of the Canadian Association of Teachers of German on May 27, 2002. I would also like to thank Professor Karin Bauer of McGill University for her comments on the essay.

tic turn where instrumental reason, a pillar of enlightenment view, valorized method over experience, so that experience that did not coincide with method was deemed irrational. Dialectical thought functions as criticism and resists affirmations that falsify the present and gloss over injustices of history. Understanding this dialectic would lead to a correction of the authoritarian nature of Enlightenment rationality. But the inability to recognize the unfolding contradiction of the Enlightenment program has pushed the modern age into a dangerous state of blindness. The gloomy tenor of this analysis needs to be seen in the context of a time when a generation was handcuffed to a raging fascism in Europe, on the one hand, and to a growing consumerism in America, on the other. The fractured myths of the Enlightenment—liberal humanism, universalism, and cosmopolitanism—emerged in grotesque reconfigurations of persecution, racism, and ultranationalism. The philosophical optimism characteristic of the nation-state shattered into p/articles of disbelief, when the first half of the twentieth century began witnessing the victimization and deportation of millions of citizens by their own governments. In Horkheimer and Adorno's view, modernity transmogrified the ideals of the Enlightenment into a massive betrayal of the masses (Horkheimer 41).

It is perhaps no coincidence that the critique of the Enlightenment and its ideals of progress, freedom from authority, and normative humanism have most rigorously been exercised by thinkers, such as Horkheimer and Adorno, Hannah Arendt, and Walter Benjamin, whose lives and careers were compromised and interrupted by exile and extremity during the Nazi reign of terror. Their reflections on and redefinitions of modernity, morality, and agency are determined to a large extent by the specific condition of exile itself. Many other European writers and philosophers—among them Primo Levi, Albert Camus, Jorge Semprún—whose lives had been inscribed by extremities of persecution, loss, and dislocation, recast the inexpressible idiom of extreme trauma into a critical reflection on the historical and sociopolitical conditions for the production of a morally impoverished Zeitgeist. Deprived of livelihood, persecuted, and hunted, they wrote, in Emily Apter's poignant words, "criticism as a kind of message in a bottle dispatched to former interlocutors whose whereabouts were unknown, whose lives were uncertain" (88).

Ironically, the bankruptcy of the bravest ideals of the Enlightenment was at least partially countered by the new critical coordinates and paradigms exile offered. Recalling Friedrich Nietzsche's affirmation of homelessness, Adorno observes, "es gehört zur Moral, nicht bei sich selber zu Hause zu sein" (it is ethical for the self not to be at home) (Adorno 43). The ethos of exile expanded the concept of cosmopolitanism and sensitized it to the reality of historical, geographical, cultural, and linguistic difference. "Ethos means to locate oneself in another place," Iain Chambers states, "[i]n the endless interplay between ethos and topos we are forced to move beyond rigid positions and locations, beyond forms of judgement dependent upon the abstract identification of values that have already been decided and legislated for in advance" (42). In a certain sense, the best intentions of the Enlightenment paradigm survived in a self-reflexive, reinterpreted, or reimagined mode in pockets and margins of exile.

Many German intellectuals and artists who fled Hitler's Germany strove to preserve something of a moral and intellectual legacy that lay in ruins. And the countries that offered these Germans refuge strove, in the interest of a genuine understanding of cosmopolitanism, to negotiate between the conflicting demands of universal hospitality and limitations on rights of residence, another paradox of political immigration that Jacques Derrida has addressed in a speech delivered at the International Parliament of Writers in Strasbourg in 1996. In a highly charged political atmosphere in the wake of mass demonstrations—condemning the violent subjugation of immigrants and undocumented aliens to the Debret laws in a country proud of its reputation as a place of refuge from persecution—Derrida takes up the question of "Cities of Refuge," where exiles and migrants can find sanctuary. He reiterates the need previously expressed by the international parliament of writers to institute autonomous "free cities," independent, as much as possible, from the state and from one another yet forming an alliance "according to laws of solidarity yet to be invented." The task of the writers would be the invention of these laws whereby free cities would "reorient the politics of the state" and "transform the modalities of membership" that join a sovereign city as sanctuary to the state (Derrida, 2001 4). Here Derrida recalls how Hannah Arendt underlined the trauma of an unprecedented number of refugees between the two wars who, without recourse to repatriation and naturalization, could not be granted any status recognized by international state laws, not even that of "stateless people" (9). The task at hand, then, is to reclaim a new meaning and identity as a sovereign entity for the "city" that would free it from the authority of nation-states in matters of hospitality and refuge. The idea of such a city, however, cannot be disassociated from its political implementation. It is in the latter that the contradictory logic of cosmopolitanism resides. On the one hand, the rule of unconditional hospitality inherent in cosmopolitanism aspires to welcome all refugees; on the other hand, certain limitations have to be imposed on rights of residence that Derrida, citing Kant's formulation of cosmopolitanism, sees as dependent on treaties between nations (20–23).

A historically noteworthy, albeit incomplete, implementation of the idea of cities of refuge was realized between the two wars in the two major cities, Istanbul, the old capital, and Ankara, the new capital of a fledgling new nation, the Republic of Turkey. Of course, these cities were not independent of the nation-state; nevertheless, the state itself managed to circumvent the letter of the international law in order to grant refuge and work to many German and Austrian academics and artists who had to flee the Third Reich (it must, of course, also be noted that the city doors were not open to all refugees from Germany but mostly to those who came with intellectual capital). The hospitality extended to the German refugees was perhaps less an expression of a cosmopolitan consciousness than a response to the demands of the cultural politics of the nation. The formative years of the Turkish Republic, which was established in 1923 after the fall of the Ottoman dynasty in the First World War, coincided with the cataclysmic events of German history commencing with Hitler's rapid rise to political power in 1933. Many German and a few Austrian academics as well as some non-academics who, either because of their political inclinations or faith or both, or marriage to a non-Aryan spouse, could hope neither to make a living nor live in Germany, accepted the invitation to teach at the universities of Istanbul and Ankara.

Many critics and historians have underlined the irreparable blow dealt to Germany's intellectual legacy as a result of the massive migration of its scientists, politicians, thinkers, writers, and artists between the years 1933 and 1945. Even though several exiles returned to their homeland after the war and some were reinstated in their former positions, many branches of knowledge and disciplines lagged behind or were altogether cut off from new advances, methodologies, and theoretical perspectives with regard to their respective fields of inquiry. In *Exodus der Kultur*, a critical historical account of the emigration of German scholars, writers, and artists, Horst Möller notes that both the German intellectuals in exile and the culture they left behind endured multiple losses. Many major thinkers and writers, such as Stefan Zweig, Walter Benjamin, and Kurt Tucholsky took their own lives in exile; others could not establish themselves in a foreign culture nor continue with their scholarly or artistic work. The best products of the Weimar culture were lost or went to waste during the transport. And perhaps most deplorably, "Ein Ende fand die zu kulturellen Leistungen von Rang führende deutsch-jüdische Symbiose, die in ihrer Größe und Eigenart unwiderbringlich ist" [the German-Jewish symbiosis characterized by cultural achievements of a high caliber and irrevocable in terms of its greatness and singularity came to an end] (Möller 118). What survived of German intellectual culture during the fateful years between 1933 and 1945 was preserved and reproduced at various sites of exile and in the invisible spaces of inner emigration.

Although the emigration of German scholars and writers to other European countries and particularly to the United States has been studied fairly extensively, the long-term sojourn of many noted academics, artists, and politicians in Turkey has received scant critical attention. Among the roughly 130 German refugees and exiles in Turkey during the twelve years of what was supposed to be a Thousand Year Reich were Rüstow, Ernst Reuter (an urban planner who before his exile was the Socialist mayor of Magdeburg and after his return to Germany the mayor of Berlin), Fritz Neumark (a prominent economist who taught at the University of Istanbul and served twice as the *Rektor* of the University of Frankfurt upon his return to Germany), Leo Spitzer, Erich Auerbach (philologists and literary critics), Georg Rohde (a classical philologist and the architect, along with the Turkish Minister of Education Hasan Ali Yücel, of a major project of translation of world classics into Turkish), Rudolf Nissen (a professor of surgery at the University of Berlin who headed the surgery department of the Medical School of the University of Istanbul between 1933 and 1939, and trained numerous Turkish professors and physicians), Rudolf Belling (a sculptor fired from his position at the Berlin Academy of Fine Arts as one of the representatives of "entartete Kunst" [degenerate art] who then was appointed by Atatürk himself as chair of the sculpture department of the Istanbul Academy of Fine Arts), Paul Hindemith (a musician and composer who helped found the Ankara State Conservatory), and Carl Ebert (a theatrical producer and director who founded and directed the Ankara State Opera Company). The list of luminaries goes on. This chapter of German intellectual history and its role in instituting a prescient transcultural and translational field of knowledge still awaits critical remembrance.

In the foreword to his anecdotally rich memoir, *Zuflucht am Bosporus: Deutsche Gelehrte, Politiker und Künstler in der Emigration 1933–1953* (Escape to the Bosphorus: German Scholars, Politicians, and Artists in Exile 1933–1953), Fritz Neumark observes that although in the years following 1933 the number of German-speaking refugees in other countries, especially in the United States, far exceeded those in Turkey, in no other place was the relative significance of German refugees as great as it was in Turkey, and nowhere else did their work leave as permanent an impact (Neumark 8–9). Although I have a personal connection through my parents' lives and careers to the story of the German academic migration to Istanbul, my interest is guided more by the suggestive force of this intellectual transport, insofar as it raises questions of translation, linguistic dislocation, national culture formation and its ideological underpinnings, as well as the problematic of tending to a cultural heritage compromised by silencing and exile.

The attempted rehabilitation of a humanistic legacy shattered by the experience of Nazi persecution became, by a strange twist of history, linked to the formation of the young Turkish republic that aspired to translate what it saw as the exemplary representation of Western education into its own discourse of nation. Multiple modalities of translation underwrote the Republic's cultural reform movement. Arguably, the first and most significant translation project was the alphabet reform, known as *harf devrimi* (letter reform) that was engineered by a commission of linguists, presided over by Atatürk himself, that painstakingly transliterated the Arabic script of Ottoman Turkish into a slightly modified Roman alphabet. The result was a very phonetic alphabet that radically raised the rate of literacy. Along with this form of translation was the attempt to translate Ottoman Turkish, a hybrid language of the court mostly composed of Arabic and Persian words and constructions, into an "essential" or "real" Turkish by replacing the former with existing Turkish words or neologisms derived from extant stems. Both these projects were later criticized for their supposed hidden agenda of creating a cultural discontinuity whereby the post-reform generations could not read or understand most of what was written as late as in the early 1920s.

The third modality of translation was to go into effect as a result of the crossed historical destinies of the mass exodus from Nazi Germany and the outbreak of the Second World War in Europe on the one hand, and the growing pains of a new nation in Asia Minor, on the other. The necessity to capitalize on the body of knowledge at their disposal led the Turkish university administrators and academics to improvise protocols of translation and writing that effectively aided a cross-fertilization of linguistic and intellectual heritages. These innovative conventions of translation were implicated in the resituation of a Western intellectual legacy in a radically different cultural geography. And finally, a fourth blueprint of translation in the most literal sense was drafted by Hasan Ali Yücel, the Turkish Minister of Education (1938–1946), himself a prolific and multilingual comparatist critic and translator. With the help of Georg Rohde, Yücel implemented a large-scale project of the translation into modern Turkish of a record number of Western and Eastern classics.[1] I shall discuss shortly the interlinked destinies of these translational moments with their larger conceptual and sociocultural contexts. However, in order to understand the critical trajectory of the association between translation and the radical transformation of a national culture, a brief detour through history is necessary.

The *Machtergreifung* of 1933 and the subsequent dismissal of numerous Jewish professors from their posts coincided with the radical reform movements Kemal Atatürk, the founder of the modern Turkish republic and its first president, had undertaken in an ambitious attempt of modernization (which was typically synonymous with Westernization in many lands of the East coming into belated nationhood). In *Zuflucht am Bosporus*, Neumark states that the departure of German intellectuals began with the passing of the bill, "Gesetz zur Wiederherstellung des Berufsbeamtentums" (Re-establishment of the Civil Service Law), a few weeks after the Nazi rise to power in 1933. This law led to the speedy dismissal of scores of Jewish and politically suspect professors from their positions (Neumark 13). Realizing that the worst was yet to come, many of them started looking for ways of leaving Germany. Among those fired from their jobs was a Hungarian born Frankfurt pathologist, Dr. Philipp Schwartz, who fled with his family to Switzerland. In March 1933 Schwartz established in Zürich the *Notgemeinschaft Deutscher Wissenschaftler im Ausland* (Emergency Assistance Organization for German Scientists) to help Jewish and other persecuted German scholars secure employment in countries prepared to receive German refugees.

Meanwhile, Atatürk and his visionary ministers were engaged in an intensive modernization of Turkish higher education. This involved the transformation of the existing scholastic-Ottoman institution of the *Dar-ül Fünun* (Arabic for "house of knowledge") into the University of Istanbul fashioned after the nineteenth-century German university model. Schwartz got in touch with interested parties in Turkey and, along with Professor Rudolf Nissen and Professor Albert Malche of the University of Geneva, he visited Turkey in July 1933 and convinced the young Turkish Minister of Education Reşit Galip that the participation of distinguished refugee professors would contribute immensely to the success of the Turkish university reform. The visiting committee left a list of names with Galip who persuaded Atatürk to personally support the project. The Turkish Minister of Health Refik Saydam, another reform-minded cabinet member, was keenly interested in inviting professors of medicine to work in the university hospitals and other medical facilities. Since Germany would have been reluctant to allow a massive exodus of scholars, it was decided that the contracts would be signed in a neutral country, in this case, Switzerland. The refugee professors were given long-term (five-year renewable) contracts, salaries that were

four or five times the amount paid to Turkish faculty, and travel and moving ex-
penses. In turn, the contract stipulated that the professors learn Turkish as soon
as possible and write textbooks and scholarly books in their fields of expertise.

Among the many competent faculty members of the *Dar-ül Fünun* there were
also those who showed up at work only to collect their modest paychecks. Like
all the fossilized elements at institutions, they were expected to put up a resistance to the reform project and the foreign "intruders." In an effort to stymie any
resistance, the architects of the university reform prepared a law that ordered the
closure of the *Dar-ül Fünun* on July 31, 1933 and the establishment of the new
university on August 1, 1933. Most German professors settled into a rather privileged and comfortable existence on the hills of Bebek, a fashionable suburb
overlooking the strait of the Bosphorus. Several newcomers were allowed to
bring along their assistants and were also assigned Turkish assistant translators.
Tutors were hired for the private education of their children. Understandably,
the hospitality extended to the refugees was not necessarily universal. The German professors, scientists, and doctors were resented by many Turkish academics
who were either dismissed as part of the university reform or were appointed as
assistants to the newcomers, when in fact they had the credentials to be appointed
to the choice positions offered to the guest professors. Turkish professors of medicine as well as doctors in private practice did not want competition from world-
renowned experts who were running the clinics of the University of Istanbul.

Although the German professors' contracts stipulated that they learn Turkish
in three years, most professors could not fulfill the language requirement of the
contract and had to rely on translators. Their dependence on translation made
them vulnerable to vocal criticism from their disgruntled colleagues. However,
translation, as a means of negotiating different cultural discourses, proved to be
an effective instrument of education. The translators, most of them professors
and distinguished academics themselves who were trained at European universities, were able not only to transform complex ideas into an accessible idiom but
also to inspire the students to learn other languages, since the translator enjoyed
the powerful status of at once messenger, interpreter, and arbiter. When prominent Turkish scholar-teachers, such as Azra Erhat, Sabri Ülgener, or Mina Urgan
translated, they did not just relate content; they brought into the language the
richness of context and offered students linguistic and cultural resources that
provided a dynamic learning setting. This mode of translation promoted a kind
of social awakening and the circulation of the material value of knowledge that
coincided with the vision of the education reform. In fact, the attempts of many
German professors to lecture in Turkish met with the disapproval of most students, who preferred expert translation to a stutter that concealed expert knowledge. In *Turkey and the Holocaust*, noted historian Stanford Shaw quotes from a
memorandum sent in July 1936 from the United States Embassy in Istanbul (it
seems that the American officials were monitoring German activities in Turkey
very closely at this time) to the State Department:

> Turkish students do not generally understand German; but both those who do and
> those who do not often find that the subject matter of the lectures is made clearer

when the professor speaks in German and has his remarks translated into Turkish by an expert interpreter than when he speaks Turkish badly. One professor has said that when he tried to speak Turkish to the students they stamped and yelled until he changed back into German. (Shaw 12)

Thus, despite the clause in their contracts, most German professors continued to lecture in German, and the lectures were translated. Since there was a shortage of competent translators of German among the faculty and the students, the professors sometimes lectured in French or English in order to make use of a larger pool of translators. In a very concrete sense, then, the Turkish higher education reform was underwritten by a massive translation project. Translation became a trope, specifically, a metaphor for higher education at the new university. Alexander Rüstow, though he never became very proficient in Turkish during his long sojourn in Turkey, inspired generations of idealistic Turkish students with his interdisciplinary imagination and method through translations of his lectures, articles, and books on economics, economic geography, sociology, and cultural history. He viewed transmission of knowledge in translation as an effective discursive practice.[2] In fact, since Rüstow's interdisciplinary critical idiom was well suited to an analytic probing of history's crises and its disjunctive, revolutionary, and transitional moments, it resonated powerfully with his students and readers who were trying to understand and come to grips with the momentous political, social, and cultural transformations they were witness to. Through his political and intellectual engagement with the host country, Rüstow made excellent use of his exile years and wrote his painstakingly thorough, historically and critically astute three-volume magnum opus, *Ortsbestimmung der Gegenwart* (Positioning the Present), that was published shortly after the war in Switzerland. Neumark considers this book a work of "visionarär Kraft" (visionary power) and "eines der bedeutendesten Werke, die von deutschsprachigen Sozialwissenschaftlern in der Emigration geschrieben wurde" (one of the most important works written by German-speaking social scientists in exile) (76).

Several German professors, among them Fritz Arndt, Fritz Neumark, and Ernst Hirsch, became fluent in Turkish and complemented their many works in translation with those written in Turkish. In a similar vein, many Turkish professors were expected to publish their works in prestigious, peer-reviewed journals as a result of the promotion criteria established at the modernized university. What this meant was that they had to publish in European and Western professional journals, in "high status" scholarly languages, such as French, English, and German. These expectations of added fluency brought German and Turkish scholars together in the framework of translational and dialogic projects. In collaboration with their Turkish colleague/translators, many German professors wrote widely used textbooks as well as major scholarly books and, for the first time in the history of the Turkish university, founded scholarly journals. One of these, edited by Leo Spitzer, *Romanoloji Semineri Dergisi* (*Zeitschrift des romanischen Seminars*), unfortunately consisted of a single issue. Spitzer's successor Auerbach founded the *Garp Filolojileri Dergisi* (*Zeitschrift für europäische Philologie*) in 1947 shortly before his move to the United States. He published a highly regarded textbook, *Einführung in die romanische Philologie*, translated by his successor Süheyla Bayrav (*Roman filolojisine giriş*). This book appeared in French translation in 1949 in Frankfurt and was also translated into English and published posthumously as *Introduction to Romance Languages and Literature* in 1961.

Istanbuler Schriften (*İstanbul Yazıları*), a monograph series that began publication in 1947 was instrumental in keeping both the exiles and Turkish scholars in contact with their colleagues in the West. The majority of the contributions were in German, but a few appeared in Turkish. Auerbach's arguably most celebrated essay, "Figura" was published in his collection, *Neue Dantestudien*, which appeared in this series. Ernst Hirsch, the youngest scholar to be invited from abroad, acquired full proficiency in Turkish and became a Turkish citizen in 1943, when Nazis took away his citizenship. He taught legal philosophy and legal sociology in both Istanbul and Ankara and wrote and published his lectures (among them *Hukuk Felsefesi ve Hukuk Sosyolojisi Dersleri* [Lectures on the Philosophy and Sociology of Law, 1949]) in Turkish. The steady scholarly output of this cross-national, translational endeavor not only established an academically solid institutional structure for the Turkish university of the early republican period, but it also secured, in Walter Benjamin's notion of translation as *Überleben* and *Fortleben* of the original text, the preservation and propagation of an intellectual legacy diminished, even impoverished by bans on ideas and by book burnings and later misplaced or lost during transit. In this case, translation in its mission of transmission and dissemination remains, true to Benjamin's vision, a redemptive practice that ensures the survival of cultural remembrances.

However, there was some disagreement among German professors with regard to the value of translated education. Like Rüstow, Rudolf Nissen, who enjoyed a very successful professional sojourn in Istanbul, maintained that translation in the hands of its capable practitioners benefited the two languages in transaction, since both the lecturer and the translator had to strive for economy and precise idiom. However, there were others who felt that since Turkish lacked the vocabulary for certain disciplinary discourses, such as astronomy, concepts were all but lost in translation (Widmann 233). Ironically, one of the reasons for the inadequate vocabulary of Turkish as a language of *Wissenschaft* can be found in the radical language reform that in its attempt to replace the Arabic and Persian words, that had become an integral part of Turkish culture with "essential" or pure Turkish words, caused a chaos of terminology. In the process, many philosophical and scientific concepts that lent Turkish its rich, albeit morphologically and semantically hybrid, conceptual grounding were systematically dropped from the language. The fight for the Turkish language, between the moderates who argued that language could not be changed by decree and the purists who considered this stance a "counter-revolutionary mentality," still goes on.[3] This "translation" project was carried on by the members of the *Türk Dil Kurumu* (Turkish language association founded by Atatürk) who researched and collected words from surviving dialects, other Turkic languages, and pre-Ottoman texts. Some of these words were readily adopted by the population, others coexisted with their "archaic" counterparts but acquired different meanings, and still others were not accepted by the speakers as adequate terms for the ones they sought to replace. One of the difficulties the German professors encountered was the Turkish students' poor command of their own language that resulted from the rushed modernization of Turkish. Thus, the professors who attempted to learn Turkish came up against the redoubled task of learning a totally unfamiliar language that itself was undergoing constant transformation. On the other hand, the alphabet reform, which was an integral part of language reform and perhaps its most radical component, was implemented with great success by Atatürk in 1928. The Arabic script was extremely ill suited to the phonetic nature of Turkish. For example, whereas Turkish has eight vowels, Arabic has only three. There was also no correspondence between consonants. Consequently, reading was guesswork. Due to the confusion caused by a script radically alien to the nature of Turkish, instruction in Turkish was so difficult that the language of instruction at the School of Medicine, established in 1827 during the Ottoman reign, was French (Güvenç 262).

There were many secondary schools in Istanbul at the time of the reform that offered instruction in other languages, including the German School. The impetus behind the various translation projects was to enrich the expressive capabilities of modern Turkish and elevate it to the status of a language of *Wissenschaft*. The slow but steady growth of Turkish as a language of ideas developed against a background of translation. What was ironic, however, was the coexistence of an extensive practice of translation with a passionately articulated uniqueness and moral superiority of Turkish nation and national identity. This paradox of the need for translation and resistance to it is eloquently expressed in Antoine Berman's *Experience of the Foreign,* a study that argues that the major translation project of German romanticism articulated a deep desire to enrich German by incorporating the other: "Every culture resists translation, even as it has an essential need for it. The very aim of translation—to open up in writing a certain relation to the Other, to fertilize, what is One's own through the meditation of what is Foreign—is diametrically opposed to the ethnocentric structure of every culture" (Berman 4). In the new Turkey of the 1930s and 1940s, the need for translation arose from the conditions of the historical moment; the Westernization reforms embraced a discourse of progress that entailed a radical translation from the *alaturka* (Turkish) to the *alafranga* (Frankish) way of life. On the other hand, as a late newcomer to the league of "Nation"s, Turkey adopted an essentialist grammar of linguistic and ethnic unity that would represent Turkish culture as an unadulterated whole. Yet the embrace of translation, as Berman has convincingly argued, is simultaneously an embrace of the foreign.

In a foreword dating from 1941 and included as a preface to all translations issued by the Ministry of Education, the then Minister of Education Yücel reconciles the desire for translation with a nationalist resistance to it by arguing that the wealthier a nation's library of translations is, the higher its status among the nations of the civilized world. Yücel, a legendary reformer and educator, undertook, with the help of classical philologist Georg Rohde, the extensive project of translation of world classics into Turkish (*Dünya Edebiyatından Tercümeler*). In collaboration with his students, Rohde published Latin textbooks for high schools. Yücel had introduced Latin instruction into the high school curriculum, and Rohde's students began teaching Latin at many secondary schools. Although the experiment with Latin instruction at the secondary school level was short-lived, Rohde's many students carried on the classical tradition with distinction at the University of Ankara where he taught from 1935 to 1949. His *Lingua Latina,* a textbook in Turkish, coauthored with one of his star students, Samim Sinanoğlu, enjoyed several reprints (Widmann 286). Azra Erhat, another student, became a leading scholar and popularized classical mythology in a series of highly informative and well-written books.

Translation always entails a contract between two parties. The terms of this contract are best fulfilled when the transaction stipulated by the contract is not only linguistically but also culturally viable. The translation project that in various guises shaped the cultural policies of the early Turkish republic cannot be understood as a mere transmission of content. The professors who contributed most substantially both to their students' *Bildung* and their own were those who chose not to reside in the ivory tower of intellectual migration. "Translation," writes Berman, "is a radical reformulation of the idea of classical Bildung: what is one's own or familiar gains access to itself or becomes conscious of itself only through the experience of the other" (Berman 162). Although Rüstow never gained mastery in Turkish, he was effective as a cultural translator, since his political past and sensibilities enabled him to understand the historical challenges facing the Turkish generation that was his charge. For many scholars biding their time in Istanbul in relative comfort and security and making little effort to communicate with their hosts, the trials of a war-torn Europe seemed like something from another planet—until the unstoppable German army came within eighty miles of the Turkish border. Franz von Papen, Hitler's ambassador to Ankara, was ordered to revoke the passports of the Jewish professors, and the Nazi anti-Semitic propaganda in Turkey backed by other non-refugee German establishments stepped up. The Turkish government, however, intervened vehemently in each case on behalf of the academics and offered all Turkish citizenship.

I need to note here, however, that the picture did not seem so rosy from all sides. A few refugees, who were dismissed due to their reluctance or inability to learn Turkish, expressed very bitter feelings toward their Turkish hosts upon landing on the greener pastures of Great Britain and the United States. A few others, among them students of Spitzer, when safely settled into the comfort of American research universities, criticized the lack of resources or the standard of living in Turkey. Shaw notes that they were quick to blame the Turks, "who had in fact given them refuge when no other country would. Part of the problem was in attitude. Most of the refugees had been leading figures in Germany and elsewhere in western Europe and had treated even their German students with considerable arrogance, something which the democratically-minded Turks simply could not accept" (Shaw 11). Nevertheless, the disgruntled voices of a handful of refugees remain insignificant in the larger context of a mutually beneficial cultural exchange. Contrary to the well-known claim that Auerbach wrote *Mimesis* in Istanbul in a vacuum where he could not consult other scholarly works, both

Neumark and Shaw state that the university was able to furnish the scholars with needed books and materials in record time, and Barry Rubin writes that Auerbach found some of the books he needed in the library of Angelo Giuseppe Roncalli, Vatican's legate in Istanbul who was to become Pope John XXIII (Rubin 44). Whereas Auerbach had serious apprehensions about the lack of intellectual community in his Istanbul exile and worried about not having access to Western libraries, Rüstow was risking his life along with Hans Willbrandt, another refugee professor in Istanbul, by collaborating under the code name "Magnolia" with American and British intelligence in Turkey against the Nazis (Rubin 172–76, 280). Ernst Reuter, who had spent two years in a concentration camp, became one of the leaders of the anti-Nazi community in Turkey. He established the chair for urban planning at the University of Ankara, a discipline that was to become an integral component of Turkish modernization. Later as mayor of Berlin, Reuter oversaw the operation of the Berlin *Luftbrücke* (crisis airlift).

Perhaps not so surprisingly, the professors that participated most actively in a dialogue with their hosts were social scientists whose critical apparatus enabled them to register and decode social change. Whether they translated their own works, or had them translated, or wrote in Turkish, which was conceived in advance as a gesture of self-translation or a form of double translation, they generated a new kinship between Turkish and German in such a way that each language became richer relative to its former self by incorporating the nuances and traces of the other. Whereas neither Leo Spitzer's brilliant textual analyses nor Auerbach's widely read and referenced *Mimesis* reveal even the faintest trace of the exilic experience and its attendant other-cultural encounters, Rüstow's *Ortsbestimmung*, in its intellectual mood and voice, bears witness to exile in a land undergoing major social transformations and trying to make sense of its peculiar destiny. In his preface to the book that was conceived and written in Istanbul, Rüstow explains the reason for undertaking this study in a most eloquent fashion. He states that the catastrophic events of history require that the sociologist and historian investigate the causes of the catastrophe and determine the place of those affected in the historical continuum. He voices his gratitude to the Turkish nation that offered him the space and the time that made the pursuit of this inquiry possible. Exile offered him the detachment from lived history necessary for a critical observation and reassessment of the latter (Rüstow xxiii).

For an exile, the acquisition of the host country's language is virtually a contractual obligation. As mentioned before, the contracts of German academic exiles actually contained a clause that required them to learn Turkish. This contract, Derrida would claim, like "[a]n agreement or obligation of any sort . . . can only take place . . . in translation, that is, only if it is simultaneously uttered both in my tongue and the other's. If it takes place only in one tongue, whether it be mine or the other's, there is no contract possible" ("Roundtable on Translation," 125). When Fritz Arndt, the chemist, Neumark, the economist, Hirsch, the legal philosopher, or Rohde, the classical philologist, wrote in Turkish, their "translated" texts no longer followed the German script. This writing as translation implied a memory without moorings ready to enter a bilateral agreement with the other. By turning to Turkish, these scholars were able to re-form and reclaim a German that was ideologically manipulated as a tool of oppression and exclusion. Neumark recalls an incident that more than anything else—the brutality of Nazism, the loss of his position, and the fear of exile—he regarded as the most devastating blow to his personal and collective identity. On that fateful day that turned out to be his last at the University of Frankfurt before going into exile, Neumark saw,

> mit tiefster Erschütterung am Schwarzen Brett einen Anschlag des NS-Studentenbundes, indem unter anderem die Forderung erhoben wurde, künftig alle Publikationen von jüdischen Professoren als "Übersetzungen aus dem Hebräischen" zu bezeichnen (eine Sprache die mir unbekannt war). Diese Diffamierung von Menschen, die nie etwas anderes als Deutsch ihre Muttersprache betrachtet und geliebt hatten, zeigte mir endgültig, daß mein Wirken an einer Institution, die nur um des äußeren Scheinens willen fortfuhr, sich "Johann Wolfgang Goethe-Universität" zu nennen, nicht mehr möglich war. (Neumark 44)

> [in profound shock on the blackboard a notice of the Nazi student union which, among other claims, stated that from now on all publications of the Jewish professors would be considered "translations from the Hebrew" [a language I did not know]. This defamation of people who had never considered anything other than German as their mother tongue and who loved it as such finally convinced me that it was no longer possible for me to work at an institution which continued to call itself the "Johann Wolfgang von Goethe University" for appearances' sake].

This painful memory is corroborated by widespread evidence that showed how Jewish intellectuals and writers were forcibly expelled from the only mother tongue they knew. A poster with the heading, "Wider den deutschen Geist" (Against the German Spirit), prepared for the Nazi campaign that began on April 13, 1933 made, among others, the following pronouncement: "Der Jude kann nur jüdisch denken. Schreibt er deutsch, dann *lügt* er" (The Jew can only think Jewish; if he writes German, then he *is lying*). The poster also stated that since the Jew was an alien (*Fremdling*), censors had to stipulate that Jewish works be published in Hebrew. If they came out in German, they had to be categorized as translation (*Übersetzung*).[4]

There are multiple ironies darkly lurking in these statements. The double etymology of *Übersetzung* shows that it means both translation and transporting or ferrying over (when its verb form is transitive) or crossing over (intransitive). The German Jewish scholars in question did not write or publish in Hebrew. Like Neumark, most probably had little or no knowledge of the language, but the Nazi ideology read in their works a translated German and not the authentic, pure one. Furthermore, in that context, the status of translation was clearly inferior to language "unadulterated" by translation. The Jews were transported out of their language and later to concentration camps. Those who crossed over the border, who were able to escape, lived a life in translation. They crossed over from one meaning of *Übersetzung* to the other, from one *Übersetzung* to another *Übersetzung*. Istanbul is a city astride two continents, separated by the strait of the Bosphorus. Although there are now two suspension bridges connecting the two shores of the strait, during Neumark's Istanbul years ferry boats were the only means of crossing the Bosporus. Since the University of Istanbul is on the European side, and Neumark, Rüstow, and some of their colleagues lived on the Asian side, they were "ferried over" every day, thus leading a life of double *Übersetzung*.

It is no small irony that although Neumark wrote most of his work in German, his mother tongue, the Nazis censured his books as translations from the Hebrew. But when he wrote in Turkish, in this case, his other tongue, his writing was, in effect, a translation from the German. In the latter context, translation is understood as a historical necessity articulated against a background of social, political, and cultural exchanges. In this historical context, translation, positioned before and after language, becomes, as the German Romantics and Benjamin have shown, a "Potenzierung" (potentiation or exponentiation) of language. In the critical space for exchange and negotiation afforded by translation, Neumark can now reclaim the language from which he was forcefully exiled. The history of German migration to Turkey illustrates the dialectic cycle of loss and restitution whereby amends are made, however gradually, for the theft of language and history. What was recovered in language and memory from the shards of a once humanist culture became a significant contribution to the educational reforms of a new nation In turn, like many countries that offered German academics refuge, Turkey placed a significant amount of German intellectual capital in escrow until it could be returned home safely—with interest.

NOTES

1. According to figures given by Stanford Shaw, between 1940 and 1950, 76 works of literature from Germany, 180 from France, 46 from England, 64 from Russia, and 13 from Italy were translated into Turkish. In addition, 28 works were translated from Latin, 76 from Ancient Greek, and 23 from Persian and Arabic. See Shaw, *Turkey and the Holocaust*, p. 8, n. 19.

2. Horst Widmann quotes from a letter Rüstow wrote to his colleague Andreas Schwarz before the latter's arrival in Istanbul. Here Rüstow reassures Schwarz that consecutive oral translation of a lecture works very well. *Horst Widmann, Exil und Bildungshilfe: Die deutsche akademische Emigration in die Türkei nach 1933* (Frankfurt am Main: Peter Lang, 1973), p. 241. Others who remember Rüstow, including Neumark and Rüstow's son, Dankwart Rustow, point to Rüstow's ease of communication with his students and hosts. Despite imperfect language skills in Turkish, Rüstow clearly shared in the discourse of his Turkish colleagues and friends.

3. For a more comprehensive historical context of Atatürk's cultural reforms, see Erik J. Zürcher, *Turkey: A Modern History*, rev. ed. (London and New York: Tauris, 1980), pp. 194–203.

4. This poster was on display at the exhibition that was a re-creation of the exhibition called "Entartete Kunst" (degenerate art) that the Nazis opened on March 19, 1937 in Munich as part of an all out attack on modern art. The discovery of some of the installation photographs of the Munich exhibition made the reconstruction of the original one possible at the Los Angeles County Museum of Art through the initiative of Stephanie Barron, curator of twentieth-century art at the museum, who assembled 150 pieces from

the original show. After its initial display in Los Angeles, the exhibition traveled to the The Art Institute of Chicago and the Smithsonian Institution. I saw the poster and copied its contents in my notebook during my visit to the Smithsonian where "'Degenerate Art': The Fate of the Avant-Garde in Nazi Germany" was on display from October 8, 1991 to January 5, 1992.

Works Cited

Adorno, Theodor W., *Minima Moralia: Reflexionen aus dem beschädigten Leben*, in *Gesammelte Schriften*, ed. Rolf Tiedemann, vol. 4 (Frankfurt am Main: Suhrkamp, 1980).

Apter, Emily, "Comparative Exile: Competing Margins in the History of Comparative Literature," in *Comparative Literature in an Age of Multiculturalism*, ed. Charles Bernheimer, pp. 86–96 (Baltimore: Johns Hopkins University Press, 1995).

Berman, Antoine, *The Experience of the Foreign: Culture and Translation in Romantic Germany*, trans. S. Haywaert (Albany: State University of New York Press, 1992).

Chambers, Iain, *Migrancy, Culture, Identity* (London and New York: Routledge, 1994).

Derrida, Jacques, *On Cosmopolitanism and Forgiveness*, trans. Mark Dooley and Michael Hughes, preface Simon Critchley and Richard Kearney (London and New York: Routledge, 2001).

———. "Roundtable on Translation," in *The Ear of the Other: Otobiography, Transference, Translation*, trans. Peggy Kamuf and Avital Ronel, eds. Christie McDonald and Claude Lévesque (Lincoln and London: University of Nebraska Press, 1988).

Güvenç, Bozkurt, *Türk Kimliği: Kültür Tarihinin Esasları* (Istanbul: Remzi Kitabevi, 1996).

Horkheimer, Max and Theodor W. Adorno, *Dialektik der Aufklärung* (Frankfurt am Main: Fischer, 1969).

Möller, Horst, *Exodus der Kultur: Schriftsteller, Wissenschaftler, und Künstler in der Emigration nach 1933* (Munich: Beck, 1984).

Neumark, Fritz, *Zuflucht am Bosporus: Deutsche Gelehrte, Politiker und Künstler in der Emigration 1933–1953* (Frankfurt am Main: Knecht, 1980).

Rubin, Barry, *Istanbul Intrigues: A True-Life Casablanca* (New York: McGraw Hill, 1989).

Rüstow, Alexander, *Freedom and Domination: A Historical Critique of Civilization*. Abbreviated Translation *of Ortsbestimmung der Gegenwart*, trans. Salvator Attanasio, ed. with a preface by Dankwart A. Rustow (Princeton, N.J.: Princeton University Press, 1980).

Rustow, Dankwart A., "Alexander Rüstow (1885–1963): A Biographical Sketch," in *Freedom and Domination: A Historical Critique of Civilization*. Abbreviated trans. of *Ortsbestimmung der Gegenwart*, trans. Salvator Attanasio, ed. with a preface by Dankwart A. Rustow (Princeton, New Jersey: Princeton University Press, 1980), pp. xiii–xxii.

Shaw, Stanford J., *Turkey and the Holocaust: Turkey's Role in Rescuing German and European Jewry from Persecution, 1933–1945* (Washington Square: New York University Press, 1993).

Widmann, Horst, *Exil und Bildungshilfe: Die deutschsprachige academische Emigration in der Türkei nach 1933* (Frankfurt am Main: Peter Lang, 1973).

Zürcher, Erik J. *Turkey: A Modern History*, rev. ed. (London and New York: Tauris, 1998).

DeLillo in Greece Eluding the Name

STATHIS GOURGOURIS

"I think fiction rescues history from its confusions." This tentative assertion in one of the rare interviews with Don DeLillo could draw a hail of objections from historians, as it insinuates, with confident and serious nonchalance (DeLillo's characteristic style), that history is confused. Elaborating, the novelist goes on to attribute to the writing of fiction a capacity of historical insight that the writing of history cannot possibly possess, a clarity of perception into history's own *things*: "[Fiction] can operate in a deeper way: providing the balance and rhythm we don't experience in our daily lives, in our real lives. So the novel which is within history can also operate outside it—correcting, clearing up and, perhaps most important of all, finding rhythms and symmetries that we simply don't encounter elsewhere."[1]

This hardly means that literature has triumphed over history. Quite the contrary, since according to this formulation the insight of fiction is achieved only as historical insight, as the alleviation of history's confusions on its own behalf. After all, history, not fiction, is being rescued. On the one hand, this rescue operation ensures fiction's implication in things historical, which goes far towards dispelling the classic notions about literature's self-referential nature at one time so dear to literary critics. On the other hand, however, DeLillo's remark also implies a particular and indeed unique quality in literature's relation to knowledge, to what makes knowledge possible *in history*, and this is the larger issue framing the discussion here.

DeLillo insists that, unlike the work of Beckett or Kafka (which he identifies as placeless and abstract and therefore more explicitly theoretical), his work is attached "to real places, to color and texture, to names, to roots and pigments and rough surfaces."[2] For him, fiction must have a locus in a literal, not merely metaphorical, sense—if for no other reason than to subvert fiction's tendency toward self-absorption. And yet, DeLillo has accomplished an exemplary body of theoretical literature in the very tradition of the great modernist experimentation he cites, which engages with great subtlety the elusive mysteries of the contemporary world, a literature of unique performative contemplation.[3] Despite easy-handed pronouncements on DeLillo's postmodern techniques (which sometimes locate his work in a tradition of alleged antiliterature), his entire

A slightly longer version of this essay forms part of *Does Literature Think? Literature as Theory for an Antimythical Era* (Stanford University Press, 2003) and appears here by permission of the publisher.

mode of interrogation points to a refined confidence in literature's capacity to theorize the mystery of the world, the elemental historical *thingness*.[4]

Since the 1980s particularly, Don DeLillo's work exhibits striking cohesion as an overall theoretical project, despite a consistently multifaceted approach to subject matter and narrative locus. Next to the extraordinary textures of *Libra* (1988)—to whose literary sophistication it serves as a precursor—*The Names* (1982) exemplifies literature's theoretical capacity with stunning richness. In this work, the capacity of fiction to abolish history's confusions is tested against the background of a foundational desire in human society to harness the power of the proper name. Therefore, the mythical undercurrent of this encounter between the world of a late twentieth-century novel and an archaic desire is none other than the transgressive legacy of the Tower of Babel: "Western" culture's generative lapse into confusion. In general, the novel derives its energy from an intersection between history's mythological core and its dissolution in the contemporary market of politics and culture. In a constant rejuvenation of the Babel experience, which is no longer simply the proliferation of languages but the negotiation of cultural rates of exchange in a globalized market, to make history may involve the struggle between naming and being named, or even more so, the chance to elude the name altogether. To render this struggle or this elusion palpable, to register it as an act in the world, requires poetic thought—in other words, the transformative contemplation of history's confused present by means of (re)staging history's mythological core.

DeLillo's strict standards of narrative locus situate this historical and philosophical crossroads in the contemporary conditions of the eastern Mediterranean basin (or what is commonly called, in terribly vague terms, the Middle East), with Greece as the central referential space and India as the outer boundary. This territorial point of reference is hardly a matter of literary convenience; it is the internal necessity of the work. *The Names* puts forth a particular geographical element as its very method of contemplation. To understand how this novel *thinks* is to recognize a certain primacy in geography, to remind oneself that the foundational questions that still animate the imaginary of today's world are associated with a specific terrain on the globe, and not merely the actual presence of this terrain but its many histories, its many names. Thus, place-names in this novel are particularly significant. They carry a critical logic: an inventory of myths, an archaeological record, but also a distinct modernity.

Though the terrain named is vast, Greece is evidently central, not merely in the narrative frame but in methodological weight. To assume that something is central is to inhabit a characteristic ambiguity, to reside simultaneously at the core and in between, at the base of things and in the interstices of things. In this respect, to be in Greece is to be simultaneously grounded and suspended—an acrobatic condition that informs both the author's own motivation (DeLillo spent four years in Greece as a "research base" for the novel) and the novel's horizon. Keeping this ambiguity in mind as a point of departure, let us consider DeLillo's own words:

In *The Names*, I spent a lot of time searching for the kind of sun-cut precision I found in Greek light and in the Greek landscape. I wanted a prose which would have the clarity and the accuracy which the natural environment at its best in that part of the world seems to inspire in our own senses. I mean, there were periods in Greece when I tasted and saw and heard with much more sharpness and clarity than I'd ever done before or since. And I wanted to discover a sentence, a way of writing sentences that would be the prose counterpart to that clarity—that sensuous clarity of the Aegean experience.[5]

Surely, one does not easily take an author's words about himself for granted, which is hardly to say that a critic's words about an author are by rule any more trustworthy. Yet, in reading this confession, one cannot help being struck by a rather folkloric representation of the Greek landscape, akin, let us say, to the manner of Odysseus Elytis in one of his own slanted references to the Aegean quality of his verse, or even more so, to a critic of Elytis enamored, if not necessarily with the poet, then surely with the words that construct the poet. Nonetheless, when we traverse this terrain of suspicion and look at the passage again, we may be struck by the same *coup de foudre* that strikes DeLillo: "the sun-cut precision." Indeed, for a Greek reading this passage, the experience is even more arresting. Precision isn't quite what a Greek would usually associate with absorbing from the sun, yet the feeling one gets from DeLillo's sketching of this space tantalizes because it succeeds at evoking something mysterious, intangible, familiar.

Having ascertained that these remarks are not in fact the remarks of a Greek praising his cultural genius or the fortitude of his distinct nature, the likely response to such perplexed reception is to invoke the memory of the next best figure to the proud Hellene: the Philhellene. Suddenly, the lyric turmoil of a Byron or a Hölderlin, the rapture of a Shelley or a Humboldt, comes pouring down on the cultural memory cells with all of its implications: Philhellenism's punitive damages. From Chateaubriand's necrophilic gaze to the antiquarian chastity in the philological and archaeological laboratory to the latter-day tourist invasion, it has always been a matter of a sun-drenched, clear-cut, postcard Greece.

So, what is there to say about one more such reiteration that underlines the notorious clarity of the Hellenic cultural landscape, that recognizes Greece as the source of sensual accuracy? What do such remarks reveal anew about the eye surveying the landscape, the beneficiary (and indeed the privileged object) of this solar surgery of the psyche? And how might this figure in the eyes of those populating the landscape, those purveyors of a specific historical and geographical element that seem to—dare I say it?—abandon themselves to the surveying gaze in what is a dangerous game of mutual seduction? The answers to such questions must retrace the multivalent trails that make the history of the region so "confusing" and, as DeLillo told us at the outset, can only reside in fiction.

The Names is remarkable for the uncanny exactitude with which it weaves together the designs of multinational capitalism with the compulsive desire of archaeology; the inanities of tourism with the genuine longing to shake loose the American cultural malaise; the writing of fiction in a world that has turned the word into a technological command with the murderous force invoked by an ancient calling for the primacy of the proper name; the abyssal and traumatic quest for one's identity with the resigned loneliness of contemporary married life. But what makes this novel even more remarkable for a Greek reading it is its capacity to actualize contemporary Greek reality (and particularly urban reality) in a way that, to my mind, is unprecedented in accounts of Greek life by expatriated cultural observers, artists or otherwise. To read DeLillo's descriptions of the Greek way of doing things is to realize instantly the artistic poverty of a Henry Miller or a Lawrence Durrell.

On the other hand, this sort of comparison can be misleading for it confines DeLillo to the quarters of those twentieth-century "lovers of Greece" whose aesthetics, unwitting in their dilettantish or adventurist pleasures, were serving the imperialist apparatus. It isn't appropriate because, for one, Don DeLillo is a novelist of international magnitude as yet incalculable in its ultimate ramifications, a writer with the keenest focus on the predicament of the present. Nonetheless, should he in this case be located (and that is a question) in the context of Western culture's psychic investment in the eastern Mediterranean world, then he cannot but inherit the weight of the vast Orientalist and Philhellenist legacy in the region.

When the novel's protagonist, John Axton, a risk-analyst working in Greece for the benefit of multinational banking (a firm selling political risk insurance), opens the narrative by confessing he has been dissuading himself from visiting the Acropolis while living in Athens, DeLillo's fiction takes on precisely that weight: "The weight and moment of those worked stones promised to make the business of seeing them a complicated one," Axton announces.[6] To see the worked stones means precisely to cross the chasm between cultural fantasy and reality and look at civilization's phantoms face to face. Freud spoke succinctly of the experience of this nearly impossible passage, an experience he identified as derealization. For him, like myriad others, climbing the Acropolis hill was and is a ritual dictated by an ultimately incomprehensible pulsion, an archaic (meaning also an *archic*—originary, compelled) sense of security in civilization. The realization of such a drive can be quite monstrous. Freud had likened the shock of seeing the Acropolis in reality to the shock of seeing the perfectly unreal Loch Ness monster. John Axton, risk analyst, knows the risk of this encounter quite well: "It looms. It's so powerful there. It almost forces us to ignore it. Or at least to resist it" (TN 5).

Surely, the terrifying power that the Acropolis exerts beneath the customary ritual of confirming the fact that it exists is rarely perceptible as such. Having been burdened so long with the task of being Western Civilization's constitutive object of fantasy, the Acropolis does not speak. It operates by means of silent coercion, exemplified in the tourist's compulsive effort to meet it face to face without quite understanding the nature of his gesture—this same coercion recognized by Axton (the antitourist) as the source of his equally incomprehensible denial: "What ambiguity there is in exalted things. We despise them a little" (TN 3).

Axton's psychic universe is constituted around the profoundly estranged observer position that his work demands. In his field of vision, objects and gestures take on distinct and disembodied qualities, casting themselves in the foreground as the co-ordinating agents of life, perfectly animate. Familiar cultural signposts fade. Suddenly, to be in Greece has nothing to do with what is expectantly Hellenic. One senses the animation of everything around. Culture takes place in the flux sustained by the barrage of conversation, the inordinate exchange of cut-up phrases, exclamations, and incidental sounds, all orchestrated by an array of gestures:

> People everywhere are absorbed in conversation. . . . Conversation is life, language is the deepest thing. We see the patterns repeat, the gestures drive the words. It is the sound and picture of humans communicating. It is talk as a definition of itself. . . . Every conversation is a shared narrative, a thing that surges forward, too dense to allow space for the unspoken, the sterile. The talk is unconditional, the participants drawn in completely. (TN 52)

In this whirlwind, John Axton, risk analyst, realizes instinctively that, from the point of view of granting insurance for multinational investment (economic but also cultural), Greece is high-risk territory. Hence his sensitivity to the defamiliarizing (derealizing) undercurrent of the culture and his resistance/denial of its projected signposts. This condition accounts for Axton's twofold consciousness: on the one hand, his extraordinary insight into which elements of the surveyed culture slip right through the net of the surveying gaze, and on the other (in a contradictory simultaneity that does not abolish either term), his absolute blocking of the significance inherent in the sort of work that brings him to Greece in the first place, the network of power that feeds on cultural surveillance. Axton is baffled when he discovers eventually that his firm is an informant front for the CIA. Breaking down the rules of the surveying gaze does not mean breaking down the identity (always autonomously alien) of the surveying subject. But Axton's irresolute cultural displacement makes certain his failure as a CIA informant (emblematic of the general failure of the CIA to ever really understand what goes on in that part of the world—the narrative takes place in the wake of the Iran hostage crisis). At the same time, however, his personal alienated condition as cosmopolitan observer, as private citizen of the world, ensures his decoding of both the psychological shards of contemporary culture as well as the psychotic patterns of a murderous cult.

Paradoxically—or perhaps not—the alertness and sensitivity generated by Axton's displacement breaks open the cultural mystery of Greece and thus opens up the long text of the West's psychic investment in the region (Philhellenism, Orientalism, etc.) so that the West's own inscriptions on the social-cultural landscape can be read. This runs counter to—indeed replaces—archaeology's incessant need to extract the traces of Greece's ancestry, to excavate (or exhume) the buried inscriptions of the past. The novel makes this clash central to its perspective. Axton's resistance to "seeing the stones" is countered by archaeology's eagerness not merely to see them but to read them. The untenability of this latter desire in a *modern* Greek world where the barrage of fragmented or unfinished discourses reigns, where inscriptions cannot be read in any final sense, is exemplified by the novel's other protagonist, Owen Brademas, the brilliant epigraphologist from Kansas and closest presence to the novel's traumatic core, who is brought into the picture having already abandoned the aims of his vocation and taken up the trail of a nomadic murderous cult.

A wide-ranging geographical mutability is interwoven in the exclusive sense of modernity that "Western culture" fosters and protects. Brademas's archaeological obsession has its geographical parallel in Axton's information gathering for multinational capitalist politics, which is why the two characters converge in their compulsive attraction to the cult. They are plugged into the same trajectory, both acting as contemporary surveyors of the ancient routes of culture, the territory that has been circumscribed as Indo-European culture. Axton's work involves deciphering the cultural inscriptions of the present. But this work also produces the traces of today's bookkeeping. It leaves behind a trail of coded inscriptions, complex accounts of an economic and cultural war whose politics is inevitably geographical. These inscriptions burning at the heart of telex machines have their own instant epigraphologists to match, which is to say that present-day culture leaves nothing to future interpreters. Today's accounting is itself subjected to the geographical mutability it serves. Perhaps its aim is to leave nothing in its wake (at least, this would be the ideal CIA mode of operation). Or rather, it signifies a form of culture that aspires to render itself and its territory unaccountable, like the occasional traveller who doesn't even take pictures. The myriad agents of capitalist politics in the region conduct their lives and business like tourists. Axton has no trouble admitting this for himself: "I began to think of myself as a perennial tourist. There was something agreeable about this. To be a tourist is to escape accountability. Errors and failings don't cling to you the way they do at home. You're able to drift across continents and languages suspending the operation of sound thought. Tourism is the march of stupidity" (TN 43).

A future epigraphologist would find it hard to distinguish between the traces of stupidity and intelligence. Not merely because the mass cultivation of stupidity has proven to be one of capitalism's most intelligent weapons, but also because the intelligence of a culture set on devouring the territory of the other (including the territory of its recorded past) has something incomparably brutal about it, a method of unaccountable obliteration, crude emptiness. One might consider that Brademas begins to seek the self-referential in ancient epigraphy because his own existence is determined by an increasingly self-referential world. It is as if the cost of globalization in the late twentieth century is a kind of cultural imploding, a deeper and deeper self-enclosure that must seek its historical alibi in the elemental, the original dissociation within language that led from hieroglyph to alphabet. The late twentieth-century epigraphologist who wants to go beyond cultural accounting to the purest traces of an archaic language is ultimately unconcerned with any other culture than his own. In an admittedly seductive way—for he is no doubt a rebel—Brademas exemplifies the bankrupt ideology of classical archaeology in the eastern Mediterranean. No matter what

the force of loyalty to the discipline might dictate, the excessive and elusive inscriptions of present life overshadow the silent signposts of the glorious past.
Classical archaeology particularly falters when the exhumation of a dead language revealed as an apparatus for a kind of archaic accounting takes place in a
world where the living language reigns as a guiltless end-in-itself, a celebration
of unaccounted repetition: "A Greek will never say anything he hasn't already
said a thousand times" (TN 4). This discrepancy, the unaccountability that lies
between the language of the past and the language of the present, holds the key
to the novel's obsession with naming.

Behind the desire to name, to couple together word and thing, there is a secret
desire to embrace the order of the particular. In a world whose *archē* is the interruption of the Babel project, such desire would be a response to the *aporia* generated before the gaze of the universal that arrives as a kind of nameless aggregate
of many names, never reducible to any one except its own. There is a categorical
multiplicity hidden in every expression of the universal, a necessary appropriation and taming of the fearful energy of the untotalized particular. The desire to
permeate the manythingness of the world, the elusive boundaries of the post-
Babelian word, propels and holds intact the universal. And yet, what sustains
the regime of the proper name, what justifies the act of naming in the last instance (at least in what is termed the Western tradition), is the most absolute of
universal signs, the monadic order itself, the last instance of the Name (which is,
of course, unnameable): God.

This paradoxical condition accounts for the double demand posed by the
proper name, the simultaneous necessity of readability and unreadability, translatability and untranslatability, pure reference and substantive essence. In his repeated meditations on this condition, Jacques Derrida has insisted on the double
bind of God himself, the double bind of the monadic institution.[7] According to
Derrida, the Tower of Babel myth is resolved with an impossible command, a gift
that is also an injunction. In a war of proper names, God interrupts the work of
the tribe that still holds intact the power to name (the traditional Hebrew name
of the tribe, Shem, means "name") by forcing upon it his own name, which is
Babel and which means "confusion": the one name for all names that can never
be reproduced. God interrupts the work on the Tower by the force of his name,
which plunges all work into confusion. Though it is beyond all particulars, it
traverses each and every particular; though it must be no one's name, it is the
name of the One. Suddenly, the work is bound to a new object: in the confusion
of tongues, the work becomes the work of translation. Derrida identifies the
arche of this new labor as God's own double bind produced by an inaccessible
gift: the untranslatable name presented with the order that it be translated—an
order produced out of a new order of things, a new order between words and
things. This is an *archic* division within the proper name: "it divides God himself. . . . God himself is in the double bind, God as the deconstructor of the
Tower of Babel. He interrupts a construction. . . . He interrupts the construction
in his name: he interrupts himself in order to impose his name."[8]

There is a double edge to this condition to whose contradictory essence we shall later return: the Babelian performance is both myth and deconstruction. For the moment, let us consider this performance as the origin of a desire that has scattered its traces all over history, a diasporic desire that has plunged history into confusion—after all, Babel is also the mythical *arche*, the governing principle, of diaspora. If fiction is to rescue this scattered history, it is because it (re)enacts both the myth and the deconstruction.

DeLillo infuses his characterization of globalized estrangement in *The Names* with a fanatic figure that extends the antinomic logic of the Babelian performance (from both ends: to name, to be named) to its utmost violence. The world of investment bankers and risk analysts, terrorists and tourists, foreign archaeologists and modern Athenians, is suddenly permeated by the Babelian logic of a murderous cult. This cult consists of a loose structure of small cells strewn throughout Greece and the Middle East and driven by a desire to merge with the most elemental terrain of culture. What binds them together is a fanatic interest in ancient alphabets, hence their geographical orientation.

The cult members travel—or more accurately, they drift—according to an instinctively mapped circuitous pattern that retraces the trajectory of the first instances of post-Babelian culture. They hover around the geographical patterns of the initial dispersal, as if magnetized by the gravitational loops of matter that follow the first explosion. This is the dispersal, the multiple (re)staging, of the original act of culture: carving out of the blank matter of nature the first sign of symbolic representation (writing) and attributing to nature's henceforth broken elements the first sign of identity (naming). Owen Brademas is able to get close to the cult because the cultists are themselves immersed in the contemplation of language and they value his knowledge.

When they address him with the question, "How many languages do you speak?" they are merely issuing their calling card, offering him their password, certain, of course, that he will respond:

> They wanted to hear about ancient alphabets. We discussed the evolution of letters. The praying man shape of the Sinai. The ox pictograph. Aleph, alpha. From nature, you see. The ox, the house, the camel, the palm of hand, the water, the fish. From the external world. What men saw, the simplest things. Everyday objects, animals, parts of the body. It's interesting to me, how these marks, these signs that appear so pure and abstract to us, began as objects in the world, living things in many cases. (TN 116)

Brademas recognizes that epigraphology runs into a dead end as a simple device of mapping ancient cultures. Risking the danger of fetishizing the object, he becomes a reader not of the content of inscriptions but of the actual existence of inscriptions as the content of human toil, the work of culture in its most elemental sense. He only wants to know languages in order to get even closer to the material energy of the human trace on the stone. And of course, the more languages one knows the more inclusive and more proximate is the encounter. It seems to be the work of civilization in reverse, a sort of time-travel, to the point where ancient inscriptions assume presence and need not be deciphered. To know many languages may be a desire to reverse Babel from the inside, to resume work on the Tower against the name. The cultists recognize in Brademas a kindred soul, at least to a certain extent. Says Andahl, the apostate member (who is in this respect even closer to Brademas, the almost member, the fellow traveller): "A man who knows languages. A calm man, very humane. He has a wide and tolerant understanding, a capacity for civilized thought. He is not hurried, he is not grasping for satisfactions. This is what it means to know languages" (TN 207).

In a Babelian universe, to know languages—to know more than one language—means simultaneously to be further immersed in the work of translation and to be increasingly free of translation. The space-time dimension of this simultaneity makes its paradox more comprehensible. Translation is metaphorically linked to the crossing of boundaries, the traversing of places, geographical movement (*translatio* literally means to cross lands). In this sense, to know languages means to travel, as much as it also means, with equal force, to have a sense of place (in each place, in many places). Temporally, it means to have access to many time frames, to work against time's linear construction, against the distance between past and present. But it also means, by the same token, to have an ample sense of time, to belong to time. Brademas, who is sketched as an aging but timeless figure, reciprocates Andahl's characterization when he recognizes the cult's enormous patience, its endless stalking of time and place, its final denial of the dynamics of space-time. Axton also reaches the same conclusions by simple observation when he runs across a cell of the cult at a remote village café in Mani: "They looked like people who came from nowhere. They'd escaped all the usual associations. . . . They were in no hurry to find another place to sit, another place to live. They were people who found almost any place as good as almost any other. They didn't make distinctions" (TN 190).

But, of course, they do make distinctions; at the very least, they aspire to an act whose arbitrary violence is based on absolute distinction. The cult survives on the obsession that the sublime violence inherent in the originary instances of writing and naming—the shattering of nature's undifferentiated whole by culture's unbounded abstract representation (what in another context we could call humanity's entrance into history)—is in fact possible to (re)enact, to live it through as pure contemporary experience. This originary violence holds over them an enchanting allure and they set out to merge with it by pursuing a series of arbitrary murders: staking out a remote territory and pouncing on the unfortunate passerby whose initials match the initials of the place. The logic is inexorable and has no other implicit or encrypted suggestion. An event forms out of nowhere, goes nowhere, just happens, all because simply "the letters matched" (TN 169, 208).

The cult insists on carrying out its arbitrary killings using the most primitive instruments: hammers, chisels, sharp stones—the archaic (*archic*) instruments of writing. Like good philologists, the cult members become perfectly versed in the media of the culture they seek to understand; they appropriate its methods, its attitudes and visions, its language. They begin to measure each act, each thought, by its corresponding philological anatomy. In this they merely follow the steps of Ernest Renan, arguably the quintessential philologist of the nineteenth century, who identified the work of philology as a "vivisection . . . , treat[ing] the living as we ordinarily treat the dead."[9] But with a crucial exception: the cult takes its act out of the laboratory and into the world, and it does so explicitly, taking the matter to its epistemological limit. It chooses to perform this vivisection in actual terms, demonstrating that the epistemic or the cultural body is indeed made out of flesh and blood. The experience has a sort of catalytic terror, a hysterical frenzy, precisely because the murderer's brutal contact with the flesh confirms the absolute finality of his own existence, but also because in another sense the flesh remains irreversibly alien, nonresistant, noncomplicit: "We hit harder because we could not stand the sound of the hammers on her face and head. How Emmerich used the cleft end of the hammerhead. Anything to change the sound. . . . Or how little blood, not at all what we expected, the blood. We looked at each other, amazed at this paucity of blood. It made us feel we had missed a step along the way" (TN 211).

As Brademas recognizes from the outset, the psychological condition of the cult is a denial of their humanity by total submission to the most elemental, desexualized, dehumanized flesh, flesh as organic dirt: "Dirt was their medium" (TN 29) or "They were involved in the most painstaking denial . . . intent on ritualizing a denial of our elemental nature. To eat, to expel waste, to sense things, to survive . . . to satisfy what is animal in us, to be organic, meat-eating, all blood-sense and digestion" (TN 175). The result is a collective autism, a totally self-enclosed universe whose invented meaning appears as perfect nature and whose teleological commitment is absolute and beyond justification: "The murder has become part of the dream pool of his self-analysis. The victim and the act are theory now. They form the philosophical base he relies on for his sense of self. They are what he uses to live" (TN 291). From the point of view of society, this condition exemplifies the dissociation of thought from the world—despite the cult's strict adherence (almost collapse) between object and word—and therefore demonstrates a deep psychosis. Of course, all cults make such behavior necessary: the psychotic clarity of a unified vision, untouched by the inconsistencies of everyday life, unburdened by the demands of the other. But here the dissociation is so profound that no apparent tradition, as cults go, can even contain their behavior as reference. This cult has nothing to do with repeating or emulating ancient rituals, which is why the discourse of human sacrifice, as it pertains to ancient cultures in the region from Babylonian to Minoan times, is altogether irrelevant. The contemporary discourse of arbitrary murders (serial killers, mass shootings, Manson-type rituals) is closer in significance but still not a matter of direct emulation, of exporting. The affinity is deeper and I will return to it shortly. For now, it is important to understand that the cultural groundwork for the ritual of murder in America—"men firing from highway overpasses, attic rooms, unconnected to the earth"—and its various pathological obsessions is alien here. "There is a different signature here, a deeper and austere calculation. We barely consider the victims except as elements in the pattern" (TN 171).[10] Like tourists passing through an alien territory untouched, the cult passes through the terrain of murder with an empty psyche: "Nothing clings to the act. No hovering stuff. It's a blunt recital of the facts" (TN 302).

The ideology of the cult's violence excludes any contemplation of what is human. The kill is just initials, letters of the alphabet. Whatever human element registers, if at all, it does at the ultimate moment of murderous violence, during the actual experience of violating helpless and unresisting flesh. Only such radical self-denial, which necessarily culminates in the denial of whatever connects them to their own death (witness the final stage of some members dying out of simple indifference to life, out of simply turning themselves off), could produce such violence empty of human signification. "The final denial of our base reality, in this schematic, is to produce a death. . . . A needless death. A death by system, by machine-intellect" (TN 175). In this respect, the indisputable madness that underlines the cult's cohesion recedes before the madness of its method, its strict structuralist madness: "Madness has a structure. We might say madness is all structure. We might say structure is inherent in madness. There is not the one without the other" (TN 210).

As with any cult, membership means absolute synchronization with the shared imaginary and the rituals it demands. In all cases, a unique idiom develops, a private language that ultimately reaches beyond its evident signification, beyond even its cultural makeup, to something vertical and practically telepathic, a self-referential symbolism. But here is the most extreme case. Language itself is dissolved to its smallest material particles: letters themselves, emancipated from communicative function, separated, fixed in sequence. Self-referential symbolism undoes any sort of recognizable symbolic order in the sense that language functions without representation. These "zealots of the alphabet" (TN 75) operate by their own admission at a preverbal level. They seek recognition at an unconscious level, an unconscious method, intuitive knowledge. Preverbal is in this sense "prelinguistic" insofar as whatever is shared exists in a space beyond or before language as such; although words are used, they are deemed worthless beyond the arbitrary letters that signify their sound.[11]

The orality associated with sound would be disturbing to the mindset of the cult. Witness the hysterical response to the sound of beating flesh to a pulp. The cult's logic originates in writing and specifically in nonrepresentational writing. What obsesses them is the strange leap from the communicative desire to represent the elements of nature to the invention of arbitrary signs that condense representation to the point of obliteration (from the ox pictograph to aleph to alpha), where communication becomes solely a matter of social convention. The cult's further obsession with a multiplicity of languages, particularly ancient "dead" languages, is owed less to a kind of linguistic fetishism than a desire to delve further into the alphabetic arbitrariness that cuts across linguistic convention between different societies and cultures. As Andahl puts it, "We are here to carry out the pattern. . . . Abecedarian. Learners of the alphabet. Beginners" (TN 210). Although the pattern refers to the alphabetic coincidence of the final act, the confession itself reveals it to stand for the desire to return to the *archē* of Babel, the violence of the first interruption by the name. The violent nature of the final act reciprocates the violence of the beginning. The cult aspires to live this violent beginning on a daily basis, drifting around between arbitrary alphabetic spaces, between initials in different languages. Living this absurd heterochronicity is what turns the archaic into the *archic*. The performance that brings each occupation of a place to an end, the death that demonstrates the life of the pattern, is the justification for the categorically determinant beginning: the alpha and the omega.

Such performance draws its energy from the originary act of social institution inherent in the advent of writing, the violent obliteration of nature by culture upon which the constitution of human society is based. But we are no longer at such a state; at least, what we recognize as our modernity is predicated on an understanding of culture as a technology of taming violence. Civilization has imposed its rule by relegating the *archic* violence of writing to the realm of collective (cultural) sublimation, and in the process holding intact (even if repressed) its universalist/monotheistic propensity. The fact that the cult is caught in this heterochronous dislocation is what accounts both for its absurdity (e.g., conducting their daily communication in Sanskrit or Aramaic) and its psychotic relation to the world. Yet, the cult's murderous performance also makes evident (as forensic proof) the foundations of contemporary culture. Something of civilization's monstrous experience is inherent in the cult's project, albeit dressed up and projected as turning ritual inside-out and sinking further into the sphere of the archaic and the elemental. Were we to strip the cult of this self-projection, it would appear in the light that distinguishes the terrorist logic of late capitalism, whether in the form of clandestine urban warfare (guerrilla groups with myriad secret cells) or the CIA's global operations with its multiple tentacles resembling points of electronic stimulus reception in a vast computer network.[12]

The cult lives and kills by naming. It lives and kills by translating names into pure signs, by denuding them of their acquired ontology and restoring their arbitrariness. The act is based on a perversely mystical materialism of language. The alphabet is elemental representation, so absolutely elemental, however, as to be itself the element that does not represent and is not representable. It becomes itself a name. Inevitably, the moment of murdering is a moment of naming. Michalis Kalliabetsos becomes Mikro Kamini and vice versa. Death becomes a means of identity; it occupies a place. The cult delegates over matters of life and death—this is what it means to name. Thus, despite Owen Brademas's objections, the cult enacts a religious order. I would argue that it is impossible to conceptualize any collective condition that bears the remotest traces of cult life outside a religious imagination. All cults are religious (even if explicitly secular) and all religion has at its basis, whether fully exercised or not, the elements of a cult community. However, because of his profound ambivalence toward religion, Brademas tries to convince himself that these are not "god-haunted people" since no god would dictate and accept such an act devoid of ritual, devoid of tradition. On the other hand, Frank Volterra, the maverick filmmaker who entertains the absurd idea of filming the cult in action, characterizes them as "secular monks" who "want to vault into eternity" (TN 203). Brademas underestimates the signifying range of religious order; Volterra over-aestheticizes an imaginary that disdains representation. Both of them never quite consider what it means to live up to an obsession with a self-referring world and the perverse desire to indulge in its ultimate consequences.

The tortured explanation of cult leader Avtar Singh is perfectly articulate and worth considering at length:

> The world has become self-referring. . . . This thing has seeped into the texture of the world. The world for thousands of years was our escape, our refuge. Men hid from themselves in the world. We hid from God or death. The world was where we lived, the self was where we went mad and died. But now the world has made a self of its own. Why, how, never mind. What happens to us now that the world has a self? How do we say the simplest thing without falling into a trap? Where do we go, how do we live, who do we believe? This is my vision, a self-referring world, a world in which there is no escape. (TN 297)[13]

To some extent all cults experience everything as an interiority. The outer boundary collapses and a profound solipsism sets in. Objective reality as an external supposition disappears, hence the radical inward devotion and impenetrable separation from all otherness. It is perfectly logical that the culmination of such conditions is often ritualized mass suicide. But here the logic has been turned inside out, although the radical self-reference is kept intact. Singh paints the picture of a world that exists in permanent cult conditions. But instead of having lost its objectivity, it has gained a self, an absolute subjectivity. Therefore, the world can no longer escape from itself; it has no space to put aside its obsessions in order perhaps to imagine itself differently, to alter itself. The language of the world has become finite and palindromic. No more words, no new words, no new meanings, no otherness, no alteration. In this total paranoid collapse of signification, Singh and his followers devise a "program" of externalizing fully, of making concrete, the implications of pure self-reference. They turn reality into an alphabetic equation between proper names. While there may be actual inscriptions with the 99 names of God—culture keeping count, accounting— the endless name of God is the alphabet itself (TN 92). So, like the ancient God who gave his endless name to a place he effectively destroyed, the cult baptizes by killing. Like the God whose self-given name was Babel, the cult seeks to inhabit the insides of language, before its outward proliferation, the radioactive fallout, before translation became the necessary resolution of its arbitrariness. These survivors of Babel gather again to seek the name, the utmost self-referent, the beginning which is complete unto itself. They seek the secrets of the name, the secret power of naming that created culture out of fissuring language and made it possible to doubt the association between word and thing: "A secret name is a way of escaping the world. It is an opening into the self" (TN 210). But what happens now that the world has a self? A way out of where? Opening to where?

The cult members kill with the blunt instruments of society's first writers; their victims are their original texts.[14] In other words, they aspire precisely to the instituting power of mythical action. But given the cult's historical and cultural dislocation in space-time, this mythological aspiration to write as if the world is tabula rasa produces an empty set of signification. The cult's act of writing is also an act of erasing; its orthographic naming is literally an *obliteration*. Driven by an anxiety to resist the regime of the universal (in their mind, exemplified in today's global culture) by taking on, like a new Adam, the act of naming, the cult becomes victim to its own logic. To name is also to obliterate. It is an act that erases an object's historically contingent characteristics by inscribing upon it a final identity. In this sense, a nomadic inscription returns head-on to the void of the monadic: the Name itself.

No cult can exist before the Tower of Babel is condemned to permanent ruin, before it acquires its name at the moment of its death. The Shem tribe embarked on this project in order to achieve the permanence of name through the permanence of place. "Let us make ourselves a name, so that we not be scattered over the face of all the earth," is the Biblical verse. In this desire for *autonymy* lies the desire for autonomy. To give oneself the name, to name oneself, is to give oneself the law. In this very fundamental way—and the matter is by no means exhausted there—the Tower of Babel incident is humanity's most profound mythical representation of heteronomy. To give oneself a name, just as much as to give oneself the law, is staged here as the first and final transgression, the very essence of transgression. This essence is grounded on a paradox. The originary desire for the name (which is also the law) reveals, by the punishment it incurs, an *archē* before the origin, an unwritten and unknown name, a law before the law is made, which turns this foundational desire for autonymy/autonomy into foundational transgression.

This transgression is foundational in a literal sense and twofold. Not only does it institute a select people insofar as God himself gives these people his Name (an other name) but in addition, because God's name is Babel ("confusion"—of tongues, of languages, of names), his response to the transgression institutes/names all others, all those who will not actually bear his name but will bear the effect of his naming. As a mythical narrative, the Babelian performance stages the story of everyone being the effect of a naming that comes from elsewhere, from an elsewhere name that retains *by law* its mysterious status as an elsewhere that cannot be named. The Babel incident is the mythical performance of heteronymy/heteronomy, of being named by the Other, which is to say, of bearing the name of the Other's law.

What is particularly relevant here is that the Babel incident also signifies an act of another naming: the totalizing submission of world culture to a monotheistic point of view of history. It is a myth of heteronymy that makes the name of the One the one and only worthy name of history. Although global history is surely composed of multiple points of view—the points of view of many different religions or even nonreligions, which is another way of saying, the confusion of names and laws of worship—to participate in global history (at least since the Crusades) requires that everyone recognize their multiplicity of names in the round mirror of a prevalent monotheistic imaginary.

This is perfectly compatible with the cult's avowed desire to exit from history, if only because its actions aspire to a reversal of humanity's *archic* historical act, an alphabetic relation to life: "This is precisely the opposite of history. An alphabet of utter stillness. We track static letters when we read . . . a logical paradox" (TN 291–92). Yet, in order to really obliterate the Name, you must obliterate it in history. Consider here the importance of stealing your enemy's name in animist societies. The existence of the cult is a clue as to what happens when this animist relation to history is infused with the weapons of a monotheistic psyche. It is tantamount to society's infantile regression, regression always being a reenactment taken as a return. For the cult is by no means primitive; its operations put into practice the tenets of computer logic.[15] The members know this and recognize it when they speak of their mode of existence (whose culmination is the murders) as "the program."

The cult provides a unique occasion for philological practice, a different sort of reading/erasing, as it involves the paradoxical condition of an archaeological epigraphy of culture's shifting present. When Owen Brademas abandons the reading of stones, he does not in fact abandon the pursuit of epigraphic history. His shadowing of the mysterious cult through its various incarnations in the expanse between Greece, the Jordanian desert, and India involves the attempt to decipher this other sort of inscription—a nomadic inscription that cuts across histories and cultures, hence ever-shifting in space and time, heterochronous and heterotopic. Reading such an inscription means traversing the space-time of its fantasy, which more or less means subscribing to the signifying demands of its project. That Brademas ultimately becomes, for all practical purposes, a member of the cult—or at least, complicit in its murderous action by virtue of deciphering their innermost signifying frame and yet remaining a passive observer—is perfectly consistent with his training as an epigraphologist, a man versed in the denuding of names. Intellectual (theoretical) curiosity is satisfied at the price of complicity to the practice.

Yet, though "gravitationally bound to the cult" (TN 286), Brademas does not entirely collapse into its mass density. He achieves the closest possible orbit at a distance decided by a mutual resistance toward being named. The cult's name continues to elude him, as he says, because he serves the purpose of the cult's first and final real interlocutor, "observer and tacit critic," an indication of the cult's demise (TN 299). By refusing to reveal its name, the cult refuses to be named, refuses to relinquish its obsessive self-enclosure. But Owen Brademas himself responds by an act of uncanny mirroring. When Emmerich asks him point blank to reveal his identity, Owen answers "No one" (TN 292). Owen ↔ No one. A curious sonoric matching, a skewed anagram of sound. Is this Odyssean inscription the magic gesture of deconstructing the cult's Babelian violence? Instead of matching the initials face to face, Owen matches them in a sonic mirror. He scrambles the sound of the syllables—the oral insides of the name—to show the void of the name: No one. He reaches behind the alphabetic stillness, behind the death of the sacred script, to utter the erasure of the name, which is subliminally inscribed in the name. The cost of this negative naming is the realization of a lost self. At this final proximity to the world of the cult, Owen realizes he is irretrievably torn from the core of his psyche—the hysteric evangelism of the plains community in Kansas—even though he also realizes that his pursuit of the cult was fueled by the desire to overcome this lack. In other words, the internal chasm is unbridgeable. It is precisely what turns Owen—so obviously closer to One—to No one.

The cult, on the other hand, names itself according to the strict idiom of its identity: *Ta Onómata,* The Names. As absurd reenactment of the long obliterated tribe Shem, the cult invokes its being in its name without qualifications. Like everything else that characterizes it, its name obeys an identitarean logic. The cult can bear no self-reflection in the sense of critique, which is why the only occasion of revealing its name is the desperate gesture of the apostate Andahl, itself actualized by the deciphering eyes of risk analyst Axton. Brademas recognizes finally the tautological nature of the cult's relation to the culture it wishes to destroy: "The killings mock us. They mock our need to structure and classify, to build a system against the terror in our souls. They make the system equal to the terror. The means to contend with death has become death" (TN 308). This is why Owen's Odyssean autonymy consists not only in the refusal to reveal his actual name but in the denuding of the cult's monotheistic propensity, whether it be the ideological service of the Name or the binary computer logic that ties zero to one.

The novel's obsession with the philosophical problem of naming is supported by two other less explicit obsessions (central, however, to DeLillo's work overall): religion and contemporary violence.[16] On the face of it, there seems to be a geographical distinction between the two. Upon his arrival to India, Brademas will recognize himself as a Christian, not as a matter of faith but as a framework of definition. The suggestion is that in Eastern societies religion becomes the language of identity, with India being the epitome of multiplicity in this respect, a veritable documentation of the post-Babelian instance. On the other hand, contemporary violence seems the sole privilege of Americans, a characteristic that has become almost natural, like consumerism. DeLillo himself has been quite explicit: "I see contemporary violence as a kind of sardonic response to the promise of consumer fulfillment in America"[17] to elaborate in another context: "The consequence of not having the power to consume is that you end up living in the streets."[18] Axton echoes him in the novel: ". . . killing in America [is] a form of consumerism. It's the logical extension of consumer fantasy. People shooting from overpasses, barricaded houses. Pure image" (TN 115).

The Names is predicated on the internationalization of this geographical distinction. Thus, the consequences of mirroring American consumer culture and the violence it entails are retraced in a region generally characterized by a deep-seated anti-Americanism, while conversely, religion is revealed as a fundamental obsession of the Western secular mind, whether in the example of the repressed evangelical chaos of Brademas's childhood or the psychotic ruminations of a murderous cult. This chiasmic translation makes it possible to reach the realist groundwork beneath the philosophical concerns of the novel. An American author has situated the demands of his fiction in the mythological present of multinational capital, international politics, and nationalist idiom. If "America is the world's living myth" and possesses "a certain mythical quality that terrorists find attractive" (TN 114), then its literature should perform at this level of mythistorical clarity, the clarity of mythical, not quotidian, violence. On the other hand, societies that bear the brunt of such mythical violence in their daily lives encounter the American present at this same level: "The Mideast societies are at a particular pitch right now. There is no doubt or ambiguity. They burn with a clear vision. There must be times when a society feels the purest virtue lies in killing" (TN 115).

No need to underline the wisdom of this last statement, nor the many times it would be applicable to American society itself. But at the narrative's specific historical juncture, to bear the cultural name *American* in the territory of the Other means more or less to stand on the other side of a gun. For it is a name that speaks the authority of one of late twentieth century's most powerful divinities: the CIA. It is consistent with the novel's unblemished theoretical mind that the CIA occupies the position of the god who destroyed the Tower of Babel by bequeathing it his name. For all those who struggle to translate the significance of American capital, culture, and politics into their own national language (as they experience the multivalent occupation of their actual and virtual territory), the acronymic reference holds all the terrible secrets. The killing of Americans abroad throughout the 1970s and 1980s was in many ways symptomatic of the failure to deconstruct the acronymic power of this contemporary myth. The CIA disseminated everywhere an image of pure and impenetrable self-reference, essentially the Yahwist logic of the untranslatable and unpronounceable name: "I am that I am."[19] Axton's failure to detect himself in the language of this name testifies to its mythological power to confuse the world and particularly the people who allegedly speak its own language: "If America is the world's living myth, then the CIA is America's myth" (TN 317).

It is interesting that DeLillo chooses to stage a terrorist shooting, which targets American capitalist politics, in Greece and not in Jordan, Israel, or India—the other geographical sites of the narrative. The novel documents with considerable precision how, subsequent to the Iranian revolution, Greece became the landing strip of various operatives of multinational capitalism and American politics during their bailing out process, the most significant such retreat since Vietnam. Likewise, the Greek popular sentiment reflected at this time the full militant extent of Greece's disengagement from direct American intervention in its social and political present, following the guidelines of the Truman doctrine (1947) and culminating in the CIA-supported military government (1967–74). As a country with strong Leftist traditions and given the antiimperialist tenets of post–'68 European youth culture, Greece also witnessed the rise of various urban guerrilla groups, the most notorious of which—still active and literally legendary, as no members have ever been identified since it began operations in 1976!—is the group *November 17*. The novel insinuates that the attempted shooting at Lycabettus may have borne this group's signature, one more occasion of DeLillo's subtle interweaving of the boundaries between history and fiction.[20]

The shot fired in broad daylight against the comic target of Americans jogging in one of the few wooded spaces in Athens—whether the intended victim was Axton or the banker David Keller is appropriately left ambiguous (they are interchangeable names: Americans and agents of multinational capital)—cannot but resound against "the sun-cut precision" DeLillo had mentioned at the outset.

After the circuitous adventure has run its course and the narrative of nomadic inscriptions has used up its alphabet, the text has returned to the *archē* of a gestural space, the centrality of which suggests that it lies both at the core and in the interstices of language. We are told early on that "the Greek specific" is a characteristic that "pits the sensuous against the elemental," a space whose abundant light brings attention to the smallest thing, to "correctness of detail" (TN 26). The microworld of the elemental encounters the boundless expanse of the sensual in the kind of embrace that requires utmost precision, otherwise the content of the world is lost. By the same dialectical attention to radical specificity Axton may conclude: "Life is different here. We must be equal to the largeness of things" (TN 89). The Greek landscape, a nature which is fundamentally social, induces a sensual clarity that seems to occupy the entire sensory apparatus of body and soul, a curious materiality of the intangible. Though paradoxical in terms of rational logic, it nonetheless registers with the uncanny precision of already incorporated knowledge. As Brademas reflects in one of his dreamlike speculative moments, one experiences in Greece a residual memory, as in a *metempsychosis*, which is hardly translated by its quotidian notion of reincarnation and is rendered instead through its etymological ground: "not only *transfer-of-soul* but reach[ing] the Indo-European root *to breathe*. . . . We are breathing again" (TN 113).

In Greece, you breathe the elemental. This seems to be what the novel argues for, what sums up its geographical mode of contemplation. The elemental was precisely what the cult also sought, as we know, but its program enforced the strictest singularity possible—no transfer-of-soul, no breathing of history, just one arbitrary shot in the desert of mind, literal alphabetic translation. The cult perceives Mani as "a place where it is possible for men to stop making history . . . [to] invent a way out" (TN 209) because it misreads its cultural reticence as tabula rasa for alphabetic inscription, while Axton recognizes the silence of Mani, though opposed to the polyglot nature of Athens, to be of the same order of precision, "a pure right of seeing" (TN 182). The cult never dares enter the space of Athens—nor any other urban space, which is where whatever psychological similarity it shares with urban guerrilla groups categorically ends—because it is terrified of the stray excess of multiple orders of language. In Athens one enters a whirlwind of language modes, which exist as if untouched by the fallout from the Babelian performance. Axton experiences collective intoxication because "the air is filled with words" (TN 79) and, as we have seen, "gestures drive the words." The gestural world exceeds the alphabetic, which is why the cult is terrified of it. The gestural, which slices the air with interruption and punctuation, eludes the deathly blows of writing instruments. This is why the cult must invent a way out. Because the intangible flux of history is contained in the gesture and in Greece, Axton reiterates with characteristic variance, "history is in the air" (TN 97).

In the everyday realm, Greek life has broken away from the regime of naming, having opted for the broken phrase, the gesture, the incidental sound, the barrage of conversing/contesting voices, the pointless and guiltless repetition.[21] It cannot be reduced to any philological grid because it has long incorporated, according to its imposed classical heritage and the conceptual rifts it entails (to which the contemporary presence of the Acropolis fragments bears material witness), a ruined logos, which is why in (modern) Greece "the ruin is managed differently" (TN 179). The book makes this enigmatic proposition one of its theoretical projects. Axton's ultimate reconciliation with the Greek element, whose symptom is to visit finally the Acropolis, is based on the realization that these "mauled stones" are not "a relic species of dead Greece but part of the living city below" (TN 330). This worldly last instance liberates the ruin from the archaeological ideal, reenters it into the flux of time, restores its historical essence. The Acropolis in ruins remains still the emblem of the city below, Athens in the modern world, a world characterized by the fact that the polis, as a social entity, is in ruins. This language of ruin spells out all the more the necessity that the play of history be elucidated by the act of fiction, which is precisely to say that history cannot be eluded. If the cult ("The Names")—or whatever agency aspires to the categorical privilege of naming—seeks to occupy "a place where it is possible for men to stop making history," eluding the name may be just that no-place where history is in the making.[22]

Such different senses of space mean that the performance of Babel would need to be reread, which means that it would need to be given a different language. Derrida suggests this path when he recognizes that Babel spells out "the need for figuration, of myth" and may be deemed "the myth of the origin of myth," while also testifying to "an internal limit to [the] formalization" that human society engages in since time immemorial, a limit that becomes the mobilizing force behind the need for myth, the need for figuration.[23] The Babelian instance is thus not an Ur-structure in symbolic time but a Möbius strip sort of figure, which is also uniquely intertwined: intertwining itself with itself. Derrida sees there—in the irreducible multiplicity of language, the incompletion of language—the groundwork of myth. Insofar as he has repeatedly presented the Babelian performance as an exemplary instance of deconstruction, he thus draws implicitly (and without ever elaborating) a *co-incidence* between deconstruction and myth.

DeLillo's novel provides precisely the theoretical elaboration of the interstitial spaces of this *co-incidence* by drawing the Babelian performance into the reality of the late twentieth-century world. This novel teaches us to perceive behind the deconstructive double bind of God's interruption of culture its other side. The other side of the double bind is the total command. To face a double bind, we know from real life, is to feel surrounded. To be the double bind, as is God's own life in this mythological instance, means to exhaust the position of deconstruction at the moment it occurs. The deconstructive command of Babel ("confusion") is itself undeconstructible. In this respect, only God can deconstruct. After him, all deconstruction becomes obedience to his double bind. There is thus only one way to disobey God: to elude his Name. This is, to my mind, the distilled significance of the *co-incidence* between deconstruction and myth in the Babelian instance.

It might also be said that this disobedience to the regime of the name is what enables us to resume the work of culture, after the scattering of languages, from the inside of history's fragmented course, from the inside of contingent action. In this respect, fiction makes history possible in a continuous sense. Or to put it otherwise, fiction provides a continuum between the realm of making history (social action) and the realm of imaginative alterity (social imagination). In an essay that might be said to preface his novel *Underworld*, Don DeLillo returns to the heart of this problem: "The novel is the dream release, the suspension of reality that history needs to escape its brutal confinements. . . . Lost history becomes the detailed weave of novels. Fiction is all about reliving things. It is our second chance."[24] Our second chance at Babel after the irreversible chasm opened by the imposition of the Name, the chasm that has opened language (and culture) to interminable multiplicity, is to recognize in this multiplicity the force that enables societies to dare imagine themselves otherwise, beyond the Name.

NOTES

1. Anthony de Curtis, " 'An Outsider in This Society': An Interview with Don DeLillo," in *Introducing Don DeLillo*, ed. Frank Lentricchia (Durham: Duke University Press, 1991), p. 56.

2. Thomas Le Clair, "An Interview with Don DeLillo," *Contemporary Literature* 23(1), 1982, p. 31.

3. DeLillo's affinities with a modernist conceptualization are recognized in the better readings of his work. See, notably, Thomas Le Clair, *In the Loop: Don DeLillo and the Systems Novel* (Urbana: University of Illinois Press, 1987), who sees in *The Names*, among other things, the tradition of the Jamesian international novel.

4. Of the slew of such postmodern readings of DeLillo, I would single out Peter Baker's "The Terrorist as Interpreter: *Mao II* in Postmodern Context" (*Postmodern Culture* 4(2), 1994. But it is indicative of the destabilizing character of DeLillo's work that he can also be read, from a postmodernist point of view, to embody a traditional romantic metaphysics. (See Paul Maltby, "The Romantic Metaphysics of Don DeLillo," *Contemporary Literature* 37(2), 1996.) The vehemence of such critiques demonstrates the strain of allegedly postmodernist categories against the uncategorizable flux, the undercurrent of poetic thought, that distinguishes literature as a unique mode of negotiation between history and knowledge. In contrast, consider the admirable readings of John McClure, particularly "Postmodern/Post-Secular: Contemporary Fiction and Spirituality" *Modern Fiction Studies* 41(1), Spring 1995, pp. 141–63.

5. de Curtis, "An Outsider in This Society," p. 60.

6. Don DeLillo, *The Names* (New York: Vintage, 1982), p. 3. Henceforth cited in the text as TN followed by page number.

7. See particularly Derrida's ruminations on the Tower of Babel myth in "Des Tours de Babel" (Joseph F. Graham trans.) in *Difference in Translation*, ed. Joseph F. Graham (Ithaca: Cornell University Press, 1985), pp. 165–207, and also in *The Ear of the Other* (New York: Schocken, 1985). Derrida's conceptualization of the double bind is drawn from Gregory Bateson's pioneering formulation: the condition of being caught between two commands, whose contradiction never tends toward the term's mutual exclusion or abolition. See G. Bateson, D. D. Jackson, J. Haley, and J. H. Weakland, "Toward a Theory of Schizophrenia" *Behavioral Science* 1 (1956), pp. 251–64.

8. Derrida, *The Ear of the Other*, p. 102.

9. Ernest Renan, "Qu'est-ce qu'une nation?," in *Discours et conférences* (Paris: Calmann-Lévy, 1922), p. 278 (my translation).

10. The words belong to Brademas, and Matthew Morris is correct in recognizing a series of misreadings on Brademas's part that serve to distance himself ideologically from the cult. Morris's characterization of Brademas is on the whole insightful, but I still believe it is important to hold on to this idea of the cult bearing a different signature, or at least, a different way of signing a pattern of destructive activity in a region whose tradition of destruction goes back centuries. The distinction is crucial, otherwise the cult, as a theoretical figure in the mythistorical staging of the novel, becomes reduced to a bunch of psychotic leftover hippies. See Matthew Morris, "Murdering Words: Language in Action in Don DeLillo's *The Names*," *Contemporary Literature* 30:1 (1989), pp. 118–20.

11. See also Dennis A Foster, "Alphabetic Pleasures: *The Names*" in *Introducing Don DeLillo*, Lentricchia, ed., p. 159.

12. "In one sense, we barely exist. It's a difficult life. There are many setbacks. The cells lose touch with each other. Differences arise of theory and practice. For months nothing happens. We lose purpose, get sick. Some have died, some have wandered off. Who are we, what are we doing here?" (TN 208). Andahl's desperate self-description is repeated as a refrain by Emmerich in India. It could easily be the weary confession of clandestine life from a member of the Italian Red Brigades or the German Red Army Faction while in ideological defeat and on the run at more or less the same historical time frame as the narrative. Again, although DeLillo constructs the cult in strict formalism, his realist sensibility endows it with a concrete historical language.

13. This point of view is echoed by Frank Volterra's stunning summation of the twentieth century:

> "Film is much more than the twentieth-century art. It's another part of the twentieth-century mind. It's the world seen from the inside. . . . This is where we are. The twentieth century is *on film*. It is the filmed century. You have to ask yourself if there is anything about us more important than the fact that we are constantly on film, constantly watching ourselves. The whole world is on film, all the time. Spy satellites, microscopic scanners, pictures of the uterus, embryos, sex, war, assassinations, everything." (TN 200)

It is indicative of Volterra's own self-enclosure that he doesn't realize the incompatibility of two tautological universes. How could the cult agree to become part of this total scopic self-reference, when its entire existence is based on exorcising historical totality by reproducing in practice its totalizing logic?

14. See Le Clair, *In the Loop*, p. 192.

15. Le Clair develops this point convincingly and connects it to the imperialism of print language. See ibid., 193–94.

16. The two may be substantially intertwined. Violence has always been a primary component of religion (certainly monotheistic religion), while the spectacle of contemporary violence assumes at times an essentially religious frenzy. Says DeLillo: "I am interested in religion as a discipline and a spectacle, as something that drives people to extreme behavior" in Le Clair, "An Interview with Don DeLillo," p. 26.

17. Anthony de Curtis, "'An Outsider in this Society,'" p. 57.

18. Maria Nadotti, "An Interview with Don DeLillo," *Salmagundi* 100, Fall 1993, p. 93.

19. This observation initially belongs to Dennis A. Foster, "Alphabetic Pleasures: *The Names*," pp. 159–60.

20. The extraordinary story of *November 17* is unique by all standards of so-called urban guerrilla warfare. Its history has unfolded like a grand serial novel within the neo-Hellenic imagination, spanning nearly three decades, and is by all accounts still unfinished. (The stunning developments in July 2002, which brought about the sudden arrest of seventeen members and has effectively led to the group's demise, figures as the serial's most recent, but hardly final, chapter). *November 17* became legendary if for no other reason than that, since 1976, when it appeared on the scene with the assassination of the CIA chief operative in Athens, no member had ever been discovered and its composition was shrouded in mystery and rumor. The legend was nurtured, not merely by the longevity of its mysterious existence, but by multipage declarations accompanying the "terrorist" actions, whose authorial erudition, incisive sarcasm, and sometimes impressive economic analysis made them alluring commodities to the mainstream press, which continued publishing them despite the fact that for a time they were considered documents of high treason and their publication a criminal act. The paradoxical complicity (almost erotic attraction) between the most visible mass media and the most phantom political entity in the country—the unbreachable mystery surrounding the identity of the group had in its heyday (the 1980s) granted them metaphysical cult status—was itself a mythistorical project on a collective scale, a huge Balzacian enterprise that implicated the imaginary of the entire nation. I elaborated on the logic of this self-fictionalization and its national(ist) values in "*Nea Taxe Thymaton*" [New Order of Victims], *Planodion* 17 (December 1992), pp. 615–24. Since the 1990s, however, the group's increasing ideological confusion (which, to no surprise, coincided with its loss of irony and subversive humor) made for rather boring fiction. This degeneration was also fed by contributions from the State Department and major American media, who, in a blatant gesture of harassment and political blackmail, kept using the mystery of *November 17* to declare Greece a terrorist haven (including the ridiculous charges that the group had links to the governing socialist party). The recent events have gone a long way to dispel both the U.S. imperialist fantasy and the Left's imaginary investment in the urban guerrilla romance. Yet the torrent of self-examination these events have brought out throughout Greek society, ranging from serious analyses to idiotic bravado in an unprecedented barrage of mass media images, suggests that the grand serial of national self-fictionalization remains unfazed.

21. Presumably, this is why DeLillo returns to Athens in *Mao II*. Athens becomes again the interstitial space where an American writer (who is such a total recluse that he has become only a name) and an Arab political radical meet in an obvious gesture of cultural negotiation. From a certain point of view, both embody a terrorist logic in respect to the culture they inherit. But their encounter can only be effectively staged in modern Athens, in the midst of a culture that takes place (actualizes itself) in the form of unaccountable street noise, a flux of "nameless things."

22. As extreme or sophistic as it might sound, this meditation could have taken place from the point of view of "DeLillo in India," although I am not the appropriate person to undertake it beyond a mere hint. Contrary to Brademas's distinction between Greece and India as spaces of precision of detail and lack of common measure respectively, the novel demonstrates a capacity to weave the two spaces together in one overarching theoretical language. It is the extraordinary talent of Don DeLillo that makes possible in the same novel, in the same framework, such different conceptualizations.

23. Derrida, "Des Tours de Babel," pp. 165–66.

24. Don DeLillo, "The Power of History" *New York Times Magazine* (Sept. 7, 1997), pp. 60–63.

PART FOUR

Beyond the Nation

Looking to the twentieth and twenty-first centuries, the essays in this section examine the role of translation in an increasingly interwoven, globalizing world.
Here, translations become exemplary "traveling texts," capable of highlighting
the complex interactions between still vital nationalisms on the one hand, and
growing local and international cultures on the other. Four of these essays explore colonial and postcolonial issues in texts from francophone Africa, India,
South Africa, and Latin America, while the fifth and final essay takes its literary
example from the war-torn Balkans. As each "thick description" suggests,
though in very different ways, translations today demand an educated reader to
evaluate their aesthetic and political implications.

Françoise Lionnet's opening essay, "Translating Grief," foregrounds "the ambiguous powers of language and education in the postcolonial world." Her reading of Maryse Condé's novel *Heremakhonon*, and her comparison of it with
Teresa Hak Kyung Cha's *Dictée*, work through a theoretically rich paradox in
translation. For if the terms "grief" and the etymologically related "grievance"
evoke different reactions to loss, their linguistic and psychological connections
make them important to consider together: "what might it mean to grieve in the
face of losses that are so easy to attribute to another's perceived failures," as
Veronica in Condé's novel does? And what might it mean, asks the Korean
American narrator of *Dictée*, to suffer loss and to grieve, as a colonial subject for
whom there can never be just one nation? Lionnet astutely reminds us that these
are questions to consider not only as we read these particularly eloquent texts,
but also as we look to the binary oppositions and conflicts that confront us as educators and readers in our contemporary, post–9/11 world.

Gauri Viswanathan takes her texts from an earlier, and equally poignant, historical moment, when an anticolonial nationalism clashed with internationalism in post–World War I India and Ireland. What, she asks, were the motives of
cultural and literary translators such as James Cousins, "the Irish poet in India,"
and the Indian poet Rabindranath Tagore, who advocated internationalism at
this troubled time? "Were they simply continuing colonial rule in a different
form? Or were they crafting a worldview that sought an ideal meeting point as

much between philosophy and politics as between a narrow, provincial nationalism and rank colonialism?" Through her historically and politically informed analysis of Cousins's failed attempt to construct a spiritual internationalism (an attempt that stumbled on its racialized foundations), Viswanathan deftly reveals the "acute difficulties [he] faced in developing an aesthetics that could accommodate politics without being subordinated to it." Perhaps, she suggests, such difficulty helps explain why today's internationalism is measured in economic rather than spiritual terms.

A keen awareness of the ongoing shuttle between local and global, national and transnational also characterizes Vilashini Cooppan's engagement with the very different writing of the new South Africa. Tracing language, theme, and political issues in J. M. Coetzee's 1986 *Foe*, Achmat Dangor's 1997 *Kafka's Curse*, and Coetzee's 1998 *Disgrace*, she notes, "to write South Africa in the texts considered here, it also becomes necessary to write the world." Not that such a feat of literary and cultural/political metamorphosis is easily performed or always recognized. But the clear resistance of these texts to unitary structures in time and space contributes to a new sense of national identity, "'something struggling to be born,' that might be the transnational nation." As Cooppan shrewdly leads the reader into the nation by traversing it, she reminds us that comparative literature and postcolonial studies do their best work when they "choose to trouble that particular trajectory that places nation first and globe after."

Yet the international critical contexts into which texts are now translated and received can certainly cause problems. Sylvia Molloy notes, for instance, the tendency in the United States to use terms such as "postcoloniality," and "magic realism" as shorthand for Latin American literature as a whole, homogenizing whole ranges of texts while eliminating others that do not fit these preconceived categories. "This is a postcolonialism that, formulated 'over here' (by this I mean the U.S. academy), signifies one thing, while 'over there' (in Latin America, itself a site of multiple enunciations), it signifies something quite different; or, better said, signifies many different things." Similarly, magic realism is "a mode *among many other modes of literary figuration in Latin America.*" If "postcolonial studies should afford a way of teasing apart differences instead of erasing them," Molloy also persuasively argues for a truly transnational discussion engaging scholars from the United States with scholars from specific Latin American settings, and for greater awareness of local modes of production, theorization, and reception. Though there may be no quick fix, Molloy calls attention to these important issues "in the hopes of generating a more thoughtful debate on Latin America from within the U.S. academy."

Focusing on Milorad Pavic's 1984 *Dictionary of the Khazars*, David Damrosch also grapples with troubling contrasts in local and global readings. Pavic's widely acclaimed novel takes translation as its explicit theme. But its own literary border-crossing highlights its political—and ethical—complexity. Though the novel is commonly read in translation as a "tour de force" of postmodern "world literature," Damrosch reminds us that it is interpreted locally as a fierce defense of Serbian nationalism. Indeed, "what the double life of *Dictionary of the Khazars* demonstrates is the major difference between a work's life in a national context as opposed to a global context." Damrosch suggests that we take Pavic's nationalist agenda seriously, and "confront the ethical choices that the novel is pressing us to make." But it is up to the reader to decide what use to make of such contextual understanding. Perhaps the best strategy is to cultivate a "detached engagement," aware of the local and the global contexts in which this, and any work of "world literature," must be read. In this brilliant encounter of texts and contexts, originals and translations, the reader becomes an educated site of freedom and ethical responsibility, where local and global meet and can sometimes decide to settle their differences.

Translating Grief

FRANÇOISE LIONNET

In her 1993 essay, "Order, Disorder, Freedom, and the West Indian Writer," Maryse Condé takes a clear-eyed position on the *créolité* movement, and on its leaders' 1989 manifesto, *Eloge de la créolité*.[1] She criticizes, in a thoughtful tone, the *mots d'ordre* or "commands" that the authors of the manifesto have felt entitled to dispense to their fellow Antillean writers. She pointedly surveys the numerous literary taboos and prejudices that have served as creative straightjackets for Caribbean writers, restricting them to themes and idioms that, in her view, deaden the imagination and stifle the ability to dream. She bemoans the continued invisibility of women writers, and of their imaginative contributions to the existing history of Caribbean literature. Her message resonates with those who have embraced her impertinent desire "to challenge conventions, and to defy dogmatisms and totalizing myths of all kinds."[2] It was inevitable that the author of *La Parole des femmes* would find it difficult to stomach some of the rhetorical excesses of the créolistes and their blindspots with regard to gender representations.[3] Since her first novel, *Heremakhonon* (1976), Condé's work has consistently focused on the complexities of gender imbalance, including the vexed issue of unresolved racial grief and the melancholic disidentifications that colonialisms produce.[4]

Condé's essay, and the volume on *Penser la créolité* that she subsequently edited, did not endear her to the créolistes.[5] They riposted in a 1999 interview with Lucien Taylor in *Transition* entitled "Créolité Bites."[6] In it, Raphaël Confiant stated that "[c]ertain Antillean authors, whose popularity is in free fall . . . are scared of being replaced by us. . . . I guess when I am sixty and see young authors . . . coming out with new works and a new theory, I'll fear that they are replacing me. . . . These Antillean authors who charge us with exoticism are worried that we are stealing their thunder" (153). Using inflammatory rhetoric to reject what they qualify as these Antillean authors' own brand of "the great feminist discourses still in fashion in the West" (154), the créolistes implicitly mock Condé as a has-been. Such literary and critical jousting is common among Parisian as well as Antillean intellectuals, and my purpose in this essay is not to survey in detail those various critical *prises de position*. Rather, I want to suspend the question of créolité altogether, and go back to Condé's early work to disprove the parochial views expressed by the créolistes, and their charge of "self-conscious cosmopolitanism" (151) against her work. Examined in light of current critical concerns about language and power, her early work not only sustains further critical scrutiny, but emerges as a poignant and lasting contribution to our understanding of both political and aesthetic issues. Condé has always engaged with large intellectual questions, from feminism to linguistic diversity, and in this paper, I want to take another look at the way language and loss are thematized in *Heremakhonon*. To develop this point, I will read *Heremakhonon* together with the Korean American writer Teresa Hak Kyung Cha's autobiographical fragments *Dictée*, a book that articulates a similar problematic in a lyrical mode that contrasts sharply with the psychological realism of Condé's style.[7]

Long before Condé stated her critical position on the various "commands decreed about West Indian literature" ("Order" 122) by her fellow male writers and critics, *Heremakhonon* contained in narrative form an implicit theory of "order, disorder, and freedom" and an imaginative engagement with colonial, neocolonial, and postcolonial history. To re-read this first novel in the critical contexts of traumatic historical events is to deepen our understanding of the originality of Condé's early vision, and her choice of a narrative strategy that links the theme of individual grief to the issue of social injustice. Foregrounding the ambiguous powers of language and education in the postcolonial world, *Heremakhonon* illuminates the role of the writer as cultural translator, border-crosser, and sexual transgressor. Reading this novel with *Dictée* will allow me to dwell on the spectral elements of both narratives, their hauntings by the ghosts of two young students whose untimely deaths set in motion patterns of disorder, unrest, and possibly freedom for the respective narrators. It is to the disappearance and death of these students that the novels ultimately bear witness, as both authors present the pedagogical as a paradoxical site, one that is linked to both creative and criminal impulses. Condé and Cha focus our attention on the role of education and its complicity with systems of order and power. They both frame experiences of authority and loss within a thematics of grief, and they use as leitmotif the incommensurability of different linguistic systems of meaning. Their sensitivity to the melancholic aspects of racial and linguistic othering reverberates with timely theoretical and cultural concerns in both francophone and American studies contexts.

In *Heremakhonon*, which was republished under the title *En attendant le bonheur* (*Waiting for Happiness*) in a second edition by Seghers in 1988, a heavy burden is placed on the figure of the "teacher" as potential enforcer or instigator, legislator or rebel. But as the title indicates, the waiting game the narrator Veronica Mercier plays makes her a failed agent of freedom for her young African students. In Teresa Cha's *Dictée*, it is education as a "site of subject formation"[8] that is foregrounded, as well as the exercise or activity of translation (the *thème et version* ritual of the French school system). Cha's novel raises the theoretical issue, now commonly discussed in translation studies, of the "ideal of equivalence" and the "*ethos* of fidelity"[9] that can mask the subtle and problematic relationship between the cultures in presence or the historical correspondence between words. Both novels carry a somewhat "hermetic" title that requires translation and explication for the reader to grasp fully the allegorical intent of the narratives. For the average francophone reader of Condé's text,

Heremakhonon is an unreadable Malinké word, whereas within the discipline of Asian American Studies, *Dictée* is an opaque title that requires elucidation.

When I first read and wrote about *Heremakhonon* in the early 1980s, I was fascinated by Condé's satirical tone, her allegorical treatment of exile and desire, and her portrayal of what she has termed (in her interview with Ina Césaire) an "anti-moi."[10] This anti-autobiographical character, Veronica Mercier, journeys to Africa in search of a (racial and cultural) genealogy, a beginning or an origin, "Un commencement possible" (18) [Possibly . . . a beginning (7)]. She goes to an unnamed country to work as "coopérante" (58) and "professeur de philo" (47).[11] Condé's ironic indictment of the "search for origins," a common theme of the literature of negritude produced by the male writers of the 1930s and 1940s, was an energizing and productive discovery. But what I did not dwell on is the role or identity of Veronica as a teacher who fails to acknowledge the social bonds that link her to the lycée students eager to engage her in political conversations. This prominent motif engages us as readers and as "postcolonial" teachers who cannot but interrogate Veronica's lack of involvement in the social and political spheres, and her sexual liaison with the controversial politician Ibrahima Sory. It also puts into relief the role of language and power in the classroom and community, thus echoing the pedagogical concerns that remain central to the field of postcolonial francophone studies.

Lost in Translation: Véronica and the Abandoned Brother

Upon disembarking from the plane that brings her from Paris to Africa, Véronica is entrusted to one of her "futurs élèves Birame III" (21) [future students, Birame III (8)] (named the "Third" because there happen to be three students "with the same name in the class from the same village"). Birame attempts, in vain, to interest her in the political situation of the country in which she has just arrived. He is also assigned the task of teaching her Mande (36/17), and calls her his "grande soeur" (90) [big sister (47)], revealing the faith he puts in her, and the possibility of kinship that as a black "coopérante" she is led to communicate. She experiences Birame's reactions as unwelcome demands, feeling overburdened by his expectations. Being too self-involved to become fully aware of the true nature of these expectations, she cannot adequately recognize, let alone acknowledge, that his wishes and his insights are mirror images of her own self-deprecating quest for identity and community. Birame plays the part of a native informant who can "translate" the local culture for her. Their relationship presents the promise and the possibility of reciprocal exchange and learning. Yet it is not until after the students' strike and the disappearance of Birame—who becomes the first "Martyr de la Révolution Africaine" (134) [Martyr of the African Revolution (73)]—that Veronica begins to pay attention to the historical part he plays in a crucial counternarrative, the one that haunts her own narcissistic quest.

When the seriousness of the situation pierces through to her lulled consciousness, she finally recalls (with a glaring sense of disconnection) her callous indifference to his earnestness about history and politics: "Bizarre comme je recommence à penser à Birame III après l'avoir longtemps tenu éloigné. J'ai rêvé de lui. Notre première sortie quand il me servait de guide à travers la ville et que je l'écoutais si peu" (238) [Strange how I'm starting to think of Birame III again after having kept him at a distance for such a long time. I dreamed of him. Our first outing across the town when he acted as my guide and I hardly listened to him (134)]. She also evokes the forty young men, her class of eager students, who had started out so well disposed and full of affection toward her, but who end up being thoroughly disappointed by her irresponsible connection with corrupt power in the person of her lover, Ibrahima Sory. Veronica's failure to be an enlightened questioner in the classroom links her to the criminals, the politicians whose reign of terror masquerades as law and order, and who perpetuate a form of violence "sourde et secrète qui s'exerçait quotidiennement et en toute impunité sous les masques de l'Ordre et de la Loi" (299) [underhand and secret, that has become a daily occurrence carried out with impunity under the guise of Law and Order" (168)].

As a pedagogue, Veronica is in the ambiguous position of having to enforce rules while also being expected to encourage her students to develop critical thinking—the task of philosophy—and to question authority in a way that can ultimately lead to disorder and revolution. Having failed to live up to this challenge, she is left with a sense of emptiness and loss, a *"Rien"* (312) [*Nothing*] (175) which, at the conclusion of the novel, leaves her trapped as a subject whose identity has been shaped on a postcolonial historical stage of guilt and shame. Although she is able to escape back to Paris, her inability to translate her experiences into the language of grief condemns her to be "Piégée . . . Parmi les assassins" (314) [Trapped . . . in the arms of an assassin (176)], who has managed to corrupt the process of independence. The novel delivers us a character that is numb, unable to grieve for the loss of her friends and students, and unable to take a stance with regard to the injuries that have been perpetrated against them. Her ironic posture incorporates an ambiguous relationship to the politics of victimization and violence, and the patterns of passivity and fatalism (252/141) that she suspects she is misreading into the behavior of the local population. She is trapped in a narrative of guilt but continues to blame others around her for her own passivity and inertia, all the while projecting a discourse of grievance onto the Africans themselves.

Veronica's experiences in Africa constitute her as a subject of law rather than as an agent of freedom because she is unable to make the imaginative leap required of her as a pedagogue. The social disorder that has erupted as a result of the strike finds no concrete or active echo in her. She remains peripheral to these events, waiting on the sidelines, justifying her passivity as a covert strategy of "investigation" and "objectivity" (270/150–51), while maintaining her posture of self-deprecation and derision. Veronica thus comes across as a teacher who upholds the order of power and fails miserably at helping her students articulate their grievances. Failure to grieve for her own sense of racial and social losses makes her unable to hear the legitimate questions that Birame III and the other students put to her, and unable to recognize the structure of grievances that is in fact their common lot. The disappearance and death of Birame III and the arrest of the proctor, her friend Saliou, provide her with tragic opportunities to ask more questions. But she is incapable of doing so and remains inert, at an impasse.

It must be noted however that the book *Heremakhonon* begins with an epigraph from the philosopher Pascal: "Je crois volontiers les histoires dont les témoins se font égorger" [I am willing to believe the stories whose witnesses have their throats cut]. This paratextual element suggests that the author is signaling to her readers the importance of making the imaginative leap that the character of Veronica cannot. As Lorraine Piroux has shown in her book, *Le livre en trompe l'oeil ou le jeu de la dédicace*, dedications and, by extension, epigraphs establish a contract between author and reader, and articulate an oppositional aesthetic that undoes the textual order of narrative representation.[12] Pascal's statement, in such a reading, would require of Condé's reader that he or she make a Pascalian leap of "faith" ("je crois volontiers") in the plausibility of the counternarratives about the deaths of innocent citizens and about the oppositional practices of the powerless under the official appearance of calm and order. The epigraph warns the reader that Veronica Mercier is an unreliable narrator whose unhappiness and subjection to official power feeds a form of melancholic narcissism.

Véronica is a classic example of the Freudian melancholic subject who maintains a stance of self-deprecation and derision because she is unable to mourn for her own lost "origins." According to Freud, the melancholic subject's "complaints are really 'plaint' [or 'plainte'] in the old sense of the word. [She is] not ashamed and [does] not hide [herself], since everything derogatory that [she says about herself] is at bottom said about someone else."[13] Freud's argument that the melancholic subject suffers from a displacement of affect points to the fundamental confusion or identification between the subject and her object of derision and resentment. When she accuses the citizens of Africa of dissimulation and cowardice, "ils sont restés derrière leurs portes closes, couchés sur leur grabat" (312) [they remained behind closed doors, lying on their lice-infested straw beds (176)], instead of engaging in massive protest against the regime of "Law and Order," it is her own passive behavior that she is implicitly and ultimately condemning.

In the end, Veronica leaves Africa behind but this "abandoned object" (Freud 248) is figuratively retained within her psychic economy in the person of the "balayeur de la rue de l'Université" (312) [streetcleaner on the Rue de l'Université (176)], whose quiet presence concludes the narrative. Her melancholic ego continues to be haunted by this figure of a "brother" who, one might argue, is but a projection of both her dead student Birame and her dead friend Saliou. Condé's novel thus thematizes a crucial link between the experience of unresolved grief and the articulation of social and political grievances. Véronica's return to Paris and her reinsertion into the present time of the immigrant experience is but a provisional solution to the dilemmas of racial and political injustice that continue to haunt and trouble her.

GRIEF, GRIEVANCE, AND PEDAGOGICAL STUTTERING

This link between grief and grievance has been explored, in the American literary context, by Anne Anlin Cheng in *The Melancholy of Race*.[14] Cheng argues rigor- ously and convincingly that the United States is "a nation at ease with grievance but not with grief" (x) and with the melancholic aspects of unresolved sorrow and suffering. But, she also concludes, this melancholic consciousness may well be pro- ductive of cultural change, and "melancholia may be the precondition—and the limit—for the act of imagination that enables the political as such" (194). Veron- ica as melancholic subject might thus be read as the enabling figure for the possi- bilities of political action. More to the point here, I would argue that the Pascal epigraph quoted above is Condé's clue as to this enabling limit and its pedagogical function within the narrative context of *Heremakhonon*. The psychological stasis of the main character and her self-deprecating language serve as screens that hide, for her, the real work of resistance as well as the actual acts of "disorderliness" per- formed by the students and the people. Her melancholia veils the Lacanian Real, the unattainable goal of freedom in a political and cultural system where order (the Symbolic) and disorder (the Imaginary) have become confused due to her ambiguous personal and social position.[15] Veronica is at once a witness and the one who veils the truth, not unlike the historical Veronica of Christian mythology whose veil kept the marks and the signs of Christ's martyred face.

What interests me here is that Condé's novel articulates a different paradigm from Anne Cheng's theorization of "the melancholy of race." Condé helps us ask another kind of question: that is, What might it mean to *grieve* in the face of losses that are so easy to attribute to another's perceived failures (as Veronica does) that the immediate reaction is blame, anger, revulsion, or flight instead of pain and mourning (as was indeed the U.S. national reaction in the immediate aftermath of 9/11)? Where does grief hide when grievance takes over? The French word *grief* (grievance) comes to mind as an interestingly ambiguous term, as one of those *faux amis* as translators like to call words that are identical in two languages, yet have different meanings in each. To grieve is *avoir du chagrin, de la peine*, whereas to have a grievance is *avoir un grief*. These terms, their common etymology, and the interesting slippages of meaning that occur between the two languages refine Anne Cheng's formulation of melancholia and racial grief, forc- ing us to bear in mind that grief and grievance are co-constitutive linguistically as well as within the psychic economy of loss. They can never be two opposed concepts. The etymology of the word *grief* in French implies that both concepts— grief and grievance—are actually contained within one another. This suggests that the work of grief and the articulation of a grievance must go together for freedom to be achieved. These two sides of the same process are, however, in constant and unresolvable tension since each functions according to a different logic, lending to this process the air of an interminable search for freedom from sorrow and, simultaneously, for compensation.

The work of translation further underscores the sliding meanings that echo through etymologically close *faux amis* such as grief and *grief,* both of which derive from *grever,* the twelfth-century Old French word the primary meaning of which is *grave* or heavy. This etymology suggests that the gravity of any injury must be addressed both on the psychic and legal levels, or both within the private and public spheres lest they dissolve into melancholic conditions that would then be "fortified by a spectral drama whereby the subject [or the collectivity] sustains itself through the ghostly emptiness of a lost [and denigrated] other" as Cheng theorizes it (10).

In our own current historical predicament, it may be important to ask, with Cheng, the following question: When we are aggrieved by catastrophic losses that seem naturally to lead us toward the articulation of a just and noble *grievance* against a putative enemy, what do we do with our feelings of sadness and confusion? What does it mean for an individual, for a nation, to suffer injury and to denounce the political and psychological consequences of that damage in a way that focuses us on the need for retaliation and all the attendant public claims of retribution and reparation? Claims of injury need to be based on the foundational binary paradigms of "perpetrator/victim," "oppressor/oppressed," and "innocent/guilty" that require both terms in the opposition to remain yoked to each other, since there can be no victim without an offender. Put another way, claims of collective injury are grounded in the definition of a "we" that is pitted against a "them" whose identity thus becomes firmly delineated in opposition to our own, our group or our nation.

Condé's novel, however, shows us that, in the case of Veronica Mercier, this binary is unavailable. The distinction between "us" and "them" is not an easy one to make for this "trans/national" citizen whose search for ancestors blurs national borders and sends her to Africa on a learning (if failed) expedition. Furthermore, her role as teacher constructs her as both innocent and guilty, situated on the side of power but as questioner of the structures she inhabits, and thus as agent of both order and disorder. The realist mode of the narrative and the use of free indirect discourse convey with exquisite audacity the tangled psychic phenomena that burden Veronica. Condé delivers her to the reader as an ambiguously "transparent mind," and ultimately as a silent one.[16] Véronica becomes aware of the limits of language and can only stammer and stutter (to use a Deleuzian term) as she attempts to grapple with the ultimate foreignness of Africa and with the ruptures in the pedagogical fabric and meaning structures of her ovelapping worlds.[17] "L'éloquence politique m'a toujours paru une chose abjecte" (278) [Political eleoquence has always seemed abject to me (155)], she declares, and her tentative attitude as a narrator who is "pas capable d'avoir une opinion" (252) [incapable of having an opinion (141)] becomes the thematic equivalent of linguistically challenged speech.

If Veronica's melancholic self-deprecation keeps her far from lyrical flights of poetic prose, that is, by contrast, the strength of Teresa Cha's *Dictée.* But this difference in style underscores a thematic similarity that has uncanny resonances for the understanding of unresolved grief. *Dictée* offers us the narrative voice of a student, a Korean-born U.S. immigrant, trapped by transcultural forces, disciplined by a traditional set of rules, from grammar to religion, history to geography. Cha's book is striking for its multiplicity of languages, characters, images, and its intricately intertwined stories that shift from prose to poetry, words to images, past to present, history to fiction. The dominant note is one of anxiety about language and representation, visible on both the levels of theme and structure.

Learning to read, write, and spell in the proverbial manner of the French school system, the narrator takes dictation, "mimick[ing] the speaking" (3) of her teachers, and the proper order of words and their punctuation. Learning to translate herself into a system of historical representation that can only accent her difference of intonation and the different modulations of her family's journey through many layers of colonial encounters with Japan, China, and France, the narrator's exile is punctuated by many losses, especially that of her brother. To deal with these losses, she chooses a path of lyrical dis-order. In the middle section of the book, titled "Melpomene Tragedy," a site of memory and trauma is linked to the figure of this brother who was killed in a 1962 student demonstration in Korea. The cadence of Cha's poetic language opens a space in which there is a sorrowful attempt to translate grief:

> *There is no surrendering you are chosen to fail to be martyred to shed blood to be set an example one who has defied one who has chosen to defy and was to be set an example to be martyred an animal useless betrayer to the cause to the welfare to peace to harmony to progress. (83)*

> You, my brother, you protest your cause, you say you are willing to die. Dying is part of it . . . My brother. You are all the rest all the others are you. You fell you died you gave your life. That day it rained, it rained for several days. It rained more and more times . . . I heard that the rain does not erase the blood fallen on the ground. (84–85)

Returning after eighteen years to the moment and place of separation and division, the narrator explains that "the war is not ended": "We are inside the same struggle seeking the same destination. We are severed in Two by an abstract enemy an invisible enemy under the title of liberators who have conveniently named the severance Civil War. Cold War. Stalemate" (81).

The geography of Korea has become one with "Imaginary borders. Un imaginable boundaries" (87), split in two and thus mirroring the narrator's own sense of internal division, her psychic split as colonial subject for whom there can never be just one (*Un* in French) country, one nation. In the landscape of the demilitarized zone, it is brother against brother, "SHE against her," North against South, as a nation at war with itself becomes increasingly swallowed up in betrayals that arrest the process of grieving, and interrupt the work of mourning. The impossibility of grief is associated with the absurdity of having to imagine one's identity as constituted through an act of belonging to *one* nation and *one* language, as has been the norm in the Western nations addressed by her narrative. This norm, in the United States, includes the ideology of *e pluribus unum* and in France, the constitutional language that states that the nation is "une et indivisible" [one and indivisible].[18] The narrator, who calls herself the *diseuse* (3, 123, 133: an ambiguous French word that can mean the one who foretells the future, the one who tattles, or simply the one who knows how to speak, how to make speeches), raises questions about her epistemological and ontological status as a subject of multiple histories in which grief, mourning, and grievance have acquired such weighty connotations that she must end, paradoxically, in "immobile silence" (179). Faced with the impossibility of choosing just "one" language, and thus of saying anything, the "diseuse" is the split immigrant subject who has journeyed from a divided nation to an arbitrarily "unified" land, and finds herself, like Conde's Veronica, at an impasse. The past becomes veiled: "Hidden. Forbidden. . . . Veil. Voile. Voile de mariée. Voile de religieuse. Shade. Shelter . . . screen . . . behind the veil . . . of secrecy . . . veiled voice under breath murmuration render mute strike dumb voiceless tongueless" (127). The rupture of the border, like the stutter of the immigrant and the punctuation of poetic speech, inflect the English language with a stammer that communicates the poignancy of her situation and the instability of rules—be they grammatical, political, or cultural. Cha makes the loss of origin and language the thematic and structural equivalents of the loss of coherence and reality that serve to destabilize normative narratives of identity. The tragedy of Korea's partition, this complete and total severance is an "incision" (79) in the map of the present. It is a form of finality in which "The submission is complete" and all protest becomes futile. Only grief remains, with its procession of *un articulable* grievances.

Condé's and Cha's works illuminate a central paradox of identity politics in the context of traumatic events, one that might be formulated in this way: How do we *listen* to expressions of *grievance* and to expressions of *grief*? And to expressions of *grievance* that are primarily displaced expressions of *grief*? How do we respond without immediately transforming the conversation into a ground for immediate or future social, legal, or political action? Can we bear witness even in the face of our inability to understand and perhaps our refusal to judge? When a personal or collective history of trauma is still in the shadow of shock and amnesia, how can it be named? Finally how do we do so without pointing the finger, since as Trinh Minh-ha eloquently writes, "every discourse that breeds fault and guilt is a discourse of authority and arrogance."[19] Ultimately, it may well be that Maryse Condé's eloquent defense of dis-order is the most appropriate response in our own troubled and troubling political times.

I want to conclude with these thoughts about pain or trauma and its aftermath because both Condé and Cha give us the means to think differently about some of the binary distinctions that I have just outlined: that is, the ones between theory and practice, between excruciating affect and dogmatic speeches, between calls for compassionate recognition and calls for justice and retribution, in other words, between the private domain of *grief* and the more public arena of collective *grievance*. Their shared experience of war and loss, and the silences of their texts are the sites of "unclaimed experiences" that highlight the affective geographies of narrative subjects who seem caught between the private inability to mourn the past and the public refusal to feel self-pity or be treated as victim.[20] Their narrative registers take their readers to a level of poetic understanding where language and meaning can "vibrate and stutter,"[21] a vantage point from which the petty lines of criticial jousting with which I began this essay begin to fade into the realm of wooden speech. The troubling question of what to do with one's unresolved grief in the face of un-articulable grievances will however continue to haunt our understanding of the conflicted sites of personal and cultural trauma, and the emotional force that can ultimately translate our *grief* into *rage*.[22]

NOTES

1. Maryse Condé, "Order, Disorder, Freedom, and the West Indian Writer," eds. Françoise Lionnet and Ronnie Scharfman, *Yale French Studies* 83, 1993, pp. 121–35; Jean Bernabé, Patrick Chamoiseau, and Raphaël Confiant, *Eloge de la créolité* (Paris: Gallimard, 1989).

2. Ronnie Scharfman, text of program copy for the Conference on "Order, Disorder, Freedom" at Columbia Univeristy, November 16, 2002.

3. Maryse Condé, *La Parole des femmes: essai sur des romancières des Antilles de langue française* (Paris: L'Harmattan, 1979).

4. Maryse Condé, *Heremakhonon* (Paris: UGE 10/18, 1976); *Heremakhonon*, trans. Richard Philcox (Washington, D.C.: Three Continents Press,1982).

5. Maryse Condé and Madeleine Cottenet-Hage, eds., *Penser la créolité* (Paris: Khartala, 1995).

6. Jean Bernabé, Patrick Chamoiseau, and Raphaël Confiant in Conversation with Lucien Taylor, "Créolité Bites," *Transition* 74 (1998), pp. 124–61.

7. Teresa Kak Kyung Cha, *Dictée* (New York: Tanam Press, 1982).

8. Lisa Lowe, "Unfaithful to the Original: The Subject of *Dictée*," in *Writing Self, Writing Nation*, eds., Elaine Kim and Norma Alarcón (Berkeley: Third Woman Press, 1994), p. 43.

9. Ibid., p. 42.

10. Interview of Maryse Condé by Ina Césaire in Condé, *Parole des femmes*, p. 125.

11. Since independence, it has been common practice for the French government to send professionals to work as "coopérants" or "collaborators" in various "developing" francophone nations, including Louisiana. Here, the narrator is sent to work as "a teacher of philosophy" (22) in a local high school that follows the general curriculum of the French lycée, in which the discipline of philosophy has a prominent place during the senior year. Richard Philcox translates "coopérante" as "expatriate" (28), which conveys the right idea about the professionals working abroad during the postindependence years; but the word also carries an ambiguous meaning as "collaborator" with the regime in place.

12. Lorraine Piroux, *Le Livre en trompe-l'oeil ou le jeu de la dédicace: Montaigne, Scarron, Diderot* (Paris: Kimé, 1998).

13. Sigmund Freud, "Mourning and Melancholia," *Standard Edition*, gen. ed. James Strachey (London: Hogarth Press, 1955), vol. 14, pp. 239–60 (248).

14. Anne Anlin Cheng, *The Melancholy of Race* (New York and London: Oxford Univeristy Press, 2001).

15. For a discussion of *Heremakhonon* in terms of the Lacanian psychoanalytic concepts of Symbolic, Imaginary, and Real, see Françoise Lionnet, *Autobiographical Voices: Race, Gender, Self-Portraiture* (Ithaca, NY: Cornell University Press, 1989), pp. 172ff.

16. See *Autobiographical Voices*, ibid. In chapter 4 (182–90), I discuss Condé's extensive use of free direct and indirect discourse using Dorrit Cohn's formulation of psychological

realism as the representation of "transparent minds." See Cohn, *Transparent Minds: Narrative Modes for Presenting Consciousness* (Princeton: Princeton University Press, 1978).

17. Gilles Deleuze, "He Stuttered," in *Gilles Deleuze: Essays Critical and Clinical*, ed. and trans. Daniel W. Smith and Michael A. Greco (Minneapolis: University of Minnesota Press, 1997), pp. 107–14. See also the editors' introduction for a succinct and clear exposition of the process of "becoming-minor" in literary language as Deleuze undertands it.

18. Article 1 of Title II of the French Constitution of 1791 states that "le Royaume est un et indivisible" (the Kingdom is one and indivisible); the Constitution of 1793 went on to state in its Article 1 that "la République est une et indivisible." The question of diversity (whether linguistic, racial, or cultural) is thus a *constitutional* one that supercedes the nature of the regime (kingdom or republic). The ideal of unification animates the collectivity and guarantees the possibility of (sovereign, unitary) identity for each and every citizen.

For an important feminist reading of some of these questions see Shu-mei Shih, "Nationalism and Korean American Women's Writing," in *Speaking The Other Self: American Women Writers*, ed., Jeanne Campbell Reesman (Athens: The University of Georgia Press, 1997), pp. 144–62.

19. Trinh T. Minh-ha, *Woman Native Other: Writing Postcoloniality and Feminism* (Bloomington: Indiana Univeristy Press, 1989), p. 11.

20. I borrow the phrase from Cathy Caruth, *Unclaimed Experience: Trauma, Narrative, and History* (Baltimore: Johns Hopkins Univeristy Press, 1996).

21. Deleuze, "He Stuttered," p. 108.

22. See for example Renato Rosaldo, "Grief and a Headhunter's Rage," in *Culture and Truth: The Remaking of Social Analysis* (Boston: Beacon Press, 1989), pp. 1–21; or William H. Grier and Price M. Cobbs, *Black Rage* (New York: Basic Books, 1968).

"Synthetic Vision": Internationalism and the Poetics of Decolonization

GAURI VISWANATHAN

By the time of home rule agitation in both Ireland and India, anticolonial movements blended into a more internationalist vision then beginning to emerge in the years following World War I. To extreme nationalists, internationalism was a complete anathema, a more refined term to prolong the evils of colonialism indefinitely under the guise of a universal humanism. However, to those who still considered themselves nationalists, but believed they had a responsibility that extended far beyond the immediate goal of liberation from colonial rule, internationalism was the only solution to a world totally sundered by ethnic fratricide. The frightening reality of states at war with each other threatened to engulf with equal devastation those states aspiring to newfound independence. Therefore, when the Indian poet and Nobel laureate Rabindranath Tagore raised his voice in India on behalf of the "expanding soul of humanity," the language of universalism that underlined his appeal for "some spiritual design of life" earned him brickbats from his compatriots, who mocked his views as hopelessly romantic and beguiled.[1]

Incidentally, Tagore was a puzzle not only to his own countrymen. He equally intrigued those in other countries who looked to Indian anticolonialism as a potential model for combating racism in their societies. For instance, a short but cryptic letter by Tagore to *The Crisis*, a periodical devoted to African American issues, which was at the time edited by W.E.B. DuBois, raised eyebrows among African American readers. They were rightly stunned that Tagore, "a colored man," should so strike a universalist note even while experiencing the most humiliating forms of racism.[2] Tagore's call to Indians and other oppressed subjects to break out of the "forced seclusion of our racial tradition," astounded those who were trying to recover all that had been suppressed by centuries of white oppression. Tagore's declaration that "we must show, each in our own civilization, that which is universal in the heart of the unique" appeared to reintroduce the colonial logic of universal humanism, just as his appeal to fellow subjects to harmonize their growth with "world tendencies" seemed to place the center of their cultural development outside themselves. Yet as DuBois admitted, in a moment of total agreement with Tagore, the struggle against racism in the African Amer-

An earlier version of this essay appeared in *Ireland and Postcolonial Theory*, ed. Clare Carroll and Patricia King (Cork: Cork University Press, 2003).

ican community was falling victim to the same provincialism that had given the defining strokes to European colonialism and American white supremacy.

Tagore's isolation, especially in India, was all the more pronounced because his stance on internationalism as the political philosophy of the future appeared to converge with that of Europeans then residing in India. Indeed, internationalism appeared to many to have become the cultural priority of European émigrés in India who, neither sympathetic to the continuance of British colonial rule nor keen on seeing a violent takeover by extremist nationalists, favored a more spiritual successor to the inevitable demise of empire. Movements with a global reach, like Theosophy, gained strength during the same period, advocating a "brotherhood of man" as a metaphysical counterpart to a British commonwealth destined to supersede empire. From our own perspective as critics of the discourses of both nationalism and colonialism, the real challenge lies in evaluating the motives and intentions of those advocating internationalism. Were they simply continuing colonial rule in a different form? Or were they genuinely crafting a worldview that sought an ideal meeting point as much between philosophy and politics as between a narrow, provincial nationalism and rank colonialism?

Among Tagore's most avid supporters was the Irish poet, James Cousins. Born in Belfast in 1873, he left a flourishing poetic career in Dublin and settled in India at the behest of the Theosophist Annie Besant, who invited him to be the new literary subeditor of her newspaper *New India*. Though Cousins's views on Theosophy were fairly unexceptional, virtually alone among Theosophists he developed a perspective on war, violence, and fratricide that allowed for a creative synthesis of spirituality and politics and brought him much closer to postnationalist forms of thinking about decolonization—views that were highly suspect at the time.[3] His sympathy for Tagore was sparked by the hostility shown by many Indians to the latter's internationalism, to which they opposed their own nationalism as the only viable response to the oppressions of British rule. To Cousins the distinction ill-served the nationalist aspirations of the vast majority of Indians. He joined his voice to Tagore's to argue that, by imposing narrowness and exclusiveness on its aims and methods, Indian nationalism proved that its true enemy was not the British but, rather, itself. Describing nationalism as an "act . . . of national selfishness," but without quite dismissing it as false consciousness, Cousins maintained that the emerging, anticolonial sentiment in India was producing a new racialism, the "enlargement of consciousness beyond mere personal interest towards the realisation of a corporate life in the geographical or racial groupings called nations."[4] Like Tagore, he maintained that nationalism's self-centeredness cut it off from world unity, turned creative energy into destructive fever, and set up antagonisms generating more antagonisms.[5] Cousins reiterated in forum after forum that the enemy of Indian nationalism was not internationalism but an alien self-absorption. Needless to say, to Indian intellectuals such statements had the inflammatory power of a "red rag to a bull,"[6] and they saw both Tagore and Cousins hijacking the agenda for freedom from British rule and turning it into a more benign form of colonialism.

LITERARY MIGRATIONS

James Cousins's advocacy of internationalism marked the culmination of a poet's career split between Ireland and India. In his native Ireland Cousins had built an established literary reputation as a prolific author of numerous collections of poems and plays, and he was at the helm of literary activities involving Ireland's cultural renewal. His standing in the Irish literary revival was undisputed, yet his name dropped out of the canon on his departure from Ireland to India in 1915. Though Cousins continued to publish poetry in the four decades he spent in India, this work, along with his voluminous output of literary criticism, has received little if any critical attention even in India where, on the other hand, his work in education and public service is remembered fondly and celebrated. As far as the rest of the world was concerned, Cousins was a failed poet who had sacrificed whatever talent he had by migrating to India and throwing his lot with an esoteric movement more interested in occult happenings than literary achievements. In a strange admixture of condescension and compatriot feeling, Padraic Colum describes his efforts to see Cousins published in America as doomed to failure from the outset. Colum writes, referring to himself somewhat pompously in the third person, "The year was 19—, and James Cousins was then on a tour of the United States. So too was Padraic Colum, but Colum already had a substantial following and was the toast of the lecture-circuit. By contrast, Cousins wore a more anonymous face, acquiring the vague appellation of the 'Irish Poet from India,' a title conferred by William Rose Benét writing for the *Saturday Review of Literature*."[7]

Colum's comradely but dismissive comments about Cousins's work might appear warranted under the circumstances. After all, the market for poetry is never a certain one, especially the poetry of a man who could not be placed in any single, comprehensible tradition of writing. How were Western critics to deal with the work of a man who fused Irish mythological heroes and Hindu deities, or whose sense of poetic location was a blur between Dublin and Madras? Yet, until Cousins left Ireland permanently in 1915, he was widely regarded as an accomplished poet who held great promise in rising to greater heights. The poetry he wrote prior to 1915 was included in a number of significant anthologies of Irish verse, such as the *Dublin Book of Irish Verse, 1728–1909* (1909), the *Oxford Book of English Mystical Verse* (1916), *Anthology of Irish Verse* (1948), *1000 Years of Irish Poetry* (1949), and the *Oxford Book of Irish Verse* (1958). And though disparaged by Yeats and Joyce as a mere versifier, Cousins was a respected member of Irish literary and intellectual circles and stood at the forefront of a movement to revive Irish arts. And indeed even Yeats's and Joyce's contempt for his poetic talents was not entirely on aesthetic grounds, since it was also laced by a nervous apprehension about his popular reach. James Joyce, for instance, carped at Cousins for being favored by publishers who at one time rejected Joyce's work and published Cousins's poetry instead. In a string of biting doggerel stanzas Joyce lampooned what he considered his rival's contrived poetical ear.[8] Yet for all the sneering by Yeats and Joyce, there was no denying the active involvement of both James Cousins and his wife Margaret in all aspects of Irish political and literary life, the full range of which is measured by their embrace of a curious blend of scientific and antiscientific interests. They were involved in such diverse topics as astrology, Theosophy, occultism, vegetarianism, agricultural cooperatives, mythology, the promotion of the Gaelic language, the revival of Irish drama, women's suffrage, anti-imperialism, reincarnation, and antivivisectionism. Whatever the perspective in writing about the central figures embracing this range of interests and heterodoxies in Dublin in the early twentieth century, it was a fact that, as one critic observes, "the same name (Cousins) drops again and again."[9]

How then did it come about that James Cousins's name virtually vanished from the Irish literary canon, allowing Padraic Colum to demote Cousins unceremoniously to the ranks of a marginal, indeed unknown, poet? Acknowledged in Ireland at one time as a promising writer and committed intellectual, Cousins remained in other people's shadows all his life, perhaps achieving some measure of personal recognition only in India, where, on the other hand, he was better known for his contributions to education and social service than for his poetry and literary criticism. Certainly Cousins's name does not even enter as a passing whisper in any of the recent books on Irish studies, some of them justly acclaimed for their revisionist, postcolonial insights.[10] The relegation of James Cousins to poetic oblivion is accepted with stoic resignation in the following comment by Alan Denson, a compiler of Cousins's published record who was evidently on a crusade to save him from oblivion: "Words written or spoken by James Cousins or his wife Margaret E. Cousins were published widespread over three continents and at least eight countries, for almost sixty years. If at all, they are remembered now only in India."[11] Yet, as the same editor notes in an unabashedly partisan burst of indignant protest against the poet's neglect, "whilst [Yeats and Joyce] lived out their lives in service to their own self-centered ideals, Cousins devoted his best energies and his subtlest intellectual powers to the education of the young and the welfare of the poor and the oppressed."[12]

One important reason for Cousins's marginalization is his own tenuous position within the Theosophical Society, as well as in India under British rule. Though Annie Besant recruited him from Ireland to run her newspaper *New India*, she abruptly dismissed him when he wrote a series of trenchant articles on the Easter Rising of 1916. As a result of these fiery articles, Cousins was closely monitored by the British authorities, who regarded him as a subversive radical threatening to extend support to Indian insurgents.[13] Though James Cousins remained scrupulously loyal to Annie Besant, his wife Margaret felt no such compulsion and lambasted Besant for her hypocrisy and political cowardice.[14] Out of a job and adrift in India, Cousins subsequently accepted a teaching position in Madanapalle College, several hundred miles north of Madras. Removed from the main center of activities in Madras, where the Theosophical Society was located, and discouraged by the daunting challenges of teaching English poetry in the provinces, Cousins felt acutely marginalized, but never without purpose. He turned his position to good advantage by immersing himself in the educational reconstruction of India, while at the same time fusing his developing theories of education with sustained work in literary and art criticism. A visiting professorship in Japan during the heyday of Japanese modernism in art and literature clarified his own thinking about the potential models India needed most as it struggled to emerge from under the shadow of the West and assert its own distinctive voice. While in Japan, he met numerous artists, pacifists, and intellectuals, such as Kakuzo Okakura, Nuguchi, Tami Koume, and Paul Richard, who were all trying to find a pan-Asian alternative to the incursions of Western Civilization. His exposure to the convulsive debates in Japan on the attractions of Western modernization convinced him that India could not go the way Japan did in its uncritcal embrace of the West as the source of its own artistic experimentations. He saw in Japan a country that had turned its back on the richness of its own traditions, sacrificing creative inspiration for a hollow imitativeness. This view was to stay with him in his exploration of indigenous alternatives to the legacies of Western culture as India emerged from colonial rule, even as he resisted nationalism as a viable political philosophy.

Cousins's marginalization in Ireland after 1915—the year he sailed to India—must also be related to the momentous event in Ireland that occurred less than a year later. That event, of course, is the Easter Rising of 1916, which profoundly affected the ways that Irish intellectuals, writers, and artists henceforth approached the question of Irish nationalism. The catastrophic aftermath of the armed struggle for Irish nationhood, the executions of civilians, and the doomed heroism of the Irish insurgents all combined to throw Irish nationalism back into the post-Parnellite factionalism of earlier, bitter days. Yeats was provoked to write to Lady Gregory: "I had no idea that any public event could so deeply move me—and I am very despondent about the future. At the moment I feel that all the work of years has been overturned, all the bringing together of classes, *all of the freeing of Irish literature and criticism from politics.*"[15]

Yeats's disappointment at the intrusion of politics into literature is a telling commentary on the shattering impact of the Easter rebellion. The conviction that Irish writers could no longer indulge in pure romance would have in itself contributed to marginalizing someone like Cousins, who long after 1916 believed that the solution to world problems could only emerge outside of a political framework. However, though Cousins may have already left Ireland by 1916 and was therefore out of the immediate circle of debate and discussion, it is quite another matter to say that his work had become dated because it could not engage directly with this pivotal event in Irish nationalism. Indeed, I have already referred to his *New India* articles on the Easter Rising, which caused his dismissal as literary subeditor and put him under the watchful eyes of the British in India.[16] Furthermore, though he did not directly allude to the bloodshed of 1916 in his poems, he did write a poem, "To Ireland, Before the Treaty of December, 1921," that, in lines like "for your night of agonies, / I give dark songs I cannot sing," reflects his silent participation in a world no longer his. Numerous references to civil warfare in other poems reveal how disillusioned he had become by the violence unleashed by the movement for Irish home rule. The most outstanding of these poems is Cousins's moving tribute to his friend and associate, Francis Sheehy-Skeffington, with whom he had collaborated in publishing the newspaper *The Pioneer* in Dublin. Sheehy-Skeffington was, as Cousins describes him, "the first sacrificial victim in the Irish struggle at Easter, 1916," who was shot without trial even though he was trying to restrain the people from disorder when arrested. "In Memory of Francis Sheehy-Skeffington" includes these sorrowful lines:

> When with dark wrongs we waged our strife. . . .
> You in the clash of iron powers
> Should fall, and, falling, shake the world.

Cousins's lament for the death of his close friend valiantly strives to balance the destructive consequences of the Irish revolt with the heroic impulses from which it arose.[17]

But Cousins expressed his most sustained response to the events of 1916 through his literary criticism. In several books on poetics and criticism published in India long after he left Ireland, he passionately argued that Ireland's civil strife was symptomatic of a deeply flawed idealism existing at the core of the Irish literary renaissance, to which he directly traced the failed promises of the Irish political struggle. He maintained that the heady idealism of Ireland's nationalists was compromised by a "self-centered realism" never able effectively to ground politics in a goal beyond itself. If the Irish literary renaissance, like the Irish political struggle, fell far short of its aims, Cousins was convinced it was because of the movement's ineffective resolution of the opposing pull between romance and realism. Although this dissatisfaction was not his alone, what was distinctive is that the Easter Rising functioned in his critical writings as a tragic counterpoint to a more fruitful, alternative model that he found in the Aryan heritage of modern Indian nationalism. In the process of setting up an antithesis between the differential paths of Irish and Indian nationalism, Cousins reintroduced a language of race that, significantly and ironically, he made it the sole goal of his criticism to transcend.

Searching for Ireland in India

Before I unfold the full scope of Cousins's complex and contradictory racial argument, let me briefly outline his path to this position. However much his cultural criticism may have grown out of his need to provide a corrective to the alignment of the arts with functionalism and pragmatism, he was all too aware of the political realities that informed his public role as critic and educator. The substantial body of his work published in India represents his attempt to work through issues of realism and idealism in art by applying theosophical principles, or what he typically called "deeper unities in literature."[18] Cousins claimed that his discovery of Theosophy led him to a discovery of Ireland itself. But the discovery is made less on the principle of connection than on an awakened perception of the scale of both Theosophy and Ireland. Whereas he had earlier learned about Theosophy primarily from "small manuals," as he contemptuously described them, just as Ireland too was dimly perceived as a place confined to the known and the familiar, subsequently Cousins came to understand place through metaphysical elaboration, mysticism, and esotericism. Partly, the gain in perspective resulted from his tendency toward dialectical thinking, which projected the density of place as a product of metaphysical abstraction.

However, his early Irish poems were starkly naturalistic rather than abstract. He claimed that A. H. Leahy's new edition of the myth of the goddess Etain, *Heroic Romances of Ireland* (1905), had set his imagination alight with the vision of an embodiment of perfection captured by the goddess Etain, whom he imagined as descending from her original state as consort of the King of Fairyland to become the wife of the King of Ireland. Cousins's interest in a legend whose trajectory of incarnation is from universal imagination to geopolitical reality was driven by the will to turn mythological fantasy into national possibility. He wrote, "Here was matter to my taste, *the circle of the cosmic life completed in a single story*, and with a nearness to the details of nature and of human psychology in its earthly phase that excited the imagination with the anticipated delight of recreating the beauties of the temporal on the background of the eternal."[19] Cousins's compulsion to contain infinite planes of meaning within the recognizable limits of linear narrative was part of his attempt to reconcile the conflicting claims of idealism and realism in his representation of Ireland.

At the time that Cousins was at work on his poem "Etain the Beloved" (1912), he was also writing a book titled *The Geography of Ireland*, intended for publication by Oxford University Press. The book was never completed, but the two projects crystallized in his mind as a common one: he described the writing of Ireland's geography—with its own national unity—as less a process of cartographic empiricism than of imaginative selection. Written over five summer vacations, each time in a different part of Ireland, "Etain the Beloved" blended the scenery from the various provinces with such control that the details of nature never went beyond those of Ireland: as Cousins phrased it, "no lion roared, no parrot shrieked."[20] He disciplined his imagery never to exceed the bounds of Ireland and so delineated the geographical outlines of the nation through principles of selectivity and synthesis of remembered details dispersed across provinces. In "Etain the Beloved" he wrote the geography book that he never completed as a scholarly project, yet in form it combined the deepest impulses of geography, mysticism, and anti-imperialism. Filled with local details, the poem nonetheless connected in ever-expanding circles to incorporate other scales of existence that defined, for Cousins, the imaginative yet controlled possibilities of an emergent Ireland.[21]

The search for the reality behind the external Ireland led Cousins, through historical circumstances, into the folkloric bases of Irish Catholicism. Although, as he himself noted, a number of the reigning writers such as Yeats, AE, Douglas Hyde, and Samuel Ferguson were Protestants, he was convinced that, notwithstanding the Protestant domination of the arts, Irish civilization and culture lay elsewhere, but he was not prepared to say it resided in Catholicism. Rather, he argued that the sectarian divide prevented Irish culture from being fully captured by either Catholicism or Protestantism and so left its preservation in a presectarian memory intact. If, for Cousins, organized Irish Protestantism had turned its back on Ireland, organized Irish Catholicism manifested a split consciousness: "Religiously it turned towards Rome, but it had eyes and sentiment for indigenous legendary remembrance."[22] Enveloped by anti-Catholic sentiments all around him and taught that all Catholicism was superstition and paganism, Cousins was transformed by the realization that superstition had a literary dimension, or, as he described it more poetically, that superstition was "rooted in the silt of a long stream of traditional imagination" (49). That discovery created a new understanding that anterior memories exceeding the history of sectarian conflict inhabited his own Protestantism. This realization marked the beginning of Cousins's turn to difference as constitutive of Irish culture. In the long run, it prepared him for the discovery of India as both Ireland's other and true self, even as it displaced the need to acknowledge Catholicism as Protestantism's "other."

Cousins's attendance at a lecture given by Annie Besant on October 1, 1908—"a red-letter anniversary in my calendar"—literally changed his life (75). Instructed as were most young Irishmen of the time that Besant was an agent of the devil, especially because of her longtime intellectual partnership with the atheist Charles Bradlaugh, Cousins might have been predisposed to dismiss her influence. But he had himself been driven closer to atheism at the time Besant arrived in Dublin, his readings in "sixpenny Rationalism" being more than a casual interest. Not only had he begun to read seriously about Theosophy, he had also turned to the heterodox sermons of those like the Reverend Frederick Robertson of Brighton, who "put Truth in a position in front of its utterance in the Bible" (75). At any rate, by the time Annie Besant delivered her lecture on "Theosophy and Ireland" on that fateful day, Cousins was open to thinking about God and nation in different ways: "I gathered the idea that clairvoyance, or revelation, or both, declared a long process of racial and cultural evolution out of which Ireland was ultimately to emerge as the spiritual mentor of Europe, even as India had long ago been to Asia" (75). The dialectical association of spirituality with race—and with the evolution through various species and subspecies—offered Cousins one point of entry into working through the problems of idealism and realism in his work. Even as a poet in Dublin, Cousins had begun to reject romanticized reveries about the Irish past and, under the influence of Huxley and Darwin, was drawn to intellectual agnosticism and scientific determinism. But soon becoming interested in mystical experience, he turned to India for inspiration, but not merely because he associated the land with mysticism. Rather, he found India to be the practical site of a resolution between romance and realism that had long eluded him. The poetry and criticism published in India marks Cousins's engagement with as well as departure from the romanticist preoccupations of his fellow Irish poets, particularly Yeats and AE, as he sought out satisfactory models to deal with the pressing questions of decolonization and home rule, especially against the backdrop of European civil strife:

I knew it would be suicidal for me to attempt to intimidate my imagination with either the personality or the poetry of AE or Yeats, though much of their early work had a permanent place in my memory. Mine must, to have any authenticity, be mine own, even if an ill-favoured thing. There was something to be sung, and a way of singing it. These should be at the highest. (216)

Though eventually Cousins came to see India as the source of a spiritual revival throughout the world, it is also evident India first offered him a way of working through problems of a narrow nationalism in Irish literature—problems he could not resolve simply by mythologizing the Irish past.[23] While, like many Anglo-Irish writers of the early 1900s, Cousins too participated in the Irish dramatic movement, writing romantic verse plays based on Celtic myth, such as "The Sleep of the King" and "The Racing Lug," he rejected mythological romance as too local and narrow. He found himself drawn to the larger project of establishing the common foundations of Irish-Indian culture as the first step toward the overthrow of colonial rule in both countries. In India he rewrote some of his earlier Celtic plays, reworking Hindu themes and legends into his new material in plays such as *The King's Wife* (1919), a poetic drama based on the life of the Hindu female poet-saint Mirabai. Such changes were not well received by Cousins's critics in Ireland, who were prone to describing Cousins's project of establishing Irish-Indian foundations as basically a "pagan" impulse, further marginalizing him from Irish intellectual life. They saw such forms of experimentation as an expression of the fashionable anti-Christian feelings then running rampant, which to his critics' minds self-consciously reproduced the tendencies against modernity, progress, rationalism, and materialism perceived to reside in the non-Western world.

Cousins's move to India during the heyday of the home rule movement enabled him to do more than merely participate in the Indians' agitation against British rule. By migrating, he also sought to shape the literary expression of Indian nationalism by importing into India the concerns of the Irish literary renaissance. But while the importation would prove salutary in some respects, it resulted in a peculiar situation where Cousins's remythologizing of the Irish past delinked him from Ireland and left him curiously removed from the realities of both place and time. The continuing use of Irish mythology in Cousins's Indian poems, sometimes with an Indian twist, leads one to ask whether Cousins was as interested in recreating the Ireland of his remembered past as in evoking a different sense of place altogether. In this evocation "Ireland" is produced not as a real place but rather a literary, philosophical, and political concept, just as India too for Cousins had a connotation that far exceeded its geographical limits.[24] By leaving Ireland Cousins did not lose his place in the Irish literary canon so much as dislocate the canon itself. Everything that he wrote in India in continuation of his poetic career in Ireland was displaced and truncated, vitiating any claim that he might have had to a place in either Irish or Indian letters. His Irish work was carried over into the Indian context, but only imperfectly and discontinuously. Indeed, it is telling that his most lasting contributions were in the area of commentaries on Sanskrit poetics, a field he virtually remade his own as if to compensate for the diminished returns on the cultural capital he had invested in Ireland.

If, on one hand, Cousins was able to widen the nationalist net to include the parallel histories of two colonized societies, on the other his attempt to reinvent a mythology of cultural identity that could accommodate both Irish and Indian histories paradoxically deracinated him from one place while rooting him even less firmly in another. His muse may have remained Celtic, as he wrote, but that could not alter the fact that "nothing was quite right with the world for the purposes of a sensitive poet."[25] The attempt to universalize the shared colonial histories of Ireland and India had the reverse effect of leading him to the recognition that local experience was too powerful to warrant such totalizing moves. Cousins realized this only when he tried to transfer the Christian concepts of atonement and incarnation first to Irish mythology and then to Hindu philosophy. He claimed that he had long suspected the doctrine of the Atonement because of its narrow interpretation of an event (the crucifixion and resurrection of Christ) for which both uniqueness and universality were claimed by the rival sects of Christianity. Yet he also felt that, under the "strange mixture of human disobedience and celestial bad temper leading to delegated crucifixion,"[26] there lay some imperfectly expressed mystery of the universe and life. This became clearer when, in his studies in the old Celtic mythology, he came upon the legends of Cuchulain who, like Jesus, had a "reputed" father, the earthly Prince Sualtam, and a "real father, Lugh, the God of Light and Master of all Arts." Cousins writes, "I came to realise that the localisation of universal truth was, in human conditions, an inescapable condition of expression; that all such expression everywhere had therefore to be interpreted by the intuition and imagination; and that any attempt to treat the local expression of universal truth as in itself final and universally obligatory was a fundamental error."[27]

It is evident in this statement how disparaging Cousins was of Christian Eurocentrism, but at the same time he resisted submitting to the view that all truth was relative. Though totally rejecting the imperialist belief that truth was "an entirely territorial and racial affair," while also contesting the "dry-rot of Christian thought and experience"[28] as the only witness of spiritual truth, he attributed an exemplary power to Eastern thought that probably went too far in the other direction. Cousins's sole logic in going this way was the simple one that, if Christianity's claims to universal truth were based on the sense of its own "racial ascendancy," then when other religions based their claims on nonracial grounds, their "truth" must be given greater credence. Therefore, when the hold of racial logic was broken, he believed it was possible to assert universal truth without submitting to the hegemonic control that racialism premised.[29] What is distinctive in Cousins's argument is that, instead of adducing a relativist position from a Voltairean rejection of Christianity, he retained a universalist emphasis by detaching race from its composition and so could assert the claims of non-Western religions to the status of truth. In a contradiction that was later to unravel his argument, race was the central category underpinning his assessment of whether truth was relative or universal. By implication, Cousins deduced, spirituality—and the internationalism that it promised—was impossible as long as the rhetoric of race continued to dominate the aspirations of both colonialists and nationalists. We can see here how closely Cousins's views mirrored Tagore's. Both their views depended crucially on distinguishing between what they believed was a contingent notion of truth and an idea of truth unshackled from the hierarchical relations of power, privilege, and patronage produced by racialism.

RACE AND SPIRITUALITY

In making such distinctions, Cousins trapped himself in a web of contradictions that exposed the shifting connotations of spirituality in the nineteenth century. In his own usage, spirituality had associations with race, as I noted earlier when I cited his references to Irish spirituality as a product of racial evolution. In one of his most significant works, *The Wisdom of the West: An Introduction to the Interpretive Study of Irish Mythology* (1912), Cousins describes the resurgence of Irish literary pride as the discovery of a common Aryanism. He emplots literary history in terms analogous to Annie Besant's and other Theosophists' deployment of a racial scheme,[30] tracing the culture of the Celts to an originary source in Asian religions. Subdivided into Aryan, Semitic, and Mongolian, these religions, he declares, had moved into Europe centuries before the birth of Christianity. Cousins cites Henry Maine's *Ancient Institutions* to argue that the "cultural tendencies" left by these older religions included Brehon laws, which, he claims, had striking affinities to Vedic laws. Like Vedic laws that were challenged by English law, Brehon laws and institutions were contested and ultimately overthrown by the Roman law of England in the seventeenth century. The intertwining of Brehon and Vedic laws, like the interweaving of Irish and Indian cultures, provided racial continuity to their common struggle against British colonialism. In a remarkable passage, Cousins writes:

> So subtly, however, had the Aryan influence intermingled with the culture of Ireland that when, once again, at the beginning of the twentieth century, the ancient Asian spirit touched Ireland through the philosophy of India, as conveyed to it through the works of Edwin Arnold and the Theosophical Society, there was an immediate response. Two poets (AE and Yeats) found their inmost nature expressed in the Indian modes. They found also the spiritual truths that Asia had given to the world reflected in the old myths and legends of Ireland; and out of their illuminations and enthusiastic response arose the Irish Literary and Dramatic Revival whose influence at its height was purely spiritual.[31]

The most striking aspect of Cousins's description of ancient Hindu influence on the Celtic renaissance is how much at variance it is with prevalent accounts of Irish-Indian cultural influences. Far from understanding this interest in terms of the Orientalist scholarship available to Irish nationalist writers, Cousins insisted on a pre-existing religio-racial mixture of Celt and Aryan. This unique mixture prepared the ground for the "discovery" of Asia's spiritual truths. The mythologies of the past are preserved and reproduced by what Cousins clearly regarded as a racial imagination. Hence he could argue that the literary revival of his time was an awakened memory of what had, in epigenetic terms, been suppressed by colonial rule.[32]

Drawing on Sanskrit poetics in an attempt to find a unifying principle of human experience that surmounted the exigencies of colonial control, Cousins's aesthetic theories anticipated and indeed even shaped attempts to construct a confederation of nations as a successor to Indian decolonization. Predicated on the Sanskrit principle of *samadarshana*, or synthetic vision, Cousins's notion of internationalism had an aesthetic character that was little understood even by his own fellow Theosophists. He took an avid interest in Indian art, challenging Walter Pater's dismissal of Indian art for its "overcharged symbols." What Pater saw as symbolic excess leading to vagueness and indeterminateness, Cousins interpreted as the capaciousness of *samadarshana* for overlapping meanings. Interestingly, Cousins saw the trend in contemporary European art verging toward the principle of *samadarshana:* Postimpressionism and cubism were essentially concerned with overlapping and enfolding visions. Taking note of Virginia Woolf's response to the first exhibition of Postimpressionist paintings held in 1910 as evidence of how human consciousness had itself undergone a revolutionary change, Cousins was totally convinced that the literature of the twentieth century would be indelibly marked by these changes in perception and understanding. Indeed, he argued that it was largely through literature and art, and *not* through the political order, that the new internationalism was being forged. Predicated on unity and composite vision, the aesthetic principles of Sanskrit literature were resurfacing in the Western poetic thought of the early twentieth century. The point of connection was synthesis, which Cousins claimed was the fundamental business of poetry. His preference for the poetry of the achieved vision rather than the analytic process of vision marked his search for a deeper unity in literature, rendering the antithesis between idealism and realism a false one. The complex delight in the process of exploration that the modern poets seemed to celebrate allowed for the unregulated, unpatterned search for unity that Cousins saw as a principle enshrined in *samadarshana*. By describing himself as an inheritor of the intellectual legacies of Sanskrit poetics, English romanticism, and Theosophy, Cousins fell back on a romanticist conception of bringing the creative intuition of the East and the critical intelligence of the West into a synthesis. Philosophically, his interest in Indian thought reflected his inner concern for the recovery of wholeness by civilizations that had forsaken spiritual growth for material progress. Politically, however, he felt such wholeness could be achieved only when colonialism was dismantled. And here resides an intractable problem in his thought, since even when he acknowledges the necessity for the dismantling of imperialism, Cousins insisted on seeking solutions outside a political framework. While internationalism was a goal of his work, both critical and creative, his attempt to realize world unity by reviving Indian nativism established a clear-cut polarity between Eastern spirituality and Western materialism. This polarity linked him perhaps self-evidently with English romanticism. Yet at the same time, his own turn to romanticism grew out of his profound revulsion from the horrors of World War I, which filled him with determination to replace narrow national prejudice with a philosophy of internationalism—a philosophy that had an aesthetic content along with a political objective.

Internationalism, "Synthetic Vision," and the New Romanticism

The central paradox is that Cousins's internationalism was mediated by his avid interest in Indian nativism, and it is in this incessant move between national and international interests that Cousins expressed the impulses of a new romanticism. Devoting himself to the recovery of indigenous literary traditions with greater energy than even the Indian nationalists of the time, Cousins was committed to the rehabilitation of Indian ideals in the fields of art, literature, and education, but less so for the sake of engendering a mood of patriotism. Confident that what he called the "unitive" vision of Indian culture and philosophy could provide an answer to world problems, he saw India—the "mother of Asian culture"[33]—as the focal point of a new world reconstruction. In a formulation borrowed from the famous axiom of the Japanese intellectual Kakuzo Okakura, who declared in *The Ideals of the East* that Asia is one, Cousins wrote, "in Asia all roads lead to India—or rather, all roads lead from India."[34] Cousins's pan-Asian faith was accentuated as much by his Theosophical belief as by his study of the works of contemporary Western pacifists and writers like AE, Edward Carpenter, Paul Richard, and Romain Rolland, all of whom affirmed that Asia could be the savior of the war-ridden West. The undermining of European imperialism therefore lay in a new romanticism whereby India's spirituality would save Europe from self-destruction and undo the effects of its sustained imperial depredations. Imperial dismantling was thus conceived less as a cataclysmic gesture of political liberation than the timely inauguration of a new era of pacificism, internationalism, and romanticism.

At this point it is useful to elaborate Cousins's very important concept of *samadarshana*, or synthetic vision, adumbrated most comprehensively in his work *Samadarshana (Synthetic Vision): A Study in Indian Psychology* (1925). This work best demonstrates Cousins's deft deployment of his skills as a literary and art critic in the service of world reconstruction. It reveals a carefully considered, if decidedly idiosyncratic, theory about the Indian renaissance. Against the grain, Cousins argues in this work that nationalism was not the driving goal of India's literary revival, as it was in the Irish. Because of a different motivation, the Indian literary renaissance followed exactly the *opposite* path of the Irish revival, with more fruitful results. While both movements were driven by a common spiritual orientation, Irish spirituality in Cousins's view had become essentially compromised by the impulses toward a "material and self-centered realism."[35] The result was a vicious internecine war whose level of violence was made possible, paradoxically, by the driving idealism of Irish nationalism.

India, on the other hand, was not hobbled by such contradictory impulses tearing between realism and idealism. What makes Cousins's argument so intriguing, and at the same time so troubling, is that he attributes India's escape from the fate of Ireland's failed idealism to the continuing vitality of its Aryan heritage. For Aryanism, in his view, had the distinct ability to turn diversity into a form of unity, a term that he also comes to accept as interchangeable with similitude. In a rather remarkable statement that glides over the pernicious history of Aryanism's racial politics, especially in South India, he observes that "the renaissances of India have been the recurrent protests of the apprehension of unity against a too elaborate diversity."[36] Thus, for Cousins, the Indian renaissance is not a moment of political awakening, but instead the timely reassertion of racial unity against an all-consuming diversity. In short, the literary renaissance is a recapitulation of the Aryan experience in India, a symbolic reenactment of the Aryan conquest of pre-Aryan India.[37] One should take note of the fact that Cousins avoids any association of the Indian literary renaissance with nationalism but rather identifies it with a movement toward aesthetic and philosophical unity. This fundamental difference between the Irish and the Indian renaissances explains for Cousins the differential path of internationalism in the two contexts. To the West, internationalism is a condition of release from political tyranny, "an event subsequent to the victory of the chained Titan over the tyrant Jove" (61). But to the East, he argues, internationalism is a metaphysical condition; it is not bound by or dependent on a linear time frame for the attainment of political freedom, but has a repetitiveness and cyclical quality releasing it from world-historical trajectories. In the ultimate analysis, the spiritual East's understanding of internationalism would have to be taken as the "measure and test of all movements that take to themselves the sacred name of freedom" (61).

And what is the nature of internationalism in Eastern thought, as Cousins understands it, and why is it a yardstick for evaluating liberation movements elsewhere? In a formulation that scrupulously avoided assigning political meanings altogether, Cousins described the struggle for freedom as essentially an expansion of consciousness.[38] Where such inner growth could be accommodated by external conditions, as at certain periods in history such as the Sung era in China between the tenth and thirteenth centuries, aesthetics and politics coexisted in perfect synchrony. During such times, human propensities for violence and coercion were kept in check as a matter of course by the refinements of cultural expression through literature, music, and art. On the other hand, where external circumstances (such as bureaucratic reason) resisted or opposed the expansive consciousness, the insistent demands of internal growth could only be met by violence. Cousins's cautionary example is the French Revolution. The violence associated with the French Revolution best exemplified for him the fraught consequences of the pursuit of liberty, equality, and fraternity, when its motivating idealism had to contend with those communitarian pressures that were essentially opposed to removing all restrictions on individual development and creating the autonomous individual. Under the weight of such pressures, the tendency to respond "with the instinct of the self" rather than by "abstract and universal thinking" compromised the possibilities of realizing the world ideal, which became in effect a group demand, an expression of tribalism, "with a tendency to return to the primitive assertion of individual freedom" (17).

The result of the friction between world idealism and political realism was the self-centered nationalism that Cousins anathematized as an aberration from the true course of human history. The French Revolution was history's prime example of the reduction of the ideal to the assertion of local, narcissistic needs. In Cousins's eloquent phrase, the demand for liberty, relieved of the logic of the complete ideal, fell "from the level of universal human speech to that of racial and national vernacular" (18). He was so convinced that the rhetoric of racial belonging thwarted the attainment of world unity that he saw his main challenge as that of asserting the world ideal without submitting it to a political framework. For when the quest for freedom is presented in political terms—or in terms of a world-historical model of progress, as it was in the case of the French Revolution—he believed it could only be expressed in the language of domination and subordination, and that in turn in the language of racialism. Thus, it is easy to see why the gains of European humanism and the European Enlightenment have consistently occurred at the expense of non-Europeans. Cousins quotes the nineteenth-century poet Francis Thompson to the effect that the "spacious century," which was born with the cry of "Liberty" in its ears and on its lips, boasted of having "seen the Western knee / Set on the Asian neck, / And dusky Africa / Kneel to imperial Europe's back." Under these circumstances, "equality" mapped out for itself a single hemisphere of the globe—the Western—and assumed a single complexion, that of whiteness. Likewise, "fraternity," with unseemly literalness, remained confined to masculinity until the new order of politically minded women in the early twentieth century challenged their exclusion from the electorate. As an era of "stultified idealism" (19), the nineteenth century had relegated aesthetic culture to a matter of taste and refinement, rather than regarding it as a means and expression of human freedom.

World War I, however, rudely shattered the expected fulfillment of the promises of liberal humanism. Employing a religious vocabulary, Cousins described the world war as a punishment for the ills of colonialism, as the world stretched out in supplication for some attitude to life, turning to the proverbial wisdom of the East to revoke the legitimacy of colonial tyranny. And indeed from this perspective imperialism is just as bad for the colonizer as it is for the colonized, imposing on the dominating group "false and selfish preoccupations that stand in the way of its attention to the natural evolution of its own national genius and pull it from the path of open rectitude into the twisted byways of dishonest thought, speech and action in the artificial defence of a false position."[39] Swayed by the power of liberal angst perhaps a little more than he may have realized, Cousins gave room for the articulation of a nationalist consciousness among the colonizers freed from reprehensible imperial possessiveness. Whatever the sources of such liberal guilt, it certainly led Cousins to believe that the cause of the world war was not confined to immediate actions of belligerence, but rather was a world-cause with world-responsibility in varying degree. In this reading, war is symptomatic of the "world malady" introduced into the world by colonialism, for which a "world remedy" had to be sought."[40]

As one of the most ardent exponents of internationalism, James Cousins urged that the horrors of the world war necessitated a model of world unity. But in developing such a concept philosophically he believed it was necessary to distinguish between a (negative) world unity forged by the domination of some countries by one master country and a more positive unity genuinely expressive of the principle of spiritual oneness. The positive notion of internationalism eschews domination as the principle of relations between nations. It offers a more egalitarian philosophy in which political freedom is attainable as a quest of the spirit. In this reworking, culture is the free space beyond religion and politics, the arena for the emergence of "truth." In elaborating theosophical principles of oneness to incorporate a view of nationalism as *internationalism*, Cousins gave expression to Theosophy as a fulfillment of romanticism.[41] Fused with Tagore's strictures on the dangers of bureaucratic rationality,[42] Cousins's Theosophy recapitulated the romanticist condemnation of nation-building at the expense of the "elastic and expansive" spirit of humanity. In Tagore's theory of nationalism Cousins found the most potent answer to the malaise spawned by the world struggle, "the point which would banish from criticism of his utterances the false antithesis of nationalism and internationalism."[43] The real struggle at every stage of human history, whether between or within nations, has been, Tagore tells us, "between the living spirit of the people and the methods of nation-organising; between the expanding soul of humanity (Indian or English) and mechanical limitations that refuse to adapt themselves to that expansion."[44] While this sounds very close to what I have described as Cousins's historical analysis of violence, Tagore was much less interested in probing historical causes for the clash between consciousness and administrative rationality. Indeed, Tagore was far more vague in his descriptions and resorted to metaphor and synecdoche to replace historical explanation, as when he described (false) nation-building through the symbol of red tape and organic nationhood through the symbol of the elastic band.

Cousins's fundamental challenges as a critic were two in number. The first goal was to detach the concepts of oneness, unity, and the common origins of all humanity from racial understandings, and the second was to reassert these notions—newly defined—outside of race. Rhetorically, it required him persistently to distinguish between two concepts of internationalism—as he did between two renaissances, two nationalisms, and so forth. On one level, such differentiation allowed him to distance internationalism from its imperial moorings. It further permitted him to expose cultural movements and migrations as a masquerade for imperialism, which, despite the pretense of forging a unity of nations, was solely driven by the impulse to dominate and appropriate. But at another level, the critique of imperialism's universalizing impulse included even his own migration to India, as well as his attempt to import the concerns of the Irish literary renaissance into another, apparently parallel setting. Cousins's autocritique is set against the backdrop of the historical course of imperialism, which clearly shows that the "plantations" of English settlers in Ireland and the coming of the East India Company were not international movements, but rather predatory excursions from the "lair" of nationalism intended to bring back as much prey as could be seized. Cousins's questioning of his own status as a cultural émigré fuses with his critique of imperialism's claims to internationalism.

But ultimately Cousins's vision of a postromantic internationalism failed him because the new, animated literary spirit that he hoped to see prevail was clearly marked in racial terms—the very terms that he claimed produced a false unity. By wishing to take the literary renaissance outside purely nationalist concerns, Cousins reintroduced Aryanism as a principle of creative change, thereby substituting one set of hierarchical relations with another. The interchangeability of philosophical unity with racial continuity may have been motivated by Cousins's overwhelming desire to prevent the appropriation of humanism by imperializing intentions. But it could not forestall the return to a hierarchical mode of cultural production, in which diversity is flattened out and replaced by sameness and oneness—all in the name of world reconstruction. "Realism" for Cousins came to mean narrow, local, narcissistic needs: it was an expression of a divisive ethnicity whose principle of difference militated against attaining the world ideal. "Idealism," on the other hand, was too rooted in conditions of temporality and political possibility to have any real meaning for Cousins. In his (misguided) reading of Indian history as an ongoing repetition of the Aryan experience—of the reassertion of unity against an all-consuming diversity—he found a way of getting beyond the limitations of realism and idealism as he had himself defined these terms. But by shifting spirituality back into the category of race (as had Ernst Renan and Matthew Arnold before him)—even though it was the very category he sought to dispel—Cousins drove his own work into oblivion, as other models of internationalism that were more overtly political and economic gained ascendancy and anti-Aryanism galvanized the twentieth-century movements of India's minority groups. If today internationalism signifies economic globalization rather than spirituality, it is a measure of the acute difficulties Cousins faced in developing an aesthetics that could accommodate politics without being subordinated to it.

NOTES

1. See Rabindranath Tagore, *Nationalism* (London: Macmillan, 1917).

2. "A Message to the American Negro from Rabindranath Tagore" *The Crisis*, 36(10), 1929.

3. Cousins's most sustained work on this subject is *War: A Theosophical View* (London: Theosophical Publishing House, 1914).

4. James Cousins, *Modern English Poetry: Its Characteristics and Tendencies* (Madras: Ganesh and Co., 1921), p. 202.

5. See Tagore's *Nationalism* for the poet's most sustained and impassioned argument against nationalism.

6. James Cousins, *Samadarshana (Synthetic Vision): A Study in Indian Psychology* (Madras: Ganesh and Co., 1925), p. 61.

7. Alan Denson, *James H. Cousins and Margaret E. Cousins: A Bio-Biographical Survey* (Kendal: Alan Denson, 1967), p. 14. Benet's article appeared in the *Saturday Review of Literature*, vol. 8 (June 4, 1932), p. 772.

8. In his 1912 broadside, "Gas from a Burner," Joyce wrote: "I printed the table-book of Cousins/Though (asking your pardon) as for the verse / 'Twould give you a heartburn in your arse." *The Essential James Joyce*, ed. Harry Levin (London: Penguin Books, 1963), p. 349.

9. John Wilson Foster, "The Interpreters: A Handbook to AE and the Irish Revival," *Ariel* 11(3), July 1980, p. 69. Quoted in D. C. Chatterjee, *James Henry Cousins: A Study of His Works in the Light of the Theosophical Movement in India and the West* (Delhi: Sterling, 1985), p. 17.

10. Among the most significant works in Irish studies that have appeared in recent years are: David Lloyd, *Nationalism and Minor Literature: James Clarence Mangan and the Emergence of Irish Cultural Nationalism* (Berkeley: University of California Press, 1987), and Lloyd, *Anomalous States: Irish Writing and the Post-Colonial Moment* (Dublin: Lilliput Press, 1993); Declan Kiberd, *Inventing Ireland* (Cambridge, MA: Harvard University Press, 1996); Seamus Deane, *Strange Country: Modernity and Nationhood in Irish Writing Since 1790* (Oxford: Clarendon Press, 1997). All fine critical studies, none of them, however, makes any mention of James Cousins.

11. Denson, *James H. Cousins*, p. 14.

12. Ibid., p. 16.

13. There were precedents for British apprehensions: Charles Johnston (1867–1931) was a key figure in the Dublin Theosophical Society who came to India as a member of the Indian Civil Service. But he was forced to leave India because of his suspected political sympathies for Indian nationalists. As D. C. Chatterjee notes, the Dublin Theosophical Lodge was a primary channel of Indo-Irish interaction (*James Henry Cousins: A Study of His Works in the Light of the Theosophical Movement in India and the West* [Delhi: Sterling, 1985], p. 153).

14. James H. Cousins and Margaret Cousins, *We Two Together* (Madras: Ganesh and Co., 1950).

15. *Letters of W. B. Yeats*, ed. Allan Wade (London, 1954), p. 613; quoted in Seamus Deane, *A Short History of Irish Literature* (London: Hutchinson, 1986), p. 158.

16. The most hard-biting of these articles included "Patriot Bards and Ballad Makers: A Page from the History of Freedom by an Irish Home Ruler," *New India*, January 11, 1916, and *New India*, January 15, 1916; "The Irish Impasse and Its Lessons," *New India*, January 29, 1916; "Nationality and Art," *New India*, April 8, 1916; "The Irish Leaders," *New India*, May 4, 1916; "The Irish Revolt," *New India*, May 10, 1916.

17. James H. Cousins, *Collected Poems, 1894–1940* (Madras: Kalakshetra, 1940).

18. James Cousins, *New Ways in English Literature* (Madras: Ganesh and Co., 1920), p. 14.

19. Cousins and Cousins, *We Two Together*, p. 217.

20. Ibid., p. 218.

21. See Catherine Nash, "Geo-centric Education and Anti-imperialism: Theosophy, Geography, and Citizenship in the Writings of J. H. Cousins," *Journal of Historical Geography* 22(4), 1996, pp. 399–411, for an illuminating discussion of Cousins's involvement in geographical education. As Nash points out (400), Cousins's interest in geography was driven in part by a need to find a common meeting point between local pride and global

unity. He saw the study of geography as an excellent way of teaching students to resist Eu-rocentric values, while avoiding xenophobic nationalism through a discipline that en-couraged an imaginative rather than separatist identification with places.

22. Cousins and Cousins, *We Two Together*, p. 49.

23. The role of one country as the site for the working out of problems presented in an-other underlies the sentiment of interparty head John Costello, who announced in 1948 that Ireland had become a republic: "As an Irishman, I have pleasure in recalling that many of my race encouraged and were encouraged by the magnificent efforts of Indians to realise the national aspirations of our own great country." Quoted in Sarmila Bose and Eilis Ward, " 'India's Cause I Ireland's Cause': Elite Links and Nationalist Politics," in *Ireland and India: Connections, Comparisons, Contrasts*, eds. Michael Holmes and Denis Holmes (Dublin: Folens, 1997), p. 70.

24. It is also the case that Cousins justified the imaginative view of India by saying that the toiling masses had become alienated from their own land not only because of colo-nialism but also because of colonialism's effacement of the Idea of India.

25. Quoted in William A. Dumbleton, *James Cousins* (Boston, MA: Twayne, 1980), p. 105.

26. Cousins and Cousins, *We Two Together*, p. 68.

27. James H. Cousins, *The Renaissance in India* (Madras: Ganesh and Co., 1918), p. 8.

28. Ibid.

29. Cf. "[Christian Europe] cannot regard a presentation of truth in another land and through other instruments of revelation, together with its resultant culture, as other than outside its own circumference. The impact of eastern thought has to meet the opposition of the old spirit of racial ascendancy, which can only exist on the illusion of the exclusive possession of a universal truth." (Cousins, *The Renaissance in India*, p. 8.)

30. See my *Outside the Fold: Conversion, Modernity, and Belief* (Princeton: Princeton University Press, 1998) for a discussion of Besant's deployment of racial rhetoric in her delineation of universal brotherhood and a commonwealth of nations.

31. James H. Cousins, *Cultural Unity of Asia* (Madras: Theosophical Publishing House, 1922), pp. 7–8.

32. Ibid., p. 133.

33. Ibid., p. 133.

34. Ibid. See Kakuzo Okakura, *The Ideals of the East* (Leipzig: Insel-Verlag, 1922); see also Kojin Karatani, *The Origins of Modern Japanese Literature*, trans. Brett de Bary (Durham: Duke University Press, 1993) for a provocative critique of Okakura's pan-Asianism and its subsequent effects on Japanese modernism.

35. Cousins, *Samadarshana*, p. 7. See also James H. Cousins, *Modern English Poetry: Its Characteristics and Tendencies* (Madras: Ganesh and Co., 1921) for an equally devastating critique of the flawed purposes of Irish revivalism.

36. Cousins, *Samadorshana*, p. 9.

37. Thomas Trautman has demolished this myth in *Aryans and British India* (Berkeley: University of California Press, 1997).

38. James H. Cousins, *The Path to Peace: An Essay on Cultural Interchange and India's Contribution Thereto with a Prefatory Note on "Modern India"* (Madras: Ganesh and Co., 1928), p. 16.

39. James H. Cousins, *Heathen Essays* (Madras: Ganesh and Co., 1925), p. 69.

40. Cousins, *Path to Peace*, p. 19.

41. James H. Cousins, *Bases of Theosophy: A Study in Fundamentals Philosophical, Psy-chological, Practical* (London: Theosophical Publishing House, 1913), p. 24.

42. Cf. Tagore: "You must know that red tape can never be a common human bond; that official sealing-wax can never provide means of human attachment; that it is a painful ordeal for human beings to have to receive favours from animated pigeon-holes, and condescensions from printed circulars that give notice, but never speak." Rabindranath Tagore, *Creative Unity* (London: Macmillan and Co., 1922), p. 109.

43. Cousins, *Samadarshana*, p. 65.

44. Ibid.

National Literature in Transnational Times: Writing Transition in the "New" South Africa

VILASHINI COOPPAN

Among the many changes we credit globalization with—including the increasing interconnection of nations, cultures, and economies, the rapid and widespread flows of persons, goods, information, and capital across national borders, and the production of new forms of identity and community—we may add the reconfiguration of academic disciplines from national to global frameworks. As a practice of critical thought, intellectual globalization is marked, as Anthony D. King notes, by "the rejection of the nationally-constituted society as the appropriate object of discourse, or unit of social and cultural analysis, and to varying degrees, a commitment to conceptualising 'the world as a whole.'"[1] But what does it mean for a discipline, particularly disciplines as rooted in the national paradigm as comparative literature and postcolonial studies, to envision the globe? Comparative literature and postcolonial studies have in common disciplinary histories that posit the nation as the founding origin, the transnational and global as the future perfect. However, disciplinary history, like history more generally, owes no special allegiance to linear plots. Indeed, scholars in both fields do most justice to the transformative energies of the present moment when, rather than taking criticism's task as the simple bypassing of national pasts on the way toward transnational futures, they instead choose to trouble that particular trajectory that places nation first and globe after.

Frantz Fanon, perhaps postcolonial studies' most iconic theorist, writing in the context of the Algerian war for independence, spoke of the "occult instability" of that moment, one in which he foresaw the nearly simultaneous triumph

Earlier versions of this essay were presented in March 2000 at the "Comparative Literature in Transnational Times" conference held at Princeton University, and at the English Department of Brown University, as well as in April 2001 at Columbia University's Southern Asian Institute. I am grateful to Sandra Bermann and Michael Wood at Princeton, Nancy Armstrong, Leonard Tennenhouse, Ellen Rooney, and María Josefina Saldaña at Brown, and Gauri Viswanathan at Columbia, for invitations to present this work and for generous and wise engagement with its substance. Brief portions of this essay were also presented at the "Peripheral Centers, Central Peripheries: Literature of the South Asian Diaspora" conference held at the University of Saarbrucken, August 2002, and published under the title "National Literature in Transnational Times: Achmat Dangor's *Kafka's Curse* and the South Asian South African Diaspora," in *Peripheral Centres, Central Peripheries: Anglophone India and its Diaspora(s)*, eds. Martina Ghosh-Schellhorn and Vera Alexander (Weimar VDG, 2004). I am grateful to the editors for permission to reprint those portions here.

of hard-won national consciousness, its dying away, and its giving way to a global consciousness.[2] Even in the mid-century apogee of anticolonial nationalism, nation already articulated itself in and to a notion of "world." I take this imbrication of the national and the transnational, the local and the global, to be one of the founding instances of postcolonial studies. Similarly, if comparative literature finds an inaugural moment in the minute anatomies of national characters and national literatures popularized by such founding fathers (and mothers) as Taine, Herder, and Stael, it looks back equally to Goethe's roughly contemporaneous elaboration of the expansively transnational concept of *weltliteratur*— texts that at once represented, traversed, and transcended particular national origins to inaugurate a literary version of global trade.[3] That the rise of nationalism as a principle of differentiation coincided with a culture of cosmopolitanism in comparative literature's history, just as the liberation of the decolonized nation coincided with the consolidation of a broader Third Worldism in postcolonial studies' history, argues for a long historical interpenetration of nation and globe.

The presence of the global in our past (and of the national, however fractured and rearticulated by globalization, in our future) reorients disciplinary history, shifting it from the diachronic line of progress to a series of more lateral connections in which the national and the transnational, the local and the global, may be seen to intersect, to overlap, and to serve as one another's conditions of possibility. Certainly we do ourselves no favors if we so truncate the complexities of our disciplinary histories as to place ourselves in the position of having to learn, from the globalized present, interconnected ways of reading to which our disciplines have inclined us from their inception. This is not to say that in the face of the contemporary imperative to think globally, scholars of comparative literature and postcolonial studies should be content to proclaim "been there, done that." If, like Benjamin's famous angel, we are condemned to look backwards at disciplinary history as we are propelled forward into our disciplinary future, surely we may hope to learn something from that position.

To the extent that there exists an affinity between the concerns and rhetorics of comparative literature and postcolonial studies and those of a contemporary globalized world marked by the twin forces of nationalism and transnationalism, it is an affinity of method. Comparative literature and postcolonial studies neither prophesy the present moment nor embody it in disciplinary form. Rather, they share with it a certain imperative to recognize connection—be it the connection of nation to globe, of one national literature or cultural context to another, or quite simply of one text to another, as echo or allegory, repetition or rewriting. The world thus sketched is one in which claims of isolated purity or national distinctiveness give way to the messy, invigorating facts of cross-pollination and hybridization, interdependence and transformation. This essay takes that world to be as much a textual phenomenon as a political phenomenon, one that has not banished the category of national literature so much as redefined and rearticulated it. What is the function and form of national literature in transnational times? And how does that question begin to demarcate a new kind of comparative literature linked, on the one hand, to a set of concerns named "global" and, on the other, to a related set named "postcolonial"?

I will approach these questions by looking closely at a single national context and a discrete historical period—South Africa in the waning years of apartheid and the early years of transition—as seen in two novels by the internationally acclaimed white writer J. M. Coetzee and a novella by the less well-known Indian writer Achmat Dangor. Reading locally, I suggest, can also constitute an act of thinking globally. For insofar as the reading of individual national texts entails connecting them with times and places, cultures and worlds not their own, such reading weaves an intertextual web that is the literary equivalent of globalization's famously interconnected world. The globalization of literary criticism demands that we work on two fronts: first, recognizing on a disciplinary level a long tradition of thinking nationally and globally in tandem; and second, identifying on a textual level the narrative strategies and reading practices that respectively express and exfoliate this imbrication of nation and globe. It is to the second project that this essay turns, seeking to find in the local case of contemporary South African writing a window onto the disciplinary formations and critical futures of comparative literature and postcolonial studies.

World and *Weltliteratur* in Late Apartheid Literature

The question of just how snugly South Africa fits into postcolonial paradigms is a vexed one, much debated in South African literary and cultural theory of the late 1980s and 1990s. By some accounts South Africa has been postcolonial many times over: with the establishment of the Union of South Africa in 1910 in the wake of the Anglo-Boer war; with the triumph of Afrikaner nationalism and the birth of the apartheid state in 1948; and of course, with the historic elections of 1994 that brought Nelson Mandela's ANC-led government to power. The obviously farcical nature of South Africa's first two "independences" places an additional burden on the third, which must be not only genuinely representative of all national constituencies but also temporally decisive. If you listen enough times, as all South Africans who lived through 1990s did, to the phrase "the 'new' South Africa," you cannot help but hear in it a deep and abiding anxiety, a rhetorical disavowal of the unspoken yet ubiquitous presence of the old. Perhaps we may speak then of "postapartheid" in a similar sense to that in which we speak of "postcolonial" or "postnational," that is, advisedly and with reservation, ever aware of the difficulties and ironies of a prefixed "post" that prematurely announces the passing of a system of domination that actually remains, albeit in residual, reconfigured forms. These remainders include neocolonialism, neoimperialism, and multinational global capitalism for the postcolonial, the ongoing interpellative force and political presence of national identification for the postnational and racialized inequities of all manner for the postapartheid. Part of the burden of a literary-critical engagement with the South African literature of transition must thus be the learning of a kind of methodological oscillation, in which the parsing of newness goes hand in hand with the naming of old-ness, in which the exploration of nationalist address goes hand in hand with the mapping of the transnational circuits that inform the nation.

Such a method seeks connection where South African literary criticism has historically sought division. During the 1980s South African literary criticism commonly distinguished two major strains of national literature: a "resistance" strain associated with Sipho Sepamla, Mongane Serote, Mbulelo Mzamane, Mtutu-zeli Matshoba, and others that reached back to the Black Consciousness move-ment of the 1970s and also encompassed the flood of black protest poetry, na-tionalist prose, and realist "people's literature" unleashed by the 1976 Soweto uprising; and, on the other hand, a "futurist" or "apocalyptic" largely white strain dedicated to imagining the end of apartheid and epitomized by such political novels as Nadine Gordimer's *July's People* (1981) and, in the different register of the parable or allegory, J. M. Coetzee's *Waiting for the Barbarians* (1981), *Life and Times of Michael K* (1983), and *Foe* (1986).[4] To his critics, Coetzee's penchant for allegory implied a concomitant refusal of the historical imagination, a refusal not only of the political here and now but equally of some nascent, struggle-born fu-ture. In Gordimer's view the allegorical form of Coetzee's early novels emerged "out of a kind of opposing desire to hold himself clear of events and the daily, grubby, tragic consequences in which, like everybody else living in South Africa, he is up to the neck, and about which he had an inner compulsion to write . . . allegory as a stately fastidiousness; or a state of shock." Even a novel like *Life and Times of Michael K*—whose story of a deformed, displaced, abandoned man actu-ally names South Africa as its setting unlike the earlier *Waiting for the Barbarians*, with its nameless, placeless, ahistorical Empire, or the later *Foe*, with its similarly extranational geography of desert island periphery and English metropole—commanded Gordimer's criticism for its contentment with the play of allegorical symbols and simultaneous "revulsion against all political and revolutionary solu-tions."[5] Gordimer herself advocated a realist mode for the telling of truth to power. Writing in the explosively riven South Africa of the 1980s, she claimed that the writer's task "can be fulfilled only in the integrity Chekov demanded: 'to describe a situation so truthfully . . . that the reader can no longer evade it.'"[6]

Coetzee, by contrast, abjured this compact between world and word. Speaking in the context of his 1987 Jerusalem Prize, he characterized South African writ-ing as "a literature in bondage," born of a situation in which there was "too much truth for art to hold, truth by the bucketful, truth that overwhelms and swamps every act of the imagination."[7] Faced with what he would later depict as a choice between writing that, in its reliance on truth-telling and fact, sought a supple-mentary status to history, and writing that sought instead to itself rival the dis-course of history, Coetzee proclaimed himself obliged to choose the latter. In a 1988 essay titled "The Novel Today," he argues that storytelling ("more venera-ble than history, as ancient as the cockroach") represents an altogether different "mode of thinking," one with its own rules and imperatives, "its own paradigms and myths."[8] In what he calls "a parable, a mode favoured by marginal groups," Coetzee goes on to catalogue the similarities between stories and cockroaches.

Both are consumable, colonizable, catalogueable, ineradicable, even instrumentalizable as the stuff of revolutions. "You can even, if you wish, dry them and powder them and mix them with high explosives and make bombs of them. You can even make up stories about them, as Kafka did, although this is quite hard" (4). Though Coetzee refers here specifically to cockroaches, the ironic disdain of his tone perfectly captures his broader reservations about the political use of literature. In a striking assertion of the distinctiveness and autonomy of literary discourse he concludes that ultimately, "there is still the difference between a cockroach and a story, and the difference remains everything." Coetzee implies that storytelling's difference emerges at precisely the point where the play of discourse resists interpretative efforts to corral and catch it in a set of allegorical equivalences as imprisoning as the carapace that Gregor Samsa wakes one day to inhabit. If Gordimer's model was Chekovian realism in the service of political change, Coetzee preferred the more Kafkaesque form of a narrative that does not record historical truth but instead offers a surreal, distorted, destabilizing version of its own—a version whose literary form exceeds its political purposes.

Though Coetzee and Gordimer have customarily been understood to mark opposite poles of a writers' debate on the place of art in politics, for the purposes of this essay I want to emphasize a relatively minor but potentially significant commonality. In the examples I have discussed, both Coetzee and Gordimer reach beyond the borders of their own national literary tradition in order to represent the unavoidable national meanings of literary expression in the 1980s. Coetzee's Kafka and Gordimer's Chekov are thus the signs not only of a particular crisis point in the history of one nation and its national literature, but also of a broader transnational system that, as Goethe foresaw, links nations and texts together across geopolitical and cultural divides. The existence of such a "world system" creates a context in which any attempt to think the national cannot help but simultaneously route itself through some version of the global. Whether in Goethe's model of the cosmopolitan exchange of the great works of world literature or in the more recent paradigm of the literary encounter of colonial texts and postcolonial responses,[9] both comparative literature and postcolonial studies can be seen to offer a version of what I will call literary transnationalism. The remainder of this essay explores this transnationalism at work in three South African texts: Coetzee's 1986 *Foe*, Dangor's 1997 *Kafka's Curse*, and Coetzee's 1998 *Disgrace*. Tracing the migratory patterns of various literary references, I reveal intertextuality to be the modality in which literary transnationalism is written. (In other words, intertextuality provides the formal expression of a geopolitical condition of modernity shaped by bordercrossing). I do not mean to suggest that transnational form is simply layered onto a uniform national archive. Indeed, as the South African case makes abundantly clear with its richly polyglot, racially and culturally diverse population, it is the very internal difference of national identity that seeks out, perhaps even requires, the external form of an intertextual transnationalism. To write South Africa in the texts considered here, it also becomes necessary to write the world.

ALLEGORIZING APARTHEID IN COETZEE'S *FOE*

Foe allegorizes late apartheid through a pointedly unoriginal, un-South African story made to bear the burden of local and particular meanings. *Foe's* reworking of Daniel Defoe's *Robinson Crusoe* (1719) would thus seem to belong alongside Derek Walcott's *Omeros* (1990), Aimé Césaire's *Une Tempête* (1968), and Chinua Achebe's *Arrow of God* (1964). All translate the internal dynamics of a contact scene in which language, subjectivity, power, history, and culture are parceled out on one side or the other of a great divide (Odysseus and the Cyclops, Prospero and Caliban, Marlow and Kurtz's Africa, Crusoe and Friday) into textual encounters in which the element that remained silent or inchoate in the original text now speaks back. But while *Foe* exhibits a properly postcolonial repertoire of strategic inversion, parody, destabilizing incorporation, and unseemly echo in its relationship with its master text, *Foe* also pointedly shies away from any imperative to give voice to the Calibans of literature. Unlike Defoe's Friday, a Carib Indian transformed into an Enlightenment icon of the educable native, Coetzee's Friday, a black slave from Africa, never speaks.[10]

Before turning to Coetzee's representation of his Friday, it will be helpful to establish the broader intertextual relationship between Coetzee's text and Defoe's. Unlike *Robinson Crusoe*, whose title page announces it to have been "Written by Himself," *Foe* is a narrative written by a "Herself," the half-English, half-French Susan Barton.[11] Like her namesake in Defoe's *Roxana* (1740), Susan is searching for her lost daughter. In the course of Susan's more far-flung travels she is shipwrecked onto an island inhabited by a man named Cruso and another named Friday. The island is at once familiar and alien, a textually uncanny place that both conjures and banishes the ghostly presence of a literary origin. Whereas Defoe's island is a territory teeming with constructive and nominative possibility, an Edenic colony with Crusoe as its "Adamic monarch,"[12] the island in *Foe* is utterly lacking in natural wonder, desolately bare of things to see or do, build or make, narrate or possess. Readers of *Robinson Crusoe* will remember how much time and attention Defoe lavishes on the description of the felling of a tree, its dragging, cutting, planing, and eventual transformation into the fences and fortifications, tables and canoes of the settler. By contrast, the scattering of "puny" trees that Susan observes on the island represents the diminishment of the luxuriant forests that stood ready for Defoe's Crusoe and the refusal of the descriptive imperium they occasioned. There are only two sustained activities on Coetzee's island: Friday's fishing, which provides the mainstay of a monotonous diet, and Cruso's stone-by-stone construction of empty terraces, the return of the Puritan ethic of Defoe's Crusoe as meaningless busywork. The terrace-lined hillside awaits the arrival, Cruso tells Susan, of "those who come after us and have the foresight to bring seed" (33). Cruso's fruitless labor, like his reference to himself in the past tense and his refusal to admit the slightest changes into the island's daily regime, render him representative of the political order that was beginning to have a sense of its own looming obsolescence in mid-1980s South Africa.

Foe expresses its South Africanness in unlikely places. It turns the blank territory of an unnamed desert island into a temple on which a familiar story of conquest and colonization is rewritten with all the tragic absurdism that late apartheid demands and a longtime student of Beckett might elect.[13] With similar disregard for national boundaries, the novel raids England for a plot synonymous with the rise of literary realism and France for a poststructuralist narrative discourse that relentlessly seeks to cut Reality, Truth, and History down to size. To this end, *Foe* moves away from *Robinson Crusoe*'s dominant genres of travelogue, adventure story, Christian conversion tale, confession, how-to manual, and emergent autobiography, all of which merge their self-authenticating registers to produce novelistic realism, and instead utilizes the equally realist but explicitly feminized forms of the memoir, the letter, and a first-person narration far too anxious about the status of the writing "I" to claim the title of autobiography.[14] Coetzee's narrator Susan is of two minds about the utility of realistic description. While on the island, she exhorts Cruso to enter the realm of what Ian Watt calls *Robinson Crusoe*'s "concrete particularity":[15]

> All shipwrecks become the same shipwreck, all castaways the same castaway. . . . The truth that makes your story yours alone, that sets you apart from the old mariner by the fireside spinning yarns of sea-monsters and mermaids, resides in a thousand touches which today may seem of no importance, such as: When you made your needle (the needle you store in your belt), by what means did you pierce the eye? When you sewed your hat what did you use for thread? Touches like these will one day persuade your countrymen that it is all true, every word . . . (18)

Following their rescue and Cruso's death on the voyage home to England, Susan takes charge of the telling and selling of the story and explicitly eschews such authenticating details. Her memoir of island life, addressed to the famous English writer Foe in the hopes of soliciting his help in publication, constitutes the first part of the novel. It mentions daily details largely to dismiss them: "There is more, much more I could tell you about the life we lived, how we kept the fire smouldering day and night, how we made salt; how, lacking soap, we cleaned ourselves with ash" (26). The second and third parts of the novel describe Susan's effort to write a publishable manuscript. Like Foe, Susan realizes that "the island is not a story in itself" (117). But whereas he professionally proposes that Susan flesh out her skeletal story in a swashbuckling fashion, peopling the island (as the real Defoe did) with cannibals and giving Cruso a gun, she prefers to tunnel into its most secret and hollow places. This is the zone of Friday, the tongueless, voiceless subject of a story that Susan can never know yet constantly desires, a story she pointedly refuses to invent. Friday's story finds its only expression in the opaque dream sequence with which the novel's fourth and final section concludes. Coetzee's *Foe* thus calls up Defoe's *Robinson Crusoe* precisely in order to banish it or, more specifically, to banish the species of novelistic realism (fiction passing itself off as fact) for which it serves as privileged sign.

Foe's refusal of realism is consistent with Coetzee's oft-criticized preference for a version of history that eschews the realm of factual truth and turns instead to the alternative space of art, in which history is rendered in discourse, as story.

Foe's politics of storytelling are nowhere clearer than in the subplot concerning Friday's silence. Defoe's Friday, we may remember, makes self-expression the very means of his subjection, from the submissive gesture with which he first kneels and places Crusoe's foot upon his head in token of his servitude, to his subsequent acquisition of an initial rudimentary vocabulary ("Friday," "Master," "YES," "NO,"), to his eventual mastery of enough English to proclaim his undying loyalty when Crusoe eventually offers to return him to his native island. *"You take, kill Friday;* (says he.) *What must I kill you for?* said I again. He returns very quick, *What you send Friday away for? take, kill Friday, no send Friday away."*[16] Friday's words are so clearly his, so marked by the syntax of servitude, that the text's markings of "says he" and "said I" are practically unnecessary. For Defoe's Friday, speech enables the issuing of a phantasmal invitation to rule, an effective conversion of the speaking subject into grammar's and dominion's object. By contrast, Coetzee's Friday resists all efforts to, as Susan says, "giv[e] voice" to him. Her efforts to communicate with him through drawing produce only "a long silence" (70); when given a flute he plays only the same phrase over and over; and when she seats him at Foe's desk and tries to teach him to write, his first gesture is to fill the slate with rows of the same hieroglyphic image, a human eye upon a human foot. In response to Susan's demand to see the slate, he wipes it clean with spit-moistened fingers, converting the gaping hole of his tongueless mouth into the means of a second silence.

Faced with the South African white writer's perennial problem of how to record the spoken discourse of black characters in such a way as to mark that speech's difference without altogether exoticizing it as a species of, quite literally, local color, Coetzee in *Foe* chooses what Gayatri Spivak and others characterize as a Derridean aporia of silence.[17] Reluctant to make the racial other speak, the novel refuses to enter the domain of black language, black history, and black subjectivity. For Kwaku Larbi Korang, Coetzee's "eccentric allegory" comes at a high cost: the simultaneous production of Friday as "the limit term of a Western historicist script" and a desubjectified, deinteriorized, agentless entity, nothing more and nothing less than "the spectacular essence, the truth, of black victimage."[18] I agree that Friday's simultaneous representation of the inaccessibility and indeterminacy of meaning and the highly specific meaning or "truth" of racial subjugation suggests a certain political untenability in Coetzee's own position, caught between his allegiances to white books and the overweening historical presence of black bodies, negotiating, as Korang puts it, "an impossible transition from a transcendent Europe to a descendent Africa" (190). But I would like to pursue a somewhat different set of consequences issuing from Coetzee's deauthorizing rewriting of the white book.

Insofar as Coetzee's *Foe* unsettles its textual predecessor with what Homi K. Bhabha in his influential account of colonial mimicry calls "the menace of resemblance," it is because *Foe* achieves a relationship to *Robinson Crusoe* that is, again in Bhabha's words, "almost the same but not quite," "almost the same but not white."[19] To seek the vanishing point of whiteness in a novel by a South African white writer is an interpretive gesture that goes against the binarized racial schemas of South African literary criticism. Is it precisely because Coetzee's Friday does not speak that his novel of (waning) empire may be said to be "almost the same but not [as] white" as Defoe's novel of (rising) empire? In other words, is Coetzee's writing not white to the extent to which it admits into its representational orbit a species of black difference that is unassimilable to the codes and imperatives of whiteness, the codes and imperatives that produce such grotesquely distorted language as *Robinson Crusoe's* "*take, kill Friday, no send Friday away*" or the "catch 'im, eat 'im" with which *Heart of Darkness* graces one of its two speaking Africans? I am not saying that Coetzee is a black writer or that he voices black opposition to a white colonial order; there is too much painfully material history at stake here to play with the fire of rendering race as metaphor. To read *Foe* through Bhabha's formulation of a menacing resemblance to colonial models that is "almost the same but not white" is to begin to grasp the subjective location of a writing that departs from whiteness only insofar as it acknowledges its own irrevocable, yet by no means final, placing within whiteness. *Foe* can thus be understood as an instance of what Coetzee calls "white writing"— "white only in so far as it is generated by the concerns of people no longer European, not yet African."[20]

In the transitional, translational space of *Foe's* white writing, empire is made to confront a silence of its own creation, the silence of subjected persons whom it can neither hear speaking nor make speak unless they speak in empire's own voice.[21] What Coetzee refuses his silent Friday is that ventriloquizing or mirroring function that Defoe accords his Friday, the ability to so flawlessly internalize the ideologies and structures of colonial address as to himself perform them. Friday's placing of Crusoe's foot upon his head can only be a mirror-scene, a phantasmal image in which colonialism thinks it is seeing its other, but is only seeing itself. Colonialism sees itself reflected back in the projected image of an other who either willingly offers himself up for colonial incorporation (*take, kill Friday*) or else presents himself in terms of such radical difference that he cries out for rule ("catch 'im, eat 'im"). *Foe's* silent Friday, by contrast, merely marks the spot of something the novel cannot even begin to imagine, namely, a third possibility for the relationship of empire to its others.

Coetzee's foreclosing in *Foe* and other novels of what Gordimer called "political and revolutionary solutions" to the atrocity of apartheid has preoccupied his critics, perhaps obscuring the extent to which his allegories *are* historical. As David Attwell points out, though *Foe* clearly privileges signifier over signified, the act of storytelling over the (his)story told, "the signifier itself is localized in allusive ways in order to make this story of storytelling responsive to the conditions that writers like Coetzee are forced to confront." The signifier of Friday's silence thus contains for Attwell at least three distinct traces: "the mark of Coetzee's unwillingness to receive the canon as the natural breath of life . . . the mark of history, and the mark of South Africa."[22] If Friday bears the mark of the national, his very presence in *Foe* is also enabled by what I have called an intertextual transnationalism. Like Susan Barton, daughter of an English mother and a French father, Friday is the strangely South African progeny of the England in whose foundational novel he first appeared and the France whose emblematic theoretician provides the hidden structure of his re-presentation in *Foe*. As the simultaneous sign of the national and the transnational, Friday's silence embodies a specific kind of national allegory in which South Africa emerges, as it were, through its own absence, deferral, or displacement, perpetually shuttled to the side but never wholly erased.[23]

To read *Foe* as an allegory of apartheid is in some sense to read against Coetzee, who has protested "the colonisation of the novel by the discourse of history" and repeatedly distinguished narrative discourse from materialist fact. For all their allegorical correlations, "in the end there is still the difference between a cockroach and a story."[24] True to its poststructuralist roots (or routes), *Foe's* model of allegory is one predicated not on closing the gap between one thing and another, but rather opening it. That endlessly open gap repeatedly resists interpretation, whether in Friday's nonreferential sequences of open eyes and written o's or in the novel's final image of Friday floating underwater in a nonnarrative space "where bodies are their own signs." His open mouth issues a stream that passes out of him, over the unnamed narrator, through the shipwreck, around the island, to "ru[n] northward and southward to the ends of the earth" (157). Taking distance not closeness as its mode, privileging the ever-expanding circuit of difference over the mirror of mimesis, this is allegory that constantly de-allegorizes itself. Just as the novel seems to approach the historical referents of South Africa and its pariah mode of governance, a self-conscious skepticism about the very possibility of referring in language to history waylays the structure of allegorical equivalence (the island is South Africa, Friday its oppressed majority, Susan the well-intentioned but ineffectual white liberal) and unleashes or frees a further set of meanings that are as wide-ranging, as unfixed, and as uninterpretable as Friday's final wordless stream.

Of course, interpretive freedom is not at all the same thing as political freedom. Even if we admit the possibility of a metaphorical connection between the two, and even if we take *Foe* as a particularly effective example of that connection (wildly disregarding Coetzee's insistent opposition of word and world, discourse and history), the fact remains that the novel fails to imagine the future. In this, Coetzee is paradigmatic more than exceptional. Elleke Boehmer's insightful survey of the endings of late apartheid narratives by white and black writers discerns a common tendency to "shut down on tomorrow," a "tailing-off, an unwillingness or an inability to comment on what might follow."[25] For example, the final scene of Serote's *To Every Birth its Blood* depicts a woman in labor while Gordimer's *July's People* concludes with the white heroine, a survivor of an apocalyptic revolution, running toward a landing helicopter bearing undecipherable markings and carrying passengers who are either "saviours or murders."

Which of the two, we will never know. No less than Serote's and Gordimer's realism, for Boehmer Coetzee's allegory also short-circuits, its "imaginative challenge . . . finally contained within end-stopped structures."

Turning her attention to the emergent literature of postapartheid South Africa, wondering if "[t]he best one can hope for the novel in South Africa is that it will not remain so painfully impaled on that two-pronged fork which is history versus discourse, or reality versus fantasy," Boehmer calls for a new kind of future-directed writing (53). She anticipates "narrative structures that embrace choice," "stories that juggle and mix generic options," a "freeing of words" and "loosen[ing] up" of writing that will invite "greater complexity, more exploration, more cross connections, more doubt" (51, 54). Writers of the period known as the transition, she concludes, will need resources "as broad as it is possible to have, for the metamorphoses that may unfold will, if nothing else, be unpredictable and astonishing" (55).[26] Achmat Dangor's 1997 *Kafka's Curse* is a case in point, taking metamorphosis as both the metaphor and the mode of transition. Written by a longtime ANC supporter who returned to South Africa from exile in order to take up a position in the new government, and first published as the title novella of a prizewinning short story collection only three years after the historic elections that brought Nelson Mandela to power, *Kafka's Curse* is animated by the clearly nationalist intent of representing the "new" South Africa. The transformations that the novella describes are both political (its cast of characters mutate endlessly across the historical divides of color, culture, and community) and textual (the narrative mixes idioms, forms, and genres from within and outside South Africa). Metamorphosis thus at once writes the new nation and, in its Kafkaesque debts and broadly connective impulses, returns us—just when we think we are most securely on national terrain—to the shifting sphere of the intertextual transnational.

TRANSITIONAL FORMS AND TRANSNATIONAL ALLEGORIES

Kafka's Curse opens by portraying its protagonist, a Muslim man of mixed descent ("Javanese and Dutch and Indian and God knows what else") as the victim of a degenerative, form-altering disease, the "Kafka's Curse" of the title. Containing quite literally "the roots of another being . . . something struggling to be born,"[27] he slowly reverts to a vegetal state and eventually becomes a tree (58). This living death is the final metamorphosis of an individual who was born Omar Khan but spent his life passing as Oscar Kahn, a white Jew married to the daughter of one of the finest English families of Natal. Omar/Oscar's grandmother was born Christian Katryn into a poor Afrikaner (Dutch-descended) family but became Muslim Kulsum when she married. Omar's white wife Anna, the victim of childhood incest perpetrated by her brother (who now preys on his own daughters), discovers yet another skewing of her family tree: her father's secret relationship and child with a colored woman. Omar/Oscar's nephew Fadiel runs away to live with Marianne, a woman raised on a small farm in the Orange

Free State, the heart of Afrikaner nationalism, who has since become a bohemian, a doctoral candidate and, in her family's eyes, a miscegenator. Omar/Oscar's brother Malik, a devout Muslim patriarch, falls in love with Amina, a woman raised as a Muslim but now married to a white, ANC-affiliated Jew. In the novella's surreal conclusion it appears that Amina, or some hybrid incarnation of her, may have murdered many of the men in her life, including Malik, just as Anna may have murdered her predatory brother. Nothing is certain plotwise. Formally, however, everything is certainly mixed.

If Coetzee's *Foe* is, in Benita Parry's trenchant observation, "little touched by the autochthonous, transplanted and recombinant cultures of South Africa's African, Asian, and Coloured populations," *Kafka's Curse* is everywhere touched by them.[28] Its characters compose a nation made from transnational movements: the Dutch settlers, English colonials, and Jewish refugees who came in successive waves to the southern tip of Africa, and the Cape Malays and Indians who were brought by the global systems of Dutch slavery and British indentured labor. The narration of individual chapters from the perspectives of different characters, each multiply inscribed by the codes of ethnicity, race, gender, sexuality, and class, effects a polyphonic form that refuses singular, homogenizing, or omniscient perspectives. The narrative's heteroglossia further extends to its incorporation of several of South Africa's fourteen official languages, including English, Afrikaans (in both its white and colored versions), Hindi, and Arabic. In a signal example Marianne, the Afrikaner free spirit, speaks to Terry, formerly Tertius, like herself a refugee from Afrikaner culture. Terry peppers his English comments with Afrikaans expressions, driving Marianne to exclaim: "this afrikaans thing of yours, you know, every sentence juiced up with your favourite *pampoenspreekwoordjies* [country proverbs], it's becoming too much. I'm really *dik* [fed up] of it." Marianne, fully aware of the irony in her recourse to an Afrikaans word to express her frustration with Terry's hybridized or metamorphosed idiom, goes on to imagine the reasons for Terry's linguistic switching. Perhaps, she muses, he was

> [t]aught this language with a precision that hurts, no verb out of line, no inappropriate adjectives, no plurals used to multiply single meanings, and an absolute must—never, never, get your genders mixed up. Anyone who used a "hy" for a "hom" or confused "syne" and "haarne" was given the cold-eyed third degree: it shrivelled you up inside and made you doubt your ancestry. Ja-nee, somewhere in this creature lurks a twisted Hotnot-tongue gene. So, like a child remembering those hateful piano lessons—this key for that scale, but the tone is all wrong, supple fingers wasted in their rigid passage over inert black and white keys—Terry delights in creating discord and clash in his language, a low-toned Capie English lit up by flashes of Afrikaans *donder-en-bliksem* [thunder and lightning]. (183–84)

This meditation on the undoing of a home language—performed in a novel written in English by an Indian from a Gujarati-speaking family—poignantly expresses the pain and possibility of transition and translation. Miniaturizing the method of Dangor's text, Marianne's description of the breaking of syntactical law mirrors the novella's formal breaking of apartheid's emblematically "black and white" law; a law that sought to keep ethnicities apart, languages separate, and communities firmly racialized.

If we take Benedict Anderson at his word, and accept an intimate bond between the imaginative constructs of novels and nations, then the interweaving of black, white, Indian, and colored characters and voices in *Kafka's Curse* teaches us, through the preoccupations of its novelistic form, to reenvision the South African nation itself.[29] Mixing up and bleeding together those same categories of identity whose minute differentiation in racial classifications and Immorality Acts constituted the very underpinnings of the apartheid state, *Kafka's Curse* portrays metamorphosis as both curse and blessing, both the cultural wages of a history scarred by the unspeakably violent politics of purity and the future promise of a diverse and democratic nation. Such a vision flirts with utopianism, particularly when contrasted to the decade following the ANC's 1994 electoral victory, a period marked on the one hand by official state discourse's celebration of the nonracialist "rainbow nation," and on the other, by the paradoxical recrudescence of differentialist ethnocultural identification.[30] The challenge facing both *Kafka's Curse* and the nation it represents is that of finding a middle ground between apartheid's confining binaries of black vs. white, *volkstaat* vs. the world, and some postmodernist democratic idyll where the plenitude of endlessly mobile and mutating difference recuperates the schisms of a brutally divided history. Metamorphosis is *Kafka's Curse*'s answer to this problem, its version of a politics of transitional translation or translational transition in which persons and texts can be seen doubly, both as the possessors of lives, histories, and voices firmly their own and as the agents of recombinant processes continually yielding something rich and strange. *Kafka's Curse* extends its metamorphic mode from the crafting of individual sentences in which competing national idioms—English, Afrikaans, Hindi, Xhosa—are rendered contiguous with one another, and of plot lines in which family trees similarly hybridize, to the larger construction of national stories of markedly mixed origins.

It is to this task that the very first chapter of the novella turns, recounting a tale of star-crossed love that Omar/Oscar, a Cape Malay Muslim passing for a white Jew, once told to his white wife Anna. In its original form, written by the renowned twelfth-century Arabic poet Niz_m_, the romance of *Layl_ u Majn_n* describes a mad lover who allows himself to be so thoroughly consumed by passion that when his beloved finally, after several years of waiting, appears before him, he cannot reconcile the real woman with his idealized image and rejects her, leaving her to die of grief.[31] Traditionally the lover Majnun is associated with the sterile desert where he flees to wait for his beloved Layli, herself associated with the fertile gardens of her father's kingdom. Although "desert triumphs over garden" in the original version, as Julie Scott Meisami observes, in Omar/Oscar's prescient retelling of the tale the reverse holds true.[32] In the version Anna remembers Omar/Oscar telling, Majnoen is a gardener who falls in love with the king's daughter, arranges to meet her in a forest so that they may elope, and when she does not arrive, waits for days, weeks, months until he eventually becomes a tree. In a subsequent chapter of the novel, narrated in her husband's own voice, he admits to "I[lying] a little more than necessary." Yes, he acknowledges, there are no forests in Arabia, and yes, no one in the original Arabic romance becomes a tree.

> "So," he asks himself, "what are the real origins of the legend? A trivial incident, sentimentalised and exaggerated to heroic proportions by slaves from India or Java or Malaysia to sustain themselves? A coping mechanism—that's what you call it, no? It might have been African? This continent is fecund—yes, fecund—with the kind of foliage which gives birth to the secret lives that are the very substance of magical parable." (21)

In this version of the romance it is not the Arab woman but the African continent that is associated with fertility and fecundity. Such a gesture typifies magical realism's popular premise that the very nature of certain parts of the world forces the word to transform itself in order to capture their descriptive abundance and fantastically protean histories. Omar/Oscar's voicing of the hypothesis that the legend "might have been African" appears to shape his story to fit a generic model first advanced by the Cuban Alejo Carpentier, canonized by the Colombian Gabriel García Márquez, and turned into a veritable industry by the Indian Salman Rushdie. But Omar/Oscar pulls back from this particular set of transnational affiliations and the style of national reading they enforce. If his wry allusion to an Africa "fecund—with the kind of foliage which gives birth to the secret lives that are the very substance of magical parable" ventriloquizes the metropolitan will to find magical realism, no less than national allegory, in the Third World text, his subsequent statement arrests that desire. "Making this tale African would have been too obvious. Everybody wants to make our little room theirs, make their destiny ours. It was Muslim, that much I know" (22). To make the tale African would be to nationalize it first in order to transnationalize it second. Read thus, *Kafka's Curse* becomes yet another instance of the creeping spread of an expressive genre turned global literary commodity and the historical and cultural specificities of its local content become a mere footnote to the homogenizing sameness of its global form.[33] As dangerous as the possibility that critics may globalize too much in their reading of national literatures, it is equally dangerous that they may not globalize enough, that they may focus so intently on the national character of these allegories that they miss their transnational cast. Once again, it is *Kafka's Curse*'s contribution to find the middle ground.

Ironically, in Dangor's South African novella it is the sign of Arabia not Africa that nationalizes. Omar/Oscar's self-proclaimed "Muslim" tale intertextually cites an Arabic tradition *outside* South Africa that is also a powerful force in the Indian and Cape Malay populations *inside* South Africa. To say the tale is Muslim is thus tantamount to saying it is South African, part of a nation defined by the histories and identities of a diverse and diasporic citizenry. This transnational circuitry in the opening pages of a novella dedicated to the imagining of a new nation also in its way constitutes a metamorphosing, a conscious blurring of oppositional schemas that render the national and transnational, the local and the global, as one another's antagonists. As a national allegory, *Kafka's Curse* re-peatedly requires transnational form, from the Arabic romance whose metamor-phosized retelling fuels one subplot, to the magical realist techniques that inform the larger story of Omar/Oscar's metamorphosis into a tree, to the implied histor-ical border crossings that bring Afrikaners and Cape Malays, Indians and the En-glish, blacks and Jews together to mix on South African soil. What *Kafka's Curse* ultimately accomplishes is a boundary-breaking, binary-confounding instance of writing that declassifies itself, writing that is neither white nor black, neither myth nor history, neither nationally territorialized nor globally deterritorialized, but rather flits between being both, all, and none in the same moment and often in the same sentence. In this mobile address and double vision, the fruit of what I have called the novella's metamorphic mode, lies its deepest debt to Kafka and all he signifies in South African and world literature.

Kafka's Forms

In *Kafka: Toward a Minor Literature* (1975), Gilles Deleuze and Félix Guattari proclaim their desire to free Kafka from his interpreters, whom they blame for re-ducing a truly revolutionary body of writing to three "themes": the transcendent power of the law, the interiority of guilt, and the subjectivity of enunciation. In contrast to this interpretive focus on tribunal, self, and speech, Deleuze and Guat-tari insist that Kafka's texts cannot be interpreted. They must instead be seen to function as "assemblages" of desire, marked, like all minor literatures, by the fol-lowing: a minority's seizure of a major language, free-floating or "deterritorialized" language, the "connection of the individual to a political immediacy," and a "col-lective assemblage of enunciation."[34] In "The Metamorphosis," a tale of Gregor Samsa's transformation into a bug, or "A Report to the Academy," a parable of an ape who becomes human, or the meditative reflections of an anthropomorphized canine in "Investigations of a Dog," Deleuze and Guattari find that an identifiable subject of enunciation—Gregor, ape, dog—gives way to a nonspecific "circuit of states that forms a mutual becoming, in the heart of a necessarily multiple or col-lective assemblage" (22). This becoming or, as they also call it, "becoming other" is not an end in itself. For Gregor becomes other, breaks out of his mind-numbing social world of work and family, and, in their terminology, deterritorializes him-self, only to die quite humanly from the grief of familial abandonment. Deleuze and Guattari read this moment precisely as Oedipal reterritorialization. Neither it nor the previous deterritorialization should be taken as the "end" of metamorpho-sis, they insist, for metamorphosis is less a trajectory from state A to state B than a ceaseless movement or flux between A and B.

In a similar vein, Walter Benjamin places Gregor within a larger Kafkaesque "tribe," all of them "beings in an unfinished state . . . neither members of, nor strangers to, any of the other groups of figures, but rather, messengers from one to the other." In the peregrinations of this tribe Benjamin discerns the symbolic presence of the law, "oppressive," "gloomy," and inescapable.[35] For Deleuze and

Guattari, however, the movement of metamorphosis names a textual process, not a textual meaning. Lacking a stable figurative meaning, "[m]etamorphosis is the contrary of metaphor" (22). I would not want simply to shout back "metamorphosis is metaphor" while waving a copy of *Kafka's Curse*. But surely there is a need and a way to name how metamorphosis operates as a metaphor for national transition, how the becoming-other of Dangor's characters describes that radical becoming-other which each South African citizen must allow if national culture is to emerge from the territorialized, classification-mad history of apartheid. Deleuze and Guattari's model of a critical engagement that tries to free the literary text from its interpreters with their themes and symbols, metaphors and allegories, certainly lends itself to the South African context where literary criticism has worked in apartheid's shadow, relentlessly binarizing, racializing, temporalizing, and territorializing cultural production into black writing/white writing, late apartheid writing/postapartheid writing, national writing/non-national writing. But to critically deterritorialize contemporary South Africa's "minor literature" we must be willing to reterritorialize it. This is to say that there can be no reading of the transformative energies at play in a text like *Kafka's Curse* without prior location of the national signifier. That these energies often route themselves through the intertextual transnational in order to return to the national suggests the necessity of learning to see neither the one nor the other but rather their moving, middle ground. For all the limitations of a theory of minor literature that largely dismisses the question of oppositional politics and relegates the Third World to the metaphorical status of a "linguistic zone,"[36] Deleuze and Guattari's focus on metamorphosis as movement nonetheless also allows us to begin to name a new kind of reading process.

At its best, this reading aspires to grasp the oscillatory movement of texts back and forth between the national and the transnational, the territorial local and the deterritorialized global. What bedevils such reading is the dilemma of how to read metaphoric meanings without claiming for certain literatures the status of metaphor per se. Transnational approaches to literary analysis can sometimes simply denationalize their objects, effectively decoupling texts from their national contexts and tacitly conglomerating them as instances of some version of the global, be it the curiously placeless, abstractly subversive concept of the "minor" or the equally amorphous "Third World." Yet the assertion of a collective, protoglobal category like "Third World" can also reinstantiate a national analytic lens, as in Jameson's notorious claim that all Third-World texts "necessarily project a political dimension in the form of national allegory."[37] Jameson's critics, exercised over his claim for a necessary nationalism to Third-World literatures, perhaps discount his rethinking of allegory, which arguably contains a more complex model for such literature's simultaneous nationalism and globalism, particularism and universalism.[38]

Jameson distinguishes his concept of allegory from the traditional model of two sets of figures and symbols read in a one-to-one correspondence and ultimately tending towards a certain fixity and unity of meaning. Instead, he claims: "[T]he allegorical spirit is profoundly discontinuous, a matter of breaks and het-

erogeneities, of the multiple polysemia of the dream rather than the homoge-
nous representation of the symbol . . . the capacity of allegory [is] to generate a
range of distinct meanings or messages, simultaneously, as the allegorical tenor
and vehicle change places. . . ." (74). In the national allegory, a "'floating' or
'transferable' structure of allegorical reference" connects the realms of the public
and the private, the national and the individual, the political and the libidinal
in a set of equivalences that "are themselves in constant change and transformation" (78, 73). The body politic imagined in *Kafka's Curse*, with its polymorphous
sexual crossings, physical alterations, and multiple social and linguistic metamorphoses, well deserves the label of national allegory. But that label brings its
own set of problems, foremost among them the suggestion that some literatures—
Third-World literatures—are more national and others—First-World literatures—
more universal. Ultimately, however, *Kafka's Curse* finds a mobility in allegory
that allows it to resist such formulaic equations in the writing of newness. Here
again, Jameson's theory of allegory provides a model. Arguing that it is only
through allegory's "complex play of simultaneous and antithetical messages, that
the narrative text is able to open up a concrete perspective on the real future,"
Jameson highlights dialectical movement as allegory's central feature, the structure that most powerfully enables its writing of the future (77). As I have suggested in my reading of *Kafka's Curse*, that movement is both temporal, linking
the national past to the national future, and spatial, connecting the national to
the transnational.

Literary transnationalism thus is not the denationalization or universalization
of texts so much as a critical mode with movement at its heart, a mode that seeks
to understand how and why one must sometimes look outside the nation in
order to write its transition, transformation, and future. Deleuze and Guattari's
pointedly nonallegorical, nonmetaphoric version of Kafka provides one model of
literary transnationalism, Jameson's allegorical Third-World literatures another.
A third, indigenous, example emerges from Coetzee's reflections on Kafka.

Commenting on an essay he wrote on Kafka's short story "The Burrow," Coetzee identifies narrative's imperative to "create an altered experience of time."[39]
This imperative has particular resonance in the South African context where,
Coetzee notes, time has been "extraordinarily static" since the 1948 triumph of
Afrikaner nationalism, which sought to remake history and the future in its own
image.[40] Kafka for Coetzee represents an alternative to this regime, an unprecedented inhabiting of language that yields a unique disordering of time. Turning
his linguist's eye on Kafka's short story "The Burrow," Coetzee catalogues the inconsistencies of verbal tense and aspect that narrate a bunkered creature's anxious anticipation of external attacks that may come at any moment. In the story,
Coetzee observes, time moves differently: there are no "transition phases" but
rather "[t]here is one moment and then there is another moment; between them
is simply a break." Constantly in a state of crisis, time exists as a "repeatedly broken, interrupted iterative present," a radically discontinuous zone in which actions are not causally linked and history's teleological plot is unavailable (227–

28). Coetzee compares this uncertain temporal state of "The Burrow"'s bunkered animal to that of Gregor Samsa, who will never know how and why he has been transformed into an insect. "[B]etween the before and the after there is not stage-by-stage development but a sudden transformation, *Verwandlung*, metamorphosis" (228). Coetzee's connection between "The Burrow"'s time without transition and the nontransitional metamorphosis of Gregor Samsa begs connection with Dangor's effort to turn Kafkaesque metamorphosis into the very image of *political* transition.

Coetzee himself attempts something of the sort in *Disgrace*, winner of the 1999 Booker Prize.[41] In contrast to the late apartheid concerns and strategies of *Foe*, *Disgrace* locates itself in the difficult moment of postapartheid South Africa. The novel seeks a narrative temporality that will be adequate to the task of representing this particular "transition phase" in national history. Coetzee's protagonist, David Lurie, a onetime professor of modern languages and now professor of communications at Cape Technical University (formerly Cape Town University College), feels himself bypassed in the new political order. Dismissed from his academic position over a sexual harassment incident, he finds himself in the rural Eastern Cape where his daughter runs a small farm. By his own admission, David is far from the life he has spent in academia, "explaining to the bored youth of the country the distinction between drink and drink up, burned and burnt. The perfective, signifying an action carried through to its conclusion" (71). Later, after his daughter's farm is attacked by three young African men, after Lucy has been raped and David locked in a bathroom and set on fire, the perfective returns in the text's description of David's "tender" scalp, "[b]urned, burnt" (97). The novel concludes by describing the corpses of the abandoned dogs that David, with new-found sympathy, for the suffering of others, has put to sleep and then incinerated—"burnt, burnt up" (220).

In the task of writing the transitional phase of a "new" South Africa, Coetzee does not turn to Kafka's repeated iterative present nor to the prophetic future of nationalism which, in Fanon's description, "stops short, falters, and dies away on the day independence is proclaimed."[42] Coetzee instead employs the perfective, the tense that at once belongs to the past and calls its finality into question. Apartheid in *Disgrace* is an action not yet carried through to its conclusion. Transition is the moment that lives the difference between the apartheid "then" and the postapartheid "now" as a break, a discontinuity between states of being rather than an either/or choice between the prefigurative fulfillment of an anticipated identity and the burial of an obsolete one. So David's "burned, burnt" scalp slowly grows hair although his scars remain, and the pathos of the final image of the dogs "burnt, burnt up" by a loving hand coexists with Lucy's decision to bear the biracial child of her rapist. With a nod to the Gramscian epigraph of Gordimer's *July's People* ("the old is dying and the new cannot be born; in this interregnum there arises a great diversity of morbid symptoms"), *Disgrace* ends by oscillating between times and states, death and birth, the past of the completed perfective and the unknown yet hopeful future to come.

Although Coetzee's sparse, minimalist prose and Dangor's lush and hallucinatory magical realism could not be more different, their common roots in Kafka's syntactic and symbolic universe make them twin representatives of what I have termed the intertextual transnationalism of national literature. Read through Coetzee's reading of Kafka, *Kafka's Curse* emerges as a national allegory of political transition that is also a particular kind of temporality, one that does not move forward in what Coetzee calls "the smooth course of narrative development" so much as veer back and forth in the oscillation "between then and now," an oscillation, he adds, that "is always a break."[43] This movement, for Coetzee the hallmark of metamorphosis, reconceptualizes the political moment of transition not as history's vaunted "end" but as a rupture in progressive temporality altogether. In this regard, *Kafka's Curse* gives up on the comforts of the teleological plots of history and fiction, of national reigns and generic evolutions. In their place it constructs a more lateral set of connections through which to map not the national rise of the novel but its transnational spread, not the forward movement of the nation but the more shifting psychic, social, sexual, and linguistic passages of its citizens across the divides of their past in that moment of national emergence described by Fanon as a zone of "occult instability."

The double placing of *Kafka's Curse* (or of *Foe* and *Disgrace*), as an instance of minor literature within national literature as well as a product of a transnational circuitry of literary influence, carries a further lesson.[44] The temporal location of *Kafka's Curse* in South Africa's putatively nonracial, postapartheid present might, if we let it, instruct us to read it as a text whose fundamental concern is newness. The novella's hybrid thematics and transnational patterns (would thus seem to) trumpet forth such categories of disciplinary renewal as the much vaunted "hybridity" that appears to rescue postcolonial studies from the charges of nationalist thinking, or the "transnationalism" that would save comparative literature from the calcifications of nation-based analysis. I began this essay by suggesting that disciplinary history does not sanction this reading. If we are to avoid the pitfalls of disciplinary presentism, and if we are to read in the literary texts of today something more than an unanchored, free-floating "newness," we might consider taking metamorphosis as our theoretical guide. In the shifting forms of *Kafka's Curse* lies an invitation to envision a practice of movement or critical metamorphosis that, rather than seeking out a place for comparative literature and postcolonial studies to go (the transnational, hybrid future), would instead apprehend the possibilities of disciplines that once again, as in their founding moments, shuttle across and between the spaces of the national and the transnational, the local and the global, the particular and the hybrid. Seeking to articulate a sense of national identity through a distinctly transnational ideology of literary form, *Kafka's Curse* proposes the intertextual transnational as a species of literary hybridity. Such hybridity changes the form of national fiction as much as that of the national subject. Protean, moving, metamorphosing, this national story and the selves it depicts recounts "something struggling to be born" (58) that more than a tree within a man, might just well be the transnational nation.

NOTES

1. Anthony D. King, "Introduction," *Culture, Globalization, and the World-System*, ed. King (Binghamton: Department of Art and Art History, State University of New York at Binghamton Press, 1991), p. ix.

2. Frantz Fanon, *The Wretched of the Earth*, trans. Constance Farrington (New York: Grove Press, 1963), p. 227.

3. For a sampling of Goethe's fragmentary accounts of the ideal of *weltliteratur*, see Goethe, "Some Passages Pertaining to the Concept of World Literature," in *Comparative Literature: The Early Years*, eds. Hans-Joachim Schulz and Philip Rhein (Chapel Hill, NC: University of North Carolina Press, 1973), pp. 3–11. For critical explications of the ideal, see: Fritz Strich, *Goethe and World Literature* (London: Routledge & Kegan Paul, 1949); John Pizer, "Goethe's 'World Literature' Paradigm and Contemporary Cultural Globalization," *Comparative Literature* 52(3), Summer 2000, pp. 213–27; and my two essays, "World Literature and Global Theory: Comparative Literature for the New Millennium," *Symplok_* 9(1–2), 2001, pp. 15–43; and "Ghosts in the Disciplinary Machine: The Uncanny Life of World Literature," *Comparative Literature Studies* 41(1), 2004, pp. 10–36.

4. There are various critical versions of this narrative. See, for example: Stephen Clingman, "Revolution and Reality: South African Fiction in the 1980s," in *Rendering Things Visible: Essays on South African Literary Culture*, ed. Martin Trump (Johannesburg: Ravan, 1990), pp. 41–60; Michael Chapman, Colin Gardner, and Es'kia Mphahlele, eds., *Perspectives on South African Literature* (Johannesburg: AD. Donker, 1992), especially essays by Mphahlele, Chapman, Green, Rabkin, Strauss, Visser, Ndebele, and Kunene; and Michael Vaughn, "Literature and Politics: Currents in South African Writing in the Seventies," in *Critical Essays on J. M. Coetzee*, ed. Sue Kossew (New York: G. K. Hall & Co., 1998), pp. 50–65. A concise summary of the period and its racial and textual divisions can be found in David Attwell, *J. M. Coetzee: South Africa and the Politics of Writing* (Berkeley: University of California Press, 1993), pp. 9–34.

5. Nadine Gordimer, "The Idea of Gardening: *Life and Times of Michael K* by J. M. Coetzee" (review), *New York Review of Books* 31 (February 1, 1984), pp. 3–6, rpt. in *Critical Essays on J. M. Coetzee*, ed. Kossew, pp. 139–44, 139, 143.

6. Nadine Gordimer, in "The Essential Gesture," in *The Essential Gesture: Writing, Politics and Places*, ed. Stephen Clingman (London: Jonathan Cape, 1988), pp. 285–300.

7. J. M. Coetzee, "Jerusalem Prize Acceptance Speech," in *Doubling the Point: Essays and Interviews*, ed. David Attwell (Cambridge: Harvard University Press, 1992), pp. 96–99, 99.

8. Coetzee, "The Novel Today,"*Upstream* (South Africa) 6(1), 1988, pp. 2–5, 3. Subsequent references appear parenthetically.

9. Peter Hulme explores this method in an excellent series of local readings in *Colonial Encounters: Europe and the Native Caribbean 1492–1792* (London: Methuen, 1986). A more generalized presentation of the paradigm can be found in Bill Ashcroft, Helen Tiffin, and Stephen Slemon, *The Empire Writes Back* (New York: Routledge, 1989). For a discussion of Coetzee's *Foe* as an instance of "writing back," see Tiffin, "Postcolonial Literatures and Counter-Discourse," *Kunapipi* 9(3), 1987, pp. 17–34.

10. Coetzee specifies the racial difference between Defoe's Friday and his own in "Two Interviews with J. M. Coetzee, 1983 and 1987," interview with Tony Morphet, *Triquarterly* (South Africa) 69, 1987, pp. 454–64.

11. Daniel Defoe, *The Life and Strange Adventures of Robinson Crusoe of York, Mariner,*

Norton Critical Edition, ed. Michael Shinagel (New York: W.W. Norton, 1994). J. M. Coetzee, *Foe* (New York: Penguin, 1987). Subsequent references appear parenthetically.

12. Manuel Schonhorn, *Defoe's Politics* (Cambridge: Cambridge University Press, 1991), as quoted in David Medalie, "Friday Updated: *Robinson Crusoe* as Sub-Text in Gordimer's *July's People* and Coetzee's *Foe*, " *Current Writing* (South Africa) 9(1), 1997, pp. 43–54, 44.

13. Coetzee wrote his 1969 University of Texas–Austin doctoral dissertation on "The English Fiction of Samuel Beckett: An Essay in Stylistic Analysis."

14. On the emergent realism of *Robinson Crusoe* see: Ian Watt, *The Rise of the Novel* (Berkeley and Los Angeles: University of California Press, 1957), pp. 60–92; Michael McKeon, *The Origins of the English Novel 1600–1740* (Baltimore: Johns Hopkins University Press, 1987), pp. 315–37; and Maximillian Novak, *Realism, Myth, and History in Defoe's Fiction* (Lincoln: University of Nebraska Press, 1983).

15. Watt, *Rise*, p. 29.

16. Defoe, *Robinson Crusoe*, pp. 163–64.

17. In a review of *Foe* Dennis Donoghue trenchantly observes that the character Foe, a writer given to statements on the multiple meanings of words, "has evidently been reading Jacques Derrida's *De la Grammatologie*." Dennis Donoghue, "Her Man Friday," *New York Times Book Review*, February 22, 1987, p. 26. Several critics have taken Friday's silence as the occasion for more substantive explorations of *Foe*'s debt to French poststructuralism. See David Attwell, *J. M. Coetzee: South Africa and the Politics of Writing*; Teresa Dovey, *The Novels of J. M. Coetzee: Lacanian Allegories* (Johannesburg: AD Donker, 1988); Michael Marais, " 'Little Enough, Less than Little, Nothing': Ethics, Engagement and Change in the Fiction of J. M. Coetzee," special issue of *Modern Fiction Studies* on "South African Fiction after Apartheid," ed. David Attwell, 46(1), 2000, pp. 159–82, 164; Gayatri Chakravorty Spivak, "Theory in the Margin: Coetzee's *Foe* Reading Defoe's *Crusoe/ Roxana*, " *English in Africa* 17(2), October 1990, pp. 1–23; and, for a forceful critique of Spivak, Kwaku Larbi Korang, "An Allegory of Re-Reading: Postcolonialism, Resistance, and J. M. Coetzee's *Foe*," *World Literature Written in English* 32(2), 33(1), 1992–93, rpt. in *Critical Essays on J. M. Coetzee*, ed. Kossew, pp. 180–97, 183, 194, n. 8.

18. Korang, "Allegory," pp. 188, 193.

19. Homi K. Bhabha, "Of Mimicry and Man: The Ambivalence of Colonial Discourse," in *The Location of Culture* (New York: Routledge, 1994), pp. 85–92.

20. Coetzee, *White Writing: On the Culture of Letters in South Africa* (New Haven: Yale University Press, 1988), p. 11.

21. I take this to be a central point of Spivak's "Can the Subaltern Speak?," in *Marxism and the Interpretation of Culture*, eds. Cary Nelson and Lawrence Grossberg (Urbana and Chicago: University of Illinois Press, 1988), pp. 271–313.

22. Attwell, *J. M. Coetzee: South Africa and the Politics of Writing*, pp. 104, 105.

23. I provisionally distinguish this version of national allegory from that famously defined by Fredric Jameson, in which Third World texts find a fulsome equivalence between the fictional stories they tell and the story of the nation: "[I]t is this, finally, which must account for the allegorical nature of third-world culture, where the telling of the individual story and the individual experience cannot but ultimately involve the whole laborious telling of the experience of the collectivity itself." Fredric Jameson, "Third-World Literature in the Era of Multinational Capitalism," *Social Text* 15, Fall 1986, pp. 65–88, 85–86. I will return to the implications of Jameson's model later.

24. Coetzee, "The Novel Today," pp. 3–4.

25. Elleke Boehmer, "Endings and new beginnings: South African fiction in transi-

tion," in *Writing South Africa: Literature, Apartheid, and Democracy, 1970–1995,* eds. Derek Attridge and Rosemary Jolly (Cambridge: Cambridge University Press, 1998), pp. 43–56, 45, 50.

26. Boehmer's vision of the future builds on ground laid by several South African commentators. In a widely cited 1990 address entitled "Preparing Ourselves for Freedom," the veteran white ANC stalwart Albie Sachs called for a five-year moratorium on the saying "culture is a weapon of struggle." The dictum, he claimed, had "impoverish[ed]" art, "narrow[ed] down" themes, "extrud[ed]" "all that is funny or curious or genuinely tragic," and "shut out" ambiguity and contradiction, effectively trapping a nation in "the multiple ghettoes of the apartheid imagination." Albie Sachs, "Preparing ourselves for freedom" (1989), rpt. in *Writing South Africa,* eds. Attridge and Jolly, pp. 239–48. The black writer and critic Njabulo Ndebele similarly described a South African literature unhappily imprisoned by the demands of the spectacular, the superficial, and the slogan—a Manichean world of good and evil, black and white, worker and boss, that refused all depth, interiority, complexity. Njabulo Ndebele, *South African Literature and Culture: Rediscovery of the Ordinary* (Manchester and New York: Manchester University Press, 1994). The white South African postcolonial critic Benita Parry urges critics of antiapartheid and postapartheid civil society not to forget the work of language, urging them to look beyond the dicta of "committed writing" to the intricacies of literary form, rich in all manner of defamiliarization, creolization, reappropriation, and subversion. Parry, "Some Provisional Speculations on the Critique of 'Resistance' Literature," in *Altered State? Writing and South Africa,* eds. Elleke Boehmer, Laura Chrisman, Kenneth Parker (Sydney: Dangaroo Press, 1994), pp. 11–24. Also see Parry, "Black Writing," review essay in *Southern African Review of Books,* December 1989–January 1990. For a parallel writer's view on the need to envision a liberation of writing from the burden of political representation, see André Brink, "Reinventing the Real: English South African Fiction Now," *New Contrast* 21(2), June 1993, pp. 44–55.

27. Achmat Dangor, *Kafka's Curse* (New York: Vintage International, 2000), p. 14. Subsequent references appear parenthetically.

28. Benita Parry, "Speech and Silence in the Fictions of J. M. Coetzee," in *Writing South Africa,* eds. Attridge and Jolly, pp. 149–65, 160.

29. Anderson, *Imagined Communities.* Although in its first South African edition (Cape Town: Kwela Books, 1997) *Kafka's Curse* appeared under the label of a novella in a collection that also included three shorter stories, the 2000 Vintage International edition repackaged the novella as an autonomous novel. Such marking of Dangor's narrative offers a marketplace version of Anderson's critical equation of novel and nation as necessarily linked forms.

30. This intensified sense of differentialist consciousness can be seen in the white Afrikaner Freedom Front's campaign for a separate white *Volkstaat* throughout the 1990s; in the highly effective efforts of the National Party (the party that invented apartheid) to bring in colored and Indian voters in the 1994 elections on an overt platform of common linguistic-cultural and economic interests and a covert appeal to reject black affiliations; and in the formation in the late 1990s of a new parliamentary Commission for the Promotion and Protection of the Rights of Cultural, Religious, and Linguistic Communities. Proclaiming their distance from apartheid while preserving and retooling its differentialist imaginary, these initiatives are in sharp contrast to rainbowism's image of a nation in which the identities of particular groups will be individually celebrated yet collectively unified. For a forceful iteration of rainbowism's trans-ethnic consciousness, see Yunus Carrim, "Minorities together and apart," in *Now That We Are Free: Coloured Communities*

in a Democratic South Africa, eds. Wilmot James, Daria Caliguire, and Kerry Cullinan
(Cape Town: IDASA, 1996), pp. 46–51. For broad historical context see Julie Fred-
eriekse, *The Unbreakable Thread: Non-Racialism in South Africa* (Johannesburg: Ravan
Press, 1990).

31. I am indebted to María Rosa Menocal's discussion of the medieval text and its
many derivations in *Shards of Love: Exile and the Origins of the Lyric* (Durham: Duke University Press, 1994), pp. 142–83.

32. Julie Scott Meisami, *Medieval Persian Court Poetry* (Princeton: Princeton University Press, 1987), pp. 159–62. The trope of the garden in late apartheid and postapartheid
South African literature probably deserves its own exegesis. Here I confine myself to simply noting the bare outlines connecting Coetzee's Michael K, quietly gardening in the
face of social abandonment; Gordimer's musings on the poverties of allegory and the social and metaphorical possibilities of gardening in her review of *Life and Times of Michael
K* (cited in note 5); Coetzee's exploration of the garden trope in South African literature
in *White Writing;* and the figure of Marianne in *Kafka's Curse,* lapsed citizen of a dying empire who retreats from her family's farm to the back garden of a house in the southern
Cape, where she waters the plants naked and couples with her colored lover.

33. An intriguing alternative is suggested by André Brink, who asserts that the traditions
of black orature have produced a peculiarly African (both black and white African) strain
of magical realism. André Brink, "Interrogating Silence: New Possibilities Faced by South
African Literature," in *Writing South Africa,* eds. Attridge and Jolly, pp. 14–28, 25–27.

34. Gilles Deleuze and Félix Guattari, *Kafka: Toward a Minor Literature,* trans. Dana
Polan, foreword by Réda Bensmaia, *Theory and History of Literature,* vol. 30 (Minneapolis:
University of Minnesota Press, 1986), p. 18.

35. Walter Benjamin, "Franz Kafka: On the Tenth Anniversary of his Death," in *Illuminations,* pp. 111–40, 117.

36. Deleuze and Guattari, *Kafka,* 27. For examples of this critique, see Caren Kaplan,
Questions of Travel: Postmodern Discourses of Displacement (Durham: Duke University
Press, 1996); and Samia Mehrez, "Azouz Begag: *Un di zafas di bidoufile* or The *Beur* Writer:
A Question of Territory," special issue of *Yale French Studies,* "Post/Colonial Conditions:
Exiles, Migrations, and Nomadisms," eds. Françoise Lionnet and Ronnie Scharfman,
82(1), 1993, pp. 25–42. In the same issue, Lisa Lowe finds a more salutary possibility, cit-
ing the theory of nomadic movement as a strategic, heterogenizing interruption of the
binary schemas of colonialism, nationalism, and nativism. Lowe, "Literary Nomadics in
Francophone Allegories of Postcolonialism: Pham Van Ky and Tahar Ben Jelloun," pp.
43–61.

37. Fredric Jameson, "Third-World Literature in the Era of Multinational Capitalism,"
p. 69.

38. See Aijaz Ahmad's well-known and forceful critique in "Jameson's Rhetoric of
Otherness and the National Allegory," in *In Theory: Classes, Nations, Literatures* (London:
Verso, 1992), pp. 95–122. Réda Bensmaia offers a contrasting model that is more attentive to the work of allegory in "Postcolonial Nations: Political or Poetic Allegories?," special issue of *Research in African Literatures* 30(3), Fall 1999, pp. 151–63.

39. Coetzee, "Interview" and "Time, Tense, and Aspect in Kafka's 'The Burrow,' " in
Doubling the Point, ed. Attwell, pp. 202–32, 203.

40. In the same interview Coetzee observes:

"I was born in 1940; I was eight when the party of Afrikaner Christian nationalism
came to power and set about stopping or even turning back the clock. Its programs in-

cluded a radically discontinuous intervention into time, in that it tried to stop dead or turn around a range of developments normal (in the sense of being the norm) in colonial societies. It also aimed at instituting a sluggish no-time in which an already anachronistic order of patriarchal clans and tribal despotisms would be frozen in place." (209)

41. Coetzee, *Disgrace* (New York: Viking, 1999). Subsequent references appear parenthetically.

42. Fanon, *Wretched* (203).

43. Coetzee, "Time, Tense, and Aspect in Kafka's 'The Burrow,' " p. 229.

44. I do not want to elide the historical differences between *Foe* and the later texts. The literary strategy of intertextuality is differently available and does different work in a late apartheid moment as opposed to a postapartheid moment. What remains consistent is the basic function of intertextuality that I have sought to emphasize here, namely its connection of the project and practice of a national literature to the world beyond.

Postcolonial Latin America and the Magic Realist Imperative: A Report to an Academy

SYLVIA MOLLOY

The first part of my title refers to the discomfort of many Latin American intellectuals when faced with a postcolonial "model" into which they feel they are expected to fit; a model whose terms have been formulated from, and in reference to, a "center" whose interventions, however well intentioned, continue to be seen as imperialistic and/or simplistic. This is a postcolonialism with which modern Latin American intellectuals and scholars have, at best, a mediated relation, one necessitating multiple reformulations and translations. Furthermore, this is a postcolonialism the nature of which very much depends on its site of enunciation, a postcolonialism that is constituted by shifting perspectives. In other words, it is a postcolonialism that formulated "over here" (and by this I mean the U.S. academy), signifies one thing while "over there" (in Latin America, itself a site of multiple enunciations), it signifies something quite different; or, better said, signifies many different things.

As a Latin American studying in France back in the early 1960s (I should say as an Argentine, therefore a Latin American: these things happen in two stages), I received a fairly traditional training in comparative literature. When the time came to write my dissertation, I gravitated toward an adviser and was practically assigned a dissertation topic: I was from Latin America, I would therefore write on the reception of Latin American literature in France, a project I remember my adviser describing as "immensely useful," although it was unclear who or what (myself, my reader, the discipline?) would benefit from my compilation, conclusions and, mainly, my conjectures. I protested I knew very little Latin American literature, having trained in French, and was curtly told: "Vous l'apprendrez." Even then, I knew I was being assigned the role of the native informant, a role I have been asked to play more than once since then, a role many scholars from other countries working in the United States no doubt find familiar.

What certainly *was* "immensely useful" to me was to study certain preconceived French notions of what Latin American literature "should" be. In other words, I noted early on how, even as Latin American literature became available in France, it was already spoken for. Thus for example Jean Cassou, as early as 1900, regretted that Rubén Darío had opted for what he, Cassou, considered derivative symbolism, instead of writing about what he termed, with considerable geographical license, "ce dont nous rêvons, sa forêt et sa pampa natales." (Molloy, *Diffusion* 58). The writer who discredited these preconceptions was of course Borges, a figure that puzzled French critics to no end because *he did not fit.* "Ne cherchons pas en lui un 'écrivain argentin'—bien qu'il aime et évoque souvent son pays—Borges n'est pas un représentant de la littérature argentine, il est un monstre et un génie," wrote a reviewer (Molloy, *Diffusion* 219). Borges did not match French expectations of a Latin American specificity and was therefore a monster (albeit a brilliant one) devoid of nationality. Darío, had he written "regional" poems, probably would have matched those expectations. Alejo Carpentier certainly did, partly because of magic realism (to which I shall return) and partly through reverse snobbery: he was erroneously believed to be Afro-Cuban. "M. Alejo Carpentier qui, sauf erreur de ma part, est un écrivain noir," wrote Max-Pol Fouchet in his enthusiastic review of *The Kingdom of This World* (Molloy, *Diffusion* 191). Parallel to the construction of the "Orient" there was here a very active fabrication of a Latin American "South," one that had to be, of necessity, free of Western alliances so that Western fantasies could generously play themselves out.

I have gone back to personal history, and to that first shock of recognition—I was, on the one hand, the native informant, on the other, the native spoken for—because some aspects of that same vexed construction of Latin American literatures and cultures (I use the plural deliberately) is often at play today in a different but not unrelated setting, that of departments of literature and/or comparative literature in the United States, intent, if not on "exoticizing" Latin America, at least on acritically, even ahistorically, "postcolonizing" it and channeling it through magic realism. The two gestures have more in common than it would, at first, appear.

Mexican anthropologist Jorge Klor de Alva has written astutely on the pitfalls of applying post-1960 constructions of colonialism, imperialism, and postcolonialism retroactively and anachronistically to the Americas in general, and to Latin America in particular. I will not go into his arguments in detail, but will retain what is obvious to historians and is often neglected by theoreticians and literary scholars, namely, the specificity of the Latin American colonial experience both temporally, politically, and ideologically. With the exception of parts of the Caribbean, Spain's colonies seceded very early in the nineteenth century; the confrontation was not between indigenous peoples and metropolitan colonizers (although it may have been that too) but between Euro-Americans (*criollos*), Westernized *mestizos*, and even some Europeans (*Peninsulares*) against other Europeans; an experience more akin, say, to the North American experience, than to that of British colonies a full century later. As Latin Americanists working on nineteenth-century literature know full well, the points of contact and friction between the two Americas, their literatures and cultures in the nineteenth century, even in their relations to Europe, are many and fruitful, yet remain largely underexplored. It is in the nineteenth century that Latin American cultures "write back," it is then that they plagiarize, translate and misread,[1] with the difference that there is no real "empire" to write back to nor to substantially dissent from. Even before secession, Spain, a decaying metropolis already superseded by its energetic colonies, was no longer a model to subvert; she had long been replaced by France (and to a point by England) in the cultural imaginary of Latin America. So, if Latin America is "writing back" anywhere—and, given the identification of its new national cultures with Enlightenment models, one wonders whether the expression applies—one could argue that it is doing it to the "wrong" address. It is not striking back, in name of a recuperated indigenous past,[2] but constructing itself afresh, as an alternate, transculturated West.[3]

The distinctiveness of Latin American postcolonialism, which does not necessarily exclude neocolonial situations within its very boundaries (a situation the United States itself should not be unfamiliar with), lacks a place, however, in the legitimating narrative the U.S. academy usually tells itself about Latin America. Instead, in that narrative, Latin American literature "begins" at another time and in another place, is made to "emerge" ("emerge" into U.S. awareness, as in "emergent" literatures that always seem to emerge when the First World discovers a need for new cultural goods) in the early 1960s, an emergence coinciding, roughly, with the Cuban revolution—a "new" beginning—and with the publication of One Hundred Years of Solitude—a "new" genre, magic realism, a genre against which all Latin American literature would be read in a sort of ahistorical, postcolonial present. This is a literature endowed with a new, snappy genealogy and new interlocutors: Perry Anderson "dates" One Hundred Years of Solitude by calling it a typically Third World "shadow configuration" of First World modernism (García Canclini 44) and relates García Márquez's novel to Salman Rushdie's Midnight's Children and Yilmiz Güney's Yol. "It is necessary to question above all the mania that has almost fallen out of use in Third World countries: to speak of the Third World and include in the same package Colombia, India, and Turkey," observes Néstor García Canclini of Anderson's homogenizing gesture (45), echoing the concerns of other Latin American critics and not a few postcolonial theorists from non-Western countries.[4] Above all, it is necessary to question the short-sighted view that García Márquez's novel, in this new configuration, is the symptom of Latin American modernism when that modernism, as García Canclini rightly argues, has been the subject of cultural reflection and aesthetic experimentation in Latin America since the turn of the century. Familiar to any Hispanic reader, this earlier modernist experimentation, however, was only spottily translated into English.

Crucial in this recycling of Latin America into a "new" postcolonial, which sacrifices the thick texture of a process to the superficial similarity of its effects, is, I think, a problem of language, more specifically, with language. Critiquing the metropolitan urge to homogenize so-called "Third World literatures" and contain their representations, levelling them with "the rhetoric of Otherness," Aijaz Ahmad reflected a good ten years ago on the problematic availability of certain cultural traditions. These texts may become available directly, through translation, wrote Ahmad; more often, however, they arrive indirectly, in critical essays about those texts that offer "versions and shadows of texts produced in other spaces of the globe" (127). Despite an admirable effort to tease apart "Third World literatures," Ahmad drew a not altogether convincing distinction between these unavailable texts (mainly from the Indian subcontinent) and Latin American literatures, whose "direct" availability he stressed:

> Literatures of South America and parts of the Caribbean are *directly* available to the metropolitan critic through Spanish and Portuguese, which are after all European languages. *Entire* vocabularies, styles, linguistic sensibilities exist now in English, French, Italian, for translations from these languages. Europeans and American theorists can either read those literary documents *directly,* or in case one is not entirely proficient in Spanish or Portuguese, he/she can nevertheless speak of their literatures with *easy familiarity* because of the *translatability* of the originals. (127; my emphases)

The notion of easy familiarity is both rich and problematic here, since it appears based on a translatability that is presented, *at the same time,* as a trope and a linguistic reality. As we know only too well in departments of foreign languages, linguistic competence is a highly charged ideological issue and nothing is "easy." If Spanish and Portuguese are "after all" European languages, they may be a little less European than others. And even if they are "after all" European, I would argue that they are certainly not considered metropolitan languages and that their complex cultural traditions, on both sides of the Atlantic, are largely ignored. In this country, the purported "easy familiarity" and "translatability" of Spanish (Portuguese, a less "familiar" language is, I would argue, in a different situation), usually work to its detriment, crediting the language with an unwarranted transparency that seriously limits its range. Rarely, if at all, does the academy view Spanish as a language of authority or of intellectual exchange: Latin American critics who have debated long and hard on postcolonialism *from* Latin America, specifically addressing Latin American difference—say Nelly Richard in Chile, Néstor García Canclini in Mexico, Jesús Martín Barbero in Colombia, to name but three—are rarely if ever brought into general debates about postcolonialism, even when their texts are available in English, that is, there are "real" translations of their works. Despite this very direct availability, their interlocutors in this country (with a few notable exceptions) seem to be other Latin Americanists working on postcolonial issues, such as Walter Mignolo, Mary Louise Pratt, George Yúdice, or John Beverley, scholars who, themselves, are not always recognized as productive participants in the more general postcolonial debates.[5]

Let me then render Ahmad's statement a little more complicated and say that Latin American texts appear to offer the *illusion* of an easy familiarity, the *illusion* of translatability, and thus create the *illusion* of cultural competence, not to mention the *illusion* of institutional expertise, usually based on a smattering of texts. This apparently "easy" translatability is further complicated by ideologies of reception that "choose," as it were, certain vehicles (but not any vehicle) for that translatability, certain representations and texts (but not any representation or text). Selected Latin American texts are thus uncoupled from their particular mode of functioning within their respective Latin American traditions *and then* turned into a corpus that purports to be "fully" representative of an "entire . . . sensibility" called "Latin America," "Third-World modernism," or "postcolonial literature." (What exactly does it represent?, Who selects the criteria of representativity?, and From where, ideologically speaking, is that selection being made?, are of course the key questions that should be asked here.) What is missing from these reductive attempts at reconstructing "entire . . . sensibilities," is the understanding of culture as *relation;* one ends up with a dehistoricized, "manageable" corpus but not with modes of reading, with cultural genealogies, or with theoretical speculation.

Several years ago Juan Goytisolo, in a melancholy piece in the *New York Times Book Review,* pondered on the politics of cultural representation in general, the reception of Spanish-language literatures in particular and their place in a dialogue of literatures and, importantly, the marketing tactics of publishers. He spoke mostly of Spain, a country, he said, that was doomed to being a single-faced culture, allowed only one image that would "translate well" in the international market and "represent" Spain. The image might change with the passing of time but there was always a quota: one image. Latin America, in itself a more fluid cultural composite, suffers from readings that are even more reductive, at least when they come from the North. Real geographical proximity seems to increase the cultural divide; the nearer the border, the more anxious the containment and policing of cultural representativity becomes.

The history of magic realism has been written elsewhere and it is not my intention here to retrace its long and tenacious life. It should be recalled, however, that from its very inception, this figuration of Latin America was a self-conscious, literary effort by a self-conscious, literary writer, Alejo Carpentier. An excrescence of French surrealism "transculturated" to Cuba and, by extension, to the rest of Latin America, magic realism was a strategical, polemical element in a transnational literary quarrel. It was Carpentier's response both to the Surrealists' conception of poetic image and to the avant-garde's discovery of "primitive" art. More than sprouting then "naturally," from Latin American "reality," as Carpentier himself, in a burst of nativistic fervor, would have his reader believe,[6] magic realism was born on the same operating table on which Lautréamont's umbrella hobnobbed with the sewing machine. A transculturated mode, in the way Fernando Ortiz and Angel Rama (two other Latin American critics rarely cited in postcolonial debates) understood the notion of transculturation, one more product of what Gustavo Pérez Firmat has called Latin America's "translation sensibility" (1), magic realism is a mode *among many other modes of literary figuration in Latin America;* yet it has been singled out by First World readerships to signify, as surely as Carmen Miranda's fruity cornucopias, "Latin America." What magic realism loses, in this cultural transaction that privileges one form of representation to the detriment of others, is precisely its relational quality. Latin American magic realism becomes a regional, ethnicized commodity, a form of that essentialized primitivism that continues to lurk in the minds of even well-intentioned First-World critics.[7] For a country that persists in representing itself as a Western country (I speak of the United States), it is also a handy way of establishing spatial distance and, perhaps more importantly, temporal distance vis-à-vis a region that may be too close for comfort, of practicing what Johannes

Fabian has called "the denial of coevalness." Magic realism is refulgent, amusing, and kitschy (Carmen Miranda's headdress; José Arcadio Buendía's tattooed penis)—but it doesn't happen, couldn't happen, here.

With its exotic connotations, its potential for stereotypical casting, its "poetic" alienation into the realm of the "magical," that is the *very far away*, the *very other*, magic realism has become, for the United States, a mode of Latin American *representation*, not a mode of Latin American *production*. As such—as representation, not as production—it is used to measure Latin American *literary* quality. It is used to both effect and confirm First-World "discoveries" of undetected Latin American talent: readerly expectation (abetted by canny publishing strategies) explains, for example, the huge success of Isabel Allende *outside* Latin America, a phenomenon akin to the reception of Jerry Lewis in France. Applied retrospectively, magic realism may be used to enhance past texts: witness the way in which, in many reviews written in the United States, magic realism rubs off on Borges, recycled as a "precursor" of sorts, the scope of his work considerably diminished. More alarmingly, magic realism serves to banish many Latin American writers to the wasteland of the "different-but-not-in-the-way-we-expect-you-to-be-different" or, even worse, to the ever-expanding purgatory of the forever untranslatable. That perception of Latin American literatures should primarily be confined to this mode seems lamentable; that, additionally, magic realism should be seen as the favored expression of a homogenized postcoloniality and as such exclusively representative of "Latin America" narrows perspective even further.[8] Postcolonial studies should afford a way of teasing apart differences instead of erasing them, of unpacking preconceived notions instead of prepackaging cultural commodities. Unfortunately, they seldom do.

I would like to mention very briefly the predicament of the Latin American writer in the complicated reception scene I have described, a scene ignoring the heterogeneous composition of Latin American literature, its distinctive, mediated relations to its diverse metropolitan centers, its transcultured Westernism. A well-meaning observer, Timothy Brennan, notes for example that among Third World writers there "has been a trend of cosmopolitan commentators on the Third World, who offer an *inside view* of formerly submerged peoples for target reading publics in Europe and North America in novels that comply with metropolitan literary tastes. Some of its better known authors have been from Latin America: for example, García Márquez, Vargas Llosa, Alejo Carpentier, Miguel Asturias [sic], and others" (Brennan 63). This notion of a metropolitan "taste" waiting to be satisfied with "an *inside view* of formerly submerged peoples," a view so redolent of the most imperialist anthropological approach, does not even contemplate (cannot even imagine) that the target reading publics of Latin American writers are, primarily, Latin American; that it is for the literary taste of those publics, and not to comply with metropolitan demands, that the Latin American writer primarily writes. Awareness of the conditions of production and reception of texts *in Latin America*, awareness of what Spivak calls "the staging of the language as the production of agency" ("Politics" 187), would show precisely how the text functions in relation to its many contexts and not as a token commodity.

I am not proposing quick fixes, just calling attention to these operations in the hopes of generating a more thoughtful debate on Latin America from within the U.S. academy, a debate (and exchange) recognizing in Latin American cultural production not only multiple representational strategies and aesthetic practices but a theoretical and critical agency that Latin America has been denied until now. This appears particularly urgent at a time when the growth of Spanish has reached uncalculated highs in this country, when it is no longer possible to dismiss it as a merely utilitarian language, although the temptation to do so may persist;[9] particularly urgent when border crossings and bilingualism are no longer "mere" sociological issues but have become, in many cases, aesthetic choices demanding competent readings; particularly urgent, finally, because Latin American literature, both as creative and institutional practice, and its relation to other literatures, is also being reformulated in specifically Latin American settings, and those "outside" reformulations ("outside" the U.S. academy) should be an integral element of a truly transnational debate. If the U.S. academy, and within it, not just departments of Spanish and Portuguese but departments of literature at large, cannot relate to such reformulations and debates and cannot engage in exchange, if only to realize the importance of the local in any transnational dialogue, then we will have little more than incidences of cultural tourism.

A parting note. The second part of my title, unmentioned until now, is less an allusion to Kafka than to an essay by the Argentine critic Claudia Gilman, titled "La literatura comparada: informe para una academia (norteamericana)," a piece critical of certain aspects of the Bernheimer report for the American Comparative Literature Association, mainly of its prepackaged multiculturalism with which it has trouble relating, perceiving it as one more attempt by the United States to dictate cultural policy. The essay, which has its own, not insignificant problems—it bypasses the issue of location, never pauses to consider the *where* (Argentina, Latin America) of its reflection[10]—closes on a rebellious, petulant phrase, one that perhaps only an Argentine would write, a phrase fully measuring the crossed connections between Latin America and the United States: "Ironically, we Third-Worlders, we 'postcolonials,' women, Jews, homosexuals, are not threatened [by this report] and can safely go on making our own mistakes. For once, we are not threatened by something" (43). The essay appeared in Buenos Aires, in the 1997 issue of *Filología* devoted to a reflection on comparative literature. By titling my own essay to echo Gilman's Kafkaesque allusion, I had initially thought that I would report to the U.S. academy about a Latin American report on a report to the U.S. academy. And perhaps, in a manner or speaking, that is what I have done.

NOTES

1. See Sylvia Molloy, "The Scene of Reading," and Doris Sommer, "Plagiarized Authenticity: Sarmiento's Cooper and Others."

2. In *The Burden of Modernity: The Rhetoric of Cultural Discourse in Spanish America*, Carlos Alonso persuasively reflects on the "narrative of futurity" that informs Latin America's secession from Spain and blots out the recuperation (or in some cases the invention) of an indigenous past: "[T]he indigenous populations received the same treatment in this ideological narrative of Creole hegemony as their erstwhile Spanish oppressors: they as well as the Spaniards were simply written out of it by being subsumed under the mantle of the preterit, by being assigned to what from the perspective of the narrative of the future could only be described as the *non-place* of the past" (16). The fact that *mestizaje* was a most distinctive effect of Spanish colonialism in Latin America, further complicates the notion of recuperating a "pure" indigenous past.

3. I take this notion of alternate Westernness from George Yúdice's excellent essay, "We Are *Not* the World," He writes:

> There is a well-founded reaction against Eurocentrism within multiculturalism that seeks to valorize other, non-Western cultural experiences. The transfer of this tendency to Latin American cultures, however, can produce serious distortions, not the least of which is to argue that Latin America is non-Western. . . . Latin American cultural experiences, I would like to argue, constitute *alternate* ways of being Western. . . . [It] is not that Latin American cultures are Western in the same way as the US or France but, rather, that they are inscribed in a transcultural relation to Western modernity just as much as, say, Eastern Europe (or for that matter multicultural US)." (209–10)

4. As Gayatri Chakravorty Spivak writes, "[A]11 the literature of the Third World gets translated into a sort of with-it translatese, so that the literature by a woman in Palestine begins to resemble, in the feel of its prose, something by a man in Taiwan" ("Politics," 180).

5. None of these names appears, for example, in the "postcolonial theory" bibliographical section of Susan Bassnett's *Comparative Literature*. As a matter of fact, there are only three entries related to Latin America in that bibliography: Carlos Fuentes (who can hardly be claimed as a theoretician), a rather old anthology of Chicano fiction (Sommers-Ybarra Fausto, 1979), and a more recent collection of essays in Chicano cultural studies (Calderón-Saldívar, 1990). The pertinence of the last two to Latin America is, at best, indirect. The inclusion of Fuentes as a Latin American postcolonial thinker is one more case of what Yúdice calls "a politics of reception of so-called Third World figures that gives priority to high profile positions and gestures and neglects the contradictions of those figures in their national settings" (204).

6. A position murkily echoed by Miguel Angel Asturias, in an interview after receiving the Nobel Prize, in which magic realism is strangely equated with social justice (See Morris).

7. To give but one example: Susan Bassnett, when speaking of Nicolás Guillén's book, *Motivos de son*, concludes that these are "'sound' poems"—misinterpreting the word *son* which refers to a highly sophisticated musical composition and not to mere sound. Carrying the primitive sound motif even further, she adds that in Alejo Carpentier's *The Lost Steps*, the protagonist is "led to the primeval forests of his origins ostensibly by the search for a primitive instrument" (84). The observation is worthy of Cassou's demand for forests and native pampas from Rubén Darío. For an acute analysis of Cuban *son* as a transculturated form, see Pérez Firmat, 67–79.

8. To quote Spivak again: "[T]he interesting literary text might be precisely the text where you do not learn what the majority view of majority cultural representation or self-representation of a nation state might be" ("Politics" 187). The apparent lack of interest

in "non-representative" Latin American texts in this country is reflected in its particularly problematic translation politics.

9. "Departments of Spanish may flourish, but not because of the attraction of Latin-American literature courses," contends William Moebius (253). While this may or may not be true, the mere possibility that cultural reasons and not base pragmatism might explain the success of Spanish departments seems to worry the author. Interestingly, in quoting the MLA statistics for English and foreign language majors from 1993 to 1994, Moebius only reports statistics for French, German, and English.

10. But then neither did the conference on "Comparative Literature in Transnational Times" at Princeton, where I first read this text. When, in a general discussion on national literatures, I asked why the issue of U.S. literature as a national literature never came up, the answers were surprisingly unsatisfactory, going from the vague ("we don't think in those terms") to the flippant ("probably because we're like a clearinghouse"). Notably, in both off-the-cuff answers a communal "we" was used. Also remarkably, no one stopped to think that while they did not think "in those terms," they were indeed being thought of "in those terms" by other cultures. For acute comments on location and cross-cultural readings, see Millington.

Works Cited

Ahmad, Aijaz, "'Third World Literature' and the Nationalist Ideology," *Journal of Arts and Ideas* 17–18, 1989, pp. 117–36.

Alonso, Carlos, *The Burden of Modernity: The Rhetoric of Cultural Discourse in Spanish America* (Oxford and New York: Oxford University Press, 1998).

Bassnett, Susan, *Comparative Literature: A Critical Introduction* (Oxford: Blackwell, 1993).

Brennan, Timothy, "The National Longing for Form," in *Nation and Narration*, ed. Homi K. Bhabha (London and New York: Routledge, 1990), pp. 44–70.

Fabian, Johannes, *Time and the Other: How Anthropology Makes Its Object* (New York: Columbia University Press, 1983).

García Canclini, Néstor, *Hybrid Cultures: Strategies for Entering and Leaving Modernity*, trans. Christopher L. Chiappari and Silvia L. López, foreword by Renato Rosaldo (Minneapolis and London: University of Minnesota Press, 1995).

Gilman, Claudia, "La literature comparada: informe para una academia (norteamericana)," *Filología* XXX(1–2), 1997, pp. 33–44.

Klor de Alva, Jorge, "Colonialism and Postcolonialism as (Latin) American Mirage." *Colonial Latin American Review* I(1–2), 1992, pp. 3–23.

Millington, Mark, "On Location: The Question of Reading Crossculturally," *Siglo XX / 20th Century Critique and Cultural Discourse* 13(1–2), 1995, pp. 13–39.

Moebius, William, "Lines in the Sand: Comparative Literature and the National Literature Departments," *Comparative Literature* 49(3), 1997, pp. 243–58.

Molloy, Sylvia, *La diffusion de la littérature hispano-américaine en France au XXe siècle* (Paris: Presses Universitaires de France, 1972).

———, "The Scene of Reading," in *At Face Value: Autobiographical Writing in Spanish America* (Cambridge and New York: Cambridge University Press, 1991), pp. 13–76.

Morris, Ira, "Interview with Miguel Angel Asturias," *Monthly Review*, March 1968, pp. 50–56.

Pérez Firmat, Gustavo, *The Cuban Condition: Translation and Identity in Modern Cuban Literature* (Cambridge and New York: Cambridge University Press, 1989).

Sommer, Doris, "Plagiarized Authenticity: Sarmiento's Cooper and Others," in *Foundational Fictions: The National Romances of Latin America* (Berkeley, Los Angeles, Oxford: University of California Press, 1991), pp. 52–82.

Spivak, Gayatri Chakravorty, "The Politics of Translation," in *Destabilizing Theory: Contemporary Feminist Debates*, eds. Michèle Barrett and Anne Phillips (Cambridge: Polity Press, 1992), pp. 177–200.

Yúdice, George, "We Are *Not* the World," *Social Text* 31–32, 1992, pp. 201–16.

Death in Translation

DAVID DAMROSCH

According to the Preliminary Notes to Milorad Pavić's *Dictionary of the Khazars*, his book is a reconstruction of a long-lost encyclopedia concerning a people who lived around the Black Sea until the tenth century, when they disappeared from history. Published in 1691 by a Polish printer in Prussia, the *Lexicon Cosri* was destroyed a year later by the Inquisition. Only two privately held copies survived. One, fastened with a golden lock, was printed in poisoned ink; it had a companion copy, not poisoned, fitted with a silver lock:

> Insubordinates and infidels who ventured to read the proscribed dictionary risked the threat of death. Whoever opened the book soon grew numb, stuck on his own heart as on a pin. Indeed, the reader would die on the ninth page at the words *Verbum caro factum est* ("The Word became flesh"). If read simultaneously with the poisoned copy, the auxiliary copy enabled one to know exactly when death would strike. Found in the auxiliary copy was the note: "When you wake and suffer no pain, know that you are no longer among the living." (6)

Pavić's book is one of a growing number of recent novels that take translation as an explicit theme. A novel in dictionary form, the *Dictionary of the Khazars* is presented as a translation of three different encyclopedias concerning the Khazars (who, unlike the poisoned encyclopedia, did actually exist). Both within the *Dictionary* itself, and in the novel's own worldly circulation, issues of translation are closely intertwined with issues of national identity—explicitly of the Khazars, implicitly of Yugoslavia and its constituent republics. This theme proves to have deep ethical implications both within the book and in its reception at home and abroad, for running through the book is a current of Serbian nationalism deeply hostile to Tito's attempt to weld Yugoslavia into a unified nation.

The book's politics, and their ethical consequences, have often been obscured by the book's status as a work of international postmodernism. Most commonly, foreign readers have celebrated the *Dictionary of the Khazars* as a tour de force of metafictional play, and this aspect of the text is certainly evident as early as the book's cover and table of contents. Its cross-referenced entries invite the reader

This is a revised version of a discussion that appears as the ninth chapter of my book *What Is World Literature?* (Princeton: Princeton University Press, 2003), pp. 260–79, where Pavić figures in a section of the book devoted to the contemporary phenomenon of works being written primarily or even exclusively to circulate abroad in translation.

to abandon the narrative progressions of ordinary novels and consider whole new ways of reading, signaled from the start by the fact that the book is published in two different editions, "Male" and "Female." As the front cover of the Female Edition dramatically announces (with corresponding language on the cover of the Male Edition):

> This is the FEMALE EDITION of the Dictionary.
> The MALE edition is almost identical. But NOT quite.
> Be warned that ONE PARAGRAPH is crucially different.
> The choice is yours.

Clearly, readers of this novel have new opportunities, and new responsibilities.

Pavić had been a respected poet and scholar of Serbian literature but was almost unknown outside Yugoslavia until he published his novel, which rapidly became a runaway success around the globe. The French rights to the novel were acquired while the book was still in press, and it was published in Paris as well as in Belgrade in 1984, by which time another dozen translations were already under way. By the late 1990s it had been translated into no fewer than twenty-six languages, including Japanese and Catalan, and had sold several million copies in all. Yet the book's international success involved the neglect or outright misreading of its political content. Presumably the book's Catalan translators were fully alive to Pavić's covert attack on national unity, but most foreign readers missed this dimension of the text, at least until Yugoslavia began to disintegrate after Tito's death. At that point Pavić began to speak out bitterly on behalf of the cause of Serbian nationalism, his international reputation giving weight to his words at home. The metaphysical magician turned out to have an angry joker up his sleeve. His novel contains a political polemic that had been hidden in plain sight from international audiences who had welcomed the novel as "an Arabian Nights romance," "a wickedly teasing intellectual game," and an opportunity "to lose themselves in a novel of love and death," as the flyleaf of the American edition describes the book. How should we read this novel now, and what can its double life tell us about the ethics of translation across national boundaries?

The nationalist undercurrent of Pavić's book could have remained invisible abroad not only through outsiders' ignorance of local concerns but also because in many ways the book appears to be a satire of any one-sided viewpoint. The three encyclopedias represent three limited, warring points of view, Christian, Muslim, and Jewish: each encyclopedia tells the story of the Khazars' conversion to *that* religion. Pavić based this multiple tale on a dialogue by the medieval poet and philosopher Judah ha-Levi, the *Kitab al-Khazari* or *Book of the Khazars*, written in Arabic in Spain in around 1140. Judah ha-Levi in turn was meditating on historical sources that told of the conversion of the Khazars to Judaism in around 740 C.E. No other case is known of a non-Jewish country ever having converted to Judaism in this way, and apparently the kingdom remained at least nominally Jewish until it was defeated and dismantled by Russian invaders late in the tenth century.

In Judah ha-Levi's account, the Khazars' heathen ruler, the Kaghan, has a dream in which an angel tells him that his intentions are pleasing to God but his deeds are not. The Kaghan decides that he must determine which of the world systems surrounding him makes the most sense, and so he summons to his court a Greek philosopher, a Christian scholastic, and a Muslim theologian, and probes the basis of their beliefs. Dissatisfied by each of their answers, he reluctantly invites a rabbi as well; "I had not intended to ask any Jew," the Kaghan remarks, "because I am aware of their reduced condition and narrow-minded views, as their misery left them nothing commendable" (Judah ha-Levi 40). The rabbi, however, gives the most persuasive arguments in favor of Judaism, stressing the events of Hebrew salvation history accepted by Muslims and Christians alike, whereupon the Kaghan and his people convert.

Pavić used this remarkable dialogue as the basis for his set of three one-sided encyclopedias. He added further entries to trace the later history of knowledge of the Khazars, centering on the efforts of a seventeenth-century Walachian nobleman, Avram Brankovich, to reconstruct these early events in the form of the original Lexicon, destroyed a year after he published it in 1691; still further entries describe several modern scholars' efforts to reconstruct Brankovich's destroyed book. They are frustrated in their efforts by the Devil—or rather, three devils, one for each major faith—who exert themselves to keep the scholars from re-assembling the three parts of the encyclopedia. Having long divided and conquered the world, the devils wish humanity to continue to see only one side of reality, each group trapped in its own partial viewpoint. Thus the struggle to create (and then to re-create) the multilingual dictionary becomes a cosmic battle to piece reality together into a whole, or to hold it apart in fragments.

The *Dictionary of the Khazars* has a multinational pedigree. It is directly descended from the imaginary encyclopedia of Tlön in Borges's story "Tlön, Uqbar, Orbis Tertius," with the ambitious twist that where Borges only described his encyclopedia, Paviæ actually writes one, or at least three hundred pages worth of the supposed fragments of its three versions. Other Borges stories, like "The Library of Babylon" and "Death and the Compass," are certainly in the background as well. Like Borges's stories, the novel also plays on Mallarmé's dream of a book as "a spiritual instrument" that would encompass the entire world within its covers. The *Dictionary of the Khazars* is also, as its cover says, "an Arabian Nights romance," complete with tales embedded within tales, references to Haroun al-Rashid, and a Scheherazade-like poet-princess, Ateh, who has blind scribes draw sacred letters on her eyelids, letters that will kill whoever sees them, so that enemies cannot surprise her in her sleep (21). If the lost language of the Khazars survives at all, it is among a group of Black Sea parrots, descendants of parrots whom Ateh taught to sing her poems. Finally, in its use of a medieval Jewish source-text, the *Dictionary* was surely inspired by Danilo Kiš's 1976 story sequence *A Tomb for Boris Davidovich*, published just two years before Pavić began his novel. Kiš's title character, Boris Davidovich Novsky, is a modern reincarnation of a skeptical fourteenth-century rabbi, Baruch David Neumann, questioned by the Inquisition as to his faith, in an extended dialogue recorded at the time and retold in modified form by Kiš, who footnotes the sources he is transforming, just as Pavić does in turn.

Kiš's book is an important precursor in the linking of nation and translation in a Yugoslavian context. On the first page, his narrator says he is about to tell a true story of the 1932 murder of a young revolutionary who is falsely suspected of informing on the activities of her cell and is consequently killed. He adds, though, that for the story

> to be true in the way its author dreams about, it would have to be told in Romanian, Hungarian, Ukranian, or Yiddish; or rather, in a mixture of all these languages. . . . If the narrator, therefore, could reach the unattainable, terrifying moment of Babel, the humble pleadings and awful beseechings of Hanna Krzyzewska would resound in Romanian, in Polish, in Ukranian (as if her death were only the consequence of some great and fatal misunderstanding), and then just before the death rattle and final calm her incoherence would turn into the prayer for the dead, spoken in Hebrew, the language of being and dying. (3)

Pavić followed Kiš in privileging Hebrew as a key language hidden with the national languages of Eastern Europe, and he followed Kiš as well in commenting obliquely on the Yugoslavian situation by writing about anywhere but Yugoslavia itself. The stories in Kiš's book are set decades (and in Rabbi Neumann's case centuries) before the present, and concern characters from a range of countries, always outside Yugoslavia. Only in the final page of the final story does a Russian character, A. A. Darmolatov—significantly, a poet-translator—come to Montenegro. He is attending a jubilee celebration for *The Mountain Wreath,* the great tragicomic drama by Petar Petrovich Njegoš, Montenegrin prince-bishop and a founder of Serbian poetry in the mid-nineteenth century. Darmolatov sits in the tall chair built for the seven-foot Njegoš, his legs dangling childishly above the floor—a comic image of the Russian's inability to fill the Montenegrin hero's shoes. This final image is the closest Kiš ever gets to direct local application, but his book was widely understood to be a critical commentary on the lingering Stalinism of Tito's Yugoslavia.

Building on his wide network of literary and historical sources, Pavić takes a further step along comparable lines, expanding Kiš's Slavic framework to give his characters a global perspective. His modern scholars form a multinational trinity: a Polish-born, Yale-trained professor, Dorothea Schultz; an Egyptian Hebraist, Abu Kabir Muawia; and a Serbian archaeologist, Isailo Suk, professor at Novi Sad, a center of Serbian culture where Pavić himself long taught literature. These characters and their earlier counterparts are all flamboyantly multilingual, sometimes using different languages for specific purposes. Already in the seventeenth century, Avram Brankovich's family "count in Tzintzar, lie in Walachian, are silent in Greek, sing hymns in Russian, are cleverest in Turkish, and speak their mother tongue—Serbian—only when they intend to kill" (25). Brankovich "cannot stay with one language for long: he changes them like mistresses and speaks Walachian one minute and Hungarian or Turkish the next, and he has begun to learn Khazar from a parrot. They say he also speaks Spanish in his

sleep, but this language melts by the time he is awake" (28). In a dream he is told
a poem in Hebrew, a language that he doesn't know; when he manages to get it
interpreted, it proves to be a famous poem by Judah ha-Levi concerning the
poet's divided self, living in Spain far from his distant homeland: "My heart is in
the East, but I am at the end of the West. / . . . Zion is in Edom's bondage, and I
am in Arabian fetters" (29). Only a reader of Hebrew can know this, as Pavić
places the reader into Brankovich's position by giving the poem only in Hebrew,
without translation, though this has long been the most widely translated medieval Hebrew poem. It is this poem that leads Brankovich to Judah ha-Levi's
Book of the Khazars, setting him off on his increasingly obsessive quest for information about the Khazars.

In a confidential report to the Viennese court, which is always on the watch
for challenges to its imperial authority, an incarnation of the Devil named
Nikon Sevast describes Brankovich's efforts to assemble materials and to create a
complete account of Khazar history and culture:

> Brankovich had eight camel-loads of books brought to Constantinople from the
> Zarand district and from Vienna, and more are still arriving. He has sealed himself off
> from the world with walls of dictionaries and old manuscripts. . . . Brankovich's card
> file, created along with the library, encompassed a thousand pages, covering a variety of
> subjects: from catalogues of sighs and exclamations in Old Church Slavonic to a regis-
> ter of salts and teas, and enormous collections of hair, beards, and moustaches of the
> most diverse colors and styles from living and dead persons of all races, which our mas-
> ter glues onto glass bottles and keeps as a sort of museum of old hairstyles. His own hair
> is not represented in this collection, but he has ordered that strands of it be used to
> weave his coat of arms with a one-eyed eagle and the motto "Every master embraces
> his own death." (45)

The dictionary may well be the death of the reader if not of Brankovich himself,
as the only surviving copies are the gold- and silver-locked volumes; a reader
who finds a copy thus has an equal chance of being enlightened or murdered by
the book on reaching the words "*Verbum caro factum est*" on the ninth page.

Isailo Suk and Abu Kabir Muawia are murdered in Istanbul in 1982, just before they and Dorothea Schultz succeed in reassembling the dictionary, and so
Pavić's 1984 novel can only be a partial reconstruction, incomplete and often at
variance with information about the original. Late in the book, for example,
Pavić actually reprints the ninth page of a Latin and Hebrew translation of
Judah ha-Levi's Arabic dialogue, published in 1660 as *Liber Cosri* and obviously
prefiguring Brankovich's lost *Lexicon Cosri*. The ninth page of Judah ha-Levi's
treatise does indeed discuss Christ's incarnation, yet the fatal words from John's
gospel can't be found there. Instead, the Christian sage paraphrases the Bible, interestingly translating within Latin itself between physical and metaphysical
terms: "incorporata (*incarnata*) est Deitas, transiens in uterum virginis" ("God
was incorporated [*incarnated*], passing through a virgin's womb," 298). Source
and reconstruction together might even complete the true dictionary's destruction: Judah ha-Levi's *Liber Cosri* and Pavić's *Dictionary* may resemble certain

Khazar mirrors, made of polished salt, which come in two varieties, slow and fast, reflecting past or future events rather than the present. Princess Ateh is said to have died when her servants foolishly brought her a pair of these mirrors before the fatal letters had been washed off her eyelids:

> She saw herself in the mirrors with closed lids and died instantly. She vanished between two blinks of the eye, or better said, for the first time she read the lethal letters on her eyelids, because she had blinked the moment before and the moment after, and the mirrors had reflected it. She died, killed simultaneously by letters from both the past and the future. (24)

. . .

To an unusual degree, Pavić's book openly anticipates its circulation in translation after publication. Indeed, Pavić actually arranges matters so that his book *needs* to be translated in order to achieve a full expression of his themes. Intent upon breaking up linear ways of reading, Pavić stresses a consequence of the multilingualism of the "lost" original: its entries would have been alphabetized differently in Greek, Arabic, and Hebrew, so that readers in each language would inevitably have been reading different books, arranged in a different order in each translation. Pavić's original novel can only describe this difference without embodying it, since he doesn't really want to limit his readership to the few people who could read those three languages, even assuming that he could write them all himself, which doesn't appear to be the case. His book is written in Serbo-Croatian throughout, though he asserts that the 1691 *Lexicon Cosri* produced by the Polish printer Johannes Daubmannus was "printed in Arabic, Hebrew, and Greek," as well as—improbably—Serbian (239). In his Preliminary Notes, Pavić describes his book's monolingualism as "the main shortcoming of the current version in relation to the Daubmannus edition," adding that at least the reader can choose to read the book's entries out of order: "it can be read in an infinite number of ways. It is an open book, and when it is shut it can be added to: just as it has its own former and present lexicographer, so it can acquire new writers, compilers, and continuers" (11).

Only a fiction in the original novel, the entries' multilingual mobility became a reality once the *Dictionary* was translated, a fact that Pavić noted with great satisfaction in a 1998 article:

> I have always wished to make literature, which is a nonreversible art, a reversible one. Therefore my novels have no end in the classical meaning of the word. . . . The original version of *Dictionary of the Khazars,* printed in the Cyrillic alphabet, ends with a Latin quotation: "sed venit ut illa impleam et confirmem, Mattheus." My novel in Greek translation ends with a sentence: "I have immediately noticed that there are three fears in me, and not one." The English, Hebrew, Spanish, and Danish versions of *Dictionary of the Khazars* end in this way: "Then when the reader returned, the entire process would be reversed, and Tibbon would correct the translation based on the impressions he had derived from this reading walk." ("The Beginning and the End of Reading" 143)

Pavić goes on to quote the closing sentences of the versions in Swedish, Dutch, Czech, German, Hungarian, Italian, Catalan, and Japanese. Foreign translations collectively create a multiple book, extending the original novel's monolingual reconstruction of Daubmannus's supposedly quadrilingual original.

Pavić's international framework and his experimental emphases reinforced each other for his international audience, leading foreign readers to overlook any local implications of his book and instead to emphasize its metafictional concerns. Even after Yugoslavia had fallen into civil war, discussions by non-East European scholars continued to focus almost exclusively on apolitical readings of the book, an approach typified in 1997 by the theorist of science and postmodernism N. Katherine Hayles, in an article flamboyantly entitled "Corporeal Anxiety in *Dictionary of the Khazars:* What Books Talk About in the Late Age of Print When They Talk About Losing Their Bodies." Giving a detailed and interesting reading of the theme of textual production and destruction, Hayles emphasizes the novel's "radical indeterminacy" (804) and the operations of "a closed self-referential loop" within it (811). She says nothing at all about the book's political themes or the cultural context of its composition and publication, apart from a passing reference in a footnote to an article by Petar Ramadanović, "Language and Crime in Yugoslavia," which she describes as taking "a sociological approach" (819n.).

In the most extended presentation of Pavić to date, the *Review of Contemporary Fiction* devoted over a hundred pages in the summer of 1998 to a cluster of a dozen pieces on Pavić's novels, centering on the *Dictionary* and including a long interview with Pavić as well as his article on "The Beginning and End of Reading." Nowhere in these pieces is there anything more than vague passing mention of the tragic events that occurred in the former Yugoslavia, beginning in 1987 when resurgent micronationalisms tore the nation apart. The articles have titles like "*Dictionary of the Khazars* as an Epistemological Metaphor" and "Milorad Pavić and Hyperfiction." Even an article entitled "Culture as Memory" concerns intertextuality and makes no reference to battles over cultural identity and memory in the former Yugoslavia of the 1980s and 1990s.

For his own part, Pavić says nothing at all about politics in his article on reading, focusing entirely on formal issues and the future of the novel. In the interview, with a Greek journalist named Thanassis Lallas, Pavić speaks mostly of his ancestors and of his metafictional concerns, mentioning only in very general terms that "For a while I was not able to publish my writing in my own country. There were political reasons for it. . . . I had to wait until 1967, when the appropriate conditions were established that allowed me to publish my first book in my country" (Lallas 133). Asked directly about his views on Serbia, Pavić replies with a kind of gentle, distanced irony that gives little indication of his personal views, even speaking of the Serbs as "they" rather than as "we": "It is a nation deprived of memory. They never forgive, but forget immediately. They are good warriors, but the worst diplomats. They win wars, and lose battles. . . . They always have their enemies in mind and they do not care a lot for their friends" (133–34). He then quickly turns the conversation to a discussion of Serbia's prominent writers and filmmakers and to his own fiction. As the interview draws to a close, Pavić sidesteps a question as to whether he has ever been a Communist, replying that "I am the last Byzantine" (140).

Nowhere in this interview, conducted in Belgrade by a foreign journalist for international consumption, does Pavić make anything resembling a direct political statement. He describes his life's goal as "to rescue as many pieces of beauty as possible. Tons of beauty sink every day in the Danube. Nobody notices. The one who notices it must do something to rescue it" (135). Asked specifically about the current situation in Serbia, he expresses a hope that the international success of novels like his may be "an assurance that love will overcome savagery in this world where there is always more beauty than love. . . . Let us for an instant count readers, not voters" (141). This is just what Pavić's personal website actually does: the home page displays a tally of how many people have visited the site to date. Reflecting an awareness of the foundation of his global appeal, Pavić's site is registered not in his own name but as "www.khazars.com." Appropriately, like the *Dictionary* itself the site comes in two parallel versions, not male and female but Serbian and English. A capsule biography on the home page says pointedly that Pavić "is not a member of any political party." Instead of party affiliation, the biography lists Pavić's membership in the Serbian Academy of Sciences and Arts and in several European cultural organizations, with no hint of the fact that the Serbian Academy was extensively involved in Serbian cultural politics in the 1980s and 1990s.[1]

Pavić's stance had been very different in the late 1980s, when Slobodan Milošević came to power vowing to restore the greatness that had once been Serbia's, with himself as the dominant unifying force. According to an account by Rajko Djurić, Milošević's party modified the traditional nationalist "four-S" slogan, "Samo sloga Srbina sparava" (only *unity* can save Serbia) to read "Samo *Slobodan* Srbina sparava." Speaking for domestic consumption, Pavić expressed his forceful support for Milošević's goals in a range of articles and interviews for Belgrade newspapers, reinforcing nationalist messages of Serbian ancestral greatness, a favorite theme of Milošević's. As Pavić declared in 1989, "In Serbia people were eating with golden forks in the thirteenth century, while the Western Europeans were still tearing raw flesh apart with their fingers" (quoted in Djurić 163–64).

Language was a crucial arena for the nationalist program of Serbian resurgence, spearheaded by activities of the Serbian Academy of Sciences and Arts, to which Pavić was elected in 1991. As Petar Ramadanović says in his article on "Language and Crime in Yugoslavia,"

> Croats, Serbs, and Muslims used to speak a common language before the war; now they speak "Croat," "Serbian," and "Bosnian." Serbo-Croat, the vanquished language, has no people, no folk anymore. But Serbo-Croat, the language of a ghost, the language of people who have lost their country, remains as a trace, as a witness of the un-speakable crime that is committed in the Balkans. (185)

Pavić, on the other hand, saw Serbo-Croatian as a political fiction created to suppress local identity, most specifically the historical greatness of Serbia and of the Serbian language. As he said in 1989, using the rhetoric of victimhood that would undergird Milošević's declarations of war against Slovenia and Croatia in 1991, "the Serbs come from the midpoint of the world, from the navel of the Indo-European peoples, and the Serbian language is an ancient language, the ancestor of all the Indo-European languages. And so everyone hates us out of envy; they sense that we are the most ancient of all the peoples between the Himalayas and the Pyrenees" (Djurić 164).

These statements give a chilling cast to one aspect of the Brankovich family's multilingualism: they use Serbian "only when they wish to kill" (25). Written words function as weapons throughout the *Dictionary of the Khazars,* from Princess Ateh's death-dealing letters to the invention of the Cyrillic alphabet by Saint Cyril. Summarizing the move from the rounded early Slavonic alphabet (Glagolitic) to the angular Cyrillic, Pavić describes the process of alphabetization in violent terms:

> While the Slavs besieged Constantinople in 860 A.D., [Cyril] was setting a trap for them in the quiet of his monastic cell in Asia Minor's Olympus—he was creating the first letters of the Slavic alphabet. He started with rounded letters, but the Slavonic language was so wild that the ink could not hold it, and so he made a second alphabet of barred letters and caged the unruly language in them like a bird. (63–64)

In order to fit the Slavonic language within the cage of their script, Cyril and his brother Methodius "broke it in pieces, drew it into their mouths through the bars of Cyril's letters, and bonded the fragments with their saliva and the Greek clay beneath the soles of their feet" (64).

The monastic theocracy on Mount Athos in northern Greece, where this scene takes place, has long been a focus of Eastern Orthodox identification; Pavić gives a further literary and heroic twist to the locale by identifying it with Olympus, a site he associates with Homer. In his interview with Thanassis Lallas, he cites Homer and the later Serbian bards as his predecessors in epic creation from oral material (138). Pavić went on to make Athos a key locale in his 1988 novel *Landscape Painted with Tea,* and well before he began the *Dictionary* he gave Athos pride of place in a poem called "Monument to an Unknown Poet," in which several of his characteristic themes are already fully evident. "My eyes are full of blood and wine like plaster on Athos' walls," the poem begins; in the second stanza, the speaker develops the link between literature and liturgy:

> My tongue three times peeled off its shirt of years
> > and three languages forgot within me
> But my tongue still recognizes the language of lost liturgies.
> My feet are tired from choosing the staff that will not break
> But my heart still makes a pilgrimage to your words set on fire.

In the poem's conclusion, these Khazar-like lost languages are redeemed in an internalized homeland:

> My tongue three times peeled off its shirt of time
> and three languages forgot within me
> But my heart has tasted the rock of your homeland
> and found in it the flavor of hearth,
> Although I was the apprentice of a poet who doesn't exist,
> a poet without a poem. ("Monument," in Simic 28)

From the eyes full of blood in the opening line to the "flavor of hearth" at the end, this poem resonates with the pre-Nazi tradition of celebrations of "Blut und Boden"—blood and ground, symbols of ethnic rootedness, typically mobilized against Jews and other newcomers who are thought to be supplanting the original inhabitants in their own land. There are, of course, no real monuments to unknown poets, just as no poet can exist without a poem: Pavić is playing on the imagery of monuments to the Unknown Soldier, here a man without a country fighting for his rightful home and hearth.

For all the ironic detachment of his interview with Thanassis Lallas, Pavić speaks rather differently on his website. To be sure, he belongs to no political party, and a brief "Autobiography" on his site insists that "I have no biography. I have only a bibliography." Yet this autobiography closes with a direct self-identification with an unjustly persecuted Serbia:

> I have not killed anyone. But they have killed me. Long before my death. It would have been better for my books had their author been a Turk or a German. I was the best known writer of the most hated nation in the world—the Serbian nation.
>
> XXI century started for me avant la date 1999, when NATO airforces bombed Belgrade and Serbia. Since that moment the river Danube on whose banks I was born is not navigable.
>
> I think God graced me with infinite favor by granting me the joy of writing, and punished me in equal measure, precisely because of that joy perhaps. *Milorad Pavić*

His website, www.khazars.com, is thus still developing the themes of writing, victimization, and divine inscrutability that pervade the *Dictionary of the Khazars*.

The novel complicates these themes by its use of a Jewish source-text. Pavić treats Jewish mysticism, in fact, with insight and sympathy as the utopian vision of an eternally displaced people. Having printed Judah ha-Levi's "Song of Zion" in Hebrew early in the book, he gives a partial prose translation two hundred pages later, describing the poet composing the poem as he finally makes his longed-for journey from Spain to the Holy Land at the end of his life:

> It was on this trip that he wrote his most mature poems, among them the famous *Song of Zion*, which is read in synagogues on the Day of the Holy Abba. He landed on the holy shores of his original homeland and died within reach of his destination. According to one account, just as he laid eyes on Jerusalem he was trampled to death by Saracen horses. Writing about the clash between Christianity and Islam, he said: "There is

no port in either East or West where we might find peace. . . . Whether Ismael wins or the Edomites"—Christians—"prevail, my fate remains the same—to suffer." (246)

The Jewish section of the *Dictionary* is the longest of the three; placed at the end, it is the section where the book's many threads are drawn together. If the true Lexicon could ever be assembled, it would represent the hidden body of Adam Ruhani or Adam Cadmon, a figure from Kabbalistic mysticism, whose instantiation would redeem the fallen universe: "The Khazars saw letters in people's dreams, and in them they looked for primordial man, for Adam Cadmon, who was both man and woman and born before eternity. They believed that to every person belongs one letter of the alphabet, that each of these letters constitutes part of Adam Cadmon's body on earth, and that these letters converge in people's dreams and come to life in Adam's body" (224–25). Samuel Cohen, a contemporary of Avram Brankovich's and compiler of the Hebrew version of the Dictionary, struggles to assemble a text that will fully embody Adam Cadmon: "I know, my Khazar dictionary includes all ten numbers and twenty-two letters of the Hebrew alphabet; the world can be created out of them but, lo, I cannot do it. I am missing certain names, and as a result some of the letters will not be filled" (229).

Far from treating Judaism slightingly or with hostility, Pavić does just the opposite: throughout his book, he implicitly identifies the Serbs *with* the Jews. Judah ha-Levi, trapped between Christianity and Islam, becomes the model for Pavić himself, a philosophical poet who records his country's fate, caught between the Austro-Hungarian Empire on one side and imperial Russia on the other. At the very beginning of the *Dictionary,* The Khazars stand in for the Balkans when their independence is brutally crushed by the Russians:

> A Russian military commander of the 10th century, Prince Svyatoslav, gobbled up the Khazar Empire like an apple, without even dismounting from his horse. In 943 A.D. the Russians went without sleep for eight nights to smash the Khazar capital at the mouth of the Volga into the Caspian Sea, and between 965 and 970 A.D. they destroyed the Khazar state. Eyewitnesses noted that the shadows of the houses in the capital held their outlines for years, although the buildings themselves had already been destroyed long before. They held fast in the wind and in the waters of the Volga. (2–3)

Before Yugoslavia plunged into civil war, it was natural enough to read such passages as expressing the heroic resistance of an indomitable nation to the oppression of imperial invaders. With Pavić identified as "Yugoslavian" and his book as "translated from the Serbo-Croatian," the *Dictionary* could be read in a way pleasing to Western liberals and conservatives alike, as a general plea for Yugoslavian self-determination in the face of Soviet repression. Such a reading would accord well with the perspective of Pavić's precursor Danilo Kiš, who did embody a liberal nationalism opposed both to Tito's authoritarianism and to divisive ethnic rivalries within the country.

This turns out not to be what Pavić had in mind. Far from defending Yugoslavia, he wanted to see it taken apart. Once in power, Slobodan Milošević and his ultranationalist allies began to disassemble Yugoslavia and even Serbo-Croatia into separate ethnic identities and languages. Formerly virtually indistinguishable from Croatian except in script (Roman versus Cyrillic), Serbian now became a distinct language, and Pavić took the opportunity to have his book "translated" *into* Serbian. Though for most books this would have meant little more than transliteration, in the case of the *Dictionary* the new version acquired a new order of entries, and the "Serbian version printed in the Latin alphabet" is one of the translations Pavić points to as differing from the original ("The Beginning and the End of Reading," 143). Christina Pribićević-Zorić's widely praised English translation is described in the British and American editions as "translated from the Serbo-Croatian," and yet when this same translation was locally re-issued in Belgrade in 1996, it was labeled as "translated from Serbian." We are used to seeing translations change linguistically as they reinterpret a common source language. Here just the opposite has occurred: the identical English version is presented as a translation of two *different* original languages, as Serbo-Croatian is torn asunder.

Within the book itself, Pavić focuses the rhetoric of suppression and victimhood on the Khazars. Modifying Judah ha-Levi's dialogue, Pavić adapts the theme of the Jews as archetypal oppressed minority to describe the Khazars as an oppressed *majority* in their own multicultural land, in a translation of Serbian nationalist resentment toward Tito's efforts to create a unified Yugoslavia. Tito's program is sharply satirized in an extended discussion of the organization of the Khazar state, in which the causes of Serbian resentments can be seen in heightened form. Whereas the Serbs, with some 40 percent of the population, were a plurality but not at all a majority in Yugoslavia, "the Khazars are the most numerous in the empire, the others all constituting very small groups. But the empire's administrative organization is designed not to show this" (146). The state is divided into districts, with more districts for the minorities than for the Khazar majority. Political representation, however, is proportional to the number of districts rather than to population. Moreover, the major Khazar region has been split up: "In the north, for instance, an entirely new nation was invented, which gave up the Khazar name, even the Khazar language, and it has a different name for its district" (146). Names are a crucial battleground:

> Given this situation and this balance of forces, promotions hinge on blind obedience to the non-Khazar representatives. Just avoiding the Khazar name is already a recommendation in itself, enabling one to take the first steps at court. The next step requires fiercely attacking the Khazars and subordinating their interests to those of the Greeks, Jews, Turkmen, Arabs, or Goths, as the Slavs are called in these parts. (147)

It will be noted that this listing makes the Khazars the oppressed majority among a total of six ethnic groups, a number corresponding to Yugoslavia's six constituent republics.

The Khazars' struggle is economic as well as cultural. In a grim parody of Tito's policy of giving preferential economic treatment to the smaller, less-developed republics, the Khazar government sells specially dyed bread to non-Khazar regions:

Dyed bread is the sign of the Khazars' position in the Khazar state. The Khazars produce it, because they inhabit the grain-growing regions of the state. The starving populace at the foot of the Caucasus massif eats dyed bread, which is sold for next to nothing. Undyed bread, which is also made by the Khazars, is paid for in gold. The Khazars are allowed to buy only the expensive, undyed bread. Should any Khazar violate this rule and buy the cheap, dyed bread, which is strictly forbidden them, it will show in their excrement. Special customs services periodically check Khazar latrines and punish violators of this law. (149–50)

The Khazar state, in Pavić's presentation, becomes the ultimate dystopia of a totalitarian multiculturalism.

The Khazars are exemplary victims geographically as well as socially, for the three hells of Christianity, Islam, and Judaism meet under their lands (52). The devils' influence continually percolates upward, though naturally the devils themselves hate what they have wrought. As one of the three devils says to Dr. Muawia at the end of the book:

> "Look at the results of this democracy of yours. Before, big nations used to oppress small nations. Now it's the reverse. Now, in the name of democracy, small nations terrorize the big. Just look at the world around us. White America is afraid of blacks, the blacks are afraid of the Puerto Ricans, Jews of the Palestinians, the Arabs of the Jews, the Serbs of the Albanians, the Chinese of the Vietnamese, the English of the Irish. Small fish are nibbling the ears of the big fish. . . . Your democracy sucks. . . ." (330)

Having expressed his views on democracy, the devil orders Muawia to open his mouth so that his teeth won't be spoiled, and shoots him in the mouth.

A novel that achieved rapid worldwide success as "an Arabian Nights romance" and "a novel of love and death" actually contains more death than love, and it even helped to usher in the death it most longed for, the destruction of a multiethnic Yugoslavia. In an article on "Pavić's Literary Demolition of Yugoslavia," Andrew Wachtel points out that Pavić's use of postmodernist techniques could be read in Western Europe as pure play or as a healthy corrective to Enlightenment certainties, whereas Pavić could deploy these techniques to very different effect in a Yugoslavia whose very creation expressed an Enlightenment ideal of unity in diversity based on a common, reasoned public discourse:

> The philosophical demolition job Pavić performed on the synthetic concept of Yugoslavia grew out of his own importation of a particular postmodernist mode of thought into Yugoslav discourse. But on Yugoslav soil, the Lyotardian vision of separate and incommensurable language games did not remain a metaphor. It was embodied, instead, in a series of nationalist micronarratives whose primary mode of communication turned out to be shooting. (640)

Perhaps we were reading the poisoned copy of the book all along?

.   .   .

Closely connected to contemporary reality, the *Dictionary* was a pointed and polemical intervention in cultural debate in the uncertain years leading up to

Yugoslavia's vicious civil war. How should we read the book in light of this new understanding, or should we continue to read it at all? Certainly a book marketed as a romantic escape into hyperfiction would have attracted fewer readers if it had been presented as "A Playful Apologia for Ethnic Cleansing." One possibility would be to regard the novel as a sort of con job. On this view, foreign readers haven't realized that they were being sold a bill of goods: nationalist propaganda was falsely marketed as international postmodernism.

To take such a view, though, risks a kind of textual essentialism, as though a book really is one thing and has one meaning wherever and whenever it is read. Few of us still believe this in theory, thanks to a generation's worth of poststructuralist theory, and yet in practice it is all too easy to fall into essentialist language in describing a book's themes and effect, even though what we are really describing may largely be our own reading of it at a given time. To realize this doesn't mean that we need to go to the opposite extreme, supposing that a book has an infinite multiplicity of meanings and perhaps no real ethical impact at all, a view that would be the equivalent of the relativistic translation theories that deny that there can ever be good and bad translations. Despite Pavić's enthusiasm for his text's reversibility, there are finally always going to be forty-five entries that collectively present the same elements for the reader to absorb. Further, individual readers don't read in a private cultural vacuum. Though a range of readings is always possible at a given time and place, this range is limited, not infinite, and the readings produced in a particular cultural context will tend to have a definite family resemblance.

What the double life of *Dictionary of the Khazars* demonstrates is the major difference between a work's life in a national context as opposed to a global context. As a work of Yugoslavian literature, written in Serbo-Croatian and printed in Cyrillic script, the Хазарски Ре★ник had one kind of impact, or a range of impacts, that began to change as Yugoslavia broke apart and the book became *Hazarski Rečnik,* written in Serbian and printed in Roman script. In both forms, it would naturally be read in a direct relation to the local literary, social, and political history that Pavić shares—and disputes—with his readers. An individual Serbian, or Bosnian, or Montenegrin reader might approve or reject Pavić's satiric implication that the Khazars are the forerunners of modern Serbs as a majority oppressed in their own country, but this theme would be strongly evident for most readers in the area, however they assessed it. Probably many readers around Eastern Europe would be attuned to this level of the text, as it would resonate so strongly with issues close to home.

Farther afield, however, *Hazarski rečnik* changed character as it became a work of world literature, whether as *Diccionario Jázaro* or as מילון הכוזרים. The novel's nationalism remained subordinate to its inter-nationalism for most foreign readers even after Milošević came to power and ethnic tensions mounted throughout the Balkans, and it didn't take the expanse of the Atlantic to induce such readings. In a 1995 survey of the French reception of the *Dictionary,* Milivoj Srebro finds French-speaking reviewers and critics consistently reading Pavić as the playful heir to Calvino, Cortázar, and Perec. She quotes a Swiss reviewer in 1988 describing the novel as "une machine infernale," but this is not at all a political assessment; instead, the reviewer concludes, "the demoniacal Pavić teaches us that reality, like truth, is a sweet illusion" (Srebro 277). The reviewer makes no reference to any Balkan realities, even though at their closest point the borders of Switzerland and the former Yugoslavia are less than a hundred and fifty miles apart.

To understand the workings of world literature we need more of a phenomenology than an ontology of the work of art: a work *manifests* differently abroad than it does at home. Yet acknowledging such differences doesn't mean that it is good to remain as clueless as the Swiss reviewer allowed himself to be, at a time when it would have behooved Western readers to pay much closer attention to the issues Pavić was raising. Having found one French critic (an Eastern European émigré) who "has even been tempted to see in this work a parable of the destiny of the Serbs," Milivoj Srebro dismisses such an interpretation as denying the book's universality. "It is precisely this universality," she adds, "that makes the difference between a masterpiece and an ordinary work" (284). Even Srebro, though, ends by admitting that French responses to the novel have been one-sided: "To be sure, if we take up the formulation of Jean Starobinski according to which 'the critical trajectory develops, so far as possible, between *accepting everything* (through sympathy) and *situating everything* (by comprehension),' one could say that the reviews of *Dictionary of the Khazars* have stayed fairly close to the first pole of this trajectory" (284–85).

It shouldn't be necessary to treat a foreign work with an uncomprehending sympathy in order to appreciate its excellence. It does no service to works of world literature to set them loose in some deracinated space, whether the "great conversation" of a 1950s-style academic humanism or the "closed self-referential loop" of recent poststructuralist metafiction. Aesthetically as well as ethically, a pure universalism of either variety is finally reductive, missing the real complexity of a work, just as much as would an opposite insistence that a work can only be read effectively in the original language, inextricably linked at all points to its local context. An informed reading of a work of world literature should keep both aspects in play together, recognizing that it brings us elements of a time and place different from our own, and at the same time recognizing that these elements change in force as the book gets farther from home.

Understanding the cultural subtext of Pavić's Khazars is important for foreign readers, as otherwise we simply don't see the point of much of the book. As Petar Ramadanović says, Pavić was composing an "appeal for compassion with the Serbian problem . . . addressed to the international community" (190). However we choose to react to that appeal, a full reading should be aware of it and should confront the ethical choices that the novel is pressing us to make. At the same time, when we read a work of world literature we have a great deal of freedom in deciding what use we will make of such contextual understanding. This freedom can most readily be seen when we are reading a work from a distant time as well as place. To take the case of Dante, for instance, it seems to me trivializing to treat the *Divine Comedy* as an essentially secular work, though various modern commentators have chosen to focus on Dante as "poet of the secular world," in Erich Auerbach's phrase. Auerbach went so far as to claim that Dante's realism overwhelmed his theology "and destroyed it in the very process of realizing it" (*Mimesis*, 202). We can dispute such a claim on both historical and aesthetic grounds, taking seriously the idea that the *Divine Comedy* may actually have been a successful Christian poem. Even so, appreciating Dante's profound religious vision does not require us to convert to Catholicism, or to take a stand on issues of Florentine politics, though both of these responses are ones that Dante might well have desired. A work of world literature has its fullest life, and its greatest power, when we can read it with a kind of *detached engagement*, informed but not confined by a knowledge of what the work would likely mean in its original time and place, even as we adapt it to our present context and purposes.

Pavić himself raises this theme repeatedly. The son of a house builder, he often uses architectural metaphors in talking about his books. He has tried, he says, to construct books with many exits rather than a single ending, so that the reader "can come out not only through one exit but also through other exits that are far from each other. . . . Slowly I lose from my sight the difference between the house and the book, and this is, perhaps, the most important thing I have to say in this text" ("The Beginning and the End of Reading" 144). We can extend Pavić's metaphor: a book offers us many ways in as well as many exits, some of which are most readily accessible from a local standpoint, while others only become visible from a distance. For Pavić, indeed, it is the reader who has the true freedom of the text; caught within a web of circumstance and fatality, the writer has far less. It is the Devil in Istanbul who declares that "your democracy sucks," but by giving this speech to the devil Pavić doesn't mean to distance himself from this viewpoint, since he regularly identifies himself with the devil. Poet of a radically fallen world, Pavić creates a book from his own passions and prejudices, expecting that like-minded readers will see it likewise but different readers may find ways out of his book that he himself cannot take or perhaps even find.

A clear stand-in for Pavić within the book is the devil Nikon Sevast, a master calligrapher who spends his time painting frescoes in Moravian churches before he goes on to encounter Avram Brankovich and serve as a copyist of the *Lexikon*. Describing his fresco technique to a fellow monk, Sevast says that "I work with something like a dictionary of colors, and from it the observer composes sentences and books, in other words, images. You could do the same with writing. Why shouldn't someone create a dictionary of words that make up one book and let the reader himself assemble the words into a whole?" (96). In so doing, the reader won't merely share in the creative process but will actually experience a freedom denied to the devil/artist himself: "It is not I who mix the colors but your own vision," Sevast tells his fellow monk: "I only place them next to one another on the wall in their natural state; it is the observer who mixes the colors in his own eye, like porridge. . . . Therefore, faith in seeing, listening, and reading is more important than faith in painting, singing, or writing" (95).

Reading gives access to a realm of freedom that provides strength to the dreamer, who is otherwise caught in the trials of the waking world. For Pavić it is world literature that typifies the possibility of escape from the tragedies of individual circumstance. Just as reciting Dante gave Primo Levi strength in Auschwitz, so too Pavić has Saint Methodius think of Homer while undergoing torture at the order of hostile German bishops:

> He was brought to trial before a synod in Regensburg, then tortured and exposed naked to the frost. While they whipped him, his body bent over so low that his beard touched the snow, Methodius thought of how Homer and the holy prophet Elijah had been contemporaries, how Homer's poetic state had been larger than the state of Alexander of Macedonia, because it had stretched from Pontus to beyond Gibraltar. . . . He thought of how Homer had seas and towns in his vast poetic state, not knowing that in one of them, in Sidon, sat the prophet Elijah, who was to become an inhabitant of another poetic state, one as vast, eternal, and powerful as Homer's own–an inhabitant of the Holy Scriptures. (88–89)

Recalling his reading of Homer and Elijah, whose overlapping empires the poet and prophet themselves couldn't perceive, Methodius can ignore the whips that seek to break his spirit.

Translation is a key to the reader's freedom. Isaac Sangari, Hebrew representative before the Kaghan in the great religious debate, is intensely loyal to his language and tradition, but not exclusively so:

> He made a point of stressing the values of the Hebrew language, but he knew many other languages as well. He believed that the differences between languages lay in the following: all languages except God's are the languages of suffering, the dictionaries of pain. "I have noticed," he said, "that my sufferings are drained through a rupture in time or in myself, for otherwise they would be more numerous by now. The same holds true for languages." (274)

The only truly free characters in Pavić's book are a select sect of "dream hunters," devotees of a cult headed by Princess Ateh, an alternative to all existing religions. The dream hunters travel from one person's dream to another, seeking pairs of people who unknowingly dream of one another; the rifts in the universe can be healed if the dream hunters can unite these pairs, who are the potential lexicographers of the full Dictionary. As a devil named Ibn Akshany remarks to one of these dream hunters, his hunt is the most privileged form of reading, and it is better than writing itself: "Anybody can play music or write a dictionary. Leave that to others, because people like you, who can peer into the crack between one view and the other, that crack where death rules supreme, are few and far between" (183).

Pavić's book enters world literature both by its translations abroad and also by opening out directly, so far as possible, into the reader's world, well signaled by the trompe l'oeil cover of the British and American edition, which appears to be an embossed dictionary cover, with a jewel set into the spine and a fly resting on the back cover. Though the Dictionary proper ends differently in different languages, in every edition Pavić follows the Dictionary with a "Closing Note on the Usefulness of this Dictionary," in which he evokes the reader, or more specifically a pair of readers, male and female. These readers will each have read one of the book's differently gendered editions and will now meet in the square of their town: "I see how they lay their dinner out on top of the mailbox in the street," he says, "and how they eat, embraced, sitting on their bicycles" (335). In the *Dictionary of the Khazars*, the nightmare of history becomes the dream of world literature, a multilingual space of freedom from the limited viewpoints that enmesh nations and individuals alike, not excluding the book's own author. The readers' meal on the mailbox, and its hinted romantic aftermath, can form an antidote to the poison with which the book itself was written.

NOTE

1. I am describing the site as of March 2003. The site has been set up and maintained by Pavić's wife, Jasmina Mihajlović, herself a critic and writer, who has written extensively on Pavić and is keenly concerned with his reception and reputation both at home and abroad.

WORKS CITED

Auerbach, Erich, *Mimesis: The Representation of Reality in Western Literature*, trans. Willard R. Trask (Princeton: Princeton University Press, 1953).

Borges, Jorge Luis, *Ficciones*, trans. Anthony Kerrigan (New York: Grove Press, 1962).

Djurić, Rajko, "Kultur und Destruktivität am Beispiel Jugoslawien," In *Suchbild Europa: Künstleriche Konzepte der Moderne* ed. Jürgen Wertheimer (Amsterdam: Rodopi, 1995), pp. 162–67.

Hayles, N. Katherine, "Corporeal Anxiety in *Dictionary of the Khazars*: What Books Talk About in the Late Age of Print When They Talk About Losing Their Bodies," *Modern Fiction Studies* 43(3), 1997, pp. 800–20.

Judah ha-Levi, *The Kuzari*, trans. N. Daniel Korobkin (Northvale, NJ: Jason Aronson, 1998).

Kiš, Danilo, *A Tomb for Boris Davidovich*, trans. Duška Mikić-Mitchell (Harmondsworth: Penguin, 1980).

Lallas, Thanassis, "'As a Writer I Was Born Two Hundred Years Ago. . . .': An Interview with Milorad Pavić." *Review of Contemporary Fiction* 18(2), 1998, pp. 128–41.

Pavić, Milorad, "Monument to an Unknown Poet," In *Four Yugoslav Poets*, ed. and trans. Charles Simic (Lillabulero Press, 1970), unpaginated.

———, *Dictionary of the Khazars*, trans. from the Serbo-Croatian by Christina Pribićević-Zorić. In Female and Male editions (New York: Knopf, 1988).

———, *Landscape Painted with Tea: A Crossword-Novel*, trans. Christina Pribićević-Zorić (New York: Knopf, 1990).

———, "The Beginning and the End of Reading—The Beginning and the End of the Novel," *Review of Contemporary Fiction* 18(2), 1998, pp. 142–46.

————, and Jasmina Mihalović. *Www.khazars.com.*

Ramadanović, Petar, "Language and Crime in Yugoslavia," in *Regionalism Reconsidered: New Approaches to the Field* ed. David Jordan (New York: Garland, 1994), pp. 185–96.

Srebro, Milivoj, "Le Coup médiatique de Milorad Pavić: *Le Dictionnaire khazar* vu par la critique littéraire française," *Revue de Littérature Comparée* 69(3), 1995, pp. 273–85.

Wachtel, Andrew, "Pavić's Literary Demolition of Yugoslavia," *Slavic and East European Journal* 41(4), 1997, pp. 627–44.

CONTRIBUTORS

Jonathan E. Abel is a PhD candidate in the Department of Comparative Literature at Princeton University, writing a dissertation entitled *Pages Crossed: Tracing Scorned Literature Through the War in Japan and America*. In addition to his dissertation topic of transwar censorship, his current research interests include the relationships of copyright, songs, and criticism to literatures. His other publications include "Different from Difference: Rereading Kurutta Ippeiji," in *Asian Cinema* (Fall 2001).

Emily Apter is editor for the books series, Translation/Transnation, published by Princeton University Press. She is a professor at New York University, teaching for both the French and Comparative Literature departments. Her books include *Continental Drift: From National Characters to Virtual Subjects*, *Fetishism as Cultural Discourse* (co-edited with William Pietz), *Feminizing the Fetish: Psychoanalysis and Narrative Obsession in Turn-of-the-Century France*, and *André Gide and the Codes of Homotextuality*.

Sandra Bermann is Chair of the Department of Comparative Literature at Princeton University and co-editor of this collection. Author of *The Sonnet Over Time: A Study in the Sonnets of Petrarch, Shakespeare, and Baudelaire*, she has also translated Alessandro Manzoni's *Del romanzo historico* into English (*On the Historical Novel*). She is currently working on a study of René Char.

Vilashini Cooppan is Assistant Professor of Literature at the University of California at Santa Cruz. She has published articles and essays on postcolonial and world literatures, globalization theory, and psychoanalysis, and is completing a book entitled *Inner Territories: Fictions and Fantasms of the Nation in Postcolonial Writing*.

Stanley Corngold is Professor of German and Comparative Literature at Princeton University. Translator of Franz Kafka's *The Metamorphosis* and *Selected Stories*, forthcoming, he is also the author of many books, including *Franz Kafka: The Necessity of Form*; *Complex Pleasure: Forms of Feeling in German Literature*; and *The Fate of the Self: German Writers and French Theory*. His most recent book is *Lambent Traces: Franz Kafka*.

David Damrosch is Professor of English and Comparative Literature at Columbia University. He is general editor of *The Longman Anthology of World Literature*, and his other books include *What Is World Literature?*, *Meetings of the Mind* (in collaboration with Vic d'Ohr Addams, Marsha Doddvic, and Dov Midrash), *We Scholars: Changing the Culture of the University*, and *The Narrative Covenant: Transformations of Genre in the Growth of Biblical Literature*.

Robert Eaglestone is Lecturer in the Department of English at Royal Halloway, University of London. He is series editor of Routledge Critical Thinkers and author of *Ethical Criticism: Reading After Levinas*, *Doing English*, and *The Holocaust and the Postmodern*, among others.

Stathis Gourgouris teaches at Columbia University. His books include *Does Literature Think?: Literature as Theory for an Anti-mythical Era* and *Dream Nation: Enlightenment, Colonization, and the Institution of Modern Greece.*

Pierre Legrand teaches law at the Sorbonne.

Jacques Lezra is Professor in the Departments of English and of Spanish and Portuguese at the University of Wisconsin, Madison. He is the author of *Unspeakable Subjects: The Genealogy of the Event in Early Modern Europe*, and has co-edited (with Georgina Dopico) a recent supplement to Sebastián de Covarrubias Horozco's *Tesoro de la lengua castellana, o española* based on a manuscript found in the Biblioteca Nacional de Madrid.

Françoise Lionnet is Chair of the Department of French and Francophone Studies at UCLA. She taught previously at Northwestern, where she held the Pearce Miller Professorship in Literary Studies. She is author of *Postcolonial Representations: Women, Literature, Identity*, and *Autobiographical Voices: Race, Gender, Self-Portraiture*; forthcoming from Duke University Press is *Minor Transnationalism*, co-edited with Shu-mei Shih.

Sylvia Molloy is the Albert Schweitzer Professor in the Humanities at New York University, where she teaches in the Departments of Spanish and Portuguese Languages and Literatures and Comparative Literature. Her books include *Signs of Borges* (a translation with Oscar Montero of her earlier work, *Las letras de Borges*), *At Face Value: Autobiographical Writing in Spanish America*, *Women's Writing in Latin America: An Anthology*, co-edited with Sara Castro-Klarén and Beatriz Sarlo, and *Hispanisms and Homosexualities*, co-edited with Robert McKee Irwin.

Yopie Prins is Associate Professor of English and Comparative Literature at the University of Michigan. She is the author of *Victorian Sappho* and has published various articles on classical Greek literature and nineteenth-century Hellenism. Currently she is writing a series of essays on Victorian poetry and prosody, tentatively entitled *The Fetish of Meter.*

Edward Said, who died in 2003, was Professor of English and Comparative Literature at Columbia University. His many books include *Orientalism*, *The Question of Palestine*, *The World, the Text and the Critic*, *Culture and Imperialism*, and *The Politics of Dispossession*. His memoir, *Out of Place*, was published in 1999 and several posthumous books are forthcoming. His work has been translated into thirty-six languages.

Azade Seyhan is Fairbank Professor in the Humanities, Professor of German and Comparative Literature, and Adjunct Professor in Philosophy at Bryn Mawr College. In addition to numerous articles, she is the author of *Writing Outside the Nation* and *Representation and Its Discontents: The Critical Legacy of German Romanticism.*

Gayatri Chakravorty Spivak is the Avalon Foundation Professor in the Humanities at Columbia University. She has translated Jacques Derrida's *De la grammatologie* and the fiction of Mahasweta Devi into English. Her books include *In Other Worlds*, *The Post-Colonial Critic*, *Outside in the Teaching Machine*, *A Critique of Post-Colonial Reason*, and *Death of a Discipline.*

Henry Staten is Professor of English at the University of Washington. In addition to numerous articles, essays, and reviews, he is the author of *Eros in Mourning: Homer to Lacan*, *Nietzsche's Voice*, and *Wittgenstein and Derrida*. He is working on a project entitled *The Transvaluation of Values in the Victorian Novel*.

Lawrence Venuti is Professor of English at Temple University. He has translated numerous works of fiction and poetry from Italian to English, including *Breath: Poems and Letters* (Antonia Pozzi), *Finite Intuition: Selected Poetry and Prose* (Milo De Angelis), *Passion* (I. U. Tarchetti), and *Restless Nights: Selected Stories of Dino Buzzati*. He has also written about the theory and practice of translation in *Rethinking Translation: Discourse, Subjectivity, Ideology*, *The Translator's Invisibility: A History of Translation*, *The Scandals of Translation: Towards an Ethics of Difference*, and *The Translation Studies Reader*.

Lynn Visson received her PhD from Harvard University and has been a staff interpreter at the United Nations since 1980. She is the author of *From Russian into English: An Introduction to Simultaneous Interpretation*, and most recently, of *Wedded Strangers: The Challenges of Russian-American Marriages*.

Gauri Viswanathan is the Class of 1933 Professor in the Humanities at Columbia University. In addition to numerous articles for journals and edited volumes, she is the author of two books, *Outside the Fold: Conversion, Modernity, and Belief*, and *Masks of Conquest: Literary Study and British Rule in India*, and editor of *Power, Politics, and Culture: Interviews with Edward W. Said*. She was guest editor for a special issue of *Ariel*, entitled "Institutionalizing English Studies: The Postcolonial/Postindependence Challenge."

Samuel Weber is the Avalon Professor of Humanities at Northwestern University. He has translated works by Theodor Adorno and Jacques Derrida into English and has done extensive work as a dramaturge. His own books include *Unwrapping Balzac*, *The Legend of Freud*, *Institution and Interpretation*, and *Mass Mediauras: Form, Technics, Media*, and *Theatricality as Medium* (Fordham UP, 2005).

Michael Wood is the Charles Barnwell Straut Professor of English and Professor of Comparative Literature at Princeton University, and is the co-editor of this collection. He writes regularly for the *London Review of Books* and the *New York Review of Books*. He is the author of books about Stendhal, García Márquez, Nabokov, and Kafka, and recently published *The Road to Delphi: The Life and Afterlife of Oracles*.

INDEX OF NAMES AND TITLES